Richard Baxter

Church-history of the government of bishops and their councils abbreviated

Including the chief part of the government of christian princes and popes

Richard Baxter

Church-history of the government of bishops and their councils abbreviated
Including the chief part of the government of christian princes and popes

ISBN/EAN: 9783337104405

Printed in Europe, USA, Canada, Australia, Japan

Cover: Foto ©Lupo / pixelio.de

More available books at **www.hansebooks.com**

Church-History
OF THE
GOVERNMENT
OF
BISHOPS
AND THEIR
COUNCILS
ABBREVIATED.

Including the chief part of the Government of Christian Princes and *POPES*, and a true Account of the most troubling Controversies and Heresies till the

REFORMATION.

Written for the use especially of them,

I. Who are ignorant or misinformed of the State of the Ancient Churches.
II. Who cannot read many and great Volumes.
III. Who think that the Universal Church must have one Visible Soveraign, Personal or Collective, Pope or General Councils.
IV. Who would know whether Patriarchs, Diocesans, and their Councils, have been, or must be the cure of Heresies and Schisms.
V. Who would know the truth about the great Heresies which have divided the Christian World, especially the *Donatists, Novatians, Arrians, Macedonians, Nestorians, Eutichians, Monothelites*, &c.

By *RICHARD BAXTER*, a Hater of false History.

LONDON:
Printed, and are to be sold by *John Kidgell* at the *Atlas* in *Cornhill*, near the *Royal Exchange*, MDCLXXX.

THE
PREFACE.

THE great usefulness of History needs not many words to prove it, seeing natural inclination it self is so much for it, and reason and experience tell men, that they cannot spare it, as to Natural, Civil, or Religious use. God himself hath highly commended it to us, by writing the Sacred Scriptures so much Historically; yea and making some of it part of the necessary Articles of our Creed. Children that yet understand not the Doctrinal part of the Bible, do quickly take delight in the Historical part; which prepareth them for the rest. Ignorant and ungodly persons that have no true sense of Sacred Doctrine, can yet understand and with lesse aversness and weariness read the history. Melancholy and sad persons who can hardly bear long Doctrinal studies, are often eased and recreated with useful History.

Man is a part of the Universe, and every man is a part of the world of mankind, and therefore thinketh the case of the whole to be much of his concerne. And were not narrow selfishnes much of our Pravity, we should take the universal and publick good, and Gods Love to it and Pleasedness and Glory in it, to be much more our end, and the object of our desire and delight, than any personal felicity of our own; It is a Monster of inhumanity in the Doctrine of the Sadducees, Spinosa, Hobbes, and their brutish followers, that they set up Individual self interest as a mans chiefest end and object of rational Love and desire; and own no Good, but that which Relatively is Good to me, that is, either my personal life and pleasure as the end, or other things as a means thereto: Though Grace only savingly cure this base inhumane maladie, yet common reason beareth witness against it, and only sense, and reason captivated by sense do patronize it. Put not the question to a reasonable man, though wicked, what he can do or doth: But what in reason he should do, and he cannot deny but that he should think of a more excellent person at the Indies, that never will do any thing for him, as more amiable than him-

A 2 self,

The PREFACE.

self, much more many thousands such; And as Goodness and Amiableness are all one, so that which is best, should be loved best: And he that would not die to save his Country is worse than sober Heathens were. And he that would not rather be annihilated than all or halfe the world should be annihilated, is so basely selfish, that I should sooner believe that analogical Reason ruleth some bruites, than that true Reason determineth this mans choice.

Spinosa taketh the Knowledge of our Union with Universal nature (which he calleth God) to be mans perfection and his chief good, in comparison of which sensual Pleasure, Riches and Honour are but troubles further then they are a meanes hereto: And if he had better known God, as the Creator and Governour and end of the material Universe which he took to be God, and had joyned [holy Uniteing Joyful Love to the Universe, and specially to the Heavenly Society, and above them all to God himself] unto this Knowledge, and extended it to the perpetuity of an Immortal state, he had been happily in the right; which missing, he became a pernicious seducer of himself and others.

But thus nature and Grace do loudly tell us, that each part should be greatly concerned for the whole, and therefore every one should desire to know as much of the whole, as he is capable, and as tendeth to his duty and delight. And how small a parcel of Time, or Men, or Actions are present or in our daies? How little knoweth he that knoweth no more than he hath lived to see? What Religion can he have who knoweth not the History of Creation, Redemption or the giving of the Holy Ghost, or the planting and propagating the Church, and also what will be when this life is ended?

But it is not all History that is needful or useful to us: There are many things done which we are not concerned to be acquainted with. But the History of the Church, of the propagation of the Christian faith, and what the Doctrine was that was then received, and how it was practised, promoted and defended, and how it was corrupted invaded and persecuted, is of so great use to posterity, that next to the Scripture and the illumination of Gods Spirit, I remember nothing more needful to be known.

When Philip Nerius set up his Oratorian exercises at Rome, as to win the people, they found it necessary to use large affectionate extemporate prayers and expositions and Sermons, so the next thing found necessary was, to bestow constantly one exercise in opening Church-History

The PREFACE.

ry to the people. And this did both entice their attentions by delight, and also by fitting reports more to the Papal interest than to the truth, did greatly bewitch them into a confident beliefe, that the Papal sect was all the true Church, and all other Christians were but sectaries and branches broken off, and withered, and therefore to be burned here and hereafter (abusing Joh. 15. 5. &c.).

And I have oft thought that the right use of such an Historical exercise, in an ordinary congregation would be of great use to the ignorant vulgar and unlearned zealous sort of Christians: For I find that for want of the knowledge of Church-History, and how things have gone before us in all former times, many errours and sins are kept up that else would more easily be forsaken. To instance in some few.

1. As it was the craft of Baronius (who performed that exercise in Nerius his Conventicles at Rome,) to write afterward his Church-History in Latin so voluminously, that few but the Clergie byassed by interest would read it, and so the Clergy might be the credited reporters of all to the vulgar; so to this day, the Papist-Priests contrive to be the Masters and reporters of Church-History as well as of unwritten Tradition, and to keep the Laity so far ignorant of it, that when they tell men confident stories for their advantage, few or none may be able to contradict them, and so their report must passe as undenyed truth. And thus false History is made the chief foundation of the Roman Kingdom.

Thus they will face you down that you are ignorant or impudent, 1. If you question whether Peter was a true Bishop at Rome, (yea or ever there, which Nilus hath shewed to be somewhat uncertain) 2. Or that he setled the Roman Bishop as his successour in a supremacy over all the Christian world, 3. Or that the Popes Primacie was over all the Churches on earth, which indeed was but (as Canterburie is in England,) in one Roman Empire only. 4. They will perswade you that this Primacie was setled by Christ or his Apostles, which was done only by Councils and Emperours of Rome, 5. They would make you believe that this was from the Apostles daies, which began long after, 6. They would perswade you that all the Christian world submitted to it, even Abassia, and all the extra-imperial Churches, which is no such matter, 7. Yea, that before Luther none contradicted the Papal power and claime, but all the Christian world were Papists. By many such lies they deceive thousands of the ignorant: And when they challenge men to dispute, by word or writing, their last refuge is to bring them

A 3   into

The PREFACE.

into a wood of History, that there they may either win the game, or end the chase: And if a Minister of Christ be not armed here, to confute their historical forgeries, they will take it for a victory and triumph; which made me write my last book against Johnson (or Terret) to shew Historically the Antiquity of our Church, and the novelty of theirs (which I could wish young Ministers unacquainted with Church-History would peruse.)

But if our people were truely acquainted how things have gone in the Church from the beginning, it would be one of the most effectual preservatives against Popery, when now the falsifications are become its strength. I have oft thought that it had been greater policy in the Papists, if they could, to have burnt all Church-History, but specially of the Councils, that the credit might have depended on their bare word: For verily once reading of Crab, Binnius, Surius, or Nicolinus would turn against them any stomack, that is not confirmed in their own disease. But they have overdone Baronius, and now made so great and costly a load of the Councils, as that the deficiency of money, time, wit and patient industry, shall save the most, even of the Priesthood from the understanding of the truth: And such Epitomes as Caranza's leave out most of the culpable part: and yet even such they can hardly tolerate.

II. The more moderate French Papists who magnifie Councils above Popes, would make us believe, that though Popes are fallible and may miscarry, yet General Councils, have been the universal Church-representative, which have a Legislative and Judicial Universal power, and that our concord must be by centring in their decrees; and all are Schismaticks at least, that take not their Faith and Religion upon their trust: But if men knew that there never was a General Council of all the Christian Churches but only of the Empire, and how wofully they have miscarried, it would do much to save them from all such temptations.

III. The overvaluers of Church grandure, and wealth, and maintainers of the corrupt sort of Diocesane Prelacy, Patriarks, &c. write books and tell the ignorant confident stories, how such a Prelacy hath been in the Church ever since the dayes of the Apostles, and that all the Churches on earth consented to it: But if the people were acquainted with Church-History they would know, that the primitive fixed Episcopacy was Parochial, or every Church associated for personal present Communion had a Bishop, Presbytery and Deacons of their own: (unfixed Itinerant General Pastors, indefinitely taking care of many Churches). And that it was the Bishops striving who should be greatest, and turning single

Churches

The PREFACE.

Churches into an Association of many Churches, and to be but Chappels or parts of the Diocesan Church (that their power and wealth might be enlarged with their Territories) and the turning of Arbitrating Bishops into the Common Judicature; which must govern all Christians, and such like, which poysoned the Church, and turned the species of particular Churches, Episcopacy, Presbytery and Discipline, quite into another thing. And to speak freely, it was the many blind volumes and confident clamours of some men, that rail at us, as denying an Episcopacy, which the universal Church hath always agreed in, which drew me to write this abridgement of the Church History of Bishops, Councils and Popes.

IV. And those that make the Ignorant believe that seditious disobedient Presbyters have in all Ages been the dividers of the Church, and the Bishops the means of Unity, concord and suppression of such Schismaticks and Hereticks, could never thus deceive the people, were but so much Church-History commonly known, as I have here collected. Read Church-History and believe that if you can.

V. And many that take up any new opinion or dotage which is but newly broached among them, would have been saved from it, if they had but known how that same opinion or the like, was long ago taken up by Hereticks, and exploded by the faithful Pastors and people of the Church.

VI. And the sectaries who rashly seperate from some Churches, because of some forms, opinions or ceremonies, which almost all Christians on earth have used, in the former purer ages, and still use, would be more cautelous and fearful in examining their grounds, and would hardly venture to seperate from any Church for that, which on the same reason would move them to separate from almost all Christians in the whole world; if not Unchurch the Church of Christ : And ancient errours and crimes would affright us from imitating them.

VII. And those that make new ambiguous words or unnecessary practices to become necessary to Church Communion, and hereticate all that differ from them, or persecute them at least, would be more frightened from such pernicious courses, if they well knew what have been the effects of them heretofore.

VIII. And it is not unuseful to Princes and Magistrates to see what hath corrupted and disturbed the Churches in former times : and what cause they have to keep the secular power from the Clergies hands, and to value those that for knowledge and piety are meet for their proper guiding office, and use of the Church Keys: but not to corrupt them by ex-

cess

The PREFACE.

cess of worldly wealth and power, nor to permit them by striving, who shall seem GREATEST, WISEST and BEST, to become the incendiaries of the Church and world, and the persecutors of the best that cannot serve their worldliness and pride.

The Reader must Note, 1. That though much of the History be taken from others, the Councils are named and numbred according to Binnius and Crabbe: 2. And that because so much evil is necessarily recited, I thought it needful in the beginning and end to annex a defence of the Pastors and their office and work, lest any should be tempted to think hardly of Religion and the Church for mens abuses. 3. And if Micrelius, Gutlerbeth, Phili Pareus, Funcius, Carion, Melancthon, Buchotzer, Scultetus, Pezelius, Helvicus, or any other that I have seen, had answered the ends which I here intend, I should have gladly saved my self this labour and have refer'd the reader to them.

The Councils are now published voluminously, and many young students want money and time to read them at large. To such this abridgement may not be unuseful; especially to men that have mistaken the case of the great heresies and hereticators, and would know what Prelacy and Councils have done to the concord or discord of the Churches. The Description of the State of Alexandria recited in the beginning as a Letter from a friend, was from Mr. Clerkson a Learned and worthy Minister (though silenced) now in London.

The Lord pardon and heal our common faultiness, and give better Teachers to his Churches when we are dead and gone, who will take warning by all our errours and miscarriages, especially to escape a worldly spirit, pride, Church-tyranny and schism, and serving the world, the flesh and the Devil, by pretence of Authority from Christ. Amen.

March 31. 1680.
London.

What History is Credible, and what not.

AS the Holy Ghost saith, *Believe not every spirit*; I may say, Believe not all Reports, or History. It was not only *Ahabs* Prophets, in whose mouths Satan was a *lying spirit*: As *lying* and *deceiving* is his work in the world, for the destroying of *Holiness*, and of *Souls*, even when he turneth himself into an Angel of Light; so is it the work of his Ministers, when they seem to be Ministers of Righteousness; when it is oft said (*Be not deceived*) and [*Let no man deceive you with vain words*;] it is more necessary advise, and hardlier followed, than most men understand. As *Truth* is Gods means to work the will to *holy love*, and lead us in a *holy life*, so *Lying* is the Devils means to oppose them: and of all Lyars, none are more pernicious than *lying Historians*, and *lying Preachers*. It is a sad *perplexity* to the world, that when men *read* and *hear*, even the more confident and plausible Histories and Reports, they know not whether they are true or false; and if they believe that to be true which is not, the effect is worse than this *perplexity*. I will tell you what I take to be credible, and what not.

I. It is presupposed that a man must believe his senses, if sound, about their proper objects: Papists that tell us that all mens senses are deceived, when they seem to perceive *Bread* and *Wine* in the Sacrament, do but tell us that no man then is to be believed, and therefore not they themselves.

II. The History of the Gospel is certainly credible, because it was confirmed by multitudes of uncontrouled Miracles wrought by Christ, and by his Apostles, and multitudes of Christians; as the Doctrine it self beareth the Image and Superscription of God.

III. The Prophets that had Divine Inspiration and Vision, had that Evidence which gave themselves a certainty, though not to others.

IV. When History delivereth a matter of fact and sense, by the common consent of all men that knew it, though of contrary minds, dispositions, and interests, it giveth us a certainty which may be called Natural; because Nature hath nothing in it that could cause such a Conspiracy in Lying: That it is so credible as to be a *Natural certainty*, that there is such a place as *Rome*, *Paris*, *Jerusalem*; that the Statutes of the Land are not Forgeries, while all Contenders plead them against each other, and hold by them their Estates and Lives: And so that there was such a Person as Jesus Christ, and that the Scriptures were written by the Prophets and Apostles, &c.

V. When the History of any person and action is proved by continued or visible effects: as that *William* of *Normandy* conquered *England*, while so many of the effects of that Conquest in our Laws and Customs are still visible: And that the *Welsh* were the Ancient *Britains*, driven by the *Saxons* into *Wales*, while their Language, Habitation, &c. shew it: And so that Christ instituted Baptism, and Church-Communion, and the Apostles separated

parated the Lords Day for holy worship, when the Christian World hath used all these publickly in all places ever since, and do still use them: And so that Temples were built for holy worship, and endowed, when we still see and possess them.

VI. That History is credible which consentingly speaketh against the known interest of the Author; for mans corrupt nature is apter to fall, boasting, than to false Confessions of Sin; against a Confessor there needs no Witnesses: And this is much of the credibility of the harsher part of the Church-History which I here recite: What I say of the miscarriages of Bishops and Councils, is mostly in their own words; and what I say against Popes, is but the recital of what is said by the greatest Defenders or Flatterers of Popes: I give you no Reports against the pride, contentions and corruptions of Patriarchs and Prelates, out of the supposed Hereticks, or Protestants; I give you not a word out of *Luther* (who *de Conciliis*) hath very much; and especially speaketh much like as I here do of *Cyril* and *Nestorius*; nor out of *Illyricus* his *Catalogus Testium Veritatis*, nor out of the *Magdeburgenses*, *Osiander*, *Sleidan*, *Carion*, *Melancthon*, *Mornay*'s *Mystery of Iniquity*, no nor out of the Collections of *Goldastus*, *Marquardus*, *Freherus*, *Ruberus*, *Pistorius*, &c. But the substance of the common History is taken out of the commonly received Church-Historians (*Eusebius*, *Socrates*, *Sozomene*, *Cassiodorus*, *Theodorite*, *Ruffinus*, *Evagrius*, *Nazianzen*, *Hierom*, *Victor*, *Nicephorus*, *Liberatus*, *Nicetas*, and such others; and the sum of the Councils and Popes is out of *Baronius*, *Anastasius*, but most out of *Binnius*, and *Platina*, and *Æneas Sylvius* (a Pope,) *Petavius*, and such other as are the greatest Papal Zealots: When these speak *for their Cause*, I leave you to just *suspition*; but when they speak *against it*, by way of confession or lamentation, they are not to be suspected.

VII. The next degree of credibility dependeth on the Veracity or credible fitness of the Reporter; some men are much more credible than others: For instance.

1. One that was *upon the place*, and *saw* what was done, or lived near, where he had full information, is (*ceteris paribus*) more credible than one that followeth uncertain reports, or hear-say.

2. A wise man is much more credible than a proud self-conceited Confident Fool.

3. One that hath made a matter his long and hard study, is (*ceteris paribus*) more to be believed in that matter, than many ignorant men.

4. One that is impartial, a lover of peace, and not ingaged by faction or interest to one side against the other, is *ceteris paribus* much more credible than a factious interested man.

5. A sober, calm, considerate man, that will stay and try before he judgeth, is more credible than a passionate or hasty judger.

6. A man of manifest honesty, conscience, and the fear of God, is much more to be believed than a worldly, wicked, bloody, unconscionable man.

7. *Ceteris*

7. *Cæteris Paribus* many agreed honest impartial men are more to be believed than one, or a few odd and singular persons, who have no more advantage than the rest to know the truth.

8. The young and unexperienced owe some Reverence to the judgment of their *Seniors*, as more credible by age and experience than their own.

9. Accordingly Children to their Parents, and Scholars to their Masters and Tutors owe such belief as is answerable to their difference, and the use of their learning of them.

By this you may see on the contrary who is not worthy of belief.

I. One that pretendeth Inspiration, Vision, Revelation, and giveth the hearer no sufficient proof of it.

II. One that pretendeth to tell you things beyond his reach; as many Philosophers do about the mysteries of Nature, spiritual and corporeal, Elements or mixt bodies, above and below, of which the Books of many are full, and malignant men, that take on them to tell you other *mens hearts*, without just proof, that they are hypocrites, and intend that which they never did, or meant ill, when they said or did well; and when false Historians will tell you with what (unproved) ill purposes or deceits, persons a thousand miles off, and perhaps a thousand years past, whom they never knew, did say and do all that is reported of them.

III. When there are but *few reporters* of things pretended to be *known publickly* in the world, especially when more *credible persons* contradict them.

IV. When the person is deeply ingaged in a Party, and carrying on all for the interest of his Party, doth give you but his word, or the report of his own Party for what he saith; so that you may perceive that interest byaffeth him to partiality.

V. When the Historian sheweth a malignant spirit, that extenuateth or denieth all the good that was in his Adversaries, and fasteneth on them as much *Odium* as he can without just proof, and justifieth all the reproach that is used against them.

VI. When the Historian liveth so far off from the place and time, that he is no competent reporter, having all his notice but by the fame of his own Faction, as uncapable as himself.

VII. When the sober moderate men of his own party contradict him, and speak well of the persons whom he reproacheth.

VIII. When the reporter is manifestly a proud, worldly, wicked, unconscionable man, especially of a bloody hurtful disposition: For as Gods threefold Influence, or the *Understanding*, *Will* and *Life* is but one, so the Devil doth usually vitiate together the *Understanding*, *Will* and *Life*; and he that is from the beginning an *Enemy*, and a *Murderer*, is also a *Lyar*: Though a *wicked, malignant*, and *cruel man*, may yet have an opinionative faith and knowledge, and preach the truth, when it is for his carnal interest; yet when his malice and interest tempteth him against it, there is no trusting his word.

a 2　　　　　　　　　　　　　　　　IX. When

IX. When an ignorant proud man thinketh that he muſt be believed meerly for the reverence and authority of his place.

X. When the reporter liveth in a time and place where carnal intereſt hath got the major Vote for falſhood, and it paſſeth commonly for truth, eſpecially where Tyranny, Civil or Eccleſiaſtical, ſilenceth the truth in Preſs, Pulpit, and Diſcourſe, that it dare not be ſpoken; by which the Papiſts have not only made their own writings and reports incredible, but by their *Indices Expurgatorios*, and baſe corrupting of ancient Writers, have weakned our certainty of much of the old Hiſtory and Fathers.

XI. When the reporter is a weak and ſilly man, that hath not wit to ſift out the truth.

XII. When he is paſſionately raſh, and of haſty judgment, and hath not patience to ſtay and ſuſpend his judgment till he hear all.

XIII. When it is a Novice or raw Student, that hath not had time, helps and experience to know what he pretends to know, and yet contradicteth wiſer men of more advantage and experience.

XIV. When preſent experience telleth us, that the party that he writeth againſt as unlearned or wicked, are men of Eminent Learning, and the fear of God; and that the party that he magnifieth as ſuch, are contrary; by ſuch marks incredible Hiſtory may be diſcerned.

Qu. *But how can we know mens wiſdome, and piety, and honeſty, and impartiality, when we never knew the men?* Anſ. Though hypocrites may much counterfeit truth and goodneſs, its hard ſo to do it, but the contrary which ruleth in them will break out, as a ſtink will get through narrow paſſages: and though truth and honeſty may be much clouded, they have, like light, a ſelf-revealing power.

To give you ſome inſtances; as among Phyſitians *Hypocrates*, and *Galen*, and *Celſus* of old; and of late *Montanus*, *Crato Fernelius*, *Platerus*, *Hildaſius*, and ſuch others, do ſpeak with that ſelf-evidencing honeſty, and many *Paracelſians* with that palpable vanity, that one of them will conſtrain belief, and the other unbelief, even in them that never heard what they were: So among Hiſtorians, *Euſebius*, though counted an *Arrian*, and *Socrates*, and *Sozomen*, though called *Novatians*, and *Theodoret*, and *Liberatus*, and ſome others, do write ſo as to conſtrain belief of things which were within their notice, and with honeſt impartiality: Among the Papiſts, what clear footſteps of underſtanding, honeſty, and impartiality, and ſo of truth, is there in *Thuanus*, and much in *Comines*, *Guicciardine*, Father *Paulus Servita* Hiſt. of *Trent* Council, and divers others: Though Doctor *James* bid us keep *Crab*, becauſe the later Councils are corrupt, and all of them muſt be taken with due Antidotes, yet becauſe moſt of the matter is fetcht from publick Acts and Records, they are more credible than moſt ſingle Hiſtory; *Acoſta* ſpeaketh impartially of the *Weſt Indies*, and *Godignus* of the *Abaſſians*, *Matth. Paris* of *England*, and the Pope, and ſo of ſome others: Of Proteſtants, ſome do but recite recorded teſtimonies, or publick acts; and the very writings themſelves of the times they ſpeak of, when others do but
tell

tell you ſtories on their bare word: *Goldaſtus, Ruberus, Freherus* and *Piſtorius*, do but give us Collections of the writings of thoſe former Ages, and nothing of their own: So doth Mr. *Ruſhworth* now in his three Volumes of Collections; and Mr. *Fuller* hath partly done ſo, and writeth moderately; Mr. *Gilbert Burnet* thus writeth the Hiſtory of the Reformation, laying not the credit on his word, but on his Evidences; and *Cambden* impartially thus writeth of Queen *Elizabeth*, and in his *Brittania*: *Uſher* hath done the like, *de ſucceſ. Eccleſ.* of the *Waldenſes*; and in his *de Primordiis Eccl. Brit.* of the *Pelagians*, not *ſaying*, but *proving* by Records, and old Evidences, what he delivereth, beſides the advantage of his known extraordinary learning, honeſty, and impartiality; ſo doth *Fox* for the moſt part in his *Martyrology* give you but the publick Record, or proved Hiſtories (though *Cope* call him lyar) *Melancthon* and *Bucholtzer* were men of ſuch known ſincerity, as conſtraineth credit to their reports.

On the other ſide, who can believe ſuch palpable Railers as *Tympius, Cochleus, Genebrard*, and many ſuch, that lye contrary to certain evidence? ſuch as make the Vulgar believe, that *Luther* learnt his Religion of the Devil, and was killed by him; that *Oecolampadius* was kill'd by the Devil; and that *Bucer* had his guts pull'd out, and caſt about by the Devil; that *Calvin* was a ſtigmatized *Sodomite* and Senſualiſt; that *Beza* died a Papiſt (who lived long after to write a Confutation) and abundance ſuch, *Melchior Adam* gathereth his Hiſtory of Lives from the Pens of thoſe that moſt intimately knew the perſons, what able, holy, laborious, and excellent ſervants of God were *Calvin, Beza, Daneus, Knox*, and many ſuch, as deſcribed by *Adamus*, and in the judgment of thoſe that were their moſt knowing obſervers: But what vile rebellious wretches were they in the judgment of Doctor *Heylin*, and ſuch as he? what excellent perſons did God uſe for the beyond-ſea Reformation? even as in *France*; and *Holland*; *Jewel, Bilſon*, and other Biſhops, defend that which *Heylin* deſcribeth as the moſt odious Rebellions: He maketh the *Geneva* Presbyterians to do that againſt their Biſhop, which Dr. *Pet. Moulin* in his Anſwer to *Philanax Anglicus*, ſheweth was done before, while they were Papiſts. Some things in *Heylins* Hiſtory of the Reformation, and the Presbyterians, I believe, which he bringeth Records for; but upon his own word I can ſcarce believe any thing that he ſaith, ſo palpably partial is he, and of ſo malicious and bloody a ſtrain, repreſenting excellent perſons as odious intollerable Rogues, and the Reformation, even of the *Lutherans*, as too bad; but that in *France, Belgia, Frieſland*, the *Palatinate, Hungary, Tranſilvania, Scotland*, to be but a ſeries of the moſt odious Rebellions, Murders, and horrid Sacriledge; and ours in *England* to be much the Spawn of King *Henries* Luſt, and thinking King *Edward 6.* his death a ſeaſonable mercy; and odiouſly repreſenting ſuch excellent Biſhops as *Grindall, Abbot*, and *Uſher*, and ſuch excellent Divines as we ſent to *Dort, Davenant, Hall, Ward, Carlton*, &c. It pleaſeth the Prelatiſts to ſay tru of me, that I am no Presbyterian, and therefore ſpeak not for the perſons in partiality, as one of their party; but I muſt ſay, as in Gods

ſight,

fight, that in my own acquaintance, I have found that fort of men, whom Dr. *Heylin* and fuch other reproach as Presbyterians and Puritans, to be the moſt ſerious, conſcionable, practical, ſober, and charitable Chriſtians that ever I knew, yea verily the knowledge of them hath been a great help to the ſtedfaſtneſs of my Faith in Chriſt : Had I known no Chriſtians but carnal, worldly, and formal men, who excel not Heathens in any thing but Opinion, it would have tempted me to doubt whether Chriſt were the Saviour of Souls, as I ſhould think meanly of the Phyſitian that doth no cures: But when I ſee holy mortified perſons, living in the love of God and man, I ſee that Faith is not a dead fancy : And when I have lived in intimate familiarity with ſuch, from my Childhood, to the ſixty fifth year of my age, and known their integrity, notwithſtanding their infirmities; and then read ſuch Hiſtories as repreſent them as the moſt odious, flagitious perſons, I ſee it is not for nothing that ſome men are called Διάβολοι in the Scripture, and the *Children of their Father the Devil*, who was from the beginning a *lying malignant Murderer*.

Two Crimes I have long ago heard the Rabble charge on thoſe whom they called *Puritans*, *Lying* and *Covetouſneſs*; whereas near two thouſand Miniſters are caſt out, and ſuffer, which they could moſtly eſcape, if they durſt but lye; and if I ask money for the Poor (of what party ſoever) I can ſooner get a Pound from thoſe called *Puritans*, than a Shilling from others far richer than they. Can I take any men to be other than malignant lyars who would make men believe that ſuch men as *Hilderſham*, *Dod*, *Rogers*, *Ball*, *Paul Bayne*, *Ames*, *Bradſhaw*, &c. were Rogues and ſeditious Rebels, or that revile ſuch as *Uſher*, *Hall*, *Davenant*, &c. ? Reader, believe not a word of any of the revilings or odious characters and ſtories, which any aſpiring worldly factious Clergy man writeth of ſuch as are his Adverſaries: lying is their too common language ; yea, if they do but once ſet themſelves eagerly to ſeek Preferment, I will never truſt them, or take their words: It hath been ſo of old, the ſame man that was a Saint to his Acquaintance, hath been deſcribed as wicked, or a Devil by others: How bad were *Origen* and *Chryſoſtome* to *Theophilus*, *Alexand.* and *Epiphanius* ? And how bad was *Theophilus* to the Hiſtorians that write his actions? How excellent a perſon was *Cyril Alex.* to the Council of *Calcedon*, and how bad a man was he to *Theodoret*, *Iſidore*, *Peluſ.* &c. *Ignatius Conſt.* was a Saint to *Nicetas*, and many others, and to *Photius* he was an *Antichriſt*, and *wicked limb of the Devil*: *Photius* was a *holy man* to his Party, and a *wicked wretch* to *Nicetas*, and others: Yea, ſee the credit of worldly Prelates; the ſame Biſhops one year cry down *Ignatius* as a *wicked man*, and call *Photius* a *holy perſon*, and the next year, or ſhortly after, cry down *Photius* for a *Rogue*, and cry up *Ignatius*; yea, and upon the next turn cry up *holy Photius* whom they had anathematized : Theſe doings were familiar with carnal Prelates.

But as Gods Spirit in his ſervants is ſo ſuited to the Doctrine of the ſame Spirit, that they reliſh it where they find it ; ſo their piety and honeſty is ſuch a ſelf-evidencing thing, that pious and honeſt men that knew them, cannot believe their lying ſlanderers.   And

And when Satan hath done his worst, the very *writings* of such men as *Calvin, Beza, Melancthon, Perkins, Hildersham, Ames, Dod, Burges, Gataker, Usher, Davenant, Hall, &c.* will not suffer men to believe their odious revilers: Even among Papists, when I read the works of *Bernard, Gerson, Kempis, Thaulerus, Sales,* and the Lives of *Nerius, Renti, &c.* I cannot believe him that would tell me they were *wicked men* though *faulty*: And the Lives written by *Adam, Clerk, Fuller, &c.* shall be believed before Calumniators.

Alas, how little are most Histories to be believed, where they prove not what they say; there are about sixty that say there was a Pope *Joan*, and near as many that say no such thing. *Hildebrand* to one half of the Bishops was the *holy Restorer of the Church*, to the other half the *vilest Rebel*. We are not agreed here in *London* who *burnt the City* in 1666. nor what *parties began the late War*, nor what *party brought the King to death*, while we are alive that saw these publick facts: Not only Lads that knew it not, but *Heylin* (the great Reproacher of the Reformers) would make men believe that it was *Presbyterians* in *England* that began the strife and War, when yet he had himself laid so much of it on Archbishops, and Bishops, and on the Parliaments complaints of Popery, Arminianism, and Arbitrary Illegalities; and after saith (Hist. Presb. p. 465. 470.) *The truth is, that as the English generally were not willing to receive that yoak; so neither did the Houses really intend to impose it on them, though for a while to hold fair quarter with the Scots, they seemed forward in it.* This appears by their Declaration of April 1646 --- Nor have they lived to see their dear Presbytery setled, or their Lay-Elders entertained in any one Parish of the Kingdome (that's false on the other side) and yet in must be done by this Parliment, as *Presbyterians, four years before*, when they were *Episcopal*, distasting only the persons and actions of Bishop *Laud, Wren*, and some other present Bishops.

If I find a man like *Schluffelburgius*, fall Pell-mell with reproach on all that differ from him, or Dr. *Heylin*, speak of blood with pleasure, and as thirsty after more (as of *Thacker, Udall, &c.*) or as designing to make Dissenters odious, as he and most of the Papists Historians do, (as the Image of both Churches, *Philanax Anglicus*, the Historical Collections out of *Heylin*) I will believe none of these revilers, further than they give me Cogent proof.

I hear of a *Scots* Narrative of the *Treasons, Fornications, Witchcrafts,* and other wickedness of some of the *Scottish* Presbyterians; and as *for me*, the *Author knoweth not what to call me, unless it be a Baxterian, as intending to be a Hæresiarcha, being neither Papist, nor of the Church* of *England, nor Presbyterian, nor Independent*, &c.

To this I say, I have no acquaintance with any *Scots* Minister, nor ever had in my life, except with Bishop *Sharp* that was murdered, and two other Bishops (and two or three that live here in *London*) therefore what they are I know not, save by Fame: But though I have heard that Country asperst, as too much inclin'd to Fornication, I never before heard the

Religious

Religious part and Ministers so accused: Either it is *true*, or *false*; if *false*, shame be to the *reporters*; if *true*, what doth it concern us here, or any that are innocent, any further than to abhor it, and lament it, and to be thankful to God that it is another sort of men that are called *Puritans* in *England*; and that in all *my acquaintance with them these* 56 *years (which hath been with very many in many Countries)* I remember not that ever I heard of one Puritan, *man or woman, save one, accused or suspected of fornication*; and that one yet living, though openly penitent, hath lived disowned and shamed to this day; but I have heard of multitudes that revile them, that make a jest and common practice of it: Try whether you can make the Inhabitants of this City believe, that the Nonconformists or Puritans are fornicators, drunkards, or perjured, and that their accusers and haters are innocent men that hate them for such Crimes! But its possible that you may make men of other Countries or Ages believe it, and believe that we wear Horns, and have Cloven Feet, and what you will; but I fear not all your art or advantages on those that are acquainted with both sides: But the misery is, that faction ingageth men to associate only with their party where they hear reproaches of the unknown dissenters, from whom they so estrange themselves, that the Neighbours near them are as much unknown to them, save by lying fame, as if they lived an hundred miles from them. I remember Mr. *Cressey* once wrote to me, that *he turned from the Protestant Religion to the Roman, because there was among us no spiritual Books of Devotion for Soul Elevations, and affectionate Contemplation:* And I told him it was Gods just Judgment on him, that lived so strange to his Neighbours, because they are called *Puritans*, and to their Writings, which Shops and Libraries abound with; had he read Bishop *Halls*, Mr. *Greenhams*, Mr. *Ri. Rogers*, Mr. *Jo. Rogers*, Mr. *Hildershams*, Mr. *Boltons*, Mr. *Perkins*, Mr. *Downhams*, Mr. *Reyners*, Dr. *Sibbes*, &c. yea or no better than my own (*the Saints Rest, the Life of Faith, the Divine Life, the Christian Directory,* &c.) or had he read the Lives of Divines called Puritans (or but such as two young men (published partly by my self) *Joseph Allen*, and *John Janeway*) he would never have gone from the Protestants to the Papists, because of our formality and want of an affectionate spiritual sort of devotion, especially knowing what excess of formality is among the Papists, and how much it is of the Clergies accusation of the Puritans, that they are for too little form, and too much pretence of spiritual devotion.

But if any called Religious, or Puritans, or Presbyterians be vicious, I know no men that so heartily desire their punishment and ejection, as those that are called by the same names: I thank God that these twenty years, while neither *Wit, Will*, nor *Power* hath been wanting against them, I have scarce heard of two men (if one) that have been judged and proved guilty of any such immorality, of all the ejected silenced Ministers in this Land: I would I could say so of their Adversaries.

II. And now I must speak to the Accusers speeches of my self; I thank you Sir that you feigned no worse against me; if I am an *Heresiarcha*, why would

would not you vouchsafe to name that Heresie which I have owned: I have given you large Field-room, in near 80 Books; and few men can so write, as that a willing man may not find some words which he is able to call Heresie: A little learning, wit, or honesty, will serve for such an hereticating presumption. 2. I never heard that *Arminius* was called an *Arminian*, nor *Luther* a *Lutheran*, nor Bishop *Laud* a *Laudian*; but if you be upon the knack of making Names, you best know your ends, and best know how to fit them to it. 3. But seriously, do you not know my Judgment? will not about 80 Books inform you? how then can I help it? 4. No, but you know not what Party I am of, nor what to call me; I am sorrier for you in this than for my self; if you know not, I will tell you, I am a CHRISTIAN, a MEER CHRISTIAN, of no other Religion; and the Church that I am of is the Christian Church, and hath been visible wherever the Christian Religion and Church hath been visible: But must you know what Sect or Party I am of? I am against all Sects and dividing Parties: But if any will call *Meer Christians* by the name of a *Party*, because they take up with *meer Christianity, Creed*, and *Scripture*, and will not be of any dividing or contentious Sect, I am of that Party which is so against Parties: If the Name CHRISTIAN be not enough, call me a CATHOLICK CHRISTIAN; not as that word signifieth an hereticating majority of Bishops, but as it signifieth one that hath no Religion, but that which by Christ and the Apostles was left to the Catholick Church, or the Body of Jesus Christ on Earth.

And now Sir, I am sorry that you are not content with meer Christianity, and to be a Member of the Catholick Church, and hold the Communion of Saints, but that you must needs also be of a Sect, and have some other Name: And how shall I know that your Sect is better than another? Were not the Papists Sectaries and Schismaticks, damning most of Christs Body on Earth, for not being subject to their Pope, I should not be so much against them. I find promises of Salvation in Scriptures to Believers, that is, Christians as such (if such sincerely,) but none of the salvation of men as *Papists, Diocesans, Grecians, Nestorians, Eutychians*, &c. I would say also [*nor as Protestants*] did I not take the Religion called *Protestant* (a Name which I am not fond of) to be nothing but *simple Christianity*, with opposition to Popery, and other such corruption. And now you know your own designs, your tongue is your own, and who can controul you, whatever you will call us; but I, and such others, call our selves MEER CHRISTIANS, or CATHOLICK CHRISTIANS, against all Sects and Sectarian names, and haters both of true *Heresie, Schisme*, and *proud, unrighteous, hereticating* and *Anathematizing*. Psal. 4. *O ye sons of men, how long will ye turn my glory into shame? how long will ye love vanity, and seek after lying? But know that the Lord hath set apart him that is godly for himself:* Psal. 12. 1, 2, 3, 4, 5. *Help Lord, for the godly man ceaseth; for the faithful fail from among the children of men: They speak vanity every one with his Neighbour*, &c. See the rest.

b   I will

I will add, that if to be serious in the belief of the Christian Faith, and the Life to come, and in seeking it above this world, and in constant endeavours to please God, whoever be displeased by it, is it that maketh a man a *Puritan*, because he is not a *formal Hypocrite*; then I would I were worthy of the Titles which your *Pseudo Tilenus* and his Brother give me, who say, I am *Purus Putus Puritanus*, and one *qui totum Puritanismum totus spirat*: Alas I am not so good and happy. But Readers, when this sort of men have described the Puritans as the most intollerable Villains, you that knew them not may conclude, that they were men no more erroneous, or worse than I, how much better soever; for Bishop *Morley* saith of me, *Ab uno disce omnes*: And of my Doctrine, I have left the world a full account; and must shortly be accountable for it and my life to God, whose pardon and grace through Christ I daily beg and trust to.

A Notice concerning Mr. *Henry Dodwell*.

MR. *Dodwell* having written a copious Discourse, asserting, that we have no right to salvation, but by Gods Covenant validly sealed by the Sacrament; and that the Sacrament is not valid, unless delivered by one that hath Ordination by such a Bishop as hath his Ordination by another Bishop, and so on by an uninterrupted succession from the Apostles, with much more such Schismatical stuff, which I fully confuted in my Books called, [*The true and only terms of the Concord of all the Christian Churches*] and I aggravated his Schismatical condemnation of the Reformed Churches, and most others (as having no true *Ministry, Sacraments, nor Covenant-title to salvation*, and as sinning against the Holy Ghost, because *he professeth himself a Protestant*: The said Mr. *Dodwell* saith, that these words would perswade men that I take him for a *Papist*, and expecteth that I therein right him: Be it therefore known to all men, that I never meant by that word to accuse Mr. *Dodwell* of being a *Papist*, but to aggravate his abuse of Protestants; and that I take my self bound to charge no man to be of a Religion which he *denieth*: And what his Religion really is, his Books may best inform him that would know.

THE

THE CONTENTS

Chap. 1. What Order and Government Christ and his Spirit settled in the Churches; and what was the appointed work of Bishops. That particular Churches, that had every one a Bishop, were associated for personal Communion of neighbours: That none on earth for about two hundred years, and none but Rome and Alexandria for longer time, can be proved to be more numerous than our greater Parishes, no nor half so big. The Case even of Rome and Alexandria examined, and the like proved even of them against the contrary arguments. How the change was made; and what change it is. How Prelacy became the diseasing tumour of the Church. Many Reasons against an ill use of the History of Councils and Prelates usurpations; that no man thence dishonour Christ, Christianity, the Ministry or Church.

Chap. 2. Of Heresies: What Errors are not damning, and what are. How the most Erroneous come to cry out against Errors: Instanced in all wicked Men, and in Papists, Arrians, Nestorius, Dioscorus, &c. What horrid Work blind Zeal against Error hath made, many instances, even good Men, as Hillary and Popes and Councils. The History of all the Councils begun. The first Councils about Easter contrary to each other. The second being at Carthage erroneous, and Tertullian, Novatus and Novatian. The Roman Presbiters govern the Church and call a Council, having no Bishop, and are said by Binius to have the care of the universal Church. Cyprians Council condemneth a dead man Victor, for making Faustinus a Presbiter, Guardian of his Sons, and so entangling him in worldly business. The Council Iconiense is said to erre, and all those Oriental Bishops excommunicated by the Pope (about Hereticks Baptism). Many other Councils for rebaptizing, with Cyprian's pleading Tradition. Bishops of Bishops there censured. Cyprian's Concession. A sad Hereticating Council at Cirta against Traditions. The Concilium Eliber Novatiani: And against Images in Churches,&c. approved by

Pope Innocent. *The beginning of the Donatists Schism for a Bishop:* Constantines *reproof of* Alexander *and* Arius *silencing their disputes.* Concil. Laodic. Silvesters *strange Roman Council.*
Chap. 3. *The Council of* Nice: Constantine *keepeth them in peace. The strange Schism between* Peter Alex. *and* Meletius: *Two Bishops and Churches in the same Cities. The sad story of* Alexanders *troubling the Meletians, and driving them to seek help of the Arrians, and so to strengthen them.* Epiphanius *good character of* Constantius *and* Valens. *His notable Character of* Audius, *and how the violence of dissolute Bishops forced him to separate; and of* Alexander *and of* Crescentius's *strife: and of some Confessours and Martyrs great faults.* Audius *banished converteth the* Gothes. *The Slander of* Eustathius Antioch. *Notes of the* Nicene *decrees: The ordination of scandalous uncapable men nullified by them.* Concil. Rom. *the people united at the making of Bishops and Priests.* Arius's *Creed and restoration at a Council.* Jerusal. Marcel. Ancyr. *Condemned at* Const. *as denying Christs Godhead, by the Arrians whom he was for the same cause against. A* Concil. Antioch. *deposed* Athanasius *and made Canons for Conformity.* Anno 344 *a fourth Creed reconciling at* Antioch: *The General Council of* Sardica *divide: The Oriental Bishops at* Philippolis *strange charge against* Athanasius, Paulus Const. &c. *and their plea for peace. The* Donatists *unjust justice. The slander and fall of Bishop* Euphratas. Anno 355 *a General Council at* Milan *where the Arrians prevail.* Hilary *banished by the Semiarian Bishops as a separatist. The Council of* Sirmium *curse* Arius, Photinians, *and condemn* Athanasius, *pretending to reconcile.* Constantius *labours union: The General Council divided at* Ariminum *and* Seleucia: *The* Arians, Orthodox, *and* Reconcilers *fall into more Sects: Ten creeds, sometimes one, sometimes another liked or condemned: The Bishops deposing and damning each other. Of* Meletius Antiochenus, *the dissention, danger and reconciliation about* hypostasis & persona, *at a Council of* Alexandria. Julian. Jovian *for peace:* Valentinian *and* Valens *charge the Asian Bishops to giveover persecuting any of Christs Labourers.* Valens *a zealous Arrian Persecutor.* Damasus *bloody Election against* Sisinnius. *The Schism at* Antioch *how ended.*
Chap. 4. *Why* Rome *was yet Orthodox.* § 1. Valens *persecution.* § 2. Gratian *and* Valentinian Junior, Theodosius. *The Council at* Constance. § 4. Greg. Nazianzens *case.* § 5. *His sad description of the Councils and madness of the Prelates of his time.* § 7. 8. *The case of* Antiochs Schism *again.* Nectarius *a Bishop and Patri-*
ark

ark before he was a baptized Christian. § 10. *The Councils decrees.* § 11. *The History of the Bishops that prosecuted the Priscillianists, and* St. Martins. § 18. 19. *A Council at* Capua *decreed that the two Bishops and Churches at* Antioch *live in love and peace.* § 20. *Bishop* Bonosus *heresie denying* Mary's *perpetual virginity.* § 21. Jovinians *heresie described.* § 23. *A wise Novatian Council.* § 24. Carthage *good Councils.* § 31. 32, 33, 34. *The History of* Melania, *and the Bishops persecution of the friends of* Origene. § 36. &c. Theophilus Alex. *story.* § 37. 38. 39. *Chrysostomes History.* § 40. *And the* Joannites. § 42. *Those that believe the Astrologers and Mathematicians cursed at* Tolet. § 47. *The* Melivitane *Councils against Appeals to* Rome, *and of Liturgies to be approved.* § 55. Pelagius *and* Celestius *absolved by one Council and one Pope and condemned by others,* § 53. &c. Pelagius *Confession,* 57. Boniface *and* Eulalius *schism at* Rome, § 59. P. Boniface's *decree that no Bishop be brought or set before any Civil or Military Judge,* § 60. *The sixth Council of* Carthage *that resisted the Popes,* § 61. P. Celestines *decree, that no Bishop be given to the unwilling.*

Chap. 5. Atticus Const. *peaceableness: The pretty story of the people deposing* Theodosius *Bishop of* Synada, § 2. Cyrils *violence; the Monks assault of* Orestes, *and the peoples cruel usage of* Hypatia, § 3. Alexand. Antioch. *and* Atticus Const. *by his Council are for restoring the Non-conformists* Joannites: Cyrils *reason against it,* § 4. *Whether* Cyril *repented,* § 5. Isidore Pelus. *words of him.* § 6. Proclus *refused Bishop at* Cyzicum *by the people,* § 7. Nestorius *chosen,* § 8. *He is a persecuter of Hereticks. His opinion* § 9. *The first* Ephes. *Council,* § 10. *They divide and condemn and depose each other and fight, and* Nestorius, Cyril *and* Menmon, *are deposed by the Emperours Command, but the two last restored. Whether* Nestorius *or* Cyril *was the Heretick, The issue of that Council,* § 12. 13. 14. Derodon *prooves that* Cyril *was an* Eutychian *and* Nestorius *Orthodox,* § 18. 19. *The truth,* § 20. *The present Churches of the* Nestorians. *That these Bishops set the world on fire about a word while they agreed in sense,* § 20. 21, &c. *The Emperour forceth the Bishops to Communion, and setteth* Simeon Stillettes *to pray down their horrid discord,* § 23. *Bowing Eastward forbidden, because the* Manichees *bowed to the Sun among them,* § 29. Leo's *Roman Council of Bishops, Priests, and Lay-men: Another against* Hilary Arelatenlis, § 31. 32.

Chap. 6. *Of the* Eutychians, &c. *The true case of the Controversie,* § 2.

The Contents.

Unity taken by one side for undivided, *and by the other for* undistinguished, *and so the world set again on fire:* The Constantinople Council *about* Eutychius, § 5. *Another* Constantinople Council *contrarily cleareth him*, § 8. Ibas *cleared at Council* Beryt, § 7. *The second Ephesine Council, under* Dioscorus. *Eutyches justified there.* Flavianus, Euseb. Dor. Ibas *and* Theodorite *condemned and deposed. All the Patriarks else and Bishops subscribe, save the Popes Legates.* Flavianus *hurt and dieth*, § 9. Leo *in a Roman Council condemneth this*, Eph. 2. § 10. Dioscorus *in a Synod at* Alexandr. *excommunicateth* Leo, § 11. *Theodosius virtue and miraculous Victory*, § 15. *His praise of the second* Eph. *Council*, § 16. Martians *reign, and the Council of* Calcedon, § 14. 17. *Turnings, mutual condemnings, recantings and rigor there*, § 17. 18, 19. *The cry of the Egyptian Bishops*, § 24. *The Abbots protestation to cleave only to the* Nicene Creed *(as* Pioscorus *did to the Nicene Council and* Eph. 1.) *and not to subscribe* Leo's *Epistle, and to contemn excommunications*, § 25. Dioscorus *not condemned for heresie*, *saith* Anatolius, § 26. Theodorites *usage by the Bishops*, § 27. *The Canon equalling* Const. *and* Rome, § 30. *The doleful issue of this Council*, § 31. *The woful work at* Alexandria. *The murder of* Proterius, § 33. 34. *The bloody Tragedy against the* Calcedon *Council and* Juvenal *(as betrayers of the Nicene Faith) by the Monks at* Jerusalem, § 36. Eudocia *and* Pulcheria *the Spring of all.* Leo *is Emperour, and for the Council of* Calcedon. *He desposeth* Timothy Ælurus *at* Alexandria, Peter Gnapheus *usurpeth* Martyrius *Seat at* Antioch: Martyrius *renounceth his rebellious clergy and people.* Gnapheus *banished by* Leo. Stephen *that is for the Council, is put in: The boyes kill him with sharp Quills, and cast him into the River*, § 37. Zeno *Emperour*, Basiliscus *usurping commandeth the Bishops to renounce the Council of* Calcedon. *Three Patriarks and five Hundred Bishops subscribe against it (before most were for it)* Basiliscus *changing his mind commandeth that the Council be owned. The Bishops obeyed this*, § 38. Zeno *restored, and being for the Council, the Asian Bishops said they subscribed to* Basilicus *first Orders for fear and asked pardon.* Zeno *by his* Henoticon *silenceth the controversie, leaving it free to all to own or disown the Council. The Bishops and people are still worse, at* Alexandria *and* Antioch, *&c.* Acacius Const. *and* Fælix. Rom *excommunicate each other*, § 39. Flavitas Const. *cheateth the Emperour that would have God by an Angel choose the Bishop*, § 40. *The Bishops of*. Alexandria *and* Antioch

tioch *successively curse the Council: And the Bishop of* Rome *and* Const. *curse them for it,* § 41. Anastatius *Emperour is for toleration: Three parties of Bishops there condemning each other in* East, West *and* Lybia, *some strict for the Council; some cursing it, and some for the* henoticon *or peace. He deposeth* Euphemius Const. *and would have deposed* Macedonius *that came next, but the people rose for him, and forced the Emperour to submit,* § 43. *Cruel bloodshed in* Antioch *of Monks and others,* § 44. Xenaias *an unchristened man made Bishop, forceth the Bishops to curse the Council,* § 45. Severus *at* Antioch *maketh men curse the Council: some Bishops repent and condemn* Severus, 45. *The Emperor against all blood for this Cause, and the Monks in* Palestine *for it,* § 45, 46. Helias *Bishop of* Jerusalem *and the Monkes resist the Emperours Souldiers, once and again,* § 46. Timothy Const. *on both sides,* § 46. Rome *under* Theodorick; *their Schism or two Popes with blood three years,* § 47. Anastatius *wearied with the Orthodox rebellions, offereth to resign his Crown: In remorse they desire his continuance,* § 48. Valentinian *maketh a Law, that Bishops (except chosen by both Parties) shall no more be Judges in any Causes, save of Faith and Religion.* Binius *reproacheth this, as being absurd, that the Sheep judge the Shepheard,* § 49. *Fully confuted. The Pope excommunicateth* Acacius Const. *with a* [nunquam Anathematis vinculis exuendus] § 58. Leo Rom. *his Decree against the* Manichees, *and all other that take the Bread without the Cup,* § 60. Gelasius: *The Popes Separatists, condemn* Euphemius *and* Acacius. Gelasius *saith any Bishop may excommunicate an Heretick Bishop (though a Patriarch) his Catalogue of Apocrypha, and canonizing* Leo's *Epistle,* § 62. *The Pope excommunicateth the Greek Emperour and Patriarch of* Constantinople, *but not King* Theodorick *the Arrian at home,* § 64. *Ordination resolved on against the Kings commands* § 65. *Council* Agath. *decreeth that if a Bishop excommunicate any wrongfully, another Bishop may receive him, &c. That if any Citizen on the dayes of great solemnity refuse to meet where the Bishop is, he is three years denied Communion (which sheweth, that the Bishops Church was no greater than our Parishes.) Lay-murderers punished with denying them the Communion, and Deacons put in Monasteries, &c.* § 67. *Council* Apannens *saith* Hereticks *Temples cannot be purged nor applied after to Holiness,* § 68. *Council* Sydon. *curse the* Calcedon *Council,* 69. *Bishops*

having

The Contents.

having the third (or fourth) part of all Church profits sheweth how big their Dioceſs or Churches then were § 72. Council Gerund of ſeven Biſhops ordered Litanies, and that the Metropolitanes Liturgy be uſed in other Churches § 73. Juſtine the Emperour againſt Eutychians reſtoreth the names of Euphemius and Acacius againſt the Pope, their Caſe opened § 75. Juſtine an Orthodox murderer. Antioch caſt down by an Earthquake, the Biſhop killed, the reſt burnt by the lightning, § 76. Euphremius the Lieutenant relieving the People is choſen their Biſhop. The Biſhops turn to the Council of Calcedon again, under Juſtine, § 77. &c. Popes proſecute the dead Biſhops of Conſtantinople. § 79. Juſtine violent againſt Arrians. Theodorick maketh Pope John go beg for them, leaſt Italy ſuffered as much: He killeth Symmachus and Boetius, impriſoneth John and maketh Felix Pope, § 80. Clergy murderers ſuſpended from the Sacrament, &c. § 81. Theodorick ſubjecteth the Clergy to Civil Judicature. Athalaricus freeth them again § 85. Juſtinian his Laws, he is againſt the Entychians, and his Wife for them, § 87, 88. Thirty thouſand kill'd by inſurrection in Conſtantinople, § 89. The miraculous ſpeaking of Preachers, when their Tongues were cut out by the Kings command, § 90. King Theodorus a lover of Books giveth up Rome, § 91. In Juſtinians time three Countries converted: The Perſians prevail: A dreadful Plague, § 92. Pope Boniface choſen by the Arrian Athalaricus, § 96. Pope Hormiſda denying that [one of the Trinity was crucified] Juſtinian ſending to Pope John who ſaid the contrary; Binius excuſe is [Weapons muſt be changed with changed enemies.] Many Notes on the excellent diſputation of Hypatius with the Eutychians cauſed by Juſtinian, opening fully Cyrils weakneſs, and that the difference was but verbal, § 99. A Council at Conſtantinople under Menna called him Patriarcha Oecumenicus, and ſet Leo after the before curſed Biſhops. Macedonius the Orthodox Biſhop put out, the People that were Orthodox ſeperate, § 103. Silverius made Pope by an Arrian, P. Vigilius the Antipope impriſoneth and famiſheth him, § 105. The Schiſm between two Biſhops and their Parties in Alexandria; one for the corruptibility of Chriſts body called Corrupticolæ; the other for the incorruptibility called the Phantaſiaſtæ; and the bloody fight between them, § 107. Paulus Alexand: Murder of a Deacon, § 108. P. Vigilius denieth two natures, § 109. P. Vigilius excommunicateth Menna, and is dragg'd with a Rope, till he repented, 110. Juſtinian called a Heretick and damned by Evagrius, § 111.

Chap.

The Contents.

CHAP. 7. *Of the Controverſie* de tribusCapitulis, *& the fifth General Council,* &c. *of the hereſie of the* Apthardocitæ, *& Juſtinians piety and hereſie; & the Biſhops appeal to* Anaſtaſius Antioch. §. 1, 2. *The converſion of the* Auxumites. Juſtinian's *puniſhing the Sodomitical Hereſie of ſome Biſhops.* §. 3. *The People dye rather than eat Fleſh in* Lent. *The Council at* Orleance *Decree that* Qui omnibus præponendus eſt ab omnibus eligatur: *Of Inceſt, Too ſtrict keeping the Lords-Day.* §. 4. Concil. Avernenſ. *Decree that men ſeek to be Biſhops by Merits, and not by Votes or Favour, yet be choſen by all.* §. 6. *All Citizen Chriſtians to be in the Biſhops Meeting at* Eaſter, &c. *by* Concil. Aurelian. §. 7. *And the Biſhop to be Ordained in that Church which he muſt overſee.* Theodor. Cæſar's *project to condemn the* tria Capitula (Theodor. Mopſueſt. Theodorite *and* Ibas:) Juſtinians *endeavours.* §. 9. *An* Orleance *Council decree that* King, Clergy *and* Laity *agree, and none be made Biſhop,* populo invito, *or forced to conſent, and that the Biſhop elſe be depoſed. The Biſhop to relieve all the Poor.* §. 12. *Null the former living. Its Emperours that call Councils, ſaith* Juſtinian. §. 13. *The fifth* Conſtant. *Council to cure the doleful ſeparations of the Biſhops* §. 13. P. Vigilius *difficulty: dare not joyn with the Council: Their ſlighting him: only two or three Weſtern Biſhops at the four firſt Generals Councils.* §. 15. Theod. Mopſ. *accuſed.* Theodorite *accuſed for ſaying that* Mary *begat not God in the nature of God, but Man as united to the God-head: that Chriſt was forſoken, ſuffered, hungred, ſlept,* &c. *as Man and not as God.* §. 17. Theodorites *virulent Ep. againſt dead* Cyril, *and the* Theopathitæ. §. 17. *The* tria Cap. *condemned* Vigilius's *ſober judgment of it.* §. 18, 19. *Inſtead of healing, this Council ſet all on fire, and* Juſtinian *on perſecution.* §. 21. Vigilius *changeth; and condemneth again the* tria Capitula. §. 22. Vigilius *is by* Binnius *called,* homo perditus, *the buyer of anothers place, a violent Invader, a Wolfe, a Thief, a Robber, not entring by the Dores, a falſe Biſhop, and* quaſi Antichriſtus, *that the lawful Paſtor yet living did add pernicious Hereſie to his Schiſm:* Tet ſanctiſſimus Papa *as ſoon as he had murdered his Predeceſſor, and had ſole poſſeſſion.* §. 24. *A* Jeruſalem *Council received the Conc.* Conſt. §. 25. *A Council at* Aquileia *condemn it, and the Weſtern Biſhops are ſeperated near* 100 *years from the Cath. Church (about the words of three dead men.)* §. 26. Juſtinian *made* Pelagius *Pope; two Biſhops & a Presbyter ordain him, the Weſtern Biſhops diſobey him & reject him, and ſo reject the Council* Conſt. V. *confirmed by a Pope: He gets* Narſes *to perſecute*

secute them. §. 28. *The* Romans *for this incline to the* Goths *again.* Justinians *Laws censured by* Binnius. §. 30. *A Council.* Parif. *confirmeth the free Election of Bishops by the People and Clerks.* §. 31. *All Hereticks that refused to eat Hearbs boill'd with Flesh.* §. 34. *Whether only the Bishop must say the* Pax vobiscum, *(and to have but one Church.)* §. 35. *King* Clotharius *forceth the Bishops to receive a Bishop of his choice.* §. 37. *Not Popes, Councils nor Bishops, but Kings divided Dioceses and Parishes, as* Bin. §. 38. *A Council at* Tours. *that Bishops may keep their Wives as Sisters for House-keepers, so they lye not with them. All condemned Malefactors that are penitent and will obey the Preacher, to be pardoned.* §. 39. *The Villanies of two Bishops quit by the Pope.* §. 40. *A Canon against reading* Apocrypha *or any thing but Canon Scriptures in the Church.* §. 42. *Pope* Pelagius *the second, got* Smaragdus *to force the Western Bishops to condemn the* tria Capitula. §. 45. *King* Gunthram *represseth the Murders and Adulteries of Bishops against the Clergies Sentence.* §. 47. *A Council at* Constantinople *calleth* JohnConst.UniversalBishop, *Pope* Pelagius *the second damneth the Title as unlawful in any, and commandeth them rather to dye than yield it. Some queries hereupon.* §. 51. *King* Gunthram *finding all grow worse and all long of the Bishops, calls a Council at* Mascon, *where the stricter keeping the Lords day is Decreed.* §. 54. *The Bishops of* Venice, Istria *and* Liguria *continue separate from* Rome *and chose* Paulinus *Bishop of* Aquileia, *their Patriarch, and supreme Bishop instead of the Pope.* §. 55. *Oft Pennance to embolden oft Sinning.* §. 57. Philoponus *against the Council of* Calcedon. §. 60. *The Factions now called* Jacobites *and* Melchites, *and why.* §. 61. *The Armenians plead Tradition for their Error.* §. 62. *The Pariarchs of* Aquileia *persecuted by* Mauritius *and Pope* Gregory. §. 65. *Dead* Gregory *fights with* Sabinian *his Successor that would have burnt his Books,* §. 68. Boniface *the third chosen by* Phocas, §. 70.

CHAP. 8, *Councils about the Monothelites and others.* Cyrus Alex. *by the word* [Deivirilis] *would heal the Divisions (in vain,)* §. 1, 2. *Pope* Honorius *called a Monothelite, for his good Council,* §. 2, 3. *The Emperour* Heraclius *a Monothelite censured by* Binnius *for using his own judgment in matters of Faith,* §. 4. *A* Constantinopolitane *Council for the* Monothelites, §. 12. *The Emperour condemned, and Pope* Honorius *commended for forbidding the names of* [One] *or* [Two] *operations and Wills,* §. 15. *The Popes Agents beaten at* Constantinople, §. 18. *Pope* Martin *imprisoned, banished and dead by the Emperour for condemning his Act of silencing* [One *and*

The Contents.

and Two] called Typus. §. 19. *His* Laterane *Council asserteth two* Operations *and* Wills. §. 20. *The King of* Spain *finding all Laws fail against Priests and Bishops Leachery, decreeth that the children of their women servants be uncapable of inheritance, and be the Churches servants, and the Concubines whipt with an hundred stripes.* §. 23. *Kings Preach to Bishops.* §. 24. 21. *Ordination without Election of* Clergy *and* People *null.* §. 25. *The Bishop of* Ravenna *reconciled to* Rome, *after long separation.* §. 30. *A* Millan *Council, and the third* Constantinople, (6 *General*) *condemn the* Monothelites, *and* Macarius Antioch, *that would have silenced* [*one*] *and* (*two*) *but not assert* [*two*] §. 34. *Their partiality.* §. 35. *Pope* Leo *confirmeth the* Constantinopolitan *Council which damned Pope* Honorius *as an Heretick.* §. 36. *A new controversie, whether* Christ *hath three substances,* Divinity, Soul, *and* Body. §. 40. *A* Toletane *Council defends it, and that* Voluntas genuit voluntatem. §. 45. *The* Concil. Trull. *called* Quini Sextum: *Railed at by* Papists: *Notes hereon.* §. 47, 48. *Called by* Binnius *Monothelites: The same men that were in the 5th Council. It forbideth Priests to put away their Wives.* §. 50. *It deposeth Bishops and Priests that were not duly Examined and Elected.* §. 50. *It equaleth the priviledges of* Constantinople *with* Rome. §. 53. *It* (*ill*) *ordereth, that wherever alteration the Imperial power makes on any* City, *the* State Ecclesiastical *follow it.* §. 54. *Other notable* Canons. §. 55, &c. *Every Parish of twelve Families must have their proper Governour* (*in* Spain.) §. 57. Paul *contradicted as to the believer and unbeliever staying together* §. 58. *A Council at* Aquileia *condemneth the 5th General at* Constantinople. §. 60. K. Wiliza *and the* Spaniards *forsake* Rome. §. 65. *A General Council of* innumerable *Bishops at* Constantinople *under* Philippicus *are for the* Monothelites. §. 67. *They condemn the* 6th *General Council that was for two* Wills *and* Operations. Binnius *note of the Bishops temporizing.*

CHAP. 9. *Councils about Images and others. Images how introduced in* England. §. 2. &c. Spelmans *proof that the old* Saxons *prayed not to* Saints. §. 3. *A* Parliament Role *recited, proving the old Popish Worshiping of Images.* §. 4. Leo Isaurus *puts down Images:* Gregory *the second rebels for it, and confederates with* Charles Martell *against his Prince, and absolveth his subjects from their allegiance.* Binnius *records it as an excellent* example *to* posteri-

The Contents.

posterity, not to permit pertinacious Heretical Princes to reign. §. 5. *The consequents of this doctrine: How the Pope ruined the* Eastern *Empire, and betrayed Christianity.* §. 5. Wilfrids *Oath to the Pope.* §. 6. *Councils* pro Imaginem cultu, Alicnſus *first calls himself* The Catholick King. §. 9. P. Zachary, *and* Charles Martell *against the Emperour:* Pipin *and the Popes Treason in* France, *and* Baronius *and* Binnius *treasonable doctrine.* §. 11. *Twenty. Queries hereupon.* §. 12. P. Zachary *and Bishop* Boniface *Excommunicate* Virgilius *for holding Antipodes: Queries hereupon.* §. 14, 15. Philaſtrius *of the stars.* §. 16. *A caution against misapplying all.* §. 17. *When Lard muſt be eaten.* P. Zachary's *decree.* §. 18. Caroloman's *Council to recover Chriſtianity, and save mens souls from false Priests.* §. 19. Boniface *finely made Arch-bishop of* Mentz: *accuseth Bishop* Adelbert *and* Clemens. §. 21, 22. *Pipin helpeth the Pope and* Deſiderius *Traytors, and maketh a Donation of Cities to the Pope.* §. 23. *A General Council at* Conſtantinople *condemn Image Worſhip as Idolatry, and swear men against it, and against praying to the Apoſtles, Martyrs, and* Virgins (*I suppose before Images.*) §. 24. *This Council and the Council of* Nice *second, determine that Chriſts glorified body is not fleſh (with* Anathema.) §. 26. *Noted as to Tranſubſtantiation and other Errours.* §. 26, 27. Pipins *Council decreeth every City a Biſhop, and joyneth the ſword or force to Excommunication, baniſhing the despisers of it.* §. 28. *The* Greeks *accuse the* Latines *for adding* [Filioque.] §. 30. *The People still chooſe Popes.* §. 29, 31. *Three Popes fighting for it: one putting out the eyes and cutting out the tongue of the other, and of his adherents.* §. 31. Conſtantines *Acts invalid, except Baptizings and Conſecrating.* §. 33. Chriſtophers *eyes and life taken away through the Pope that he ſet up.* §. 35. Deſiderius *fighteth against the Pope,* Charles M. *overcometh him, and maketh Pope* Adrian *grater than any before him.* §. 37. *Why Deacons moſtly made Popes: No Biſhop might be made Pope, or removed.* §. 39. *The termes of Papiſt Writers expounded.* §. 40. *Putting penance on Murderers for hanging, fill'd the Church with Rogues.* §. 41. *The Hiſtorians give the lie to each other about the power given* Carol. M. *in making Popes and Biſhops.* Baronius *Argument against it vain. That the People and Clergy by the* French *Conſtitutions ſtill chooſe Biſhops.* §. 42. Irene *ſet up Images again:* Women *and Rebels ſet up Popes.* §. 46. *The Fable of* Sylveſters *baptizing* Conſtantine, *and the*

The Contents.

the Images shewed him. §. 48. *Pope Adrian owneth the* whole Council *of* Calcedon. §. 47. *Many notable old Canons sent by* Adrian *to Carol.* M. *A Bishop neglecting to convert Hereticks, he was to have them that delivered them,* &c. §. 51. Ch. Mag. *forceth the Saxons to profess themselves Christians and swear perseverance, which they oft broke.* §. 52. *Eight more old Canons collected by* Adrian, *e. g.* The Bishops sentence void, not confirmed by the presence of the Clergy. The judgment of a Bishop in anothers Parish void, for none is bound by the sentence of any but his own Judge. Foreign Judgments forbidden: All to be judged by Men chosen by themselves. No Clergy-man to be judged without lawful accusers present, and leave to defend himself. Bishops tyrannical judgments null: Constitutions contrary to good manners of no moment. Delators, *that is,* qui ex invidia produnt alios, to have their tongues cut out, or their heads cut off. The danger of the Judge greater than of the judged, &c. And let no man receive a Lay-mans witness against a Clergyman. (*No wonder if the Clergy were unpunished and wicked.*) §. 53. Irene *calls a Council at* Constantinople *for Images. The old Souldiers of the former Emperours not enduring it, routed them. She and* Tarasius *agreeing call them to* Nice. *The Bishops that were sworn against Image-worship, presently turn generally for it, by a Womans and a Patriarchs known will.* §. 49. 54. *How could the Iconoclast Emperours be Hereticks, unless the use of such Images were an Article of Faith?* §. 55. *The Empress and Emperour called* The Governours of the whole World: They are the callers of that Council. §. 56. Basil Ancyr. *and other Bishops that were Leaders against Images in the former Council, lament it, and curse all that are not for Images, and all that favour such,* &c. Theodosius *Bishop of* Amoricum *also curseth himself, if ever he turn again, and curseth those who do not from their hearts teach Christians to venerate Images of all Saints, praying for their intercession,* &c. *Queries hereon. When General Councils curse each other, is the whole Church cursed?* &c. §. 59. *A crowd of changling Bishops crying mercy,* Tarasius *puts them hard to it, what made them of the contrary mind heretofore, and what reason changeth them?* §. 60. *Whether these penitent Hereticks should be restored to their Bishopricks.* Tarasius *faith,* Arians *and these against Images and all Heresies and Evils are alike. But another,* That this was

greater

The Contents.

greater than all other Heresies, subverting Christs Oeconomy. *The instance of the* Calcedon peccavimus omnes *prevaileth.* §. 62, 63. *A shrewder doubt raised, Whether all these were truly ordained by former Hereticks* (Iconoclasts-) *The Popes Vicar denyeth it.* Tarasius *durst not so unpriest almost all the Christian world of the* East, *and is contrary.* By a cunning argument *he prevailed;* Viz. The Fathers agree among themselves: *Ergo,* all the rest are of the same mind with some before cited. §. 64. Gregory *Bishop of* Neocæsaria *next recanteth, a Leader of the* Iconoclasts. §. 67. *Iet* Tarasius *and this Council disclaim giving* Latria *to Images of creatures. Yea honour them but as* memorative. §. 67, 70. *The* Constantinopolitan *Councils Arguments against Images.* §. 68. &c. *Bread not Transubstantiate.* §. 72. *The two Councils contrary about Tradition of Images.* §. 73. *The* Nicene *Council curseth from Christ all that are not for saluting and adoring Images.* §. 76. *Bishops and Priests made by Magistrates Election, or that use the Magistrate to get the place, are void. A Canon against silencing Preachers and shutting up Churches.* §. 77. *A sober Council at* Horojulium. §. 80. Fœlix Urgelitanus, *and* Elepandus, *condemned, for saying Christ was Gods natural Son in the Deity, and his adopted in his Humanity.* §. 81. Claudius Taurinensis *against Images.* §. 82. Car. Mag. *Book, and the Council of* Franckford *against Images.* §. 82, 84. Fœlix *and* Elepandus *condemned, for saying Christ was a Servant.* §. 85. *The* Frankford *Council decreeth that Christ was not a Servant subject to God by penal servitude.* §. 89. *Pope* Leo's *eyes put out, and tongue cut out, and restored, and he made great by* Charles the Great. §. 92. *Kissing the Popes Foot.* §. 93. Irene *killeth her son, and is banished her self.* §. 94. Filioque *added by the* Spanish *and* French *Bishops without the Pope.* §. 96. Carol. Mag. *being dead the People Rebel against the Pope; till* Ludovicus *subdued them.* §. 97. *A Council at* Constantinople *for the Emperours Adultery: And another against* Plato *and* Theodorus Studita, *that were against it; which saith* Binnius *passed the sentence of* Anathema *on the whole* Catholick-Church. *And decreed that Gods Laws can do nothing against Kings, nor is any man a Martyr that suffereth (as* Chrysostome) *for opposing them for truth and justice.* §. 98. *A Council at* Arles, *and another at* Tours *have good Canons, One that is for the old prohibition of genuflexion*

flexion on the Lords daies. §. 104. *Charles M. restoreth Learning: A Council at* Chalones *decreed against the Oath of Canonical obedience.* §. 105, 106. *Another against Arch-Deacons ruling Presbyters, and taking Fees of them.* §. 107. *Others for the old Excommunication, and about Confession to God and Man, and against trust in Pilgrimages.* §. 108, 109, 110. *Another Council at* Constantinople *curseth that at* Nice, 2d, *and pull down Images, and the Bishops turn again.* §. 113. *The murder of Bishops punished by payments at last.* §. 114. Ludovicus Pius, *Emperour, Bishops with* Bernard *rebel,* Stephen *made Pope without him, pardoned.* §. 115. *His care of lost Learning: A pious Treatise out of the Fathers; against Bishops domination, and for their equality with Presbyters in Scripture-times.* §. 116. *Against Clergy sins, and Womens company. Against genuflection on the Lords days:* Augustines *contempt of appeals to Councils and* Rome: *A strange temperance of the Canonical Monks, that were tyed to four pound of Bread and five pound of Wine in a day; or in scarcity, to three pound of Wine and three pound of Beer; or in greater scarcity, to one pound of Wine and five of Beer.* §. 118. Ludovicus Pius *maketh the Pope greater than ever.* §. 120. Michael Balbus *murdering* Leo, Armenus *sendeth to* Ludovicus Pius *about Images: An Assembly at* Paris *called by him judge the judge of the World, and the* Nicene *second Council saith* Bellarmine. §. 124. *Now both East and West judged the Pope and his General Council to erre; yea this Emperour that made him Great.* §. 125. *A book of concord by the Pope and Emperour, that Images are neither to be contemptuously broken, nor adored.* Bellarmines *words against it. He revileth the Popes words, that Princes are Governours of the Church.* §. 127, 128. *Confuted. Faith and Love may be without Images.* §. 129. *It was the right of the Empire to consent or not, to the chosen Pope.* §. 132. Platina *wisheth for a* Ludovicus *to reform the luxurious Clergy then.* §. 133. *A* Paris *Council write an excellent Book: They tell of some struck with Thunderbolts, Convulsions, &c. for and as working on the Lords day. And say* Beati Petri vicem gerimus. §. 136. *The Emperour making his three Sons Kings, they Rebel: He conquereth* Pipin, Lotharius *rebelleth again.* Ebbo *and a Council of Bishops wickedly depose him absent and unheard, and force him to resign his Scepter on the Altar, and thrust him into Prison: Thus was the best of Princes that most advanced the Clergy used by them.*

The Contents.

them, on Religious pretense Ludovicus *restored the second time.* Lotharius *rebelleth still, till pardoned.* Ludovicus *dyeth.* §. 137. *The form of his condemnation by the Bishops at large; with all the Articles of Accusation and his penance at the Bishops high Court of Justice.* §. 139. *The Emperour restored by force, the Bishops recant and he forgiveth them,* Ebbo *resigning.* §. 140. *The Wars between* Ludovicus *Sons:* Lotharius *justly conquered.* §. 145. *The Bishops depose him upon impeachment as they did his Father by his will.* §. 146. *Images restored at* Constantinople *by* Theodora *a Woman: she sped as* Irene. Photius *Patriarch* §. 148, 149. *The Bishops suddenly turn again.* §. 150. *Strife for the Popedom* §. 151. Lotharius *and his brothers agree.* §. 153. *The Archbishop of* Rhemes *fled and the seat vacant was ten years Governed by two Presbyters.* §. 152. Carolus Calvus *alienateth Church-lands.* §. 153. *Pope* Leo *and his City* Leonina: *He writeth Massing Rules, and deposeth Priests that cannot read till they amend.* §. 154. *Singing Liturgies the occasion of imposed forms.* §. 155. *A Council at* Mentz *punisheth murder even of Priests, but with putting them from the communion.* §. 157.

CHAP. 10. *Councils about* Ignatius *and* Photius, *with others.* Hincmarus's *description of* Godescalcus *and his Heresie.* §. 1. *Canons, that Arch-Presbyters examine every Master of a Family personally, &c. That none denyed Communion have any Office civil or Military,* §. 3. *Whether unconstrained sufferers are Martyrs.* §. 4. *A hard case about the nullity of* Ebbos *Ordinations: Two Popes differ.* §. 5. Ignatius *case.* §. 8. Remigius *and eleven more at* Valence *make notable decrees about Predestination, Redemption, Perseverance, and choice of Bishops.* §. 9. *The Clergy and People to choose Bishops.* §. 9, 10. Lotharius *turneth Monk.* §. 11. *No Pope* Joan. §. 12. *Two strive for the Papacy:* Anastasius *against Images, repulst.* §. 13, 14. *Thunderbolts in the Church.* §. 16. John *Bishop of* Ravenna *forced to submit to the Pope.* §. 17. *The Schism between* Ignatius *and* Photius. §. 18. *Bishops for the Emperours divorce, censured by the Pope, despise him.* §. 19. *Pope* Nicolas, *against* Hincmarus: *Against the* Greek *Emperour: His notable Epistle: He maketh the greater number of Bishops and People no sign of truth; nor fewness of errour.* §. 21. *Baptism valid by one that is no Priest nor Christian.* §. 22. *None proper Patriarchs but Apostles Successours.* §. 22. *All other Churches*

The Contents.

ches and Dignities made by Rome, *and* Rome *by Chriſt.* §. 24. *Peter had the Empire of Heaven and Earth. Ill choſen Popes not Apoſtolical,* § 25. *Many other Papal Uſurpations, againſt Oaths, Princes, &c.* § 26, *&c. People ſtill chuſe Biſhops,* § 29. *None may hear Maſs of a fornicating Prieſt,* § 30. *Lay men muſt not judge or ſearch the lives of Prieſts. K.* Charles *ſaith none but the Biſhops may depoſe him,* § 32. Photius *ſetled by Councils,* § 31, 33, 35. *Divers Councils for K.* Lotharius *divorce againſt the Pope,* § 38, 39, 40. *The Pope curſeth them,* § 41, *and curſeth his Legates at* Conſt. § 42, *and at* Metz, § 46. Hincmarus *and the Pope's Contention,* § 43, 44. *Hiſtorians ſay the Papacy was void eight years, and others but ſeven days,* § 50. Photius *and his Cornſels deſpiſed the Pope. His depoſition by* Baſilius *a Murderer,* § 51. Baſilius *craveth the Popes pardon for the Biſhops, becauſe they had almoſt all been deceived or falſe, by following the upper Powers, and the Churches would elſe be left deſtitute,* § 52. *What nullifying Ordinations hath done,* § 53: *Men wrongfully excommunicated to be received by other Biſhops: Presbyters to annoint the ſick, becauſe the Biſhops cannot viſit all,* § 56. *A* Conſt. *Council ejecteth* Photius; *where the Biſhops that were for him, turn again and condemn him, crying* peccavimus; *ſave ſome few: Subſcriptions denyed, and why,* § 57. *This eighth General Council decreeth equal honour to Chriſts Image as to the Goſpel: Forbiddeth Patriarchs to require Biſhops to ſubſcribe to them, but only to the Faith, and depoſeth them that do it,* § 58: *Curſeth them that ſay man hath two Souls: All Biſhops to be worſhipped by Princes, and not go far to meet them, nor light from their Horſes to them, nor Petition them, on great Penalties,* § 58. *Princes as profane may not be preſent at Councils; nor have been,* (impudent!) § 58. *No Lay man may diſpute Eccleſiaſtical Sanctions, be he never ſo wiſe or good: But a Biſhop muſt not be reſiſted though manifeſtly deſtitute of all virtue of Religion,* § 59. *They decree that* Photius *be not called a Chriſtian,* § 60. *Biſhops above Kings, as Heaven above Earth,* § 61. *The Pope but one Patriarch cannot abſolve them that many Patriarchs condemn,* § 62. Nicetas *Life of* Ignatius *in brief,* § 63. *The Pope depoſed by a* Conſt. *Council. The Biſhops wrote not* Photius *condemnation with Ink but with Chriſts blood, and yet reſtored him and honoured him as the Emperour turned.* Photius *depoſeth and re-ordaineth, and requireth ſubſcription to him,* § 63. *Votes hereon,* § 64. *The Contention between* Rome *and* Conſt. *for ruling the* Bulgarians,

The Contents.

and the effects, § 65. *The Pope's Monarchy then unknown*, § 66, 68. *The* French *Bishops against the Pope gave* Ludovicus's *Kingdom to* Charles Calvus, § 70. *The King,* Hincmar. *and Bishops against the Pope,* § 71, 72. *Deposing and blinding* Hincmaru's *Laudunenfis. The* Romans *imprison Pope* John, § 75. *His Acts; decree for perjury,* § 76, 77. *Going to* Rome *merits the pardon of Murder,* § 77. *Service in the* Sclavonian *Tongue forbidden them,* § 78. Auspertus *Bishop of* Milan *refuseth to obey the Pope:* Sclavonian *Service yielded to: The Bishop of* Vienna *rejecteth a Bishop of* Geneva (Aptandus) *sent by the Pope, because he was never baptized, made Clerk, nor Learned: The Pope tells him that he himself had none of these when he was consecrated Bishop of* Vienna, § 77. *Whether the Right of Emperours was only by the Pope's Guift,* § 78. Binius *resolution: One Church had two Bishops,* § 81. *A General Council at* Constant. *restoreth* Photius, *expungeth* filioq; *condemneth the last General Council there; yet both approved by Popes,* § 83. *The Council accuse* Rome, § 87. Rome's *jurisdiction excluded,* § 87. *Adders to the Creed* (filioq;) *anathematized: Pope* Martin *and* Hadrian *condemn* Photius, *and enrage the* Greek *Emperour against them,* § 89, 91. *Bishops and Lords depose* Carolus Crassus; *he is put to beg his bread,* § 92. *The Pope above Emperours as Heaven above Earth; Kings are Servants, and not above the Clergie their Masters,* § 93. *A King ruling ill decreed to be a Tyrant: Bishops and Priests lying with their own Sisters, restrained: but no Bishop is to be accused by a Presbyter, nor judged under seventy two Witnesses, nor Priests under forty two, &c. He that would lye with his Sister before so many deserved blame: Murderers of Priests denyed Flesh, Wine, Coaches, &c.* § 96, 97. Formosus *perjured, was the first Bishop that ever was made* Pope, § 99.

CHAP. 11. *The Progress of Councils, till* Leo *the* 9th, *especially in the* West.

The Bishops depose Odo, *and set up* Charles. §. 1. *The Virgin* Mary's *Smock works wonders.* §. 2. *Bloud and confusion in* Italy. §. 3. *Bishops to be obeyed before Earls and Magistrates. Clergy-men must not be put to swear. No Presbyter to be depos'd, but by six Bishops,* §. 5. *Two wicked Popes at once:* Stephen *Judgeth, Dismembreth, and drowneth dead* Formosus, *and re-ordaineth those ordained by him,* §. 7, 8. *The Bishops in Council approve it; yet now Papists detest it.* §. 9. *When Popes are Infallible.* §. 10. *Popes undo what their Predecessors*

cessors did. §. 12, 13, 14, 15, 17. Platina's *description of a Malignant Pope.* §. 14. *Popes Crown for fear, and uncrown, and Crown others.* §. 15. *Bishops turn and return, and cry* Peccavimus. *Reordinations forbidden.* §. 16. *Bad Princes the cause of bad Bishops.* §. 17. *Wicked Christians on whom the Pope durst not use Discipline.* §. 17. *Schismes and violence on Popes.* §. 18, 19, 20. Sergius *made Pope the third time, keeps it; by Whores and Whoredom the most wicked of men, saith* Baron. *and* Bin. §. 22. Formosus *again executed dead,* §. 23. *Questions to the Papists of their holyness and Succession.* §. 24. Photius *last deposition, and the Murders, of Emperours at* Constant. §. 26. *A Whore Ruleth at* Rome, § 21. *She maketh her Fornicator Pope;* Baronius *and* Binnius. *hard put to it* §. 62. *Earl* Heribert's *Son, not five years old, made Archbishop fo* Rhemes. §. 30. *Ratified by Pope* John, *lamented by* Baron. *that by this Example other great men did the like:* John's *end by a Whore,* §. 30. *None to marry within the seventh degree, as incest.* §. 31. Sergius *bastard-Son under age made Pope* John *by a Whore, and destroyed after a Monster saith* Binnius. §. 35. *None to fast privately, but by the Bishops consent.* §. 36. *The King of* Denmark *made Christian by* Henry *King of* Germany. §. 39. *St.* Peter *made the example for many Bishopricks to one Bishop.* §. 40. Albericus *ruleth, and mangle th the Pope.* §. 41. *The Bishops judge the Infant before the perjured Monk to be Bishop of* Rhemes, § 43. *The treasons and changes in* France, § 44. Tryphon *illiterate finely cheated of his Patriarchate* Const. § 46. *Councils do and undo between the two Bishops of* Rhemes, § 48, 49, 50. John XII *Lawful Pope wanted all things necessary to a Pope, say* Baronius *and* Binnius, § 51. *Notes hereon,* § 52. *Pope* John *dismembreth his Cardinals,* § 53. *He fled,* § 53. *The Bishops depose him, and make another by* Otho's *means,* § 54. *The horrid charges against Pope* John *sworn,* § 53. Baronius *and* Binnius *against his condemnation answered,* § 56. *Two Popes and Churches,* § 57. *Not yet known who was the true Pope,* § 59. John *killed in Adultery,* § 60. *Another Antipope perjuriously chosen,* § 61. *A Martyr,* § 62, 64. *An interruption of the Succession by* Baronius *and* Binnius *account,* § 65. Otho *saveth them. The next imprisoned and strangled,* § 67. Boniface VII. *runs to* Constantinople *with the Church Treasure,* § 69. *Two more Popes,* § 69, 70, 72. Boniface *murders another Pope, and gets in; dyeth, and is drag'd about the Streets,* § 74. John XV, *durst not dwell at* Rome, § 75. Hugo Capet *turneth the Bishops,* § 78. *Popes fighting.* John XVII, *blinded,*

The Contents.

blinded, mangled, disgraced, kill'd, § 84. *Seven Electors of the Emperour settled,* § 85. *Gerbert how made Pope,* § 87. *The King of* Hungary *Converts the* Transilvanians, § 87. *Good Kings,* § 90. Leutherius *Archbishop of* Seus *against Transubstantiation,* § 91. *Two Popes fighting. The King of* Hungary *converted by the Emperour* Henry, § 95. *The first burning of Hereticks* (Manichees.) § 97. Henry *the Emperour leaveth his Wife a Virgin,* § 100. Benedict. IX. *a debosh boy-Pope: put out again,* § 103. *Gets in again: A third enters at once.* The Cerberus *hired all out by dividing the Church-rents between them; do resign; but the hirer as pacificator is made Pope,* § 103. *Six that had been Popes alive at once: One honest Pope that could not read made a fellow Pope to do it,* § 104. Gregory VI. *The illiterate reconciling Pope variously described: put out with the other three, and a Fifth chosen,* § 107. Benedict. *gets in the third time,* § 107. *Another gets in by* Poyson, *and dyeth the* 23. *day,* § 110. Baron. *answered,* § 111. *The Monster* Bened. 9. *is he that condemned* Berengarius, § 112. Leo 9th. *of the Resurrection: Renounceth the Title of Universal Patriarchs, as of the bawd of Antichrist:* Peter *not Universal Apostle. Bishops equal; varied by City priviledges, save in* Africa *by seniority. The Romish Church usurped by no Pastors,* § 205. Michael Patr. *of* Const. *Rebaptizeth Papists, saith they had no true Baptism, or Sacrifice,* § 205. *A* Roman *Council pardon simoniacal Bishops and Priests, lest the Church be utterly destitute,* § 206. *The Popes hold a Council in* France *against the King's will: A Bishops horrid Crimes, and a miracle there. Still Clergie and People must chuse every Bishop* 207.

CHAP. 12. *The continuation till the Council of* Constance: *Councils against* Berengarius, § 2, &c. *Adulterous and* Symoniacal *Bishops: A miracle,* § 4, 9. Hildebrand, *a Sub-deacon, presideth in Councils, and deposeth Bishops, and Excommunicateth,* § 9, 10. *Bishops by Excommunication rule K.* Ferdinand, § 12. Milan *separated from* Rome 200 *years,* § 16. *Another Schism,* § 17, 18. Hildebrands *new Foundation of Popes (by Cardinals Election)* § 22. *Notes hereon,* § 22. *A* Roman *Council forbids hearing a Fornicator Priest,* § 23. *Bloody fights between two Popes: Five years schism,* § 25. P. Alexander *giveth* England *to* William the Conqueror, § 27. *Councils for each Pope,* § 28, 29. *Gods word affirmed violable,* § 30. Hildebrands *War in* Rome: Italian *Bishops against him. His hard work. Obedience to the Pope forbidden by a Council at* Mentz. *He deposeth the Emperour for seeking to diminish the Majesty of the Church:*
and

The Contents.

and absolveth his sworn Subjects: An Antipope made that sate 21 *years, (the* 23d *schism.) The Emperour barefoot in frost three days begs pardon, and promiseth obedience. He is again cursed by the Pope in Council, as having power to take away Kingdoms, and all that men have,* § 41, 42. *The Siege of* Rome: *Two Popes:* Gregory's *death,* § 42. *He threatneth to depose the King of* France: *claims* Hungary, &c. §23. Binnius *record of* THE POPES DICTATES, *telling in* 27 *Articles* WHAT POPERY IS, § 44. *He claimeth* Spain, § 46. *and* Dalmatia, § 49. *A great part of the Bishops against him,* § 49. *Pronounceth unsincere repentance fruitless,* § 50. *Denyeth Divine Service in the* Sclavonian *tongue,* § 51. *Ill weather imputed to the ill Lives of Priests: The* Armenians *errours what,* § 51. Apulia, &c. *the Popes,* § 51. *One man turned an hundred thousand men in* Spain *from the Pope. He threatneth to Excommunicate and depose the King of* Spain, *as an Enemy to the Christian Religion,* § 52. *He newly found St.* Matthews *body,* § 54. *He will expose the Prince of* Sardinia *unless he obey him in making all Priests shave their beards,* § 55. *Notes hereon. The* French *convert the* Sweeds, *and the Pope would reap the fruit,* § 56. *His notable Epistle to prove Popes, Priests, (and Exorcists) above Kings,* § 57. *Answered,* § 58. Peter-pence, § 59. *An Arch-bishop suspended for not visiting* Rome, § 60. *A pious Lie for Peace is a sin,* § 61. *The old* Spanish *Liturgy partly contrary to the Christian Faith till now,* § 62. *His respect to* William the Conquerour, &c. § 64, 66. *The* German *Bishops hereticate the Pope, for forbidding Marriage,* § 67. Matthew *is forsaken,* § 68. Philip *King of* France *and many great Bishops excommunicate,* § 69. *Divers Councils excommunicating contrarily; the Antipopes,* § 69, *to* 74. *Ordinations null that are made* pretio, precibus vel obsequio, *and not by the common consent of Clergy and People,* § 75. *He excommunicateth the* Greek *Emperour usurping,* § 76. *The* Greek *affairs summ'd up,* § 77. *The power of Pope and Bishops to depose Kings,* § 79. *A Council Character of* Gregory, § 80. *A Council make Loyalty to be* Hæresis Henriciana, § 87. *The Disciple is not above his Master, answered,* § 87. Wecilo's *heresie, that men obey not unjust Excommunications, but may by others be received,* § 88. *The* 23d. *Schism,* § 91. Victor's *Soldiers conquer* Clement's, § 92. *Lay Princes presentations or Investitures are Heresie: every Heretick is an Infidel: It's better be without visible Communion than have it with such,* § 93. *Consectaries overthrowing* Rome, ib. *A*

new

The Contents.

new Pope marrieth Mathildis *to* Welpho *on condition they use not carnal Copulation,* § 94. *A* Jerusalem *expedition causeth peace at home.* Conrade *rebelleth against his Father,* § 94. *The Emperour commits Fornication,* § 101, 103. *Wrongs on Monday, Wednesday, or Thursday, no breach of holy peace: No Bishop or Priest must swear or promise Allegiance to a King, nor take Preferment from any Lay-man,* § 104. *None to communicate in one kind,* § 105. *All the Bishops of* England *save* Rochester *renounce obedience and society with* Anselme *Archbishop of* Canterbury, *because he would not renounce the Pope, saying, he blasphemed the King, setting up any in his Kingdom without his consent,* § 106. *Time given the King of* England *to repent,* § 109. *The Anti-Pope* Clement *digg'd up and burnt:* Paschal 2. *Council Decree that all Bishops of the* Henrician *Heresie (Loyalists) if alive be deposed, if dead, digg'd up and burnt (that is, most of the Western Bishops,)* § 112. *The Schism continued,* § 113. *The Pope set up young* Henry *against his Father, who taketh him Prisoner to the death: He keeps his Fathers Corps five years unburied, because Excommunicate. Yet proveth* Hereticus Henricianus, *Imprisoneth the Pope till he grant him Investitures. The Pope absolveth himself,* § 114, 115. *Cases on* Binnius, § 116. *Note that Investitures supposed the* People *and* Clergies *free choice of Bishops,* § 117. *The Bishops usage of old* Henry *to the last,* § 118. *To take the Popes Excommunications as not obligatory is a Heresie,* § 119. *The dangerous Doctrine of* Fluentius *Bishop of* Florence *(that Anti-Christ was come)* § 120. *Only the Church made* Henry *rebell,* § 121, 122. Tybur *coloured with bloud: The Earl of* Millans *Flesh given to Dogs: The Popes sacramental Covenant broken,* § 127. *God will have no involuntary service,* § 129. *The same is a* Henrician *Heresie in others which is none in the Pope,* § 132. *He may forswear for the People of God.* § 132. *Two Popes contending and excommunicating: The Emperour giveth up Investitures,* § 135 *to* 138. *Four Doctrines of* Guilb. Porretane *condemned in Council;* 1. *That* Divinitas *and* Deus *are not the same (in signification:)* 2. *That the three Persons are not* unum aliquid: 3. *That there are eternal Relations besides the Persons:* 4. *That it was not the Divine Nature that was incarnate. Two more Popes,* § 138, 142. *A Preacher murdered at* Rome, § 144. *Two more Popes, the succession from the wrong,* § 145. *They fight for it,* § 146. *How Clergy and People first lost their Votes in choice of Popes,* § 147. *Two Popes still striving,* § 149, &c. *Many Castles in* England *built*
by

The Contents.

by two Bishops, § 160. *Abailard condemned unheard*, § 161. *Cælestine* II. *the first Pope without the Peoples election*, An. 1143. *Rome against the Pope: Bishops are his strength*, § 168. *Porretane again accused, and puzzled the Council*, § 170. *He is again accused by Bernard, whom the Cardinals accuse for writing his Faith and getting Bishops hands to it*, § 171. *The Romane people excommunicate by Pope* Adrian 4. *They are for a Preacher called by him an heretick*, § 174. *Rome fighteth with Pope and Emperour: They fight again, and expel the Pope*, § 174. *The 27 pair of Popes: Wars between the Emperour* Frederick *and Pope: The Crown of England held as from the Pope: Yet* Rome *receiveth him not: The Emperour submitteth, being deserted, &c.* § 175. *The setling the choice of Popes by Cardinals: The Pope no Bishop by the Canons*, § 177. *The* Roman *Succession is from* Alex. 3. *when the Clergie, People, Emperour, Princes, and a Council of* innumerable Bishops *were for* Victor, § 176. *Parliaments called Councils*, § 179. Ireland *the Popes*, § 180. *The* Albigenses *Henricians*, § 181. *No Bishop may suspend a Presbyter without the judgment of his Chapter: A perjured Clergie-man perpetually deprived: Doubtful words to be understood as usually*, § 182. *The Popes Party in* Rome *have their Eyes put out*, § 183. Frederick *drowned in* Asia, § 187. *The Kingdom of* France *interdicted*, § 190. *The Pope sets up an Anti-Emperour, who prevaileth*, § 192. England *interdicted six years and three months*, § 194. *The famous twelfth General Council at the* Laterane *under* Inoc. 3. *for Transubstantiation, exterminating hereticks, deposing Princes, absolving Subjects, forbidding unlicensed* Preachers, &c. § 195. Almaricus *burnt dead*, § 196. Stephen Langton *and King* John, § 197. *Ten Queries upon this Council*, § 198. *The Canons of this Council true: Mr.* Dodwel's 17 *Arguments for it*, § 199. *The Papists excuses answered*, § 180. (*misnumbred.*) *The bloody Execution*, § 181. Oxford *Canons, that* every great Parish have two or three Presbyters, &c. § 183. *Against Preaching when silenced*, § 184. *The Pope twice banished by the* Romans*: The Emperour excommunicate and deposed; fights it out: The Pope dyeth*, § 186. *A mortal sin to have two Benefices, if one will maintain him*, § 187. *The Emperour again excommunicate: A merry Excommunication*, § 191. *Rebellions*, § 192. Conrade *and King* Henry, § 193. *Bishop* Grosthead's *notable Letter to the Pope, and its reception*, § 195.

The Contents.

§ 195, 196. *Obedient disobedience: All Power for edification,* ib. *The Pope calls the King of* England *his Slave, whom he can imprison, &c.* § 196. *The Cardinals Speech to quiet the Pope: A Defection foretold,* § 196. Grosheads *death: He taketh them for Hereticks that tell not great men of their sin, &c. The Pope Antichrist, for destroying souls. The Popes pardoning Letter: The Pope described,* § 198. *Miracles at* Robert Grosheads *death: The Pope would have burnt and damned his Corps: In a vision he mortally woundeth the Pope,* § 198, 199. H. III. *pawneth his Kingdom to the Pope,* § 200. *The* 13th *General Council at* Lyons *excommunicateth and deposeth the Emperour and absolveth his Subjects,* §. 202. Guelphus *for the Popes,* Gibelius *for the Emperour,* § 203. *The* English *Parliament demand the choice of the Lords Justice, Chancellour and Treasurer,* § 204. *The Plot of King* Henry *and the Bishop of* Hereford, *to get money by the Pope,* §. 206. *The Parliament resist it:* M. Paris *talks too boldly of the King,* § 206. *Buying Bishopricks:* Brancaleo *at* Rome *mastereth the Pope,* § 208, 209. Sewale *Archbishop of* York *against the Pope: doth Miracles,* § 212. Rome *not ruled by the Pope,* § 214. *Near three years vacancy of the Papacy,* § 219. *Cardinal* Portuensis *jeast,* 220. *The foolish Pope* John *sadly confuted,* § 224. *King* Peter *of* Arragon *deposed,* § 226. *The Popes Tenth peny denyed,* § 228. *Two years more vacancy. The* Greeks *enmity to* Rome, §. 229. *Pope* Celestine *cheated to resign, and imprisoned,* § 233. Boniface *the* VIII. *his conflict with the King of* France *: taken prisoner, and dyeth:* Platina's *good Counsel to all Rulers,* § 224. *The Clergy not to be taxed by Princes,* § 235. *The Pope setled in* France *by* Clement V. *Continueth* 70 *Years,* § 236. *Above* 2 *years vacancy,* ibid. 40. *Articles of the King of* France *against* Boniface VIII. *Three Herisies of* Petrus Joannis, 1. *The rational soul, as such is not* forma corporis humani. 2. *Grace habitual, not infused in baptisme to Infants.* 3. *The Spear pierced Christ before his death,* § 242. *The Heresie of the* Beguines *and* Beguardes *for perfection,* § ibid. *Pope.* Clements *Decrees,* De fide. 1. *Of the form of the body (the soul.)* 2. *Infants infused Grace.* 3. *Usury a sin.* 4. *To be restored. The contrary to suffer as* Hereticks, § ibid. *The falshood of some of these new Articles of Faith,* § 243. *Magistrates excommunicated that disgrace wicked,* Priests, § 247. *Or compel them to answer to them,* § 248.

Popes

The Contents.

Popes and Councils condemn each other as Hereticks, § 250. *The Pope claimeth the Empire by Escheate,* § 251. *The Priest to take the name of every Parishoner, that being confessed and confirmed they may communicate only by his counsel*, § 252. *The* Greek *affairs*, § 256. *A* Toletane *Council Decree that their Provincial Constitutions bind only* ad pœnam, *not* ad culpam, *lest Christians Consciences be burdened,* § 257. *After seventy years residence at* Avignion, *forty years more there were two Popes (and sometime more) one at* Avignion *and one at* Rome. *Discord chooseth an honest Pope, but Concord an Anti-Pope. Their Wars: The Pope drowneth Cardinals in Sacks, and makes twenty nine new ones in one day,* § 260. *Italy still the most unpeaceable warring place of the World,* § 262, 263. *The Popes bloody way of curing Schism,* § 263. *The Council of* Pisa *thinking to have but one Pope made a third,* § 267. *Who Deposed King* Ladislaus, § 268.

CHAP. 13. *The Councils of* Constance, Basil, &c. *That at* Constance, *called by Pope* John 21 (alias 22 *or* 23 *or* 24) *by* Sigismund *the Emperours means, Councils above the Pope,* § 3. Wickliffs *Articles,* § 6. *One is, that they are Traytors to Christ, who give over preaching, and hearing Gods word, for mens Excommunications,* § 6, 54. *heynous Articles against Pope* John, *commonly called* The Devil incarnate: *An obstinate Heretick, denying the life to come,* &c. § 8. *He ratifieth all himself, and with other two Popes is deposed,* § 9. *A decree against giving the Sacramental Cup, though Christ and the Ancient Church used it,* § 10. *Articles against* John Hus *as* Wickliff's; *More as his own,* § 12, 13. *Excommunication must not make us leave off Preaching. Against* Hierome *of* Prague *breaking safe Conducts,* § 14, 15. *The third Pope depos'd,* § 16. *Decrees for frequent General Councils: Popes Elections regulated: A new Pope chosen,* § 17. *The Fate of P.* John *and the rest,* § 18, 19. *Continued Wars at* Rome, *against the Pope, and in* Italy, § 23. *The Council at* Basil. *The* Bohemians *case: Their four Articles,* 1. *For the full Sacrament.* 2. *For correcting publick Crimes.* 3. *For liberty to preach Gods Word.* 4. *Against the Clergies civil Power; all eluded,* § 24. *Bishop* Augustinus *de* Roma's errours *(Phanatick) Pardon of all sins confest with a contrite heart, sold for money and fasting,* § 27. *Their Catholick Verities:* 1. *For Councils Supremacy.* 2. *They may not be dissolv-*

e   *ed,*

The Contents.

ed, removed, prorogued, but consenting. 3. Its Heresie to oppugn these, § 28. P. Eugenius deposed as a pertinacious Heretick, &c. § 22. Queries hereon, § 30. The immaculate Conception decreed, § 31. Two Popes again, § 32. Epistles of and against the Pope, § 33. Four Treatises against the Bohemians four great Articles, § 34, 35. God only pardoneth the fault, and the Pope part of Church Penances. Whether silenced Preachers must cease: Unjust Sentences not regardable, confessed: The Council confirmed, § 35, 36. A Council at Briges confirmeth this, § 37. The Council at Florence: Two General Councils at once, § 38. The Romans still fight against the Pope, § 39. Constantinople lost, ib. P. Pius 2. his Character and Sentences: For Priests Marriage: Yet for Rome's Universal Headship to be received as necessary to salvation, § 44. P. Paul 2. a just and clement Simoniast and Tyrant: Tormenteth Platina and many others: Accuseth them of Heresie for praising Plato and Gentile Learning, &c. Against Learning, § 45. P. Sixtus Wars and treachery, § 46. Denying the Decrees of a General Council de fide (of the immaculate conception of B. M.) no Heresie, § 47. P. Inoc. 8. fights to be King of Naples, § 49.

Pope Alexander the Sixth his ugly Character, and his Son Cæsar Borgia's Villanies: Both drinking the poyson prepared for others: The Pope dyeth of it, § 50. Pius 3. § 51. P. Julius 2. Italy in blood still by him, § 52. Councils against the Pope: The King of France excommunicated, § 53, 54. The Anti-Council at Lateran, against the Pisane, against the French pragmat. Sanction: The notable Titles of the Pope, § 55. Decreed that Simoniacal Election of Popes is null, and giveth no Authority, (which nullifieth the Roman succession) § 56. Decrees about Souls, § 57. Leo 10. a Cardinal at 13. and an Archbishop in his Childhood: His Wars and bloodshed, § 58. Luther: The Reformation: The end of Charles 5. § 59. Leo's death, § 60. Reformers drive the Papists to Learning, § 61. All Papist Princes owe their safety, Crowns, and deliverance from Papal deposition to the Reformation; and Italy its peace, § 62. The History of the Reformation, and of Papists Murders of Martyrs passed by, § 63. Freder. of Saxony refuseth the Empire and Money, and chose Charles, § 64. Thirty five cases for which men must be denyed Communion in the Eucharist, § 65. Later Reforming Papist Councils, § 66, &c. The Conclusion, what this History specially discovereth,

The Contents.

discovereth. § 70. *A Poem of Mr.* George Herbert's, *called* The Church Militant.

CHAP. 14. *A Confutation of Papists and Sectaries, who deny and oppose the Ministry of the Reformed Churches.*

CHAP. 15. *A Confutation of the prophane Opposers of the Ministry.*

CHURCH-

An Account of some Books lately Printed for, and to be Sold by *Thomas Simmons*, at the *Prince's Arms*, in *Ludgate-street*.

A *Supplement to Knowledge, and Practice*: Wherein the main things necessary to be known and believed, in order to Salvation, are more fully explained, and several new Directions given for the promoting of real Holiness, both of Heart and Life: To which is added a serious dissuasive from some of the reigning and Customary sins of the Times. *viz.* Swearing, Lying, Pride, Gluttony, Drunkenness, Uncleanness, Discontent, Covetousness, and Earthly-mindedness, Anger, and Malice, and Idleness; by *Sam. Cradock, B. D.* late Rector of *North-Cadbury*, in *Somersetshire*: *Useful for the instruction of private Families*: Price bound 4 *s.*

De Analogia, sive Arte lingua Latina Commentariolus: In quo omnia, etiam reconditioris Gramaticæ, Elementa ratione nová tractantur, & ad brevissimos Canones rediguntur: In usum Provectioris Adolescentiæ. Opera *Wilhelmi Baxteri* Philistoris, Price bound 1 *s.* 6 *d.*

The lively *Effigies of the Reverend Mr.* Mathew Pool: So well performed as to represent his true Idea, to all that knew him, or had a Veneration for him: Design'd on purpose to befriend those that would prefix it to his *Synopsis Criticorum*, Price 6 *d.*

Moral Prognostications: 1. What shall befall the Churches on Earth, till their Concord, by the Restitution of their Primitive Purity, Simplicity, and Charity: 2. How that Restitution is like to be made (if ever) and what shall befal them thenceforth unto the end, in that Golden Age of Love: Written by *Richard Baxter*, when by the *Kings Commission*, we in vain treated for Concord, 1661. and now Published 1680, Price 1 *s.*

The *Nonconformists Advocate*; or an Account of their Judgment in certain things in which they are mis-understood: Written principally in Vindication of a *Letter from a Minister to a Person of Quality, shewing some Reasons for his Nonconformity*, Price 1 *s.*

There is Published every Thursday, a Mercurius Librarius, or *A Faithful Account of all Books and Pamphlets Published every Week*: In which may be inserted any thing fit for a Publick Advertisement, at a moderate Rate.

Directions to the Binder of Baxter's Church History, &c.

After the Title Sheet follows a, b, c, d, e; then B, C, D, E, F, G, H, I, K, L, M, N, O, P, Q, R, S; then AA, BB, CC, DD, EE, FF, GG, HH, II, KK, LL, MM, NN, OO, PP; then SS, TT, VV, XX, YY, ZZ, AAA, BBB, CCC, DDD, EEE; then GGG; and so on to QQQ; which Signiture ends the Book.

Church-History
OF
BISHOPS
And their
COUNCILS
ABRIDGED, &c.

CHAP. I.

Of the sacred Ministry, Episcopacy and Councils, necessary Premonitions: and of the Design of this Book.

§. 1. GOD that could have enlightned the Earth without the Sun and Stars, could immediately alone have taught his Church, and communicated knowledge to mankind: But as he is the most communicative good, he was pleased not only to make his Creatures receptive of his own influx, but also to give them the use and honour of being efficient sub-communicants under him, and causes of good to themselves and to one another: And as his *Power* gave *Being* and *Motion*, his *Wisdom* gave *Order* and *Harmony*, and his *Love* gave *Goodness* and *Perfection*, *felicity* and *love*, as he is the creating and conserving Cause of Nature; and this in much inequality, as he was the free disposer of his own; so in the Kingdom of Grace he doth by the Spirit of *Life*, *Light*, and *Love*, 1. Quicken and strengthen the dead and weak souls, and awaken the slumbering and slothful; 2. Illuminate the dark with Faith and Knowledge; and 3. Sanctifie the malignant Enemies of holiness, by the power of his communicated love, making them friends and joyful lovers: This Spirit first filled the Humane Nature of Christ our Head; who first communicated it to some chosen persons in an eminent manner and degree, as Nature maketh the heart and brain and other principal parts to be *organical*, in *making*, *preserving*, and *governing* the rest. To these he gave an eminence of Power to work Miracles, of Wisdom to propagate the Word of life, and infallibly by Preaching and Writing promulgate and record his sacred Gospel, and of *holy love* to kindle the like by zealous holiness in the hearts of others. To these *organical persons* he committed the Oeconomy of being the *witnesses* of his *words* and *actions*, his resurrection and ascension, and of recording them in writing, of planting his first Churches, and sealing the truth of their testimony by many Miracles, promising them his Spirit to perform all that he committed to their trust, and to bring all to their remembrance, and to lead them into all truth, and to communicate instrumentally his Spirit to others, the sanctifying gifts by blessing their Doctrine, and the miraculous gifts by their imposition of hands.

§. 2. By these principal Ministers the first Church was planted at *Jerusalem*, (fitliest called the Mother-Church) and after by those that were sent thence many Churches were gathered in many Kingdoms of the world, darkness being not able to resist the light. The Apostles and Evangelists and Prophets delivered to them the Oracles of God, *teaching them to observe all things that Christ had commanded them*, and practically teaching them the *true Worship of God, ordering their Assemblies*, and *ordaining* them such Officers for sacred Ministration as Christ would have continued to the end of the world, and shewing the Churches *the way* by which they *must be continued*, and describing all the work of the Office appointed them by Christ.

§. 3. The Apostles were not the Authors of the *Gospel*, or of any essential part of the Christian Religion, but the *Receivers* of it from *Christ*, and *Preachers* of it to the *world*: Christ is the *Author and finisher*, or perfecter of our faith. But they had besides the power of *infallible remembring*, *knowing* and *delivering* it, a double power about matters of Order in the *Church*: 1. By the special gift of the Spirit's inspiration, to *found and stablish such Orders* as were to continue to the end, and none that came after them might change, they being the *Ordinances* of the *Holy Ghost* in them. 2. Temporarily, *pro re nata*, to make convenient mutable Constitutions, in matters left by the great Legislator to humane prudence, to be determined according to his general regulating Laws. In this *last* the Apostles have Successors; but not in the *former*: No other have their *Gift*, and therefore not their *Authority*: No men can be said to have an Office that giveth them Right to exercise abilities which they never had nor shall have.

§. 4. Christ summed up all the Law in LOVE to God and Man, and the works of Love; and all the Gospel in *Faith*, and *Hope*, and *Love* by them

them kindled and exercised by the Spirit which he giveth them; even by the Belief and Trust of his Merits, Sacrifice, Intercession and Promises, and the *prospect* of the future Glory promised, fortifying us to all holy duties of obedience, and diligent seeking what he hath promised, and to patient bearing of the Cross, conquering the inordinate love of the world and flesh and present life, and improving all our present sufferings, and preparing for his coming again, and for our change and entrance into our Masters joy.

§. 5. Christ summed up the Essentials of Christianity in the Baptismal Covenant, in which we give up our selves in Faith, Hope, and consenting Love, to God the Father, Son, and Holy Ghost, our Creator, Redeemer, and Sanctifier, and in which God receiveth us in the Correlations as his own. And all that are truly thus baptized are Christened, and are to be esteemed and loved as Christians, and to be received into Christian Communion in all Christian Churches where they come, until by apostasie or impenitency in certain disobedience to the Laws of Christ, in points necessary to Christian Communion, they forfeit that priviledge. Nor are men to deprive them of the great benefit thus given them by Christ, on pretence of any *wit* or *holiness*, or *power*, to amend Christs terms, and make the Church Doors narrower, or tie men to themselves for worldly ends. Yet must the Pastors still difference the weaker Christians from the stronger, and labour to edifie the weak, but not to cast them out of the Church.

§. 6. The sacred Ministry is subordinate to Christ in his *Teaching*, *Governing*, and *Priestly* Office, and thus essentiated by Chrifts own institution, which man hath no power to change: Therefore under Christ they must teach the Church by sacred Doctrine, guide them by that and sacred Discipline, called *The power of the Keys* (that is of judging who is fit to enter by Baptism, to continue, to partake of the Communion, to be suspended or cast out) and to lead them in the publick Worship of God, interceding in Prayer and speaking for them, and administring to them the Sacraments or holy Seals of the Covenant of God.

§. 7. The first part of the Ministers Office is about the *unbelieving world*, to convert them to the Faith of Christ; and the second perfective part about the *Churches*. Nor must it be thought that the first is done by them as meer private men.

§. 8. As Satan fell by *pride*, and overthrew man by tempting him to *pride* (*to become as Gods in Knowledge*) so Christ himself was to conquer the Prince of *pride* by *humility*, and by the *Cross*, by a life of *suffering*; contemned by the blind and obstinate world, *making himself of no reputation, despising the shame* of suffering as a Malefactor (a Traitor and Blasphemer:) And the *bearing of the Cross* was a principal part of his Precepts and Covenant to his Disciples, without which they could not be his Followers. And by Humility they were to follow the Captain of their Salvation, in conquering the Prince of *pride*, and in treading down the Enemie-world, even the *lust of the flesh*, the *lust of the eyes*, and *pride of life*, which are not of the Father but of the world.

§. 9. Accordingly Christ taught his chief Disciples, that if they were not so *converted as to become as little children, they could not enter into the Kingdom of Heaven*, *Matth.* 18. 3. His School receiveth not masterly Disciples, but humble *teachable Learners*, that become *fools* that they may be *wise*.

And when they were disputing and seeking which *of them should be greatest*, he earnestly rebuked all such thoughts, setting a *little child* before them, telling them that the Princes of the Earth *exercise authority*, and are called *Benefactors* (or by big Names) but with them it should not be so; but *he that would be the greatest must be servant of all*, *Luk.* 22. shewing them that it was not a *worldly grandeur*, nor *forcing power* by the Sword (which belongeth to Civil Magistrates) which was to be exercised by the Pastors of the Church: But that he that would be the Chiefest, must be most excellent in Merit, and most serviceable to all, and get his honour and do his work by *meriting* the respect and love of Volunteers. The *Sword* is the *Magistrates*, who are also Chrifts Ministers; (for all Power is given him, and he is Head over all things to the Church.) But they are eminently the Ministers of his *Power*; but the *Pastors* and *Teachers* are most eminently Ministers of his *Paternal and saving love and wisdom*. And by *wisdom* and *love* to do their work. The Word preached and applied generally and particularly (by the Keys) is their Weapon or Arms, and not the *Sword*.

The *Bohemians* therefore knew what they said, when they seemed damnable Hereticks to the worldly Clergie that destroyed them, when they placed their Cause in these four Articles: 1. *To have the whole Sacrament, Bread and Wine.* 2. *To have free leave for true Ministers to preach the word of God* (without unjust silencing of proud worldly men that cannot stand before the truth.) 3. *To have Temporal Dominion* (or Government by the Sword, and power over mens Bodies and Estates) *taken from the Clergie*. 4. *To have gross sin suppressed by the lawful Magistrate by the Sword.*

§. 10. Had it been necessary to the Churches Union against *Schism* or *Heresie* for Christians to know that *Peter* or some one of his Apostles must be his Vicar-General, and Head of his Church to whom all must obey, who can believe that Christ would not only have silenced so necessary a point, but also at a time when he was desired or called to decide it, have only spoken so much against it, to take down all such Expectations. Yea we never read that *Peter* exercised any Authority or Jurisdictions over any other of the Apostles, nor more than other Apostles did; much less that ever he chose a Bishop to be Lord of the Church, as his Successor. Nay he himself seemeth to fore-see this mischief, and therefore saith, 1. *Pet.* 5. 1, 2, 3. *The Elders which are among you I exhort, who am also an Elder and a Witness of the Sufferings of Christ, and also a Partaker of the Glory,*

Glory that shall be revealed. (These are his Dignities.) *Feed the Flock of God which is among you,* (not out of your reach and hearing in a vast Diocess) *taking the oversight, not by constraint, but willingly* (and on willing men) *not for filthy lucre, but of a ready mind; neither as being Lords over Gods Heritage, but being Examples to the Flock; and when the chief Shepherd shall appear, ye shall receive a Crown of Glory that fadeth not away.*

§. 11. Nothing is more certain than that the Church for above 300 years had no power of the Sword, that is, forcibly to meddle with and hurt mens Bodies or Estates, (except what the Apostles had by miracle): And to this day no *Protestants,* and not most *Papists* claim any such Power as of Divine Institution, but only plead that the Secular Powers are bound by the Sword to destroy such as are judged *Hereticks* by the Bishops, and to punish such as contemn the censures of the Church.

§. 12. He that would see more for the Power of Princes vindicated from the Clergies Claim and Usurpation, may find much in many old Treatises, written for the Emperours against the Pope, collected by *Goldastus de Monarch.* and in *Will. Barclay,* but much better in Bishop *Bilson,* of *Obedience,* and in Bishop *Andrew's Tortura Torti,* and in Bishop *Buckridge Roffensis* of the Power of Kings, and much in *Spalatensis de Repub.*

§. 13. The *Universality of Christians* is the *Catholick Church,* of which Christ is the only Head or Soveraign; but it is the duty of these to worship God in solemn Assemblies, and to live in a holy Conversation together; and to join in striving against sin, and to help each other in the way to life; therefore Societies united for these ends are called, *Particular Churches.*

§. 14. When the Apostles had converted a competent number of Christians, they gather'd them into such Assemblies, and as a Politick Society, set over them such Ministers of Christ, as are afore described, to be their Guides.

§. 15. These Officers are in Scripture called sometime *Elders,* and sometimes *Bishops,* to whom *Deacons* were added to serve them and the Church subordinately. Dr. *Hammond* hath well described their Office in in his *Annotat.* which was *to preach constantly in publick, and private, to administer both Sacraments, to pray and praise God with the People, to Catechize, to visit and pray with the sick, to comfort troubled Souls, to admonish the unruly, to reject the impenitent, to restore the penitent, to take care of the poor,* and in a word, *of all the Flock.*

§. 16. The Apostles set usually more than one of these Elders or Bishops in every Church, not as if one might not rule the Flock where no more was necessary, but according to their needs, that the work might not be undone for want of Ministers.

§. 17. They planted their Churches usually in Cities, because Christians comparatively to the rest were few (as Sects are among us) and no where else usually enough for a Society, and because the Neighbour-scattered Villages might best come to the Cities near them; not but that it was lawful to plant Churches in the Country, where there were enough to constitute them, and sometimes they did so, as by *Clemens Roman. ad Corinth.* by History appeareth.

§. 18. *Grotius* thinketh that one City at first had divers Churches and Bishops, and that they were gathered after the manner of the Synagogues; and Dr. *Hammond* thinketh that for some time there were two Churches and Bishops in many Cities, one of Jews and one of Gentiles; and that in *Rome Paul* and *Peter* had two Churches, whom *Linus* and *Cletus* did succeed, till they were united in *Clemens.*

§. 19. There is great evidence of History that a particular Church of the Apostles setling was essentially only [" a Company of Christians, Pa-" stors and People associated for *personal holy communion* and mutual help " in holy Doctrine, Worship, Conversation, and Order.] Therefore it never consisted of so few or so many, or so distant as to be uncapable of such *personal help and Communion* : But was ever distinguished as from accidental Meetings, so from the Communion of many Churches or distant Christians, which was held but by Delegates, Synods of Pastors or Letters, and not by personal help, in presence.

Not that all these must needs always meet in the same place: but that usually they did so, or at due times at least, and were no more nor more distant than could so meet : Sometimes Persecution hindred them; sometimes the Room might be too small: Even Independent Churches among us sometimes meet in divers places : and one Parish hath divers Chappels for the aged and weak that are unfit for travel.

§. 20. *Scotus* began the opinion (as *Davenport, Fr. a Santa Clara* intimateth) and *Dion Petavius* improved it, and Dr. *Hammond* hath largely asserted it, that the Apostles at first planted a single Bishop in each Church, with one or more Deacons, and that he had power in time to ordain Elders of a different Order, Species, or Office, and that the word Elder and Bishop and Pastor in Scripture never signifie these subject Elders, but the Bishops only, and, saith he, there is no evidence that there were any of the subject sort of Presbyters in Scripture-times: Which concession is very kindly accepted by the Presbyterians; but they call for proof that ever these Bishops were authorised to make a new Species of Presbyters which were never made in Scripture-times? and indeed they vehemently deny it, and may well despair of such a proof.

§. 21. But for my part I believe the foundation unproved (that then there was but one Elder in a Church) and think many Texts of Scripture fully prove the contrary. But I join with Dr. *Hammond* in believing that in Scripture-times there was no particular Church that had more stated meetings for publick Communion than one : For if there was so long but one Elder, there could be but one such Assembly at once ; for they had no such Assemblies which were not guided by a Presbyter or Bishop, in Doctrine, Worship, Sacraments and Discipline: And they used to have the Eucharist every Lords day at least, and often much more. And one man can be at once but in one place. §. 22.

§. 22. I have elsewhere fully proved, that the ancient Churches that had Bishops were no bigger than our Parishes (and few a quarter so big as the greatest of them) and consisted of no more than might have such present personal Communion as is before described ; the proofs are too large to be here recited. *Ignatius* is the plainest, who saith, that this was the note of a Churches Unity, that [*To every Church there was one Altar, and one Bishop, with his Fellow Presbyters and Deacons:*] And elsewhere chargeth the Bishop to take account of his Flock whether they all come to Church, even Servant-men and Maids.

Clemens Romanus before him intimateth the like, mentioning even Country Bishops.

Justin Martyr's Description of the Christian Assemblies plainly proveth it.

Tertullian's Description of them and many other passages in him prove it more fully. He professeth that they took not the Lord's Supper save only *from the hand of the Bishop* (*Antistitis manu*) who could give it but to one Assembly at once.

Many Canons also fully shew it (elsewhere cited) some appoint all the people to joyn with the Bishop on the great Festivals of the year, even above 300 years after Christ.

The Custom also of choosing Bishops sheweth it, where all the people met and chose him : Yea in *Cyprian*'s time the Exercise of Discipline proveth it, when even in such great Churches as *Carthage* it was done in the presence of the people, and with their consent.

§. 23. The only Churches in the World, that for about 200 years after Christ, if not more, had more than one ordinary Assembly, for Church-Communion, though but like our Parish-Chappels, were *Rome* and *Alexandria*, as far as I can learn in any History: For that at *Jerusalem* for all the numbers had no more stated Members than oft met in one place (excepting occasional absents). And I find no reason to believe that ever these two (the chief Cities of the Empire,) had so long more than some *London* Parishes (which have above sixty thousand souls as is supposed) no nor near (if half) so many. And because elsewhere I have only excepted these two Cities, I will yet add somewhat to shew, that even there the case was not as many now imagine.

§. 24. *Cornelius* in an Epistle to *Fabius* of *Antioch* (in *Euseb. Hist. l. 6. c. 43. alias* 42.) saith that " in the Church of *Rome* were 46 Presbyters, " 7 Deacons, and of other Officers 94. that is, 42 Acolites, 52 Exor- " cists and Readers, with Porters, Widows, and impotent persons a- " bove 1050 souls, who are all relieved by the grace and goodness of " Almighty God, &c.] This is the chief testimony in the third Age to prove that this one Church had more than could either meet in one place, or hold personal Communion.

§. 25. But let it be considered, 1. That partly for the honour of qualified persons, and partly that all the Church might in season have the help of all mens gifts, they were so far in the ancient Churches from having so few as Dr. *Hammond* and *Petavius* imagine, that they multiplied Officers, and dignified, and so employed a great part of the Church that had useful gifts: Insomuch that a most credible Witness shortly after, even *Gregory Nazianzen*, saith, *Orat.* 1. *Pag.* 45. that by the intrusion of men for dignity and maintenance, "*The Church-Rulers were almost more than the Subjects.* The words are Ἡγεῖσθαι ὑπὲρ τῶν ἄλλων, &c. *Of* "*others I am ashamed, who when they are no better than others, (and* "*I wish they were not much worse) thrust themselves upon the most holy My-* "*steries, as we say, with unwashen hands and prophane minds, and before* "*they are worthy to approach to holy things, ambitiously enter the Vestry it* "*self (or Chancell) and press and thrust themselves about the holy Table,* "*as if they judged this Order not to be an example of Virtue, but an occasion* "*and help of getting maintenance, and not to be an Office lyable to give Account,* "*but a Command in which they may be free from Censure: Who being misera-* ☞ "*ble (or pitiful persons) as to Piety, and unhappy as to Splendour, that is,* "*low in the World and Parts) do now in number almost exceed those whom* "*they are over (or are to govern).* [This would make one suspect that "there were then many Ruling Elders that preach'd not; but it's plain "they had an Office about the Sacraments.] *Therefore this Evil increasing* "*and getting strength with time, it seems to me that they will have none under* "*them to rule, (or guide) but that all will turn Teachers and will Prophesie, in-* "*stead (as was promised by God) of being all taught of God: So that of old* "*the History and Parable said,* Saul *also is among the Prophets. For there* "*neither now is nor ever was so great plenty of any other thing as there is now* "*of these frequent Shames and Criminals; for other things, as they have their* "*flourishing time, have also their decay. And though to repress their impetu-* "*ousness be a work above my strength, yet certainly to hate it and be ashamed is* "*not the least part of Piety.*

Judge by this, what numbers of Officers or Clergy-men then the Church had.

§. 26. Next for the *Poor*, consider their proportions in and by other Churches; *Chrysost. in Matth. Edit Savil. p.* 421. supposeth the Poor of the Church of *Antioch* (whence he came) to have been about the *tenth part* and dividing the City into three Ranks, he accounts a tenth part rich, and a tenth part poor, and the rest of a middle Estate between both. Now in *Chrysostom*'s time the Church was so high, being owned by the greatest Emperours as we may well suppose almost all or most of the rich came in: Whereas at *Rome* in the time of *Cornelius* it being under reproach and cruel persecution, we may well conclude, that most of the rich stood out, and they might say with *Paul*, not many Great, not many Noble are called; few rich men comparatively receiving the Gospel, it's most likely that the poor were then far more than a tenth part, if not the greater part of the Church. But suppose them a tenth part, which is not probable, the whole Church of *Rome* then would be but 10500 Souls, which

which is about the fifth part or sixth as big as *Martins* Parish, and about a quarter as big as *Stepney* Parish, and about a third or fourth part as big as *Giles Cripplegate* Parish, and not half so big as *Giles* in the *Fields* and other Parishes. Moreover *Chrysostome, Hom.* 11. in *Act. p.* 674. computes the poor at *Constantinople* to be about half as many as all the other Christians, and this in the most flourishing City and Age. And by this measure they would yet fall further short.

It may be you will say, that these were not the poorest of all that were kept by the Church: But it's known that ever since the times of extraordinary Community, the Churches relieved all the needy according to the several degrees of their wants; and these were such as were in want, though not equally, and they are such poor as were distinguished not only from the Rich, but also from the middle sort; and such as the Church took care to relieve.

§. 27. And as for *Alexandria*, the greatest City of the Empire next *Rome* (as *Josephus* saith, *de bello Jud. l.* 5. *c. ult.* it is certain that in the third Century the Christians had more Meeting Places for Divine Worship than one, and in the fourth Century had many: *Epiphanius* nameth divers, *Haeref.* 69. *p.* 728. *Arius* having one wherein he preached, had that advantage to propogate his Heresie. But all know that the building of Temples began after Emperours were Christians, and the fair Churches which, *Eusebius* faith, they had in *Dioclesians* time (till he destroyed them) were but like our Tabernacles or private Churches, and grew to Number and Ornament but a little before, as *Eusebius* intimateth. It was a good while before there were two Churches, even in *Constantinople*. Indeed, it is noted, as a singularity, that they had *two Churches*: But they mistake, that apply that to *two Meeting Places*, which is spoken of two Societies, because in *Meletius* time they had two Bishops.

§. 28. But yet let us see how big the Christian Church was in this great City, even when it had many Chapels; even in *Athanasius* time, in the fourth Century, *Tom.* 1. *Ed. Commel. p.* 531. in his Apology to *Constant.* you may find (in words too large to be all transcribed) that he being accused for assembling the People in the Great Church, maketh this part of his Defence, ['*The confluence of the People at the* Easter *Solemnity was so great,*
'*that if they had met in several Assemblies* (or by parties) *the other Churches were*
'*so narrow or small that they would have been in danger of suffering by the Crowd;*
'*nor would the universal Harmony and Concord of the People have been so visible*
'*and efficacious if they had met in Parcels; Therefore he concludeth it better for*
'*the whole Multitude to meet in that great Church,* (being a place large enough
'*to receive them altogether,) and to have a concurrence of the People all with one*
'*Voice* (in Symphony :) *For if according to Christ's promise where two shall agree*
'*of any thing it shall be done for them — how prevalent will be the One-voice of so*
'*numerous a People assembled together, and saying, Amen, to God? Who therefore*
'*would not admire? Who would not count it a happiness to see so great a People*
'*met together in one place? And how did the People rejoyce to see one another,*

'*whereas*

'*whereas formerly they assembled in several places.*] Thus plainly *Athanasius*.

I do not hence gather that every Man, Woman, and Child was present: In our Parish Churches that hold the Assembly, some are there, and usually some stay at home and come by turns: But it seemeth hence plain that even in *Alexandria* the Christians were no more than that the main Body of them at great Solemnities could meet and hear in one Assembly. Which in many of our Parishes they cannot do.

§. 29. Add to this, that *Athanasius* tells them that his Predecessor *Alexander* did as much as he had done, on such occasions assembling their whole Multitude in one Church before it was dedicated, *pag.* 532.

§. 30. I add a further Argument from the City it self, as offered me also while I was writing this, by a learned Friend in his own Words.

This City was, by Strabo's *description of it, like a Souldiers Coat, whose length at either side was almost thirty furlongs, its breadth at either end seven or eight Furlongs,* Geogr. li. 17. p. 546. *So the whole compass will be less than ten Miles. A third or fourth part of this was taken up with publick Buildings, Temples, and Royal Palaces,* ibid. *Thus is two miles and a half, or three and a quarter taken up. I take this to be that Region of the City which* Epiphanius *calls* Ϲρύχιον *(where he tells us was the famous Library of* Ptolomy Philadelphus) *and speaks of it in his time as destitute of Inhabitants, de ponder. & mensur.* n. 9. p. 166. *A great part of the City was assigned to the* Jews. *So* Strabo *indefinitely, as* Josephus *quotes him,* Antiqu. Jud. l. 14. c. 12. *Others tell us more punctually that their share was two of the five Divisions (*Ushers *Annals Lat. p. 859.) Though many of them had their habitations in the other Divisions, yet they had two fifth parts intire to themselves: And this is I suppose the* τόπος ίδιος *which* Josephus *saith the Successours of* Alexander *set apart for them,* Bell. Jud. l. 2. c. 21. *Thus we see how six or seven miles of the ten are disposed of. The greatest part of the Citizens (as at* Rome *and other Cities) in the beginning of the fourth Age were Heathens. Else* Antonius *had wronged their City, who in* Athanasius *time is brought in thus, exclaiming by* Jerome, Vit. Paul. p. 243. Civitas meretrix in quam totius orbis Dæmonia confluxère, *&c. A charge thus formed supposeth the prevailing Party to be guilty. But let us suppose them equal and their proportion half of the five or four miles remaining. Let the rest be divided between the* Orthodox, *and the* Arians, *and* Novatians, *and other sorts. And if we be just, a large part will fall to the share of* Hereticks *and* Sectaries. *For (not to mention others) the* Novatians *had several Churches and a Bishop there, till* Cyrils *time,* Vid. Socrat. Hist. l. 7. c. 7. *The* Arians *were a great part of those that professed Christianity,* Sozom. Hist. li. 1. c. 14. *And if we may judg of the Followers by the Leaders, no less than half: For whereas there were nineteen Presbyters and Deacons in that Church (* Theodor. Hist. li. 4. c. 20.) *(Twelve was the number of their Presbyters by their ancient Constitution, and seven of their Deacons as appears by* Eutychius, *here and at* Rome, *and elsewhere) six Presbyters with* Arius, *and five Deacons fell off from the* Catholicks, Sozom. Hist. li. 1. c. 14. *But let the* Arians *be much fewer, yet will not the proportion of the* Catholick *Bishops part in this City be more than that of a small*

Town,

Town, one of eight or twelve Furlongs in compass. And so the number of Christians on this account, will be no more than might well meet for Worship in one place.

If the Reader will peruse *Epiphanius* History of the Fraction between *Alexander* and the Followers of *Meletius* in *Alexandria*, how *Alexander* was impatient with their separate Meetings, when *Meletius* was dead (though till then two Bishops and Churches lived quietly in one City) because they came not to his Church; with the rest of the story, he will easily see what a Church was then even in *Alexandria*.

Thus you see the difference of a just computation, and the hasty accounts of men, that judg of Places and Persons as they are in their misled imaginations, and not as they were indeed and truth. Mr. *Dodwell* in a Letter to me layeth so much on the number of the Officers and Poor before mentioned, as if it proved undoubtedly a Diocesane Church, when the conclusion ariseth from an erroneous comparing their Cities and times with ours, and their Presbyters with our Parish-Priests and Curats.

And when all's done a grand Patriarchal Church is not the measure of a Diocesane, or of every Bishops Church: their Presbyters had other work than our Curates have: They met in the same Assembly with the Bishop, and sate in a Semicircle on each side him, and were as a Colledge of Governours to rule one Church, and that only by the Word (applyed by the Keys) and not by the Sword, till *Cyril* first usurped it, for which by Historians he is noted. If our times tempt you to marvel how so many Officers or Clerks were maintained by so few People, Church-History affordeth you matter enough to resolve your doubt.

§. 31. But if these two great Cities had indeed had yet more Altars and Churches, *Orbis major est Urbe*, saith *Hierome*: Two singular Cities may not over-weigh the contrary case of all the Churches: If any other had been like them it would have been *Antioch* the third Patriarchate, when as in *Ignatius* time, as is aforesaid, the Churches unity there and else-where was notified * by [εν συνασκειν η ως επισκοπος], *One Altar* (or Altar-place) *and One Bishop with his Presbyters and Deacons.*]

And hence came it to be the note of a Schism, to set up *Altare contra Altare* because one Bishop and Church had but one Altar. Mr. *Mede* (no injudicious nor Factious man) saw this, and asserteth it from the plain words of *Ignatius*.

§. 32. How the case came to be altered it is easie to know: But whether it was well or ill done, is all the controversie, or the chief.

I confess there want not some that think that the Apostles had their several assigned Provinces, and that they left them to twelve Successours, and this is the foundation of Patriarchal or Provincial Churches, with such unproved Dreams: 1. We doubt not but that the Apostles wisely distributed their Labours: But we believe not that they divided the Countreys into their several Dioceses, or Provinces: nor that two of them (*e.g. John* and *Paul, Peter* and *Paul, James* and other Apostles) might

* *That a local Altar is here meant, I elsewhere prove against there that lay it as but one communicating Body, cohearing to one Bishop.*

not and did not do the work of an Apoſtle in the ſame Country and City. Much leſs do we believe that one of them (*e. g.* *James* at *Jeruſalem*, whether an Apoſtle or not I contend not) was a Biſhop over the Apoſtles when they reſided there.

2. Nor do we believe that they left any ſuch divided Provinces to their Succeſſors: If they had, it's ſtrange that we had not twelve or thirteen Patriarchal or Provincial Churches hence noted. Which were they, and how came they ſo ſoon to be forgotten and unknown? And why had we firſt but three Patriarchs, and one of thoſe (*Alexandria*) accounting from no Apoſtle, but from S. *Mark*, and the other two reckoning from one and the ſame Apoſtle, ſave that *Rome* reckoned from two at once, *Peter* and *Paul*, when as one City muſt (ſay they) have but one Biſhop?

§. 33. The caſe is known; that, 1. When Chriſtians ſo multiplyed, that one Aſſembly would not ſerve, but they became enough for many, the Biſhops greatneſs and wealth increaſing with the People, they continued them all under their own Government, and ſo took them all to be their Chapels, ſetling divers Altars but not divers Biſhops in one Church. 2. And herewith their work alſo, by degrees, was much changed; and they that at firſt were moſt employed in Guiding the whole Church in Gods publick worſhip, and exerciſed preſent diſcipline before them, and were the ſole uſual Preachers to them all, (the reſt of the Elders Preaching but when the Biſhop could not, or bid them,) did after become diſtant Judges, and their Government, by degrees, degenerated to a ſimilitude of Civil Magiſtracy. 3. And then they ſet up the old exploded queſtion; which of them ſhould be the chief or greateſt: And then they that had the greateſt Cities being the richeſt and greateſt Biſhops in intereſt, becauſe of the greatneſs and riches of their Flocks, they got the Church Government to be diſtributed, much like the *Roman* Civil Government within that Empire; And where the Civil Magiſtrate had moſt and largeſt command, they gave the Eccleſiaſtical Biſhop the like: And ſo they ſet up the Biſhops of the three chief Cities as Patriarchs, *Rome* being the firſt, becauſe it was the great Imperial Seat, as the *Chalcedon* Council giveth the true reaſon. Afterwards *Conſtantinople* and *Jeruſalem* being added, they turned them into five: And *Carthage* and other places, not called Patriarchal Seats, had exempt peculiar Juriſdictions with a power near to Patriarchs. And the reſt of the Biſhops ſtrove much for precedency, and got as large Territories as they could, and as numerous Flocks and many Pariſhes, though ſtill the name *Parœcia* was uſed for the whole Epiſcopal Church when it was turned into a Dioceſs.

§. 34. I conceive that this Change of *One Altar* into a *Dioceſane Church* of *many Altars* and *Pariſhes* was not well done, but is the thing that hath confounded the Chriſtian World, and that they ought to have increaſed the number of Churches as the number of Chriſtians did increaſe, as the Bees ſwarm into another Hive. My Reaſons are, 1. Chriſt and the Holy Ghoſt in the Apoſtles having ſetled a *Church Species* and Order

(like

(like that of the Synagogues, and not like that of the Temp'e,) no man ought to have changed that Form: Becaule they can prove no power to do it: and becaufe it accufeth the Inftitution of Chrift and the Holy Ghoft of infufficiency or errour, which muft fo foon be altered by them. Perfective addition, as an Infant groweth up to Manhood, we deny not. But who gave them power to abrogate the very *Species* of the firft Inftituted Churches? That the *Species* is altered, is certainly proved by the different ufes and *Termini* of the Relation. For a Church of the firft Inftitution was a *Society joyned for perfonal Communion in Doctrine, Worfhip, and holy living*: But a Diocefs confifting of many fcore or hundred Parifhes that never fee or know or come near one another, are uncapable of any fuch prefent perfonal Communion, and have none but Mental, and by Officers or Delegates.

2. By this means, all the Parifh-Churches being turned into Chapels and un-Churched, are all robbed of their Right; feeing each one ought to have a Bifhop and Prefbyters, and the benefit of that Office and Order, which is now denied them, and many hundred fuch Parifhes turned into Chapels have no Bifhop to themfelves but one among them all to the Diocefs.

3. Becaufe by this means true Difcipline is become impoffible and unpracticable; by the diftance and multitude of the people, and the diftance and paucity of Bifhops: What Chrift commandeth, *Mat.* 18. being as impoffible to be done in many hundred Parifhes, by one Bifhop and his Confiftory, as the Difcipline of fo many hundred Schools by one Schoolmafter (though each School have an Ufher) or the care of many hundred Hofpitals by one Phyfician, perhaps at twenty, or forty, or eighty, or an hundred miles diftance.

4. Becaufe it altereth the antient Office of a Bifhop and of a Prefbyter, and fetteth new ones in the ftead: As a Bifhop was the Bifhop of one Church, fo a Prefbyter was his Affiftant, *Ejufdem Ordinis, in the Government of the Church*, who now is turned into a meer Ufher, or *Worfhipping-Teacher*, or *Chaplain*.

5. Becaufe it certainly divideth the Churches: For Chriftians would unite in a *Divine Inftitution*, and the *exercife of true Difcipline*, that will never unite in a *humane Policy* which abrogateth the Divine, and certainly deftroyeth commanded neceffary Difcipline.

§. 35. The very work alfo of the Bifhop, and fo the Office came thus to be changed: Chrift having appointed no other Church Governours (befides Magiftrates) but fuch (as Philofophers in their Schools) who were appointed to fet up Holy Societies for Divine Doctrine, Worfhip, and Holy Living, and to Guide them accordingly, by Teaching, Worfhip, and Government by the Word, forbidding them the Sword or Force, they are faid to have the *Keys of the Church* and the *Kingdom of Heaven*, becaufe as Grace is Glory in the feed, the Church is Heaven in the feed, and the Paftors were the Adminiftrators of Sacraments and Church-priviledges, and therefore the Judges who were fit for them, who fhould be Baptized, who

fhould

should Communicate, and in what rank, and who should be denied these, admonished or excluded, and who should, as far as belongeth to others, be judged meet or unmeet for Heaven: And so the Christian Societies were to be kept clean, and not to be like the polluted World of Infidels. And the Pastors had no other power to use; but were to judge only those within, and leave them without to Gods own judgment, and to the Magistrate, who was not to punish any one for not being in or of the Church, or for departing from it, which is a grievous punishment it self.

But Magistrates being then Heathens, the Christians were hard put to it for the decision of their quarrels: For the love of the world and selfishness were but imperfectly cured in them. They went to Law before Heathen Judges with each other; and this became a snare and a scandal to them. S. *Paul* therefore chideth them for not ending differences by Christian Arbitrators among themselves, as if there were none among them wise enough to Arbitrate. Hereupon the Churches taking none to be wiser or trustier than their Pastors, made them their Arbitrators, and it became a censurable scandal for any to accuse a Church-member to a Magistrate, and to have Suits at Law. By this means, the Bishop becoming a Stated Arbitrator, thereby became the Governour of the Christians, but with his Presbyters and not alone. But because Bishops had no power of the sword, to touch mens bodies or estates, but only to suspend them from Church-Communion, and Excommunicate them, or impose penitential Confessions on them, therefore they fitted their Canons (which were the Bishops Agreements) to this Governing use, to keep Christians under their Government from the Magistrates. And so they made Canons, that a Fornicator or Adulterer should be so long or so long suspended, and a Murderer so long, and so of the rest.

§. 36. And when *Constantine* turned Christian, he had many reasons to confirm this Arbitrating Canonical power to the Christian Bishops by the Civil Sanction. 1. Because he found them in possession of it as contracters by mutual consent; and what could a Christian Prince do less than grant that to the Christians which they chose and had. 2. Because the advancement and honour of the Teachers and Pastors he thought tended to the honour of their Religion, and the success of their Doctrine upon the Heathens with whom they dwelled. Grandure and Power much prevail with carnal minds. 3. Because he had but few Magistrates at first that were Christians, and none that so well knew the affairs of Christians as their own chosen Bishops. And he feared lest the power of Heathen Magistrates over the Christians might injure and oppress them. 4. He designed to draw the Heathens to Christianity by the honouring of Christians above them. 5. And withal his interest lay most in their strength; For they were the fastest part of his Souldiers and Subjects, that for Conscience and their own Interest, rejoyced to advance and defend him to the utmost, (when he lost many of the Pagans) and they were not of the spirit of the old Pretorian Souldiers, that set up and pulled down Emperours

at

at their pleasure. Had *Constantine* faln, the Christians had much faln with him, and had the Christians been weakned he had been weakened: They were become his strength. And he foresaw not the evils that afterwards would follow. Some must govern, and there were then no wiser nor better men than the Bishops and Pastors of the Churches. And their interest in the Christian people (that chose them) was greatest: As now all differing parties of Christians among us (Papists, Presbyterians, Independents, Anabaptists) would desire nothing as more conducing to their ends, than that the King would put the greatest Power (especially of Religion) into the hands of those Teachers whom they esteem and follow; even so was it with the Christians in the days of *Constantine*: And hereupon Laws were made, that none should compel Christians to answer in any Court of Justice, saving before their own Bishops, and so Bishops were made almost the sole Governours of the Christians.

§. 37. By this means it is no wonder if multitudes of wicked men flock'd into the Church and defiled and dishonoured it: For the Murderer that was to be hanged if he were no Christian, was but to be kept from the Sacrament if he were a Christian, and do some confessing penance; which was little to hanging or other death; And so proportionably of other Crimes. Bad Christians by this device were multiplyed. The Emperour also being a Christian, worldly men are mostly of the Religion of the Prince or highest powers.

§. 38. And no man that can gather an effect from an effectual cause could doubt, if neither *Nazianzen*, or any Historian had told it him, but that proud and worldly men would strive then to be Bishops, and use all possible diligence to obtain so great preferment: Who of them is it that would not have Command and Honour and Wealth, if he can get it? While the great invitation to the sacred Ministry was the winning and edifying of Souls, those that most valued Souls, desired it (yet desired it to be kept from such Poverty and Persecution as exposed them to hinderance and contempt). But when Riches, Reputation and Dominion were the Baits, who knoweth not what sort of Appetites would be the keenest? Christ telleth us, how hardly Rich men are good and come to Heaven. Therefore when Bishops must be all Great and Rich, either Christ must be deceived, or it must be as hard for them to be honest Christians as for a Camel to go through the Needles eye. And thus, *Venenum funditur in Ecclesiam*.

§. 39. The World being thus brought into the Church without the cure of the worldly mind, and the Guides being so strongly tempted to be the very worst, no wonder if the Worldly Spirit now too much rule the Church, and if those that are yet of the same Spirit, approve, plead, and strive for what they love and despise the business of the Cross, and Christian Humility, and Simplicity to this day: And if Bishops have done much of their work accordingly, ever since *Constantine* (and much before) it hath been the Devils Work to carry on his War against Christ and Piety, under

Christ's

Chrift's own name, and the pretence of Piety, as an Angel of Light and Righteoufnefs and Unity, and to fet up Paftors over the Church of Chrift, that hate the Doctrine and Life, and Crofs of Chrift, that by pleading for Godlinefs and Concord, may be the effectual Enemies of both, and may fight againft Chrift in his own Livery, under his Colours, and with his own Arms. *Whofe God is their Belly, who glory in their fhame, who mind earthly things, being Enemies to the Crofs of Chrift*: The Hiftory of whom you will find in the following part of this Treatife.

§. 40. But here I muft above all remember the Reader, that he is not for this Corruption of the Clergy, and Government of the Church, to think that the Church here ceafed to be a true Church, or that the Miniftry was loft, or that it became unlawful to hold Communion with any fuch Churches; much lefs to think hardly of Chriftianity it felf, as if it were no better than falfe Religions, becaufe fo many of its Paftors were fo bad. None of God's Counfels were fruftrate by mans fin: None of his Promifes to his Church have failed. For all this Chrift is the Saviour of the World, the Prince of Righteoufnefs and Peace, that came to deftroy the Works of the Devil, and to fave his people from their Sins; and all that are given him of the Father fhall come to him, and he will caft none of them out, nor fhall any take them out of his hands?

§. 41. I. Let it be ftill remembred, that as the Chronicles of Kingdoms mention only the publick Actions of Princes and great Men, but name not the poor and private fort, fo alfo our Church-Hiftory of Councils and publick things, fay little of godly private Chriftians, but of Patriarchs and great Prelates, who yet are themfelves but a very fmall part of the Chriftian World.

II. Note alfo that every Bifhop had many Presbyters; whofe work was not to ftrive for fuperiority, nor trouble the world in Councils (where ufually they came not) and fo had not a quarter of the temptations that the Bifhops had: And though we find mention fometimes of the Presbyters alfo that were naught, yet the number fo reproved and proved bad, is not proportionable to the number of Prelates compared among themfelves, that mifcarried in Councils. The Presbyters that ftaid at home and followed their work in private with the Flock, and came not on the Stage in publick affairs, kept up the fubftance and practice of Religion.

III. And the private Chriftians had yet lefs temptation, and were not fo overwhelmed with worldly things, nor carryed away by pride and ambition and covetoufnefs, as the ruling party were.

IV. And the Monks, and other retired Chriftians, that faw the Prelates fin and fnares, (though many of them had their failings too, yet) no doubt kept up much ferious piety, and a holy life.

V. And no doubt but very many of the Bifhops themfelves were humble holy faithful men, that grieved for the mifcarriages of the reft. Though fuch excellent perfons as *Gregory Neocefarea, Gregory Nazianzen, Gregory Nyffen, Bafil, Chryfoftome, Auguftine, Hillary, Profper, Fulgentius*, &c.

were

were not very common, no doubt but there were many that wrote not Books, nor came so much into the notice of the world, but avoided contentious and factious Stirs, that quietly and honestly conducted the Flocks in the ways of piety, love, and justice. And some of them *(as S. Martin)* separated from the Councils and Communion of the prevailing turbulent sort of the Prelates, to signifie their disowning of their sins.

VI. And oft times, when the Prelates were at the worst, God raised up some very Godly Princes, that maintained Religion more than the Clergy, and were an honour to it when the Bishops dishonoured it.

VII. And it is not to be contemned, that much piety was kept up among great numbers of Christians, whom (for some mistake) the rest reviled and condemned as Schismaticks or Hereticks. Little know we how many holy souls were among those that are in *Epiphanius* Catalogue. Of the *Audians* and some others he seemeth to confess as much himself. The *Novatians* were tolerated in almost all the Empire, and had their Churches and Bishops, having the testimony of the Orthodox that they were usually of sound faith and upright lives, and stricter than other Christians were. And God pardoneth the infirmity of a small mistake in judgment, when men are sincerely addicted to his service. Now and then a cruel Prelate did prosecute them, but so did not the gentler sort *(as Atticus, Proclus, &c. at Constantinople, &c.)* nor the Emperours themselves, save when so instigated.

VIII. And though the Churches in the *Roman* Empire kept up this grandure of Patriarchs, Metropolitans, and rich Prelates, that after over-topped Kings, it was not so in other parts of the Christian world, but the Clergy lived more humbly and quietly. The *Scots* under *Columbanus* and their other Presbyters, long lived in great piety without any Bishops. And when the *Scots* Presbyters *Finan, Aidan,* &c. ordained Bishops in *Northumberland*, they were commonly humble, holy men, like themselves. And both *Scots* and *Britains* so much misliked the *Romane*-grandure and way, that when *Augustine* the Monk came in, they would not subject themselves to the Pope, or any Foreign Prelates, nor so much as eat and drink with the Missionaries. And the like we may say of some other *Extra-imperial* Churches. The *Spaniards* themselves not only while *Arian Goths* (of whom see the testimony of *Salvian*, to the shame of the Orthodox) but after *Recaredus* days, for many ages, lived in great quietness, while *Italy, France,* and *Germany* were employed in Hereticating, Cursing, Excommunicating, or bloudy Wars. The great Empire of *Abasia* (as the credibleſt History saith) never had Bishops to this day, but only one called the *Abuna*, while the whole Clergy are exercised (though in too much ignorance) in their Priestly Office. *Brocardus*, that lived at *Jerusalem*, testifieth that those *Eastern* Christians, called by the Papists, *Nestorians, Jacobites, Eutychians,* were commonly plain honest Religious people, free from Heresie, and of better lives than even the Religious of the Church of *Rome*, and that there were not worse men at *Jerusalem* than the *Roman*

See Mr. *Jones* Hearts Soveraign, excellently describing the *English* Succession.

Catholicks. The *Armenians* have many Bishops, and one chief, but live (though too ignorantly and superstitiously, yet) in great austerity of life.

IX. In all ages since Prelacy swelled to the corruption of the Churches, and annoyance of the Peace of Kings and Kingdoms, there have been still a great number of pious lamenters of the Corruptions of the Church, that have groaned and prayed for reformation: Insomuch, that Dr. *Field* maintaineth, that even in the Church of *Rome* there have been still considerable numbers of Doctors, that owned truth and piety, and misliked the Papal usurpations and errours. The *Waldenses* and *Albigenses* (exceeding numerous) said, they had continued from the Apostles, and so from the days of *Sylvester* (or *Constantine*) had dissented from the *Roman* pride, and corruptions. And God hath made the Protestant Churches since the Reformation, as his Vineyard, where truth and piety have prospered, though Satan hath been still at work, and here also had too much success.

X. And it must be remembred, that God hath made use of many proud and turbulent men, to propogate and defend the truth of the Gospel: And their Gifts have served for the good of the sincere. As the husk or chaff and straw is useful to the Corn; so many worldly Prelates and Priests have been learned Expositors and useful Preachers, and taught others the way to life, which they would not go in themselves. Besides that, their very Papal power and grandure, which hath corrupted the Church, hath yet been a check to some, that would have assaulted it by force; and as a hedge of thornes about it. Worldly interest engageth Pope, Patriarchs, and Prelates, to stand up for the Christian Religion, because they gain by it (as *Leo* the 10th is said to have odiously confessed.)

§. 42. And the old Fathers, till *Constantines* time, did most of them think that the last thousand years would be a time of fuller glory to the Church; as many yet think, though I confess my self unskilful in the Prophesies.

But I make no doubt, but though this earth be so far deserted by God, the Glorious Kingdom which we shall shortly see, with the new Heaven and Earth, wherein dwelleth righteousness, will fully confute all our present temptations to think hardly of God or the Redeemer, because of the present corruptions and dissentions of this lower world.

§. 43. We may conjecture at former times by our own: We see now, that among the most Reformed Churches, too often the most worldly part are uppermost, and perhaps are the persecuters of the rest, and though they may be the smaller part, it's they that make the noise, are the noted part that carry the name, and that Histories write of. A few men got into places of power, seem to be all the Church, or Nation, by the prevalency of their actions, which few dare contradict: They may give Laws; They may have the power of Press and Pulpit, so that nothing shall be published but what they will; They may call themselves
the

the Church, and call all that obey them not Schifmaticks and Sectaries, and ftrangers may believe therefore, that it is but fome few in-
confiderable fellows that are againft them, when yet the far greateft
part may utterly diffent and abhor their pride. I have lived to fee fuch
an Affembly of Minifters, where three or four leading men were fo prevalent as to form a Confeffion of Faith in the name of the whole party,
which had that in it which particular members did difown. And when
about a controverted Article, *One man* hath charged me deeply, for que-
ftioning the words of the *Church*, others that were at the forming of that
Article, have laid it all on that fame man, as by his impetuoufnefs putting
in that Article, the reft being loth to ftrive much againft him, and fo it
was he himfelf that was the *Church*, whofe authority he fo much urged, at
leaft the effectual fignifying part. We cannot judge what is commoneft by
what is uppermoft, or in greateft power. In divers Parifhes now, where
the Minifter is conformable, perhaps ten parts of the people do diflike it;
and fometimes you may fee but three or four perfons with him at the Com-
mon-prayers; And yet all know, that Diffenters are talkt of as a few
fingular Fanaticks. I compare not the Caufes, but conclude, that fo alfo for
the *Numbers*, humble Godly perfons might be very numerous, though only the
actions of worldly Prelates do take up moft of the Hiftory of the Church.

Yea, I believe, that among the Papifts themfelves, five to one of the
people, were they free from danger, would declare their diflike of a great
part of the actions and Doctrines of their Prelates, and that the greateft
part that are named Papifts, are not fuch throughly and at the heart.

When the Rulers, Scribes, and Pharifees were againft Chrift, and perfecuted him and the truth, the common people fo much adhered to him,
that the perfecutors durft not feize on him openly by force, but were fain
to ufe a Traytor, to apprehend him in the night, and in a folitary place, left
they fhould be ftoned by the people, who faid, Never man fpake as this
man fpeaketh.

§. 44. Let us not therefore turn Church Hiftory into a temptation, nor
think bafely of the Church, or Chriftianity, or Chrift, becaufe of Papal and
Prelatical pride and tyranny. God can make ufe of a furly porter to keep
his doors; yea, a maftiff-dog may be a keeper of the houfe; and his
Corn hath grown in every Age, not only with ftraw and chaffe, but with
fome tares: And yet he hath gathered, and will gather, all his chofen.

§. 45. Nor is the Miniftry it felf to be therefore difhonoured: For as
at this day, while a few turbulent Prelates perfecute good men, and much
of the Miniftry is in too many Countries lamentably corrupted, yet is Religion, piety, and honefty kept up by the Miniftry, and never was well kept
up without it: For the Faithful Minifters labour ftill, and their very fuffer-
ings further the Gofpel, and what they may not do publickly they do privately.

Yea, their very Writings fhew, that ftill there are fuch as God doth
qualifie to do his work, even among the Papifts, he that readeth the pious

Writings of such men as *Gerson*, and *Gerhardus Zutphaniensis*, and *Thaulerus*, *Thomas à Kempis*, *Ferus*, and many such others, will see that Gods spirit was still illuminating and sanctifying souls. And he that readeth such Lives as *Philip Nerius*, persecuted by the Bishop as an ambitious Hypocrite, for setting up more serious Exercises of Religion than had been ordinarily used among the Formalists, (to say nothing of such privater men as M. *de Renty* and many others) will see that it is not all Church-tyranny and corruption, though very heinous, that will prove that Christ hath not a Holy Generation whom he will save.

§. 46. Yea among the very corrupted sort of the Clergy, many that are overcome with temptations in that point, and take usurpation and tyranny, and worldly pomp and violence for Order, Government, and the interest of the Church, have yet much good in other respects: Even among the Cardinals there have been such men as *Charles Boromæus*, *Baronius* (*Nerius*'s companion) *Bellarmine*, and others, that would Preach and practise the common Doctrines of serious piety: Yea, among the Jesuits there have been divers that have Preacht, Written, and lived very strictly; much more among their Fryars: and such Bishops as *Sales*: And though their times and corruptions blemished their piety, I dare not think they nullified it.

§. 47. And it sheweth the excellency of the Sacred Office, 1. That Christ did first make it as the noble Organical part of his Church, to form the rest. 2. That he endued the first Officers with the most noble and excellent gifts of his spirit. 3. That he founded and built his Church by them at first. 4. Yea, that he himself preached the Gospel, and is called The Minister of the Circumcision, the chief Shepherd, and the Bishop of our Souls. 5. That he hath used them to enlarge, confirm, preserve, and edefie his Church to this day. 6. That he maketh the best of them to be the best of men. 7. That he putteth into the hearts of all good Christians a special love and honour of them. 8. That he useth even the worser sort to do good, while they do hurt; especially some of them. 9. That Satan striveth so hard to corrupt them and get them on his side. 10. That Religion ordinarily dyeth away, or decayeth, when they fail and prove unable and unfaithful. 11. That Christ commandeth men so much to hear, receive and obey them, and hath committed his Word and Keys to them, as his Stewards. 12. And hath promised them a special reward for their faithfulness: and commanded all to pray for them and their preservation and success. And the nature of the things tells us, that as knowledge in lower things is not propagated to mankind, but by Teachers (man being not born wise;) so much less is heavenly wisdom. And therefore it is, that God is so regardful of the due qualification of Ministers, that they be not blind guides, nor novices, nor proud, nor careless sluggards, nor self-seeking worldlings, but skilful in the word of truth, and lovers of God and the souls of men, and zealous, and diligent, unwearied, and patient in their holy work. And when they prove bad, he maketh them

most

moſt contemptible and puniſheth them more than other men, the corruption of the beſt making them the worſt.

§. 48. Therefore let us make a right uſe of the pride and corruption of the Clergy, to deſire and pray for better, and to avoid our ſelves the Sin which is ſo bad in them, and to labour after that rooted Wiſdome and Holineſs in our ſelves that we may ſtand, though our Teachers fall before us. Let every man prove his own Work, and ſo he ſhall have rejoicing in himſelf, and not in others only, *Gal.* 6. But let us not hence queſtion the Goſpel, or diſhonour the Church and Miniſtry; no nor any further ſeparate from the Faulty than they ſeparate from Chriſt, or than God alloweth us, and neceſſity requireth: As we muſt not deſpiſe the needful helps of our Salvation, nor equal dumb or wicked men with the able faithful Miniſters of Chriſt, on pretence of honouring the Office; ſo neither muſt we deny the good that is in any, nor deſpiſe the Office for the Perſons Faults.

§. 49. Eſpecially let us take heed that we fall not into that pernicious Snare that hath entangled the *Quakers* and other Schiſmaticks of theſe times, who on pretence of the faults of the Miniſters, ſet againſt the beſt with greateſt fury, becauſe the beſt do moſt reſiſt them, and that revile them with falſe and railing language, the ſame that Drunkards and Malignants uſe, yea worſe than the prophaneſt of the Vulgar; even becauſe they take Tythes and neceſſary Maintenance, charging them with odious covetouſneſs, calling them Hirelings, deceivers, and what not. Undoubtedly this Spirit is not of God, that is ſo contrary to his Word, his Grace, and his Intereſt in the World. What would become of the Church and Goſpel, if this malignant Spirit ſhould prevail to extirpate even the beſt of all the Miniſtry? Would the Devil and the Churches Enemies deſire any more? The very ſame Men that the Prelates have ſilenced (near 2000) in *England* theſe fifteen or ſixteen years together, are they that the *Quakers* moſt virulently before reviled, and moſt furiouſly oppoſed.

§. 50. Nor will the Clergies corruption allow either unqualified or uncalled Men to thruſt themſelves into the Sacred Office, as if they were the Men that can do better, and muſt mend all that is amiſs. Such have been tryed in Licentious Times, and proved, ſome of them, to do more hurt than the very Drunkards, or the ignorant ſort of Miniſters, that did but read the holy Scriptures. Pride is too often the reprehender of other Mens Faults and Imperfections, and would make other Mens Names but a ſtepping-ſtone to their own aſpiring Folly: As many that have cryed out againſt bad Popes and Prelates, that they might get into the places, have been as bad themſelves when they have their Will: No wonder if it be ſo with the proud revilers of the Miniſtry.

§. 51. There is need therefore of much Wiſdome and holy care, that we here avoid the two extreams; that we grow not indifferent who are our Paſtors, nor contract the Guilt of Church-corruption, but mourn for the reproach of the ſolemn Aſſemblies, and do our beſt for true and needful

ful Reformation, that the Gospel fail not, and Souls be not quietly left to Satan, nor the Church grow like the Infidel World; and yet that we neither invade nor dishonour the sacred Office, nor needlesly open the nakedness of the Persons, nor do any thing that may hinder their just endeavours and success; we must speak evil of no man either falsly or unnecessarily.

§. 52. I thought all this premonition necessary that you make not an ill use of the following History, and become not guilty of diabolism or false accusing of the Brethren, or dishonouring the Church: And that as God hath in Scripture recorded the Sins of the ungodly, and the effects of Pride and of malignity, and Christ hath foretold us that Wolves shall enter and devour the Flock, and by their Fruits (of devouring, and pricking as Thorns and Thistles) we shall know them, and the Apostles prophecied of them; I take it to be my duty to give you an Abstract of the History of Papal and aspiring Prelacy, usurping, and schismatical, and tyrannical Councils, as knowing of how great use it is to all to know the true History of the Church, both as to good and evil.

§. 53. Yea Bishops and Councils must not be worse thought of than they deserve, no more than Presbyters, because of such abuses as I recite; The best things are abused, even Preaching, Writing, Scripture, and Reason it self, and yet are not to be rejected or dishonoured. There is an Episcopacy whose very Constitution is a Crime, and there is another sort which seemeth to me a thing convenient, lawful, and indifferent, and there is a sort which I cannot deny to be of Divine Right.

§. 54. That which I take to be it self a Crime, is such as is aforementioned, which in its very constitution over-throweth the Office, Church, and Discipline, which Christ by himself and his Spirit, in his Apostles, instituted: such I take to be that Diocesane kind which hath only one Bishop over many score or hundred fixed Parochial Assemblies; by which, 1. Parishes are made by them *no Churches,* as having no Ruling Pastors that have the Power of Judging whom to Baptize, or admit to Communion or refuse, but only are Chapels, having preaching Curates. 2. All the first Order of Bishops in single Churches are deposed, as if the Bishop of *Antioch* should have put down a 1000 Bishops about him, and made himself the sole Bishop of their Churches. 3. The Office of Presbyters is changed into semi Presbyters. 4. Discipline is made impossible, as it is for one General without inferiour Captains to Rule an Army: But of this before.

§. 55. Much more doth this become unlawful, 1. when deposing all the Presbyters from Government by the Keyes of Discipline, they put the same Keyes, even the Power of decretive Excommunication and Absolution into the hands of Laymen, called Chancellours, and set up Courts liker to the Civil than Ecclesiastical. 2. And when they oblige the Magistrate to execute their Decrees by the Sword, be they just or unjust, and to lay Men in Goals and ruine them, meerly because they are Excommunicated by Bishops, or Chancellours, or Officials, or such others, and are not reconciled:

conciled: And when they threaten Princes and Magistrates with Excommunication (if not Deposition) if they do but Communicate with those that the Bishop hath Excommunicated. 3. Or when they arrogate the power of the Sword themselves, as *Socrates* saith *Cyril* did: Or without necessity joyn in one person the Office of Priesthood and Magistracy, when one is more than they can perform aright.

§. 56. And it becometh much worse by the tyrannical abuse, when (being unable and unwilling to exercise true Discipline on so many hundred Parishes) they have multitudes of Atheists, Infidels, gross ignorants, and wicked livers in Church-Communion, yea, compel all in the Parishes to Communicate on pain of Imprisonment and ruine, and turn their censures cruelly against godly persons, that dare not obey them in all their Formalities, Ceremonies, and Impositions, for fear of sinning against God. And when conniving at ignorant ungodly Priests that do but obey them, they silence and ruine the most faithful able Teachers, that obey not all their imposing Canons, and swear not, and subscribe not what they bid them.

§. 57. Undoubtedly Satan hath found it his most successful way, to fight against Christ in Christs own name, and to set up Ministers as the Ministers of Christ, to speak indirectly against the Doctrine, Servants, and interest of Christ, and as Ministers of Light and righteousness, and to fight against Church-Government, Order, Discipline, and Unity, by the pretences of Church Government, Order, Discipline, and Unity: and to cry down Schism to promote Schism, and to depress Believers by crying up Faith, and Orthodoxness, and crying down Heresie and Errour: Yea, to plead God's Name and Word against himself, and to set up Sin, by accusing Truth and Duty as Sin.

§. 58. II. That which I take for Lawful Indifferent Episcopacy is such as *Hierome* saith, was introduced for the avoiding of divisions, though it was not from the beginning: When among many Elders in every single Church, one of most wisdom and gravity is made their President, yea, without whom no Ordinations or great matters shall be done. The Churches began this so early, and received it so universally, and without any considerable dissent or opposition, even before Emperours became Christians, that I dare not be one that shall set against it, or dishonour such Episcopacy.

§. 59. Yea, if where fit men are wanting to make Magistrates, the King shall make Bishops Magistrates, and joyn two Offices together, laying no more work on them than will consist with their Ecclesiastick work, though this will have inconveniencies, I shall not be one that shall dishonour such, or disobey them.

§. 60. III. The Episcopacy, which I dare not say is not of Gods institution, (besides that each Pastor is *Episcopus Gregis*,) is that which succeedeth the Apostles in the Ordinary part of Church-Government, while some Senior Pastors have a supervising care of many Churches, (as the Visiters
had

had in *Scotland*,) and are so far *Episcopi Episcoporum*, and Arch-bishops, having no constraining power of the Sword, but a power to admonish and instruct the Pastors, and to regulate Ordinations, Synods, and all great and common circumstances that belong to Churches. For if Christ set up one Form of Government in which some Pastors had so extensive work and power, (as *Timothy*, *Titus*, and Evangelists as well as Apostles had) we must not change it without proof, that Christ himself would have it changed.

§. 61. But if men on this pretence will do as *Rome* hath done, pretend one Apostle to be the Governour of all the rest, and that they have now that Authority of that Apostle, and will make an Universal Monarch to rule at the Antipodes, and over all the World, or will set up Patriarchs, Primates, Metrapolitans and Arch-bishops, with power to tyrannize over their Brethren, and cast them out, and on pretence of Order, and imitating the Civil Government, to master Princes, or captivate the Churches to their pride and worldly interests, this will be the worst and most pernicious tyranny.

§. 62. And as it is not all Episcopacy, so it is not all Councils that I design this History to dishonour. No doubt but Christ would have his Church to be as far One, as their natural political and gracious capacities will allow: And to do all his work in as much love, peace, and concord as they can: And to that end, both seasonable Councils, and Letters, and Delegates for Concord and Communication, are means which nature it self directeth them to, as it doth direct Princes to hold Parliaments and Dyets. In the multitude of Councellours there is safety: Even frequent converse keepeth up amity: In absence slanderers are heard, and too oft believed: A little familiarity in presence confuteth many false reports of one another, which no distant defences would so satisfyingly confute. And among many we may hear that which of few we should not hear. How good and pleasant is it for Brethren to dwel together in Unity? And the Concord of Christians greatly honoureth their holy profession, as discord becometh a scandal to the world. But all this, and the measures and sort of Unity and Concord which we may expect, and the true way to attain it, I have fullier opened in a Treatise entitled, *The true and only terms of the Concord of all Christian Churches*.

§. 63. When Christians had no Princes or Magistrates on their side, they had no sufficient means of keeping up Unity and Concord for mutual help and strength, without meetings of Pastors to carry on their common work by consent. But their meetings were only with those that had nearness or neighbourhood: And they did not put men to travel to Synods out of other Princes Dominions, or from Foreign Lands, much less did they call any General Councils out of all the Christian Churches in the world. But those that were capable of Communion by proximity, and of helping one another, were thought enough to meet for such ends.

§. 64. And

§. 64. And indeed neither nature nor Scripture obligeth us to turn such occasional helps into the forms of a State-policy, and to make a Government of friendly consultations. And therefore though where it may be done without fear of degenerating into tyranny, known times of stated Synods or meetings of Pastors for Concord are best, (as once a month in lesser meetings, and once a quarter in greater,) yet where there is danger of such degeneracy, it is better to hold them but *pro re nata*, occasionally, at various seasons and places.

§. 65. The lesser Synods and correspondency of Pastors before there were Christian Magistrates were managed much more humbly and harmlesly than the great ones afterward: Because that men and their interest and motives differed. And even of later times, there have been few Councils called General, that have been managed so blamelesly, or made so many profitable Canons, as many Provincial or smaller Synods did. Divers *Toletane* Councils, and many others in *Spain*, *England*, and other Countries have laboured well to promote piety and peace: As did the *African* Synods, and many others of old. And such as these have been serviceable to the Church. And the Greater Councils, though more turbulent have many of them done great good, against Heresie and Vice; especially the first at *Nice*: And nothing in this Book is intended to cloud their worth and glory, or to extenuate any good which they have done: But I am thankful to God that gave his Church so many worthy Pastors, and made so much use as he did of many Synods for the Churches purity and peace.

§. 66. But the true reason of this Collection, and why I have besides good products, made so much mention of the errours and mischiefs that many Councils have been guilty of, are these following.

I. The carnal and aspiring part of the Clergy, do very ordinarily, under the equivocal names of Bishops, confound the Primitive Episcopacy with the Diocesane tyranny before described: And they make the ignorant believe, that all that is said in Church-Writers for Episcopacy, is said for *their Diocesane Species*: And while they put down an hundred or a thousand Bishops and Churches of the Primitive Species, they make men believe that it is they that are for the old Episcopacy, and we that are against it, and that it is we and not they that are against the Church: while we are submissive to them as Arch-bishops, if they would but leave Parishes to be Churches (or Great Towns formerly called Cities at least) and make the Discipline of all Churches but a possible practicable thing.

§. 67. II. And to promote their ends, as these men are for the largest Dioceses and turning a thousand Churches into one only, so they are commonly for violent Administration, ruling by constraint, and either usurping the power of the sword themselves, or perswading and urging the Magistrate to punish all that obey not their needless impositions, and reproaching or threatning (at least) the Magistrates that will not be their Executioners. And making themselves the Church snuffers, (or made without the Churches confent) their Office is exercifed in putting out the Lights, fometimes hundreds of faithful Minifters being filenced by their means in a little time. And they take the fword of Difcipline or power of the Keys as the Church ufed it 300 years to be vain, unlefs prifons or mulcts enforce it. And to efcape the Primitive poverty, they overthrow the Primitive Church, Form, and Difcipline, and tell men, All this is for the Churches honour and peace.

§. 68. Yea all that like not their arrogances and grandure, they render odious as *Aerian* Hereticks or Schifmaticks, provoking men to hate and revile them, and Magiftrates to deftroy them, as intolerable. And by making their own numerous Canons and Inventions neceffary to Miniftry and Church-Communion, they will leave no place for true unity and peace, but tear the Churches in pieces by the racks and engines of their brains and wills.

§. 69. III. Yea worfe than all this, there are fome befides the *French* Papifts, who tell the world, *That the Univerfal Church on Earth is one vifible political body, having a vifible Head or Supreme vicarious Government under Chrift, even a Collective Supreme, that hath univerfal Legiflative, Judicial and Executive power.* And they make this Summa Poteftas Conftitutive *of the Church Univerfal, and fay that this is Chrifts body out of which none have his Spirit nor are Church-members, and that there is no Unity or Concord but in obeying this fupreme vifible power ; And that this is in General Councils and in the intervals in a* College *of* Bifhops *Succeffors of the Apoftles,* (I know not who or where, unlefs it be all the Bifhops as fcattered over the earth) *and that they rule* per literas formatas: (as others fay, *It is the Pope and* Roman *Clergy or Cardinals.)*

§. 70. And when our Chriftianity, Salvation, Union and Communion, yea, our Lives, Liberties and mutual forbearances, and Love, is laid upon this very form of Church-policy and Prelacy, and Chrift is fuppofed to have fuch a Church as is not in the World, even conftituted with a Vifible Vicarious Collective Soveraign, that muft make Laws for the whole Chriftian World, it's time to do our beft to fave men from this deceit.

§. 71. I muft confefs, If I believed that the Whole Church had any Head or Soveraign under Chrift, I fhould rather take it to be the Pope than any one, finding no other regardable Competitor. He is uncapable of ruling at the Antipodes and all the Earth; but a General Council is much more uncapable, and fo are the feigned College of Paftors or Bifhops, (none knoweth who.)

§. 72. IV. And a blind zeal againft errour, called *Herefie*, doth cry down the neceffary Love and toleration of many tolerable Chriftians; And fome cry, down with them, and away with them that erre more themfelves, and by their meafures would leave but few Chriftians endured by one another in the World: Thus do they teach us to underftand *Solomon*, Eccl. 7. 15. *Be not righteous and wife overmuch*: fo much are thefe men for *Unity*, that they will leave no place for much Unity on earth. As if none

fhould

should be tolerated but men of one Stature, Complexion, &c.

§. 73. Briefly, they do as one that would set up a *Family Government*, made up of many hundred or thousand Families dissolved and turned into one, and ruled supremely by a Council of the Heads of such enlarged Families, and then tell us, that this is not to alter the old Species of Families, but to make them greater that were before too small: Keep but the same name, and a City is but a Family still. And when they have done, they would have none endured, but cast out, imprisoned or banished, as seditious, that are for any smaller Family than a City, (or any lesser School than an University:) And these City Governours must in one Convention rule all the Kingdom, and in a greater all the World.

§. 74. I shall therefore first tell you, what errour must not be tolerated, and then by an Epitome of Church-History, Bishops and Councils and Popes, shew the ignorant so much of the Matter of Fact, as may tell them who have been the Cause of Church-corruptions, Heresies, Schisms and Sedition, and how: And whether such Diocesane Prelacy and grandure be the Cure, or ever was. And, if God will, in a Second Volume shall prove the sinfulness and novelty of that sort of Prelacy, and answer the chief that have defended it.

CHAP. II.

Of Heresies, and of the first Councils.

§. 1. THe Apostle *James* saith, ch. 5.19,20. *Brethren, if any one of you do erre from the truth, and one convert him, Let him know that he that converteth a sinner from the errour of his way, doth save a soul from death, and hide a multitude of sins.* By which it is implyed, that *Errour* tendeth unto *Death:* But what *Errour is it?* Is it all? Who then can be saved? It is of great use to know, what Errours are mortal, and what not.

§. 2. There are errours that are *no sins,* and errours that are *sins.* Those which are not voluntary either in themselves, or in their antecedent causes, are no sins: Those which are not voluntary either by the act or by the omission of the will, are no sins. Those which are unavoidable through a necessity which is not moral but natural, are no sin: As if Infants, Idiots, Mad-men, erre in matters of which they are uncapable: Or if any erre for want of any revelation of the truth. As if the Papists did rightly charge those with errours whom they burnt for denying Transubstantiation, yet it could be no *sinful errour,* because it is necessary and unavoidable. For the first discerning principle is sense: And if we are deceived while we judge that to be *Bread and Wine,* which all the sound senses of all men in the World perceive as such, we have no remedy. For whether sense be fallible or infallible, it is certain that we have no other faculties and organs to perceive immediately sensible things by. I can see by nothing but my eyes, nor hear any other way than by my ears. If they say, that we must believe that all mens senses are deceived when God telleth us so? I answer, If we do not presuppose that by sense we must perceive things sensible, it is in vain to talk of Gods telling us any thing, or of any of his Revelations, or faith therein: For I know not but by sense, that there is a *Bible,* or a *Man,* or a *Voice* or *Word,* to be believed. And as *humanity* is presupposed to *Christianity,* so is sense and reason to faith and the objects accordingly. And to say, that all mens sound senses about their due placed objects are fallible, is but to say, that no certainty can be had.

§. 3. Of those errours that *are sins,* it is not all that are effectively mortal or damning sins: Else no man could be saved. There is no man that hath not a multitude of errours, that hath any actual use of reason.

§. 4. Errours are of three sorts: 1. Errours of *Judgment* (to say nothing

thing of sense and imagination.) 2. *Of Will*; 3. *Of Life*, or practice. The *Judgment* is to *Guide* the *Will*; and the *Will* is to command our *practice*. Therefore those errours are least dangerous that least corrupt the *Will* and *practice*, and those most dangerous that most corrupt them. But every errour contrary to any useful truth is bad, as it is a corruption of the *judgment*, tending to corrupt the *will* and *practice*.

§. 5. 1. No errour is effectively damning which turneth not the Heart or Will in a predominant degree from the Love of God to the Love of the Creature, from the Love of Heaven and Holiness to the prevalent Love of Earth, and sinful pleasure, riches or honour therein; from things Spiritual to things Carnal: For God hath prepared unconceivable glory for them that Love him: The Kingdom of God consisteth not in meats and drinks, but in righteousness, peace and joy in the holy Ghost: And he that in these things serveth Christ, doth please God, and is acceptable to (good) men, *Rom.* 14. 17, 18.

§. 6. 2. I think no errour is effectively damning which a man doth sincerely desire to be delivered from at any rate, and when he that hath it doth faithfully endeavour to come to the knowledge of the truth, in the use of such means as God vouchsafeth him: He that searcheth the Scripture with a Love to truth, and sincerely prayeth for Gods illumination, and sincerely practiceth what he already knoweth, and is willing to hear what any man can say to his further information, God will hide nothing necessary to his salvation from such a man. For this is a work of such dispositive Grace, as shall not be received in vain.

§. 7. Obj. *But may not one that believeth not in God, or Christ, or the Life to come, say all this, that he desireth and endeavoureth to know the truth?*

Ans. 1. These things are so *Great*, so *Evident*, and so *Necessary*, that they cannot be unknown to one that hath the Gospel, who hath the foresaid sincere desires and endeavours. And as for them that have not the Gospel, I have spoken to their case before. 2. God that giveth so much grace doth thereby signifie his willingness to give more.

§. 8. Obj. *This intimateth that Grace is given according to Merits.*

A s. 1. Not the first Grace: But to him that hath (and improveth it) shall be given, and from him that hath not (such improvement) shall be taken away even that which he hath. 2. No Grace or Glory is given according to *Merits* in point of Commutative Justice, as *quid pro quo*, as if it did profit God. But to him that asketh it shall be given. We must have a Beggers Merit: Begging and thankful accepting; And yet that also is of antecedent Grace.

§. 9. On the contrary, 1. All errour is damning which excludeth the life of *faith, hope, love* and *sincere obedience*: For these are of necessity to salvation: without holiness none shall see God, *Heb.* 12. 14. The wisdom from above is first pure, and then peaceable, and must be shewn out of a good conversation by works with meekness of wisdom, *Jam.* 3. 13, 17. He that Loveth not God, Heaven, and Holiness, with a predominant Love, doth damnably erre.

§. 10.

§. 10. Second.y, Therefore all errour of judgment which *effectively excludeth the belief* of any of the *Essentials of Godliness*, or of *Christianity* where the Gospel is, is damning errour: Because a Mans *Will* and *Life* can be no better than his *belief* or *judgment* is. No man can love that God that he believeth not to be amiable, nor obey him whom he believeth not to be his Governour; nor seeks for a happiness which he believeth not; And it is in the face of Christ, a Redeemer, and Saviour of lost Sinners, that Gods amiableness suitably appeareth unto man: And it is by his Word and holy Spirit that Christ reneweth Souls.

§. 11. And an ungodly carnal worldly man (though he be a learned Preacher of the Truth) is damnably erroneous, and hath really the sum of manifold Heresies: 1. He erreth about the greatest and most necessary things: He taketh God to be less amiable than the Creature, and Heaven than Earth, and Holiness than the Pleasure of Sin. 2. His errour is practical and not only notional: 3. It excludeth the contrary truth, and is predominant; so that what contrary truth he acknowledgeth, he doth not soundly, practically, and prevailingly believe.

§. 12. Were it not besides my present purpose I might manifest that every carnal ungodly man among us, 1. Doth not truly believe any one Article of the Creed with a serious practical belief; 2. Nor doth he consent to the Baptismal Covenant; 3. Nor sincerely desire and put up one Petition of the Lords Prayer, rightly understood; 4. Nor sincerely obey one of the Ten Commandements; 5. Nor can sincerely receive the Sacrament of the Lords Supper; Nor, 6. Is a sincere Member of the holy Catholick Church, nor can sincerely hold Communion with the Saints: He is an Hypocrite and damnably erroneous, even while he seemeth to be Orthodox and pleadeth for the Truth, and cryeth out against Heresies and Errours; which he may easily and ordinarily do.

§. 13. It hath still been one of Satans effectual Snares to deceive and damn ungodly men by, to hide their own practical errour and wickedness from their Consciences, by seeming to be *Orthodox*, and crying down Errours and Heresies in others: But alas, how unfit persons are they for such Work? And how dreadfully do they condemn themselves? It is a pitiful thing to hear a man that is false to the very essence of his Baptismal Vow, to revile and prosecute a poor *Anabaptist* (though erroneous) for holding that Baptism should be delayed till years of discretion that it may be the better kept: Or to hear a man that obeyeth not God himself, but his fleshly Lust, to cry out against every Dissenter, how conscionable soever, for *not obeying the Church* in some questionable points: or to hear a man that sticketh not at any wickedness that maketh for his worldly ends or pleasure, to cry out against those that in fear of Perjury or Lying or other sinning against God, dare not take some Oath, Subscription, Profession, or Covenant which is imposed: As these notorious Hypocrites who live quite contrary to the Christian Religion which they profess, do use to call those Hypocrites that labour in all things to please God,

God, if they do but miflike any thing in their Lives. So alfo while they are drowned in damnable Errour, they cry out againft Errour in thofe that practically hold all the Effentials of Chriftianity, and are certainly in the way of Life, if they do differ in any thing from them, or are ignorant of any thing which they know. He that never puts up a fincere Prayer to God for his Grace, nay, that would not have it, to make him holy, and deprive him of his finful pleafure, will yet call others *erroneous* and Schifmaticks, if they pray not by his Book, or in all his Circumftances; while his Heart and Family are prayerlefs, and God's Name ofter heard in Oaths and Curfes than in Prayer.

§ 14. Becaufe *bare opinion* may confift with worldlinefs and *fleshly lufts*, therefore it hath long been the trick of the ungodly to feem zealous for the true *Church*, and for *right opinions*, and to over-do here to quiet their Confciences in Sin: And it hath been a Snare to many confcionable People, to tempt them to fufpect and diflike the Truth, becaufe ungodly Men thus ftand for it; and to think it muft be fome bad thing which wicked men feem fo zealous for: when as they do it but for a cover for their Sin, as Hypocrites and Oppreffors ufe *long Prayers*, which would not ferve their turn if there were not fome good in it.

§. 15. And yet Errour is fuch a blinding thing, that it's very ufual even for grofly erroneous men, to cry out moft fiercely againft Errour: For they know not themfelves, and they are proud and felf conceited, and oft by malignity apt to fufpect and condemn others. What did the Jews perfecute the Chriftians for? For fuppofed Herefie and Errour: What did the Heathens caft them to wild Beafts and Torments for? For fuppofed Impiety and Errour: becaufe they would not erre in their Idolatry as they did. What hath difquieted and torn in pieces the Chriftian World, but erroneous and worldly Popes, Patriarcks, and Prelates inordinate out-crys againft fuppofed Errours? For what have they filenced hundreds and thoufands of faithful Minifters of Chrift? for Errour. For what have they racked, tormented, burnt to afhes, and flain by the Sword fo many thoufand, and hundred thoufands? O, it was for Herefie or Errour. And are not thefe men perfectly free from Errour themfelves, that have fo great a zeal againft it? No, fo grofly erroneous are they, that they deny credit to all mens Senfes, and know not Bread and Wine when they fee, and touch, and tafte it; and would have all thofe deftroyed that will not deny b.lief to fenfe as well as they: So erroneous are they, that they pretend a mortal man to be the Church Governour of all the Earth; fo erroneous, that they think God well Worfhipped by praying in words not underftood; and dare deny half the Sacrament of the Lords Supper to the People, which they confefs that he inftituted, and all the Church did ufe; fo erroneous, that they think the flames of Purgatory will help them the better to love that God that doth torment them. How foul and many are their Errours that kill, and burn, and damn others as erroneous? But S. *James* hath told us, *Jam.* 3. *That the Wifdom is not from:*

from above, but is earthly, senſual, and devilliſh, which hath an envious ſtriving zeal; and that if it work not by meekneſs of wiſdom, and be not pure, peaceable, gentle, eaſie to be intreated, full of mercy and good fruits, without partiality and hypocriſie, ſowing the fruit of righteouſneſs in peace, by peace-making, but hath bitter contention, it is not of God, but bringeth confuſion and every evil work.

§. 16. The *Arians* were cruel Perſecutors, on pretence of zeal againſt Errour, as they accounted it: They baniſhed godly Paſtors; they killed them, they cut out the Preachers Tongues; they reproached them. The Emperours *Valens* and *Conſtantius* were more fierce than the *Arian Goths* themſelves.

Macedonius that denyed the Deity of the Holy Ghoſt, was a great pretender to Orthodoxneſs, and a great decryer and perſecuter of others, as erroneous and Hereticks.

Neſtorius (though ſomewhat worſe judged of by *Cyril* than he deſerved) was juſtly condemned, were it but for his heat and fierceneſs againſt others: He fell preſently upon the *Novatians* and other Parties, and began with this overdoing zeal at his entrance, *O Emperour, give me a Church without Hereſie, and I will give thee Victory over the Perſians*: that is, Deſtroy all theſe diſſenting Parties and God will proſper thee: And very quickly was he depoſed, condemned, and at laſt baniſhed even to miſery and death as an Heretick (whether juſtly or no I ſhall ſay more anon.)

The *Eutychians* were as great Zealots againſt Errour and Hereſie as any of the reſt: They took *Cyril* for their Captain whom *Theodoret* and *Iſydore Peluſiota* that knew him, deſcribe as heynouſly proud and turbulent, and *Socrates* as the firſt Biſhop that himſelf uſed the Sword. *Dioſcerus* raged at the ſecond Council of *Epheſus* againſt diſſenters, and all in Zeal againſt *Neſtorian* Hereſie. But what dreadful work his *Eutychian* Party and Succeſſors made, I have elſewhere ſhewed: And all as againſt Hereſie.

The *Anthropomorphite* zealous *Egyptian* Monks thought it was Errour and Hereſie which they ſo furiouſly oppoſed, when they forced *Theophilus Alexand.* to diſſemble to ſave his Life.

It was zeal againſt *Origens* Hereſie and Errour which ſet *Epiphanius* and *Theophilus Alexand.* upon their irregular and inhumane oppoſition to *Chryſoſtome*.

What abundance of groſs Errours doth *Philaſtrius* vend while he thinks that he reciteth other Mens Errours: I have given a Catalogue of them elſewhere. Beſides the inconſiderable Errours which he calleth Hereſies.

It was zeal againſt the *Arian* Hereſie which made *Lucifer Calaritanus* occaſion the Schiſm between two Biſhops at *Antioch*, and after become the Head of a ſeparating Party, becauſe he would not receive the returning *Arians* into Communion as others did.

And it was zeal againſt Hereſie that made others for this account him a Heretick, and call his Followers *Luciferians*.

It was zeal againſt Errour which made both the *Novatians* and the *Donatiſts natifts* run into Errour, and keep up their Parties as more pure from the Crimes of Idolaters, Traditors, Libellaticks, and other Criminals.

Sulpitius Severus describeth *Ithacius* as a man that cared not what he said or did, and the rest of the Synod of Bishops about him as unfit to be communicated with; that would bring Christianity it self into reproach by their furious opposition to Hereticks: And who would have thought but these Bishops had been very good men themselves, that were so zealous against the *Priscillianists*, as to procure the Death of some, and the Banishment of others, and bring *Martin* himself, and other strict abstemious people into the suspicion of *Priscillianism*?

It was a zeal for Christ, and against supposed Errour, which raised the doleful contention about the corruptibility of Christ's Body; one Party calling the others *Phantasiasticks*, and the other calling them *Corrupticolæ*; into which Errour the Emperour *Justinian* himself did lapse and become a zealous Heretick, as the Orthodox Party called him.

And even S. *Hilary Pictav. l.* 10. *de Trinit.* seemeth not free, when, p. 205. he saith [*In quem quamvis aut ictus incideret, aut vulnus descenderet, aut nodi concurrerent, aut suspensio elevaret, afferrent quidem hæc impetum passionis, non tamen dolorem passionis inferrent, ut telum aliquod aut aquam perforans, aut ignem compungens, aut æra vulnerans: Omnes quidem has passiones naturæ suæ infert, ut perforet, ut compungat, ut vulneret; sed naturam suam hæc passio illata non retinet; dum in natura non est vel aquam forari, vel pungi ignem, vel æra vulnerari, quamvis natura teli sit vulnerare & compungere & forare: Passus quidem Dominus Jesus Christus dum cæditur, dum suspenditur, dum crucifigitur, dum moritur; sed in Corpus Domini irruens passio, nec non fuit passio, nec tamen naturam passionis exercuit: Cum & pœnali ministerio illa desævit, & virtus corporis sine sensu pœnæ vim pœnæ in se desævientis excepit.*] Yet it was against Heresie that the good Father defended this (worse than many of *Philastrius*, yea or *Epiphanius*'s Heresies.) *Pag.* 208. saith he, *Metum Domino hæresis ascribit:* ——*Timuisse tibi, O Hæretice, Dominus gloria passionem videtur* ——Pag. 216. *Non vis, impie hæretice, ut transeunte palmas clavo Christus non doluerit, neq; vulnus illud nullam acerbitatem teli compungentis intulerit. Interrogo, cur pueri ignes non timuerint nec doluerint*—

So p. 217, 218. you see how little heed is to be given oft to good mens outcries against Heresie: He spake much better, ibid. *pag.* 231. *In simplicitate fides est; in fide justitia est; in confessione pietas est: Non per difficiles nos Deus ad beatam vitam quæstiones vocat; nec multiplici eloquentis facundiæ genere solicitat. In absoluto nobis ac facili est æternitas, Jesum suscitatum à mortuis per Deum credere, & ipsum esse Dominum confiteri.*] And *Lib.* 11. p. 332. *initio* [*Non enim ambiguis nos & erraticis indefinita doctrinæ studiis dereliquit, vel incertis opinionibus ingenia humana permisit, statutis per se & oppositis obicibus in libertatem intelligentiæ voluntatisq; concluders, ut sapere non nisi ad id tantum quod prædicatum à se fuerat, nos sineret, cùm p r definitam fidei indemutabilis constitutionem, credi aliter atque aliter non liceret.*]

§. 17. And

§. 17. And it is not only particular persons, but many General Councils, that have erred and persecuted others; as if all the while they were but cleansing the Church of the most odious Heresies.

The many Councils of the *Arians* I may after touch upon, *viz.* at *Tyre*, *Ariminum*, *Syrmium*, &c. I will before its time here mention that of *Sardica:* What horrid Heresies and Villanies do they lay to the charge (not only of *Marcellus*, but) of *Athanasius*, of *Paulus Constant.* of *Julius* Bishop of *Rome*, of *Prothogenes*, and others, whom they excommunicate as if they had been the very plagues of the earth? See the Copies of their Epistle in *Hilary Pict.* Fragments, *p.* 414, &c.

§. 18. And because Papal Approbation is made by the Papists the mark of an unerring and infallible Council, note that even the *Arian* Council of *Syrmium* was expresly approved by Pope *Liberius* in his Exile, as you may see in *Hilary*, ibid. *p.* 426, 427. saying, [*Itaq; annoto* Athanasio *à communione omnium nostrum, cujus nec Epistolia à me suscipienda sunt, dico me parem cum omnibus vobis,* & *cum Universis Episcopis orientalibus, seu per universas provincias pacem* & *unitatem habere: Nam ut verius sciatis me verâ fide per hanc Epistolam ea loqui, Dominus* & *frater meus communis* Demofilus, *qui dignatus est pro suâ benevolentiâ fidem* & *catholicam exponere quæ* Syrmium *à pluribus fratribus* & *co-episcopis nostris tractata, exposita,* & *suscepta est, ab omnibus qui in præsenti fuerunt, hanc ego libenti animo suscepi; in nullo contradixi; consensum accommodavi, hanc sequor, hæc à me tenetur; sanè petendum credidi Sanctitatem Vestram, quia tam pervidetis in omnibus me vobis consentaneum esse, dignemini communi auxilio ac studio laborare, quatenus de exilio dimittar,* & *ad sedem, quæ mihi divinitùs credita est, revertar.*] In reciting of which *Hilary* thrice saith [*Anathema tibi, Liberi prævaricator*]——If they say that *Liberius* did this in his Exile through fear or suffering, I answer, his Sufferings were small; and *Hilary* annexeth another of his Epistles to the *Arian* Bishops, in which he sweareth or calleth God himself to witness, that it is not for his Sufferings which are not great, but for the Peace of the Church, of which he knew those Bishops to be Lovers, and which is better than Martyrdom, that he did what he did.

§. 19. I. Before these there were many Provincial Councils called to decide the Controversie of the time of *Easter*; and as that at *Rome*, in *Palestine*, *Pontius*, and one in *France* went one way; so that of *Asia*, under *Polycrates Ephes.* went another way, professing to stick therein to the Gospel, and the Tradition of their Fathers: For which *Victor* would needs excommunicate them, which *Irenæus* sharply reprehendeth. Its worth the noting, That as the wrong party pleaded Tradition, so the right party pleaded Reason and Scripture, as you may see in *Beda*'s Fragment of the *Palestine* Council, *sub Theoph. Cæsar. Bin. T.* 1. *p.* 132. And that the main argument used was the Divine Benediction of the Lords day: which they may note, that question the ancient observation of that day.

§. 20. II. The next Council recorded (*Bin. p.* 135.) is one at *Carthage*, under

under *Agrippinus*, which decreed the re-baptizing of those that were baptized by Hereticks: For which they are commonly now condemned.

§. 21. And *Binnius* noteth that they had this from their Countryman *Tertullian*, whose zeal against Hereticks was so hot, that he would have nothing, no not Baptism, common with them; so *Baron. an.* 217. *n.* 1, 2, 3. & *an.* 258. *n.* 19, 20. Yet is this man now numbred with Hereticks.

§. 22. III. The *Concilium Labesitanum* is the next in order, where one *Privatus* was condemned for an Heretick (mentioned by *Cyprian*, *Epist.* 55.) But, saith *Binnius*, what his Heresie was is not known nor mentioned.

§. 23. IV. Next we have an *Arabian* Council, in which the Errour of the *Souls Mortality* (allowing it only to rise again with the Body at the Resurrection) was excellently oppugned and expugned by *Origen*; but it was by that *Origen* who himself is called a blasphemous Heretick.

§. 24. V. The next mentioned Council (*Bin. p.* 158.) was at *Rome*, about the restoring of the Lapsed upon *Cyprian*'s motion. A business that made no small dissention, while *Lucianus* and some others made the Church-door too wide, and *Novatus*, and *Novatianus* made it too narrow, and *Cyprian* and the *Roman* Clergy went a middle way: bitter and grievous were the Censures of each other, and long and sad the Schisms that did ensue, the rigour of the *Novatians* being increased by their Offence at other mens sinful latitude and tepidity.

§. 25. By the way it is worth the considering by some *Papists*, who make both a Bishop Essential to a Church, and a Pope to the Church-Universal, and deny Church-Government to Presbyters, that this Council is said to be called by the *Roman* Clergy (the Presbyters and Deacons) when the Church had been a year or two without a Bishop (through the sharp persecution of *Decius* upon *Fabian*'s Death). And it is to the *Roman* Clergy (Presbyters and Deacons) that *Cyprian* at this time wrote divers of his Epistles, as they wrote to him; insomuch that *Binnius* sticketh not to say, *that in this interregnum the* Roman *Clergy had the care or charge of the Universal Church*.

Quær. How far their Government, even of Bishops (whom they Assembled in this Council) was Canonical or valid?

§. 26. VI. After this there was another Council at *Carthage*, and two at *Rome*, and one in *Italy*, and another at *Carthage*, about the same Controversie; where it was determined that the Lapsed should be received to Repentance, and after a sufficient space of Penance, should communicate, but not sooner: And that the Bishops that lapsed should be uncapable of Episcopacy and communicate only with the Laity upon their penance: Yet *Cyprian* in time of a renewed Persecution thought meet to relax this, and take in the Penitent presently, lest they should be discouraged under Suffering. But *Fælicissimus* one of his Deacons made himself the Head of a Faction, by taking men in by his own Authority too soon, and *Novatus* and *Novatian*, as is said, being against their taking into Communion at all, the Councils excommunicated them all as Schismaticks. Where note, that *Novatus* an *African* Priest, that went to *Rome* and got *Novatian* ordained Bishop, did not deny them Pardon of Sin with God, but only Church-Communion. 2. Nor did he deny this to other great Sinners repenting, but only to those that lapsed to Idolatry or denying Christ. But the *Novatians* long after extended it to other heynous Crimes, as upon supposed parity of Reason.

§. 27. VII. Next this we have *Cyprians African* Council in which (after the censuring of some that reproached a Pastor) they condemn a Dead Man called *Victor*, becaufe by his Will he left one *Faustinus* a Presbyter the Guardian of his Sons, which the Canons had forbidden, becaufe no Ministers of God should be called from their sacred Work to meddle with Secular things : Therefore they Decree that *Victors* Name shall not be mentioned among the Dead in Deprecation, nor any Oblation made for his Reft. *(Non eft quod pro dormitione ejus apud vos fiat oblatio, aut deprecatio aliqua nomine ejus in Ecclefia frequentetur.)* The cafe of the Clergy is much altered fince then; And whether the penalty had more of Piety, as to the end, or Errour in the rigor, and the matter (as if it were a Punishment to the Dead, not to be offered for, or prayed for) I leave to further confideration, *Cypr. li. 1. Epift. 66.*

§. 28. VIII. The next Council we meet with is *Concil. Iconienfe an.* 258. where the Bishops of *Cappadocia, Cilicia, Galatia*, and other Oriental Provinces at *Iconium* in *Phrygia*, Decreed that the Baptifms of Hereticks, their Ordinations, Impofition of Hands, and other sacred Actions were invalid. For which, faith *Baronius an.* 258. *n.* 14, 15, 16. Pope *Stephen* Excommunicated all these Oriental Bishops, and Reprobated the Council, and would not receive or hear their Legates: Of which *Firmilianus Cafar. Cappad.* writeth to *Cyprian* againft him.

§. 29. IX. At the fame time, *Eufeb. lib.* 7. *c.* 6. tells us, there was alfo a Synod at *Synadis*, yea, divers in other places, that all decreed the fame thing, for rebaptizing those that were baptized by Hereticks; and that this had been the Bishops opinion of fo long time before, that *Eufebius* durft not condemn it. *Vid. Baron. Anno* 258. *n.* 17. But it is now commonly condemned.

§. 30. X. If they had confined their opinion of rebaptizing to fuch Hereticks as are ftrictly fo called, that renounce any effential Article of the Faith, they might have made the Controverfie hard; But as Hereticating increafed, fo their own difficulties increafed. And now the *Novatians* were pronounced Hereticks, it grew a hard queftion, whether all that the *Novatians* had baptized muft be rebaptized. And for this an *African* Council, *Anno* 258. concluded affirmatively: Becaufe all that are baptized are baptized into the Church : But Hereticks are not in the Church, and fo baptize not into the Church: therefore fuch muft be rebaptized. *Cyprian* and many very Godly Bifhops confented in this errour.

§. 31. XI. To try this bufinefs further, *Cyprian* gathered another Council of above 70 Bishops out of *Africk* and *Numidia*, and all were defired to declare:

declare what was the Tradition of their Fathers; And they all agreed that according to Scripture, and Tradition, the Baptism of Hereticks was a Nullity, and it was no rebaptization to baptize such as they baptized: (see here what strength is in the Papists argument of Tradition in such cases.) But this Council and their Doctrine Pope *Stephen* condemned: But they never the more altered their judgments, not believing his Infallibity or power to judge between them in such matters of Faith.

In this Council is set down every Bishops Reason of his Judgment.

§. 32. XII. When Pope *Stephen* had condemned these Bishops, *Cyprian* calleth yet a greater Council of 87 Bishops, who confirmed the same Doctrine, and rejected the Popes opinion and his arrogancies, that would make himself to be a Bishop of Bishops, and by tyrannical terrour and abuse of Excommunication, force others to his opinion. And with the *Africans* in this judgment joyned *Firmilian*, with 70 *Asian* Bishops, and saith *Binnius*, *Dionysius Alexandrinus* also.

§. 33. But I must here tell the Reader, that I mention not these instances to breed ill thoughts in him of these *African* and *Numidian* Bishops: For as far as I can discern by their Writings and by History, they were the Godliest, Faithful, Peaceable company of Bishops that were found in any part of the World since the Apostles times: *Cyprian*'s style and the testimony of all just History which concerneth him, as well as his Martyrdome, declare him to be a Saint indeed. (*Nazianzen* declareth the strange occasion of his Conversion; *viz.* That he loved or lusted after a Christian Virgin, and when he could not obtain his will, being given to Magick, he agreed with the Devil to procure his desire; but when he saw that the Devil confest himself unable to do it, and so that he was too weak for Christ, he forsook the Devil and turned Christian:) The Papists (*Binnius, Baronius, &c.*) conjecture that *Cyprian* before his death reformed this Errour, but their conjecture meerly tells us what they wish, without any reason, but that he dyed a Martyr and his Successours honoured him. As if none might so die and be honoured that had any errour, which no man living is without. 2. And this may be said to excuse their errour. 1. That the strictest men oftner erre on the stricter side against sin, than the complying Carnal Clergy. 2. That they thought it the safer way to baptize such again, (on the same reason as we do in case of uncertain baptisme, with a *si non baptizatus es, baptizo te*;) not knowing why there should be any danger in the mistake: Much like as in *England* now, the Bishops are for the re-Ordaining of all such as were Ordained by others that were not Diocesanes, and yet do not call it re-Ordaining. 3. That in those times of Heathenisme and persecution, the Christians had no way to maintain their strength but by the Churches Concord; nor could they otherwise have kept up so strict a discipline as they did, having no forcing power of Christian Magistrates: Therefore they were necessitated to be severe with dividers. 4. And the ambiguity of the word [*Heresie*] was not the least occasion of their errour. The *Nicene* Council afterward rebaptized such as those Hereticks

reticks Baptized, who corrupted the substance of baptisme it self, but not others. And Christians at first had more wit and charity than to call every errour a Heresie, (else there had been none but Hereticks:) such as denyed some essential point of faith or practice, and drew a party to maintain it, were called Hereticks in the former times; but afterward every Schism or Party that gathered by themselves, and set up *altare contra altare* upon the smallest difference, was called a Heresie. And so the same name applyed to another thing, deceived them. The Bishops were men of eminent piety and worth.

§. 34. XIII. *Anno* 263. They say there was a Council at *Rome* to clear *Dionysius Alexand.* of the imputation of Heresie, occasioned by some doubtful words which he wrote against *Sabellius.*

§. 35. XIV. *Anno* 266. They say there was another at *Antioch* against their Bishop *Paulus Samosatenus*, a gross Heretick: But he renounced his errour in words, and for that time kept his place.

§. 36. XV. *Paulus* returning to his Heresie and a bad life, *Anno* 272. another Council at *Antioch* deposed him; but he would not go out of the Bishops house, and the Emperour *Aurelian* a Heathen put him out.

§. 37. XVI. *Anno* 303. The next Council was at *Cirta* in *Numidia*, *Secundus Tigisitanus* being chief and calling them. Here *Secundus* accused the Bishops one by one as Traditors (delivering the sacred books to be burnt in persecution to save themselves, which was then judged perfidiousness.) The Bishops partly excused, partly confessed it, and asked pardon; Till at last *Secundus* ready to judge them, accused a Bishop *Purpurius* of murdering his own Sisters Sons: who told him that he should not think to terrifie him as he had done the rest; He had killed, and would kill those that make against him, and askt him whether he had not been a Traditor himself, and beginning to evince it, bid him not provoke him to tell the rest: Whereupon *Secundus* his Nephew told his Unkle, You see that he is ready to depart and make a Schism, and not he only but all the rest, and you hear what they say against you: And then they will joyn and pass sentence on you, and so you will remain the only Heretick (*Hereticating went then by the Vote*) *Secundus* was nonplust, and askt two others, what it was best to do? And they agreed to leave them all to God, and so the Bishops kept their places. *Augustin. cont. Crescon. l. 3. c. 26, 27.*

§. 38. XVII. Next they deliver us *Consilium Sinuessanum*, whether true or forged is too hard a controversie. It was of *three hundred* Bishops (how big were their Dioceses think you above our Parishes?) who all came secretly together to a Town now unknown, and met in a Cave that would hold but 50 at a time, for fear of persecution: The business was to Convict Pope *Marcellinus* of Idolatry, for offering sacrifice to *Hercules, Jupiter*, and *Saturn*: which he confessed.

§. 39. XVIII. *Anno* 305. Was held a Council of 19 Bishops at *Illiberis* in *Spain*: where many good things were agreed on: But not only to the Idolatrous Lapsed, but to other heinous crimes they denyed Communion

to

to the death, notwithstanding repentance. And that these Bishops should be Orthodox, and yet the *Novatians* Hereticks, it is not easie to give a reason of. Their distinction of *Penance, Sacrament,* and *Communion,* will not well perform it. Therefore *Melch. Canus* chargeth them with Errour *lib.* 5 *c.* 4. and *Bella mine* much more, *lib.* 2. *de Imag. c.* 9. That it is *Concilium non confirmatum, frequenter errasse, &c.* A Bishop, Priest or Deacon in Office, that hath committed Fornication, was not to have Communion, no not at death: and divers others. No Bishop was to receive any Gift from any one that did not Communicate. It poseth the Papists themselves to expound Can. 34. *Cereos per diem placuit in Cœmiterio non incendi: Inquietandi enim Sanctorum spiritus non sunt: Binnius* will have it to be the Spirits of the living Saints, that are not to be disquieted with trouble about Lights set up by day. But I wish that he the meaning. But the 36 Can. more troubleth them, *Placuit pictiras in Ecclesia esse non debere, ne quod colitur aut adoratur, in parietibus depingatur.* Can. 38. A Lay-man, in case of necessity, is enabled to Baptize. Can. 39. Gentiles unbaptized may be made Christians at last, by Imposition of hands. Can. 65. If a Clergy-man's Wife play the Whore, and he do not presently cast her out, he must not be received to the Communion to the last. Can. 73. If a Christian turn Accuser (*Delator*) and upon his accusation any one be banished or put to death, he is not to be received to Communion, no not at last. Can. 75. Nor he that falsly accuseth a Bishop, Presbyter, or Deacon, and cannot prove it. Can. 79. He that playeth at Dice, or Tables, was to be kept from the Communion. Many other Canons favour, some of Piety, and some of the *Novatians.* Thirty six Presbyters sate with these Nineteen Bishops. Pope *Innocent* approved these almost *Novatian* Canons, and *Binnius* excuseth them, *p.* 246.

§. 40. XIX. *Anno* 306. A Council at *Carthage* of about 70 Bishops began the Schism of the *Donatists*, contending who should have the Bishoprick of *Carthage*: One party had chosen *Cæcilianus* to succeed *Mensurius*; The other party accusing him as being a Traditor, and Ordained by *Fœlix* a Traditor, and had forbidden bringing food to the Martyrs in prison, they ordained one *Majorinus* Bishop in his stead: *Cæcilianus* had the countenance of the Bishop of *Rome*, and stood it out, and kept the place: Hereupon the Church being divided, the division run through all *Africk*, and *Numidia*, while the accusing party renounced Communion with *Cæcilianus*; so that for many years after (two hundred at least) they did with plausible pretence claim the title of *Catholicks*, though they were after called *Donatists* (from *Donatus* a very good Bishop of *Carthage* heretofore, whom they praised, and not from *Donatus à Casis nigris,* as some think.) *Secundus Tigisitanus* Primate of *Numidia*, furthers the breach, and the Ordination of *Majorinus* fixed it. Thus the doleful Tragedy of the *Donatists* began by Bishops divided about a *Carthage-*Bishop.

§. 41. XX. *Anno* 308. Another Council was held at *Carthage*, where no less than 270 *Donatist* Bishops, for moderation, agreed to Communicate with penitent Traditors, without rebaptizing them, and so did for 40 years. §. 42.

§. 42. XXI. *Anno* 313. The Schism continuing, the *Donatists* cleaving to *Majorinus*, appealed against *Cæcilianus* to *Constantine* (now Emperour.) He first appointeth three *French* Bishops to judge the Cause, but after 19 Bishops (called a *Roman* Council) met at *Rome* to hear both Parties: where *Melchiades* and the rest acquitted *Cæcilianus*, and condemned *Donatus à Casis nigris* (a promoter of the *Donatists* Cause) as guilty of Schism. But the *Donatists* accusing *Melchiades* also as a Traditor, the Schism was never the more ended: A motion was made that both the Bishops should remove (*Cæcilianus* and *Majorinus*) to end the Schisme; But the *Donatist* Bishops were so very many in number, that they thought they were to be called the *Church*, and the *Cæcilianists* the Schismaticks, and therefore would not so agree. Thus Bishops about Bishopricks set all the Country on a flame.

§. 43. XXII. Next *Constantine* would hear the Cause of these contending Bishops at a Council at *Arles* in *France*, (before 200 Bishops at least) where *Cæcilianus* was again acquitted; and the *Donatist* Bishops cast, by the witness of their Scribe *Ingentius*, who (being racked) confessed that he was hired to give false witness in the Case. Several good Canons were here made for Church-Order.

§. 44. I have heard many Popish Persons liken the Separatists among us to the *Donatists*: But so unlike them are they, That, 1. The said Separatists are against all Episcopacy, but the *Donatists* were Bishops, and contended for the highest Places of Prelacy. 2. The Separatists are confessedly a Minor Part departing from the Major Part. But the *Donatists* were the Major Part of the Bishops casting out the Minor Part as Delinquents. The Truth is, in those times the Bishops being usually in contention and Church-Wars among themselves, (especially when *Constantine* had given them peace and prosperity,) the strife was, Who should get the better, and have their will: 1. Sometime the strife was about Opinions, who was in the right, and to be called Orthodox, and who was to be accounted the Heretick. 2. The other part quarrel who should be the Bishop, or who should have the highest places. 3. And the next quarrel was whose side should carry it in setting up any Bishops, or in judging and deposing them, and who should have their Heads or Friends brought in. And the way to get the better, was, 1. At the first, by the majority of the peoples Votes in chusing Bishops, and of the Bishops in deposing them. 2. But after, most went in chusing and deposing by the majority of the Bishops Votes in the greater Seats, (the peoples consent still required,) at least if a Council did interpose. 3. And at last, it went by the favour or displeasure of the Court; either the Emperour, or the Empress, or some great Officers. The *African* Bishops it seems were far the greatest number against *Cæcilian*, (when 270 met at one Council, and *Melchiades* Council at *Rome* had but 19, and that at *Illiberis* 19, and that at *Ancyra* 18 Bishops.) Therefore the Bishops thought that majority of number gave them right to the Title of Catholicks, and that those Dissenters must be called *Hereticks*, as was too usual. And seeing they lived in the Country where many Councils under *Agrippinus* and *Cyprian*, and *Firmilian*, had voted that *Hereticks* were not of the Church, and those that they had baptized, were to be rebaptized; they thought that they did but keep up this Tradition; and so they said that they were all the Church of *Africa*, and that the *Cecilians* were *Hereticks* and *Separatists* from the Church, and that all that they baptized were to be rebaptized, as was formerly held. So that indeed the *Donatists* did but as the *Papists*, and their worldly Clergy still have done, who take the advantage of a *majority* to call themselves the *Church* and *Catholike*, and to call the Dissenters *Schismaticks* and *Hereticks*, save that they added *Cyprian*'s rebaptizing. And when it was for their advantage they communicated 40 years with Traditors; but when the power of the Court and the Bish. of *Rome* bore them down, they kept up their party by pretended strictness, and reproaching the others as a Sect, and as Heretical and persecuters of the Church. So that it was the Multitudes and Councils of the Prelates that set up *Donatism*. *And no General Council had judged against them, for there had been none.*

§. 44. XXIII. The next was *an.* 314. at *Ancyra* in *Galatia* of eighteen Bishops, who met to determine how many years the Lapsed should repent (or do penance) before they were admitted to Communion. *Can.* 17. forbad those, that were ordained Bishops to any people and were not accepted by the Parish to which they were ordained, to thrust themselves on other Parishes, or raise Sedition, but allowed them to continue Presbyters. *Can.* 21. Wilful Murderers were to communicate at last only.

§. 45. XXIV. The Churches having now peace under *Constantine* a Council of 13 Bishops that had been before most at *Ancyra* met at *Neocesarea*; but the small number did better work than many greater Councils did, making some good Canons against Adultery and Fornication; Though the 7*thCan.* that forbids Priests to dine at the second Marriages of any, because such must repent, be of doubtful sense and truth: The first *Can.* is against Priests marrying and Fornication. The last, that the number of Deacons must be just seven, be the City never so big.

§. 46. XXV. Next a *Roman* Council is mentioned by *Binnius* p. 279. for a Conference with *Jews* before *Constantine*, but he saith the Acts that now are extant are full of falshoods.

§. 47. XXVI. *An.* 315. They place us a Council at *Alexandria* in which *Alexander*, with many Bishops, condemned *Eusebius Nicomed.* with *Arius* and that the rest adhered to them, especially as holding that Christ was not Eternal, but was a Creature that had a beginning, and that the *Wisdom* and *Word* of God was not the *Son*, but made the Son.

§. 48. XXVII. Another Council at *Alexand.* they tell us of, against the *Arians*, and the *Melitian Schismaticks*: but the Acts are not known. To this is annexed an Epistle of *Constantine* to *Alexander* and *Arius*, recorded by *Euseb. Cæsar in vita Constant.* in which *Constantine* chideth them both for their Contention, and seemeth to take the Question for unsearchable and to be disputed, saying, "I understand that the foundation of the Controverse

" verfie was hence laid, that thou *Alexander* didſt ask queſtions of the Pref-
" byters about a certain Text of Scripture; yea, about a certain idle Par-
" ticle of a Queſtion didſt enquire, what every one of them thought? And
" thou *Arius* didſt inconſiderately blurt out that which thou hadſt not be-
" fore thought of, or if thou hadſt thought of it, thou oughteſt to have
" paſt by in ſilence: Whence diſcord was ſtir'd up among you, and the
" meeting hindered which is wont to be made in the Church, and the
" moſt holy people diſtracted into ſeveral parts, is divided from the
" compagination of the whole body of the Church. Therefore both of
" you, forgiving one another, approve of that which your fellow-ſervant
" doth not without cauſe exhort you to: And what is that? That to
" ſuch Queſtions you neither Ask, nor Anſwer, if asked: For ſuch Que-
" ſtions as no Law or Eccleſiaſtick Canon doth neceſſarily preſcribe, but
" the vain ſtrife of diſſolute idleneſs doth propoſe, though they may ſerve
" to exerciſe acuteneſs of wit, yet we ought to contemn them in the inner
" thought of the mind, and neither raſhly to bring them out into the
" publick Aſſemblies of the People, nor unadviſedly to truſt them to the
" Ears of the Vulgar. For how few are they that can accurately enough
" perceive the force of things ſo weighty, and ſo involved in obſcurity?
" But if there be ſome one that is confident that he can eaſily do and reach
" this, yet I pray you, how ſmall a part of the multitude is it, that he
" can make to underſtand him? Or who is there, that in the curious ſearch
" of ſuch Queſtions, is not in danger of a fall?

The reſt is well worth the Reading, as to the common caſe of Theological Controverſies, though it ſeems that *Conſtantine* made too light of the *Arian* errour. But I dare not be ſo injurious to *Euſebius* as to queſtion whether he faithfully recited the Epiſtle, when *Binnius* himſelf backs his doubt with a *dicere non auderem*: And if we give away the credit of that one Hiſtorian, it will leave much of Church Hiſtory under doubt, that now goeth for certain: Perhaps *Peters* being ever at *Rome*, &c.

§. 49. XXIX. The next mentioned is the Council of *Laodicea* in *Phrygia Paccat*, (not *Syria*) of 32 Biſhops, gathered by *Nunechius* a Biſhop of *Phrygia*. They were ſo few that without contention they made divers good Canons: The 46 Canon requireth that the baptized ſhould learn the Creed, and on the Friday of the laſt week repeat it to the Biſhop or Presbyters. (By which you may conjecture how large a Biſhoprick then was.) And Can. 56. The Presbyters were not to go into the Church before the Biſhop, but with him. (For then every Church had a Biſhop, though ſome Chapels far off had Presbyters only.) And Can. 57. It is ordered, that *Biſhops ſhould not be Ordained in ſmall Villages and Hamlets*, but *Viſitors* ſhould be appointed them. But *ſuch (Biſhops) as had been heretofore there Ordained, ſhould do nothing without the Conſcience of the City Biſhop*. Which ſheweth that before Biſhops were made in Villages; as *Socrates* ſaith then they were in *Arabia*, and the *Phrygian Novatians*, &c. The laſt Can. reciteth

the

their Councils abridged. 43

the same Canonical Scriptures that we receive, save the *Apocalyps*, which is left out.

§. 50. XXIX. Next we have a great *Roman* Council of 275 Bishops, saith *Crab*, under *Sylvester*, which hath 7 Canons: The last saith, That no Bishop shall Ordain any, but *with all the Church united.* But whether this was before or after the *Nicene* Council, is uncertain.

And another he mentioneth under *Sylvester* at *Rome*, which *Binnius* hath, where *Constantine* baptized of *Sylvester* was present and 284 Bishops. (Whether it be true or a fiction is uncertain.) But if true, it was a very humble Council: For they all professed only patience, renounced giving their judgment at all, but only heard what *Sylvester* would say, professing none fit to judge but he. But they all with Presbyters and Deacons subscribed what he said (if true.) What he said I do not well understand, supposing much of it to be scarce sense: I am sure it is far from *Cicero*'s Latine. 139 Bishops came, *ex Urbe Remá vel non longè ab illà*, *Out of the City of Rome, or not far from it:* (How big were their Dioceses?) Here, Cap. 2. three men are cursed, (anathematized:) One was a Bishop, *Victorinus*, that *being ignorant of the course of the Moon*, contradicted the right time of *Easter*. It's well the *Makers* and *Approvers* of our Imposed *English* Liturgy fell not under *Sylvester*'s severity, who have (alas, mistakingly) told us, that [*Easter-day, on which the rest depend, is always the first Sunday after the first full Moon, which happens next after the one and twentieth day of* March: *And if the full Moon happen on a* Sunday, Easter-day *is the Sunday after.*] This is one of the things that about 2000 Ministers are silenced, for not *Declaring Assent*, Consent and Approbation of; yea to the *use of it*, and so to keep *Easter* at a wrong time. But how *Sylvester* came to have power to say all, and to banish men, and *Constantine* sit by and say nothing, I know not: *Dedit eis anathema & damnavit eos extra urbes suas.*

Cap. 3. He Decreed, that *no Presbyter shall accuse a Bishop, no Deacon a Presbyter, &c.* and no Layman, *any of them*: *And that no Prelate shall be condemned but in 72 Testimonies*, nor the chief Prelate be judged of any one, because *it is written, The Disciple is not above his Master. And no Presbyter shall be condemned but in 44 Testimonies; no Cardinal Deacon but in 36, &c.* And what may they not then do or be?

Cap. 5. He Decreed *clarâ voce*, that no Presbyter should make Chrisme, *because Christ is so called of Chrisme.*

The 12. Cap. is, *Nemo det pænitentiam, nisi quadraginta annorum petenti.* Let no man give repentance (or penance) *but to one that seeketh forty years.*

Cap. 14. *Let no man receive the witness of a Clergy-man against a Layman.*

Cap. 15. For no man may examine *a Clergy-man but in the Church.*

Cap. 16. *Let no Clerk, Deacon, or Presbyter, for any Cause of his enter into any Court, because* Omnis Curia à Cruore dicitur, *every Court is so called from blood, and is an offering to Images; For if any Clergy-man enter into a Court,*

G 2 *let*

let him take his *Anathema*, never returning to his Mother the Church.

Cap. 17. *Let no man put a sinning Clergy-man to death, no Presbyter, no Deacon, no Bishop, that is over a Clerk or Servitor of the Church, may bring him to death. But if the Clergy man's cause so require, let him be three days deprived of honour, that he may return to his Mother-Church.*

Cap. 18. *No Deacon may offer against a Priest a Charge of filthiness.*

Cap. 20. *No man shall judge of the Prime seat; because all seats desire justice to be tempered of the first seat.* The *Subscribers* were 284 Bishops (what did the other 57?) 45 Priests, and 5 Deacons, and *the two following, and* Constantine *and his Mother* Helena. O brave Pope and Clergy! O patient Council that subscribed to one man, and pretended to no judgment! O humble *Constantine*, that subscribed to all this, and said nothing! And a womans subscription perfecteth all. And O credulous Reader that believeth this!

CHAP.

CHAP. III.

The Council of Nice, *and some following it.*

§. 1. XXX. WE come now to the first General Council: General only as to the *Roman World* or *Empire*, as the History and Subscriptions prove, and not as to the *Whole World*, as the Papists with notorious impudence affirm: which I have elsewhere fully proved. This Council was called, as is probably gathered, *Anno* 325. in the 20th year of *Constantine* (though others assign other years.) That they were congregate about the *Arian* Heresie and the Eastern Controversie is commonly known: As also what wisdom and diligence *Constantine* used to keep the Bishops in peace: Who presently brought in their Libels of accusations against each other; which he took and burnt without reading them, earnestly exhorting them to peace, and by his presence and prudent speech repressing their heats and contentions ; whereby the Synod was brought to a happy end as to both the controverted Causes: And *Eusebius Nicomed.* and *Arius* were brought to counterfeit repentance and consent to the *Nicene* Faith ; which *Constantine* perceiving, being set upon the healing of the divided Bishops and Churches, he commanded that *Arius* should (as reformed) be received to Communion ; which *Athanasius* refusing caused much calamity afterward.

§. 2. Because the Case of the *Meletians* is brought in by this Council, I think it useful (for our warning in these times) to recite the sum of their story out of *Epiphanius*, p. 717, &c. *Hær.* 68.

Meletius (saith he) was a Bishop in *Thebais* in *Egypt*, of sincere Faith even to the death. In *Diocletians* Persecution, *Peter* Bishop of *Alexandria*, and he, were the chief of the Bishops that were laid in Prison, as designed to Martyrdom ; while they were there long together with many fellow-prisoners, many called to Tryal before them were put to death, and many for fear subscribed to Idolatry, or denyed Christ : And when they had done, professed repentance and craved peace of the Church : As it had been in *Novatus* his Schisms, so it fell out here ; Peter Bishop of *Alexan.* was for peace and pardon ; *Meletius* and most of the other suffering prisoners were against it, and said, If they may thus revolt to save themselves, and be presently pardoned, it will tempt others to revolt : *Peter* seeing his opinion was rejected, rashly took his Cloak and hang'd it like a Curtain over the midst of the prison-room, and said, *Those that are for me, come to me on this side, and those that are for* Meletius *go on that side to him :* Whereupon far most of the Bishops, Priests, Monks, and people that were in prison went to *Meletius*, and but few to *Peter*. (A fouler Rupture
than

than that of the *English* Fugitives at *Frankford*.) This unhappy word and hour began the misery, among good men, expecting death: From that hour they keep all their meetings separate. Shortly after *Peter* was Martyred, and *Meletius* was judged to the Mines: As he went thither through the Country, he every where made new Bishops and gathered new Churches, so that there were *two in the several Cities:* Those old ones that followed *Peter* called their Meeting, *The Catholick Church*; The other called theirs, *The Martyrs Church*: But yet they held a Unity of Faith. Even the sufferers that laboured in the Mines divided, and did not pray together. At last *Meletius* and the rest were restored unto peace, and at *Alexandria, Alexander* and he lived in familiarity, and *Meletius* was he that detected *Arius* and brought him to *Alexander* to be tryed. But when *Meletius* was dead, *Alexander* grew impatient at the private separate Meetings of his followers, and troubled them, and vexed them, and began to use violence against them, and would not have them depart from his Church: They refused still, and this bred stirs and Tumults. *Alexander* persecuting them, and following them yet more sharply, they sent some men, eminent for piety and parts, to the Emperours Court, to Petition for Liberty for their private Meetings, without impediment. Of these *Paphnutius* and *John* their Bishop, and *Callinicus* Bishop of *Pellusium* were chief: who when they came to Court, being named *Meletians*, the Courtiers rejected them and drove them away, and they could not get access to the Emperour. On this occasion being put to wait long at *Constantinople* and *Nicomedia*, they fell into acquaintance with *Eusebius*, Bishop of *Nicomedia*, the Head of the *Arians*, who pretending repentance was become great with the Emperour, who was all for the Clergies peace and concord. To *Eusebius* they open all the matter: He craftily took the advantage of their suffering and long waiting, and promised his help, on condition they would but Communicate with *Arius*, who feigned repentance. The temptation overcame them, and they yield; They that had gathered separate Churches, because they would not Communicate with the repenting Lapsed (to Idolatry;) yet yielded to Communicate with *Arius*, that they might be delivered from the persecution of a Godly Bishop, and keep their Meetings. They are brought to *Constantine*, who being all for peace, though against Schism, grants them the freedom of their Meetings; And thus joyning with the *Arians* for the liberty of their Assemblies, this became the greatest support to the *Arians*, without which (saith *Epiphanius*) they could not have stood. (So much doth Bishops tyranny or severity cross its own ends, and destroy the concord which they think by such tearing means to force; And so hard is it for men that could suffer Martyrdome from Heathens, innocently to bear the persecution of their Brethren, and so greatly doth it tempt them to use unwarrantable means for their preservation: Just as if the Non-conformists at this time should seek, by the favour of the Papists, to be delivered from the silencing and destroying Prelates, upon condition of a common liberty: The Cases are not much unlike.) *Neque enim* (saith *Epiphanius*) *consistere*

Arius,

Arius, aut fiduciam ullam habere potuisset, nisi cum esset occasionem nactus; qua pessimam inter illos ad hodiernum usque diem concordiam devinxit. (But O, Father *Epiphanius*, why took you not warning by this, when you un-Bishoplike and un-Canonically set your self against holy *Chrysostome*?)

Alexander being dead, and *Athanasius* shortly succeeding him, he could not bear the *Meletian* Churches in his City: And after fair means he used foul: And going himself to look after such Meetings, with his Retinue, one of his Deacons in the *Meletian* Meetings broke a certain Vessel, which occasioned some chiding and fighting, which occasioned Accusations of the *Meletians*, and Calumniations of the *Arians* against *Athanasius* as a Man of Violence and Tyranny; which *Constantine* abhorring in a Bishop, and *Euseb. Nicomed.* representing the Matter as worse than it was, the Emperour (having granted the *Meletians* liberty for their Meetings, which *Athanasius* violently denyed them) in great anger commanded a Synod to be held at *Tyre* to examine the Matter, and *Eusebius Cæsariens.* with some others to preside or order it: Where *Potamo* Bishop of *Heraclea* seeing *Eusebius Cæs.* sit as Judge and *Athanasius* stand, with Passion and Tears inveyed against *Eusebius*, saying, *Who can endure to see thee,* Eusebius, *sit and judge innocent* Athanasius? *Were not thou and I in Prison together in time of Persecution, and when I lost an Eye for the Truth, thou camest out unmaimed? And how came that to pass, if thou didst not promise some wicked deed or other to the Persecutors, or do some?* Eusebius hearing this, suddenly rose and dismissed the Council, saying, *If you dare carry it thus here, your Adversaries Accusations are to be believed: For if you play the Tyrants here, you do it much more in your own Country.* Hereupon two *Arian* Bishops *Ursahus* and *Valens* are sent into *Egypt* to enquire after the Truth of the Matter, who coming back with Calumnies against *Athanasius*, he fled from the Council by Night to the Court to the Emperour to give him information; who taking *Athanasius* for false and Tyrannical would not believe him, but upon Letters from the Council, and upon the provocation of *Athanasius*, who told him God would judge him for believing his Accusers, banished him, where he remained (in *Italy*) twelve or thirteen years, even till after *Constantins* Death. And when *Constans* had compelled his Brother *Constantius* to restore him, he was again banished; For *George* that had been made Bishop by the *Arians* (and by *Constantius*) was killed by the Heathen People in *Julians* time, and his Corps burnt, and the Ashes scattered into the Wind, which increased the suspicion of Tyranny against *Athanasius*: But in *Jovians* Reign he was again restored; And after his Death, he conflicted with Infamies again: And when *Athanasius* was Dead, the Emperour *Valens* set *Lucius* over them, who afflicted the People that had followed *Athanasius*, and *Peter* whom they had chosen for their Bishop, and by Banishment, Death and Torments, made them know what Church-Tyranny was indeed.

Thus far *Epiphanius* giveth us the History of the *Meletian* Schism, and the effects of good Bishops impatience with Dissenters.

§. 3. But

§. 3. But I must not conceal from the Reader that *Baronius* and *Dion. Petavius* say, that *Epiphanius* is deceived in all this History, and maketh the case of the *Meletians* better than it was; and that some *Meletian* knave beguiled him: But, 1. They give us no proof of any such knaves beguiling him at all : 2. And he that was so apt to *over-do* in suspecting and aggravating Heresies, (as in *Origen*'s and *Chrysostome*'s Case,) was not likely to make the Case here so much better than it was : 3. And how much nearer was *Epiphanius* in time and place, than *Baronius* and *Petavius* ? and how easie was it then for him to have true notice of such publick things? 4. And if they make *Epiphanius* so fallacious in such a story as this, so near him, what a shake doth it give to the Credit of his copious History of the many other Heresies, which he had less opportunity to know : and consequently to the Credit of much of Church-History? Yet I confess, that the man seemeth not to be very accurate in his Disputes, nor all his Narratives; But rather by far to be suspected of making things worse than they were, than better. And I believe that some passages in this History are mistaken by him (as that the *Meletians* joyned with the *Arians* before the death of *Alexander*:)but that maketh their Case the better. *Petavius* saith also, p. 286. *Animad. in Epiph. Multum in Historiâ* Meletii *lapsum esse suprà vidimus*; *Largius* in Arianæ *Hæresis descriptione peccavit vir alioqui diligentissimus.* And in his instance of the time of *Arius* death it's undeniable. But if in such famous Histories, we must read him with such suspicion and allowance, how much more in the many little ones that were more obscure?

§. 4. As to the *Arians* Heresie, the two Epistles of *Arius* recorded by *Epiphanius* tell us much of the truth of his mistake : And the *Arians* Arguments by him are at large recorded and answered. He that denyeth the Deity of Christ, denyeth his Essence : And he that denyeth his Essence, denyeth Christ, and is no Christian. But the *Samosatenians*, the *Photinians*, and our late *Socinians*, are far more perniciously Heretical than the *Arians*. For the *Arians* maintained, that *Tres sunt hypostases, Pater, Filius & Spiritus Sanctus*; and that God did *ante sempiterna tempora unigenitum filium gignere, per quem & sæcula & reliqua procreavit omnia*; *viz., subsistentem illum suapte voluntate condidisse, ejusmodi ut neque converti neque mutari possit, perfectam Dei creaturam, sed non tanquam rerum creatarum aliquam*; *fœtum itidem, sed non tanquam unum è cæteris.* They thought that before God made the rest of the creatures , he made one super-angelical perfect Spirit, by which he made all the rest, and that this is Christ; and that he received no other soul but a body only at his Incarnation, and this super-angelical spirit was his soul. This was the dangerous heresie of *Arius*.

§. 5. *Dion. Petavius* truly telleth us, that his great advantage was, that many of the Fathers of that Church had spoken in such kind of words before him, the Controversie being not then well considered : p 285. *ad Hæres.* 69. having spoken of *Lucian*, the Martyr's giving advantage to *Arius*, he addeth, *Quod idem plerisque veterum Patrum cùm in hoc negotio, tùm in aliis fidei Christianæ capitibus usu venit, ut ante errorum atque hæreseon, quibus*

bus ea singillatim oppugnabantur, originem, nondum satis illustrata ac patefacta rei veritate, quædam suis scriptis asperserint, quæ cum orthodoxa fidei regula minimè consentiant. (And yet the Papists swear, not to expound Scripture, but according to the unanimous consent of the Fathers.) *Nè ab hac Trinitatis mysterio ac quæstione discedam, obser vavimus jamdudum* Justinum Mart. *Dialogo cum* Tryph. *de filio Dei idem propemodùm cum* Arianis *sentire.* And in his Books, *De Trinit.* he at large citeth the very words of him and many other Fathers. But he here giveth them this gentle excuse, *Sed ab omni culpâ tam hic quam* Lucianus *aliique liberandi sunt, qui nondum agitatâ controversiâ, panem de eâ commodè pronunciasse videntur. Simile quiddam de* Dionys. Alex. *tradit.* Basilius, Ep. 41, *&c.* But it is enough to think charitably, that they were saved, without going so far as to say, they were *without all fault.* For Christianity is the same thing before such Controversies and after: And it's hard to think how he can be a Christian, that denyeth Christs Essence: But God is merciful, and requireth not knowledge alike in all, that have not equal means of knowledge. Which charity must be extended to others aswell as to these Fathers. Yet the same *Petavius* cannot endure *Camerarius*, for saying, that *Athanasius*, though a valiant Champion of the truth, did *sometime indulge his own desires, and mix some ill with sacred things:* But if he were not at all to be blamed, *Constantine* was much the more to be blamed for banishing him; And why should not his honour be of some regard? The truth is, the *Alexandrian* Bishops and People were long more violent and troublesome than others, as not only *Socrates*, but many other Historians note: And as it was noted with dishonour in *Theophilus* and *Cyril*, and *Dioscorus*, &c. so it can hardly be believed by them that read the History throughout, that *Alexander* and *Athanasius* wanted not something of the humble patience, meekness, and healing tenderness and skill that their Case required: For who is perfect? And how apt are great Bishops to be too violent against Dissenters, instead of healing them with Love and clear convincing Evidence?

§. 5. Happy had it been if Prudence had silenced this Heresie betimes, for never any one did so great mischief to the Church. The badness of it, was the honour of the *Nicene* Council that suppressed it, as far as in them lay. But alas, the Remedy seemed quickly conquered by the Disease: As *Constantine* had work enough to keep Peace among the Bishops in the Council, by his presence and reproofs; so when the *Arians* profess'd repentance, his peaceableness caused him too far to indulge them; by which some of them got such interest in his Court, as proved the following Calamity of the Church. And it is the sadder to think on, that the two great Emperours, *Constantius* and *Valens*, that were deceived by them, and drawn into violent Persecution, are noted to be otherwise none of the worst men. *Epiphanius* saith, p. 737. *Accessit & Imperatorum favor cujus initium à* Constantio *Imperatore profectum est: Qui cùm cæteris in rebus perhumanus ac bonus esset,——& alioquin pius ac multis probitatis ornamentis præditus, hac unâ re aberravit, quod non impressa à parente fidei vestigia secutus est: Quod ipsum tamen*

men non illius culpâ factum, sed nonnullorum fraude, qui in die Judicii rationem reddituri sunt; qui specie & nomine tenus Episcopi, sinceram Dei fidem labefacta-runt.———*Et beati* Constantii *in errorem ab illis inducti, qui rectæ fidei regulam ignoravit, eidemque ignoranti ad illorum se utpote sacerdotum Authoritatem accommodavit, quod ipsum error illorum, ac ea itas, depravataque fides & ex diaboli profect aconsilio, lateret. Accessit & alia causa quæ huic serpenti officinæ plurimum adjecit virium,* Eusebius *scilicet, qui callide se insinuans,* Valentis *aures pii ac religiosi Imperatoris, ac Divini numinis amantissimi, corrupit. Qui quod ab illo baptismo sit initiatus, ea causa fuit cur hæc factio stabilis ac firma consisteret.* If *Epiphanius* say true, we see what men these Persecuting Emperours were.

§. 6. As to the other part of the Councils work, the fixing of *Easter*-day, had not the Bishops been sinfully fierce about it, against each other, it had never been taken for a Heresie to mistake the time, nor had it been a work so necessary and great to determine it: seeing as *Socrates, Sozomen*, &c. tell us, many Churches differed in this, and matters as great as this, without condemning or separating from each other: And the *Asians* erred by the Motive of Tradition, and *Irenæus* had long before censured the *Roman* Bishop for his violence in condemning them. And many good Christians even after the Councils determination, durst not forsake their old Tradition, nor obey them: Among whom, how long our *Britains* and the *Scots* stood out, *Beda* telleth us. And though the *Audians*, that also disobeyed, were called Hereticks, I would all Adversaries to Hereticks were no worse men.

§. 7. And because these *Audians* rose about that time, I think it worth the labour to add the sum of their History out of *Epiphanius*, that the World may better perceive what spirit the Hereticating Prelates were then of, and how some called Hereticks were made such, or defamed as such, and who they were that did divide the Churches and break their peace.

"*Epiph. l. 3. Tom. 1. p.* 811. *Of the Schism of the* Audians, which is the 50*th*
" or 70*th* Heresie: The *Audians* live in Monasteries, in Solitudes, &c. *Au-*
" *dius* their Founder arose in *Mesopotamia*, famous for his integrity of life,
" and ardent zeal of Divine Faith. Who oft seeing things ill carried in
" the Churches, feared not to their faces to reprove and admonish the Bishops
" and Priests, and say, These things should not be so done: You should
" not thus Administer: As a Lover of Truth, he used to do such things as
" these, which are familiar with men of exquisite honesty, who through
" their excellent study of Godliness, use this great liberty of Speech: There-
" fore when he saw things ill carried in the Churches, he sometimes spake
" his thoughts, and could not forbear blaming them. As if he saw any of
" the Clergy over covetous of Money, be it Bishop or Priest, he would re-
" prehend them: or if any abounded in luxury and pleasures; or if they
" corrupted any part of the Doctrine or Discipline of the Church, he
" would not bear with them, but blame them. Which was troublesome to
" men

"men of a diffolute life: And therefore he underwent the greateſt con-
"tumelies, being exagitated by the hatred and malicious words of them all.
"But he being thus tolled about, and beaten and reproached, did bear it
"all with an equal mind; and thus long continued in the Communion of
"the Church; Till ſome that were more vehemently offended with him for
"theſe Cauſes, caſt him out: But yet he patiently bore all this, but being
"more earneſtly intent for the promoting of the Truth, he ſtill ſtudied not
"to be drawn away from the Conjunction and Society of the Catholick
"Church. But when he and his friends were ſtill beaten, and ſuffered un-
"worthy uſage, groaning under theſe evils, he took Counſel of the vio-
"lence of theſe calamities and contumelies: And ſo he ſeparated himſelf
"from the Church, and many falling away with him, a new Divorce was
"hereby made. For he did not in any thing depart from the *right faith*,
"but he with his partakers held in all things ſincere Religion. Though in
"one ſmall matter they are too ſtiff. About the Father, Son, and Holy
"Ghoſt they judg excellently, and as the Catholick Church, and ſwerve not
"a jot: and the reſt of the order of their Lives is truly moſt excellent
"and admirable; ſo that not only He himſelf, but even the Biſhops, Prieſts,
"and all the reſt of them, live by the labour of their hands.

Indeed they had a conceit that the Body did partake of the Image of God, and they thought that to pleaſe *Conſtantine*, the *Nicene* Council had altered the Cuſtom and Tradition of the Church about *Eaſter*: But theſe were not the cauſes of their departure from the Church, but the *violence of diſſolute Biſhops*, that caſt them out, as being impatient of their ſtrictneſs and oppoſition to their ſin.

§. 8. About *Eaſter*, ſaith *Epiphanius*, p. 821. *Neque cruditis ignotum eſt, quàm ſæpe diverſis temporibus de illius feſti celebritate varii Eccleſiaſticæ diſciplinæ tumultus ac contentiones obortæ ſint: præſertim* Polycarpi *ac* Victoris *ætate, cùm Orientales ab Occidentalibus divulſi, pacificas à ſe invicem literas nullas acciperent. Quod idem & aliis temporibus accidit: velut* Alexandri *Epiſcopi* Alexandrini *&* Creſcentii; *quemadmodum contra ſe mutuò ſcripſerint & acerrimè pugnaverint. Quæ animorum opinionumque diſtractio, ex quo ſemel poſt Epiſcopos illos qui ex circumciſione ac Judæorum ſecta ad Chriſtum ſe converterant, agitari cœpit, ad noſtra uſque tempora eodem eſt tenore perducta.* By which we ſee, 1. With what caution Tradition muſt be truſted: 2. How early Biſhops began to divide the Church about things indifferent.

§. 9. That men that all, in the main, fear God, ſhould thus contend, abuſe, and perſecute one another, is ſad, and hath even been a hardening of Infidels: But, alas, the remnant of corruption in the beſt will ſomewhat corrupt their converſations. It is a ſad note of *Epiphanius, ib.* p. 816. ["I
"have known ſome of the Confeſſours, who delivered up Body and Soul
"for their Lord, and perſevering in confeſſion and chaſtity, obtained great
"eſt ſincerity of faith, and excelled in piety, humanity, and Religion, and
"were continual in faſtings, and in a word, did flouriſh in all honeſty and
"virtue: yet the ſame men were blemiſhed with ſome vice; as either they
"were

"were prone to reproach men, or would swear by the name of God, or
"were over talkative, or prone to anger, or got gold and silver, or were
"defiled with some such filth, which yet detract nothing from the just
"measure of virtue."]

§. 10. But as God made a good use of the falling out of *Paul* and *Barnabas*, so he did of *Audius* his unhappy case. Being cast out of the Church, he took it to be his duty to Communicate with his own party, and a Bishop that suffered for the like, made him a Bishop, and the Bishops accused him to the Emperour, that he drew many people from the obedience of the Church, and hereupon the Emperour banished him into *Scythia*. Dwelling there, he went into the inner parts of *Gothia*, and there instructed many of the barbarous in the principles of Christianity, and gathered many Monasteries of them, who lived in great religious strictness, *p.* 827. But it is hard to stop short of extreams, when men are alienated by scandal and violence: They came to so great a dislike of the Bishops of the common Churches, that they would not pray with any man, how blameless soever, that did but hold Communion with the Church. *Uranius* a Bishop and some others joyning with them, made Bishops of the *Goths*. (Note out of *Epiphanius*, p. 827, 828. what Country was called *Gethia* in those times.)

§. 11. It is not to be past over that at the *Nicene* Council, the first speaker, and one of the chief against the *Arians*, was *Eustathius* Bishop of *Antioch*. And when *Eusebius Nicomed.* was made Bishop of *Constantinople*, he pretended a desire to see *Jerusalem*, and passing through *Antioch* secretly hired a Whore to swear, that *Eustathius* was the Father of her child: and getting some Bishops of his Faction together, they judged *Eustathius* to be deposed, as an Adulterer; and got the Emperour to consent and banish him: And after, the Woman in misery, confessed all, and said, that it was one *Eustathius* a Smith, that was the father of her child.

§. 12. In *Pisanus*'s *Concil. Nic. Bin.* p. 332. this *Eustathius* is made the first Disputer against a Philosopher: And whereas the great cause of the *Arians* Errour was, that they could not conceive how the Son could be of *one substance* with the Father, without a *partition* of that substance, *Eustathius* tells the Philosopher that took their part and urged, *Faciamus hominem ad Imaginem*, &c. that *The Image of God is simple, and without all composition, being of the nature of fire*: but he meaneth sure but *analogically*:

§. 13. In the same *Pisanus, lib.* 3. p. 345. *Bin.* the description of the *Church* is, *There is one Church in Heaven and Earth*; in this the Holy Ghost resteth; *But Heresies that are without it*—are of Satan.— Therefore the Pope was not then taken for the Head of the *Catholick Church*; For he pretendeth not to be the Head of them that are in *Heaven*. See what the *Catholick Church* then was!

☞ §. 14. Note that, 1. the Council of *Nice* nameth none Patriarchs. 2. They nullifie the Ordination of scandalous and uncapable men. Can. 9. and 10. Which will justifie Pope *Nicholas* forbidding any to take the Mass of a Fornicating Priest. 3. That Rural Bishops were then in use, and

and allowed by the Council, *Can.* 8. 4. That no Bishop was to remove from one Church to another, *Can.* 15. (which *Euseb. Nicom.* soon broke.) 5. Even in the *Arabick* Canons the 4th. *si populo placebit*, is a Condition of every Bishops Election. 6. The 5th *Arab.* Canon, in case of discord among the people, who shall be their Bishop or Priest, it is referred to the people to consider which is most blameless: And no Bishop or Priest must be taken into anothers place, if the former was blameless. (So that if Pastors be wrongfully cast out, the people must not forsake them, nor receive the obtruded.) 7. Those Ordained by *Meletius* were to be received into the Ministry where others dyed, *If by the suffrage of the people they were judged fit, and the Bishop of* Alex. *designed them.* Sozom. l. 1. c. 23.

§. 15. XXXI. The next Council in *Binnius* (and in *Crabs* Order) is said to be at *Rome* under *Sylvester*, with 275. Bishops: But this is confessed to be partly false, if not all: And is the same that is before mentioned; which ordered that no Bishop should ordain any Clerk *nisi cum omni adunatâ Ecclesiâ, But with all the Church united*, or gathered into one: (Which Canon seemeth made when a Church was no more than could meet together, and when the People had a Negative Voice.)

But the *Concil. Gangrense* is *Binnius's* next (though *Crab* put afterward some of the forementioned also) said to be in *Sylvesters* days; (and yet *Sozomen* and some others, say that the Council of *Nice* was in *Julius* days, though most say otherwise.) Here were sixteen Bishops, who condemned some Errours of *Eustathius* of *Armenia*, or rather one *Eustaãus*, as *Bin.* thinks, who was too severe against Marriage, as if it were sinful, and against eating Flesh, and against receiving the Sacrament at the Hands of a married Priest; he made Servants equal with their Masters, he set light by Church-Assemblies, he drew Wives to leave their Husbands for Continency, and on pretence of Virginity despised married Persons; These superstitions they here condemned.

§. 16. XXXII. *An.* 335. The Council at *Tyre* was held for the Tryal of *Athanasius*, where he was unjustly condemned, and thereupon by *Constantine* banished, though his innocency was after cleared: Had not his severity against the *Meletians* driven them to joyn with the *Arians* against him, *Epiphanius* saith, they had not been able to make head thus against him.

Constantines Epistle to the *Alexandrians*, lamenting and chiding them for their Discords, is well worth the translating, but that I must not be so tedious: See it *Bin.* p. 391.

§. 17. XXXIII. The next is a Council at *Jerusalem, An.* 335. where *Arius* Faith was tryed, approved, and he restored to *Alexandria* and the favour of *Constantine.* The Creed which he gave in, was this.

We believe in one God the Father Almighty, and in the Lord Jesus Christ his Son, begotten of him before all Ages, God, the Word, by whom all things were made which are in Heaven and in Earth: Who came down, and was Incarnate,

and

and Suffered, *and* Rose again, *and* Ascended to the Heavens, *and shall come a-gain to* Judge *the Living and the Dead :* And in the Holy Ghost *:* The Resurrection of the Flesh *:* The Life of the World to come, *and the* Kingdom of Heaven *:* In one Catholick Church of God, extending it self from one end of the Earth unto the other.

Arius with this, protesting against vain Subtilties and Controversies, desireth the Emperour to accept of this as the Evangelical Faith; and the Council and the Emperour receive him, as for the joyful restoration of Unity and Peace, and so would undo what was done at *Nice.* The Emperour was so greatly troubled at the continued divisions of the Bishops, that he was glad of any hope of Unity and Peace: But this proved not the way.

§. 18. XXXIV. *An.* 336. A Council was called at *Constantinople*; in which they accused, condemned, and banished *Marcellus Ancyranus*, an Adversary to the *Arians*, as if he had denyed the Godhead of Christ, (upon some wrested word) though it was their denying it that offended him : Here also *Arius* was justified and *Athanasius* condemned: But *Arius* dyed shortly after.

§. 19. XXXV. The next is a Council of 116 Bishops at *Rome*, in or about *An.* 337. under *Julius*; in which the *Nicene* Creed was owned, and the *Arians* condemned, and nothing else done that is recorded.

§. 20. XXXVI. The next was a Council at *Alexandria* which vindicated *Athanasius* from his Accusations, when *Constantinus* junior sent him home from his Banishment.

§. 21. XXXVII. The next was a Council at *Antioch* of near 100 Bishops (of which 36 were *Arians*) the most Orthodox (and the holy *James* of *Nisibis* one :) yet they deposed *Athanasius*, and the *Arians* (it's like by the Emperours favour) carryed it ; In his place they put *George* a *Cappadocian* suspected to be an *Arian*, whom, (as I said before) the People murdered, burnt, and scattered his Ashes in the Wind, and he was one of the *Arians* Martyrs. (Unless *England* had ever been *Arian*, I cannot believe them that say that this is the St. *George*, that the *English* have so much honoured.)

§. 23. This *Arian* Council finding that the Emperours favour gave them the Power, made many Canons against *Non-Conformists.* The first *Can.* is against them that keep not *Easter* at the due time. The second against them that come to the hearing of the Word, but communicate not publickly in the Lords Supper and Prayers, and against them that keep private Meetings, and that communicate with them. *Can.* 4. Was to make their Case hopeless that exercise the Ministry after they are Silenced, or Deposed, be they Bishops, Priests, or Deacons. *Can.* 5. Was that if any Priest or Deacon gathered Churches or Assemblies against the Bishops Will, and took not warning, he was to be Deposed : And if he go on, to be oppressed by the exteriour Power as Seditious. (There is their Strength.)

Can.

Can. 6, and 7. None suspended by his own Bishop was to be received by another, nor any Stranger without Certificates. *Can.* 8. Country-Priests may not write Canonical Epistles, but Rural Bishops may. *Can.* 9. No Bishop must do any thing without the Metropolitane, save what belongeth (by Ordination and Guidance) to his own Church. *Can.* 10. Though the rural Bishops are consecrated as true Bishops, yet they shall only govern their own Churches, and Ordain such lower Orders as they need, but not Ordain Presbyters or Deacons without the City-Bishops, to whom they are subject. *Can.* 11. Casteth out all Bishops or other Clergy-men, that go to the Prince without the Metropolitane's Counsel or Letters. *Can.* 12. Deposed or silenced Ministers must not go to Princes for relief, but appeal to a Synod. *Can.* 13. Bishops must not go or ordain in other Diocess, unless sent for by the Metropolitane; else their Ordinations there to be null. *Can.* 15. A Bishop condemned of all may not appeal. *Can.* 16. A vacant Bishop leaping into a vacant Bishoprick without a Council (the Metropolitane present) is to be ejected, though all the people chuse him. *Can.* 17. If any Bishop be ordained to a Church, and refuse or neglect the Office, let him be excommunicate till he receive it. *Can.* 18. If any Bishop ordained to a Parish neglect it, because the people will not receive him, let him enjoy the honour, and be heard in a full Synod. *Can.* 19. The Ordination of a Bishop is null, which is done without a Synod, and the Metropolitane. *&c.*

§. 24. XXXVIII. Another Council at *Rome* under *Julius* undid what this former did, and acquitted *Athanasius, Marcellus*, and other injured Bishops: (perhaps *Eustathius*, saith *Bin.*)

§. 25. XXXIX. *Athanasius* being sent back when *Gregory* was put in his place, the City being ready to be in an uproar, *Athanasius* retired to *Rome* (or hid himself) foreseeing it; till fire and blood had proclaimed the Calamity of this Episcopal strife. And Pope *Julius* called another Council at *Rome*, to answer the Letters of the Oriental Synod, which charged him with usurpation and despised him.

§. 26. XL. *Anno* 344. Another Council was held at *Antioch*, by those called *Arians* by some, Reconcilers by others, and Orthodox and Catholicks by themselves; in which they renounce *Arius* and his sayings, but yet leave out the word ὁμοούσιος [of one substance.] This they did in a new-made Creed; fitted purposely, as they said, to reconcile; as others, to deceive: To which end four had been made before, and not availed.

§. 27. XLI. A Council at *Milan* examined this Creed, and rejected it, for leaving out [*of the same substance*] and because the *Nicene* Creed was sufficient.

§. 28. XLII. The next is called an Universal Council, of 376 Bishops at *Sardica*, which cleared *Athanasius, Marcellus*, and others. And yet *Augustine*, and many others, reject this Council. It hath divers good Canons, but one among them for Appeals to *Rome*; which three Popes
urged

urged to *Aurelius, Augustine* and the other *Africans*, as a Canon of the Council of *Nice:* And whenas neither any of these Popes, nor the *African* Bishops once took notice that those words were in the Council of *Sardica*; the Papists answer, 1. That the *Africans* knew not of this Councils Canons, but had lost them, (though *Gratus* Bishop of *Carthage* was one.) 2. And that the Popes took the Canons of *Sardica* to be but Explications of the *Nicene*, and so they were but as one. (But why did they give no such answer?)

Bishops are here condemned that remove to any other Church; and they that are above three days non-resident; and especially they that go *ad Comitatum*, to the Palaces of Princes or great Prelates; but if they have just business they are ordered to send it by a Deacon.

§. 29. XLIII. The Oriental Bishops departing from *Sardica* came to *Philippopolis*, and gathered a Council by themselves, and condemned those whom the other had absolved, and others for Communicating with them. Yet they renounced *Arius*, but also cast out the word [ὁμοούσιος, *of the same substance*] as not Scriptural; and are called *Semi-Arians*.

The Persons excommunicated by them were *Athanasius, Osius, Marcellus, Protogenes, Asclepas, Gaudentius, Maximinus, Paulus Const.* and Pope *Julius*. They write a circular Epistle, specially sent to *Donatus Carthag.* in which they so vehemently speak for peace and piety, and lay such Crimes to the charge of *Athanasius, Paulus*, and *Marcellus*, as would astonish the Reader, and confound his judgment, whom to believe. Cruel Persecution, bloudy Murders, Profaneness, burning a Church, and such like they charge on *Athanasius*; and say that they offered the Western Bishops of *Sardica* to send five of their Bishops with six of theirs to the place where these things were done, and if they prove not true they yield to be condemned. On *Marcellus* they charge written Heresie (which *Basil, Chrysostom*, and others believed.) On *Paulus Const.* they charge that he was guilty of flames and Wars, and that he caused Priests to be drag'd naked into the Market-place, with the Body of Christ tyed about their necks; and that before a concourse of people he caused the consecrated Virgins to be stript naked in the open Streets, unto horrid shame. And for such Reasons they require all good Christians to abhor their Communion. Thus the Reader is called to grief and shame to hear Bishops thus odiously reviling each other, and tempting Infidels to take them all for wicked and utterly unpeaceable men.

§. 30. XLIV. *An.* 348 or 349. was a Council at *Carthage* (called the first:) It was gathered against the *Donatists*, whose Bishops pretended to be the only Catholicks; and their Circumcellions being violent Reformers, taking from the rich that they thought had wronged any, and righting the injured, and unjustly doing justice; and resisting the Emperour *Constans* his Officers, so that they were fain by Souldiers to suppress them, and cast out *Donatus Carth.* and by gifts reconciled the people that followed them.

Many

Many good Canons for Church Order were made by this and most of the *African* Councils, no Bishops being faithfuller than they. Several passages in their Canons shew that their numerous Bishops had Churches of no more people than our larger Parishes. And Can. 12. of this Council ordereth that where the Bishops by Contract divide their several People, one take not from the other.

§. 31. XLV. *Anno* 350. A Council at *Milan* received the repentance of *Ursatius* and *Valens* that had accused *Athanasius*, and gave them Letters of reconciliation.

§. 32. XLVI. *Constans* constrained *Constantius* to recall *Athanasius*, but was himself murdered by *Magnentius* before he came thither: But at *Jerusalem* a Council was held in the way, which judged his reception, and wrote to *Alexandria* to that end.

§. 33. XLVII. Among the friends of *Athanasius*, *Euphratas* Bishop of *Collen* was one, that was sent on a Message into the *East*; where *Stephen* an *Arian* Bishop of *Ant.* got a Whore to go in to him: When she saw an old man, instead of a young one, which she expected, she immediately confessed all, and Bishop *Stephen* was cast out for it. But *Euphratas* after all, turned *Photinian* and denyed Christ to be God, and a Council at *Colen* deposed him.

§. 34. XLVIII. They talk of 3 *Concilia Vasensia*, or *Vasatensia*, and that they ordered [*As it was in the beginning*] to be added to the *doxologie*: But there is nothing of moment certain of them.

§. 35. XLIX. *Anno* 352. *Liberius* had a Council at *Rome* about *Athanasius*, and sending a Message to *Constantius*.

§. 36. L. *Anno* 353. At a Council at *Arles*, *Athanasius* is condemned, and the Popes Legate forced to subscribe it, with other Bishops, and some banished that refused it.

§. 37. LI. Pope *Liberius* desired a *General Council*, which the Emperour granteth, and it's held at *Milan*. Above 300 *Western* Bishops were there, most of the *East* (where the *Arians* reigned) could not come (*an.* 355.) *Athanasius* his Condemnation (*Ursatius* and *Valens* revolting, and again accusing him) and Communion with the *Arians*, were the things there urged by the Emperour: *Lucifer Calaritanus* (after called a Heretick) and *Eusebius Vercellensis*, and a few more, refused to subscribe, and were banished; as *Liberius* after was; and *Fœlix* made Pope: But most of the Bishops for fear, and desire of peace, subscribed. The Emperour himself wrote to *Euseb. Vercel.* to be there (who had refused) with great profession of zealous piety, and desire of the Churches peace. But this scandal and miscarriage of the Bishops, and success of the *Arians*, was the effect of this General Council.

§. 38. LII. The *Semi-Arians* pretending to Universal Concord, thus prevailing by the Emperour and a General Council, *Hilary Pictav.* (a Marryed Citizen made Bishop) drew some Orthodox Bishops of *France* to separate from the *Arian* Bishops, and renounce their Communion; The *Arians* (or *Semi-Arians*) taking these for separatists, and injurious to them, (especially *Saturninus*) procured a Council at *Byterris*, to condemn them as Schismaticks; where *Hilary* was condemned and banished, *an.* 356.

§. 39. LIII. The General Council at *Sirmium* I out of order began with. *Anno* 357. *Constantius* resolving by all means to bring all the Bishops to one Communion, was present himself; There were above 300 Bishops out of the *West*, besides all the *Eastern* Bishops: The confusion was so great, that men knew not who were or were not Hereticks. *Photinus* denying the Godhead of Christ, the Bishops called *Arian*, desired this Council to accuse and condemn him, as they did: They drew up two or three Confessions themselves: The first was not Heretical directly, save by the Omission of the [ὁμοούσιον:] which some perswaded the Emperour, being new and no ancient Scriptural or Symbolical word, was the Cause of all the divisions of the Bishops, and were that left out, all would be healed. This Council called *Arian*, passed 27 Anathema's against the *Arians* and *Photinians*: Pope *Liberius* subscribed to it and approved it, as the forcited words of his Epistle in *Hilary* shew. (And yet many Papists call it a Reprobate Council.) Old *Osius*, that presided at *Nice*, was forced by stripes, to subscribe to it, and to the condemnation of *Athanasius*.[*That the Son was in all things like the Father*,] was the substitute Form here used. In their second Form they say, that [*Quia multos commover vox, substantia, velusia, hoc est, ut diligentius cognoscatur illud quod ὁμοούσιον dicitur, ant ὁμοιούσιον, nullam earum vocum mentionem debere fieri neque de iis sermocinandum in Ecclesia censemus, quod de iis nihil scriptum sit in sacris literis, & quod illa hominum intellectum & mentem transcendant, & quod nemo posset generationem filii enarrare, ut scriptum, Generationem ejus quis enarrabit? solum enim Patrem, scire quomodo filium suum genuerit, certum est —— & nemo ignorat duas esse personas Patris & Filii, ac proinde Patrem majorem, Filium ex Patre genitum, Deum ex Deo, Lumen de Lumine* ———] Many thought this a necessary reconciling way: The words [*Person*] and [*Substance*] stumbled the *Arians*: For they knew not how to conceive of *three persons* that were not *three substances*; nor how the Son could be of the *same substance* with the Father, unless that *substance* were divided: And at last wearied with contending, they thought thus to end all, by leaving out the name [*substance*,] and professing the Generation of the Son *unsearchable*.

The third *Sirmian* Creed had, [*in unigenitum filium Dei, ante omnia secula & initia & ante omne tempus quod in intellectum cadere potest existemem; & ante omnem comprehensibilem substantiam, natum impassibiliter ex Deo, solum ex solo Patre, Deum de Deo, similem Patri suo qui ipsum genuit, cujus generationem nemo novit nisi solus qui eum genuit, Pater. Vocabulum vero substantiae quia simplicius à Patribus positum est, & à populis ignoratur, & scandalum affert, eo quod in scripturis non continetur, placuit ut de medio tolleretur, & nullum posthac de Dei substantiae mentionem esse faciendam.*

§. 40.

§. 40. LIII. The Oriental Bishops offended at the second Confession at *Sirmium*, for leaving out the word *substance*, gathered in Council at *Ancyra*, *an*. 358. and rejecting the *Arians*, were called *Semi-Arians*, because yet they were not for [ὁμοούσιον] but the [ὁμοιούσιον;] Not [*the same substance*,] but [*Like substance*.] These after turning *Macedonians* (for *Macedonius* was one of them) deny the *Holy Ghost to be God*.

§. 41. LIV. *Constantius* finding that all his endeavours missed their end, and that instead of bringing all the Bishops to Concord and one Communion, the very *Arians*, and the *Semi-Arians*, divided and subdivided among themselves, did summon another General Council at *Nicomedia*: But the City suddenly perishing, he called the *Western* part to *Ariminum*, and the *Eastern* to *Seleucia*, taking them yet but as one Council. Above 400 Bishops met at *Ariminum*, who were to determine first Doctrinal and then Personal Controversies, and then send ten Legates of each part to the Emperor, with the results: The most were Orthodox, but the *Arian* Legates were better speakers, and prevailed; so that the Emperour delayed them because of an Expedition that he had in hand against the Barbarians; In the mean time some Assembled at *Nice*, and drew up Another Confession: And when the Legates returned to *Ariminum*, the *Arian* Party of Bishops, by the Emperours countenance, so far prevailed, as that almost all the Orthodox subscribed to them. *(Gaudentius* Bishop of *Ariminum* was murdered by the Souldiers.) *Binnius* and some others, would have this Council at *Ariminum* to be two; the first Orthodox, the second *Arian*: *Bellarmine* and others called it but one: which was Orthodox in the beginning, but for fear and complyance fell off at the last.

§. 42. LV. Whether the Council at *Seleucia* shall be taken for one of it self, or but for part of that at *Ariminum*, though far distant, I leave to the Reader. But here the Heterodox Bishops carried all, but so as to divide among themselves; One party called *Acacians* were for forbearing the word [*substance*.] The *Semiarians* condemned both them and the *Arians*, and were for [*Like substances*.] They excommunicated and deposed many *Arians*, who appealed to the Emperour, and craved yet another Synod. So that the further he went for concord, the further he was from it, the Bishops dividing and subdividing more and more; and the Emperours and Bishops, by diversity of Judgment, and by Heresie, became now to the Church what Heathen Persecutors had been heretofore.

Sulpitius Severus tells us, that one thing that drew many to subscribe to the *Arian* and *Semiarian* Creeds, was a certain liberty of their own Additions or Interpretations, which was granted the Orthodox to draw them in. [Subscribe in your own sence. *q. d.*] And so conditional subscriptions quieted their Consciences, and when the *Arians* thought they had the Victory, and had made the rest *Conformists*, it proved otherwise, for they did not in sence and with approbation subscribe.

But though the Filth of the *Arian* Heresie justifie all just care and endeavours to keep it out, the multitudes of new Creeds, then made by one and the other Party became such a snare and shame to the Church, that *Hilary*, among others, greatly lamented it, even in these sad expressions.

Post Nicenam *Synodum nihil aliud quàm Fidem scribimus ; dum in Verbis pugna est ; dum de novitatibus quæstio est ; dum de ambiguis, dum de authoribus querela est ; dum de studiis certamen est ; dum in consensu difficultas est ; dumq; alter alteri Anathema esse cœpit, propè jam* Nemo est Christi. *Proximi anni fides quid immutationis habet? Primum decretum Homousion decernit taceri : sequens rursus Homousion decernit & prædicit :* Tertium usiam simpliciter à Patribus præsumptam per indulgentiam excusat ; *Postremum quartumque non excusat sed condemnat : Tandem eò processum est ut neq; penes vos, neq; penes quenquam ante nos sanctum exinde aliquid atq; inviolabile perseveret. Annuas atq; Menstruas de Deo Fides decernimus : decretis pœnitemus ; pœnitentes defendimus : defensos Anathematizamus ; aut in nostris aliena, aut in alienis nostra damnamus, & mordentes invicem jam absumpti sumus ab invicem.*

Is not this a doleful description of the Bishops so soon after their wonderful deliverance and exaltation?

The cause of all he tells us was partly forsaking the simple Form of Baptismal Faith as not sufficient, and partly following Votes and worldly Powers. *Dum à quibus ea requiritur sua scribunt & non quæ Dei sunt prædicant, orbem æternum erroris & redeuntis in se semper certaminis circumtulerunt. Oportuerat humanæ infirmitatis modestia omne cogitationis divina sacramentum illis tantum conscientia suæ finibus contineri quibus credidit : Neque post confessam & juratam in baptismo fidem in nomine Patris, Filii & Sp. sancti, quicquam aliud vel ambigere vel innovare.* And speaking of mens perverting the sence, he addeth. *Scribendæ & innovandæ fidei exinde usus inolevit : Qui postquam nova potius cœpit condere, quam accepta retinere, nec vetera defendit, nec innovata firmavit, & facta est Fides temporum potius quam Evangeliorum : dum & secundum annos scribitur, & secundum confessionem baptismi non tenetur. Periculosum admodum nobis & miserabile est tot nunc Fides existere, quot voluntates : & tot nobis doctrinas esse quot mores, & tot causas blasphemiarum pullulare, quot vitia sunt ; dum aut ita fides scribuntur, ut volumus, aut ita ut volumus intelliguntur. Et cum secundùm unum Deum, & unum Dominum & unum baptisma fides una sit, excidimus ab ea fide quæ sola est ; & dum plures fiunt, ad id cœperunt esse ne ulla sit.:* (referring to *Nice.*)

Fides enim quæritur quasi fides nulla sit : Fides scribenda est quasi in corde non sit : Regenerati per fidem nunc ad fidem docemur ; quasi regeneratio illa sine fide sit : Christum post baptisma discimus, quasi baptisma aliquid esse possit sine Christi fide : Emendamus ; quasi in spiritum sanctum peccasse sit venia. Sed impietatis ipsius his vel præcipue causa perpetua est, quod fidem Apostolicam septuplo preferentes, ipsi tamen fidem Evangelicam volumus confiteri ; dum impietates nostras nobis in populis multiloquiis defendimus magniloquentiæ vanitate aures simplicium verbis fallentibus illudimus, dum evitamus de Domino Christo ea credere, quæ de se

their Councils abridged. 61

se docuit credenda ; & per speciosum pacis nomen in unitatem perfidiæ subrepimus, & sub rejiciendis novitatibus rursum ipsi novis ad Deum vocibus rebellamus & sub scripturarum vocabulo non scripta mentimur. Tutissimum nobis est primam & solam Evangelicam fidem confessam in baptismate, intellectamq; retinere nec demutare quod solum acceptum atq; auditum habeo bene credere : Non ut ea quæ synodo Patrum nostrorum (the *Nicene*) *continentur, tanquam irreligiosè & impiè scripta damnanda sint ; sed quia per temeritatem humanam usurpantur ad contradictionem; quod ob hoc sub nomine novitatis, Evangelium negaretur impericulosè, tanquam sub emendatione innovetur. Quod emendatum est, semper proficit ; & dum omnis emendatio displicet, emendationem omnem emendatio consequuta condemnet, ac si jam, quicquid illud est, non emendatio aliqua sit emendationis, sed cœperit esse condemnatio.*

And as to the second Cause, he saith, *Ac primum misereri licet nostræ ætatis laborem & præsentium temporum stultas opiniones congemiscere ; quibus patrocinari Deo humana creduntur, & ad tuendam Christi Ecclesiam ambitione sæculari laboratur. Oro vos, Episcopi, qui hoc vos esse creditis : quibusnam suffragiis ad prædicandum Evangelium Apostoli usi sunt? Quibus adjuti potestatibus Christum prædicaverunt, gentesq; ferè omnes ex idolis ad Deum transtulerunt? Anne aliquam sibi assumebant è palatio dignitatem, hymnum Deo in carcere inter catenas & post flagella cantantes?* —— *At nunc proh dolor! divinam fidem suffragia terrena commendant ; inopsq; virtutis suæ Christus, dum ambitio nemini suo conciliatur, arguitur.*

Add what he saith of the Causes of Errour, *Lib. 10. de Trin. initio. Non est ambiguum omnem humani eloquii sermonem contradictioni obnoxium semper fuisse, quia dissentientium voluntatum motibus, dissentiones quoq; sit sensus animorum : Cum adversantium judiciorum affectione compugnans, assertionibus his quibus offenditur, contradicit. Quamvis enim enunc dictum veri ratione perfectum sit, tamen dum aliud aliis aut videtur aut complacet, patet veritatis sermo adversantium responsioni : quia contra veritatem aut non intellectam aut offendentem vel stultæ vel vitiosæ voluntatis error obnititur. Immoderata enim est omnis susceptarum voluntatum pertinacia, & indeflexo non adversandi studium persistit, ubi non rationi voluntas subjicitur, nec studium doctrinæ impenditur, sed his quæ volumus rationem conquirimus, & his quæ studemus doctrinam coaptamus. Jamq; nominis potius quam naturæ erit doctrina quæ fingitur, & jam non veri manebit ratio, sed placiti. Cætera ibi videat Lector.*

But having been long in this Citation of *Hilary*, I return to the History, of what followed these Councils and Creeds aforesaid.

§. 43. LVI. In the mean time *Constantius* calleth a Council of 50 Bishops to *Constantinople*, where *Ætius* was condemned, and a ninth Creed since the *Nicene* formed, which excluded both the word *substance* and *hypostasis* or *subsistence*. The *Semi-Arians* detesting this, condemned and banished the Authors. But another Form sent from *Ariminum* was preferred, and imposed to be subscribed on all the Bishops of East and West.

§. 44. LVII. *An.* 360. *Meletius* Bishop of *Antioch* being put in by the *Acacians* proved Orthodox contrary to their expectation : And being
preach-

preaching for the Trinity his Archdeacon stopt his Mouth, and he preached by his Fingers, holding forth *One* and *Three* : And for this was ejected, contrary to some former Covenants. Wherefore they were fain to call a Council at *Antioch* to justifie his ejection. Here they made yet another Creed, the worst of all before it.

§. 45. LVIII. *Constantius* being dead, *Julian* the Apostate is made Emperour (would not this end the Quarrel of Christian Bishops?) *Athanasius* returneth to *Alexandria* after the third banishment, and five years hiding, *an.* 362. *Gregory* the Bishop being as is aforesaid murthered by the Heathen, and burnt to Ashes. He calls a Council at *Alexandria*: Here besides the receiving of those that unwillingly subscribed to the *Arians*, divers new Controversies are judged. 1. *Eunomius, Macedonius*, and the *Semiarians* denyed the Godhead of the Holy Ghost, which was here asserted. 2. *Apollinaris* thought that Christ took but a Body at his Incarnation, his Divine Nature being instead of a Soul, which was here condemned. 3. The Orthodox *Greeks* and *Latines* could not agree by what name to distinguish the Trinity: The *Greeks* said there were *three hypostases*, which the *Latines* rejected, as signifying three *substances*: *Hierome* himself could not away with the word *Hypostasis*. The *Latines* used the word [*Person*.] The *Greeks* rejected that as signifying no *real distinction*, (and are the Schoolmen for a real distinction yet?) For they thought *Persona* signified but the *relation* of one in Authority or Office. And thus while as *Jerome* said, *Tota Græcorum prophanorum Schola discrimen inter hypostasin & usiam ignorabat* (*Ep.* 57.) and the sense of the word [*Person*] was not well determined, the danger was so great of further dissention among the Orthodox Bishops themselves, that as *Greg. Naz.* saith (*de laud. Athanas.*) *The matter came to that pass, that there was present danger, that together with these syllables the ends of the World* (East and West) *should have been torn from each other, and broken into parts.* But the Synod agreed that the Greek *hypostasis* and the Latine *Persona* should henceforth be taken as of the same signification. (But what that signification is, it was not so easie to tell.) Yet (saith *Binnius*) *Augustine de Trinit. l.* 5. *c.* 8, 9. and the *Latines* afterwards, were displeased with this reconciliation, and *Hierome* himself, who yet obtain'd of *Damasus, Ep.* 57. that the conciliation being but of a Controversie *de nomine*, might be admitted.

§. 46. LIX. *An.* 362. *Julian* reigning (several *French* Councils besides) one then at *Paris*, were employed in receiving the repentance of the Bishops that under *Constantius* had subscribed to the *Arians.*

§. 47. LX. At *Julians* death *Athanasius* calleth some Bishops to *Alexandria*, betimes to send to the Emperour *Jovianus* their Confession, to prevent the *Arians*, and other Hereticks.

§ 48. LXI. A Council also was called at *Antioch* on this occasion. The *Semiarians* petitioned *Jovianus* that the *Acacians*, as Hereticks, might be put out, and they put in their places: The Emperour gave them no other Answer, but that *he hated contention, but would love and honour those that*

that were for concord: They feeling his pulse, got *Meletius* to call a Council at *Antioch*, where they seemed very found, and twenty seven *Arian* Bishops without any stop subscribed the *Nicene* Creed: So basely did these Bishops follow the stronger side; and, faith *Binnius, of so great consequence with Bishops is the Emperours mind.*

§. 49. LXII. *An.* 364. *Valentinian* being Emperour left the Bishops to meet when and where they would themselves. And a Council was held at *Lampsacus*, where the *Semiarians* condemned the *Arians.* And though some call it Orthodox (*Basil*, and some good men being there) *Binnius* faith, that the *Macedonians* here vented their denyal of the God-head of the Holy Ghost, and that the Hereticks pretending to own the *Nicene* Faith were recieved by *Liberius.*

§. 50. LXIII. A Council in *Sicily* owned the *Nicene* Creed.

§. 51. LXIV. Some Bishops at *Illyricum* restored the *Nicene* Creed, the Emperour being now for it. And *Valentinian* and *Valens* wrote to the *Asian* Bishops to charge them to cease Persecuting any of Chrifts labourers.

§. 52. LXV. *An.* 365. At a Synod in *Tyana Cappadoc.* *Eustathius Sebast.* by Pope *Liberius* Letters was restored to his Bishoprick; and after cursed the *Homoufion,* ('the *Nicene* Creed) and denyed the Godhead of the Holy Ghost: By their means *Basil* returned from his Wilderness to *Cæsarea*, whence he fled to avoid the enmity of *Eusebius* the Bishop; who received him upon his profesed resolution for Peace, which he would buy at any rates.

§. 53. LXVI. The Emperour *Valens* (unhappily taken in to *Valentinian*) after the conquest of *Procopius*, desired Baptisme, and having an *Arian* Wife, was baptized by *Eudoxius Constant.* an *Arian* Bishop; who engaged him to promote the *Arian* Cause; which he did with a blind religious zeal, persecuting not only the Orthodox and *Novatians*, but also the *Semiarians* and *Macedonians.* And a Council of Bishops in *Caria*, rejected [*Consubstantial,*] and restored the *Antiochian* and *Seleucian* Creed as the best.

§. 54. LXVII. *An.* 366. Some *Arian* Bishops at *Singedim* in *Mysia*, restored the *Ariminum* Creed [*of Like substance*] and solicited *Geminius* the *Semiarian* Bishop to consent, but prevailed not.

§. 55. LXVIII. Two Councils were held at *Rome* by *Damasus*; one to condemn *Valens* and *Ursatius*, old *Arian* Bishops: Another to condemn *Auxentius* Bishop of *Milan,* and *Sisinius* as a Schismatical Competitor with himself: For when *Damasus* was chosen, the people were divided, and *Damasus* his Party being the more valiant Warriors, they fought it out in the Church, and left one day an hundred thirty seven dead Bodies behind them, to shew that they had no Communion with them. And because *Sisinius* and his Party still kept Conventicles, he was banished, and many with him, and now again condemned.

§. 56.

§. 56. LXIX. Another Council at *Rome* he had to condemn *Vitalis* and the *Apollinarians* (that took Chrifts Godhead to be inſtead of a Soul to his Body) and the *Millenaries*.

§. 57. LXX. A Council was called at A*ntioch* to end a Schiſm, there being three Biſhops, two Orthodox, *Meletius* and *Paulinus*; and one *Arian*, *Euzoius*: They ended the Schiſm, by agreeing that *Meletius* and *Paulinus* ſhould both continue, till one dyed, and then the other alone ſhould ſucceed him; the Presbyters being ſworn not to accept it while one of them lived. But *Meletius* dying firſt, *Flavianus* a Presbyter was ſaid to break his Oath, and was choſen in his ſtead, while *Paulinus* (an excellent perſon) lived: And ſo the Schiſm was continued.

CHAP.

CHAP. IV.

The First General Council at Constantinople, *and some following.*

§. 1. THe reason why the *West* with *Rome* was freer from the *Arian* Heresie than the *East*, was not, as the Papists say, because Christ prayed for *Peter* that his Faith might not fail, but because the Emperours of the *West* were Orthodox, while those in the *East* were *Arians*: And the Bishops much followed the Emperours Will. That this last was the Cause, is notorious in the History: That Christs foresaid promise was not the Cause, is certain. Because whatever promise Christ maketh, he fulfilleth: But he hath not kept all the Bishops of *Rome* from failing in their Faith: Therefore he never promised so to do. The *minor* is certain by History: To pass by *Marcellinus* and *Liberius* and *Honorius* falls, (which were but like *Peters*) all those wicked men whom Councils deposed as Infidels, or Hereticks, Simoniacks, Murderers, Adulterers, one as a Devil Incarnate, and all those that *Baronius* and *Genebrard* stigmatize as Apostatical, and not Apostolical, (50 together) had not this promise fulfilled: Nor *Sixtus Quintus*, if *Bellarmine* judged truly, that he was damned: For it was not *a dead faith*, but a *saving faith*, which Christ promised *Peter* should not fail; such a faith as had the promise of life; *He that believeth and is baptized shall be saved: Whoever believeth in him shall not perish, but have everlasting life: a faith that worketh by love*: Else *Peter* might have been a wicked man, and damned, notwithstanding this Prayer of Christ, and Promise. If the faith of *Constantine senior & junior, Constans, Valentinian, Theodosius, Honorius, Gratian*, &c. had failed, the General Councils at *Milan*, and *Ariminum*, tell us, how failing the Bishops faith was like to be; when *Jerome* said, that the *whole world groaned to find it self turned Arian*.

§. 2. The blind zeal of *Valens* made him restless in Persecuting the Orthodox in the *East*: At *Antioch* he vexed those that would not Communicate with *Euzoius* the allowed *Arian* Bishop: At *Cyzicum Eunomius* was put in *Eleusius* place; but his followers built them a separate Church without the Walls. (*Socrat. lib.* 4. c. 6, 7.) He Persecuted the *Novatians*, and exiled *Agelius* their Bishop at *Const*. He banished *Eustathius Antioch*. and *Evagrius*, chosen by the Orthodox Bishop of *Const*. against *Demophilus* the *Arian*. Fourscore Bishops sent to crave Justice of him, were put to Sea in a Ship there set on fire, and were both burnt and drowned together. (*Socr. l.* 4. *c.* 13.) In all the *East* he deposed, abused, murdered many that would not forsake the *Nicene* Creed. He set his Officers to suppress their

Conventicles. At *Alexandria* he imprisoned *Peter* that succeeded *Athanasius*, and banished his Presbyters, and set up *Lucius* an *Arian* Bishop. He persecuted the Monks of the Wilderness of *Egypt* (*Nitria* and *Scitis*) and destroyed their Houses: Banished *Macarius* of *Egypt*, and *Macarius* of *Alexandria*, their Leaders. He persecuted *Basil* at *Cæsarea*: He went in person at *Antioch*, to disturb and scatter the Conventicles of the Orthodox; And when he had banished one of their Bishops (*Meletius*, enduring *Paulinus*) the Presbyters kept the Meeting: when he drove them away, a Deacon kept it up: At last *Themistius*, a Philosopher, made an Oration before him, bidding him not marvel that the Christians had such differences, for they were nothing to those of the Philosophers, who were of three hundred different Opinions; and that God would be honoured even under diversity of Opinions: This somewhat asswaged him; and shortly after in the 50th year of his age, he was slain.

§. 3. *Gratian* (and *Valentinian junior*) coming to the Empire, Liberty of Conscience and Restoration was given to all Sects, except the *Eunomians*, *Photinians*, and *Manichees* (*Socrat. l. 5 c. 2.*) He took *Theodosius* into the Empire with him: And so the Orthodox Party got up again: and the *Arians* after this went every where down, save among the *Goths*.

§. 4. LXXI. *Theodosius* called a General Council at *Constantinople*, where the chief things done, were, 1. the setting up of *Gregory Nazianzene* as Bishop, 2. The condemning of the *Macedonians*, 3. The giving of the second Patriarchate to *Constantinople*, because it was the Imperial Seat; putting under him the Dioceses of *Pontus*, *Heraclea* and *Asia*: 4. The putting down of *Nazianzene* again, and putting *Nectarius* in his stead. 5. The setling *Flavianus* at *Antioch*.

§. 5. Some would perswade us that it was two Councils and not one that did these things: But the question is but *de nomine*. In the beginning they dispatch'd part of their work; and before they departed *Meletius* the Bishop of *Antioch* dying, the Bishops returned to Council, and more *Egyptian* Bishops came and did the rest.

§. 6. The Case of *Gregory Naz.* was thus: A Council at *Antioch* in the reign of *Arianisme*, sent him, with three more able speakers to go visit the Churches, and draw them from *Arianisme*. He came to *Constantinople*, and an *Arian* being in possession, he got into a little empty Church, and there so long Preached, till he had recovered much of the City from *Arianisme*. Hereupon *Peter*, Bishop of *Alexandria*, signified by Letters, that he would have him be Bishop of *Constantinople* (against the *Arian* Bishop:) The Orthodox Party chose him: One *Maximus*, that of a Philosopher turned Christian, and insinuated into *Gregories* familiarity; by money first, and threats after, gets *Peter* of *Alexander*, and the *Egyptian* Bishops, to make him Bishop of *Constant.* supposing *Gregory* not yet lawfully settled: *Meletius Antioch:* being at *Const.* Ordaineth *Gregory* Bishop. The Council, when Convened, Confirm him, and cast out *Maximus* (that never had possession:) *Theodosius* owneth *Gregory*, and putteth out the *Arian* Bishop, and possess-

possesseth him of the Great Church. The *Antiockian* Controversie falling in at the death of *Meletius*, *Gregory* was against *Flavian*; The *Egyptian* Bishops being for him, set against *Gregory*, and resolved to cast him out and choose another: He seeing their resolution, and offended at their furious carriage in the Council, resigneth to the Emperour, and departeth: some make it, as if his resignation was unconstrained; but his own words shew, that he did it but to prevent the deposition which they resolved on: Else he durst not have deserted his Flock that lamented his departure. In his place they chose *Nectarius* a Pretor, that was no Christian, *in foro Ecclesiæ*, as being not yet baptized; and so was indeed uncapable, and the choice null: But the man was honest; And *Nicephorus* saith, that they put down his name in a Paper with others, leaving it to the Emperour to chuse one of them, and that he chose *Nectarius*.

§. 7. The description of this Council, and the good Bishops of his time, by *Gregory Naz.* in his Poems and his Orations, is very doleful; How implacably factious and contentious they were, how fierce and violent, leaping and carrying themselves in the Council like mad-men. He describeth the People as contentious, but yet *endued with the love of God*, though *their zeal wanted* knowledg: *Page* 528. *Orat.* 32. "The Courtiers, "he saith, whether true to the Emperour he knew not, but for the most "part perfidious to God: And the Bishops as sitting on adverse thrones "and feeding adverse opposite Flocks, drawn by them into factions, like "the clefts that earth-quakes make, and the pestilent diseases that "infect all about, and distracting and dividing all the World, separa-"ting the East from the West, by the noise of *meus & tuus*, *Antiquus & "Novus*, *nobilior & ignobilior, multitudine opulentior aut tenuior*; raging like "furious horses in battle, and like mad-men casting dust into the air, "and under their several Heads *(or Leaders)* fulfilling their own contenti-"ons, and becoming the determiners of wicked ambition and magnificence, "and unrighteous and absurd judges of matters: The same men (saith he) "are to day of the same throne and judgment as we are, if so our Leaders "and chief men carry them; To morrow, if the wind do but turn, they "are for the contrary Seat and Judgment: Names *(or Votes)* follow ha-"tred or friendship: And which is most grievous, we blush not to say con-"trary things to the very same hearers; Nor are we constant to our selves, "being changed up and down by contention: You would say we are tossed "like the waving *Euripus*. Therefore he professeth, that it is unseemly for "him to joyn with them, in their Councils; as it were to leave his studies "and quietness, to go play with the Lads in the Streets, *Page* 524.

The like he hath in his Poem, *De vitâ suâ*, Page. 24, 25, 26, 27. Οἱ γὰρ προεδρίαι, &c.

> *Etenim Magistri Plebis atque Antistites*
> *Sancti datores Spiritus, & qui thronis*
> *Fundunt ab altis verba queis patitur salus,*
> *Cunctisque pacem jugiter qui prædicant,*

> *In æde mediâ vocibus clarissimis*
> *Tanto furore se petunt sibi invicem,*
> *Tumultuando, contrahendo copias,*
> *Carpendo sese mutuò linguâ efferâ,*
> *Saliendo, mentis ut solint sanæ impotes,*
> *Prædando quos quis ante prædari queat*
> *Rabida Imperandi dum tenet mente sitis*
> *(Quinam ista verbis, & quibus dignè eloquar ?)* .
> *Orbem universum prorsus ut divulserint ;*
> *Ortumque jam & Hesperum scindit magis*
> *Ardens simultas, quam loci vel climata :*
> *Namque illa si non finis, at media uniunt ;*
> *At hos ligare vinculum nullum potest :*
> *Non Causa Pietas (Bilis hoc excogitat,*
> *Ad mentiendum prona,) sed Lis ob Thronos :*
> *Quidnam hoc vocârim ? Præsules ? Non præsules: &c.*

Are not these lamentable descriptions of the Bishops of those happy times, and excellent Councils: Even in the days of good *Theodosius* ; when the Church recovered from under *Arianisme*, and came newly out of the fire of Persecution? The truth is, All times have had some few such excellent persons as *Nazianzene*, *Basil*, *Chrysostome*, &c. But they have ordinarily been born down by the violent stream of a more ignorant, selfish, worldly sort of men.

All this here cited out of *Gregory*, is much less than he saith in his last Oration, De Episcopis, Vol. 2. too large and sharp to be now recited: Therefore I leave it to the perusal of the Learned Reader.

One Papist saith to me, that it was the *Arian* or *Macedonian* Bishops that *Gregory* meant : But the whole tenor of his writing speaketh the contrary; and that he spake of this first Council at *Constantinople*, one of the four which is equalled to the four Evangelists: And in his 59th Epist. to *Sophronius*, Page 816. he saith, *Si eos inveneritis non ob fidei doctrinam, sed ob privatas simultates inter se distractos & divulsos, quod quidem ipse observavi*, &c.

But some may say that passion moved him to the satyrical exaggeration of his own received injuries : But, 1. He speaketh not of this Council only, but of others also : 2. He acknowledged, that till the *Egyptian* Bishops came, he had the Council Vote for his place. 3. His spirit and all his endeavours were for peace, and not to make things worse than they were; And for peace he quit his Seat. 4. And in his Epistles to the Civil Magistrates he afterwards wrote earnestly to them to keep the Bishops at the next Council in peace, lest they should make Religion a contempt and scandal. So that few men could worse be charged with abusive invectives than this Pious, Learned, peaceable Bishop.

§. 8. In:

§. 8. In his 55*th* Epist. to *Procopius*, *page* 814. refusing to come to their Council, he saith, "If I must write the very truth, I am of the mind to fly "from (or avoid) every Meeting of Bishops: For I never saw a joyful and "happy end of any Council; nor any that gave not more addition and "increase to evils, than depulsion (or reformation:) For pertinacious con- "tentions and the lusts of Domination (or Lording,) (Think me not "(saith he) grievous and troublesome for writing this,) are such, as no "words can express: And a man that will (there) be a Judg of others, shall "sooner contract dishonesty himself, than repress the dishonesty of others.

They that say he speaketh only of Heretical Councils defie the light, and will be believed by none that know the History.

§. 9. The Case of *Antioch*, briefly, was this: *Meletius* was a good man, but of a healing disposition, made Bishop by the *Arians* mistaking him, and put out by them when they knew him, yet he held Communion with repenting *Arians*. *Euzoius* an *Arian* was put into his place, and he kept Conventicles. The grand Controversie of all the foregoing Ages, was about Communion with the Lapsed, that yielded to Idolatry, or Heresie: some over zealous were too proud of their own sufferings, and were very rigid against receiving such Penitents, saying they were Time-servers, and receiving them would encourage others to save themselves in suffering, and then repent: Others were too wide in receiving them upon unsatisfactory professions of Repentance: The Wisest went a middle way. Many *Antiochians* separated from *Meletius*, because the *Arians* chose him, and he received penitent *Arians*: And *Lucifer Calaritanus*, and *Eusebius Vercellensis* of *France* going to settle the Peace at *Antioch*, *Eusebius* disliked their opposition to *Meletius*, and left them. *Lucifer* a good Man, but rigid and hot against the *Arians*, said that *Meletius* could be no Bishop, and ordained them *Paulinus* (and so there were three as is aforementioned.) The Bishop of *Rome* who would have a finger in all, encouraged *Lucifer*; *Paulinus* was a man of extraordinary goodness: but yet the Canon nullified the Ordination of a Bishop into a fore-possessed Seat; And when half cleaved to *Meletius*, and half to *Paulinus* (both very good Men,) a Synod (as is aforesaid) ended the difference, by tolerating both till the death of one, and then making him sole Bishop: The *Presbyters* (it's said) were sworn to this. *Meletius* dyeth first; yet *Flavianus* a Presbyter that had stuck to them in *Valens* Persecution, is chosen Bishop by the *Meletians*, who will not joyn with *Paulinus* as a Schismatick. The Pope owneth *Paulinus*: The Council at *Constantinople* own *Meletius* first, and *Flavianus* after: *Gregory Nazianzene* and others were against *Flavianus*, because they said he came in by Perjury, having sworn not to accept it: Some say he did not Swear. *Lucifer Calaritanus* that Ordained *Paulinus*, forsook the Party called the Catholick Church, and gathered separated Churches, and became the Head of a Schism, called since *Luciferian Hereticks*, meerly because the Churches received the confessing returning *Arians* to Communion, and he owned *Flavianus*. And thus even good Bishops

Bishops could not agree, nor scape the imputation of Heresie.

§ 10. *Baronius* and *Binnius* after him, say, *Nazianzenus hanc discordiam suâ abdicatione compositum iri arbitratus, sedi* Constantinopolitanæ *cum consensu Imperatoris, non sine magno Bonorum ac populi fletu renunciat, atq; statim post habitas in Synodo aliquot actiones, comitantibus optimis quibuscunq; Orientalibus, in* Cappadociam *discedit. Tum qui supererant ibi Episcopi ac Sacerdotes Nundinarii, in locum Christiani perfectissimi, Theologi absolutissimi, Monachi castissimi, Nectarium hominem nondum Christianum sed adhuc Catechumenum, rerum Ecclesiasticarum penitus imperitum, in voluptatibus saeculi & carnis hactenus versatum, suffecerunt.*

§. 11. This Council added to the *Nicene* Creed some words about the Holy Ghost. The advancement of the *Constantinopolitane* Bishop by this Synod with the reasons of it, bred such a jealousie in the Bishops of *Rome*, as hath broken the Churches of the *East* and *West*, which are unhealed to this day.

§. 12. LXXII. Two Bishops, *Palladius* and *Secundianus*, complained to *Gratian*, that they were unjustly judged *Arians*, and desired a Council to try them. *Ambrose* perswaded him not to trouble all the World for two Men. A Council of 32 Bishops is called for them at *Aquileia*. They refuse to be accountable to so few, and are condemned.

§. 13. LXXIII. *An.* 381. Twelve Bishops met at *Cæsaraugusta* against the *Priscillianists*: These Men had divers other Councils in those times. *Ithacius* and *Idacius* were the Leaders. The whole Story you may find in *Sulpitius Severus* in the Life of *Martin, &c.* The sum is this: *Priscillianus*, a rich Man, of much Wit and learning, was infected with the Heresie of the *Gnosticks* and *Manichees*. Many followed him; his party was much in Fasting and Reading: The Bishops in Council excommunicated them. Yet they kept up. The Bishops in Council sought to the Emperour *Gratian* to suppress them by the Sword: A while they prevailed: But the *Priscillianists* quickly learned that way, and got a great Courtier to be their Friend, and *Gratian* restored them. *Gratian* being killed, when *Maximus* was chosen Emperour by his Army, the Bishops go to *Maximus* for help: The *Arians* having got Head against *Ambrose* at *Milan*, and these Sectaries troubling the Churches in *France*, *Spain*, and *Italy*, *Maximus* (a Man highly commended for Piety by most Writers, saw that being forced by his Army to accept the Empire, he was a Usurper) being once engaged, thought the defence of the Orthodox would strengthen him: So he forced *Valentinian* by Threats to forbear wronging *Ambrose*; And to please the Bishops he put *Priscillian* to death, and banished some of his Followers. *Martin* Bishop of *Tome* (being a Man of small learning, but of great Holiness, and austerity of Life, living like a Hermite in the poorest Garb and Cabbin, lying on the Ground, faring hard, praying much, and working more Miracles, if *Sulpitius*, his Schollar and Acquaintance may be believed, than we read of any since the Apostles, even than *Gregory Thaumaturgus*) did abhor drawing the Sword against Hereticks, and dis-

swaded

swaded the Bishops and Emperour but in vain : The prosecution was so managed by the Bishops, that in the Countreys, those that did but Fast and Read much were brought under the suspicion of *Priscillianism*, and reproached : This common injury to Piety from the Bishops grieved *Martin* yet more, so that he renounced the Communion of the Bishops and their Synods : whereupon they defamed him to the Emperour and People, as an unlearned Man, a Schismatick, suspected of favouring *Priscillianism*! But *Martins* holiness and Miracles magnified him with the Religious sort. At last a great *Priscillianist* being sentenced to death, *Martin* travelled to the Emperour *Maximus* to beg his Life. *Maximus* told him, he would grant his desire if he would but once communicate with the Bishops : *Martin* preferring Mercy before sacrifice, yielded, and did once communicate with them. But professed that in his way home, an Angel corrected him and threatned him if he did so any more : and that from that time his gift of Miracles was diminished : and so he never communicated with them more to the Death : *Sulpitius* his Narrative puts the Reader to a great difficulty, either to believe so many and great Miracles as he reports, or not to believe so learned, pious, and credible an Historian, who professeth to say nothing but what he either saw himself or had from the Mouth of *Martin*, or those that saw them, and who speaketh his own knowledg of his eximious Piety. He speaketh hardly of the Bishops, not only as complying with an Usurper, but that *Ithacius* in particular of his knowledge, was one that much cared not what he said or did The Bishops would have denied that the death of *Priscillian* was by their means: Is it not strange that the Church of *Rome* should Canonize *Martin* for a Saint, believing his great Miracles, and yet themselves go an hundred times further against the blood of Dissenters, than the Bishops did whom Saint *Martin* therefore opposed and separated from to the death ?

The Churches in *Spain*, and elsewhere, were disturbed and scattered or endangered by Souldiers to please these Bishops, not (as some forge) that *Maximus* did persecute the Christians for the Prey : For most Writers magnifie his Piety and Defence of *Ambrose*, and the Orthodox that condemn his Usurpation, though he said, the Souldiers in *Britain* forced him to it.

§. 14. LXXIV. A General Council was called to *Rome* by the Emperour and *Damasus* ; but the Oriental Bishops would not come so far, but met at *Constantinople* : Here *Damasus* owned *Paulinus* at *Antioch*, as the Council of *Const.* had owned *Meletius* : And so neither would be obedient to the other ; the General Council, nor the Pope. But *Damasus* durst not excommunicate *Flavianus*, but permitted two Bishops to continue at *Antioch* ; accounted a Schism, which continued long.

§. 15. LXXV. The Oriental Bishops that would not come to *Rome*, meeting at *Constantinople*, wrote to *Rome* to tell them their Case and Faith, & minded them that it was according to the Canons that *Neighbour Bishops* (and not Strangers) should Ordain Bishops to vacant Seats (to justifie their

their setting up *Flavianus* when *Rome* set up *Paulinus*:) And they give account of the advancement of *Const.* and *Jerusalem* and call *Jerusalem* [*The Mother of all other Churches.*]

§. 16. A Synod held at *Syda* against the *Massalians*, little is known of.

§. 17. LXXVI. A Council at *Bourdeaux* condemned *Instantius Priscillian.* who thereupon was slain at *Trevers.*

§. 18. LXXVII. *An.* 380. A Council at *Rome* under *Syricius*, repeated some of the old Canons.

§. 19. LXXVIII. *Theognostus* having excommunicated *Ithacius,* and reprehended the Bishops, as irregular and bloody for procuring the Death of *Priscillian,* a Council called at *Trevers* did justifie and acquit him: Unjustly, say, even *Binnius* and *Baronius*: who here repeat out of *Sulpitius Martins* once communicating with the Bishops there, to save two Mens Lives, and the Words of the Angel to him [*Merito,* Martine, *compungeris : Sed aliter exire nequisti: Repara virtutem; resume Constantiam, ne jam non periculum gloriæ, sed salutis incurras: Itaque ab illo tempore satis cavit cum illa Ithacianæ partis communione misceri: Caterùm cum tardius quosdam ex ergumenis, quam solebat, & gratiâ minore curaret; subinde nobis cum lachrymis fatebatur, se propter communionis illius malum, cui se vel puncto temporis necessitate, non spiritu, miscuisset, detrimentum virtutis sentire: sexdecim post vixit annos, nullam Synodum adiit, &c.*

Is it not strange that Papists blush not to recite such a History with approbation, which expresseth a testimony from Heaven against far less than their Inquisition, Flames, Murders, Canons *de hereticis comburendis & exterminandis,* and Deposing Princes that will not execute them. And which sheweth such a Divine justification for separation from the Bishops and Synods of such a way, yea, though of the same Religion with us, and not so Corrupt as the Reformation found the *Roman* Papacy and Clergy ?

§. 20. LXXIX. The two Bishops continuing at *Antioch,* *Evagrius* succeeding *Paulinus,* and *Rome* owning him, and the *East Flavianus,* a Council is called at *Capua*: *Flavian* refuseth to come: The Council had more wit than many others, and Ordered that both Congregations (*Flavian's* and *Evagrius's*) being all good Christians, should live in loving Communion. (O that others had been as wise, in not believing those Prelates that perswaded the World that it is so pernicious a thing for two Churches and Bishops to be in one City, as *Peter* and *Paul* are said to be at *Rome!*) And they referred the Case to *Theophilus Alex.*

§. 21. But this Council condemned a new Heresie (Hereticating was in fashion;) *viz.* of one Bishop *Bonosus*, denying *Mary* to have continued a Virgin to the death. And they condemned Re-baptizing and Re-ordaining, and the Translation of Bishops.

§. 22. LXXX. Next comes a Provincial Council (or two) at *Arles,* which doth but repeat some former Canons.

§. 23. LXXXI. Next we have a strange thing, a Heresie raised by one that was no Bishop: But the best is, it was but a very little Heresie: *Hierome*

Rome is the describer of it, who writing againſt the Author, *Jovinian* a *Milan* Monk, no doubt according to his ſharpneſs, makes the worſt of it: At the worſt it containeth all theſe: 1. *That Virgins, Widows and Marryed Women, being all baptized* (or waſhed) *in Chriſt, and not differing in any other works, are of equal merits.* 2. That thoſe that *pleni jide* with a *full faith are born again in baptiſme, cannot be ſubverted by the Devil.* 3. There is no difference of merit between *abſtaining from meat, and receiving it with thanksgiving.* 4. *That there's one Reward in Heaven for all that keep their baptiſmal vow.* Siricius catching *Jovinian* hid at *Rome*, ſends him to *Milan*, where a Council Hereticateth him.

§. 24. LXXXII. It's ſtrange that *Binnius* vouchſafeth next to add out of *Socrates, l.* 5. *c.* 20. (when he Hereticateth him alſo) a Council of the *Novatians*; *Socrates* and *Sozomen* are called *Novatians*, by the Papiſts, becauſe they rail not at them ſo valiantly as the Hereticators do; And it may be they will call me one, if I ſay that I better like this Councils Canon, than burning men for ſuch a Hereſie. They decree that as from the Apoſtles the different time of keeping *Eaſter* was not taken for ſufficient cauſe for Chriſtians to renounce Communion with each other, ſo it ſhould be eſteemed ſtill, and it ſhould be ſo far left indifferent, that they live in love and Communion that are herein of different minds. And I would ſay, as lowd as I can ſpeak, *If all the proud, contentious, ambitious, hereticating part of the Biſhops had been of this Chriſtian mind, O what ſin, what ſcandal and ſhame, what cruelties, confuſions and miſeries had the Chriſtian world eſcaped!* But yet men will ſcorn to be ſo far *Novatians*, in deſpight of Scripture, reaſon, humanity and experience, whatever ſin or miſery follow: (As I ſaid before) in *England* the Convocation and Parliaments overſight hath determined of a falſe rule to know *Eaſter*-day, and ſilenceth Miniſters for not Aſſenting, Conſenting to it, and approving the Uſe of it, even the Uſe which conſiſteth in keeping *Eaſter* at a wrong time, which makes us Hereticks.

§. 25. LXXXIII. *An.* 393. A great Council was called at *Hippo*, where *Auſtin*, yet a Presbyter was there. Good men will do well: Here was nothing but pious and honeſt, for reformation of Diſcipline and Manners; And moſt of the *African* Councils were the beſt in all the world. Their Biſhopricks were but like our Pariſhes, and they ſtrove not who ſhould be greateſt, or dominecr.

§. 26. LXXXIV. Next a Council at *Conſtant.* decideth a Crontroverſie between two men ſtriving for a Biſhoprick, *Bin. p.* 539.

§. 27. LXXXV. *Concilium Adrumetinum* did we know not what.

§. 28. LXXXVI. *An.* 394. A Council of *Donatiſts* was held at *Caverne*, about a ſchiſm between two men ſet up for Biſhops againſt each other.

§. 29. LXXXVII. At *Bagai* another Council was called by the *Donatiſts*, for the ſame Cauſe, where *Primianus Carthag.* having 310. Biſhops, condemned *Maximianus* his Competitor, abſent. Note here, 1. How
great

great a number the *Donatists* were, and on what pretence (as over-voting them) they called others Hereticks and Schifmaticks. 2. How fmall Bifhopricks then were, the number tells us.

§. 30. LXXXVIII. A Synod was held at *Taurinum* in *Savoy*, where a difference was decided between the Bifhops of *Arles* and *Vienne*, ftriving which fhould be greateft : And he was judged to be the greateft, whofe feat was proved to be the *Metropolitan* : And a cafe of Communicating with one *Fœlix* a Partner of *Ithacius* and the bloody Bifhops was debated.

§. 31. LXXXIX. Another *Carthage* Council called the fecond, which *Binnius* faith, was the laft, is placed next ; which decreed feveral Church Orders, fome of which fhew, that a Bifhops Diocefs had then but *unum altare*; As when reconciliation of Penitents, (as well as Chrifme, and Confecrating Virgins) was to be done by the Bifhop only, except in great neceffity. And when Chriftians were multiplyed, they that defired a Bifhop in a place, that had none before, might have one. And the prohibition *erigendi aliud altare*, &c. was repeated.

§. 32. XC. Another *Carthage* Council called the third, hath many good "Orders: One is Can. 26. "That the Bifhop of the firft Seat, fhall not be "called the Chief Prieft (or Bifhop) or any fuch thing, but only the Bi-"fhop of the firft Seat. To avoid all ambitious defigns of fuperiority : Whence *Binnius* elfewhere noteth, that *Carthage* had not an Archbifhop. No doubt they had a fenfe of the fin and mifery, that came by the Patriarchall and other ambitious ftrifes.

§. 33. XCI. Another *Carthage* Council hath the like Canons, adding to this aforefaid, as *Gratian* citeth it, [*Univerfalis autem nec etiam* Romanus *Pontifex appelletur*.] To which *Binnius* hath no better an anfwer than, 1. That it is only fwelling titles, and not the fuperiour power that is forbidden. 2. That the *Africans* had no power to make Laws for *Rome*; But, 1. Sure the Name is Lawful, if the Power be Lawful. 2. They that could make no Laws for *Rome*, might declare their Judgment of Gods Laws, and that *Rome* might make no Laws for them. This Council alfo forbiddeth going beyond Sea with Appeals.

§. 34 XCII. The next *Carthage* Council hath 104 Canons for Difcipline : moft very good. Divers Canons lay fo much on the Bifhop, as plainly fhew each Bifhop had but One Altar. *Can.* 14. "That the Bifhops "Cottage be not far from the Church : *Can.* 15. That the Bifhop have but "vile or cheap houfhold ftuff, and a poor table and diet ; and feek his au-"thority or dignity by his faith and defert of life. 16. The Bifhop muft "not read the Gentiles Books ; 19. Nor contend for tranfitory things, "though provoked. 20. Nor take on him the care of Family (or common) "bufinefs, but only be vacant to the Word and Prayer. 23. The Bifhop "fhall hear no Caufe but in the prefence of his Presbyters ; elfe it fhall be "void that is fentenced without them, unlefs confirmed by their prefence. "28. The unjuft condemnation of Bifhops is void. 30. And judgments "againft the abfent. 35. The Bifhop to fit higher than the Presbyters at
"Church

"Church and their Meetings, but at home know that they are his Col-
"leagues. 51. A Clerk how Learned foever in Gods Word, muſt get his
"living by a trade. 52. That is, by a trade or husbandry, without de-
"triment to his Office. 53. All Clerks that are able to work, fhould learn
"both trades and Letters. 55. The Bifhop muſt not admit an accuſer of
"the brethren to Communion; Nor to enter into the Clergy, though he
"amend. Many againſt Clergy-men that are flatterers, betrayers, foul-
"tongued, quarrellers, at difcord, fcurrilous, of filthy jeaſts, that fwear
"by creatures, that fing at feaſts, of former fcandal, &c. 83. The poor
"and the aged of the Church to be honoured before the reſt. 88. He that
"goeth to any Shows or Sights, on publick days, inſtead of going to the
"Church-aſſembly, let him be Excommunicate. 98. A Lay-man muſt not
"teach when the Clergy are prefent, unlefs they bid him. 100. A woman
"muſt not baptize.

§. 35. XCIII. *An.* 398. Another Council was at *Carthage* of 73. Bifhops for Difcipline.

§. 36. XCIV. *An.* 399. *Theophilus* held a Synod at *Alexandria*, againſt a dead man, *Origen*. The occaſion *Baronius* and *Binnius* thus deliver: *Melania*, a Woman of greateſt Nobility in *Rome* in *Valens* the *Arians* Pefecution, hid five thouſand Monks, and a while fuſteined them, and when they were banifhed, with great zeal, followed them to maintain them out of her fubſtance (or eſtate:) When they were reſtored from banifhment, fhe built for her felf a Monaſtery at *Jerufalem*, in which, befides fifty Virgins that dwelt with her, fhe entertained and maintained holy Foreign Biſhops, Monks, and Virgins, twenty feven years: Whereby it happened that both fhe and *Ruffinus*, were by *Didymus Alexandrinus*, (a man blind, but of great learning and fame, too great an admirer of *Origen*'s works) entangled (as their accuſers faid) in *Origen*'s errours, and received and divulged his Book, called *Periarchon*: After 25 years abfence in *Egypt* and *Paleſtine*, returning to *Rome* with great fame of Holinefs, and bringing with them a piece of the Crofs, they with fraud bring to *Rome Origen*'s *Periarchon*, (that is, Tranflated and Corrected by *Ruffinus*.) Another Woman, *Marcella*, accufeth them of *Origen*'s errours, which they deny, and getting Communicatory Letters from Pope *Siricius*, forfake *Rome*, (where fuch Merits and Holinefs would not procure an aged Lady a quiet habitation, without being Hereticated, becauſe fhe highly valued *Origen*'s Works, which had divers errours; and who hath not?) Hereupon *Pamachius*, and *Oceanus*, write to *Hierome* to publifh *Origen*'s *Periarchon* entire, and detect his errours; which he did, fhewing that *Ruffinus* had mended fome, and left others unmended: This occafioned ſtirs againſt *Hierome*, and a Council call'd at *Alexandria*, *an.* 399. where *Origen* is condemned. *Theophilus* by his Legates expells *Origen*'s followers out of *Egypt* and *Paleſtine*: Being expelled they go to *Chryfoſtome* to *Conſtantinople*, and complain of *Theophilus* as perfecuting them that were innocent Catholicks, and defired his help: He undertaketh to reconcile them to *Theophilus* : *Epiphanius* followeth them to *Constantinople*, and requireth *Chryfoftome* to Excommunicate them and Expel them; *Chryfoftome* durſt not do it, againſt people profeſſing truth and piety, without a Synod: Whereupon *Epiphanius* irregularly accuſeth *Chryfoftome*, and publickly inveyeth againſt him in his own Church; of the proceſs of which, more anon.

§. 37. For the better underſtanding of theſe matters, I will inſert ſomewhat of *Theophilus* and *Chryfoftome*, out of *Socrates*, becauſe he is a moſt credible Hiſtorian, and ſaith, they were things done in his own days. *Theophilus* was noted for a Lordly Prelate; *Iſidore Pelufiota* ſaith more: When *Chryfoftome* was to be Ordained Biſhop of *Conftantinople*, *Theophilus* refuſed to Ordain him, becauſe he would have preferred to it, one *Iſidore*, a Preſbyter of his own; But *Eutropius*, a Courtier, having got Articles againſt *Theophilus*, ſhewed them to him, and bid him chooſe, whether he would Ordain *Chryfoftome* Biſhop, or ſtand at the Bar and anſwer thoſe crimes: *Theophilus* was ſo afraid at this, that he preſently Conſecrated *Chryfoftome*: *Socr. l. 6. c. 2.* But preſently after began buſily to deviſe how he might work him miſchief, which he practiſed privately by Word, and by his Letters into foreign Countries: But was vexed that his malicious practices had not better ſucceſs, for he thought to bring in this *Iſidore* (*cap. 5.*)

§. 38. One of the Articles againſt *Theophilus* was this: When *Theodoſius* was going to fight againſt *Maximus* the Tyrant, *Theophilus* ſent preſents by this *Iſidore* to the Emperour, with two Letters, charging him to give the preſents and one of the Letters to him that ſhould have the upperhand. *Iſidore* got him to *Rome*, to hearken after the Victory: But his Reader that kept him company, ſtole away his Letters: Whereupon *Iſidore* in a fright took his heels preſently to *Alexandria*.

§. 39. Another thing to be fore-known to this ſtory is in *Socrat. l. 6 c. 7.* The ſchiſme of the *Anthropomorphites* now roſe from *Egypt*: ſome of the more unlearned thought that God had a body and the ſhape of a man, but *Theophilus* (and the Judicious) condemned them, and inveighed againſt them, proving that God had not a body. The Religious of *Egypt* hearing this, flocking in blind zeal to *Alexandria*, condemned *Theophilus* for a wicked man, and ſought to take away his life: *Theophilus* very penſive, deviſed how to ſave his life: He came to them courteouſly, and ſaid, *When I faſten mine eyes on you, methinks I ſee the face of God.* Theſe words allayed the heat of the Monks; who ſaid, *If that be true that thou ſayeſt, that the face of God is like ours, then curſe the Works of* Origen *which deny it: If thou deny this, be ſure thou ſhalt receive at our hands the puniſhment due to the impious and open enemies of God*: O brave diſputing! Were theſe mortified Monks? *Theophilus* told them, he would do what they would, for he hated the Books of *Origen*.

But that which ripened the miſchief was, that the Religious Houſes of *Egypt* having four brothers, excellent men, for their overſeers, *Theophilus* was reſtleſs till he got them away to him; one of them, *Dioſcorus*, he made a Biſhop; others living with him perceived *that he was ſet upon heaping and hoarding money,*

money, and that all his labour tended to gathering, [Dr. *Hammer* translating this, puts in the Margin, *This Bishop hath more fellows in the World.* And noting how *Theophilus* to revenge himself persecuted his own Opinions, faith, *This is a sin against the Holy Ghost.*] would dwell with him no longer, but returned to their Wilderness. *Theophilus* prone to anger and revenge, endeavoured by all means to work them mischief; And the way he took was to accuse them to the Monks, for saying to him, that God *had not a body*, nor *humane shape*: And he himself was of the same Opinion, yet to be revenged of his Enemies, he stuck not to oppugn it; and sent to the Monks, not to obey *Dioscorus* or his Brethren, for they held that God had *no body*, whereas Scripture faith, that he hath *eyes, ears, hands and feet, as men have*; which with *Origen* they deny: By this treachery he set them all together by the ears; one side calling the other *Origenists*, and the other them *Anthropomorphites*; so it turned to bickering among the Monks, yea, to a deadly battel: And *Theophilus* went with Armed men and helped the *Anthropomorphites*.

So you see, if *Socrates* say true, how wickedly this Sainted Patriarch lived, and how he came so much engaged against the *Origenists*, whose errours doubtless were worthy blame: but many good persons who honoured *Origen* for his great worth, and owned not his errours, were called *Origenists*, because they honoured him: And that which was erroneous in him, was consistent with far greater Learning, Piety, and Honesty, than *Socrates*, *Isidore Pelus.* and others thought there was in *Theophilus*: Either *credible Socrates*, and others were gross Lyars, or this Patriarch and Saint was a downright knave, or acted like one.

§. 40. Now we are upon it, let us prosecute *Chrysostome's* History further. He was a studious holy Monk of a House, near *Antioch*: After *Nectarius* death he was chosen Bishop for his meer piety and worth: He was a man of great piety and honesty and an excellent tongue, and as good a life, but bred in a Cell and not to Courtship, knew not how to flatter Courtiers and Court-Prelates: He was naturally sharp and cholerick, and his conscience told him, that a Bishop must not be a dawber, nor flatter the greatest wicked men: (For Bishops in that Age were the Preachers,) not having a thousand Congregations to preach to.) He saw even the Clergy addicted to their appetites: and he kept a Table for them, but eating with great temperance he always eat alone; He rebuked the Luxury of the Court, and particularly of the Empress, who conceived a deadly hatred against him: And the Custome of the Court was, for the Women much to influence both Emperour and Courtiers, and then what Bishop soever was too precise for them and bold with their sins, to get a pack of the Worldly Clergy presently to meet together and depose him: (For Synods of Bishops (not the Pope) had then the power.) They would not be seen in it themselves, but a Patriarch of *Alexandria* should call a Synod, and do it presently. *Chrysostome* was a man of no Courtship to take off their edges; but the worse Courtiers, Bishops, and Priests were,

the

the worse he spake of them; And all the honest plain people believed and loved him; but the rich and great Prelates abhorred him. His own Clergy hated him, because he would reform them: Those that would not amend, he Excommunicated: Which they could not bear: so that one of his Deacons *Serapion*, openly said to him, *O Bishop, thou shalt never be able to rule all these as thou wouldst, unless thou make them all tast of one whip.* Every one was his Enemy who was his own, and was engaged by guilt against his Discipline and Doctrine.

The Guilty hated him: His Hearers loved him: Swift-Writers took his Sermons, which tell us what he was to this day: And it was honesty and policy in *Innocent* Bishop of *Rome* to own him, who had worth to add to the reputation of his defendants. Among other of his accusations, one was, that *Eutropius* an Eunuch, Chamberlain to the Emperour, procured a Law against Delinquents taking the Church for a Sanctuary. And shortly after being to be beheaded, for a crime against the Emperour, he took the Church for a Sanctuary himself; And *Chrysostome* from the Pulpit Preached a Sermon against him, while he lay prostrate at the Altar. Also he resisted *Gainas* the *Arian*, who turned Traytor and was destroyed.

Another cause of *Chrysostome's* disturbance was, that one *Severianus* Bishop of *Gabale* in *Syria*, came into *Constantinople*, and Preached for Money, and drew away the hearts of the People, while *Chrysostome* was about choosing a Bishop for *Ephesus*: *Serapion* a turbulent Deacon quarrelled with the *Syrian* Bishop, and would not reverence him: The Bishop said, *If* Serapion *die a Christian, Christ was not Incarnate.* Serapion tells *Chrysostome* the last words without the first: *Chrysostome* forbids *Severianus* the City: The Empress taketh his part, and importuneth *Chrysostome* to be reconciled to *Severianus.* But the Core remained, *Socrat. l. 6. c. 10.*

§. 41. *Socrat. c.* 11. Shortly after *Epiphanius* (the Collector of Heresies) came from *Cyprus* to *Constantinople*, and there irregularly in *Chrysostomes* Diocess played the Bishop, ordained a Deacon, and called together the Bishops that were accidentally in the City, and required them to Condemn the Books of *Origen*; which some did, and some refused, saith *Socrates, cap.* 12. "Obscure men, odd Fellows, such as have no Pith or "Substance in them, to the end they may become famous, go about most "commonly to purchase to themselves Glory and Renown by dispraising "such men as far excel them in rare and singular Virtues. *Chrysostome* bore patiently *Epiphanius*'s fault and invited him to take a Lodging at his House. He answered him, "I will neither Lodg with thee, nor Pray "with thee, unless thou banish *Dioscorus* and his Brethren out of the City, "and subscribe with thy own Hand the Condemnation of the Works of "*Origen*: *Chrysostome* answered, that such things are not to be done without deliberation and good advice. *Epiphanius* in *Chrysostome's* Church at the Sacrament, stands forth and Condemns *Origen*, and Excommunicateth *Dioscorus* a Bishop, and reproveth *Chrysostome* as taking their part.

Chrysostome

Chryſoſtome ſent word by *Serapion* to *Epiphanius* that he did violate the Canons, 1. In making Miniſters in his Dioceſs ; 2. In adminiſtring the Communion without his Licence, and yet refuſing to do it when he deſired it. Wherefore he bid him take heed leſt he ſet the People in an uproar, for if ought came amiſs, he had his remedy in his Hands. *Epiphanius* hearing this, went away in fear, and took Ship for *Cyprus :* The report goeth (ſaith *Socrates, cap.* 13.) that as he went he ſaid of *John, I hope thou ſhalt never dye a Biſhop*: And that *Chryſoſtome* anſwer'd him, *I hope thou ſhalt never come alive into thy Countrey*. And it ſo fell out : For *Epiphanius* dyed at Sea by the way ; and *Chyſoſtome* dyed depoſed and baniſhed.

§. 42. The Empreſs *Eudoxia* was ſaid to ſet *Epiphanius* on work. *Chryſoſtome* being hot, made a Sermon of the faults of Women ; which was interpreted to be againſt the Empreſs. She irritated the Emperour againſt him ; and got *Theophilus* to call a Council againſt him, at *Quercus* near *Chalcedon*, and *Conſtant*. Thither came *Severianus*, and many Biſhops that *Chryſoſtome* had depoſed, and many that were his Enemies for his ſtrictneſs ; but eſpecially time-ſervers that knew the will of the Empreſs, if not the Emperours: When they ſummoned him to appear before them, He anſwered, that by the Canon there muſt be more Patriarchs, and he appealed to a General Council, yet not denying to anſwer any where, if they would put out his Enemies from being his Judges, and that in his own Patriarchate. But they ſentenced him depoſed, for not appearing: The People were preſently in an uproar, and would not let him be taken out of the Church : The Emperour commanded his baniſhment : To avoid Tumult, the third day he yielded himſelf to the Souldiers to be tranſported : The people hereupon were all in an uproar, and it pleaſed God that there was an Earthquake that night : Whereupon the Emperour ſent after him to intreat him to return. When he came back he would not have officiated, till his Cauſe was heard by equal Judges, but the People conſtrained him to Pray and Preach ; which was after made the matter of his Accuſation. *Theophilus* was hated as the cauſe of all, and *Severianus* as the ſecond. After this *Theophilus* turned his Accuſation upon *Heraclides*, Biſhop of *Epheſus*, put in by *Chryſoſtome :* They condemned him unheard, in his abſence : *Chryſoſtome* ſaid that ſhould not be : The *Alexandrians* ſaid, *It was juſt* ; They went hereupon together by the Ears, and ſome were wounded and ſome were killed, and *Theophilus* glad to fly home to *Alexandria* ; but was hated by the People.

§. 43. After this a Silver Image of the Empreſs was ſet up in the Street, and Plays and Shows about it, which *Chryſoſtome* perhaps too ſharply reproached : This provoked the Empreſs to call another Council ; which depoſed *Chryſoſtome*, for ſeizing upon his place before a Council reſtored him : He ceaſed his Office : The Emperor baniſhed him : His People in paſſion ſet the Church on Fire, which burnt down the Senatours Court ; for which grievous ſufferings befell them. Upon this they forſook the Church and the new Biſhop (*Arſacius*, an old uſeleſs man) and gathered Conventicles

venticles by themselves, and were long called *Joannites* from his Name, and taken for Schismaticks: But they never returned till the Name and Bones of *Chrysostome* were restored to Honour.

§. 44. The *Novatians* quarrelled with *Chrysostome* as too loose in his Doctrine and too strict in his Life, because he said in a Sermon, If you Sin an hundred times, the Church Doors shall be open to you, if you repent. And *Chrysostome* angry with *Sisinnius* the *Novatian* Bishop, told him, There should not be two Bishops in one City, and threatned to silence him from Preaching: He told him that he would be beholden to him then for saving him his labour. But *Chrysostome* answered him, *Nay, if it be a labour, go on.*

§. 45. XCV. A Council in *Afick* to renew the Priviledges of Churches for Sanctuary; that none that fled to them for any Crime, should be taken out by force: Justice was taken for Wickedness.

§. 46. XCVI. Two Councils met, one at *Const.* to judg *Antoninus*, Bishop of *Ephesus*, for Simony, and many other Crimes: Another at *Ephesus* to judg six Bishops for Simony.

§. 47. XCVII. About *An.* 400. A Council of 19 Bishops at *Toletum* repress the *Priscillians*, and make divers Canons for Discipline; as that a Clergy-Man shall have power over his offending Wife by force, but not to put her to death; that a man that hath no Wife but one Concubine shall not be kept from Communion (though some think that this Concubine is truly a Wife, but not according to Law, but private Contract, and more servile.) Many other better there be.

There is adjoyned a *Regula fidei* of many Bishops approved by Pope *Leo*, in *Bin. p.* 563. To which are adjoyned Anathematisms against the *Priscillians*: One of them is, *If any one say or believe that other Scriptures are to be had in Authority and Reverence, besides those which the Catholick Church receiveth, let him be Anathema.* (Yet the *Papists* receive more.) Another is, *If any one think that Astrology or Mathematicks is to be believed* (or trusted) *let him be anathema.*

There are in *Bin.* divers Fragments cited, as of the *Tolet.* Councils. One saith that Arch-Presbyters are under the Arch-Deacons, and yet have *Curam animarum* over all the Presbyters. Another determineth that there shall be but one Baptismal Church, which is there called, *The Mother Church*, with its Chapels, in the Limits assigned: And another distinguisheth of Offerings made at the Parish Church, and Offerings at the Altars; which sheweth that then there were no Altars but where the Bishop was.

§. 48. XCVIII. Two Councils were held at *Carthage* about 401. The later about the *Donatists*.

§. 49. XCIX. *An.* 402. Was the Council *Melevitan.* about certain Bishops quarrels, and who should be the highest Bishop in *Numidia*.

§. 50. C. *An.* 403. Was the Synod *ad Quercum*, which deposed *Chrysostom.*

§. 51.

their Councils abridged. 81

§. 51. Cl. *An.* 403, 404, &c. There were seven Councils in *Africk*, against the *Donatists*, to procure *Honorius* to suppress them by the Sword, not as a *Heresie*, but because they rose up by *Fire and Sword* against the Catholicks, and abused and killed many. But when *Attalus* invaded *Africk*, the Emperour proclaimed Liberty for them, to quiet them; which he after recalled. Another Synod was held against them at *Cyrta*. One at *Toletum* about Ordinations; and one at *Ptolemais* to Excommunicate *Andronicus*, an oppressing Governour.

§.52. CII. The *Donatist* Bishops held a Council, decreeing, that when a sentence of banishment was passed on them, they would not forsake their Church, but rather voluntarily die, as many did by their own hands: For they took themselves to be the true Church and Bishops, and the rest persecuting Schismaticks.

§. 53. CIII. The *Concilium Diospolitanum* of 14 Bishops in *Palestine* acquitted *Pelagius* upon his renouncing his Errours.

§. 54. *An.* 416. A Council at *Carthage* of 67 Bishops condemned *Pelagius* and *Celestine*; whom the former had absolved.

§. 55. CV. A Council of 60 Bishops at *Milevis* condemn *Pelagius*. The 22. Canon galleth the Pontificians: *If Presbyters, Deacons, or other inferiour Clergy, shall in their Causes complain of the Bishops, the neighbour Bishops shall hear them and end the business; being used by the consent of their Bishops: But if they see cause to appeal from them also, let them appeal to none but to* Africane *Councils, or to the Primates of their Provinces: But if any will appeal to any places beyond the Seas, let none in* Africk *receive them into Communion.*

In this Council was *Aurelius, Alypius, Augustinus, Evodius*, and *Possidenius*, and these very great with Pope *Innocent*, one of the best and wisest Popes (who excommunicated *Theophilus, Arcadius* and the Empress, &c. for *Chrysostomes* cause.) Yet did this pass then without contradiction. *Can.* 12. of this Council Liturgies were made necessary approved by Councils left any Heresie should be vended.

§.56. *Celestine* and *Pelagius* being condemned by the *Africans*, especially upon the Accusations of *Lazarus* and *Herotes* Bishops, said to be holy men; *Innocent* joyned with the *Africans*, but after his death Pope *Zosimus* having a fair Appeal of *Celestine*, &c. to him, absolveth them both and condemneth their Accusers. He writeth an Epistle, had the cause been good, very honest against rash condemning innocent men, telling them how greatly they were rejoyced at *Rome* to find them Orthodox; and what false and bad men *Lazarus* and *Herotes* were: It was *Lazarus* custome to accuse the Innocent, as in many Councils he had done Saint *Britius* a Bishop of *Tours*; that he got by Blood into the Bishops Seat, and was the shadow of a Bishop, while a Tyrant had the Image of Empire, and then his Patron being slain, voluntarily deposed himself. The like he saith of *Herotes*; and that neither of them would come personally to *Rome*, but lay in Bed and sent false Letters of Accusation: Therefore he admonisheth the *Africans* (among whom was *Augustine*) to believe such

M whisper-

whisperers no more against the innocent: But *Binnius* out of *Prosper* maketh the accusers holy men, and the other wicked: *Bin. p. 607*.

§. 57. *Pelagius* sent *Zosimus* a Confession of his Faith, and therein condemning all the late Heresies, professeth, *That he so holdeth free-will, as yet that we always need the help of God*; *and that they erre who say with the* Manichees, *that a man cannot avoid sin, and they that say with* Jovinian, *that a man cannot sin*; *for both deny the freedome of the will: But he holdeth, that always a man can sin and can forbear sin, so as he still holdeth the freedome of the will*.

But subtile *Augustine* and the rest, sent back many harder questions to put to *Pelagius* and *Cælestine* for their tryal, upon which they after past for Hereticks.

§. 58. CVI. Therefore 217 Bishops in a Council at *Carthage* having received *Zosimus* Letters, decreed to stand to their former judgment and *Innocents*, against *Pelagius* and *Cælestine*, till they should confess certain points (for Grace) drawn up by *Paulus Diaconus*.

§. 59. CVII *Zosimus* being dead, *Boniface* and *Eulalius* strove for the Popedome: Both were chosen: The Emperour *Honorius* was sent to for both: This Case being too hard for him, he referreth it to a Council at *Ravenna*: It proved too hard for them. Therefore the Emperour commanded them both to remove from the City, and another Bishop to officiate, till it was decided by another Council. But *Eulalius* disobeying the Emperours Command, and coming into *Rome* at noon-day, occasioned a tumult, and the people were neer to fight it out. Which the Emperour hearing, expelled *Eulalius*, and a Council obeying him confirmed *Boniface*.

§. 60. Among the Decrees of *Boniface* one is, *That no Bishop shall be brought or set before any Judge Civil or Military, either for any Civil or criminal cause*. So that a Bishop had the priviledge of a bad Physician; he might murder and not be hanged; For any *crime*, he was to answer but before Bishops, who could but Excommunicate and Depose him. But another Decree is better, against *Bishops that fall out and desire to hurt their Brethren*: But, alas, to how little effect?

§. 61. CVIII. Another Council at *Carthage*, (called the sixth, and by some the fifth) had the famous contention with three Popes, *Zosimus*, *Boniface*, and *Cælestine*, successively, against Appeals to *Rome*, and the Popes sending Legates into *Africa* to judge. The Popes alledged the Council of *Nice* for it. The *African* Bishops knew no such Canon: They take time for Tryal, and send to *Constantinople* and *Alexandria*, to *Atticus* and *Cyril*, for their true Copies of the Councils: None of them have any such Canon: The Fathers write to the Pope to take better heed what he affirmeth for the time to come, and to forbear such pride and usurpation: alledging that by the Canons all strifes were to be ended by their neighbour Bishops and Councils.

Here the Papists sweat about these answers and the event. Some say
(as

(as *Harding*) that the *Africans* continued long, (some say almost 100 years) in Schism: And an Epistle under the name of Pope *Boniface* the second to *Eulalius* saith the same: Others wiser (as *Binnius*) see that to lose *Augustines* authority and have him and all the *African* Bishops (the best of the World) against the Papal power, would be to heavy a burden for them: Therefore they say, that the *Africans* were no Schismaticks, that the Canon not found was in the Council of *Sardica*; and that That went for the Council of *Nice*: That the *Africans* did not deny the Popes power of judging them, but only of sending Souldiers and doing it violently by force, and such other shifts, which the express words of the *African* Council and Letters plainly confute: If any dispute it, I appeal to the very words.

Either another Council or a second Session of the same is called the seventh at *Carthage*.

§. 62. CIX. All this while the Schism continued at *Rome*, and *Eulalius* partly would not Communicate with the rest, each side saying, that theirs was the True Bishop, and the other an Usurper and Schismatick. But *Theodosius* was for *Celestine*. In his time another *Carthage* Council made up their Canons 105. Among which are: 6. *That no Bishop be called the chief Bishop.* 33. *To deal gentlier with the* Donatists. 36. *To send to them for peace.* 53. *That Bishops latelier ordained may not dare to prefer themselves before those that were Ordained before them.* 68. *For pacifying the Churches of* Rome *and* Alexandria, &c.

§. 63. It fell out well for *Austin* against the *Pelagians*, that by the means of *Prosper* and *Hilary* Pope *Celestine* was wholly on *Austins* side, and condemned the *Pelagians*. And among his own Decrees one was *Nullus invitis detur Episcopus: Cleri, plebis & ordinis Comm. sensus ac desiderium requiratur*. Many Canons of those times shew that the Bishops Churches were no bigger, than that All the Laity could meet to choose or accept the Bishop, and have personal Communion.

§. 64. CX. An *Eastern* Council against the *Massalians*.

§. 65. CXI. Next cometh the *Nestorian* War: Pope *Celestine* provoked by *Cyril Alex.* called a Council at *Rome*, and condemned *Nestorius*, unless he recanted in ten days.

§. 66. CXII. *Cyril* calleth his Council at *Alexandria*, and passeth the same sentence, having got *Celestine* to back him, and sends it with many Anathematismes to *Nestorius*, calling for his abjuration. The whole cause is opened at the next Council at *Ephesus*.

M 2 CHAP.

CHAP. V.

The First General Council at Ephesus, *with the Second, and some other following.*

§. 1. THe Church at *Constantinople* growing to be the greatest, by the presence of the Court (which was the spring or poise of most of the Bishops courses, and indeed did rule,) it became the envy and jealousie, especially of the two great Patriarchs, *Rome* and *Alexandria*. *Alexandria* being under the same Emperour had more to do with *Const.* and made the greater Stirs; For when the Empire was divided, *Rome* being under an Orthodox Emperour, had little trouble at home, and little opportunity for domination in the *East*: Yet keeping up the pretence of the prime Patriarchate, and the *Caput Mundi Romani,* the Pope watch'd his opportunity to lay in his claim, and to keep under the stronger side, and while they did the work in the *East* against one another, he sent now and then a Letter or a Legate, to tell them that he was somebody still: And indeed the hope of help from the *Western* Emperour by the countenance of the Pope, made the *Eastern* Churches still vexed with Heresie and Persecutions and Divisions, to seek oft to *Rome* and be glad of their approbation, to strengthen them against their adversaries.

§. 2. When *Arsacius* was dead, *Atticus* succeeded him at *Constantinople,* a wise and pious healing man, who greatly thereby advanced that Church and all the *Eastern* Churches. He dealt gently with the *Novatians* and lived in peace with them. He encouraged Hereticks by kindness to return to the Communion of the Church. At *Synada* in *Phrygia Pac.* was a Church of *Macedonians*: *Theodosius* Bishop of the Orthodox Persecuted them with great severity: And when he found that the Magistrates of the place had not power to do as much as he expected, he got him to *Constantinople* for greater power: while he was there *Agapetus* the *Macedonian* Bishop turned Orthodox, and all the Church adhered to him, and *set him in the Bishops chair.* When *Theodosius* came home with power to persecute him, he found him in his place, and the people shut the doors against *Theodosius*: Whereupon he went back to *Const.* and made his complaint to *Atticus* how he was used. *Atticus* knew that it fell out for the best, for the concord of the Church, and he gave *Theodosius* good words, and perswaded him only to be patient.

Socrat. l.7. c. 3.

§. 3. *Cyril* at that time succeeded his Unkle *Theophilus* at *Alexandria,* in place and in unquiet domination, taking more upon him than *Theophilus* had done, even the Government of temporal affairs: He presently shut up the *Novatian* Churches in *Alex.* rifled them of all their Treasure, and bereaved

Socr. ib. c. 7.

bereaved *Theopemptus* their Bishop of his substance. The Jews at that time falling out with the Christians, murdered many of them. *Cyril* executed some, and banished them all. *Orestes* the Governour took this ill: Fifty Monks of Mount *Nitria* come to take *Cyril*'s part, and assault the Governour, and wound him in the head with a stone: The people rise and put the Monks to flight, but take him that did the Fact, and he is tormented and put to death: *Cyril* pronounced the Monk a Martyr, but the people would not believe him one. At that time there was a Woman, *Hypatia*, so famous for learning, that she excelled in all Philosophy, and taught in the Schools (which *Plotinus* continued:) so that she had Scholars out of many Countries, and was oft with Princes, and Rulers, and for her modesty and gravity was much esteemed. *Orestes* the Governour oft talking with her, the people said, It was long of her that he was not reconciled to *Cyril*: They laid hold of her; drew her into a Church, stript her stark naked; rase the skin, and tare the flesh off her body with sharp shells till she dyed: they quarter her body and burn them to ashes: which turned to the great dishonour of *Cyril*.

Socr. c. 15.

§. 4. All this while the followers of *Chrysostome* remained Nonconformists and Separatists at *Constantinople*, and were called *Joannites*, and kept in Conventicles of their own. *Atticus* knew that love was the way to win them, and he purposing to take that way, writeth to *Cyril Alex.* that the restoring of *Chrysostome*'s name in the Church-Office would tend to heal their sad division, and give the Churches peace: He told *Cyril*, that *Populus majori ex parte per factionem scissus extra muros conventus egerit, & plerique sacerdotes & collega nostri Episcopi & a mutua communione discedentes, bonam plantationem Domini parum abest quin avulserint, &c.* "Most of the people "were gone and had separate meetings without the Walls; Priests and "Bishops separating from one another were like to destroy the Church, and "that if he consented not to restore the name of dead *Chrysostome*, the peo- "ple would do it without him, and he was loath that Church-administra- "tion should so fall into the hands of the Multitude, and therefore he "would take in *Chrysostom*'s name.

Alexander, a good Bishop of *Antioch* put him upon this way: But *Cyril* did vehemently oppose it (How did he obey *Rome* then, when the Pope had Excommunicated *Chrysostom*'s persecutors?) And first he pleaded, that the Schismaticks were but few (as if their own Bishop knew not better than he;) and that *Chrysostome* being ejected dyed a Lay-man, and was not to be numbered with the Clergy, that *Atticus* had the Magistrates on his side, that would bring them in by force (*Reader, there is nothing new under the sun: the things that have been are.*) And a little time would reduce most of them to the Church (though they increased;) That by favouring the Schismaticks he would lose the obedient (Conformists,) and would get nothing by pleasing such disobedient men, but strengthen them; That the Conformists (or obedient) were the far more considerable part, even the Bishops and Churches of *Egypt*, *Libia*, &c. and threatned that he would seek a reme-

Niceph. l. 14. c. 17.

dy

☞ dy himself; And reproaching *Chryfoſtome*, he telleth *Atticus*, That Conformity to the Canons was more to be obſerved than the pleaſing of ſuch Schiſmaticks, and that violating the Canons would do far more hurt than pleaſing ſuch men would do good; And that ſuch men will never be ſatisfied by reaſons, nor judge truly of themſelves: And he likened the reſtoring of *Chryſoſtome's* Name, to the putting in the name of the Traytor *Judas* with *Matthias*. He added, That if ignorant wilful fellows will forſake the Church, what loſs is it? And therefore that a few mens talk muſt not draw *Atticus* to pluck up the Church Sanctions. And as for *Alexander Antioch*. who perſwaded him to it, He was a bold-faced man that had deceived many; but his diſeaſe muſt not thus prevail, but be cured. Thus *Cyril* to *Atticus*: How oft have I heard juſt ſuch language? Reader, How hard is it to know what Hiſtory to believe, when it comes to the characterizing of adverſaries? How little is a domineering Prelates accuſation of ſuch men as *Chryſoſtome* to be credited? And how ordinary is it with ſuch, to call their betters, not what they are, but what they would have them thought, if not what they are themſelves?

But *Atticus* was wiſer than to take this Counſel; but obeyed the Wiſdom which is from above, which is firſt pure and then peaceable, gentle, &c. And God had ſo much mercy on *Conſtant*. as to defeat the evil Counſel of *Cyril*, and turn it into fooliſhneſs: For *Atticus* reſtored the name of *Chryſoſtome*, and uſed the Nonconformiſts kindly, and they came into the unity of the Church: And when *Proclus*, after him, fetch'd home his bones with honour, the breach was healed.

§. 5. No credible Hiſtory telleth us, that either *Theophilus* or *Cyril* did repent of this; (Though the Papiſts ſay, that the Pope Excommunicated *Theophilus* for it; yet they are now honoured, becauſe the Pope did own the Cauſe againſt *Neſtorius*.) *Theodoret's* Epiſtle to *Joh. Antioch.* upon the death of *Cyril*, taking his death for the Churches deliverance from a turbulent enemy of Peace, intimates, that he repented not: But (God only knoweth:) *Nicephorus* out of *Nicetas* the Philoſopher, tells us a report, that after all this, before he dyed, a dream did cure him; viz. That he ſaw Chryſoſtome *drive him out of his own houſe, having a Divine company with him; and that the Virgin* Mary *intreated for him, &c.* And that upon this *Cyril* changed his mind and admired *Chryſoſtome*, and repented of his imprudence and wrath, and hereupon called another Provincial Synod to honour him, and reſtore his name. (O *ductile Synods*! And O *unhappy Churches*, whoſe Paſtors muſt grow wiſe, and ceaſe deſtroying, after ſo long ſinning, and by an experience which coſteth the Church ſo dear!) And *Nicephorus* ſaith, that *Iſidore Peluſiota's* reproof conduced much hereto, *Niceph. lib.* 14. *cap.* 28.

§. 6. *Iſidore Peluſ.* words you may ſee at large in his Epiſtles: *Nicephorus* reciteth thus much of them, *lib.* 14. *c.* 53. *Cyrillum ſane ut hominem turbulentum refellens hæc ſcribit: Favoris affectio acutum non videt: Hoſtilis vero animi odium nil prorſus cernit: Quod ſi utroque, hoc vitio te purga-*
re

re ipsum & liberare vis, ne violentas sententias extorqueto, sed justo judicio causas committe: — *Multi qui* Ephesi *tecum congregati fuerunt, publicè te traducunt, quod inimicitias tuas persecutus sis, & non ritè & ordine juxta recta fidei sententiam ea qua Jesu Christi sunt quasiveris:* Theophili, *inquiunt, cùm ex fratre nepos sit, mores quoque illius imitatur: sicut ille apertam insaniam in sanctum & Deo dilectum* Joannem *effudit, ita & iste gloriam eodem affectat modo.* And after other sharper words, he addeth. *Ne ego ita condemner, & ne tu ipse etiam à Deo condemneris, contentiones sopito: Nec injuriæ propria vindicta quæ ab hominibus provenit, videntem Ecclesiam per æstuas actiones, fallas.* And of *Theophilus*, he saith. *Eum quatuor administris seu potius desertoribus suis circumvallatum, qui Deum amantem, Deumq; prædicantem virum* (Chrysost.) *hostiliter opprimeret, quum occasionem & causam impietatis suæ arripuisset.* Thus *Isidore* speaketh of them.

§. 7. *Atticus* dying, the Clergy were for *Philip* or *Proclus*, but the Laity choosing *Sisinnius* prevailed : He was a good and peaceable Man, and sent *Proclus* to be *Bishop* of *Cyzicum* ; but the People refused him and chose another. Socr. l. 7. c. 28.

§. 8. After the death of *Sisinnius* to avoid strife at home the Emperour caused *Nestorius* to be chosen, a Monk from the House by *Antioch*, whence *Chrysostome* came. He was loud, eloquent, and temperate: But hot against the liberty of those called Hereticks: He began thus to the Emperour, *Give me the Earth weeded from Hereticks, and I will give thee Heaven: Help me against the Hereticks and I will help thee against the Persians.* This turbulent hereticators must have the Sword do the work that belongeth to the Word: Princes must do their Work, and they will pretend that God shall for their sakes advance those Princes: But he was rewarded as he deserved. He presently enraged the *Arians* by going to pull down their Church, and they set it on Fire themselves to the hazard of the City. So that he was presently called a *Firebrand*. He vexed the *Novatians*, and raised stirs in many places, but the Emperour curbed him. *Antony* Bishop of *Germa* vexing the *Macedonians*, they killed him : whereupon they were put out of their Churches in many Cities. Ser. c. 29. c. 31.

§. 9. At last his own ruine came as followeth. *Nestorius* defended his Priest *Anastasius*, for saying, that *Mary was not to be called* Θεοτόκος, *the Mother of God*: This set all the City in a division, disputing of they well knew not what, and suspecting him of denying the Godhead of Christ : But he was of no such Opinion, but being eloquent and self-conceited read little of the Ancients Writings, nor was very learned ; and thought to avoid all extreams herein, and so would not call *Mary* the *Mother of God*, nor the *Mother of Man*, but the *Mother of Christ who was God and Man*. c. 32.

At that time some Servants of some Noble Men impatient of their Masters severities fled to the Church ; and with their Swords resisted all that would remove them, killed one Priest, wounded another and then killed themselves. c. 33

§. 10.

88   *Church-History of Bishops and*

§. 10. CXIII. The Emperour *Theodosius* jun. a Religious Peaceable Prince, weary of this Stir, called a General Council at *Ephesus*, and gave *Cyril* order to preside, (the Papists pretend that he was Pope *Celestine*'s Legate, who indeed joyned with him by his Letters, when he saw how things went.) Both *Cyril* and *Nestorius* desired the Council (Letters before having made no end.) *Celestine* nor the *Africanes* could not come, *Augustine* was dead: *Nestorius*, *Cyril*, and *Juvenal* of *Jerusalem* came: *John* of *Antioch* was thirty days journey off, and his Bishops much more, and stayed long. *Cyril* and *Memnon* of *Ephesus* would not stay for him: *Nestorius* came the first day; But *Cyril* and the rest being sharp against him, for not calling *Mary* the *Parent of God*, he said to them, *Ego bimestrem aut trimestrem Deum non facile dixerim: Proinde purus sum à vestro sanguine: in posterum ad vos non veniam.* That is, *I will not easily say, that God is two or three months old: I am clean from your bloud, and will come to you no more.* Some Bishops going with him, they met by themselves. *Cyril* summoneth him: He refuseth to come till *John* Bishop of *Antioch* came. They examine his Sermons and Witnesses, and condemn and depose him, as blasphemous against Christ. Three or four days after, *John* of *Antioch*, and his *Eastern* Bishops come: He took it ill that they stayed not for him: He joyneth in a distinct meeting with *Nestorius*: *Theodoret* accuseth *Cyril*'s Anathematismes of errour: They depose *Cyril* and *Memnon*: *Cyril*'s Synod citeth *John*: He refuseth to appear: They depose him and his adherent Bishops: And thus two Synods sate deposing and condemning one another: Both Parties send their Agents to the Emperour: His Officer *Candidianus* took part with *Nestorius*: He sendeth another *Johannes Comes*, with charge to depose the heads of both the deposing Parties, and so to make good both their depositions, viz. *Nestorius*, *Cyril*, and *Memnon*: *Candidianus* before had told the Emperour, how all was done in violence and confusion, and he had pronounced all Null, and charged them to begin all a-new. When *Johannes Comes* came, he wrote to the Emperour, that *All being in confusion, and Cyril and Memnon fortifying themselves, he summoned them all to come to him; And lest they should fall together by the ears, (which he feared, by reason of their strange fierceness) he ordered their coming in so, that it might not be promiscuously:* Nestorius *and* John *of* Antioch *being come first,* Cyril *and his company (except* Memnon*) came next, and presently a great tumult and stir began,* Cyril*'s Party saying, that the sight of* Nestorius*, whom they had deposed, was not to be endured: They would have the Scripture read: But those that favoured* Cyril*, said, that the Divine and terrible Scriptures were not to be read without* Cyril*, nor while* Nestorius *and the Oriental Bishops were present; and for this there was a Sedition, yea, a War, and Fight: The same said the Bishops that were with* John*, that* Cyril *ought not to be present at the Reading of the Scriptures, he and* Memnon *being deposed: The day being far spent thus, he attempted, excluding* Cyril *and* Nestorius*, to read the Emperours Orders to the rest; But* Cyril*'s Party would not hear them, because they said* Cyril *and* Memnon *were unlawfully deposed: He had much a-do to perswade them at last, (and indeed thrusting out* Nesto-

Bin.p 786.

Nestorius and Cyril by force) so much as to hear the Emperours writing. But he made them hear it: In which Nestorius, Cyril, and Memnon, were deposed. Those that were with John heard it friendly, and approved it: The other clamoured, that Cyril and Memnon were wrongfully deposed: To avoid Sedition, Nestorius was committed to Candidianus Comes, and Cyril to Jacobus Comes (and Memnon after.) He concludeth, *Quod si pientissimos Episcopos videre implacatos & irreconciliabiles,* (*Nescio unde in hanc rabiem & asperitatem venerint,*) &c. This was his Description of the carriage of this Council.

Both Parties sent several Bishops, as their Delegates, to *Constantinople:* The Emperour would not permit them to come nearer than *Chalcedon,* (which is as *Southwark* to *London.*) While they wait there, *Theodorite,* one of *John's* Party against *Cyril,* wrote back, that the Court was against *Nestorius,* but most of the People were for them. It's said that *Pulcheria,* the Emperours Sister, was much against him. At last Pope *Celestine's* Legates came to the Council and took *Cyril's* Part. The Emperour saw how great the breach would be, if *Cyril* were deposed, and he revoked the deposition of him and *Memnon,* but not of *Nestorius,* and wrote a threatning Letter to *Cyril* and *John,* to charge them to agree and joyn in Communion, and not divide the Churches, or else what he would do to them both. These terrible words cured them both of Heresie: They presently consulted, and sent each other their Confessions, and found (good men) that they were of one mind and did not know it. And so having their will upon *Nestorius* and his adherents, the rest united. But so, that *John* and *Theodorite* took *Cyril* for a Firebrand to the last.

§. 11. *Nestorius* being deposed retired quietly to his Monastery by *Antioch,* and lived there in honour four years, but then was banished and dyed in distress: (some Fable that he was eaten with Worms.)

§. 12. The event of this Council was, that a Party of the Orientals adhered to *Nestorius*, took *Cyril* and this Council for Hereticks, and to this day continue a numerous Party of Christians, called Hereticks by the *Pontificians,* because they are not for them: And the *Eutychians* on all occasions accused their Adversaries the Orthodox to be *Nestorians,* and the Churches were inflamed by the dissention through many Ages following.

§. 13. And what was really the Controversie between them? Some accuse *Nestorius* as asserting two persons in Christ as well as two natures, which he still denyed: Others accuse *Cyril* as denying two Natures: But his words about this were many, but he affirmed two Natures before the Union, (and so did the *Eutychians*) but one after: *David Derodon* a most learned *Frenchman* hath written a Treatise *De Supposito,* in which he copiously laboureth to prove that *Nestorius* was Orthodox, holding two Natures in one Person, and that *Cyril* and his Council were Hereticks, holding one Nature only after Union, and that he was a true *Eutychian,* and *Dioscorus* did but follow him, and that the Council of *Chalcedon* condemned *Nestorius* and stablished his Doctrine, and extolled *Cyril* and condemned

N his

☞ his Doctrine. But for my part I make no doubt that, *de re, they were both fully of one mind, and differed only about the aptitude of a phrase:* Whether it were an apt Speech to call *Mary* the *Parent of God*, and *to say that God was two moneths old, God hungred, God dyed and rose, &c.* which *Nestorius* denyed, and *Cyril* and the Council with him affirmed. And what hath the World suffered by this Word Warr. But which was in the right.

We commonly say that *forma denominat, & locutio formalis est maximè propria.* And so *Nestorius* spake most properly: But Use is the Master of Speech, which tyeth us not always to that strictness, and so *Cyril* well interpreted spake well: especially if the contrary side should intrude a duality of Persons, by their denying the Phrase: While *Nestorius* accuseth *Cyril* as if he spake *de abstracto*, he wrongeth him: while *Cyril* accuseth *Nestorius* as if he spake *de concreto*, he wronged him: They both meant that *Mary* was the Mother of *Christ who was God,* and of the *Union* of the Natures, but not the Mother of *Christ as God*, or of the Deity. So that one speaking *de concreto*, and the other *de abstracto*, one *materially* and the other *formally*, in the heat of Contention they hereticated each other and kindled a flame not quenched to this day, about a word while both were of one mind.

§. 14. If any say it is arrogancy in me to say that such men had not skill enough to escape the deceit of such an ambiguity, I answer, humility maketh not men blind: The thing proveth it self. Judg by these following words of *Nestorius* and *Cyril* what they held.

§. 15. Nestorius *Epist. ad* Cyril: *Nomen hoc, Christus, utramque naturam, patibilem scilicet & impatibilem in unica Persona denotat. Quò idem Christus patibilis & impatibilis concipi queat; Illud quidem secundùm humanam naturam, hoc verò secundùm Divinam.* ☞ *— In eo non injuria te laudo quod distinctionem naturarum secundùm Divinitatis & humanitatis rationem harumque in unâ duntaxat personâ conjunctionem prædicas. — Et quòd Divinitatem pati non potuisse disertè pronuncias: Hæc enim omnia & vera sunt & Orthodoxa; & vanis omnium hæreticorum circa Domini naturas opinationibus quàm maximè adversa sunt. Non dicit, solvite Divinitatem meam & intra triduum exsuscitabo illam; sed solvite Templum hoc, &c. — Ubicunque Divinæ Scripturæ Dominicæ dispensationis mentionem faciunt, tum incarnationem, tum ipsam mortem & Passionem, non Divinæ, sed Humanæ Christi naturæ semper tribuunt. Ergo si rem diligentius consideremus, sacra Virgo non Deipara, sed Christipara, appellanda erit (*which signifieth that She is the Parent of the Humane nature, receiving the Divine in Union of Person.*) — Quis ita desipiat ut unigenitii Divinitatem Spiritus sancti creaturam esse credat. — Sunt innumeræ sententiæ quæ Divinitatem neque nuper natam, neque corporeæ perpessionis capacem esse testantur. — Rectum Evangelicæque traditioni consentaneum est, ut Christi Corpus Divinitatis Templum esse confiteamur, illudque nexu adeò sublimi Divinoque & admirabili ipsi conjunctum esse statuamus, ut Divina natura ea sibi vendicet, quæ Coporis alioqui sunt propria: Verùm propter eam sive communicationis sive appropriationis notionem, nativitatem, passionem, mortem cæterasque carnis propietates Divino Verbo*

Verbo afcribere, id demùm, mi frater, mentis eſt paganorum more verè errantis aut certè infani Apollinarii & Arii aliorumque hæreticorum morbo aut alio etiam graviore laborantis. Nam qui appropriationis vocabulum ita detorquent illos Deum verbum lactationis participem & ſuccedanei incrementi capacem & ob formidinem Paſſionis, &c.—

Neſtor. *Epiſt.* 2. *ad* Cæleſt. *Quidam de Eccleſiaſticis quandam contemperationis imaginem ex Deitate & Humanitate accipientes, corporis paſſionei audent ſuperfundere Deitati unigeniti, & immutabilem Deitatem ad naturam corporis tranſiiſſe confingunt, atque utramque naturam qnæ per conjunctionem ſummam & inconfuſam* Unica Perſona *unigeniti adoratur, contemperatione confundunt.*

Neſtor. *Epiſt. ad* Alexand. Hierapol. *Concil.* 5. *Act. Seſſ.* 6. *Oportet manere naturas in ſuis proprietatibus, & ſic per mirabilem & eminem rationem excedentem unitatem unum confiteri filium. Non duas perſonas unam facimus, ſed una appellatione* Chriſti *duas naturas ſimul ſignificamus.*

In Scriptis Neſtorii *recitatis in Concil.* Epheſ. 1. *Tom.* 2. *c.* 8. *Idem omnino & Infans erat & Infantem habitabat.* Item, *Deus Verbum ante incarnationem & Filius erat & Deus erat; At verò in noviſſimis temporibus ſervulem quoque formam aſſumpſit; Cæterum cum antè Filius eſſet, Filius appellaretur, attamen poſt Carnem aſſumptam, ſeorſim per ſe Filii nomine appellari non debet, ne duos Filios videamur inducere.* — *Item, voce* Chriſti *tanquam utriuſque naturæ notionem complectente accepta, citrà periculum illum aſſumpſiſſe ſervi formam aſſeverat & Deum nominat; dictorum vim ad naturarum dualitatem manifeſte referens.*

Cyril *lib. de recta fide ad Reginas* pag. 53. *de* Neſtorianis, *Verbum & humanitas (ut ipſi loquuntur) in unam Perſonam concurrunt: Unionis enim quæ eſt ſecundum naturam & quæ una eſt, nulla apud eos habetur ratio* — *Et p.* 66. *de* Neſtor. *Si Chriſtus ſola unione ſecundum Perſonam cum Dei Verbo conjunctionem habeat, (ſic enim illi loquuntur) quomodo in illis qui pereunt Evangelium Dei abſconditum eſt?* By which Cyril ſpeaketh for one Nature, and Neſtorius for one Perſon.

Cyril. *l.* 1. *adverſ.* Neſtor. p. 16. thus reporteth Neſtorius ſaying, *Hic qui videtur Infans, hic qui recens apparet, hic qui faſciis corporalibus eget, hic qui ſecundum viſibilem eſſentiam recenter eſt editus, Filius univerſorum opifex, Filius qui ſuæ opis faſciis diſſolubilem creaturæ naturam aſtringit.* — Item, *Infans enim eſt Deus liberæ poteſtate; tantum abeſt (*Arie*) ut Deus Verbum ſic ſub Dei poteſtate.* — Again, *Novimus ergo Humanitatem infantis & Deitatem; Filiationis Unitatem ſervamus in Deitatis humanitatiſque natura:* ſaith Derodon, I dare boldly ſay no Chriſtian hath hitherto ſpoke trulier and plainer of the Unity of Chriſts Perſon in two Natures, than Neſtorius.

Ex lib. Cyril 2. *Cont.* Neſtor.*p*.4. He thus reporteth Neſtorius, *Hoc quod Chriſtus eſt nullam patitur διαίρεσιν, ſed Deitatis, & Humanitatis eſt διαίρεσις: Chriſtus qua Chriſtus eſt ἀδιαίρετος; neque enim duos Chriſtos habemus neque duos Filios: Non eſt enim apud nos primus & ſecundus, neque alius & alius, neque rurſus alius Filius & alius rurſus; ſed ipſe ille unus eſt duplex non dignitate, ſed natura.*

Cyril faith that *Nestorius* was the Disciple of *Diodorus Tarsensis* from whom he learnt his Heresie, *Epist. ad Succes.* and that he was the hearer of *Theodorus Mopsuest* condemned in Council, for the same Heresie as *Nestorius*. But faith *Derodon, Facundus toto lib.* 4. largely proveth that *Diod. Tarsensis* was Orthodox by the testimonies of *Athanasius, Basil, Chrysostome, Epiphanius, &c. Et lib.* 3. *&* 9. he proveth the same of *Theod. Mopsuest.* citing the places where he asserteth two Natures in one Person, *Vid. Facund. l.* 3.*c*.2. *& l.*9.*c.*3.*&* 4. And *Liberatus in Brevior. c.* 10. faith: *Diod. Tarsensis & Theod. Mopsuest. & alii Episcopi contra* Eunomium *&* Apollinarem *unius Naturæ assertores libros composuerunt, duas in Christo ostendentes naturas in una persona* ! & ibid. *Duas* Joh. Antiocheni *Epistolas, primam & tertiam, laudes* Theod. Mopsuest. *continentes* Chalced. *Synodus Oecumenica per relationem suam Martiano Imperatori directam, suscepit & confirmavit.*

§. 16. By all this it is evident that *Nestorius* was Orthodox; and owned two Natures in one Person: And that the Controversie was *de nomine*, unless *Cyril* was an *Eutychian*. And that it is a more accurate cautelous Speech *à formâ* to say that God did not increase, hunger, die, rise, *&c.* than to say God did these; because it seemeth to intimate that Christ did suffer these, *quà Deus, As God*, which is blasphemy. But that it is a true speech that *God did suffer these*, meaning not *quà Deus*, but *Christus qui Deus*: and that one Syllable of distinction between *quà* and *qui* might have saved these Councils their odious Contentions and Fighting, and the Churches for many Ages the Convulsions, Distractions and mutual Condemnations that followed, and the Papists the odious violation of Christian Charity and Peace in calling the Eastern Followers of *Nestorius, Nestorian* Hereticks to this day. Judge how much the World was beholden to *Cyril, Cælestine*, and this Council.

§. 17. Obj. *By this you make the Bishops and Councils to be all Fools, that know not what they do, and to be the very plagues and shame of humane nature, that would kindle such a flame not yet quenched about nothing.*

Answ. 1. If we must measure, *fidem per personas*, yea, judge of matter of Fact by respect of persons, judge so by the Councils at *Ariminum, Syrmium, Milan, Tyre* also; Judge so by the Second Council of *Ephesus*, and abundance such: How shall we know which of them so to judge by? 2. Good men have foul Vices: Faction, and Contention, and Pride, have undeniably troubled the Churches: When *Concil. Carthag.* 6. forbad Bishops to read the Books of *Gentiles*, it is no wonder that the number of Learned Bishops was small; And when no Bishop was to be removed from place to place, but all Bishops made out of an Inferiour degree, usually of the same Parish; Yea, and when Academies were so rare, it is past doubt that Learned Bishops were rare: When *Nectarius* must be the great Patriarch, that was yet no Christian, and when *Synesius*, because he had Philosophical knowledge, is chosen Bishop, even before he believed the Resurrection; When they were such, as credible *Nazianzene, Isidore Pelusiota*, and long after *Salvian* describes. It is not I, but these knowing

Witnesses,

their Councils abridged. 93

Witnesses, and their own actions, that characterize them. Doth not *Socrates*, that knew *Nestorius*, say, that he was not Learned? And he, and others, that *Cyril* was high and turbulent? *Theodoret* was a Learned man, and he thought no better of his Adversaries.

The Objections against *Nestorius* and *Theodo^rus Mopsuest*, are largely answered by *Derodon*, *ubi supr.à*.

§. 18. The same *Derodon* laboureth to prove, that *Cyril* was an Heretick, the Father of the *Eutychians*, and so were the *Ephes*. Council, and Pope *Celestine*. His proofs against *Cyril* are reduced to these Heads. 1. His express asserting *One Nature* only in Christ. *Epist.* 2. *ad success. Diocesar. Quæ igitur necessitas ipsum pati in propriâ naturâ, si post unionem dicatur una verbi Natura incarnata?*

Item, Ignorant rursus qui rectè pervertunt, quòd juxta Veritatem una sit natura Verbi incarnata: si enim unus est filius naturâ & verè Verbum quod ineffabiliter ex Deo Patre est genitum, & si idem per assumptionem carnis non exanimis sed animatæ animâ intelligente processit homo de muliere —— *Non enim de solis simplicibus Unum secundum naturam verè dicitur, sed etiam de iis quæ juxta compositionem conveniunt, ut est* v.g. *homo, qui constat anima & corpore, hæc enim inter se differunt specie, veruntamen unta unam naturam hominis absolvunt, quamvis adsit ratione compositionis differentia secundum naturam rerum, in unitatem concurrentium: superfluè igitur sermonibus immorantur qui dicunt, si una est natura verbi incarnata, sequitur ut permixtio confusioque generetur.*

Nestorius third Objection was from Christs voluntary passions; *Ergo duas naturas subsistere post unionem indivisè.* Cyril answereth, *Adversus rursus hæc eorum propositio nihilominus iis qui dicunt unam esse Filii naturam incarnatam idque velut ineptum volentes ostendere, ubique duas naturas subsistentes conantur astruere; sed ignorant quæcunque non distinguuntur solâ mentis consideratione, ea prorsus etiam in diversitatem distinctam omnifariam ac privatim à se mutuò segregari: c. g. Homo —— duas in eo naturas intelligimus, unam animæ, alteram corporis, sed cum sola discreverimus intelligentiâ & differentiam subtili contemplatione secernentis imaginatione conceperimus, non tamen seorsim ponimus naturas, sed unius esse intelligimus. Ita ut illa duæ jam non sint duæ, sed ambæ unum animal absolvunt. Tandem ita concludit.* ☞ *Hæc igitur ex quibus est unus & solus filius Dominus Jesus Christus cogitationibus complexi, duas quidam naturas unitas asserimus; post unionem verò tanquam adempta jam in duas distinctione unam esse credimus filii naturam tanquam unius, sed inhumati & incarnati.* It's strange, how *Cyril* and the *Eutychians* meant, that Christs Natures were two before the Union. Did they think that the Humanity existed before the Union?

So *Epist.* 1. Cyril. *ad success. Nihil injusti facimus dicentes ex duabus naturis factum esse concursum in unitatem; post unionem verò non distinguimus naturas ab invicem, nec in duos filios unum & individuum partimur, sed dicimus unum filium, & sicut Partes alterum erant, Unam Naturam Dei Verbi incarnati.*

Eadem dicit Epist. ad Acacium Melet. *Post unionem sublata iam in duas distinctione*

☞ *stinctione unam esse credimus filii naturam, tanquam unius, sed inhumati.*

Cyril. *Epist. ad Eulog. Presb. Nos illas (duas naturas) adunantes unum filium, unum Dominum confitemur, deinde & unam per naturam incarnatam, quod & de communi homine dicendum.——Dum unitatem confitemur, non distinguuntur amplius quæ sunt unita: sed unus jam est Christus & una est ipsius tanquam incarnati Verbi natura.*

Cyril. *lib. cont.* Nestor. p. 31. *Hic recentissimæ impietatis inventor quamvis Christum unum se dicere simulet, attamen ubique naturas distinguit.*

Et p. 45. *Quomodo Christum unum & individuum dicis esse duplicem natura?*

Cyril. *lib. de recta fide ad reginos* p. 63. *Assumitur in unum Deitatis Naturam unus Christus Jesus per quem omnia.*

Cyril. *Dialog. Quod unus sit Christus.* [*Unum porro filium & unam ipsius Naturam esse dicimus, licet carnem anima intelligente præditam assumpserit.*]

Many more such passages are in Cyril. Here *Derodon* proveth, 1. That Cyril took not φύσις for *Persona.* 2. That he took not διαίρεσις for *Division* but *Distinction*: If he did, it was an ill quarrel, when *Nestorius* asserted not a Division, but a Distinction. 3. That Cyril still reproveth *Nestorius* for asserting only a union *secundùm personam*, and not *secundùm naturam*. 4. That Cyril (as *Dioscorus*) declares what union he meaneth, not by Confusion, Commixtion or Transmutation, but by Composition, (and so said the *Eutychians.*)

The second order of *Derodons* proofs is from all the places where Cyril pleads for one *hypostasis*, and he sheweth that by *hypostasis* Cyril meant *natura* or *substantia singularis.* The citations are too long to be repeated.

3. His proofs are from all the Texts where he saith the *Word*, and *Humanity* concurred εἰς ἕν.

His fourth proof that Cyril was an *Eutychian*, is from all those places where he saith, that the Godhead and Manhood are made *one nature* as the *soul and body of man are.*

His fifth order of proofs is from the words where he oft attributeth the same operations, and the same attributes to both nature.

His sixth proof is from the testimony of *Ibas Edes. apud Facund. l. 6. c. 3. Gennad. Const. ibid. l. 2. p. 77, 78. Johan. Antioch. Theodoret, &c.*

§. 20. For my part, I again say, past doubt, that neither *Nestorius* nor Cyril were Heretical *de re*; but that they were of one mind, and that one spake of the *concrete*, and the other of the *abstract*; that one spake of *Christus qui Deus*, and the other of *Christus quà Deus*. But (pardon truth, or be deceived still) ignorance, pride, and envy, and faction, and desire to please the Court, made Cyril and his Party, by quarrelsome Heretication, to kindle that lamentable flame in the World. But sin serveth the sinners turn but for the present, and becometh afterward his shame. All the Bishops would not follow Cyril. At this day the falsly Hereticated *Nestorians* (saith Breerwood *Enquir.* p. 139.) inhabites a great part of the *East*, for besides the Countries of *Babylon, Assyria, Mesopotamia, Parthia*, and *Media*, they are spread far and wide, both *Northerly* to *Cataya*, and *Southerly* to *India*: Marcus Paulus

Paulus tells us of them and no other Christians in *Tartary*, as in *Caſſar*, *Sarmacham*, *Carcham*, *Chinchintalas*, *Tanguth*, *Suchir*, *Ergimul*, *Tenduc*, *Caraim*, *Mangi*, *&c.* so that beyond *Tigris* there are few other Christians. The *Perſian* Emperours forced the Christians to *Neſtorianiſme*; Their Patriarch hath his Seat at *Muſal* in *Meſopotamia* or the Monastery of St. *Ermes* near it, in which City the *Neſtorians* have 15 Temples: They are falſly accuſed still to hold two Persons in Christ: They ſay as *Neſtorius* himſelf ſaid, *You may ſay that Chriſt's Mother is the Parent of God, if you will expound it well, but it is improper and dangerous.* They take *Neſtorius*, *Diodorus Tarſenſis* and *Theodorus Mopſueſt*, for holy Men ; They renounce the Council *Epheſ.* and all that owned it, and deteſt *Cyril*. They Communicate in both kinds: They uſe not auricular Confeſſion : nor Confirmation : nor Crucifixes on their Croſſes : Their Prieſts have liberty for firſt, ſecond, or third Marriages, &c. *Breerwood, ibid*, p. 144.

§. 21. I need no other proof for my opinion, that theſe Biſhops ſet the World on fire about a Word, being agreed in ſenſe, than the reconciliation of the Patriarchs *Cyril* and *John* when forced, and their Parties, profeſſing that they meant the ſame and knew it not. *Obj.* But they all condemned *Neſtorius*. *Anſ.* To quiet the World, and to pleaſe the Courtiers and violent Biſhops. And the Emperour himſelf (ſaith *Socrates*, l.7.c.41. one that excelled all the Prieſts in modeſty and meekneſs, and could not away with perſecution,) was the more againſt *Neſtorius* becauſe he was a perſecutor himſelf.

Read *Theodoret*'s Homily againſt *Cyril*, *Bin.* p. 907. and *Johan. Antioch. ibid.* But neither the one ſide [*Neſtorius hæreſiarcha impiiſſimus*,] nor the other ſide [*Cyrillus ſuperbus & blaſphemus*] ſhould ſignifie much with men that know what liberty adverſe Biſhops uſed.

§. 22. As for them that ſay, *Neſtorius did diſſemble when he aſſerted the Unity of two Natures in one Perſon: and is not to be judged of by his own words*, I take them to be the firebrands of the world, and unworthy the regard of ſober men, who pretend to know mens judgments better than themſelves, and allow not mens own deliberate profeſſion to be the notice of their Faith.

§. 23. When the Emperour ſaw that there was no reconciling the Biſhops, but by force, he authorized *Ariſtolaus*, a Lay-Magiſtrate, to call *Cyril* and *Joh. Antioch.* to *Nicomedia*, and keep them both there till they were agreed : whereupon *John* communed with his Biſhops, and they yielded, having no remedy, to the depoſition of *Neſtorius*, the Ordination of *Maximinianus* in his ſtead, and communion among themſelves. This is called another Council.

It would grieve one to read the Emperour *Theodoſius* importuning *Simeon Stylites*, a poor Anchorite, to try whether by Prayer and Counſel he could bring the Biſhops to Unity, and concluding, [*This diſcord doth ſo trouble me, that I judge that this only hath been the chief occaſion of all my calamities.*] *Bin.* p. 928.

§. 24. CXIV. *An.* 433. There was a Council called at *Rome* to clear
Pope

Pope *Sixtus* from an accusation of one *Bassus*, of ravishing a Nun.

§. 25. CXV. There is talk of a Council at *Rome* to clear one *Polychronius* Bishop of *Jerusalem*, of accusations of *Simony*: But contradictions make this (and the former) to be altogether uncertain.

§. 26. CXVI. The *Armenians* in Council are said to condemn *Nestorian* Books.

§. 27. CXVII. A Council was held at *Constant.* to decide the Controversie between the *Alexandrian* and *Constant.* Bishops, which should be greatest, and rule the East; where it was carried for *Constant.* And *Theodoret* pleading for *Antioch*, *Dioscorus* (the *Alex.* Agent) hated him ever after, (as he saith *Epist.* 86.)

§. 28. CXVIII. *An.* 439. A Council at *Regiense* of 13 Bishops did somewhat about Ordinations, &c.

☞ §. 29. About this time *Leo* at *Rome* was fain to forbid bowing toward the *East*, because the *Manichees* joyned among them, and bowed to the Sun, and could not be else distinguished from the Orthodox, *Bin. de Leone.*

§. 30. CXIX. A Council at *Arausican* repeated some old disciplinary Canons.

§. 31. CXX. *Leo* held a Council at *Rome* of Bishops, Priests, and Laymen, to detect the wickedness of the *Manichees*, and warn men to avoid them.

§. 32. CXXI. *An.* 445. *Leo* held a Council at *Rome* against *Hilary* Bishop of *Arles*, for disobedience to his Decrees.

§. 33. CXXII. A Council called *General* in *Spain*, recited the Profession of Faith against the *Priscillianists*.

CHAP

CHAP. VI.

Councils about the Eutychian Herefie *and fome others.*

§. 1. CXXIII. *Cyril* had by many words fo carried the bufinefs at *Ephefus* againſt *Neſtorius*, and himſelf fo often ſaid, that after the *Union*, the *Natures were one*, that his Admirers took that for a certain truth : But when that quarrel was over, Truth was truth ſtill, and the Orthodox would not fly from it, for fear of being called *Neſtorians*; for they diſclaimed *Neſtorius*, but diſowned the Doctrine of *One nature*. *Eutyches* an *Archimandrite*, and *Dioſcorus*, Succeſſour to *Cyril*, belived that they did but tread in his ſteps, and hold to the *Ephef.* Council. But that would not now ſerve, when the Scene was changed.

§. 2. Reader, It is uſeful to thee, to know truly the ſtate of this Tragical Controverſie, which had more dividing and direful effects than the former. The *Eutychians* ſay, that *Chriſt before their Union by incarnation had two natures*, that is, conſidered mentally, as not united; but *after the union had but one nature.* They took up this as againſt *Neſtorianiſme*. The truth is, Though they ſtill go for deſperate Hereticks, I verily believe that all the quarrel was but about ambiguous words : ſome of them underſtood the word [*Nature*] in the ſame ſenſe as their Adverſaries took the word [*Hypoſtaſis*] or [*Perſon.*] And (it's ſad that it ſhould be true, but) moſt of them confounded [*Unity undiſtinguiſhed*] and [*Uniting undivided.*] The *Eutychians* thought, How can that be called *Unity* which maketh not *one of two*? And no doubt the *Natures are One*; But *One what*? Not *One Nature*, but *One Perſon*; Yet (to bring off *Cyril*) it may be ſaid that even the *Natures are One*, in oppoſition to *Diviſion* or *Separation*, but not *One* in oppoſition to *diſtinction.* He that had but diſtinguiſhed theſe two clearly to them, and explained the word [*Nature*] clearly, had better ended all the Controverſie than it was ended. It's plain that *Cyril* and the *Eutychians* allowed *mental diſtinction*, though not that the Mind ſhould ſuppoſe them *divided :* And it's certain that the Orthodox meant no more.

§. 3. He that readeth but Philoſophers, Schoolmen, and late Writers, (ſuch as *Fortun. Licetus de natura, &c.*) will ſee how little they are agreed about the meaning of the word [*Nature*,] and how unable to procure agreement in the conception. They that ſay it is *principium motus & Quietis*, are contradicted, as confounding divers *Principia* : and as confounding *Active Natures*, and *Paſſive*, the *Active* only being *Principium Motus*, and the *Paſſive*, *Principium quietis.* And on ſuch accounts the *Eutychians* pleaded for *One Nature*; becauſe in Chriſt incarnate they ſuppoſed that

O the

the Divine Nature was the *Principium primum motus*, and that all Chrifts actions were done by it, and that the humane foul, being moved by the Divinity, was but *Principium fubordinatum*, which they thought was improperly called *Principium*, (As moft Philofophers fay, that *Forma generica* is improperly called *forma hominis*, becaufe *one thing* hath but *one form*, fo they thought that *one perfon* had but one proper *Principium motus*.

§. 4. Alas how few Bifhops then could diftinguifh as *Derodon* doth, and our common Metaphyficks, between, 1. *Individuum*, 2. *Prima fubftantia*, 3. *Natura*, 4. *Suppofitum*, 5. *Perfona*, 6. and have diftinguifhed, a right *effence* and *hypoftafis*, or *fubfiftence*, &c. and defined all thefe. *Nature* faith *Derodon de fuppof.* p. 5. is taken in nine fenfes; But the *fenfe* was not *here agreed on*, before they *difputed of the matter*.

Even about the *Nature of Man*, it is difputed, whether he confift not of *many natures*? Whether every Element (Earth, Water, Air, Fire) retain not its feveral *Nature* in the Body, or whether the Soul be Mans only *Nature*, and whether as intellectual, and fenfitive and vegetative, or only in one of thefe? And is it not pity that fuch queftions fhould be raifed about the perfon of Chrift by felf-conceited Bifhops, and made neceffary to falvation, and the world fet on fire, and divided by them? Is this good ufage of the Faith of Chrift, the Souls of Men, and the Church of God.

§. 5. But to the Hiftory: At a Council of *Conftantinop*. under *Flavianus*, *Eufebius* Bifhop of *Dorileum* accufed *Eutyches*, for affirming Heretically as aforefaid, (that *after the Union Chrift had but one Nature*.) *Eutiches* is fent for: He refufeth to come out of his Monaftery; After many Citations, he ftill refufing, they judge him to be brought by force: He firft delayeth: Then craveth of the Emperour the prefence of Magiftrates, that he be not calumniated by the Bifhops. He is condemned, but recanteth not.

§. 6. A meeting of Bifhops at *Tyre* cleared *Ibas Edeff.* from the accufation of *Neftorianifme*, made by four Excommunicate Priefts, two of them perjured; and reconciled him to fuch Priefts for Peace fake.

§. 7. Another meeting of Bifhops at *Berythum*, cleared *Ibas* from a renewed accufation of *Neftorianifme*, being faid to have fpoken evil of *Cyril*. An Epiftle of his to *Maris* a Bifhop, was accufed, which the Council at *Calcedon* after abfolved, and the next General Council condemned.

§. 8. CXXIV. Another Council is called at *Conftantinople*, by the means of fome Courtiers, in favour to *Eutiches*, where, upon the teftimony of fome Bifhops, that *Flavianus* Bifhop of *Conftantinople* condemned him himfelf, before the Synod did it, and that the Records were altered, all was nullified that at the laft Synod was done againft him.

§. 9. CXXV. *Theodofius* calleth a fecond General Council at *Ephefus* *an*. 449. and maketh *Diofcorus* Bifhop of *Alex*. Prefident. *Diofcorus* forbad *Ibas* and *Theodoret* to be there, as being *Neftorians*: The Emperour himfelf was fo much for peace, and fo deeply before engaged in *Cyril*'s caufe cause against *Nestorius*, that he thought it levity to pull down all so soon again, the *Eutychians* perswading him that they stuck to *Cyril* and the *Ephesine* and *Nicene* Council. *Dioscorus* thinking the same, that *Eutiches* and *Cyril* were of one mind, and that it was *Nestorianisme* which they were against, carried matters in this Synod as violently as *Cyril* had done in the former. The Bishops perceiving the Emperours, the Courtiers, and *Dioscorus* mind, could not resist the stronger side. The Bishop of *Rome* was commanded by the Emperour to be present. He sent his Legates; with his Judgment in Writing of the Cause. The Emperour forbad those to be Speakers that had before judged *Eutyches*. The *Roman* Legates excepted that *Dioscorus* presided: (It seemeth the *Eastern* Empire and Church, then believed not that the Popes precedency was *jure divino*.) *Dioscorus* declareth, that the Council was not called to decide any matter of Faith, but to judge of the proceedings of *Flavianus* against *Eutyches*. The Acts of the *Constant*. Synod (after the Emperours Letters) being read, *Eutyches* is absolved: *Domnus*, Patriarch of *Antioch*, *Juvenal*, Patriarch of *Jerusalem*, the Bishop of *Ephesus*, and the rest, subscribed the absolution, (which after they said they did for fear, when another Emperour changed the Scene.) This being done, the Acts of the former *Ephes*. Council were read, and all Excommunicate that did not approve them. (So that this Council of *Eutychians* thought verily the former was of their mind.) Four Bishops, *Flavianus*, *Eusebius*, *Doryl*, *Ibas Edes*. and *Theodoret Cyri*, are condemned and deposed: All the Bishops subscribed except the Popes Legates; so that, saith *Binnius*, *In hoc tam horrendo Episcoporum suffragio, sola navilula Petri incolumis emergens salvatur*, p. 1017. Judge by this, First, Whether Councils may erre, Secondly, Whether they are the just Judges or Keepers of Tradition, Thirdly, Whether all the World always believed the Popes Infallibility, or Governing power over them, when all that Council voted contrary to him.

Flavianus here offering his appeal, was beaten and abused, and dyed of the hurt, (as was said in *Concil. Calced.* and by *Liberatus*.) But this was no quenching, but a kindling of the fire of Episcopal Contentions: *Theodosius* missed of his end.

§. 10. CXXVI. *Leo* at *Rome* in a Synod condemneth this *Ephesian* Council.

§. 11. CXXVII. *Dioscorus* in a Council at *Alexandria*, Excommunicateth *Leo*.

§. 12. CXXVIII. *Theodosius* the Emperour being dead, *Martian* was against the *Eutychians*: *Anatolius* at a Synod at *Constantinople*, maketh an Orthodox Profession of his Faith, like *Leo*'s.

§. 13. CXXIX. And at *Milan* a Council owneth *Leo*'s judgment.

§. 14. CXXX. Now cometh the great Council at *Calcedon*, under the new Emperour *Martian*, where all is changed for a time; Yet *Pulcheria* who married him and made him Emperour, and whose power then was great, was the same that before had been against *Nestorius* in her Brothers

thers reign: Never was it truer than in the Cafe of General Councils, that the Multitude of Phyficians, exafperateth the Difeafe, and killeth the Patient. The word [δυσνοχθ] the [one nature after union] the words [one will and one opperation] had never done half fo much mifchief in the Church, if the erroneous had been confuted by neglect, and Councils had not exafperated, enraged, and engaged them, and fet all the World on taking one fide or another. One skilfull healing m in that could have explicated ambiguous terms, and perfwaded men to Love and Peace, till they had underftood themfelves and one another, had more befriended Truth, Piety, and the Church, than all the Hereticating Councils did.

§. 15. If what *Socrates* writeth of *Theodofius junior* be true, (as we know no reafon to doubt) God owned his Moderation by Miracles, notwithftanding his favouring the *Eutychians*, more than he did any ways of violence. *Socrates* faith, *l. 7. c. 41, 42*, that *Theodofius* was the *mildeft man in the World, for which caufe God fubdued his enemies to him without flaughter and bloodfhed*; as his Victory over *John* and the Barbarians fhew: Of which he faith, Firft, Their Captain *Rugas* was kill'd with a thunder-bolt; Secondly, A Plague killed the greateft part of his Soldiers; Thirdly, Fire from Heaven confumed many that remained. And *Proclus* the Bifhop being a man of great Peace and Moderation, hurting and perfecuting none, was confirmed by thefe providences in his lenity, being of the Emperours mind, and perfwading the Emperour to fetch home the bones of *Chryfoftome* with honour, wholly ended the Nonconformity and Separation of the *Joanites*.

§. 16. Before *Theodofius* dyed, *Leo* Bifhop of *Rome* fet *Placidia* and *Eudoxia*, to write to him againft *Diofcorus*, and for the caufe of *Flavianus*: Yea, and *Valentinian* himfelf. *Theodofius* wrote to *Valentinian* (and "the like to the Women,) "That they departed not from the Faith and "Tradition of their Fathers, that at the Council of *Ephefus* fecond "things were carried with much liberty and truth, and the unworthy "were removed and the worthy put into their places, and it was the "troublers of the Church that were depofed, and *Flavianus* was the "Prince of the Contentions, and that now they lived in Concord and "Peace.

§. 17. The Council at *Calcedon* was called, *an.* 451. *Diofcorus* is accufed for his *Ephefine* General Council, and for his violence, and defence of *Eutiches*, and the death of *Flavianus*. He alledgeth the Emperours Order to him [*Authoritatem & Primatum tuæ præbemus beatitudini*, (If the Popes Univerfal Rule be effential to the Church, then the pious and excellent Emperour *Theodofius*, and the General Council that confented, were none of them Chriftians that knew it, but went againft it.) *Eos qui per additamentum aliquod, aut imminutionem conati funt dicere, præter quæ funt expofita de fide Catholica à fanctis Patribus qui in Nicæa, & poft modum qui in* Ephefo *congregati funt, nullam omnino fiduciam in fancto Synodo habere patimur, fed & fub veftro judicio effe volumus*.] Here *Binnius* accufeth the good Emperour

perour as *giving that which he had not but by usurpation, and this through ignorance of the Ecclesiastical Canons.* But were all the Bishops ignorant of it also? Or was so good an Emperour bred up and cherished in ignorance of such a point pretended by the Papists to be necessary to the Being of a Church, and to salvation; The Bishops of *Jerusalem* and *Seleucia* also partook of the same power by the Emperour's Grant. *Dioscorus* answered that *All the Synod consented and subscribed as well as he, and* Juvenal Hierof. *and* Thalassius Seleuc.

The Bishops answered, that they did it against their wills, being under fear; Condemnation and Banishment was threatned; Souldiers were there with Clubs and Swords: Therefore the Oriental Bishops cryed out to cast out *Dioscorus*. *Stephen* Bishop of *Ephesus* (who had been *Dioscorus* chief Agent there) cryed out, *that fear constrained them:* The Lay-Judges and Senate asked, *who forced them? Stephen* said *Elpidius* and *Eulogius*, and many Souldiers threatned him. They asked, *Did* Dioscorus *use violence with you?* He said that he was not suffered to go out till he had subscribed. *Theodorus* Bishop of *Claudiopolis* said, that *Dioscorus, Juvenal,* and the leading men, led on them, as simple ignorant men, that knew not the Cause, and frightned them with defaming them as *Nestorian* Hereticks. Thus they cryed out that they were frightned.

Bin.Tom 2. P. 7, 8.

The *Egyptian* Bishops answered, that *A Christian feareth no man,* (and yet they were afraid before they ended) *A Catholick feareth no man; we are instructed by flames: If men were feared, there would be no Martyrs.*

Dioscorus noted what Bishops those were that said they *subscribed to a blank Paper,* when it was about a matter of Faith: But asked, who made them by their several interlocutions to speak their consent? Hereupon the Acts of the *Ephes.* Council were read, among which were the words of *Dioscorus,* Anathematizing any that should contradict or *retract any thing held in the* Nicene *or the* Ephesine *Synods*: Adding, *how terrible and formidable it was, If a man sin against God, who shall intercede for him? If the Holy Ghost sit in Council with the Fathers, he that retracteth cashiereth the Grace of the Spirit.* The Synods answered, *We all say the same: Let him be Anathema that retracteth;* (these Bishops that curse themselves will easily curse others,) *Let him be cast out that retracteth.* *Dioscorus* said, *No man ordereth things already ordered:* The holy Synod said, *These are the words of the Holy Ghost, &c.* *Theodorus* denyed these words recorded. *Dioscorus* said, they may as well say they were not there.

§. 18. Here also *Eutyche*'s Confession at *Ephesus* was read, in which he professeth to cleave to the former *Ephesine* Council, and to the blessed Father *Cyril* that presided, disclaiming all additions and alterations, professing that he had himself Copies in a Book which *Cyril* himself sent him, and is yet in his hands; and that he standeth to the definition of that Council with that of *Nice.*

Eusebius Bishop of *Doril.* said, *He lyeth; that Council hath no such Definition.*

Dioscorus

Dioscorus said, *There are four Books of it, that all contain this Definition. Do you accuse all the Synodical Books? I have one, and he hath one, and he hath one; Let them be brought forth.* *Diogenes* Bishop of *Cyrilum* said, *They deceitfully cleave to the Council of* Nice: The Question is of additions made against Heresies. The Bishops of *Egypt* said, *None of us receive additions or diminutions: Hold what is done at* Nice: *This is the Emperour's Command.* The Eastern Bishops clamoured [*Just so said Eutyches.*] The *Egyptian* Bishops still cryed up the *Nicene* Faith alone without addition.

Dioscorus accused the Bishops for going from their words, and said [*If Eutyches hold not the Doctrine of the Church, he is worthy of punishment and fire,* (ex ore tuo) *My regard is to the Catholick and Apostolick Faith, and not the Faith of any man: I look to God himself, and not to the person of any man, nor care I for any man, but for my soul and the true and sincere Faith.*] The *Egyptian* Bishops cryed out [*Let no man separate him that is indivisible. No man calleth one Son two.*] The Eastern Bishops cryed, [*Anathema to him that divideth.* *Basil Seleuciæ* said, Anathema *to him that divideth two natures after the union; and* Anathema *to him that knoweth not the property of the natures.* The *Egyptian* Bishops cryed out, [*As he was born he suffered: There is one Lord, and one Faith: None calleth one Lord two.* This was *Nestorius* voice. The Eastern Bishops cryed, *Anathema to* Nestorius *and* Eutyches. The *Egyptian* Bishops cryed, *Divide not the Lord of Glory, that is indivisible.*

Basil Bishop of *Silcuc.* reported how rightly he had spoken at *Ephesus*, and how the *Egyptians* and Monks with noise opposed, and cryed [*Cut him in two that saith* Two Natures, *he is a* Nestorian.] The Lay Judges asked him, *If he spake so well, why did he condemn* Flavianus? He said, *Because he was necessitated to obey the rest, being* 130 *Bishops.* *Dioscorus* said, ☞ *Out of thy own mouth art thou condemned, that for the shame of men hast prevaricated and despised the faith.* *Basilius Seleuc.* said, *If I had been called to Martyrdom before the Judges I had endured it; but he that is judged of a Father useth just means: Let the Son dye that speaketh even things just to a Father.*

But the Eastern Bishops better cryed out, [*We have all sinned, we all beg pardon.*] And *Thalassius, Eusebius,* and *Eustathius,* (leading Bishops) cryed the same, [*We have all sinned, we all crave pardon.*] After this the Acts of *Ephes.* and *Const.* were read.

§. 19. By what I have recited out of *Binnius,* and others, these two lamentable things are undeniable:

1. That this doleful Contention, Anathematizing, and ruining each other, was about the sense of ambiguous words, and that they were of ☞ one mind in the matter, and knew it not: The *Egyptians* (*Eutychians*) took *two Natures* and *two Sons* to be of the same sense, which the others did not. And they thought that the rest had asserted a *Division* of the Natures, when they meant but a *Distinction*: And the rest thought that the *Egyptians* had denyed a *Distinction,* who denyed but a *Partition* or *Division.*

their Councils abridged. 103

II. And it is plain, that while all sides held that *Nestorius* did hold that there were *Two Sons*, which he expresly denyed, that they cursed *Nestorius* in ignorance, and maintained his Doctrine (except of the aptitude of the phrase συναφ⊖,) while they curse his person or name. The Doctrine of this Council is found, and *Nestorius*'s was the same, for *two natures* in *one person*, and *one Son*. This is true, whatever Faction say against it.

III. That these Bishops (though we honour them for all that was good in them) were so far from the Martyrs Constancy, that they turned as the Emperours Countenance, and the Times, and worldly Interest turned; voting down Things and Persons in Councils, and crying *omnes peccavimus* in the next: Only *Peter*'s Ship, faith *Binnius*, scaped drowning at *Ephesus*, and yet here at *Calcedon* under *Martian* all are Orthodox.

IV. But that which is worst of all is, that yet the same men that cry *peccavimus* are here violent against any mercy to the *Egyptian* Bishops and Monks with whom they had joined at *Ephesus*.

§. 20. When an Epistle of *Cyrils* was read, the *Illyricane* Bishop cryed out, *We all believe as* Cyril *did*: *Theodorete* (that had been for *Nestorius* against *Cyril*, and cast out by *Dioscorus*) spake more warily, and said, *Anathema to him that saith there are two Sons*: *We adore our Lord Jesus*, &c. All the Bishops cryed, *We belive as* Cyril. Had not *Cyril*'s name better hap than *Dioscorus* and *Eutyches*, that followed him as far as they could understand him, and spake the same words as he?

The *Orientals* cryed, *We belive as* Cyril. The *Egyptians* cryed, *We believe as* Cyril, *We are all of the same opinion and mind*; *Let not Satan get place and advantage among us*. The *Eastern* Bishops cryed, *Leo* and *Anatolius are of this mind*; *The Emperour and Senate are of this mind*: The lay Judge, Senate, and all the Council cryed, *The Emperour, the Empress, and all of us are of one mind*: The *Egyptian* Bishops cryed, *All the World are of this mind*; *We are of a mind*. (And who would think that yet they were disagreed, even to Hereticating and Deposing, Persecuting one another.

O but say they to the *Egyptian* Bishops, *If you are all of this mind, Why did you communicate with* Eutyches, *and condemn* Flavianus? *Dioscorus* appealed to the Records. And here *Eustathius Beryl*, shewed what labour *Cyril* used to explain his own meaning, in his Epistles to *Acacius*, *Valerianus*, and *Successus* Bishops, and that these are his words; *We must not understand that there are two natures, but one nature incarnate of God the Word*: And this saying he confirmed by the Testimony of *Athanasius*. The Oriental Bishops cryed out, *This is the saying of* Eutyches *and* Diofcorus (yet these men just now were all of *Cyril*'s mind.) *Dioscorus* said, *We affirm neither confusion of natures, nor division, nor conversion*; *Anathema* to him that doth. Doth not this shew that they all agreed in Distinction of Natures? as also *Cyril* did. The Judges say, Tell us whether *Cyril*'s Epistles agree to what is here reported of them (by *Eustathius*,) *Eustathius* sheweth the Book, and faith; *If I have said amiss see the Book*; *Anathematize* Cyril's ril's *Book* and *Anathematize* me: The *Egyptians* applaud *Euſtathius*, ſaying, *Euſtathius* reporteth *Cyril*'s words, in which were, *We muſt not underſtand two natures, but one incarnate nature of God the word.* And *Euſtathius* added, *He that ſaith there is but one nature ſo as to deny Chriſts fleſh which is conſubſtantial with us, let him be* Anathema: *And he that ſaith there are two natures to the Diviſion of the Son of God, let him be* Anathema. (one would have thought this ſhould have ended their quarrel.) And *Euſtathius* added of *Flavianus* himſelf, that he received theſe *naked words*, and gave them the Emperour; *Let it be ordered that his own hand be ſhewed.* The Judges ſaid, *Why then did ye depoſe him?* *Euſtathius* anſwered, *Erravi, I erred.*

§. 21. Let it be here noted, that theſe *Eutychian* words of *Cyril* are here openly proved, paſt denial: yet ſhamelesly doth *Binnius* ſay, that this is *Euſtathii allegatio peſſima & hæretica:* What, to repeat a mans Words? ☞ Secondly, Is it not here plain that they were all of a mind, and did not, or through faction would not know it? when *Euſtathius* by a clear diſtinction had proved it, and none of them did or could contradict him.

§. 22. *Dioſcorus* ſaid that *Flavianus* in the words following contradicted himſelf, and was depoſed for holding two *natures after the union*; adding, *I have the teſtimony of the holy Fathers,* Athanaſius, Gregory, Cyril, *in many places, that we muſt not ſay, that after the union there are two natures, but one incarnate nature of God, the word, I am ejected with the Fathers; I defend the Fathers ſayings; I tranſgreſs not in any thing; I have their Teſtimonies, not ſimply or tranſitorily, but in Books.*

§. 23. *Æthericus,* Biſhop of *Smyrna*, being queſtioned about his ſubſcription, ſaid, he did as he was bid. In the ſecond Action *Dioſcorus* delivering his opinion ſaith, *Ex duabus ſuſcipio, duas non ſuſcipio.* That Chriſt ☞ is [*of two natures*] but not that he [*is or hath two natures.*] *Euſebius Doryl.* tells him of his wrong to *Flavianus* and him; *Dioſcorus* confeſſeth, ſaying, *Then offer ſatisfaction to God and you,* meaning repentance. But *Euſebius* ſaith, that he muſt ſatisfie the Law; And ſo the Verbal quarrel turneth to Perſonal revenge.

Baſil Seleuc. (though before accuſed of Hereſie) well reconcileth the Controverſie at laſt, if they would have heard him, ſaying, *Cognoſcimus* ☞ *duas Naturas, non dividimus; neque diviſas, neque confuſas dicimus.*

Eutyches words at *Conſtantinople* being recited, he ſaith, that he followeth *Cyril, Athanaſius* and the Fathers. After *Dioſcorus* and others had denyed what each other ſaid in the *Epheſine* Council, the ſaying of all the Biſhops were read, each one abſolving *Eutyches,* in words and reaſons at large. After which the Biſhops cry again, *Omnes erravimus; omnes veniam mereamur.*

In the third Action many things were read that concerned their proceedings, and among the reſt a Law of *Theodeſius jun.* for the confirming of the ſecond *Epheſine* Council, and the condemnation of *Neſtorius,*
and

their Councils abridged.

and of *Flavianus, Domnus, Eusebius,* and *Theodoret,* as *Nestorian* Hereticks, deposing all of their mind, forbidding any upon pain of Confiscation to receive them, and commanding that none read the Books of *Nestorius* or *Theodoret*, but bring them forth to be burnt, &c. So far could fierce and factious Prelates prevail with a pious and peaceable Prince, by the pretences of opposing Heresie and Schism. *Martian* made Laws also clean contrary for the justifying of the men before condemned.

§. 24. In the fifth Action the *Egyptian* Bishops Petition was read (who were accounted *Eutychians*, adhering to *Dioscorus*:) They professed their adherence to the Council of *Nice* and *Ephesus* 1. and to *Athanasius, Theophilus,* and *Cyril.* The Bishops cryed out, Why do they not curse the opinion of *Eutiches*? They offer us their Petition in imposture: They would delude us, and so depart. Let them curse *Eutyches* and his Opinion, and consent to *Leo*'s Epistle. While they cryed out to them to curse *Eutyches,* they answered (by *Hieracus,*) *If any, whether Eutyches, or any other, hold contrary to the things contained in our Profession* (the *Nicene* and *Ephes.* Councils) *let him be accursed. But for* Leo's *Epistle, we must not go before the sentence of our Archbishop* (of *Alexandria*,) *for we follow him in all things : The Council of Nice ordered that the Bishops of Egypt do nothing without him.* Enfebius Doryl. said, *They lie.* Others bid them *prove it.* Other Bishops cryed out, *openly curse the opinion of* Eutyches: *He that subscribeth not* Leo's *Epistle to which all the holy Synod consenteth is a Heretick*: Anathema to Dioscorus, *and to them that love him: How shall they chuse them a Bishop* (instead of *Dioscorus*) *if they judge not right themselves: The* Egyptian Bishops said, *The question is about Faith,* (not men:) But they cryed out so long, *Curse* Eutyches *or you are Hereticks,* that at last the *Egyptians* said, [*Anathema to* Eutyches *and to them that believe him,*] The Bishops cryed to them [*Subscribe* Leo's *Epistle, else you are Hereticks*: The *Egyptian* Bishops answered, *We cannot subscribe without the will of our Archbishop.* Some said, *All the Synod must not attend for one man: They that at* Ephesus *disturbed all things, would here do so too: we desire that this may not be granted them, but they may consent to the Epistle, or receive a Canonical damnation, and know that they are Excommunicate.* Photius Bishop of *Tyre* said, *How endeavour they to ordain* (their Arch-Bishop) *who are not of the same mind with the Synod? If they think rightly let them subscribe the Epistle, or be Excommunicate.* The Bishops cryed, *We are all of this mind.* The *Egyptian* Bishops said, *We came not hither without a just profession of our Faith. But* (as to Leo's Epistle) *we are but few* (12 Bishops) *and the Bishops of our Country are very many, and we cannot give you all their minds, or represent their persons: We beseech this holy Synod to have mercy on us,* (There is no mercy where the Bishop of *Rome* is concerned) *and do but stay till we have an Arch-bishop, that according to the ancient Custome of our Country, we may follow his Judgment: For if we break presumptiously the the Canons and Custome, and do any thing without his will, all the Regions of* Egypt *will rise up against us; therefore have mercy on our age: have mercy on us, and put us not to end our life in banishment.* The same Egyptian

Bishops cast down themselves on the Earth, and said, *You are merciful men, have mercy on us:* Cecropius Bishop of *Sebast.* said, *The whole Synod is Greater and worthier of credit, than the Country of* Egypt. *It is not just that ten Hereticks be heard, and* 1200 *Bishops be past by: We bid them not shew their Faith for others but themselves.* The Bishops of *Egypt* cryed, *Then we cannot dwell in the Province; Have mercy on us:* Eusebius Dor. said, *They are procurators for the rest: The Popes* Legate said, *If they erre, let them be taught by the magnificence of your footsteps, &c.* The *Egyptians* cryed, *We are killed; Have mercy on us:* The Bishops all said, *You see what a Testimony they give of their Bishops,* saying, *we are killed there:* The *Egyptian* Bishops cryed, *We die by your footsteps: have pitty on us, and let us die by you, and not there. Let but an Archbishop here be made, and we subscribe and consent, Have mercy on our grey hairs. Give us an Archbishop here:* Anatolius *knoweth that it is the Custom of our Countrey that all the Bishops obey the Archbishop: Not that we obey not the Synod, but we are killed there in our Country: Have mercy on us; You have the power, We are subjects; We refuse not. We had rather die by the Lord of the World* (the Emperour) *or by your magnificence, or by this holy Synod, than there. For Gods sake have pity on these grey hairs; spare ten men: We die there: It is better die here.* All the most Reverend Bishops cryed out, *These are Hereticks.* The *Egyptian* Bishops said, *You have power on our lives; spare ten men; Lords are Merciful:* Anatolius *knoweth the Custome; We are here till an Archbishop be chosen: If they would have our Seats, let them take them: We are not willing to be Bishops: Only let us not die. Give us an Archbishop, and if we gainsay, punish us: We consent to these things which your power hath decreed; We contradict not; but choose us an Archbishop: We here stay till it's done:* All the most Reverend Bishops clamoured, *Let them subscribe to the damnation of* Dioscorus.

Thus the poor *Egyptian* Bishops that had the upper hand under *Theodasius,* were in a streight between the mercilefs Bishops in the Synod (that had lately at *Ephesus* joyned with them) and the furious Bishops and people of their own Country that would have killed them when they came home (too common a Case at *Alexandria.*) But when all their dejected cryes and begging could get no mercy from the Bishops, the Lay Judges had some, and moved that they may be made stay in the Town till their Archbishop was chosen (of whom you shall hear sad work anon.) The Popes Legate requested, *That if they would needs shew them any humanity, they should take sureties of them, not to go out of the City, till they had an Archbishop.* And so it was ended.

§. 25. The next businefs was with the Abbots of the Monks: They had petitioned *Martian,* that a General Council might be called, to end their lamentable broils, and that without *turbations, forced subscriptions or persecutions by the secret contrivances of the Clergy, and casting men out before due judgment.* And they gave in a profession of their Faith, and petitioned that *Dioscorus* might be called, becaufe the Emperour had promifed them that nothing but the *Nicene* Faith should be imposed, which he professed: The Bishops
all

all clamoured out their repeated Curse against *Diofcorus*, and their *Tolle injuriam à Synodo, Tolle violentiam à Synodo, Tolle notam à Synodo, Iftos mitte foras.* that is, *Away with them*; and would not hear their petition; But the Lay Judges made it to be read: In which the Monks profess to hold to the *Nicene Creed*, and that the Church might not have discord by imposing more: *Protesting that if their Reverences, abusing their power, resisted this, as before God and the Emperour, the Judges, the Senate, and the Consciences of the Bishops, that they shake their garments against them, and put themselves beyond their Excommunication: For they would not be Communicators with those that thus refuse the* Nicene *Faith.* The Council still urged them to subscribe *Leo's* Letter. *Carofus* and *Dorotheus* in the name of the rest of the *Abbots* said; *They were Baptized into the* Nicene *Faith*; *They knew no other: They were bid by the Bishop that Baptized them Receive no other: We believe the Baptismal Creed: We subscribe not the Epistle: They are Bishops; They have power to Excommunicate and to Damn, and to do what they will more: But we know no other Faith:* The Arch-Deacon urged *Carofus* to *Subscribe to* Leo's *Epistle* as Expository of the *Nicene* Faith, and to Curse *Nestorius* and *Eutyches*: *Carofus* answered, *What have I to do to curse* Nestorius, *that have once, twice, thrice, and often cursed and damned him already.* Æ*ticus* said, *Dost thou curse* Eytiches *as the Synod doth or not?* Carofus replyed. *Is it not written, Judge not that ye be not judged?* Again he repeated, *that he believed the* Nicene *Creed into which he was baptized*; *If they said any thing else to him he knew it not:* The Apostle saith, *If an Angel from heaven preach another Gospel, let him be accursed: what should I do?* If Eutyches *believe not as the universal Church believeth*; *let him be accursed.*

§. 26. At last there was a dissention, whether *Leo's* Phrases should be put into their Definition of Faith (now drawn up a new.) A while it was cryed down, but at last yielded to, when the *Illiricane* Bishops had first slighted *Rome*, and cryed, *Qui contradicunt (diffinitioni)* Nestoriani *sunt: Qui contradicunt Romam ambulent.*

And *Anatolius* Bishop of *Constantinople* openly declared, *That* Dioscorus *was not condemned for matter of belief, but because he Excommunicated* Leo, *and when he was thrice summoned did not appear.*

6. 27. After this *Theodorets* turn came, that had been for *Nestorius*, and the Bishops all cryed out, *Let* Theodoret *curse* Nestorius. *Theodoret* desired that a Petition of his to the Emperour and to *Leo's* Legate, might be read; that they might see whether he were of their belief or not. They cryed out, *We will have nothing read*; *presently curse* Nestorius, *Theodoret* told them that he had been bred of the Orthodox, and so taught, and preached; *and was against not only,* Nestorius *and* Eutychus, *but all men else that held not the right.* The Bishops interrupted him, clamouring, *speak out plainly, cursed be* Nestorius *and his Opinions*; *cursed be* Nestorius *and those that love him.* Theodoret answered, *I take not my self to say true, but I know I please God: I would first satisfie you of my belief*; *for I seek not preferment, I need not honour, nor come hither for that: But because I am calumni-*

ated, I come to satisfie you that I am Orthodox; *and I Anathematize every Heretick that will not be converted, and* Nestorius *and* Eutyches, *and every man that saith, there are two Sons, or thinks so, I Anathematize.* The Bishops again took this for dawbing, and cryed out, say plainly, *Anathema to* Nestorius, *and them which hold that which is his.* Theodoret said, *Unless I may explain my own belief, I will not say it. I believe*—Here they interrupted, and all cryed out, *He is a Heretick, He is a* Nestorian: *cast out the Heretick:* Reader, would a man have believed that were not forced by Evidence, *That this Council was of* Nestorius's *mind, and confirmed his own Doctrine of the Unity of Christs person and two Natures,* who thus furiously cryed down *Theodoret?* (except as to the aptitude of the word Σιοτκ&c.) And is it not a doleful Thought that the worthy Bishops of the Church, even in a General Council, should no better know the way of peace? And do not these words here translated out of *Binnius*, p. 92. and 106. agree too well with *Greg. Nazianzen*'s Character of Bishops and Councils? Not but that the Church had always some Learned, Godly, Wise, and Peaceable Men, (such as *Gregory Naz.* and *Theodoret* were, and many more, especially in *Africk*;) but you see that they were born down by the stream of unskilful, worldly, temporizing, violent Men; after once worldly greatness made it the way to preferment, and it became their business to strive who should be uppermost and have his will.)

But *Theodoret* when he found that there was no hope of so much as a patient hearing of his Explication and Confession, was fain to yield, and say, *Anathema to* Nestorius, *and to him who saith not that the Virgin* Mary *was the Parent of God, and who divideth the only begotten Son into two Sons*; which was yet cantelously expressed; as if he said, *supposing that* Nestorius *did so (which himself denyed) let him be accursed*: And so *Theodoret* was absolved and counted worthy to be a Bishop.

§. 28. *Juvenal Hierosol. Thalassius,* and the rest of the Leaders, at *Ephes.* Council 2, were pardoned: *Ibas* his Epistle to *Maris* against *Cyril* was acquit, or at least the Bishop upon the reading of it. It is a sad Narrative of the Calamitous Divisions which these Prelates and their Councils made. He said that *Cyril* writ against *Nestorius* that there was but *one nature in Christ*, &c. *Hæc omnia impietatis plena*: He tells how *Cyril* prepossessed the Bishops before they met, and made his hatred of *Nestorius* his Cause. How he condemned *Nestorius* two days before *John* of *Antioch* came: How afterward they condemned and deposed one another: How *Nestorius* was in hatred with the Great men of *Constantinople*, which was his fall: How *John* and *Cyril*'s Bishops or Councils would not Communicate with each other: How they set Bishops against Bishops, and People against People, and a mans Enemies were those of his own household: How the Pagans scorned the Christians hereupon: *For* (saith he) ☞ *no man durst travel from City to City, or from Province to Province, but each one persecuted his neighbour as his enemy: For many not having the fear of God,*

God, by occasion of Ecclesiastical zeal, made haste to bring forth the hidden enmity of their hearts against others: (he instanceth in some Persecutors) and sheweth how *Paulus Emissenus* helpt to heal them.

§. 29. In the eleventh Action two Bishops strive for the Bishoprick of *Ephesus, Bassianus* and *Stephen* (that had been *Dioscorus* Agent) *:* And in their Pleas each of them proved that the other intruded by violence into the place, both he that first had it, and he that thrust him out and took his Seat, and one of them made his *Clergy swear to be true* to him and not forsake him; And while the Bishops were for one of them, the Judges past Sentence to *cast out both*, and all consented.

§. 30. But after all the crying up of *Leo's* Epistle, this Synod set so light by *Leo*, as that, some say, against his Legates Will, they made a Canon, (28.) *That every where following the Decrees of the Fathers, and acknowledging the Canon which was lately read made by the* 150 *Bishops, we also Decree the same, and determine of the Priviledges of the holy Church of* Constantinople *new* Rome: *For the Fathers did give* (or attribute) *rightly the Priviledges to the Throne of old* Rome, *because that City ruled* (or had the Empire) *And moved by the same consideration the* 150 *Bishops Lovers of God, gave* (or attributed) *equal Priviledges to the Throne of New* Rome; *rightly judging that the City which is honoured with the Empire and the Senate, and enjoyeth equal Priviledges with ancient Queen-*Rome, *should also in things Ecclesiastical be extolled and magnified, being the second after it.* The Popes Legates hand *Boniface* is subscribed to all; and *Eusebius Doril.* thus subscribed *Sponte subscripsi, quoniam & hanc regulam sanctissimo Papæ in Urbe* Roma *ego relegi præsentibus Clericis* Constantinopolitanis, *eamq; suscepit.* And this Council was after over and over approved by the Roman Bishops.

§. 31. It is in this Canon notorious, 1. That the whole General Council and so the universal Church did then believe, that the Popes or Roman Priviledges were granted by the Fathers (that is, by Councils) and stood not by divine appointment. 2. That the reason that the Fathers granted them, was because it was the Imperial Seat. Had they believed that the Apostles had instituted it, they had never said that the *Fathers did it for this reason*; and that *Constantinople* should be equal or next it for the same reason. 3. The Church of *Constantinople* never claimed their Prerogative *jure divino* as succeeding any Apostle, and yet *jure Imperii* claimed equal Priviledges. By all which it is undeniable that the whole Church in that Council, and especially the *Greeks,* did ever hold *Rome's* Primacy to be a humane institution, upon a humane mutable reason. What the Papists can say against this, I have fully answered against *W. Johnson* in a Book called, *Which is the true Church.*

§. 32. The Question now is, *What concord did those latter Councils procure to the Churches?*

Ans. From that time most of the Christian World was distract'd into Factions hereticating, damning, deposing and too many murdering one another. One party cleaved to *Dioscorus* and were called by the other *Eutychians;*

chians; These cryed up the Sufficiency of the *Nicene Councils Faith*, as that which they were baptized into, and would have no addition nor diminution; and condemned the *Calcedon* Council, and excommunicated and deposed those that would not Anathematize it: Those that were against them they called *Nestorians*.

On the other party were those that had cleaved to *Nestorius* by name, and had been persecuted for his Cause; And these were a separate Body, and cryed down the other as *Eutychians*.

Those called *Orthodox* or *Catholicks* cryed down *Nestorians* and *Eutychians* by name, indeed defending the same Doctrine as *Nestorius*, except as to the fitness of the word Διδ']οκος. And the chief of *Nestorius* his first adherents perceiving that indeed they were of one judgment, united with these against the *Eutychians*. I have shewed that all of them seemed to make all this stir but about some Words which one party took in one sense and the other in another. For these words the Bishops cast the Christian World into confusion, destroyed Love and Unity under a pretence of keeping the Faith; so that the Church was lamentably militant; Bishops against Bishops, in continual enimity and rage. The Emperours at their wits end not knowing how to end the Ecclesiastical odious Wars: And the Heathens hardened and deriding them all and their Religion.

§. 33. When the Council was ended, and *Proterius* made Bishop of *Alexandria* in *Dioscorus* stead, the City was in so great discontent that the Emperour *Martian* was fain to send a Lay-man to mollifie them; for they would not endure a *Calcedonian* Bishop: They set more by *Dioscorus* than before (so that *Binnius* incredibly saith, they offered him Divine Honour.

§. 34. It was not long till *Martian* dyed, and then they let the World know that it was Emperours and not Popes or Councils that they regarded. They thought then they might shew their minds, and what they did *Liberatus in Breviario*, *Evagrius*, *Nicephorus* and others tells us at large: But I will give it you in the words of the *Egyptian* Bishops which conformed to the Council, *Bin.* p. 147. One *Timothy Elurus* of *Dioscorus* Party who had gathered separated Congregations before, since the Council of *Calcedon*, got some Bishops of his own Party to make him Archbishop: The people soon shewed their minds though it deposed their Archbishop. They set up *Timothy*, and he "*presently made Ordinations of Bishops and Clerks*, &c. "while he thus went on, *a Captain*, Dionisius, *came to drive him out of the* "*City*: The people rage the more against *Proterius*: *He gets into the Bap-* "*tistry to avoid their rage*, a place reverenced even by the *Barbarians* and "the fiercest Men: But these furious people, set on by their Bishop *Ti-* "*mothy*, neither reverencing the Place, the Worship, nor the Time, "(which was *Easter*) nor the Office of Priesthood, *which is a Mediation be-* "*tween God and Man, did strike the blameless Man, and kill him cruelly, with* "*six more; and dragging his wounded Carkess every where, and cruelly drawing* "*it about, almost through all the parts of the City, did mercilesly beat the sense-*
"*less*

"*less Corps, and divided his Parts, and spared not to tast his Entrails with their*
"*Teeth like Dogs; whom they should have thought the Mediatour of God and*
"*Man; and casting the rest of his Body into the Fire, they scattered his Ashes*
"*into the Wind, transcending the fiercenefs of all Beasts : And the Architect of*
"*all this was* (their new Bishop) *Timothy* ; first an Adulterer (taking ano-
"thers Church) and then a Murderer, doing it in a manner as with his own
"hands, in that he bid others do it : *This man ruleth the Alexandrian*
"*Church*, and going on doth worse.

This is in the Epistle to the Emperour *Leo* ; The like they write in ano- Bin p. 151.
ther to *Anatolius*, adding, "that he Anathematized the Council of *Calce-*
"*don* and all that *communicate with it, and received none that receive it, till*
"*they renounce it.*

§. 35. On the other side Bishop *Timothy*'s Adherents wrote to *Leo* in
praise of their new Bishop, professing the *Nicene* Faith, and declaring
what great Concord and Peace their City now had, and craving the Emperours approbation of him.

§. 36. In *Palestine* also the same Fire kindled : The Monks that had been
at *Calcedon* returned lamenting that the *Nicene* Faith was there betrayed,
and stirred up their Fraternity to rescind the Acts; They got together
and expelled *Juvenal* Bishop of *Jerusalem*, as a Traytor to the Catholick
Faith and a Changer. The Empress *Eudocia*) saith *Nicephorus*) took their
part; and strengthned them ; At *Schythopolis* they killed *Severianus* the
Bishop, they compelled men to joyn and communicate with them. At *Je-*
rusalem they killed *Athanasius* a Deacon for contradicting them, and gave Niceph. l.
his Flesh to Dogs. *Dorotheus* the Emperous Lieutenant would have kept 15.c.19.
the Peace, and they compelled him to joyn with them : But after twenty
moneths *Juvenal* was restored. Thus in many Countreys the War went
on ; And they that knew not the *Arcana Imperii* thought all this was done
by Bishops and Monks : But the truth is *Eudocia Theodosius*'s Widow, and
Pulcheria Theodosius's Sister and *Martian*'s Wife, were of two sides : And
Women had great power with Emperours, and consequently with Bishops : But at last *Pulcheria* procured the conversion of *Eudocia* to her
side, and then she owned the Council, and then others owned it. This
was in *Martians* days.

§. 37. The great number of Letters sent from the Bishops to *Leo* when
he was made Emperour, which were sent in answer to his own to them,
engaged him the more for the Council Party, and against *Timothy Ælu-*
rus : He deposed him and put *Timothy Salophaciolus* in his place : But the
City was all in confusion between the two *Timothies*, Bishops. The *Egyptian* Niceph. l.
Bishops write to the Emperour against *Timothy* and *Eutychians*. The Em- 15.c. 17,
perour sends forth his circular Letters, commanding all to own the *Calce-* 18, 19.
don Council. At *Antioch Petrus Cnapheus* ambitious of the Archbishoprick
got into *Martyrius* place; by *Zeno*'s help : And thinking they were still
managing only the Controversie against the *Nestorians*, and taking the
Orthodox for *Nestorian* Hereticks, all were accursed by Anathema's
that

that would not say that *God was crucified and suffered* (The Orthodox doing the same,) and thus they increased the Confusions. *Martyrius* their true Bishop when he saw that he could do no good upon them, forsook them, with these words, *Clero rebelli, & populo inobedienti, & Ecclesiæ contaminatæ Nuncium remitto. I renounce a rebellious Clergy, a disobedient People, and a defiled Church.* *Petrus Cnapheus* kept the Bishoprick, and reviled the *Calcedon* Council. *Leo* the Emperour banisheth him: *Stephanus* a friend to the Council is put into the place: That you may know how the Council had united the people, even the Boys were set on to kill this new Bishop with sharp Quills.

Common execution was too easie a death; Being killed they cast his Corps into the River, for favouring the Council of *Calcedon*, and succeeding their desired Bishop: But *Calendion* succeeding him, made them Anathematize the same *Peter Cnapheus*.

§. 38. While *Martian* and *Leo*, reigned thus, the Council of *Calcedon* was kept up, and almost all the Bishops were brought to subscribe to it; But death changeth Princes, and thereby Bishops. *Leo* dyeth, and dissolute *Zeno* succeedeth him: He would fain have had his peace among them in sensuality: *Basiliscus* taketh the advantage of his dissolute life, and usurpeth the Empire, and maketh use of the Bishops Schism and contentions to get him a party: (For the Bishops Schisms greatly serve Usurpers ends.) And first he publisheth his Circular Letters against the Council of *Calcedon*, requiring all the Bishops to renounce it, (because his Predecessours had been for it.) To this, saith *Nicephorus, lib. 6. cap. 4.* three Patriarchs, and no fewer then five hundred subscribed, and renounced the Council. (And yet how violently they damned all that would not receive it, and writ for it to *Leo*, but a little before you have heard.) But quickly after, *Acacius* Patriarch of *Constantinople*, and *Dan. Columnella*, perswaded *Basiliscus* to write clear contrary Circular Letters, Commanding all to own the Council: For they convinced him that this was the more possible way: And these also were obeyed. But *Zeno* was shortly after restored to the Empire, who was for the Council: And then the *Asian* Bishops turned again, and wrote to get their Pardon, saying, That they subscribed to *Basiliscus* first Letters, not voluntary, but for fear! (O excellent Martyrs.) *Niceph. l. 16. c. 9.*

§. 39. Upon this the Council was up again, and the Bishops became Orthodox once more: Till at last *Zeno* thought (as the *Acacians* did about laying by ὁμοούσιον) that the only way to unite these Bishops, was to leave all free, neither forbidding any to own the Council of *Calcedon*, nor yet compelling any to it. And so he wrote an Edict of Pacification, silencing the case, which he called his *Henoticon*: For he thought that the Bishops would never agree either *for* it or *against* it. But yet this ended not the quarrels: The fire still flamed: Liberty contented not the Bishops: They were zealous for God as against his Enemies the Hereticks: And every Party were these Hereticks and Enemies in the judgment of
the

the rest. All must be damned and ruined that would not be for God, that is, that was not of their minds. When Liberty was once up, the people were significant, and their mind was soon known. At *Antioch*, *Calendion* was cast out of his Seat, and *Peter Cnapheus* got in again. (For a Combat for a Bishoprick was a War which they scrupled not.) And at *Alexandria* the whole City was in confusion while *Peter Moggus* and *John* strove who should be Bishop. *Moggus* of *Alexandria* anathematizing the *Calcedon* Council, and persecuting Dissenters, the Emperour laboureth to reconcile them. *Acacius* at *Constantinople*, though supposed Orthodox, Communicateth with *Peter Moggus*: whether in obedience to *Zeno*'s *Henoticon*, or weary of hereticating, and why, is not known. (O how common were separatist Bishops in those days!) *Felix* Bishop of *Rome* condemneth *Acacius* Bishop of *Constantinople* for this: *Acacius* had equal priviledges given by the *Calcedon* Council, and had the presence of the Emperour and Senate, and he again condemneth *Felix*; blotting his name out of the sacred *Albe* (their Book of life.)

§. 40. *Acacius* shortly dying, the Emperour found it too hard a task to choose a Patriarch, that should not keep up the Sedition; Therefore he will refer the choice to God: To that end he putteth a blank paper on the Altar, and another by it, requesting of God that an Angel might write there the name of him that God would have to be Patriarch: The doors are fast locked, and forty days Fasting and Prayer commanded, to prevail with God: The Keys are committed to a sure and great Courtier, but one that was subject to Angels: One *Flavitas* bribeth him, and he writeth *Flavitas*'s name in the paper, and sealeth up the doors: And so there was an Arch-bishop chosen by an Angel. This man joined with *Peter* of *Alexandria* by Synodal Letters, to command all to curse the Council: and yet wrote to the Bishop of *Rome*, that he renounced Communion with *Peter*; and he wrote to *Peter* that he renounced Communion with the Bishop of *Rome*. But its fearful sporting with God and Angels: He dyed within four Months.

§. 41. After *Flavitas* succeeded *Euphemius*: He joined with the Bishop of *Rome*, and rased *Peter*'s name out of the Church Book: *Peter* and *Euphemius* as two Generals were about gathering Synodical Armies against each other, and against, and for the Council. But the Foot that spurneth abroad and spoileth the Designs of Worldlings, even Death presently removed *Peter*. One *Athanasius* succeedeth *Peter*, and fain he would have reconciled and united his Clergy and People, but he could not: Holy zeal is too easily quenched, but not contentious carnal zeal. *Palladius* succeedeth *Peter Cnaphens* at *Antioch*: Both these great Patriarchs join together to curse the Council of *Calcedon*; and down went the Council. But death again maketh a turn, they both dye, and *John* succeeded at *Alexandria*, and *Flavianus* at *Antioch*. Yet these must be of the mind of the *major* part, and both join also to curse the Council: And the Patriarchs of *Rome* and *Constantinople* curse them, and are for the

Council: And thus Cursing was the Religion of the Age.

§. 42. But now *Zeno* the Emperour dyeth, and *Anastasius Dicorus* is chosen Emperour. *Nicephorus, lib.* 16. *c.* 25. saith, that he being a man of peace, and desiring the ceasing of Contentions, followed *Zeno's Henoticon*, and left all to their liberty to think of the Council as they pleased. Hereupon the Bishops fell into three Parties; some fervent for every word of the Council; some cursing it; and some for the *Henoticon* or silent peace. The East was one way: the West another: and *Lybia* another. Yea the Eastern Bishops among themselves, the Western among themselves, and the *Lybian* among themselves, renounced Communion with one another. *Nicephor. c.* 25. *Tanta confusio mentium_q; caligo* (saith the Historian) *orbem universum incessit*, (it is not my censure) *so great confusion and blindness of mind befell the whole world:* This was the Effect even of Liberty.

§. 43. The Emperour resolving to keep peace did purpose to fall on the most unpeaceable whoever, even on both sides. At *Constantinople* he put out *Euphemius*: (as some thought upon a personal dislike or quarrel:) For before his inthronizing they say he had given under his hand to *Euphemius* a promise that he would stand for the Council; and when he had possession he demanded up his Writing: *Euphemius* denyed it him, and was cast out: *Macedonius* succeeded him, and got the Writing: The Emperour demanded it also of him; he also denyed it: The Emperour would have also put him out: The people rose up in Sedition, and cryed, *It is a time of Martyrdom, let us all stick to the Bishop*: And they reviled the Emperour, calling him a *Manichee*, and unworthy of the Empire. The Emperor was forced hereby to submit to *Macedonius*, lest he should have lost all: The Bishop sharply rebuked him as the Churches Enemy. But these things made the Emperour more against the Council, partly as more against him; and when he saw time, he remembred *Macedonius*, and cast him out: yea he put *Timothy* in his place, and burnt the Councils Acts. *Timothy* pulled down the Images of *Macedonius*. The Patriarchs of *Alexandria*, *Antioch*: and *Jerusalem*, were all cast out.

§. 44. *Peter Cnapheus Antioch* had made one *Zenaius* a Persian Servant and unbaptized, Bishop of *Hierapolis.* This man was against Images and against the Council. He brought a Troop of Monks to *Antioch* to force *Flavianus* the Bishop to curse the Council; *Flavianus* refuseth: The people stuck to the Bishop, and disputed the case with such unanswerable arguments, that so great a number of the Monks were slain, as that they threw their Bodies into the River *Orontes*, to save the labour of burying them. *Niceph.* 16. *c.* 27. But this endeth not the dispute; another Troop of Monks of *Cœlo-syria*, that were of *Flavianus* and the Councils side, hearing of the tumult, and the danger of the Bishop, flock to *Antioch*, and made another slaughter, as great (saith *Nicephorus*) as the former.

§. 45. The

§. 45. The Murders done by Bishops and Christians were sometimes punished by Excommunication, but not by Death in those prosperous times of the Church: The Emperour hereupon did banish *Flavianus*, which his followers took for persecution; *Peter Alex.* being dead the Bishops of *Alex. Egypt*, and *Lybia*, fell all into pieces among themselves, each having their separate Conventions. The rest of the East also separated from the *West*, because the *West* would not Communicate with them, unless they would Curse *Nestorius*, *Eutyches*, *Dioscorus*, *Moggus* and *Acacius*: And yet saith *Nicephorus*, l. 16. c. 28. *Qui germani Dioscori & Eutychetes sectatores fuere ad Maximam paucitatem redacti sunt*. *Xenaias* bringeth to *Flavian*, the Names of *Theodore*, *Theodorite*, *Ibas* and others as *Nestorians*; and tells him, *If he* Curse not all these, he is a *Nestorian*; whatever he say to the contrary: *Flavian* was unwilling, but his timerous fellow-Bishops perswaded him, and he wrote his Curse against them, and sent it to the Emperour. *Xenaias* then went farther, and required him to Curse the Council. The *Isaurian* Bishops were drawn to consent to Anathematize it: The refusers are all renownced as *Nestorians*. And thus the Council that Cursed *Nestorius*, is Cursed of *Nestorian*: The *Eutychians* perceiving how near they were agreed.

After *Flavian*, one *Severus* got to be Bishop at *Antioch* (a severe Enemy of the *Nestorians*, and of the Council.) The first day when he was got in, he cursed the Council, though 'tis said that he had sworn to the Emperour that he would not: *Niceph. lib.*16.*cap.*29.

In *Palestine* the Condemnation or Ejection of *Flavianus* and *Macedonius* renewed their distractions and divisions.

About *Antioch*, *Severus* grew so earnest, and wrote such Letters to the Bishops under him, as frighted many against their Judgements, to Curse the Council, and those that held *two Natures*, as Hereticks: Some Bishops stood out and refused; some fled from their Churches for fear. The *Isaurian* Bishops, when they had yielded, repented, and when they had repented they Condemned *Severus*, that drove them to subscribe. Two stout Bishops, *Cosmas*, and *Severianus*, sent a Sealed Paper to *Severus*; and when he opened it, he found it was a Condemnation under their Hands. The Emperour had notice of it, and he being angry, that they presumed to Condemn their Patriarchs, sent his Procurator to cast them out of their Bishopricks, (himself at last being against the Council.) The Procurator found the People so resolute, and bent to Resistance, in defence of their Bishops: That he sent word to the Emperour, that these two Bishops could not be cast out, without bloud-shed. The Emperour sent him word, that he would not have a drop of bloud shed for the business; for he did what he did for peace.

§. 46. *Helias*, Bishop of *Jerusalem*, found all the other Churches in such Confusion, the Bishops Condemning one another; that he would Communicate with none of them, save *Euphemius* of *Constantinople* (before his Ejection) *Niceph. c.* 32. The Monks were engaged for the Council by such a means as this. One *Theodosius*, a Monk (or Abbot) gathering a great assembly, lowdly cryed out in the Pulpit to them. [*If any man equal not the four Councils, with the four Evangelists, let him be Anathema.*] This Voice of their Captain, resolved the Monks; and they thenceforth took it as a Law, that the four Councils should be *sacris libris accensenda*, added or joyned with the sacred Books. And they wrote to the Emperour, [*Certamen se de eis ad sanguinem usq; subituros*, that they would make good the Conflict for them, even to blood: Thus Monks and Bishops then submitted to Princes. These Monks went about to the Cities to engage them to take their side for the Councils. The Emperour hearing of this, wrote to the Bishop *Helias* to reform it: He rejecteth the Emperours Letters, and refuseth: The Emperour sendeth Souldiers to Compell or restrain them. The Orthodox Monks that were for the Council, gathered by the Orthodox Bishops, tumultuously cast the Emperours Souldiers out of the Church, *Niceph*. c. 34. After this, they had another Contention, and there Anathematized those that adhered to *Severus*. The Emperour more provoked by all this, sent *Olympius* with a band of Souldiers to Conquer them: *Olympius* came, and cast out Bishop *Helias*, and put in *John*. The Monks gather again, and the Souldiers bieng gone, they come to *John*, and make him engage himself to be against *Severus*, and to stand for the Council, though it were unto Blood: He yielded to the Monks, and ingaged himself to the Council, and brake his Word made to *Olympius*. The Emperor is angry with *Olympius* for doing his Work no better; and puts him out, and sendeth another Captain *Anastatius*; who came and put the Bishop *John* in Prison and Commanded him to despise the Council: *John* consulting with another Bishop craftily promised to obey him, if he would but let him out of Prison, two days before, that it might not seem a forced act. This being done, the Bishop on the contrary in the Pulpit before the Captain and the People, cryeth out *If any man assent to Eutyches, and Nestorius, (Contraries) and Severus, and Soterichus, Cæsariansis; let him be Anathema: If any follow not the Opinions of the four Universal Synods let him be Anathema.* The Captain seeing himself thus deluded, fled from the Multitude and was glad to save himself, the Emperour being offended more at this. The Bishops write to him, *that at* Jerusalem *the Fountain of Doctrine, they were not now to learn the truth*, and that *they would defend the Traditions* if need *be even to blood*, Niceph. 16. c. 34.

At *Constantinople* the Bishop *Timothy* would please both sides, and pleased neither: To some he spake for the Council, to others he Cursed it. Being to make an Abbot, the Man refused his Election, unless he consented to the Council of *Calcedon*: *Timothy* presently Cursed those that received not the Council. His Arch-deacon hearing him, reproached him, that like *Euripus* roled every way. The Emperour hearing it, rebuked him: And *Timothy* washt away the Charge, and presently Cursed every one that received the Council, *Niceph*. l. 8. c. 35.

§. 47. But what did *Rome* all this while? It were too long to recite their

their proper Hiſtory: They were for the Council, and they had other kind of Conflicts: The *Goths* held them in Wars, and had conquered them, and *Theodorick* reigned there as King, and ſo they were broken off from the Empire: *Arians* ruled them, who yet if *Salvian* ſay true, did (after) ſhame the Orthodox in point of Temperance, Truth, and Juſtice.

But beſides their following greater Schiſms, this Schiſm alſo did reach to them. *Feſtus* a *Roman* Senator was ſent by *Theodorick* to the Emperour on an Embaſſie: which having done, he deſired of the Emperour that *Conſtantinople* might keep the Feſtival days of *Peter* and *Paul* (which they did not before) as they did at *Rome*; and he prevailed: And he ſecretly aſſured the Emperour, that *Anaſtaſius* Biſhop of *Rome* would receive the *Honoticon* (to ſuſpend the conſenting to the *Calcedon* Council) and would ſubſcribe it. When this Ambaſſadour came home the Pope was dead. To make good his Word to the Emperour, he got a party to chooſe *Laurentius* Pope, who would receive the *Honoticon*: The People choſe *Symmachus* their Biſhop. And ſo there were two Popes ſettled, and the ſedition continued three years, not without Slaughter, Rapines, and other Calamities: *Nicephor. cap.* 35. *Theodorick* an *Arian*, more righteous than the Popes, would not deprive them of their liberty of choice, but called a Synod, to judge which was the rightful Biſhop, and upon their judgment confirmed *Symmachus*: But *Laurentius* loth to loſe the prey, ſtirred up the People to Sedition, and thereupon was quite degraded. This was a beginning of Schiſms at *Rome*.

§. 48. The Emperour at *Conſtantinople* favouring the addition [*Qui crucifixus eſt pro nobis*,] the People who diſliked it, ſeditiouſly cut off a Monks head, and ſet it upon a pole, inſcribing [*An Enemy to the Trinity*.] The Emperour overcome and wearied with their Confuſions, and Orthodox Murders and Rebellions, called an Aſſembly, and offered to reſign his Empire, deſiring them to chooſe another: This ſmote them with remorſe, and they deſired him to reaſſume his Crown, and promiſed to forbear Sedition: But he dyed ſhortly after.

§. 49. *Anno* 452. *Valentinian* the *Roman* Emperour attempted a great alteration with the Biſhops, by a Law recalling the Judicial Power of the Biſhops in all Cauſes, except thoſe of *Faith* and *Religion*, unleſs the parties contending voluntarily choſe them for the Judges. This *Binnius* (and the other Papiſts) take for a heinous injury to the Church. *In all mens judgment,* ſaith *Binnius, it is abſurd that the Sheep ſhould judge his Shepherd: If to day the Pretor ſtand at the Tribunal of the Biſhop, and to morrow the Biſhop may be called to the Pretors Bar? That an Earthly judge may take and puniſh the ſervants of the higheſt judge, and conſecrated men: who will not ſay that this is moſt abſurd?*

Anſw. This ſheweth what Church-grandure and power theſe men expect; If they have not the Civil power, and be not Magiſtrates or Lords of all, the Church is wronged. This Clergy-pride is it that hath ſet the World on fire, and will not conſent that it be quenched.

1. By

1. By this rule all Christians should be from under all Power of Kings and Civil Rulers: For are they not all [*the servants of the highest Judge es*] Hath God no Servants but the Clergy?

2. By this rule both Princes and People should be free from the Bishops judgment: For are not these Bishops Men as well as Princes? and are not Christian Princes and People the *servants of the highest Judge*, and therefore should not be judged by Bishops.

3. But what a wicked rebellious doctrine is intimated in the distinction, that *Princes are Earthly Judges*, and *Prelates are the servants of the highest Judge*? Are not Prelates Earthly *Judges* as well as Princes, in that they are men that judge on Earth? And are not Princes Judges of Divine appointment and authority as well as Prelates? Yea, and their power more past all dispute?

4. And what absurdity is it, *that every soul be subject to the higher power?* And that he that's one of your Sheep in one respect, may be your Ruler in another? Why may not the King be the Ruler of him that is his *Physician* or his *Tutor*? And why not of him that is his *Priest*. Was not *Solomon* Ruler of *Abiathar* when he displaced him? May not one man judge who is fit or unfit for Church Communion, and another judge who is punishable by the sword? Did Christ come to set up a Ministry instead of a Magistracy? He that saith, Man who made me a Judge, came not to put down Judges: He that saith, By me Kings reign, came not to put down all Kings.

Obj. *Christ sets up a Kingdome of Priests, or a Royal Priesthood.*

Answ. But his Kingdom is not of this World, or Worldly: It is a spiritual Kingdome, conquering sin and Satan, putting down the World out of our hearts, and making us hope for the everlasting Kingdom which we shall shortly enjoy. The Disease of the Disciples that strove who should be greatest, and sit at the right and left hand, and said, Lord wilt thou at this time restore the Kingdom to *Israel*, hath prevailed after all this warning on a Worldly Clergy, to the great calamity of the Church. And what wonder, when even then St. *Paul* saith, *All seek their own* (too much) *and none the things of Jesus Christ* (so naturally as *Timothy* did) and so zealously as they ought. Too many Popes haue been *Peters* Successours in the Character given him, *Mat.* 16. *Get thee behind me Satan, Thou art an offence unto me*; *For thou favourest not the things that be of God, but those that be of men.* I understood not who were the spring of our late Fifth-Monarchy mens diseases, till I read *Campanella de Regno Dei*, and some such Papists, where I see that *Christs reign by his Vicar the Pope over all the Princes and People of the World*, is the true Fifth-Monarchy Heresie; For which they bring the same Prophecies as the Millenaries do for their Expectations.

Obj. *But the Pope, Prelates and Clergy (called the Church) are not to reign by deposing Kings, but by Ruling them and being above them: As Love is above the Law, which yet is made for the ungodly that want Love, and must be ruled*

ruled by fear; so Princes are for the World of unbelievers, but not for the Church and Spiritual persons who live above them in the life of Love.

Answ. 1. This was one of the first Heresies which the Apostles wrote against: Many tempted Christians then to think that Christianity freed them from service and subjection and made all equal: But how plainly, frequently and earnestly, do *Paul* and *Peter* condemn it? Is it not a shame to hear such Papists as cry up such a Heresie as this, cry down and damn a *Nestorian*, or an *Eutychian*, or a *Monothelite*, for an unskilful use of a word? *Paul* saith, He that teacheth otherwise (against subjection) is proud, knowing nothing, but doting.

2. Love doth indeed set us above Fear, and Legal threats so far as it prevaileth: But it is imperfect in all, and Fear still necessary.

3. And this taketh not down either the Law or Magistracy to us, but only maketh us less need such means. It's one thing to love and live so holily and justly as never to need or fall under the sword of Magistrates; and another thing to be freed from subjection and obligation.

This increaseth in many the opinion, that the Papal Kingdom is Antichristian, in that they set up themselves above Rulers that are called Gods.

3. But why must this priviledge extend to the Clergy only? Have not other Christians as much holy love, and spirituality, as most of them? And must Princes rule only Infidels?

Some suspect none as inclining to Popery, but those that take up some of their Doctrines of Transubstantiation, Purgatory, Images, &c. But they that on pretence of the raising of the Church, and defending its power, do first call the Clergy only the Church, and then seek to make themselves the Lords of Princes, by the pretences of an Excommunicating Power, and plead themselves from under them, and take it for their priviledges to be free from subjection to them and their penal Laws, are doubtless levened with that Popish Heresie, which hath done much of all the mischiefs, which the forecited History describeth.

§. 50. CXXXI. Besides some little contention at *Alexandria*, under *Proterius*, before he was murdered; the next in *Binnius*, is said to be at *Angices* (*Andegavense*,) which saith over again some of their old Canons against Priests living with Women, and removing from place to place, and such like. And the Papists say that this Council was to contradict the Emperour *Valentinians* Law, and to vindicate the rights of the Church, as not being lyable to Civil Judicatures, or under Kings.

§. 51. CXXXII. *Anno* 453. A *French* Venetick Council was called about Ordinations, which repealed some former Canons, and was so strict, that the first Canon kept Murderers and False Witnesses from the Sacrament, till they repented (instead of hanging them.) And the second

Canon denyed the Communion to Adulterers that unlawfully put away their Wives, and took others. (O strict Laws.)

§. 52. CXXXIII. *Ann.* 459. A Council at *Constantinople*, forbad Simony.

§. 53. CXXXIV. *Ann.* 467. A Council at *Rome*, of 48 Bishops; decreed that men that had two Wives, or the Husbands of Whores should not be ordained: That they that *could not Read*, and they that were maimed or dismembred, or the Penitent, should not be made Ministers, &c.

§. 54. CXXXV. *Ann.* 482. Ten Bishops at *Tours*, made such honest Canons, as if they yet reteined somewhat of S. *Martins* Piety. They earnestly disvvade the Clergie from their Fornication: They go a middle way between them that forbad Priests to get Children, and those that turn them loose, and decree that married Priests that continue to get Children shall be advanced no higher: They forbid the Clergie to be drunk: And to take in strange women: They forbid them to forsake their Ministerial Function: (but what if Prelates silence them) They keep those from the Communion that lye with Nuns (devoted to Virginity) till they Repent: They keep Murderers from the Communion, till they penitently confess. (This is not hanging them in Chains: But who shall answer for that Blood, and for the next that this man killeth?) others such honest Canons those vertuous Bishops made (oft made before)

§. 55. CXXXVI. They say *Fœlix* called a Council at *Rome* to admonish, and Exccommunicate *Peter Cnaph. Antioch* About the time time that he Excommunicated *Acacius Const.* and *Acacius* damned him again.

§. 56. In this storm against *Acacius*, the Pope engaged other Bishops, one was *Quintianus*, who sent *Peter* a dozen Curses for his Cure: Of which one reached *Cyril* being against those that say [*Unam Naturam*] Another was [*Siquis Deum-hominem, & non magis Deum & homineum dicit, damnetur*] that is, If any one say *God-man*, and *not rather God* and *Man, let him be damned.* How careless are Papists, and Protestants, that so commonly venture on the Word ⲥⲁⲣⲇⲉ̄ⲱ̄⊕ to their damnation: If our Neighbours, that commonly these thirty years last use the word [*God damn me* had but put *Thee*] instead of [*Me*] I should have suspected that the Councils and Bishops had made their Religion.

§. 57. CXXXVII. They say that *Ann.* 483 *Acacius* (as bad as the Pope, made him) call'd a Council at *Constantinople*, to Condemn *Peter Cnapheus*.

§. 58. CXXXVIII. *Fœlix* called 77 Bishops to *Rome*, on this occasion:
He

He sent his peremptory Letters to *Acacius,Const.* and some to the Emperour *Zeno,* by two Bishops, *Misenus* and *Vitalis*: The Emperour took away their Letters; and (not knowing then the Popes Soverainty) laid them by the Heels, till he made them glad to Communicate with those Bishops that they came to Condemn: For this *Felix* and his Bishops, cast them out of the Episcopal Office; and they presumed to excommunicate *Acacius,* as aforesaid, even with this Clause, *Nunquam Anathematis vinculis exuendus*: *Never to be absolved from the Curse!* What no Repentance, for one that was no Heretick! but falsly so called, for obeying the Emperour, in dealing gently with some *Eutychians*; were not this Council and Pope *Novatians*?

§. 59. CXXXIX. Yet *Ann.* 487. The same *Felix* is said in a Council of 38 Bishops, to decree Communion to the Lapsed, and Re-baptized, penitent *Africans.*

§. 60. At this time, and before [in Pope *Leo*'s time; some *Maniches* in *Rome*, would not be Recusants, but Conformists, and come to Church, and take the Sacrament; but they took only the Bread, and not the Wine. *Leo,* Serm. 4 *de Temp. quadrag.* writeth this against them. *When to cover their Infidelity, they dare be present at our Mysteries, they so temper themselves, that they may falsely lye hid, in the receiving of the Sacraments, that they with an unworthy mouth, receive Christ's Body, but refuse to drink the blood of Redemption. Which we would have your holiness to understand; that such men may be known to you by these marks: And that when their Sacrelegious dissimulation is discerned, b'ing discovered they may by the Priestly Authority be driven from the Society of the Saints.* Hereupon the Pope decreed that none should Communicate, but in both kinds: The Words of the Canon *dist.* 2. *de Consecrat.* are these. *We find that some taking only a portion of the holy body, abstein from the Cup of the holy blood: Because I know not by what superstition they are taught to be thus bound; let such either receive the whole Sacrament, or be driven from the whole: Because a division of one and the same mystery, cannot come but from heynous Sacriledge.* Reader, Is *Rome* constant in their Religion? And have they no Innovations? Is not *Binnius* impudent in calling it foolish to cite this Canon of their own Pope, against them. Consider it and Judge.

And as impudent is he, *p.* 232. in expounding these words of *Gelasius. Non desinit substantia vel natura panis & vini,* That is, *The substance or Nature of the Bread, and Wine ceaseth not:* As if it speaks only of *the substance and nature of the Accidents:* As if *Accidents* had *substance,* and *Nature* of their own: What words, what evidence can he so plain as to convince such men.

§. 61. Among the Epistles of *Gelasius*; one is to *Euphemius* Bishop of *Constantinople*, denying him Communion, till he put the name of *Acacius* out of the Dypticks, both of them being Orthodox; only because *Acacius* *And more largely, Ep. 13. ad Episcop.*

Communi-

Church-History of Bishops and

☞ Communicated with an *Eutychian*; even when he is dead, those that Condemn him not must be excommunicated; were there ever greater separatists than these. And is it any wonder if now the Pope separate from most of the Christian World.

There is also his *Commonitorium* written to *Faustus* the Embassador of *Theodorike* at *Constantinople*; in which he insisteth on the same way of Separation. All the world must be in an Ecclesiastical Episcopal War, if they will not damn and separate from every one that speaketh an unapt word, if a Council or Pope will but call it Heresie.

But here the Papists would have us believe that excommunicating in those days was a proof of superiority: But *Gelasius* himself here tells them otherwise. It was objected against him by *Euphemius Constant*. That *one man may not excommunicate Acacius* a Patriarch. And he answereth, 1. That it was the act of many; that is, of the Council which condemned the *Eutychians* in general. But is this good Law, or Divinity? Is every offender condemned, *ipso jure*, before his personal guilt is Judged? Because the Law condemneth all Thieves, may every man Judge, and hang them. *Acacius* is confessed to be no *Eutychian*, but to have obeyed his Prince, in Communicating with one : *Euphemius* was no *Eutychian*, but would not disobey his Prince at the Popes command, by blotting out *Acacius* Name. But his ☞ Second Answer is, *Quod non solum Præsuli Apostolico facere licet, sed Cuicunq; Pontifici ut quoslibet & quemlibet locum, secundum regulam hæreseos ipsius ante damnatæ, à Catholica Communione discernant*. That is, *It is Lawful not only to an Apostolical Prelate, but to any Bishop to exclude from Catholick Communion, any Persons, and any place, according to the Rule of his fore-damned Heresie*. And accordingly, others have excommunicated the Pope, and lower Prelates have Excommunicated Patriarchs; and the lower Patriarchs the higher: Excommunication, as it is an Act of Government, is done only by a Governour: But as all Christians are commanded to avoid scandalous Christians, so in their several places they may practice this, the guilt being proved; I may tell him that I have no rule over, *I will have no Communion with you*: But I cannot thereby oblige all others to do the like.

This *Gelasius* also oft (*Epist: ad Anastas. Imperat. &c.*) setteth up the Priest above the Prince, as Gods Laws are above mans: As if Kings were not to Govern by Gods Laws? and as if the Bishops Canons were not *mans Laws* (if they be Laws.)

§. 62. CXL. It's said that 70 Bishops at *Rome* under *Gelasius* determined of the Canon of the Scripture, and also of accepted and rejected Books. In the Canon they put a Book called *Ordo Historikrum*; with one Book of *Tobias*, one of *Judith*, one of the *Maccabees*, *Nehemias* is left out. Among the approved Books the Epistle of *Leo* to *Flavian Const.* is thus imposed, ☞ [*The Text whereof if any man shall dispute, even to one iota (or tittle) and doth not venerably receive it in all things, let him be accursed.*] A multitude of of heretical and rejected Books are named: Eighteen pretended to be by or, of some Apostles, and such other: And among others the History of *Eusebius* (yet before approved, unless here he mean only *de vita Const.*) The Works of *Tertullian, Lactantius, Arnobius, Clemens Alexand. Africanus, Cassianus, Victorinus Pictav. Faustus Rhegiens. &c.* Of the Canon of Scripture Bishop *Cousins* hath collected the true History from greater Antiquity.

§. 63. CXLI. *Vitalis* and *Misenus*, the Popes Legates at *Constantinople*, having been Excommunicated for Communicating with *Acacius*, &c. *Vitalis* dyed so, but after eleven years *Misenus* repented, and was absolved by a Council of 55 Bishops: (might not the Pope alone have done it?)

§. 64. CXLII. You have heard before how *Festus* got *Laurentius* the Arch-presbyter chosen Pope at *Rome*, and more chose *Symmachus*: *Theodorick* an *Arian* being King was just, and had so much wit as to please the Clergy while his Kingdom was unsettled. The Pope, under his protection, excommunicated both Emperour and Patriarch of *Constantinople*, for Communicating with Hereticks; but he never excommunicated *Theodorick* at home, though an *Arian*: There was reason for it: Interest is such mens Law. But while the Schism between *Symmachus* and *Laurentius* divided the Senate, the Clergy, and the People, five or six several Councils are called at *Rome*, mostly to heal this rupture: For at first the *Laurentians* laid some Crimes to the charge of *Symmachus*; and when the Councils would not cast him out, they fell to rapine, violence, and bloodshed, many being killed, and all in confusion: So that it was work enough in three years for King and Council to end the Schism.

§. 65. CXLIII. When the *Arian* Persecution abated in *Africa*, *Thrasamundus* the King, contriving which way to root out the Orthodox without violence; he commanded that when any Bishop dyed, no other should be ordained in their places. Hereupon the Nonconformists seeing the Churches like to decay, *ann.* 504. held a Synod, in which they decreed that though they suffered death for it they would go on, and ordain, and do their Office; concluding that either the mind of the King would be mollified, or else they should have the Crown of Martyrdom. This is called *Concilium Byzacenum*.

§. 66. It is greatly to be noted, that many following Councils in *Spain*, *France*, and other parts of *Europe*, which were held under the *Gothish* Kings, were more pious and peaceable than the rest fore-described. The Reasons seem to me to be these: 1. These Kings being conquering *Arians*, the Bishops durst not damn them for Hereție, for fear of their own necks; and so were greatly restrained from the hereticating work of Councils. 2. These Kings having a narrower Dominion than the Empire,

pire, and being jealous of their new gotten Conquests, were nearer the Bishops, and kept them more in awe than the Emperour did 3. And these Councils being small (of a few Bishops) had no such work for arrogancy and ambition, as the great General Councils had. 4. And the great proud pretending Patriarchs that set the World in a continual War, were not here to strive who should be the greatest. The Pope himself was seldom mentioned in the *Spanish* and *French* Councils, or the *African*.

§. 67. CXLIV. One of these honest Councils is *Agathense* by the permission of *Alaricus*, by 35 Bishops, *Cæsarius Arelatensis* being chief: Where many Canons for the Clergy were made or repeated.

The 3d Canon is, that if *Bishops wrongfully excommunicate any one, other Bishops shall receive them.* (Did the Popes observe this with *Acacius, Euphemius,* &c.) Can. 63. *If any Citizens on the great solemnities, that is, Easter, the Lords Nativity, or Whitsuntide, shall neglect to meet where the Bishops are,* (seeing they are set in Cities for Benediction and Communion,) *let them be three years deprived of the Communion of the Church.* (Doth not this prove that the City Churches then met all in one place, and so were but one Assembly at those times? How else could all the Citizens be with the Bishop at one time?) But even these Canons forbid Clergy-men to sue any before a Secular Judge, or to appear or answer at anothers suit, Can. 32. Otherwise both are to be excommunicate, Can. 37. It punisheth those that kill men, but with denying them Communion. Can. 50. Only if a Bishop, Presbyter, or Deacon, commit a *Capital crime, he shall be deposed and put into a Monastery, and have but Lay-communion.* (When Murderers are hang'd, and Traytors also quartered, this Canon is laid aside.) I thought a *Monastery* had been a *desirable* place, and not bad enough to serve Traytors and Murderers instead of the Gallows.

§. 68. CXLV. A Council at *Apanna* under *Sigismund* King of Burgundy, recited such like Canons as the former: save that there is one just such as our Fanaticks in *England* would have made, who would not worship God in any Temple which the Papists had used to their Mass: so saith Can. 33. *The Temples (or Churches) of Hereticks, which we hate with so great execration, we despise to apply to holy uses, as judging their pollution to be such as cannot be purged away. But such as by violence they took from us we may recover.* This is just *Down with the Idolatrous Steeple-houses*. But if they would give the Nonconformists in *England* leave to Preach in such places, they would be thankful, and think God will not impute the sin of others to us.

§. 69. CXLVI. A Council at *Sidon* of 80 Bishops, was called by the Emperour *Anastasius*, where they agreed to curse the Council of *Calcedon*,

don, and *Flavianus Antioch*, and *Johan. Paltenf.* were banished for refusing. This was about the time when the forefaid Fight was between the Monks and the *Antiochians*, when the Carkaffes of the *Eutychian* Monks were caft into the River.

§. 70. About this time was the fall and rife of the Papacy. The fall, in that the *Eastern* Empire made little ufe of Popes, but did their Church work without them. Their rife, in that the *Western* Empire and *Africa* being divided between many late conquering Kings, they all labour to fettle themfelves in a peaceable poffeffion by pleafing the Clergy, who, as they found, had no fmall intereft in the People.

§. 71. CXLVII. *Hincmazus* in the life of *Remigius*, tells us of a ftrange thing done at a Council at *Rhemes*; that one *Arian* Bifhop challenged all the reft to difpute, and when *Rhemigius* came in would not rife to him, but upon the fhaddow of *Remigius* paffing by him, he was ftruck dumb, and falling at *Rhemigius* feet, by figns askt pardon, and was fuddenly cured of his dumbnefs and Herefie, confeffing the Deity of Chrift.

§. 72. CXLVIII. Becaufe *Johan. Nicopolit.* did but call fome of his Bifhops to flatter the Pope, and to curfe all Herefies and *Acacius*, this is put in among the Councils. But the *Concil. Tarracenfe*, *Anno* 516. feems more regardable (under *Theodorick*) where the Clergy are reftrained *from buying cheaper and felling dearer* than others, (this it feems grew to be a part of their priviledges:) and *from judging caufes on the Lords day*: And it is ordered that the Bifhop fend a Presbyter one week, and a Deacon another, to the Country Congregations, and to vifit them himfelf once a year, becaufe by the old cuftome he is to have a third part of all the Church profits.

Quer. Whether a Bifhops Diocefs then was any bigger than one of our Corporations with the Neighbour Villages? And if one of our Bifhops that have above a thoufand Parifhes, or many hundred, fhould have the third part of all (or as other Canons fay the fourth,) Would not our Bifhops be yet richer men than they are? Efpecially if they that confine Bifhops to Cities, could get a Prince to call no Corporation a City but one or two in a Kingdom, and be as the *Abuna* is in *Ethiopia*, that hath the thirds of all the Ecclefiaftical benefits in the Empire. This Council had ten Bifhops.

§. 73. CXLIX. The *Concilium Gerundenfe* is next, *Anno* 517. under *Theodorick*; It confifted of feven Bifhops, (Bifhopricks began to grow fo big, that they could not fo fuddenly meet by the fcores and hundreds as when every Church was known by one *Altar* and one *Bifhop* at *Ignatius*.

natins speaks.) The seven men made Canons, that the same Liturgy should be used in the other Churches of that Province as were used in the Metropolitan Church. (For formerly every Bishop in his own Church did pray as he thought best, without Imposed or agreed Uniformity of many Churches, much less of all in a Nation.) They Decree also that Litanies be used on the Kalends of *November*. A Litany then signified a solemn supplicating of God by the People Assembled, Fasting, Walking, Singing, and Praying, as is used here in the Rogation Week: sometime they walked to the Memorial of some Martyr, sometime about the streets, oft bare-foot, continuing it with Fasting for certain times. The Last Canon is, *That the Priests say the Lords Prayer twice a Day, Morning and Evening*. (That was a short Liturgy.)

§. 74 CL. When *Justin* was made Emperour, the Bishops turned in the *East*, and down went the *Eutychians*, and a Synod of 40 Bishops at *Constantinople* resolved, that the Names of *Euphemius* and *Macedonius* should be restored into the Dyptick (their Book of life) and that *Severus* should be condemned with his Adherents.

§. 75. The Case hath been oft intimated before ; In those times when all the Empire was in confusion between *Eutychians*, and the Orthodox, and some Emperours took one side, and some the other, and some in vain endeavoured peace : The Churches of *Antioch* and *Alexandria* were more *Eutychian* than *Constantinople*, though the Emperour that favoured the *Eutychians* were present : *Acacius* was Orthodox, but pleased the Emperour so far as to Communicate with, or not curse and excommunicate the Bishops of *Antioch* and *Alexandria*. For this, as you have oft heard, the Pope Excommunicated him, and he so dyed (having done as much for the Pope.) *Euphemius* and *Macedonius* that succeeded were both Orthodox, and commanded by the Emperour to Communicate with the *Eutychians*, and persecuted, and both cast out by him, for not obeying him, as is before described in that and another such matter : The Pope had required them to blot *Acacius* name out of the Dyptick: The Court, Clergy, and People were against it, thinking it arrogancy in one man, to Excommunicate the Patriarch of the Imperial City that was Orthodox, upon his personal revenge or quarrel: They obeyed not the Pope: The Pope is against them for not cursing a dead Orthodox Bishop *Acacius* : The Emperour was against them for being against the *Eutychians*, as the Pope was for not being more against both them, and all that did not curse them as much as he did. Were not these Bishops in a hard case ? Both agree to their extirpation, and when they were dead to damn their names : But the Clergy and People agreed not. The *Eastern* and *Western* Churches were hereby divided. (that is, *Constantinople* and *Rome*.) Is not the Christian World beholden to such Tyrants and proud pretenders for its distractions and calamities? That will rather divide the Christian World, than endure the names of

Ortho-

Orthodox perfecuted Bifhops to be honoured, when they are dead, becaufe they would not blot out and abhor the name of another dead Orthodox Bifhop their Predeceffour, when the Pope curfed him for Communicating with an *Eutychian*. I know the Papifts will cry up, *The prefervation of the Faith and Purity*; But if ever any did overdo the Pharifees, that reproved Chrift for eating with Publicans and Sinners: If ever any became Plagues of the World, by being *Wife, Orthodox, and Righteous overmuch*, and made ufe of the name of *Faith*, to deftroy *Faith, Love, Humanity*, and *Peace*, and cryed up the *Church*, and *Unity*, as *Catholicks*, to deftroy the Church and Unity, and crumble it into Sects and Factions; it is certainly thefe men.

But the *Eaft* and *Weft* that thus began their feparation by the fpirit of Pride and Envy that *Rome* had againft the growing greatnefs of *Conftantinople*, continue their Divifion to this day; And it hath been no fmall caufe of the ruin of the Empire and the Chriftian Caufe, and delivering all up to the *Mahometans*: Which the good Pope feemed to judg more tolerable (with all the ftreams of Blood that went before and after) than that he fhould not have his will upon an Orthodox dead mans name. Sure *fiat Juftitia & ruat Cœlum*, was devifed by thefe precife over righteous Popes!

§. 76. *Evagrius* (*lib.* 3.) faith, that *Juftin* came to the Empire as followeth: *Amantius* was one of the Greateft men, but uncapable of the Empire, becaufe he was an Eunuch: He gave a great fum of Money to *Juftine*, to hire the Souldiers to choofe *Theocritus*, his bofom friend: *Juftine* with that Money hired them to choofe himfelf, and quieted *Amantius* and *Theocritus*, by murdering them both. And becaufe *Vitalianus* (that had ufurped and laid down,) was then great, he drew him in to be a Commander near him, and fo got him killed. But he becometh Orthodox, and faith *Binnius*, p. 374. *The great Patron and Defender of the Catholicks, by the fingular favour of God obtained the Empire*. So zealous was he, that he caufed the tongue of *Severus* the Eutychian, Archbifhop of *Antioch*, to be pulled out of his head, for curfing fo oft the Council of *Calcedon*, and fuch like things. *Paulus* fucceeded him and dyed, and *Euphrafius* fucceeded him, who was buried in the ruines of the City, it being caft to the ground by a terrible Earthquake, and the remnant burnt with fire from Heaven, in the lightning that went with the Earthquake. But *Euphremius* Lieutenant of the *Eaft*, did fo charitably relieve the People, that in reward they chofe him for their Bifhop. Reader, Was not a Bifhoprick then grown a confiderable preferment, when the Emperours Lieutenant of the *Eaft* took it for fuch, even to be Bifhop of a City that lay on heapes? *Evagr.l.3! cap. 4. Evagr.l.6. cap. 6.*

§. 77. CLI. Things being now on the turn, a Synod at *Jerufalem* votes up the Council of *Calcedon*, and cry down *Severus*.

§. 78.

§. 78. CLII. And another at *Tyre* doth the like.

§. 79. CLIII. And another Council at *Rome* again decreeth the damnation of the three dead Bishops of *Constantinople, Acacius, Euphemius*, and *Macedonius*: What, never have done with dead men? Methinks stark dead might satisfie Pride and Malice.

Ann. 518.

Binnius saith, that the *Eastern* Church yielded to blot out of the Dypticks the names of *Acacius, Euphemius* and *Macedonius* (not the Heretick) and the Emperours, *Zeno*, and *Anastasius*: The Pope maketh himself the Governour of Hell; where he thought these Emperours and Bishops were. But it is worse than Savage malice that will not cease towards dead men! And if the Empire yielded, they shewed more love of Peace than *Rome* did, but not much wit, in giving a Prelate of another Princes Dominion such power to defame, and force them to defame their Emperours and Patriarchs at his pleasure.

§. 80. The zeal of *Justin* to eradicate the *Arians*, and take all their Churches from them, provoked *Theodorick* (though a just man, that gave the Orthodox liberty, protection, and encouragement, yet an *Arian*, and gave the *Ariens* liberty also) to resolve, that he would use the Orthodox in *Italy*, as *Justin* did the *Arians* in the *East*: Whereupon *John*, Bishop of *Rome*, with some others, went as his Ambassadours to *Constant.* to mediate with *Justin* for the *Arians* ease. *Anastasius* in *lib. Pontif.* saith he obtained it: *Binnius* out of *Gregor. Turon.* saith the contrary: which is more probable. However by going on such a Message for real Hereticks, it appeareth with what sincerity the Popes prosecuted the dead names of the three Orthodox *Constant.* Bishops, on pretence of zeal against Heresie: ☞ When their interest urgeth them, *Let the World be set on fire rather than you shall speak favourably of an* Eutychian: But when interest changeth, *Rather than they in* Italy *shall suffer*, John goeth to Constantinople *for favour to the* Arians. Suppose he did not speed: What went he thither for? On this provocation, *Theodorick*, on other quarrels, put to death *Symmachus*, and his Son-in-law *Boetius*, *Roman* Senators and excellent men, and imprisoned *John* when he returned, and in the prison he dyed: And when he was dead the *Arian* King chose *Felix* the fourth Pope: Was this Election valid? If yea, he that is strongest, though a Heretick may choose the Pope? If not, than their succession was then interrupted.

§. 81. CLIV. We have next a great Council called *Ilerdense* of eight Bishops under *Theodorick* to mend some faults of the Clergy, *viz.* That they that Minister at the Altar abstain from mans blood, *Can.* 1. That they that commit Adultery, and take Medicines, or give them to cast the Birth, or that Murder the Child, shall abstain from Communion seven yeas s: And if they be of the Clergy, must be content with the Communion and the Chore without their Office, *Can.* 2. None shall draw an

offender

offender, though a Servant out of the Church, (nor say other Canons out of the Bishops house) that flyeth thither for any Crime (The Church and Bishops Houses had the priviledge to be the harbour for murderers, Thieves, Traytors, &c.) But *Can.* 11. alloweth the Bishop to punish them more than others (with longer forbearing the Sacrament) if those of the Clergy murder one another: O severe Laws!

§. 82. CLV. Next we have a Council (not all so great, having but six Bishops) under *Theodorick*, that ordered that the Epistle should be read before the Gospel, and some things like others.

§. 83. CLVI. And four ordinary sayings, were said over again by fifteen Bishops at *Arles*.

§. 84. It seems the *Semepelagians* then much prevailed: For one *Lucian* made a Recantation of his Errors to a Council of 27 Bishops at *Lyons*, as urged by them: One of his supposed errors was, that *Some are deputed to death, and others predestinate to Life*; and another, that *none of the Gentiles before Christ were saved by the light of Nature*: And now he owneth: *That in the order of times, some were saved by the Law of Grace, others by the Law of Moses, and others by the Law of Nature ; But none ever freed from Original Sin, but by holy blood.*

And *Faustus Rheg.* against the *Prædestinarians* was owned by the foresaid Council at *Arles, Bin. p.* 386.

§. 85 *Theodorick* made the Clergy Subject to Civil Judicatures; allowing them their liberty of Religion: When he dyed (of whose Soul in Hell they pretend visions) his successours *Athalaricus*, for the quiet possession of his Kingdom, at the Clergies Complaint of this as an injury, was pleased to restore them to their Dominion, and Freedom from subjection.

§. 86. *Justinian* succeeding *Justin*, (by his choice) Compileth the Laws into better order then before, and to the great advantage of the Orthodox Clergy, and against Heresies: And yet two things trouble the Papists in them. 1. That he seemeth to pretend to a Power over the Church Laws: But their shift is to say that he did it but as a defence and Confirmation of the Bishops Laws. 2. That he restored the Names of his Predecessors' *Zeno*, and *Anastasius*, with Notes of Piety and Honour; whom the Popes had presumed to damn as *Eutychians* or *Tolera'ers* of them: But for this they say; It was the doing of *Tribonianus*, a Heathen Lawyer, that did the work: As if *Justinian* would let him do what he disliked, and not correct it.

§. 87. When *Justinian* resolved to set up the Council of *Calcedon*; he
Cursed

Curfed *Severus*, and depofed the two Patriarchs, *Anthimius* of *Conftantinople*, and *Theodofius* of *Alexandria*, for they were both *Eutychians*: *Severus* had perfwaded them rather to forfake all worldly intereft, than the Faith (as he called it.) But here I cannot fee how the Hiftorians (as *Evagrius*) will be reconciled with themfelves; that fay, *Juftin* caufed *Severus* Tongue to be pulled out; and yet, that he afterward perfwaded *Anthimius* at *Conft*. unlefs he did it only by writing.

§. 88. So far was *Juftinian's* refolution, and power, from reconciling the Bifhops of the Empire, that he could not keep Unity, in his own Houfe or bed : For his Wife *Theodora*, was firm to the *Eutychians*; and cherifhed them; as he did the Orthodox, and both with fo great conftancy, that *Evagrius* fufpecteth they did it politickly, by agreement, (for the peace of the Empire) that each party might be kept in dependance on them.

§. 89. An Infurrection in *Conftantinople* occafioned the killing of about thirty thoufand, faith *Evagrius c.* 13. out of *Procopius*.

Evag.l.4. c.10.11. and Nicep. l.17.c.7.

§. 90. About this time a miracle is fpoken of fo credibly, that I think it not unfit to mention it : *Hunnerikus* in *Africa*, being an *Arian*, *Goth* perfecuted the Orthodox Bifhops, efpecially on pretences that they refufed to fwear fidelity to him, and his Son : (fay fome) They were forbidden to preach, and for not obeying, or for Nonconformity; the Tongues of many were cut out, who they fay did fpeak freely after as before : It were hard to be believed; But three Hiftorians I have read that all profefs that they faw, and heard the men themfelves, *viz*. *Victor Uticenfis Æneas Gazæus de Anima*, & *Procopius in Evagrius, l.* 4. *c.* 14. Who yet addeth that two of them upon fome finfulnefs with Women, loft their fpeech and remained dumb. *Nicephor*. faith *Rem cum fœminis habuiffent* : Alas, that miracles will not prevent Sin.

§. 91. In the eleventh year of *Juftinian*, *Athalaricus* being dead, and *Theodatus* a Kinfman fucceeding, this man loving books better than War, yielded up *Rome* and the Crown to *Bellifarius Juftinians* General; and fo after the *Gothes* had kept it 60 years, it was reftored without a drop of blood, faith *Evagrius l.* 4. *c.* 18. But when *Bellifarius* went away *Totilas* came and recovered *Rome*: And *Bellifarius* returning, recovered it from the *Gothes* again, *c.* 20.

§. 92. Three feveral Countries about that time, received the Chriftian Faith, much through the Reverence of *Juftinians* power, *viz*. The *Heruli*, the *Abafgi*, and they of *Tanais*, *Evagr. c.* 19. 21. 22. But the grievous Wars and Succeffes of *Cofroes* the *Perfian* in the Eaft, and a plague of fifty two years continuance, which deftroyed a great part of mankind, took down much of the *Roman* Glory.

§. 49.

their Councils abridged. 131

§. 93. CLVII. A second *Concilium Aransicanum* Condemned *Semepelagianisme*, propagated by *Faustus* Bishop of *Rhegrim*, after *Prosp.* who had been of the contrary mind.

§. 94. CLVIII. A *Concilium Vasense* of ten Bishops, decreed that Parish Priest should breed up young Readers, who may marry at age; that the parish Priests shall preach, or in their absence, the Deacon read a Sermon: That *Lord have mercy on us* be often said: That *Holy, Holy, Holy*, be oft said: That, *As it was in the beginning*, &c. be oft said.

§. 95. CLIX. A Synod of 16 Bishops at *Carpentoracte* decreed that the Bishop of the City should not take all the Countrey Parish maintenance to himself.

§. 96. CLX. As *Felix* was chosen Pope by *Theodorick*; so *Athalaricus* claiming the same power, chose after him *Boniface* the second: An *Arrian* Heretick made the Pope: Others not willing of the Kings Choice, chose *Dioscorus*; so there are two Popes: But *Dioscorus* quickly dyeth; and *Boniface* Condemneth him when he is dead, on some pretence of money matters, as Simoniacal; and calling a Synod, appointeth *Virgilius* a Deacon, his Successor. After he calleth another Synod, to undo this Choice, upon his Repentance; and shortly after dyeth himself. *Agapetus* that followed him, absolveth the dead man *Dioscorus*, whom *Boniface* Cursed: such work did Church-Cursing then make, as the Engine of Ambition.

§. 97. CLXI. A Council of 8 Bishops at *Toletane*, said somewhat again to keep Bishops from Women, and from giving their Lands from the Church.

§. 98. CLXII. *John* was put by *Justinian*, to call a Council at *Rome* on an odd occasion (which sheweth what it was that Bishops then divided the the World about) In the days of *P. Hormisda*, there was a Controversie *(de nomine)* whether it might be said: *One of the Trinity was Crucified*: *Hormisda* declared against it, because they that were for it, were suspected of *Eutychianisme*, (and condemned after) But the *Nestorians* laid hold of this, and said: *If we may not say that one in the Trinity was Crucified*; then we may not say: *Mary was the Parent of one in the Trinity*: *Justinian* sent about this to *John*; and he and his Synod said contrary to *Hormisda*: *That we may say, that one of the Trinity was Crucified*. Doth not this plainly confess the bloud and doleful divisions, caused by Bishops and Monks for so many Ages about *Nestorianisme*, and *Eutychianisme*, was but about a *Word* which in one sence is *true*, and in another false; which one Pope saith, and another unfaith. When *Binnius* after *Baronius* hath no more to say for excuse of this; but that *Ita mutatis hostibus arma mutari necesse fuit*: O for honesty: *Against divers Enemies we must use divers Weapons.* But Sir may you use *contrary assertions*, as Articles of Faith? Or do you not here undenyably tell us

S 2   that

that *Ambiguous words*, and *Clergy Jurisdiction*, have been the causes of almost all the Divisions, and Ruines of the Church for 1300 years?

§. 99. *Justinian* took a better Course to Convince, and Reconcile dissenters, than violence. There is in *Binnius*, p. 409. &c. The recital of a disputation, or Friendly Conference between the *Eutychian* Bishops, and *Hypatius*, with others of the Orthodox: The most clear, rational, and moderate of any thing, that I find before that time explaining their Controversie: And which fully proveth what I have all along said as my Opinion, that indeed the world was confounded by unskilful men about *hard Ambiguous words* and by a *Lordly, selfish, imposing Spirit*, in too many of the Captains of those Militant Churches: And that *clear distinguishing explication of Terms*, with *humble Love*, would have prevented most of those divisions.

In that Conference, these things are specially notable. 1. That the Oriental Bishops called *Eutychians*, condemned *Eutyches*, and yet honoured *Dioscorus*, who defended him; so that it was a quarrel more about Men, Names, and Words, than Doctrine. 2. That *Hypatius*, and the Orthodox (though they were not willing to suspect Corruption in *Cyril*'s Epistles, yet) could not deny but *Cyril* used *Eutyches* words, that is *asserted, one Nature of God Incarnate*, after the Union. 3. That yet they proved that *Cyril* also held two Natures: (but say the *Eutychians*, he only held two before the Union considered intellectually) so that either *Cyril* was an *Eutychian*, or else his unskilful speaking, as both parties did, set the world together by the Ears. 4. That unrighteous partiality greatly prevailed with the Orthodox Bishops, and Councils of these times; when they could (as *Hypatius* here did) put a Charitable Construction upon the same words of *Cyril*, for which they condemned so many others, who as his obedient followers, held what they did of *Cyril*'s. *Unam naturam Dei incarnati:* They say, *We neither Condemnit, nor Justifie it.* If they had used that moderation with all others, all had been in greater peace. 5. That they say so much of the falsifying of *Athanasius* Epistle to *Epictetus*, of *Appollinaries* Epistle fathered on *Julius*, of the falshood of the *Dyonysius Areopag.* &c. As he tells us, that we must not be over credulous in trusting to writings ascribed to the Ancients. 6. That *Nullus ex antiquis recordatus est ea*; was thought a good argument against the Authority of *Dyonisius Areopagita.* 7. They instance in the difference between the Greeks and Latins about the words *Hypostasis*, and *Persona*, which set the Latins on condemning the *Greeks* as *Arrians*, and the *Greeks* it on condemning the *Latins* as *Sabellians*, till *Athanasius* that understood both Tongues, perswaded them, that their meaning was the same (And necessity urged *Athanasius* to reconcile them) which *Greg. Nazianzene* and other peaceable men afterward promoted; And yet *Hierome* was judged a *Heretick* after, for disliking the word *Hypostasis.*) And yet must *Hard ambiguous words* confound and divide the Churches still?

8. They confess that *Cyril*, [*idem dicebat esse substantiam, quod naturam vel subsistentiam*] & *ideo in duodecim Capitulis suis pro duabus substantiis vel naturis duas subsistentias posuit*. Reader, If this great Learned Voluminous
Pre-

Prelate had no more accurateness of Speech than to confound *substance*, *nature*, and *subsistence*, and put them one for another; what could be expected from the multitude of poor unlearned Prelates, that took his name for their guide, and cryed out in Council, *Great is Cyril; We believe as Cyril*: And what then? Could the confusions of the World be caused by (between *Nestorians*, *Eutychians*, *Severians*, *Monothelites* and *Catholicks*) such a strife about words as *Cyril* had occasioned?

9. Note that *Hypatius* and the Orthodox here maintain, that *Flavianus* himself subscribed as much for one Nature as *Dioscorus* could have desired: And that the Controversie lay in a syllable, Whether Christ were one Person? *Ex duabus naturis*, or, *In duabus*; the *Eutychians* said *Ex*, and the rest said *In*: and *Flavian* yielded to *Ex*, and the Synod of *Calcedon* accepted both: *Neque illi istos reprehendunt, neq; isti illos tanquam unius honoris arbitrati voces utrasque, quando & unam naturam Dei verbi incarnatam, non renuit beatus* Flavianus *in confessione quam propria manu subscripsit, dicere, &c.* Where *Flavians* words are recited to *Theodosius, Et unam Dei verbi naturam incarnatam tamen dicere non negamus, quia ex utrisque unus idemque Dominus Jesus Christus est*. And would not this much used to all other, have healed all the Churches?

10. Note that *Hypatius* and the Orthodox make not *Cyril* infallible, but say, that his *Synodical Epistles* they receive, *not as his, but the Synods*: But for the rest; *Neque damnamus eas, neque suscipimus*.

11. That the Controversie was Logical (*p.*413.) how *Unition* maketh or denominateth one.

12. Note that they expresly say, *Ubi Unitio dicitur, non Unius significatur rei conventus* (so all say) *sed duarum vel plurium & diversarum secundum naturam: Si erga dicimus Unitionem, procul dubio confitemur, quod carnis animatæ & verbi: sed & hi qui duas naturas dicunt, idem sentiunt.* And if this be true, were they not all of a mind and knew it not?

13. Note that the *Eutychians* took *Theodorets* Anathema, *Nestorio & Eutycheti*, with a *Valete* added for a slur, and a deceit: and *Hypatius* was fain to intimate a blame on the Council, that had not the patience once to hear such a man as *Theodorite* to open his judgment, but cryed out only, *Curse them, curse them*, and he interprets *Theodorets Valete*, as saying, *Now take my Bishoprick if you please*.

14. In a word, had this *Light* and *Love* been used by the Bishops, which this Conference expresseth, it had prevented much Confusion in the Churches, scorn against the Bishops, hardening of the Infidels, and destruction of Christian Love and Peace. And though the *Eastern* Bishops yielded not, many of their followers did.

§. 100. CLXIII. They say an *African* Council sent to *Justinian* to procure the restoration of their Liberties, which the *Vandali Arians* had taken away (*Justinian* having recovered *Africa*.)

§. 101. Pope *Agapetus* was forced by King *Theodatus* to go on an Embassie baffle to *Juftinian*, to turn by his Armies from *Italy*: which he did, and not prevailing (having rejected *Anthimus*) he dyed there, *Anno* 536.

§. 102. CLXIV. *Menna* being made Bishop of *Conft.* a Council was there called. Sure no *Roman* Presided; for there was then an *Inter-regnum*: But was it then a good Council? As please the Pope! Yet so impudent is *Binnius* as to say, that *Menna* was the Popes Vicar, and his Legates presided, when there was no Pope on Earth.

The work of this Council was to condemn and curse *Anthimus*, (a Bishop of *Conft.* got in by the Emprefs, and put out by the Emperour) with *Severus* late Bishop of *Antioch*, and *Peter* Bishop of *Apamea*, and *Zoaras* a Monk, as being *Acephali*, that is, *Severians*, or *Eutychians*, as they were variously called: *Severus* and *Peter* have cruel persecutions also laid to their charge, (for persecution hath but its time.) The Emperour hereupon maketh a severe Law against them, sending them by banishment to solitude, and condemning their Books to the fire, and judging their hands to be cut off that writ them. (We may see whence our Church-History mostly cometh, even from the stronger side, that had power to burn all which they would not have known.)

☞ Two things in this Council offend the *Romanifts*: 1. That *John* Bishop of *Conftantinople* is called *Patriarcha Oecumenicus*: 2. That *Euphemius*, *Macedonius*, and *Leo* are named, and *Leo* laft: the two firft having been damned by the Popes so oft since they were dead. And they have no better remedy, but to say that some ill *Greek* hand hath falsified the Councils. (Is that all the certainty w... .ave of recorded Councils.) If you suspect the *Greeks*, why may we not also suspect the *Romans*; especially in the days of wicked Popes?

The People cryed out here, *Quid manemus in communicati?* *Binnius* noteth, that *from the time that* Macedonius *their Orthodox Bishop was ejected, the faithful Catholicks withdrew themselves from the Communion of impious* Timothy *that was put into his place.* Note 1. that this *Macedonius* is he that the *Roman* Pope so often damned alive and dead: 2. That the Peoples separation from bad possessours of the Bishops Seats, was then an usual and justified thing.

§. 103. CLXV. A Council at *Jerusalem* having notice of what was done at *Conft.* do the same against *Anthinus*, *Severus*, *Peter*, and *Zoaras*.

104. *Anaftasius* in *lib. Pontific.* faith that the *Arian* King *Theodatus* corrupted with Money, made *Silverius* Pope, And at the same time the Empress *Theodora* promised the Popedom to *Vigilius*, on condition he would restore *Anthimus* and those that the Council had damned: which he promising, the Emprefs sent him with Letters to *Bellifarius* to see it done. *Silverius* was but a Sub-Deacon, and *Vigilius* an Arch-Deacon, son to Pope *Hormifda*: *Silverius* was accused by many witnesses of *Treafon* in offering to let in the *Goths* into the City, and was banished, and *Vigilius* put
in

their Councils abridged.

in his place, and had the keeping of him and famished him to death, and succeeded him. So that here were a while two Popes at once, one chosen by an *Arian*, and the other a perfidious Murderer, that undertook to restore those that were ejected as Hereticks: And was this man to be communicated with any more than *Acacius*, *Euthymius*, or *Macedonius*?

§. 105. *Theodosius* a Bishop of *Alexandria* refusing to subscribe to the *Calcedon* Council, was ejected and banished by *Justinian*, and *Paulus* as Orthodox put into his place: who being accused of Murder was also put out and banished, and *Zoilus* put into his place.

§. 106. But *Theodosius* is said by *Liberat.* and others, to have first deserted the place, being wearied with the Peoples Wars: The case was this: A new controversie was started, whether the body of Christ was *corruptible* or *incorruptible*? The division about this was so great, that the Church divided, and chose two Bishops: Those that were for the *incorruptability*, had *Gainas* for their Arch-Bishop, and were called by the other *Phantasiasta*, and *Gainites*: Those that were for the *corruptability*, had *Theodosius* for their Arch-Bishop, and were called by the other *corrupticola*, and *Theodosians*. Most communicated with *Gainas*; but the Souldiers were for *Theodosius*. *Liberatus Breviar. c.* 20. faith, that they fought it out, and *The People fought for* Gainas, *many days*; *and being slain by the Souldiers lost their greatest part: but yet a greater number fell of the Souldiers: And* Narses *was overcome, not with Arms, but with the concord of the Citizens: The women cast stones on them from the tops of the Houses*; *But the Souldiers did that by Fire which they could not do by Arms.* And faith Liberatus, *That City is divided with that Schism to this day*, some being called *Gainites*, and *Phantasiasts*, and the other *Theodosians*, and *Corrupticola*.

§. 107. The Case of the Orthodox *Paul* that succeeded him, is described by *Liberatus*, *c.* 23. He intending to put out *Elias* the Master of the Souldiers as a Heretick, by a power received from the Emperour, one of his Deacons discovered it to *Elias* by Letters. *Paulus* fearing the fate of *Preterius*, and getting the Letters, got *Rhodo* the Emperours *Augustal* Magistrate to secure the Deacon, who by one *Arsenius* Murdered him: For which alledging the command of *Paulus* the Bishop, and the Emperours command to obey *Paul*, the Emperour put to death the Magistrate *Rhodo*, and deposed *Paulus*, and put *Zoilus* in his place.

§. 108. There is in *Liberatus*, *c.* 22. An Epistle of Pope *Vigilius*, in which he performeth his promise to the Empress, and owneth Communion with *Anthimus*, &c. and denyeth *two natures*, &c. But *Baronius* and *Binnius* take it for a forged Epistle; when as we have scarce a more credible Writer than *Liberatus*.

§. 109. *Niceph. l.* 17. *c.* 26. faith, that *Vigilius*, when *Rome* was again taken

taken by the *Goths*, fled to *Constantinople*; There he fell out with *Mennas* the Orthodox Patriarch *(Cui Agathon Papa, quod nunquam antea factum est, manus imposuit,* faith *Niceph. c. 9.*) and *eo insolentia progressus est*, he grew so insolent that he Excommunicated *Menna* for four Months: which so provoked *Justinian*, that he sent men to apprehend him, and when he fled to the Altar, they drag'd him away, and *Anastasius* in *lib. Pontif.* faith, They tyed a rope about his neck and drag'd him about the streets till the evening, and made him glad to communicate with *Menna*. But at last he was restored to his Bishoprick.

§. 110. Two heinous crimes *Evagrius* chargeth *Justinian* with: 1. Insatiable covetousness and extortion. (But he used to do very great good works.) 2. Encouraging Murderers (see *Evagr, l. 4. c. 31.*) so that men were no where safe, but they that killed them, as in an act of manhood were protected.

§. 111. And though he was the great Zealot for the Orthodox against all Hereticks, he dyed a reputed Heretick; in so much that *Evagrius* over boldly pronounceth, *That when he had set the whole World on tumults and sedition, and at last received what was due for his lewd practices, he departed into endless torment prepared for him by the just judgment of God, l. 5. c. 1.* An arrogant sentence. And will Orthodox Zeal for the Church do no more to save a Soul from Hell.

CHAP

CHAP. VII.

Of the Controversies de tribus Capitulis, *and the Fifth Council called General, and many other.*

§ 1. **E***vagrius l. 4. c. 38.* tells us, that *Justinian* fell from the right Faith, affirming, *That the Body of Christ was every way incorruptible; and that he wrote an Edict, in which he said, That the Body of the Lord was not subject to death or corruption; that it was void of natural and unblameable affections,* &c. *which Opinions he purposed to compel both Priests and Bishops to subscribe: but they put him off, as expecting the Opinion* (not of the Pope, but) *of* Anastasius *Bishop of* Antioch, *then famous for his skill and gravity: But* Anastasius *would not be moved, and* Justinian *threatning to banish him, dyed before he did it, or published his Edict.* So hard was it then to escape Heresie.

§ 2. So hot was *Justinian* in this Error, that he ejected *Eutychius* that resisted him at *Constantinople,* saith *Niceph.l.17.c.29. Julianus Halicarnaf.* and *Gainas* raised this, holding that *Christ's hunger,thirst and suffering, were all immediately voluntary,and not as ours by natural necessity.* They said that as we all hold *Christs Body incorruptible after his resurrection, so did they before it, yet consubstantial with ours.* The Orthodox distinguished of Corruption:
1. Blameless Passions of Hunger, Thirst, Weariness, &c. 2. Dissolution of the Bodies Elements. The first they said Christ was subject to before the Resurrection, but not after (nor we:) The later not at all. The Hereticks that held the contrary, were called the *Aphthartodocitæ,* saith *Nicephorus,* [*Quá multi mortales correpti sunt, non solum ex eis qui honores & magistratus gesserunt, sed etiam Hierarchæ primarii, & Monachi vita illustres, & ex sacerdotali ordine alii, ut ipse Imperator* Justinianus.] The *Hereticators* and *Damners* are divided about *Justinian's* soul and name; some place him yet in Heaven, and others in Hell. If it be true that *Nicephorus* saith of him, my Vote should go against the *Damners,* viz. [*Nil tale de Christo propter summum ipsius erga illum amorem & desiderium audire constituerit: Princeps etenim iste tanto in Christum pietatis ardore flagrasse, ab eis qui res illius memoriæ posteritati mandarunt, dicitur, quanto alius, qui ante eum imperium obtinuerunt,nemo, termaximo illo* Constantino *semper excepto: Itaque propter vehementem in Christum amorem illius gratiâ multâ etiam violenter fecit,* &c. And if it came from vehement love to Christ, all I will say is, 1. Let him that is without Error, be the first in damning him. 2. But it was just with God to leave him to be numbered with Hereticks, who was so blindly zealous in executing the Sentences of Hereticating Prelates: (The Case of *Nestorius,* and many others before.)

§ 3. In his time the *Indian Auxumites* turned to Christ, and *Justinian* joyfully sent them a Bishop.

And I take it for more dishonour to the Bishops than to him, that *Nicephorus*

Some late Historians tell us of incredible numbers of the Egyptian Christians whom Justinian destroyed in this blind zeal for Christ, but I find no such thing in the old Historians though it was too bad.

faith, c. 32. [*In Pontifices quos admodum de Sodomorum hæresi insanire compererat, acerbe, seu potius sæde,* Justinianus *animadvertit.—*
And it is noted (*ibid.*) that in a *Famine* he commanded Flesh to be sold in *Lent*; but the People would dye rather than buy it, and break their Customs.

§ 4. CLXVI. *An.*540. A Council of 25 Bishops at *Orleance*, made some Canons of Discipline. The 3d Canon about Ordaining Bishops, layeth down the old Rule, [*Qui præponendus est omnibus, ab omnibus eligatur,*] that is, of the Clergy and People: (The Churches yet were no greater than that all the People could join in choosing the Bishop.) The 10th Canon dissolveth incestuous Marriages made after Baptism, but not those made before (as if the reason were not the same!) The 27th Canon finding some too *Jewish* in keeping the *Lord's-day*, that would not use a Horse or Chariot to carry them, nor would dress Meat, or do any thing to the adorning of their Houses, or themselves, forbiddeth only grosser labours, which hinder the holy duties of the day.

§ 5. CLXVII. The *Canones Barcinonenses,* speak of the order of Liturgy, that Clerks must cut their Beards, but not shave their Beards, and such like.

§ 6. CLXVIII. (To pass the *Concil. Byzazenum,* as having nothing noted of it) Anno 541. a *Concil. Arvernense* decreed (under King *Theodebert*) one Canon, which, if practised, had been worth many Kingdoms, Ca. 2. [*That no one seek the sacred honour of a Bishop by Votes, but by Merits: nor seem to get a Divine Office,* rebus, sed moribus: *and that he ascend to the top of that eminent dignity,* by the ELECTION of ALL, and not by the FAVOR of a FEW: *That in choosing Priests there be the greatest Care, because they should be irreprehensible, who must rule in correcting others,* &c.

§ 7. CLXIX. *An.* 545. Another Council at *Orleance* under King *Childebert*, among other Orders, saith, *Can.* 3. that the Synod *forbiddeth the Citizens to celebrate Easter out of the City; because they must keep the principal Festivities in the presence of the Bishop, where the holy Assembly must be kept. But if any have a necessity to go abroad, let him ask leave of the Bishop.*] This Canon, and many other to the same purpose tell us, that then the Infidels were still so many, that a Bishop's City-Church could all meet *in his presence in one place.*

The 5th Canon decreeth, that a Bishop shall be ordained in his own *Church which he is to oversee*; which implieth, that then ordinarily there was but one Episcopal Church. And indeed it was long before the Countrey meetings were any other than Oratories or Chappels that had no Altars, nor any but the Bishops Church.

Much ado many Councils made to keep Priests and Bishops from Wives, and to restrain them from Fornication.

§ 8. CLXX. In a Synod at *Constantinople,* An. 547. the business was debated *de tribus Capitulis.*

§ 9. Here the occasion of this stir must be noted. One *Theodorus* Bishop of *Cæsar. Cap.* was an *Eutychian,* but for his skill in business, was great with the Emperor. He thought if he could but cast any slur on the *Calcedon* Council, it would justifie their Cause: And the Emperor being speaking against the *Eutychians,*

tychians, (or *Acephali*) *Theodorus* told him that he might easily bring them all in, if he would but condemn *Theodorus Mopsuestenus*, and the Writings of *Theodoret*, and the Epistle of *Ibas* against *Cyril*, which the Council had received, it would satisfie them. This seemed to the Emperor a happy way of concord (the Empress putting him on) and so he set himself earnestly to effect it. These three men had been accounted *Nestorians*, and two of them had written smartly against *Cyril* as heretical and turbulent; but yet renouncing *Nestorius* they were received, and justified at *Calceden* against their Accusers. And if one may judge impartially by the Evidence that is left us, they seem to have been far wiser and better men than the majority of the Bishops of those times: But neither Learning, Piety, nor soundness in the Faith, is any security in such times, against Hereticaters, that can but get the upper hand and major vote. And Ignorance usually is most proud and loud, most confident and furious; and such can easilier make wise men pass for Hereticks, than learn of them to be wise. But the final judgment sets a strait.

When *Justinian* was earnestly set upon this Project, the Defenders of the *Calcedon* Council perceived themselves in a difficulty; should they condemn these three men, they would seem to condemn the Council (about which there had been such a stir in the Empire:) And they should seem to justifie the *Eutychians*, and to strengthen them: And if Council were against Council, it would dishonour Councils: And if they should refuse the Condemnation, they would seem to desert *Cyril*, and the first *Ephesian* Council, and perhaps might be called *Nestorians*; but, worst of all, they should displease the Emperor, and might occasion his favouring the *Eutychians*. Therefore they took this prudent course, to put off the business to a General Council, and to delay till then the Emperors attempts.

But the Emperor did first publish his Edict, in which after the Confession of his Faith, and praise of the four Councils, he addeth ten Curses (Anathematisms, according to the Custom and Religion of those times) of which the three last are against the *tria Capitula*, or the Councils seeming approbation of the three forenamed men. The Bishops resisted a great while, but at last were forced to submit.

§ 10. CLXXI. To this purpose *Vigilius Romanus* had a meeting of about 30 Bishops, where *Vigilius* yielding was called a Desertor, as prevaricating to please the Emperor; he got them to give in their reasons on both sides in writing, and then gave all to the Emperor's party, and perswaded the rest to silence and communion till a Council, because it was not a Controversie about Faith, but about Persons. *Consant. An. 547.*

§ 11. The Emperor's Party (acted by *Theodore Cæsar*.) got some Bishops to assemble at *Mopsuest*. *An. 550.* to prepare a Condemnation of their former Bishop *Theodore*, by saying that his name was not in their Book.

§ 12. CLXXII. King *Childebert* called another Council at *Orleance*, where many old disciplinary Canons were repeated: Among others, Can. 9. *That no Lay-man be made a Bishop without a years time to learn his Function*. (You may conjecture what Scholars they were then!) Can. 10. *That none get a Bishoprick* by gifts, or seeking; but with the will of the King, by the election of the Clergy and the Lay-people. Can. 11. Also (as the ancient Canons have decreed) let none be made Bishop to an unwilling People (or without the Peoples consent) nor let the People or the Clergy be inclined to consent, by the oppression of persons in power, which is not lawful to be spoken :) But if it be otherwise done, let the Bishop be for ever deposed from his obtained honour of Pontificate, who is ordained rather by force, than lawful decree. C. While one Bishop is living, let not any other be there made Bishop; unless perhaps in his place, who is ejected for some capital Crime. Can. 21. Though all Priests, and others, must be careful to relieve the Poor with necessaries, yet especially every Bishop must from the Church-house as far as they can, administer necessaries for food and rayment to such as are in weakness both in his Territories and his City, &c.]

Note I. Were those Bishopricks any bigger than our Parishes of Market-Towns with the Chappelleries? where 1. All the Laity met to choose the Bishop. 2. Where the Bishop could know and relieve all the Poor. 3. And this from the *domus Ecclesiæ*, which was but one.

II. Our Nonconformists plead, that according to these ancient Canons, 1. Those Bishops are no Bishops who came not in by any *choice* or *consent* of the People or Clergy, but by *power are imposed on the most unwilling.* 2. That those Ministers that were never deposed for any Crime, are not to be forsaken by their Flocks, nor imposed persons thrust into their places, accepted by the People, while the first hath true right.

§ 13. CLXXIII. We come now to that which they will needs call the fifth General Council at *Constantinople, An.* 553. of 165 Bishops. In which let these particulars be noted. 1. That *Justinian*'s Letters or *Formulæ* were first read, in which he expresly affirmeth, that it was the Emperors that called the former General Councils, and he that called this. 2. That he lamenteth the divisions which former Councils had left unhealed: saying, [*The followers of* Nestorius *and* Eutyches *made so great trouble in the holy Churches of God, that divisions and schisms were made in them, and the Churches had no Communion with one another: For no man that travelled from one City to another, did presume to communicate, nor any Clerk that went from one City to another, to go into the Church.*] Here was lamentable separation indeed. 3. That *Justinian* was made believe, that these divisions would be healed, if the *tria Capitula* of the Council of *Calcedon* were but condemned: For the *Eutychians* did so much boast of *Cyril*, being confident that they did but follow him, and his first *Ephesian* Council, that if he were vindicated, he thought they would be satisfied. 4. And he thought that the three Bishops were indeed so far to be condemned, having disgraced *Cyril*, and favored *Nestorius*, and the other was *Nestorius*'s Master. 5. That the *receiving* and the *cursing* of the Council of *Calcedon*, having hitherto been the great Contest among the Bishops, some were loth now to cast so great a dishonour upon it, and to give the *Eutychians* so much cause to boast; supposing they would but be the more confirmed in their opposition.

§ 14. Note also, that *Vigilius* Bishop of *Rome* was then at *Constantinople*, but came not to the Council, nor sent any Legate to it: But the Emperor tells the

Council, "*That when* Vigilius *Bishop of* Rome *came to that City, the Emperor* "*exactly opened to him all things about the* tria Capitula, *and asked him what he* "*thought of them; and that* Vigilius *not once nor twice, but often in writing,* "*and without writing, anathematized the impious* tria Capitula.] *And that he had* "*shewed that he was ever of the same judgment,* &c.

And they had made *Justinian* believe, *that* Ibas *in his Epistle denieth God the Word to be made man, and the Virgin* Mary *to be the Mother of God.*]

§ 15. The Emperor's Writing being read, at the next meeting the Council sent to *Vigilius* to sit with them, but he still refused, alledging, *That there were few of the Western Bishops there.* To which their answer is notable, that [*The meeting of all the rest ought not to be delayed for the Western Bishops: For in all the four General Councils, there was never found a multitude of the Western Bishops, but only two or three Bishops, and a few Clerks. But now you are here, and many* Italian *Bishops are at hand, and many of* Africa, Illyricum, &c. *And if he would not meet them, they must do it without him.* They urged him also with the Emperor's words, that *he being alone, had oft in writing, and without writing, condemned the* tria Capitula, and the Emperor desired him but *to do that with others, which he had done by himself.* But yet *Vigilius* would not come: Whether it was because he understood not *Greek*, and so should be a contemned Cypher (for he saith, *They all knew that he understood it not*) or whether it was to avoid the Censure that he had before incurred, or both, is not known. For you must understand, that *Vigilius* had suffered defamation at *Rome* already, as a Revolter from the *Calcedon* Council, for joining herein with the Emperor in the beginning, and his chief interest lay at home.

§ 16. *Theodorus Mopsuestenus* Writings are searched; and though he is highly extolled by many good Authors, yet many passages recited in the Council, and after by *Vigilius*, do shew either the error of his judgment, or his unskilfulness in speaking; for they are not justifiable. But if every Papist voluminous Writer should be damned as a Heretick, whose Writings have more and greater Errors than the Council gathered out of *Theodore Mopsuestenus*, it would be a hard reward for their exceeding labours. When such men as *Testatus, Aquinas, Scotus, Ockam, Durandus,* &c. *Bellarmine, Baronius, Suarez, Valquez, Cajetane,* &c. have spent their days in diligent labours, how easie a matter is it for a proud idle Drone that doth nothing or worse, to gather as many and as great Errors out of their Works, as were in many then counted Hereticks. But the approbation of God, who pardoneth failings, will be the comfort of such as improve their Talents; when the slothful, unprofitable Servant shall be condemned, and quarrelling with the imperfections of the diligent will not save them.

It is evident that *Theodore* and *Nestorius* acknowledged Christ's Godhead and Manhood, Soul and Body, and the personal Union of them. But they were none of them perfect in Logick and Metaphysicks, nor so spake as that no man could blame their words.

§ 17. Next the words of learned *Theodorite* are scanned; and many very smart passages against *Cyril* are recited: Many verbal Controversies are repeated. *Theodorite* is accused for saying, *That* Mary *begat not God in the nature of God*, but

but Man as united to the Godhead ; That Christ was forsaken, suffered, hungered, slept, was ignorant of that day and hour, &c. *as man, and not as God : That it was not God that was ignorant,* (he meant *not as God,* or not *the Deity*) *but the form of a Servant, which knew no more than the Deity revealed :* And so of many other properties or acts of the Humanity, he saith, *It was not* Deus Verbum *that wept, that learnt obedience,* &c. meaning only not *quâ Deus,* or not *Deitas,* for want of care in speaking. And *Ep. ad Job. Antioch.* (*Bin.* p. 559.) it's apparent that he also misunderstood *Cyril,* and thought he held that by *Unity of Natures,* the *Deity* was properly become very flesh. A severe *Epist. ad Joan. Antioch.* against *Cyril* after his death is there charged on him, in which he with great saltness rejoiceth in his death, [*Miserum illum nec ad similitudinem aliorum dimisit nostrarum animarum gubernator diutius eorum potiri, quæ videntur esse delectabilia ; sed crescentem quotidie viri malignitatem sciens & corpori Ecclesiæ nocentem, quasi pestem quandam amputavit & abstulit opprobrium à filiis* Israel : *Lætificabit superstites ejus discessio : Contristavit verò forsitan mortuos, & timor est ne prægravati ejus conversatione, iterum ad nos remittant, vel illos diffugiat qui eum abducunt, sicut ille tyrannus Cyri Ciliciam : Procurandum est igitur, & oportet tuam Sanctitatem maxime hanc suscipere festinantiam, & jubere collegio mortuos asportantium lapidem aliquem maximum & gravissimum Sepulchro imponere, ne iterum huc perveniret & instabilem voluntatem iterum demonstraret : Infernis nova dogmata adferat : Ibi diu noctuque sicut vult sermocinetur : Non enim timemus ne & illos divideret—silet miser invitus: Nudata illius facta alligant linguam, obstruunt os, fræ- nant sensum.—Ideo plango miserum & ploro : Nec enim puram mihi delectationem feci: mortis ejus denunciatio, sed dolore permixtam : Lætor & jucundor ejusmodi pestilentiâ commune Ecclesiæ videns liberatum : Contristor vero & ploro cogitans quod nec requiem malorum miserabilis susceperit, sed majora & pejora pertentans defunctus est ; somniavit enim, ut dicunt, & regiam urbem perturbare, & tuam Sanctitatem accusare, utpote ea colentem : Sed vidit Deus & non despexit : Immisit fimum in os ejus, & frænum in labia ejus,* &c.

Binnius thinketh some bad man fathered this falsly on *Theodoret,* I would hope so too : But it's strange that the Council fathered it on him, and none did vindicate him. And the next Charge (*Bin.* p. 559.) rebuketh his Charity, *viz.* his Speech at *Antioch* in the presence of *Domnus,* [*Nemo neminem jam cogit blasphemare—non jam est contentio: Oriens & Ægyptus sub uno jugo est : Mortua est invidia ; & cum eo obruta est contentio: requiescant* Theopathitæ.] Is not this of the same kind ? And this is not denied to be his. Whosoever it was, it was sad that Bishops should have such minds, and use such words of one another, especially if it be as I confidently believe, *viz.* that not distinguishing the *concrete* from the *abstract,* and *Qui Deus,* from *Quâ Deus,* they both meant the same thing, and differed but about the aptitude of words, for want of explication and distinction.

§ 18. In brief, After the reading of many Papers, and *Ibas* Epistles, the *tria Capitula* were condemned, viz. *Theodore Mopsuest.* and the writings of *Theodoret* against *Cyril,* and *Ibas* Epistle. And so the Emperor found the Council as obedient as he desired.

§ 19.

§ 19. But *Vigilius* Bishop of *Rome*, who would not come to the Council, now giveth in his *Constitutum*, or his own judgment upon the whole Case, and that with great moderation. He first reciteth many passages of *Theodore Mopsuest.* which he renounceth; and he dispraiseth the passages of *Theodoret* and *Ibas*, but he refuseth to join in the anathematizing of them, alledging that good men have their errors, and instancing in many whose errors were noted, and yet their persons not condemned, especially when they had either recanted them, or better explained their words: And he noteth that it would be a great injury to the *Calcedon* Council, to have its own members now thus condemned, that were by them accepted. [*Quid enim aliud est mendaces aut simulantes professionem rectæ fidei Patres in sancta Calced. Synodo residentes ostendere, quam dicere aliquos ex eis similia sapuisse Nestorio; quorum judicio Nestorium ejusque dogmata fuisse damnata.*]

And soberly he saith, [*It is not lawful to pass any new judgment on the persons of the dead, but we must leave all men in the case that death found them, and in special* Theodore Mopsuest. *what the Fathers did is evident from what is said; I dare not condemn him by my sentence, nor yield that any one else condemn him: but far be it from me to admit his wrong opinions.*]

This was the right way: If they had all dealt as wisely and Christian-like, Counsels had not been the Confounders of the Churches.

§ 20. *Nicephorus* nameth many of *Origen's* Errors that were condemned in this Council, but it is not found in the Acts. *Binnius* doubteth not but the *Origenists* stole them out, and falsified the Records, and also forged those Epistles of *Vigilius*, in which the opinion of *One Operation* is asserted. But will they allow us equally to suspect such Records as have been kept at *Rome*?

§ 21. What good this Council did, and how the peaceable Emperor attained the end that *Theodore Cæsar* promised him, of uniting Dissenters, I shall tell you but in the words of *Binnius* (who followeth *Baronius* in almost all) " *Whate* " Theodore Cæsar *promised, that the* Eutychian *Hereticks called* Hesitants, *when* " *the three* Capitula *were condemned, would receive the holy* Calcedon *Council, was* " *not obtained, when this was ended; but rather a most grievous mischief was ad-* " *ded to the Church: For when the Defenders of the three* Capitula, *with* Vigilius " *the Pope did not acquiesce in the Councils decree, the whole Catholick Church was* " *torn by Schism; and which is worse, the Emperor stir'd up Persecution, in which* " *he deposed or banished* Vigilius *(holding to his* Constitutum) *Victor. Afric. and* " *others.*

§ 22. I do impartially commend *Vigilius's* moderate *Constitutum*, but I must needs say that there needeth no other instance than *Vigilius*, that *Interest* is a Law to some *Roman* Bishops, and that their pretences of Infallibility, Tradition and Antiquity, notwithstanding they have changed their very Faith, or judgment of Councils at least, as their worldly motives changed. *Vigilius* first flattered the Emperor, and joined with him against the *tria Capitula, Conc. Calced.* that is, against *Theodore Mopsu. Theodoret* and *Ibas* three Bishops, saith *Binnius* p. 608. "[*Seeing therefore that before this Council a Schism arose in the* Western *and* Afri- " cane Church, *because* Vigilius *had consented to the Emperor's opinion, it became*
" *necess-*

" *neceffary, for the avoiding of Schifm, Sacriledge and Scandal, that he should pub-*
" *lifh his* Conftitutum, *in defence of the* tria Capitula, *by vertue whereof the*
" *Weftern Churches fhould be united, and the contempt of the* Calcedon Council
" *fhould be avoided, which the Impugners of the* tria Capitula *did fraudulently con-*
" *trive; and that the Univerfal Church should learn by this example, that no man*
" *that dyed in the true Faith, fhould be condemned when he is dead: But, (did*
" Vigilius *ftop here ?*) *No, faith* Binnius, [*But when after the end of his Council*
" *the Church received yet greater damage, and the Emperor perfecuted them that*
* And   " *contradicted the Synod* *, *and it was feared that the whole Eaft would be divi-*
would   " *ded and feparated from the* Roman *and* Weftern *Church, unlefs the Bifhop of*
notPapifts " Rome *approved the fifth Synod, then Pope* Vigilius, *in a Caufe which could bring*
havePrin- " *no prejudice to the Orthodox Faith, did well and juftly change his former fen-*
ces do fo? " *tence, and approved the Synodal Decree, for condemning the* tria Capitula, *and*
" *revoked and made void his* Conftitutum, *which he before publifhed in defence of*
" *the* tria Capitula. *The prudent and pious Pope (that came to the Popedom by*
" *Bribery, Tyranny, and Murder of his Predeceffor) did in this prudently imitate*
" *St.* Paul *about Circumcifion,* &c.

O what certainty and conftancy is here in the Papal judgment; For a Pope about one Caufe to judge for it, againft it, and for it again in fo fhort a time? And all this upon reafon of Policy and State. Did the fame fo often change, and prove firft true, and then falfe, and then true again?

But the Papifts excufe is, that it was *de Perfonis, non de Fide*. *Anfw*. But 1. Is it lawful to take the fame thing for true and falfe, good and bad *de Perfonis*, as our intereft requireth? 2. Why are the Perfons condemned but on fuppofition that their Faith was condemnable? 3. You confefs that it was for the advantage of the *Eutychian* Faith, and the depreffion of the Faith of the *Calcedon* Council, that the *tria Capitula* were condemned.

Reader, If all this will not tell thee how much need there is of a furer and more ftable fupport of our Faith than Popes and Councils, yea and better means of the Churches Unity and Concord, I muft take thee for unteachable: what have fuch Councils done, but fet the Churches together by the ears?

§ 23. *Liberatus* in his Breviary faith, (c. 3. 10. 24.) that *Theodore Mopfu.* his Works were approved by *Proclus, Johan. Antioch.* the Emperor, the Council of *Calced.* &c. But *Binnius* faith, *Nimis impudenter & incauté* : Yet all acknowledge *Liberatus* a moft credible Hiftorian, and lived in *Juftinian*'s time. He faith alfo, that *Nefandiffimum hæreticum* Theodoretus *&* Sozomenus *laudarunt adeo ut hac de cauſa uterque magnam nominis fui jacturam paffus fuerit,* &c. But wife men are apt to think as hardly of fuch as can cry out *Nefandiffimum hæreticum* againſt all that fpeak as unskilfully as this man did, us of charitable men that praife them for what is good, while they difown their frailties and imperfections : If it be as he faith, many thought that *Theodoret* affumed his own name from this *Theodore*, by reafon of his high efteem of him, it's like he had fome fpecial worth, though he hath many culpable expreffions. And *Sozomen* is an Hiftorian of fo deferved reputation, that it feemeth to me no argument of Pope *Gregory*'s Infallibility, that he faith, lib. 6. cp. 95. *Sozomenum ejufque Hiftoriam fedes Apoftolica*
recipere

their Councils abridged.

recipere recusat ; quoniam multa mentitur, & Theodorum Mopsuestiæ *nimium laudat, atque ad diem obitus sui magnum Doctorem Ecclesiæ fuisse perhibet.*] I think the Author of *Gregory*'s Dialogues did *plura mentiri ,* and yet that *Gregory* was *Magnus Ecclesiæ Doctor.*

§ 24. The Controversie whether *Vigilius* were the Author of the Epistle to *Menna,* I pass by : But, methinks, *Binnius* is very partial to justifie so much what he did after *Silverius*'s death, as beginning then to have right to his Papacy, and to give him so differing a Character (from *Sanctissimus Papa*) before, while he possessed the same Seat, as these words of his express, [*Cum omnium, &c. seeing that Villany* (or *Crime*) *of* Vigilius, *did exceed the Crimes of all Schismaticks, by which making a bargain with Hereticks, and giving money by a Lay-man , he by force expelled* Silverius *Bishop of the prime Seat, and spoiled of his Priestly indiments* (*or attire*) *banished him into an* Island, *and there caused him to dye , it should seem no wonder to any man, if a desperate wretch* (homo perditus, *) the buyer of another's Seat, and a violent Invader, a Wolf, a Thief, a Robber, not entering by the true door, a false* (*or counterfeit*) *Bishop, and as it were Antichrist, the lawful Pastor and Bishop being yet living, did add most pernicious Heresie to his Schism.*] Yet this man became the *most holy Pope, by the vertue* of his place, as soon as he had but murdered *Silverius,* and was accepted in his stead, and then it became impossible for him to err in the Faith.

§ 25. CLXXIV. *Anno* 553. A Council was called at *Jerusalem* by *Justinian*'s Command, who sent to them the Acts of the *Constantine* Council *de tribus Capitulis,* to be by them received; the Bishops all received it readily , save one *Alexander Abyssi,* who was therefore banished, and coming to *Constantinople,* say *Baronius* and *Binnius,* was swallowed up, and buried by an Earthquake. If this was true, no marvel if it confirmed the Emperor in his way : But I doubt the obedient Bishops were too ready to receive such reports.

§ 26. CLXXV. The same year 553. the *Western* Bishops held a Council at *Aquileia,* out of the Emperor's power, where, as Defenders of the Council of *Calcedon,* they .*condemned the fifth* Constantine *Council aforesaid,* and (so saith *Binnius*) separated themselves from the Unity of the Catholick Church , and so continued for near an Hundred years, till the time of Pope *Sergius,* who reduced them. Were not these great Councils and Bishops great Healers of the Church, that about condemning some written Sentences of three dead men, thus raise a War among the Churches ? Were Hereticks or Hereticaters the great Dividers ?

§ 27. But here followeth a Case that raiseth a great doubt before us, Whether the Pope alone, or all his *Western* Bishops, when they differ from him, are the Church ? After the death of *Vigilius,* the Secular Power procured *Pelagius* the Archdeacon to be made Pope ; the *Western* Bishops disclaiming *Justinian*'s Council, and *Pelagius* obediently receiving it (and the Popedom,) there could not be three Bishops got that would ordain him, as the Canons required, so that a Presbyter *Ostiensis* was fain to do it.

Besides the Question(Which now was the Church?) here are other hard Questions to be solved.

B b

Qu. 1. Whether *Justinian's* Election of a Pope was valid? And if so, Whether other various Electors may do it as validly?

Qu. 2. Whether a Presbyter's Ordination of a Bishop or Pope was valid? If so, Whether Presbyters may not ordain Presbyters?

Qu. 3. Whether this Pope was truly Head of the Catholick Church, when his Bishops obeyed him not?

Qu. 4. Whether it was then believed at *Rome* itself, and in the *West*, that a General Council, approved by the Pope, was either infallible, or necessarily to be obeyed?

Qu. 5. Whether it be true which *W. Johnson*, alias *Terret*, often tells me, *That it is not possible that there can be any Schism in the Catholick Church, because of the essentiality of its Union?*

§ 28. Note that this Pope *Pelagius*, because his Bishops rejected him and the Council, got *Narses* the General to *compel them*: And then who can doubt but he was Pope, and they his Subjects?

But *Narses* scrupled it, lest he should be guilty of Persecution; *Justinian's* Pope *Pelagius* telleth him, it is no sin, and bids him not fear it; for it's no Persecution which compels not men to sin: but all that separate from the Pope, and assemble separatedly do sin, and are damned Schismaticks; therefore he desireth him to send the Bishops of *Aquileia, Milan,* and the rest that yield not, Prisoners to *Constantinople*. *Narses* obeyeth the Pope and Emperor; the Bishops excommunicate *Narses*; the Pope writeth to him, that it is no news for erring Bishops to take themselves for the Catholick Church, and to forbid others their Communion, and counselleth him to go on and repress them. And the Civil Sword and the Ecclesiastical were thus engaged in a *Roman* War; one Bishop *Sapandus* of *Ares* in *France* the Pope got specially to stick to him, whom therefore he commended to King *Childebert*, &c.

§ 29. CLXXVI. A Council at *Paris* deposed Bishop *Saphoracus* for some great Crime.

§ 30. While the *Romans* were resolving to subject themselves to the *Goths* again, because the Pope made *Narses* their Persecutor, *Narses* took it so ill, that he * went away from them, but the Pope drew back, and he * shortly died. *Bellisarius* also was ruined, and *Justinian* himself shortly dyed. *Binnius* faith it is reported that he had no Learning, and thinketh that his Civil Laws were *Tribonian's*, and his Ecclesiastical *Theodorus Cæsariensis's*. And saith that the Church rejecteth his Laws of *Usury, Churches* and *Ecclesiastical Persons*, as arrogant Usurpations. *Qu.* Whether the *Roman* Power was then understood by Princes or People?

* *Baronius* contradicteth *Anastasius* & others in this point.

§ 31. CLXXVIII. Another Synod at *Paris* repeated nine old Canons: The 8th was, [*No man may be ordained a Bishop against the will of the Citizens; nor any but whom the election of the People and the Clerks, shall seek with plenary will; none shall be put in by the command of the Prince*, &c.

* *Baronius* thinks that *Theodomire* was Father to *Ariamire*.

§ 32. CLXXIX. *An.* 563. in the time of Pope *John* 3d. (not he, but) *Theodomire*, alias * *Ariamire* King of the *Sueves*, called a small Council at *Bracara* in *Galicia*, where eight Bishops opened so much of the *Priscillian* Heresie, as

may

their Councils abridged. 187

may tell us it was worthy to be detested (not much unlike the *Manichees*;) and many old Canons they recited: But I could have wished that they had not made a mans diet the note of his Heresie, and a sufficient cause of his conviction and damnation. The *Priscillianists* (as these say) would not eat flesh, nor herbs boil'd with flesh This Council ordered that if any that abstained from flesh, did not eat herbs boiled with flesh, he should be taken for an Heretick. This is not conformable to *Paul*'s Rules or Spirit.

§ 33. This Council ordered that none should be buried within the Church, which *Binnius* well sets home. And whereas *Priscillian* taught that in the Liturgy [the *Pax vobis*, Peace be unto you] should be said only by the Bishop, and *Dominus vobiscum* by the Priest, the Council contradicted him.   1. We see here what Trifles divided men! 2. We see that yet the Churches usually were no bigger than met in one place with the Bishop, or might do: For it is supposed that every Church-Assembly had a Bishop present to say his part.

§ 34. *Theodomirus* the *Suevian* King, under whom this Council was held, was the first of that race that turned Orthodox; all the *Sueves* before him (with the *Goths*) having been *Arrians*.

§ 35. CLXXX. *Anno* 566. The contest about choice of Bishops grew sharp. King *Clotharius* made one *Emerius* Bishop *Santeniensis*; the Canons had before decreed that Kings should choose none, but all the *People* and the Clerks, and the *Metropolitan* ordain him. The King's Bishop is deposed by a Council. *Santeniense*, of which *Leontius* of *Bourdeaux* was chief. They sent the King word of it by a Presbyter: The King filled a Cart with Thorns, and laid the Priest on them, and sent him into Banishment, and forced the Bishop to submit to his will.

§ 36. That it may be known that neither Popes, Councils, nor consenting Bishops divided Dioceses and Parishes, here *Binnius* giveth us at large, first *Constantine*'s divisions in *Spain*, and next the fuller division of King *Wamba*. Bin. p. 649, &c.

§ 37. CLXXXI. At *Tours* in *France* (eight Bishops) in a Provincial Council, revived many Canons of the old matter, (to keep Bishops and Priests from Women) Can. 13. *The Bishop may keep his Wife as a Sister, to govern his house:* But Can. 20. *Priests that will keep Wives, must have some Witnesses to lie in the same Chamber, to see that they lie not with them.* And Can. 14. *Episcopum, Episcopam non habentem, nulla sequatur turba mulierum,* &c.

Can. 21. They say, [*Those that the Law commandeth to be put to death, if they desire to hear the Preacher, we will have to be convicted unto life,* (that is, not to dye:) *For they are to be slain with the sword of the mouth, and deprived of Communion, if they will not observe the Decrees of the Seniors left them, and do despise to hear their Pastor, and will not be separate.*] Some Sectaries among us are of the same mind, against putting penitent Malefactors to death.

§ 38. CLXXXII. *Anno* 570. There was a Council at *Lyons* of Fourteen Bishops, who recited six Canons to restrain the Vices of the Clergy. *Binnius*, out of *Greg. Turon.* tells you the occasion was, that one *Salonius* and *Sagittarius*, as soon as they were made Bishops, being then at their own will, broke out into

B b 2   Slaughters,

Slaughters, Murders, Adulteries, and other wickedness. And *Victor* Bishop of *Tricaſ.* keeping his Birth-day, they sent a Troop with Swords and Arrows, who cut his Cloaths, beat his Servants, and carried away all his Provision, leaving him with reproach: The King *Gunthram* hearing of it, called this Synod, which found them guilty, and deposed them: They tell the King that they are unjustly cast out, and get his leave to go to the Pope, *John* 3d. The Pope writeth to the King to have them, as wronged men, restored, (this was the Papal Justice and Reformation:) The King chideth, but restoreth them; but they grew never the better afterward, but asking pardon of Bishop *Victor*, he forgave them, and for that was afterward excommunicate.

§ 39. CLXXXIII. *An.* 572. a Council was called under King *Ariomire* at *Braccara* of 12 Bishops: They are mostly forbidding Bishops to take money for their Ordinations, Consecrations, and other Actions. And the first Canon requireth them to *walk* to all their Parishes, and see that the Clerks did things rightly; that *Catechumens* learnt the Creed, and to preach to the People to forbear Murder, Adultery, Perjury, False-witness, and other mortal Sins, to do as they would be done by, and to believe the Resurrection, Judgment and Recompence according to Works.

§ 40. CLXXXIV. *An.* 572. a *Concilium Lucense* did receive from *Martin* Bishop of *Braccara* 84. old Canons, of which the 67th was against *reading Apocrypha*, or any thing but the Canon of the Old and New Testament in Church.

§ 41. After *Justinian's* death, his Sisters Son *Justinus* was Emperor, a sensual and covetous man, who murdered presently a Kinsman of his own name, upon suspicion that he was too great; yet he drew up a good Profession of Faith, exhorting all the Bishops to agree in it: But *Chosroes*, King of *Persia*, invaded his Empire, because the *Greater Armenia* (which was then under the *Persians*, as the *Lesser* was under the *Romans*) to avoid the *Persians* persecutions, had revolted to the Empire, and destroyed their Rulers: The *Persians* conquered so much of the *Eastern* part of the Empire, and *Justine's* Soldiers made so little resistance as drove him out of his wits; and his Wife, by intreaty, got the *Persians* to make a Truce. *Tiberius* was then made *Cæsar*, and afterward Emperor upon *Justine's* death; and *Justinian* his Captain repelled the *Persians*, and recovered much of what they had conquered.

§ 42. *An.* 576. Divers Kings of *France* by War among themselves destroyed Churches, and confounded all; and a Council at *Paris* was called, but in vain, to have perswaded them to Peace.

§ 43. After *Benedictus*, *Pelagius* 2d was Bishop at *Rome*; *Tiberius* an excellent Emperor quickly dyed, and by his choice *Mauritius* succeeded him. *Pelagius* (by *Gregory* his Deacon) wrote against the Bishops that would not condemn the *tria Capitula*: And when all his writings prevailed not, he got *Smaragdus* the Exorchate to force them by the Sword: (The great remedy which *Rome* hath trusted to.)

§ 44. CLXXXV. *Meroveus* Son and Heir to *Chilperic* King of *France*, marrying his Uncles Widow, offended his Father, and fled to St. *Martin's* Church
at

at *Tours*, and forced Bishop *Gregory* to give him the Sacrament. The King could not get the Bishop to deliver him up; he fled, and the King called a Synod at *Paris* to judge *Pretextatus* a Bishop, whom he accused for marrying him, and confederating with him.

§ 45. CLXXXVI. The two Bishops forenamed, *Salonius* and *Sagittarius*, being again accused of Adultery and Murder, and being freed by professing Repentance, King *Guntheramus* called a *Cubilene* Synod, and accused them of Treason, and so deposed and banished them.

§ 46. CLXXXVII. *An.* 582. King *Guntram* called a Synod at *Mascon*, to revive the old Canons for restraining the Lust and Vices of the Bishops and Clergy.

§ 47. CLXXXVIII. *An.* 583. A *Concil. Brenacense* is called, to try *Gregory* Bishop of *Tours*, falsly accused of charging the Queen of living in Adultery with a Bishop; an Archdeacon and a Deacon bore false Witness: but all came to light, and *Gregory* was cleared by his Oath.

§ 48. CLXXXIX. *An.* 587. A Council at *Constantinople* increased the Church-divisions which continue to this day, wherein *John* Bishop of *Constantinople* was decreed to be called, *The Universal Bishop*, which Pope *Pelagius* could not endure. O what hath this Question done to the World, *Who shall be the chief or greatest*? So much of the image and work of Satan hath been found in the professed Servants of a crucified Saviour, and in those that have worshipped the Cross!

In this Synod *Gregory* Bishop of *Antioch* was tryed, and acquitted of a false Accusation of Incest with his Sister another man's wife.

§ 49. *Pelagius* writeth against *John*'s *Universal* Title, saying, [*Universalitatis nomen quod sibi illicitè usurpavit, nolite attendere*, &c. *Nullus enim Patriarcharum* * *hoc tam profano vocabulo unquam utatur: quia si summus Patriarcha Universalis dicitur, Patriarcharum nomen cæteris derogatur. Sed absit hoc, absit à fidelis cujusquam mente hoc sibi vel velle quempiam arripere, unde honorem fratrum suorum imminuere ex quantulacunque parte videatur. Quapropter Charitas vestra neminem unquam suis in Epistolis Universalem nominet, ne sibi debitum subtrahat cum alteri honorem offert indebitum. Adversarius enim noster Diabolus qui contra humiles sæviens sicut Leo rugiens circuit, quærens quem devoret, non jam, ut cernimus caulas circuit.—Omnia qui soli uni Capiti cohærent, videlicet Christo, per electionem pompatici sermonis ejusdem Christi sibi studeat membra subjugare. Nec mirum quod ille tentator qui initium omnis peccati scit esse superbiam,* &c. And so he goeth on, exhorting them rather to dye, than to submit to the Title *Universal*, and resolving Excommunication against the User of it.

* No not the *Roman*.

§ 50. *Binnius* saith, It is ridiculous hence to impugn the Primacy of the Church: But *Qu.* 1. Is it not impudent after this, for them to use the Title of *Universal*? *Qu.* 2. Doth not this allow us to separate from them that usurp it? *Qu.* 3. Doth not *Pelagius* here plainly distinguish between the place of Prime *Patriarch* which he claimeth, and *Universal Bishop* or *Patriarch* which he damneth. *Qu.* 4. Doth he not describe this damned Usurpation, to be a *subjecting all Christ's members to himself*? *Qu.* 5. Doth not the Pope now use both the *name* and *thing* as far as he can attain it? *Qu*. 6. Did not *Pelagius* and *Gregory* know that *John* did no more intend to put down all other Patriarchs or Bishops by this Title, than the Pope doth? *Qu*. 7. Doth not the Pope now claim that as by Divine Right, which *John* claimed but as of Humane? Modesty can deny none of this.

§ 51. CXC. *An*. 587. Nine Bishops at *Lyons* repeated six old Canons about Women, &c.

§ 52. CXCI. *An*. 589. King *Gunthram* finding all things grow worse, and that all was long of the *Bishops onely*, (saith *Binnius*) called a Council at *Mascon*, where the stricter keeping of the *Lords-day* was commanded.

§ 53. Here *Binnius* noteth that *Priscus* is called Patriarch, and that the Bishops of *Venice*, *Istria* and *Liguria*, continuing still separate from *Rome*, chose *Paulinus* Bishop of *Aquileia* their Patriarch, [*Quem sibi loco summi Pontificis supremum Antistitem constituerent.*] *Qu*. Did the Bishops then believe that the Pope's Universal Government was essential to the Catholick Church? And that none were the Church but his Subjects?

§ 54. CXCII. King *Gunthram*, An. 589. by a Council at *Valence*, setled his Benevolences on the Churches.

§ 55. CXCIII. *An*. 589. At *Toletum* King *Recaredus* called a Council, and renounced *Arrianism*, and recited several Canons; among others, that Bishops and Priests Wives might dwell with them, but not lie with them. And they lament and condemn the practice of such as kill their children, appointing them sharp discipline without capital punishment. (Had the Church power to free Murderers from death, as they long did, Was this holy Reformation?)

The 11th Canon saith, *That they found that in many Churches of Spain, men filthily and not regularly did Penance, that they might sin as oft as they would, and be as oft reconciled by the Priests,* &c. Many reforming Canons were here made. There were 67 Subscribers besides the King, and of divers Cities two Bishops, which was unusual.

§ 56. CXCIV. (Passing by a meeting at *Rome*) Another Council at *Narbon* was held by *Recaredus*, who brought over the *Goths* from *Arrianism*.

§ 57. The Emperor *Mauritius*, though a great and excellent person, was ruined by the mad and uncurable mutinies of his Soldiers, and at last, with his Family, cruelly murdered by *Phocas*, one of his Captains; a terrible warning to Princes not to trust too much to Armies.

§ 58. All this while the opposers of the *Calcedon* Council kept up, and were divided in the *East* into many Parties among themselves: Among others, the great Peripatetic *Johan.Philoponus* was their most learned Defender, writing with such subtilty, that the Natures really two, were to be called *One Compound Nature*, as the Soul and Body of a man are, as (saith *Nicephorus*) was not easie to be answered (by which, how much of the Controversie was *de Nomine & de Notione Logicâ*, let the Reader further judge;) he that will see some of his words, may read them in *Niceph. l.* 18. *c.* 45, 46, 47, 48. his Notions made men call him a *Tritheite*.

§ 59. *Jacobus Zanzalus* being a great Promoter of the Party, many ever since

since have from him been called *Jacobites*: And the divided Parties that opposed the Council, called the other *Melchites*, that is *Royalists*, because they took them that followed the Council, to do it meerly in obedience to the Emperor, (for it was not the Pope then that was the Master of Councils.

§ 60. Among the *Armenians* also some raised the like Heresies about the Natures of Christ, some thinking his Deity was instead of a Soul to his Body, &c. To which they added superstitious Fasts, and worshipping the Cross, and such like, not *pleading Reason, but old Tradition* for their Errors, saying they had them from *Gregory*, vide *Niceph. l.* 18. *c.* 53, 54. But I must go forward.

§ 61. *Pelagius* dying, *Gregory* called *Magnus*, succeeded him at *Rome*: He continued the Controversie about the Title of *Universal Bishop*, writing many Epistles against it: He flattered *Phocas* the murderous Tyrant, with a *Lætentur Cœli & exultet Terra*, &c. yet was one of the best and wisest of their Bishops. He sent *Augustine* into *England*, who oppressed the *British* Church, and converted the *Saxon* King of *Kent*. He introduced more Superstitions, and greatly altered the Liturgy. Of which read Mr. *T. Jones* of the *Hearts Sovereign*.

§ 62. CXCIV. A *Concilium Hispalense* of eight Bishops recited three Canons.

§ 63. CXCV. *Mauritius* before his death, desired *Gregory* to call a Synod at *Rome*, to draw in the *Western* Bishops that separated, and to cast them out if they disobeyed: which he did, and they refusing his Summons, *Severus* of *Aquileia*, and other Bishops were ruined. They thought God destroyed *Mauritius* for persecuting them. *Gregory* thought God would have them destroyed as Schismaticks. The Bishops of *Rome* for near an hundred years were forced the more to please the Emperor, because their own Bishops had cast them off, and set up another Head against them.

§ 64. CXCVI. *An.* 590. A *Concil. Antisiodorense* made divers Canons against Superstitions, and some too superstitious (as that Women must not take the Sacrament in their bare hands, &c.)

§ 65. I find it so tedious to mention all the little Synods, that henceforth I shall take but little notice of them, but of the greater only.

One under *Recaredus* at *Cæsar-Augusta*, made three Canons about the *Arrians*.

One in *Numidia* displeased *Gregory*.

§ 66. A Council at *Poitiers* was called on occasion of two Nuns, daughters to the King of *France*, that broke out of the Nunnery, with many more, and accused the Abbess, and got men together, and stript her stark naked, and drew her out, and set all *France* in a Commotion, and were forced to do Penance.

A Council was called at *Metz*, to reduce the Bishop of *Rhemes* convict of Treason (for Bishops that were Traytors or Murderers were not to dye.)

A Synod at *Rome* under *Gregory* absolved a Priest of *Caleedon* condemned by *John* of *Constantinople*; what one did, the other undid.

An. 597. Under King *Recaredus*, 13 Bishops made two Canons for Priests Chastity, &c.

Another.

Another under him, *An.* 598. A *Concil: Oftieufe* made two such more.
An. 599. A Council at *Conftantinople* did we know not what.
An. 599. Under King *Recaredus,* 12 Bishops at *Barcinon* made four Canons against Bishops Bribery, &c.
A Council of 20 Bishops, 14 Presbyters, and 4 Deacons at *Rome* made a Canon for Monks.
Another there, *Ap.* 601. against a false Monk.
Another at *Byzacen* against a Bishop.
Another in *Numidia* about a Bishop and a Deacon.

§ 67. *Gregory* dying, *Sabinian* succeeded him, who reproached him, and would have had his Books burnt as unsound, saith *Onuphrius*: And, saith *Sigebert, Gregory* appeared to him in a Vision, and reproving him for that and Covetousness, knockt him on the head, and he dyed.

§ 68. *Boniface* 3d succeeded, chosen by *Phocas* the Murderer, who hating his own Bishop of *Conft. Cyriacus,* ordered that *Rome* should be the chief Church.

§ 69. A Council at *Rome* forbad chusing a Pope, till the former had been three days dead, because they sold their Votes for money.

§ 70. *Boniface* the 4th is made Pope, and *Phocas* giveth him the *Pagan* Temple, called *Pantheon,* for Christian Worship. In his time, *Phocas* was killed by *Heraclius,* as he had kill'd *Mauritius.*

§ 71. *An.* 610. A Council at *Toletum,* under King *Gundemar,* about the Bishop of *Toletum's* Primacy, which the King setleth by Edict.

§ 72. A Council at *Tarraca* under King *Sifebutus* took the shortest way, and only confirmed what had been before done for Priests Chastity.

§ 73. *Deus dedit* was next Pope, in whose time the *Perfians* conquered *Jerufalem,* and carried away the Bishop, and (they say) the Cross.

§ 74. *Boniface* 5th succeeded: *Heraclius* the Emperor is worsted by the *Perfians,* who would not give him Peace, unless the Empire would renounce Christ, and worship the Sun; *Heraclius* overthroweth them; *Mahomet* now riseth, and maketh a Religion of many Heresies.

§ 75. At a Synod at *Mafcon, Agreftinus* accused *Columbanus* of Superstition, for Crossing Spoons, &c. but was refelled.

§ 76. Seven or eight Bishops at *Hifpalis,* condemned the *Eutychians,* and called them *Acephali.*

CHAP.

CHAP. VIII.

Councils held about the Monothelites, *with others.*

§ 1. BEing come to the Reign of Pope *Honorius* at *Rome*, who was condemned by 2 or 3 General Councils for a *Monothelite* Heretick, (as *Vigilius* was by his own Bishops for an *Eutychian*) and having shewed you what work both the heretical and hereticating Bishops and Council made in the world about (not only ὁμοῶν , but ϛασιν, *one Nature,* and the *condemning of dead men*;) I shall next shew you what work they made also about the words, [*One Operation,* and *One Will,*] or [*Two Operations,* and *Two Wills.*] Reader, Wouldst thou think that there were venom enough in one of these words, to poyson almost all the Bishops in the world with the Plagues of Heresie, or Heretication and Contention?

§ 2. The old Controversie still keeping the Churches all in pieces, some being for two Natures after Union, and for the *Calcedon* Council, and others against it, and but for one Nature after Union: *Cyrus*, Bishop of *Alexandria,* was told, that it would unite them all, if they would confess *One Operation,* and *One Will in Christ,* or at least lay by the talk of *One* and *Two,* and use the words, [*Dei virilis Operatio.*] The *Operation* (and *Will*) of *God-man.* CXCVII. He therefore called a Synod at *Alexandria*, in which this was decreed (called *Satisfaction.*) For they said that *Dei virilis* signified two Natures, and so they thought they had at last hit the way of concord, which neither the General Council of *Ephes.* 1. *Ephes.* 2. *Constant.* 2. *Calcedon. Constant.* 3. had found out: but all set the Bishops but more by the ears.

Cyrus sent his Decrees to *Sergius* Bishop of *Constantinople*, *Sophronius* Bishop of *Jerusalem* perswaded the silencing of the names of [*One*] or [*Two*] *Operations* or *Wills.* *Sergius* sent the Case to *Honorius* to *Rome*; *Honorius* rationally perswaded them to use neither the *one* word, nor the *other,* (*One* or *Two*) foreseeing that a new quarrel was arising in these words, and (little knowing how for this he was by General Councils to be Hereticated, when he was dead) perswaded them to a silent Peace. It is but few Popes that were so wise and peaceable; and this one must be a Heretick for it, or General Councils be fallible, and much worse.

§ 3. Because (knowing the effect of the old unhealed Cause) I foresee that such men will go near to Hereticate me also when I am dead, for condemning Hereticating Incendiaries in the *Nestorian*, *Eutychian*, and *Monothelite* quarrels; I will recite the words of *Binnius* himself, who saith the same that I have said from the beginning, (though I justifie him not from selfcontradiction.)

Tom. 2. p. 992. [*Honorius,* fearing (*which after came to pass, and which he knew had fallen out in former Ages about the word* Homoousion *and many others*) *lest that Contention should grow to some great Schism, and seeing* withall that Faith might be safe without these words, he was willing to reconcile both Opinions, and withall to take cut of the way the matter of Scandal and Contention. Writing therefore to Sergius, he advised him to abstain from the word [*One Operation*] lest they should seem with Eutyches to assert but One Nature in Christ; and yet to forbear the word [*Two Operations*] lest with Nestorius, they seemed to assert Two Persons. (A Slander contrary to his words.) I again say, If all the Hereticating Bishops and Councils had followed this discretion and moderation, O what had the Church escaped!

Yet they are fain to stretch their wits to excuse his words elsewhere, [*Unde & Unam Voluntatem fatemur Domini nostri Jesu Christi.*] But it's certain that in some sense it is *One*, and in another sense *Two*.

§ 4. The Emperor *Heraclius* interessed himself in the Controversie, *Binnius* saith by the fraud of *Anastasius* Patriarch of the *Jacobites*, he was deceived, *Animo defendendi Concilium Calcedonense*. The *Jacobites* were *Eutychians*, the greatest enemies of the *Calcedon* Council; and it's strange then how they deceived him, to defend it by destroying it.

But, saith he, [*While he, besides his place and office, by the persuasion of the Devil, was wholly taken up in defending questions of Faith by his own judgment,* &c.] Here you may see what the Papists Clergy would make of Kings and all Lay-men: If they be *wholly taken up in defending questions of Faith by their own judgment,* they pronounce them to be persuaded to it *by the Devil*. Error is from the Devil; but sollicitous searching after the defence of Truth, is liker to be of God. But they must not do it by *their own judgment*: By whose then? By the Bishops no doubt; What Bishops? General Councils. And had not the Emperors long enough followed Councils, and banished such as they condemned, till, while they almost all condemned one another, the world was scandalized at the odious Divisions and Cruelties of the Church? But must they follow Bishops without using *their own judgments* about the Case? What, as their meer Executioners? Must the Princes of the world act as Brutes, or Idiots, or Lictors? Was this the old Doctrine, *Let every Soul be subject to the higher Power,* &c?

§ 5. CXCVIII. King *Sisenandus* (the second that had all *Spain*) called a Council at *Toletum* of all his Kingdom, *An.* 633. of 70 Bishops, who made many good Canons for Faith, Order, and Reformation; the last is a large defence of the King against Rebellion: But they order that when a King is dead, the *Prime Men of the whole Nation, with the Priests, by common consent, chuse another, that retaining the Concord of Unity, there should be no strife through Force or Ambition.*

And they decree the Excommunicating of wicked Kings that live in great sin; which I doubt whether the fifth Commandment forbid them not to have done, it being a purposed dishonour.

§ 6. CXCIX. Another at *Toletum* was called 636, by King *Chintillane*, which went the same way; Kings were Rulers here, and not Popes.

§ 7. CC. Another at *Toletum*, *An.* 638. by the same King to the same purposes.

§ 8.

§ 8. The Emperor *Heraclius* published an Edict for the *Monothelite* Opinion, called his *Echtesis*; and *Sergius Const.* joined in it.

§ 9. *Sergius* dyeth, and *Pyrrhus* a *Monothelite* succeedeth him.

§ 10. *Severinus* is chosen Pope, but being not Confirmed (as was usual) by the Emperor's consent, he is plundered of his wealth.

§ 11. The *Saracene Arabians* conquer *Persia*, and the *Eastern* parts of the Empire.

§ 12. *Sergius* before his death called a Council at *Constantinople*, which confirmed the Emperor's Faith, and the *Monothelite* Opinion.

§ 13. *An.* 640. *John* 4th was made Pope, who condemned the Emperor's *Echtesis*; and, it's said, the Emperor disowned it, and said that *Sergius* made it, and desired it might be published in his name.

§ 14. *Heraclius* dyeth, *Constantine* succeedeth him, and dyeth in 4 months. *Heracleo* succeedeth: After six months the Senate depose him, and cut off his Nose, and cut out his Mother's Tongue, on suspicion that they poysoned *Constantine*, whose Son *Constans* is next set up.

§ 15. *Pyrrhus*, thought guilty of *Constantine's* death, flieth into *Africa*, and *Paulus* a *Monothelite* hath his place. *Pyrrhus* seemeth converted by *Maximus* in *Africa*, cometh to *Rome*, and is owned by the Pope against *Paulus*. *Paulus* persuadeth the Emperor to publish a *Typus*, requiring all the Bishops to lay by the Controversie and Name of *One* and of *Two Wills* and *Operations of Christ*. But this which was approved in Pope *Honorius*, is cryed down as Heretical in the Emperor.

Pyrrhus returneth to his Opinion, and *Paul* dying, he is again put in his place at *Constantinople*.

Binnius no better answereth the Objection, [that the *Emperor's Edict* said but what Pope *Honorius* said,] than by saying, that *the time made the difference*. It was good in *Honorius's* time, and bad after to be quietly silent in such a Case.

§ 16. They say there was a Council in *Numidia*, another at *Byzacene*, at *Carthage* another of 68 Bishops, about the *Monothelites*.

§ 17. CCI. Another Council was at *Toletum* under King *Chindasermdus*.

§ 18. CCII. The Pope, with one of his little Councils at *Rome*, (for the foresaid *Italian* Bishops yet disowned him, and obey the Patriarch of *Aquileia*) presumed to condemn *Paulus Const. & Pyrrhus*, and the Emperor's Edict, (*Typus*:) Wherefore his Agents at *Constantinople* were cast out, beaten, their Altar overthrown, &c.

§ 19. *Martin* is made Bishop at *Rome*: He condemneth the Emperor's Edict of Silence (as to *Two Wills and Operations, or One.*) The Emperor sendeth for him, he is brought Prisoner to *Constantinople*, laid in Irons under several Accusations; banished and dyed.

Here the Pope pretendeth that *Truth* must not be silenced: The Emperor saith, *Peace must not be broken for needless words*: *Quer.* Whether he be a Martyr that suffers for oppugning such Peace?

§ 20. CCIII. His *Laterane* Council, *An.* 642. is very largely recorded, in which the Emperor's Edict, with *Cyrus Alex. Sergius, Pyrrhus & Paulus Constant.* are condemned, and two *Operations* and *Wills* asserted.

§ 21. CCIV. (Passing by a Synod at *Orleance*) *An.* 653. another Council was held at *Toletum* against incontinent and ignorant Priests. Kings here used to preach to the Bishops by their Letters and Decrees. Dukes and Lords here subscribed.

§ 22. *Eugenius* is Pope, and dyeth ; *Vitalianus* succeedeth him : *Constans* the Emperor cometh to *Rome*, giveth them gifts, and communicateth with them. It's said he kill'd his Brother *Theodosius*, and after was kill'd himself : *Mezentius* usurpeth the Empire. *Constantine Pogonatus*, Son to *Constans*, conquereth him, and reigneth. Pope *Vitalianus* helpeth him, and therefore expecteth his help. *Rome* stood so much between the *Eastern* Empire, and the *Western* Kings (*Goths, Lombards, Franks,* &c.) that both sides flattered the *Roman* Clergy, (though they oft suffered from both.) The Empire to keep them from turning to the *Goths*, &c. and the *Goths* to keep them from turning to the Empire. And they that had most need of the Popes, most advanced them ; and they that had least need and most dominion, kept them under.

§ 23. CCV. Another Council at *Toletum*, *An.* 655. called by K. *Recessuinthus*, (not the Pope,) made divers good Canons for Church-order ; among which the tenth is, that because all the Canons oft made, could not keep Bishops and Priests from Lechery, they tryed this additional way, to decree that all their Children begotten of their Servants, Maids, &c. should be uncapable of inheritance, and should live in continual servitude to the Church.

King *Recaredus* made a Law, that Bishops and Priests Concubines should be whipt with an hundred Stripes ; and others, that they should be sold for Slaves.

§ 24. CCVI. The King of *France* (*Clodoveus*) called his Bishops together at a Village called *Clypiacum*, and made a Sermon to them, and they applauded him.

§ 25. CCVII. He called another Synod at *Cabilone* for Church-order, where *Can.* 10. it was decreed, that all *Ordination of Bishops should be null,* that was otherwise made than by the election of the *Comprovincials*, the *Clergy,* and the *Citizens.* (A threefold Lock is not easily pickt) Let *England* understand this, to be the old Canons and Custom.

§ 26. CCVIII. A *Concil. Emeritense,* called by King *Recessuinthus,* made more Orders for regulating Bishops and Priests, &c.

§ 27. CCIX. A Synod at *Rome* justified a Bishop of *Crete*, wronged by his Archbishop.

§ 28. CCX. Another at *Toletum* under King *Wamban, An.* 675. sought to reform the Bishops and Clergy.

§ 29. CCXI. *An.* 675. the same King *Wamban* had a Synod at *Braccara,* for reforming the Clergy. *Can.* 5. was to correct the Bishops that had turned

Piety

Piety into Pride and Vanity; going to the Solemnities of the Martyrs, with Reliques hanged about their necks, carried in Chairs by Deacons in white, &c. O what hath the Pride of Prelates done in the world!

§ 30. Pope *Adeodatus*, and after him *Donus* reigned at *Rome*, and the Patriarchs of *Constantinople* and *Antioch* were *Monothelites*, and *Constantine* needing the *West*, having lost the *East*, took part with *Rome*.

After *Donus* came *Agatho*, in whose time the Bishop of *Ravenna*, after long rejecting the Bishop of *Rome* as heretical, returned to communion with him. *Constantine* sent to *Rome*, to require the Bishop to keep Missionary Legates at *Constantinople*, and intreated them to lay by Philosophical Controversies, and preach the pure Scripture, that the Churches at last might have Peace. (But alas how long was that counsel vain!)

§ 31. CCXII. *Beda* saith, an *English* Council met, *An*. 679. under *Theodorus*, to own the Catholick Faith, *Bed. l. 4. c.* 13.

§ 32. CCXIII. The same year 679. A Council at *Milan* told the Emperor their opinion for *Two Wills and Operations*.

§ 33. CCXIV. A Synod at *Rome* prepared matter for the General Council against the *Monothelites*. This tended to please the separating Bishops of *Italy* that divided from the Pope, for seeming to desert the *Calcedon* Council by condemning the *tria Capitula*.

§ 34. CCXV. Now cometh the 3d Council of *Constantine*, called the 6th General Council, in which 289 Bishops condemned the *Monothelites*, that were for *One Will and Operation*. *Constantine Pog.* being against them, *Macarius* Patriarch of *Antioch* was the chief of them, who would have consented to name neither *One nor Two*, but when they had done all, professed that he would be cast into the Sea, before he would say *there were in Christ two Wills and Operations*; thinking that he held to *Cyril*, and the first *Ephesian* Council against *Nestorius*. *George* Bishop of *Constantinople* deserted him, and he was deposed and banished (to *Rome*; no hard Banishment but for ill company.)

§ 35. A long stir there was among them, perusing former Writings; *Macarius* and his Party producing many, which others said were falsified (so little certainty is there oft of Copies.) The Epistles of *Sergius Const. & Honor. Rom.* are read, which I should think peaceable and honest; but the General Council damned and cursed them both as Hereticks. The Papists say, General Councils may err in matter of Fact: How much more then in matter of Faith, which is more obscure? and matter of Fact is much of the matter of our Faith.

No Man's name had so strange a Fate against Hereticaters, as the great Hereticater *Cyril*'s; who (in this Council in *Cyrus artic.* and many others) was fully proved to assert *One Nature of God incarnate after the Union*] and yet called Orthodox, and those that said as he, and much less, were damned Hereticks.

Some that confessed *two Natures*, yet denying *two Wills* after the Resurrection, supposing the Humane Will called Natural had been laid by, were here damned with the rest.   § 36.

§ 36. CCXVI. *An.* 681. King *Ervigius* held another Council at *Toletum*, for the Royal Power, and reforming the Clergy.

The Pope had so little to do, and the Kings so much in all these *Spanish* Councils, that it's strange *Spain* is now become so servile to the Pope. *Binnius* is forced to confess here (*To.* 3. *p.* 110.) that [*The study and labor of chusing fit men to be made Bishops, was in the power or hands of the* Gothish *Kings, which by the indulgence of the* Roman *Popes is in the* Spanish *Kings even to our times*] which he proveth. (O indulgent Popes, who let go what they cannot keep!)

An. 682. Some Synods in *France* did, we know not what.

§ 37. *Leo* 2d is made Pope by the Emperor; and because he confirmed the Acts of this Council, which damns *Honorius* as an Heretick, the Papists know not which way to turn themselves. *Baronius* would have *Leo's* Epistle forged. *Binnius* will have either the Acts corrupted by *Theodore Const.* before they were sent to *Leo*, or that necessity compelled him to this hard condition by the iniquity of the times, and that Heresie else would have revived, &c. so that by their reckoning, they that relie all on Tradition and Fathers, leave not Fathers, Councils or Traditions certain for one Age.

§ 38. CCXVII. *An.* 683. K. *Ervigius* had another Synod of 48 Bishops at *Toletum*, for restoring some guilty of Treasons, securing the King, &c.

§ 39. *Constantine Pogon.* restored to *Rome* the power of making Popes without the Emperor, which the *Gothish* Kings and other Emperors had long denied them.

§ 40. *Benedict* 2d is made Pope: A new Controversie in his time is raised. The *Spanish* Bishops write an Epistle, in which they assert *Three Substances in Christ*, *his Divinity, his Soul and his Body*, and say withall that a *Will begat a Will*, that is, *the Divine Will begat the Humane*. The numbers of *One, Two,* and *Three*, had so confounded Men in those times, that the words frightned the Pope, and he expostulated and warned them to take heed in what sense they used them; which hath made it a question whether this Pope were not erroneous himself.

Bin. pag. 127.

§ 41. CCXVIII. Another Council at *Toletum* against the *Monothelites*.

§ 42. Pope *John* 5th was the first Consecrated without the Emperor since the liberty granted.

Theodoric King of *France* called a Council, *An.* 685. in which he deposed several Bishops.

§ 43. *Constantine Pog.* dying, *Justinian* 2d his Son is Emperor. *Binnius* faith, he was not found in the Faith (a hard thing then!) And that he repented of the liberty granted in chusing Popes, and so ordered that the Exarch of *Ravenna* approve them, by which Bribery was used with the Exarch. And while the Soldiers and Clergy could not agree, they were fain to consent to a third, *Conon*, to be Pope.

§ 44. *Conon* being dead, *Theodore* and *Paschal* strove for the Popedom, and

and got their Parties to stand it out for them. *Paschal* promised the Exarch a great Sum of Gold to make him Pope. When they could not agree, *Sergius* a third was chosen. The Exarch forced him to pay the Gold, and to he got the Soldiers love and the Popedom.

§ 45. CCXIX. *An.* 688. Another *Toletan* Council writ a defence of their assertion, that Christ had *three Substances*, and that *Voluntas genuit Voluntatem*.

§ 46. CCXX. A Council at *Cæsar-Augusta*, made five Canons; the last was, that when the Kings dyed, the Queens should lay by their civil Habits, and be put into a Monastery, and profess Chastity.

§ 47. CCXXI. *An.* 692. Was the famous great Council called the *Quini-Sextum* at *Constantinople*, by *Justinian* 2d's Order; why it should not be called a 7th General Council, I know not. It was called by the persuasion of *Callinicus Constant.* to make a full Body of Canons for Practice, because the 5th and 6th Councils made none. *Binnius* saith, It could not be a General Council, because the Pope was not there by himself, or his Legates, and yet confesseth that neither was he or his Legates at the first *Constantine* Council, and yet it was universal. And why doth not another Bishops absence (*E. G. Alexand. Jerusal. &c.*) null a General Council as well as the Popes? The Papists rail at this Council as a *Convention of Malignants*, (*Bin.* p. 154) and against *Balsamon*, that defendeth it as a wicked *Greek* Impostor; (the word [*wicked*] in these Mens writings is a term of art and interest, and no *moral* term.) They recited abundance of old Canons, many of great use. One would wonder whence the anger against them ariseth. It was *per summam nequitiam*, saith *Binnius*, that they called themselves a General Council: And the *Holy Ghost was not with them*, because the Pope was not with them, (*p.* 154, 155.) and they ordained many things contrary to Apostolical Constitutions, and the Canons of General Councils. Reader, you see here, 1. How little trust Papists lay on that part of Tradition which dependeth on Councils? 2. That it is the Pope (one Man) that is the *certainty of Tradition and Judgment*, without whom Councils are nothing. 3. That if the Pope be absent, all the other Bishops assembled in Councils by the command of Emperors, may be called Knaves and wicked Malignants. Alas how few Bishops adhered to the Pope, (when *Italy* was not yet cured of Separation from him) in comparison of those that met in these *Eastern* Councils which they revile! 4. You see here, how far they are from truth, that say the Universal Church still cleaved to the Pope, when most (by far) of the Bishops in the world forsook him! you see *Luther* was not the first.

§ 48. Note that *Toarasius* Bishop of *Constantinople*, *An.* 692. in the 2d Council of *Nice*, tells them, that *it was the same Bishops* that met in the 6th General Council at *Constantinople*, who met again here under *Justinian*. And were not the Bishops of the place so near the time competent Judges of the matters of so notorious Fact? And were the same Bishops an infallible General Council at the 6th Council, and yet all wicked Schismaticks or Knaves,

and

and wicked Men, when they meet again but to make Church-Canons for Reformation? If this do not tell you how truly *Binnius* faith, in their own judgment [that *Councils have just so much authority as the Pope giveth them*] what can tell it you?

§ 49. Yea, *Binnius* makes this Council to be *Monothelites*: And were the same Men Orthodox in the 5th or 6th Council ten years before, and Hereticks in this? Is this the constancy of the Church and Bishops Faith?

§ 50. The 13th Canon is one that displeaseth them; in which the practice of the Church of *Rome* in separating Priests from their Wives, is expresly renounced; and it is decreed that no Priest be required to separate from his Wife, (so be it they abstain at Fasts and necessary Seasons) nor any Priest endured to put away his Wife, on pretence of piety; else he must be deposed.

§ 51. Another is the 16th Canon, that maketh Deacons like Overseers of the Poor.

§ 52. The 22d is a hard Canon that Bishops and Priests, ordained with money, and not by *examination* and *election*, be deposed, and they that ordained them.

§ 53. The 36th Canon displeaseth them also, which confess the Church of *Constantinople*'s Priviledges as equal with *Rome*.

§ 54. The 38th Canon containeth one great cause of the old Confusions, *viz.* *That whatever alteration the Imperial Power makes on any City, the Ecclesiastical Order also follow it.* Did God make this Law? Are not as many Souls in a Town that's no City as capable of being a Church as Citizens? It is in the Princes power to make and unmake Cities: May he accordingly make or unmake Churches? What if a King will have but one City in his Kingdom, must there be no more Churches or Bishops? What if there be no Cities (as in many *American* and *Arabian* Countries) must there be no Churches? What if the King will disfranchize most of the Cities, and another will make every Market Town a City; must Churches be altered accordingly? If so, O that our King would make us so many Cities, as the work and the souls of Men need true Bishops, that one might not have a thousand Parishes without any subordinate Bishop! But if this hold, the Emperor might have taken down *Rome*, and set up *Constantinople*, or any other at pleasure.

§ 55. *Can.* 50. Forbad Clergy and Laity to play at Dice, on pain of Deposition, or Segregation.

And *Can.* 51. forbids going to Shews, Jesters, Stage-Plays, Huntings.

The 55th Canon commands the Church of *Rome* to amend their Customs, and not to fast on Sabbath-days.

Can. 62. Forbids Womens Publick Dancings, and Mens and Womens together, and their putting on Masquers or Players Apparel, or Persons, &c.

Can. 63. Commandeth the burning of false Histories of the Martyrs, as tending to bringing Religion into reproach.

Can.

their Councils abridged. 201

continual joyful Praises to God, and holy Exercises, and to use no Horse-Races, &c.

The 67th Canon is against eating Blood.

Can. 72. Nullifieth Marriage with Hereticks. (Alas, good Bishops, did you think the Papists would have Hereticated you as *Monothelites*, and nullified all Marriages with you by this Canon? But two Hereticks Marriage is not null.

Can. 78. Commandeth all the *illuminate* (baptized) to learn the *Belief*, and *every Friday to say it to the Bishop and Presbyters*. (How many Parishes or hundred Parishes had the Bishop then to hear? Not so many as ours.)

§ 56. The 82 Canon offends the Papists, forbidding the Picture of a Lamb to be made for Christ as the Lamb of God.

The 90th Canon is (an old one) *Not to kneel on any Lord's-day*, and that this begin on the evening before.

P. 155. *Binnius* reproveth them for calling *Cyprian* Archbishop, and he proveth that *Africa* then had no Archbishop or Primate.

§ 57. CCXXII. *An.* 693. was another *Toletan* Council, called by King *Egica*: Before it the King writeth a Sermon for them, wherein he tells them, *That every Parish that have twelve Families, must have their proper Governor: But if less, it must be part of anothers charge.*

§ 58. CCXXIII. *An.* 694. was another *Toletan* Council under the same King *Egica*: (One would wonder that the Legislative vertue of the Church should be continued to such fertility and multitude of Laws, as must follow if in all Countries there be every year a Council: How great must the Volumes of Laws be at last?) *Binnius* in his Notes on this Council tells us, *That though* Paul *would have the believing Husband or Wife stay with the Unbeliever, in hope of Conversion, yet many hundred years experience hath taught us the contrary, (that it tendeth rather to hurt than good) and therefore now it must be otherwise, and they must separate.*

§ 59. CCXXIV. Even to those days the number of *Pagans* and *Infidels* in most Countries was the greatest, and the care of good men was to convert them: (And therefore we read still of so many baptized at age.) A Council at *Utrecht* decreed (*Willebrood* (or *Willifrid*) and *Suibert* being Leaders) that the best Preachers should be sent from the Neighbor Churches to convert the Heathens, (that was better work, than striving who should be chief, or raging about hard words.)

§ 60. CCXXV. A Synod at *Aquileia, An.* 698. condemned the 5th General Council at *Constantinople*, for condemning the *tria Capitula* of the Council of *Calcedon*. (O what Concord Councils caused!)

§ 61. Pope *Sergius* refusing to own the Council of *Constant.* at *Trul.* under *Justinian* 2d, the Emperor commanded that he should be brought Prisoner to *Constantinople*. The Soldiers of *Ravenna* (*Sergius* having paid them the 100 *l.* of Gold) hearing of it, rose up and rescued him, and made the Emperor's Officer in fear beg for his life. By such Obedience *Rome* kept up.

D d § 62.

§ 62. *Tiberius* the 2d depofed *Juſtinian* the 2d, and cut off his Nofe, and baniſhed him. *Juſtinian* was reſtored, and expofed *Tiberius* to ſcorn, and killed him, and baniſhed Biſhop *Calliniens* to *Rome* for unfaithfulneſs to his Prince. *John* the 6th was now Pope.

§ 63. *John* the 7th is made Pope (another Council at *Toletum* under King *Witiza* I paſs by) he was a *Greek*. CCXXVI. He gather'd a Synod at *Rome*, to debate *Juſtinian*'s Order for the receiving the *Trull. Concil.* And our Engliſh *Willifrid*, accufed by his King, was here juſtified, as a Son of that Church: And a Synod in *England* received him, when the King was dead.

§ 64. *Sifinnius* made Pope lived but 20 days, and *Conſtantine* ſucceeded him, who was ſent for to *Conſtantinople*, and honoured by *Juſtinian*.

☞ § 65. About this time (*An.* 708.) *Spain* was conquered by the *Saracens*; *Binnius* faith, *Becaufe King* Witiza *forſook the See of* Rome. By which we ſtill fee that *Rome* was forſaken even by the beſt Church, ſuch as *Spain* then was, and was not the Ruler of the World.

§ 66. *Bardanes Philippicus* by Rebellion depofed *Juſtinian*, and was made Emperor ; and within two years was ſo ufed himſelf by *Anaſtaſius*, (his eyes put out, and he baniſhed.)

§ 67. CCXXVII. The Emperor *Philippicus* and *Joh. Conſtant.* called General Council at *Conſtantinople* ; I may well call it General, when *Binnius* faith, *There were innumerable Biſhops*, which is not ſaid of any other Council. They all condemned the 6th General Council, and their Opinion of *two Wills*, and *two Operations*. Where it is manifeſt,

1. How great a part of the Church regarded not the Authority of *Rome*.

2. Nor thought a General Council infallible, when *innumerable Biſhops* are againſt both.

3. And how ſtrong the *Monothelite* Party was.

4. And alas, how bad too many Biſhops, that can change as faſt as Emperors will have them. For ſaith *Binnius* (after *Baronius*) [*Thus at the beck of the Emperor, and at the will of a Monothelite Patriarch, the holy ſixth Synod is condemned, and what they decreed of two Wills in Chriſt, and two Operations, and all retracted by the Decree and Subſcription of very many Oriental Biſhops, that were in one moment turned from being Catholiques, to be Monothelites.*] Is this the conſtancy of Biſhops, and the certainty of their Tradition? But why have we not the Acts of this great Council, as well as of the reſt?

C H A P.

CHAP. IX.

Councils called about Images and some others.

§ 1. **P**Ope *Gregory* the 2d is the Man that must set up Image-worship against all opposition, rebel against his lawful Sovereign, and confederate with other Princes to alienate the *Western* Empire, when the *East* was almost ruined before, and so to weaken the Christian Power, that the *Turk* might shortly win the Empire.

§ 2. To have recited all along as we went on, what new Ceremonies, Formalities and Orders were invented and brought in by the Popes, and how Doctrine and Practice grew corrupted, being a thing done already by many others, would have been tedious here, and besides the design of this writing, which is but to shew how Prelates have used the Church by their contentions about JURISDICTION and HARD or AMBIGUOUS WORDS; and what hath been the work especially of General Councils. But we cannot tell you well the work of the following Councils, without telling somewhat of the occasion of the matter.

The Primitive Christians used not Images in the Worship of God, (read *Dalæus de Imaginibus*.) But the contempt of Christianity by the Heathens, occasioned many to oppose their contempt by glorying in the Cross of Christ, and by making the transient sign of it with their fingers; and thence they grew to use the fixed sign of it; and thence to speak of and believe many Miracles wrought by it; and thence to make the Image of Christ crucified, (which yet *Epiphanius* condemned;) and thence by degrees to make the Images of the Apostles and Martyrs; and thence to make in their Churches the Images of their deceased Bishops, (till an Excommunicater arose of another Opinion, that pull'd any of them down.)

And abundance of Dreams, Visions, Apparitions and Revelations were the pretended Proofs that prevailed for many such Superstitions, but especially for *Images*, and *Purgatory*, and *Prayers for the dead*. Among others, an *English* Monk, *Egwin* of *Eveshohne*, chosen Bishop of *Worcester*, must lead the way, by pretence of a Vision, (a Dream, no doubt) see *Spelman*'s Concil. p. 209. in his own Chart *Egwin* faith, [*That the Virgin* Mary *first appeared to a certain Shepherd called* Eoves, *and afterward to himself with two Virgins, holding a Book in her hands, and told him in what place she would have him build her a Monastery*. The crafty Dreamer divulged the Vision, and some good Men opposing it, the Pope must have the hearing of it. The Pope put it to the Oath of *Egwin*, whether ever he saw such a Vision or not? *Egwin* sware it, and the matter was past doubt, (just as honest *Commenius* took *Daubritius*'s Prophesies to be of God, because the melancholy Man sware that they were true.) Hereupon *Egwin* is sent home, and a Council called to take *Egwin*'s words again that he had such a Vision, (and in the end

end was added, *That the Virgin* Mary's *Image must be set up in the place.*) The Pope sent to King *Kenred* and King *Offa* by Bishop *Brithwald*, to grant what the Vision intended; who obediently make over a great part of the Countrey to that Monastery, as you may see described in *Spelman, Conc.* p. 209, 210. *in Charta* Kenredi & Offæ *Regum*. And p. 211. *in Charta* Egwini, who saith himself, that [*God being propitious to him*, *he had in a little time got for the said Church an hundred and twenty Farms given, as is written and confirmed in the Charter of that Church.* Many Villages are there named, and some great ones, in the fattest and richest part of the County of *Worcester*. Was not this a profitable Dream or Vision? And should we not have many *Dreamers* and *Swearers*, if they could get as much by it as *Egwin* did? And herewith Images are set up.

§ 3. But *Baronius* and *Binnius* question whether *Naucler* and *Bale* say true, that this Council first brought Image-worship into *England*, because it came in before with *Austin* the Monk. To which *Spelman* * well answereth, That the use of the Cross in banners and otherwise was here before, and some Images for Instruction and Commemoration, as *Beda*'s own words intimate ; but not any worship of Images, or worshiping before and towards them.

*Pag.217, 218. vide cæter.s.

And Sir *H. Spelman* saith, (proving that Image-worship was not then in use among the *Saxens*) that even praying to the Saints themselves was not then in use, mentioning an old *Psalter* of his written about the time of the 2d *Nicene* Council, in which there were an hundred seventy and one Prayers inserted between the *Sections* of the 119th *Psalm*, and in them all not one name of any Saint, or the Virgin *Mary*, much less any Prayer directed to them.

§ 4. If one talk now with our *English* Papists, they are so loth to own their own Doctrine and Practice, that they will tell you they hold not the worshiping of the Image, but of the Person signified by it. But to tell them how commonly their Writers defend worshipping Images , (if *Colere* and *Cultus* signifie Worship) and what *Aquinas* saith of giving the worship of *Latria* to the *Image of Christ*, and to the *Cross*, though undeniable, yet will not be taken for sufficient proof. I shall therefore give you here the sense of the Papal Church in *England*, in the form of Abjuration which they prescribed to those that they then called *Lollards*, as it is found in the *Tower* Records; and you must take it in the old *English* in which it is written, because I do but transcribe it, and must not alter it, the sense of it being plain and obvious.

Ex

their Councils abridged.

" *Ex Rotulo Clauſax. de Anno Regni Regis Ricardi secundi* 19 *membr.*
" 18 *dors.*

MEmorand. *quod primo die Septembris Anno Regni Regis Ricardi se-*
" *cundi post Conquestum decimo nono Willielmus Dynel & Nicholaus*
" *Taillour, Michaelus Poucher, & Willielmus Steynour, de Nottingham in Can-*
" *cellar. ipsius Regis perſonaliter constituti Sacramenta divisim prestiterunt sub*
" *eo qui sequitur tenore.* [I *William Dynel befor yhow worchipifull Fader and*
" *Lorde Archbyſhop of Yorke and yhowr Clergie, with my free will and full*
" *avyſide ſwere to Gode and to all his ſeyntes uppon this holy Goſpelle that fro*
" *this day forthwarde I ſhall* Worſhip Ymages *with preying and offering unto*
" *hem in the worſchip of the ſeintes that they be made after   and alſo I*
" *ſhall never more deſpyſe pygremage ne ſtates of holy Chyreke in no degree. And*
" *alſo I ſhall be buxum to the lawes of holy Chirche and to yhow as myn Arch-*
" *byſhop and to myn other ordinares and Curates and kepe yo lawes uppon my*
" *power and meynten hem. And alſo I ſhall meynten ne techen ne defenden*
" *errours conclusions & techynges of the Lollards ne ſwych conclusions and*
" *techings that men clepyth Lollardes doctryn Ne I ſhall her bokes ne ſwych*
" *bokes ne hens or any ſuſpect or diffamed of Lollardery reſceyne or company*
" *with all wyttyngly or defende in yo matters   and if I know ony ſwych I ſhall*
" *with all the haſt that I may do ghowe or els your mr Officers to wyten and*
" *of her bokes.   And alſo I ſhall excite and ſtirr all tho to good doctryn that*
" *I have hinder'd with myn doctryn up my power.   And alſo I ſhall ſtonde to*
" *yhour declaration wych es hereſy or errour and do theraftur and alſo what*
" *penance yhe wel for that I haue don for meyntenyng of this falſ doctryn*
" *menyne   and I ſhall fulfill it and I ſubmit me therto up my power.   And*
" *alſo I ſhall make no other gloſe of this myn eth bot as the werdes ſtonde.*
" *And if it be ſo that I come agayn or do agayn this eth or any party thereof*
" *I holde me here cowpable as an heretyke and to be punyſhed by the law as an*
" *heretyk and to forſeit all my goodes to the Kynges will wyth outen any othr*
" *proceſſe of lawe.   And therto I require the Notarie to make of all this tho*
" *whych is my will an inſtrument agens me ut ex habundanti idem Willielmus*
" *Dynel eodem die voluit & recognovit quod omnia bona & catalla ſua mobilia*
" *nobis ſint forisfacta in caſu quo ipſe juramentum prædictum ſeu aliqua us*
" *eodem juramento contenta de cetero contravenerit ullo modo.*

Here you ſee whether Papiſts worſhip *Images*, and whether they take it not for Hereſie (which is death) not to worſhip them, and whether they leave it to mens liberty or not.

§ 5. *Leo Iſaurus* being Emperor, he took the *worſhipping of Images* to be *Idolatry*; and his Empire being invaded by the *Saracens*, who were ſcandali-
zed.

zed by the Christians Images, he thought it was a warning to him to reform them; and he published his Edict accordingly against the Religious adoration and use of the Images of Angels, Martyrs, or Saints. *Gregory*, Bishop of *Rome*, resisted him, and made Men believe that this was to fight against Christ, and impiously to despise the Saints. The Emperor commanded his Obedience on pain of Deposition. He would neither obey nor suffer. The Emperor sent Men to apprehend him, (some say to kill him,) but he escaped them. The *Lombards* were stirred up to make War against the Emperor as an Enemy of Christ: [*The Pope* (saith *Binnius*, p. 177. out of *Zonaras*) entered into a League with Charles Martell *King of* France, that, if there were need, he should defend the Church of Rome against the Emperor (their proper Sovereign) which League being prudently made, the Emperor abstained for fear of Charles, who by great Victories was become famous.---But when the Emperor would not obey the Pope's pious warnings, but used Tyranny in the East against the Orthodox, then the Pope anathematized him as a known declared Heretick, and exhorted all his Subjects in Italy to depart from his obedience.]

Note how Rebellion is the work and strength of the *Roman* Papacy: But do not our Papists now disown all this, and profess themselves to be the Loyallest Subjects?

Answ. If they do, let them join Restitution with Confession. If the Father seize on another mans Inheritance, and the Son keep it, and disclaim his Fathers act, this is but a dead Confession.

But hear the next words in *Binnius*, and judge what Doctrine yet they hold, [*Quo facto Sanctissimus Pontifex clarissimum posteris suis reliquit exemplum; ne in Ecclesia Christi regere permittantur hæretici Principes, si frequenter moniti errori pertinaciter adhærescant.*] That is, BY WHICH FACT (deposing the Emperor in *Italy*, and absolving all his Subjects from their Obedience) THE MOST HOLY POPE LEFT HIS POSTERITY A MOST CLEAR (or Famous) EXAMPLE, THAT HERETICAL PRINCES MAY NOT BE PERMITTED TO RULE, IF BEING OFT WARNED THEY PERTINACIOUSLY ADHERE TO ERROR.]

Note this ye Princes and Rulers that hear of Papal Loyalty.

1. It is not lawful for them, if they can help it, to permit any of you to reign over Christians, if they do but judge you Heretical. To tolerate you is against their Consciences, if to depose you be not above their strength.

2. By this Rule you see, that they were virtual Rebels to most or many Emperors, when they durst not actually rebel. 1. When *Constantine* the Great banished *Athanasius*, it's like they would have taken him for an Heretick. 2. *Constantius* and *Valens* being *Arrians*, the Pope did virtually rebel against them, and depose them (if then they were of the same mind as now.) 3. *Theodosius junior, Zeno, Anastasius*, and other Emperors they virtually deposed as *Eutychians*. 4. *Justinian* the first they virtually deposed as a *Phantasiastick*.

tafiaftick. 5. *Philippicus,* and many more Emperors are called by them *Monothelites*. 6. *Leo* and *Conftantine,* and others, are called *Iconoclaftæ.* 7. Many Chriftian Princes and States, now are called by them *Proteftant* or *Lutheran* Hereticks. All thefe, they fay, are fuch as may not be permitted, and therefore they have interpretatively and virtually rebelled, and depofed them.

3. You fee how great a matter this *Excommunication* is, and how impoffible it is, by it for Kings and States to continue long in any right to their Dominions: For all men err; and while there are fo many Patriarchs, Prelates, if not Priefts that have the power of Excommunicating, all men may expect it: For he that is orthodox in the judgment of one Patriarch, will be a Heretick in the judgment of another: while *Rome, Conft. Alexand. Antioch, Jerufal.* are fo feldom of one mind. If with the repenting *Lollard* (aforefaid) you will fwear to hold that for Error which the Archbifhop of *York* faith is fuch, perhaps the Archbifhop of *Canterbury* may be of the contrary mind: Thofe called *Arrians, Neftorians, Eutychians, Menothelites, Iconoclafts,* &c. have in their turns had moft of the known Chriftian World. And he that is Excommunicate by one, muft be received by none.

4. But if it be the Popes prerogative, that though more may Excommunicate Kings and Emperours, none but he can *depofe* them, and *difoblige* all their Subjects, it's pity but thofe Princes that are in love with fuch a Papacy fhould know by experience what they love: For he that will take Satan for his Ruler, muft bear the inconveniences of his Government.

5. You fee here how the Empire was weakned, and fo expofed to the Turk; even by the Rebellion of *Rome* cutting off the *Weftern* Empire from it.

6. And you fee what true Subjects they were to the *Arrian, Gothifh* Kings, at *Rome, Spain,* &c. who would have depofed them if they could. What wonder if the *Goths* kept down the Pope.

§ 6. In thefe times the Pope met with an *Englifh* Bifhop *Wilfrid,* who extraordinarily flattered and adored him, and he accordingly made him Bifhop of *Mentz,* and his great agent (even about this forefaid Englifh Council which was to fet up Church-Images:) and recommended him to many Chriftian Princes: And why was a'l this? and what was his rare merit? He took this Oath to the Pope (*Bin. p.* 178) [" *In the name of the Lord Je-*
" *fus Chrift our Saviour, in the Reign of* Leo *the great Emperour &c. I* Boni-
" face, *Bifhop by the Grace of God, do Promife to thee,* Peter, *Prince of the Apo-*
" *ftles, and to thy Vicar Pope* Gregory *and his Succeffors, by the Father, Son and*
" *Holy Ghoft, the infeparable* Trinity, *and this muft Holy Body of thine, that*
" *I will exhibite all faith and purity of holy Catholick faith, and in unity of*
" *the fame faith, God operating, will perfift, in which all the falvation of*
" *Chriftians is proved undoubtedly to confift; and will no way confent,*
" *whoever perfwadeth me, againft the unity of the common and univerfal Church,*
" *but, as I faid, will exhibite my faith and purity and concourfe to thee and to*
" *the Profits of thy Church, to whom by the Lord the Power of binding and*

" *loosing is given, and to thy aforesaid Vicar and his Successors in all things,*
" &c.]

Nothing is more meritorious with a Pope, or any Prelate of that Spirit, than to be absolutely devoted to him, and swear obedience to him: Indeed they that are fully fallen from God (as Satan is) would be as Gods to the world themselves, and have all men depend upon them, and obey them.

§ 7. What Arguments moved the Emperor to be against Images, (specially the 2d Commandment) and how *Gregory* thought that it was not the Images of God and Christ, and Angels and Saints that were forbidden, you may see in his *Epistles* too long to be here recited.

§ 8. Here *Binnius* inserteth three *Roman* Councils. One cursing unlawful Marriages. Another persuading *Corbinianus* to keep his Bishoprick, who would fain have laid it down. And a third for Images, against the *Iconoclasts* (the Emperor's Heresie.)

§ 9. *Gregory* 3d succeedeth *Gregory* 2d. He sendeth his Epistles for Images to the Emperor. The first Messenger durst not deliver them. The rest were stopt at *Sicily*, and kept Prisoners. The *Lombards* infested *Italy* and *Rome*. The Pope importuneth the *French* King for help. *Alphonsus* is made King in *Spain* against the *Saracens*, and first called himself [*Catholick King.*] Two Councils, *Binnius* saith, were held at *Rome* for Images. The Title of the second is, [*Pro Imaginum Cultu*, for the Worship of Images: *An.* 732. Image-worship was then avowed. But the *Eastern* Churches did more obey the Emperor.

§ 10. Pope *Zachary* coming next, in whose time *Italy* was distressed by *Luitprandus* King of the *Lombards*, who took four Cities from the Pope, because he protected *Trasimundus* Duke of *Spoleto* : The *Romans* helped *Trasimund*, on condition he would restore to them the four Cities ; he performeth not his promise : wherefore Pope *Zachary* turned to *Luitprand*, and to win him, *Salutaria illi prædicavit*, saith *Anastasius* ; and he promised him to restore the four Cities. For the performance whereof, this Pope travelled to him himself, (noted by *Anastasius* as a great act of self-denial, as venturing his life for the Cause of God, that he would go to the King to ask for four Cities) which he happily obtained.

§ 11. In this Pope's time the Crown of *France* was translated from the King and his Line, to a Subject, his *Major Domûs*.

Charles Martell the great *French* Conqueror was the Pope's Patron against the Emperor who was his Sovereign. *Gratian. d.* 16. *q.* 1. *post Can.* 59. tells it us as a matter of Church-credit, that when he was dead, he was damned to Hell (*much blood*, and *defending Popes that rebel against their Sovereign are a very likely proof.*) *Carolomannus* succeeded him, who, after two years Reign, resigned his Crown, and chose a Monastery. *Chilperic* that came after, proved very *dull* and *sensual*, and giving himself to his pleasure, let the business of Government lie most on the hands of *Pepin* , who was his *Major Domûs*, who thereby got the *power* and the *respect* that was proper to

the

their Councils abridged. 209

the King, while the King grew into contempt. (And if Kings cannot keep up their Power and Honour by the meer dignity of their place, without *personal worth and performance*; why should Popes, Prelates and Priests, (whose Power and Honour, as a Physicians, depend upon their Worth and Work) expect to keep up their Power and Honour meerly by their Offices?) *Pepin* won first the Nobles of *France*, and then the Pope; For, as *Baronius* and *Binnius* (*p.* 197.) tell us, "[*It seemed to the most Potent* Pepin (Major " *Domus*) (*) *and to the rest of the chief Men, and to all the People, that* (*) No " *he that had not the Matter and Force of the Kingdom, should not have* wonder. " *the name of a King; and on the contrary, he that had the Riches, Power* " *and Virtue, should also have the name of King: And because these Princes* " *and People were Christians, they judged that these their Councils would nei-* " *ther stand ratified to Posterity, nor be acceptable enough to God, unless they re-* " *ceived Authority and Force from the common Father and Pastor of the* " *Christian Church, the Vicar of the Lord Christ, and Successor of St. Peter.* " *Therefore they send Legates to* Rome *to* Zachary, *of whom Bishop* Burchardus " Herbipol. *was the chief, who were to ask the things aforesaid of him. He* " *consented, and decreed, and wrote back, that* Chilperic *being thrust into a* " *Monastery*, (*) *St.* Boniface *should declare and anoint* Pepin *King in Ger-* (*) Were " *many and* France : Boniface, *Bishop of* Mentz, *obeyed Pope* Zachary, *and* notMonks " *by the Authority of the See Apostolic, deposed* Chilperic, (*called also* Childe- holy men " *ric*) *and placed* Pepin *in his stead.* Thus *Jeginhart in Vit. Car. Mag.* then ? " *Annal. Franc. an.* 751. *Paul. Diac. li.* 22. *Marianus Scotus li.* 3. *Regino* " *li.* 2. *an.* 749. *Sigebert in Chron.* Lambert *in Hist. Germ. Otho Frising.* " *li.* 5. 21. *Ado. ætate* 6, *fol.* 213. *Aimoinus li.* 4. *c.* 65, &c. *Yea* (say they) " *the Hereticks of our times deny not the History.--But they sharply impugn two* " *circumstances: The first is, that it was a great wrong to* Chilperic, *that the* " *Kingdom was taken from him: The second, that the said Translation was* " *made by the consent of the Council, Nobles and Commons, without the Autho-* " *rity of the Apostolic Seat* *. Serarius *proveth that the cause of the Transla-* • If you " *tion of the Kingdom was just.* 1. *Because all the best men did desire and* will " *wish it, and did by their counsel and help co-operate to it.* 2. *Because St.* needs " *Bishop* Burchardus *did, as Legate, sollicite the Pope for it.* 3. *Pope* Zachary have the " *commanded it to be done*; 4. *And the most Holy* Boniface *at the Pope's* honour of " *command did execute it.* 5. *And being approved by Divine Testimony, it* so had a " *is recited in the sacred Canons,* 15. *q.* 6. *c. alius.* 6. *And by none of the* work, " *old Historians not praised, or disallowed: Only our new Hereticks, that love* 'that you " *Novelty, Arrogance and Rebellion by their perverse judgment by* Centumalies lower to " *and Lyes disallow it. And that it was by the Authority of the Apostolick* the " *Seat, that the Kingdom was translated from* Chilperic *to* Pepin, *the fore-* like, take " *said Historians do so expresly say, that it's a wonder with what front the in-* it. " *novating Hereticks dare call it in question. Lastly, It is here to be noted, that* " *it was by this same Pope* Zachary *that the nomination or postulation of Bishops* " *for the vacant Churches in his Kingdom, was granted to King* Pepin. *There-* " *fore if elsewhere you read that the Kings of* France *give Bishops to the Churches,*

E e " *remember*

" *remember that it is not done by their own Right, but by the Grant of the*
" *Apoſtolick Seat: In vain therefore do the innovating Hereticks glory in this*
" *Argument, who endeavor to ſubject the Church to Kings.*] So far *Binnius*
after *Baronius*.

§ 12. From this Story and theſe words, let the Reader think how to anſwer theſe Queſtions.

Queſt. 1. Had not Kings need to take heed of making any one man too great, if greatneſs and exerciſe of Government, give him ſo much right to the Kingdom?

Qu. 2. Had not Kings need to look to their manners, for their Crowns ſake, as well as their Souls; if Luſt, Senſuality and Dulneſs forfeit their Kingdoms?

Qu. 3. Did not Wars and weakning of the Empire make a great change with Popes, when they that were ſet up and baniſhed at the Emperor's pleaſure, can now firſt depoſe the Emperor in the *Weſt*, for being againſt Images and Perſecuting, and then can tranſlate the Crown of *France*?

Qu. 4. Was not an ambitious Pope a fit Tool for *Pepin* and his Confederates to work by, to put a pious gloſs on their Conſpiracy?

Qu. 5. Did not the Pope riſe thus by ſerving the turns of Conſpirators, and of Princes in their quarrels with one another?

Qu. 6. Are Subjects Judges when a King's Sins make him unworthy of the Crown?

Qu. 7. Yea, is the Pope Judge, and hath he power to depoſe Kings, if he judge them ſuch Sinners, and unfit for Government?

Qu. 8. Is it a good Reaſon that a King is juſtly depoſed, becauſe *Good Men and Holy Biſhops are the Deſirers and Promoters of it*?

Qu. 9. Would not this Reaſon have ſerved *Maximus* againſt *Gratian*? Was it not *Cromwel's* Plea? If he had but had the Pope and People on his ſide, you ſee how it would have gone.

Qu. 10. Is it the mark of an Innovating Heretick, to ſay *that the Church ſhould be ſubject to Kings*; when *Paul* and *Peter* ſaid it of all Chriſtians ſo long ago?

Qu. 11. Is it a Note that Proteſtants love *Rebellion*, becauſe they are againſt Popes depoſing Kings? Or is there any heed to be taken of the words of impudent Revilers, that dare ſpeak before God and Man at this rate? Is depoſing Kings the Papiſts freedom from Rebellion, and is our oppoſing it a character of Rebels?

Qu. 12. Is it any wonder that Biſhop *Burchardus* deſired it, and that Biſhop *Boniface* executed the Pope's command, who had been tranſlated from *England* by him to ſuch dignity, and had ſworn Obedience and Service to him?

Qu. 13. Is it any wonder that the Pope made theſe Biſhops *Saints*?

Qu. 14. I hope they were really godly Men: But is it any wonder that ſome good Men at ſuch a time as that, did think it had been for the intereſt
of

of Religion, to have all Power in the Clergies hands, especially being themselves Bishops that were to have so great a share? How few Bishops are afraid of too much power, or ever do refuse it!

Qu. 15. If the King of *France* had his Kingdom by the Pope's gift, what wonder if he had the power of nominating Bishops also by his gift?

Qu. 16. Whether he that hath power to give, hath not power to take away, and be not Judge when the Cause is just?

Qu. 17. With what face do Papists at once make these claims, and yet profess Loyalty to Kings?

Qu. 18. Whether it concern not Kings to understand on what terms they stand with the Pope and his Clergy, that must not be subject to them, but have power to depose them?

Qu. 19. If there be any Party among them that hath more Loyal Principles, is it a sign of the concord of their Church, that agreeth not in matter of so great moment? Or a proof that the Pope is the infallible Judge of Controversies, that will not determine so great a Point on which the Peace of Kingdoms doth depend?

§ 13. About the same time they persuaded *Rachis* King of the *Longobards*, Successor to *Luitprand*, for the love of Religion to lay down his Crown, and go into a Monastery; so that Monasteries are places for the worst and the best; some too bad to reign, and some too good, lest they should overmaster the Clergy.

§ 14. It may be you will think that this Pope *Zachary*, and his sworn Vassal St. *Boniface*, were some very profound Divines, that could by their wisdom and piety thus master Kingdoms. Doubtless they were zealous Adversaries to Heresies (except their own) and Successors of the Hereticating and Damning Fathers. For *Epist.* 10. (*Bin. p.* 206, 207, 208.) Zachary writeth to *Boniface*, to expel *Virgilius* from the Church and Priesthood, for holding *Antipodes*, viz. that Sun-shine, and Moon-light, and Men are under the Earth, as well as here which we call over it. The words are, [*De perversa ante n & iniqua doctrina, quæ contra Dominum & Animam suam locutus est, si clarificatum fuerit ita eum confiteri, quod alius mundus & alii homines sub terra sint, seu Sol & Luna; hunc habito Concilio ab Ecclesia pelle Sacerdotii honore privatum.*] That is, "*But as to the perverse and unjust Doctrine* "*which he hath spoken against the Lord and his own Soul, if it be made clear* "*that he so confesseth, that under the Earth there is another world and other* "*Men, and Sun and Moon; call a Council, and depriving him of the honour* "*of Priesthood, drive him out of the Church.*] That by [*another world*] is meant *Antipodes*, or the other side of the Earth inhabited, is doubtless.

§ 15. *Qu.* 1. Did God make Popes to be the Governors of the *Antipodes*, for so many hundred years, before they knew that there was any *Antipodes*? And when they excommunicated and silenced those that affirmed it?

Qu. 2. Were these Popes and Bishops Men of such wisdom, as were fit to hereticate Dissenters as they did?

Qu. 3. Do we not see here what some Councils were, and did in those times?

Qu. 4. Do we not see what Heresie signified at *Rome*, and how little heed there was to be taken of their outcry against some Heresies?

Qu. 5. Whether was all the World, or all the West bound to avoid Communion after with *Virgilius*?

Qu. 6. Do we not see here of what Infallibility the Pope is, in judging of matters of Faith, and how happy the World is to have such a Judge, and of what credit his Heretications and Excommunications are?

Qu. 7. Do we not see how Religion hath been depraved and dishonoured by the Pope and his Clergy, calling Good Evil, and the most certain Truths by the name of [*Perverse and unjust Doctrines, against the Lord, and Mens own Souls?*] What heed to take of these Mens words, when they seem zealous against Sin and Error?

§ 16. Perhaps you will ask, How could any but Idiots be so ignorant? Whither did they think the Setting-Sun went? Or what did they think the Earth stood upon?

Answ. The easiest things are strange to Men that never learnt them; it's pity that it should be true, that *Lactantius* and other Ancients, yea, *Austin* himself were ignorant of the *Antipodes*; but yet they had more Modesty than to hereticate and excommunicate them that affirmed it. Few Bishops had much Philosophy then. *Origen* and *Apollinaris* that were most Philosophical, had been hereticated and disgraced it. *Clemens* and *Tatianus* sped not much better. Councils had forbid Bishops to read the Books of Heathens. *Austin* had a truly Philosophical head, being the Father of School-Divinity; but he was αὐτοδίδακτος, and had little from his Teachers. You may see in a great Hereticater *Philastrius*, what they thought then of the course of the Sun, by what he saith of the Stars: As it was one Heresie to *call the Stars by the names of living Creatures,* so it was another to deny *that the Stars were Luminaries arbitrarily moved, that by Angels were set out at night to light the World, and at morning retired inwards, or were taken into their place again, as Men set out lights to the street at night, and take them in again.* I confess that no General Council declared this, (as they have done worse things;) but you see what kind of Men were hereticated by Pope *Zachary, St. Boniface,* and *St. Philastrius,* and such Bishops; and how little it signifieth in such Writers, whether you read a Man called a Saint, or a Sinner; an Orthodox Catholick, or *Nefandissimus Hæreticus,* as they use to speak: I speak it only of such Men.

§ 17. For, Reader, I must still remember thee, that this Folly, Pride, and almost Fury, was not the *Genius* or Character of the true spiritual Ministers and Church of Christ, but of a worldly, ignorant, domineering sort of Men, that made it their business to get Preferment, and have their wills. God had

all

all this while abundance of faithful Ministers that sate down at the lower end; and humble holy People, that set not up themselves in worldly Grandure, and came not much on the Stage, but approved themselves in secret, and in their several Places and Conversations to God, some Lay-men, some Priests, some Bishops, some of their names are come down to us in History, but those are few. They strove not for great Places, nor did their Works to be seen of Men, nor looked to Men for their Reward.

§ 18. Some of the Canons and Councils of these Universal Pastors were answerable to their Excommunications. In *Zachary*'s 12th *Epistle* to his Vassal *St. Boniface*, he giveth him the resolution of many doubts. One is, [*After how long time Lard may be eaten?* And it is resolved by the Pope, *That there is yet no Canon or Law for this by the Fathers, but he determineth himself,* 1. *That it must not be eaten before it be dried in the smoke, or boiled, (or basted) with fire: But if you list to eat it raw, it must be eaten after the Feast of* Easter.] *Binnius, p.* 209. (What would become of the Church, if there were not a Judge of such Controversies, and an infallible Determiner of such Questions?)

§ 19. CCXXV. I told you before how the Pope commanded *Boniface* to call a Council to eject him that asserted the *Antipodes*; I must next add a *French* Council called by King *Carolomannus*, to Reform the Clergy (*an.* 742.) and *to recover Christian Religion, which in the dayes of former Princes* dissipata corruit, *being dissipated, was ruined; and to shew the People how they may come to save their Souls, who have been hitherto deceived by false Priests.* (They are the words of the King and Council, *Bin.* p. 210. c. 2.) Where it was decreed that Priests be not Soldiers, (unnecessarily:) That they keep not Hounds to go an hunting with, nor Hawks: That every Religious Fornicator shall in the Jayl do Pennance with Bread and Water. If the Fornicator be a Priest, he shall be **fo** scourged, and then remain in Prison two years: But if an inferior Clerk or Monk so fall, he shall be whipt, and then do Pennance a whole year in Prison, and so the Nuns.

This was somewhat like a **Reformation**: Had it not been done by a King, it might have past for Heresie. It was at *Ratisbonne, Boniface* presiding.

Such another Council called *Leptinense*, there was under *Carolomannus*.

Another Council at *Rome* repeated the oft repeated Canons, to keep Bishops and Priests from Nuns and from Fornication.

§ 20. *An.* 744. Another *Synodus Sueffion.* under *Chilperic* governed by *Pepin*, condemned again *Aldebert* (that set up Crosses in several places, and drew People to himself) and another as Hereticks.

§ 21. Another Council in *Germany, an.* 745. handsomly set *Boniface* the Pope's Agent in the Archbishoprick of *Mentz*. First *Geroldus* the Archbishop is sent out against the *Saxons* with an Army, and he and most of them killed: Then *Gervilio* his Son, a Lay-man, is made Archbishop to comfort him. At another War he pretends a Conference with him that kill'd his Father, and murders him; this is past by as blameless: But *Boniface* saith, *That a Man that had his hand in Blood, must not be a Bishop*; and so got him

him out, and was made the chief Archbishop of *Germany* himself in his place. Judge whether he served the Pope for nought.

§ 22. Yet *Boniface* had not done with the two Hereticks, *Aldebert* and *Clemens*, a *French* man and a *Scot*. *Boniface* sendeth to *Rome* (*Bin.* p. 216.) to desire the Pope, that as he had himself condemned these two Hereticks, the Pope would also condemn them, and cast them into Prisons, where none might speak with them. (Thus the Pope obtained his Kingdom, and edified the Church. The motive was, that *Boniface* prosecuting them, had suffered much for their sakes, the People saying that he had taken from them holy Apostolick Men, (but this was not a Prison.) The Crimes which he chargeth on *Aldebert* a Bishop are, that he was an Hypocrite, (an open Crime!) that he had said an Angel appeared to him, and he had some rare Reliques, and that he said he was Apostolick, and wrought Wonders ; that he got some unlearned Bishops to make him a Bishop absolutely, against the Canons. He would not consecrate any Church to the memory of an Apostle or Martyr ; and spake against visiting in Pilgrimage the Temples of the Apostles : He made Churches to his own honour, and set up Oratories and Crosses up and down, and drew People from other Bishops to himself. That he gave his nails and hair to be honoured with the Saints Reliques, and would not hear Confessions, saying he knew their sins already.] If all this was true, (which I know never the more for this Accusation) he seemed an Hypocrite indeed, but whether an Heretick, I know not.

The *Scot* Heretick is accused as denying the Church Canons, and the meaning of some Fathers, despising the Synods Laws, saying that he may still be a Bishop (for so he was) though he had two Sons, (in Adultery, saith *Boniface*, perhaps in Marriage ;) and (as he saith) holding that a Man may marry his Brothers Widow, and that Christ at his Descent delivered all Souls out of Hell.] This was a foul Error indeed, if truly charged. These were charged by *Boniface* and the *Roman* Synod, to be forerunners of Antichrist, (and how like are *Aldebert*'s Pretensions to many *Roman* Saints!) A Prayer also of *Aldeberts* was read, in which he prayed to Angels under several strange names : Bishops and Presbyters had Votes in this Council, and subscribed the Hypocrites condemnation. *Bin. p.* 218. But there is no certainty that he named more than three Angels.

§ 23. *Stephen* the 2d was chosen Pope by ALL THE PEOPLE after *Zachary*, and dyed four days after suddenly.

§ 24. *Stephen* the 3d was chosen by all the People (saith *Anastasius*.) *Aistulphus*, King of the *Longobards*, threatned *Rome*, took their Gifts, and demanded their Subjection. The Pope (after *Gregory* the 2d's Rebellion) was glad to send to the Emperor, to crave an Army to save *Rome* and *Italy* ; when he could get no help from *Constant.* he sent to *Pepin* King of *France*. One that he had made King by Rebellion, was obliged to help him, and by an Army forced *Aistulphus* to covenant to restore *Ravenna*, and many other *Italian* Cities, (not to the Emperor, whose Agent claimed his right, and was denied by *Pepin* ;) but to the Pope, (to reward him, and get the pardon of

his

their Councils abridged. 215

his fins.) *Aistulphus* broke his Covenants. *Pepin* with another Army forceth him to deliver them, and returneth. *Aistulphus* dyeth ; *Desiderius* a Captain by Usurpation invadeth the Kingdom, *Radchis* that had been King before, and went into a Monastery, and the Nobles of the *Longobards* resist the Rebel. He sendeth to the Pope, offering him all that he could desire (more Cities) to help him : The Pope maketh his own bargain with him, as he did with *Pepin*, (and *Charles Martell* before) and by the help of the *French*, setleth the Rebel *Desiderius* in the Kingdom. *Pepin* maketh a Deed of Gift of all the foresaid Cities to the Church of *Rome*, (Was this *Constantine's* Gift?) He gave away another Mans (the Emperor's) Dominions, and with *Desiderius's* additions, now the Pope is become a Prince.

§ 24. CCXXVIII. We come now to a great General Council of 338 Bishops at *Constantinople*, *An*. 754. under *Constantine Copronymus* against the worshiping of Images: The Adversaries of it will not have it called the 7th General Council, because divers Patriarchs were absent, and it decreed, say they, against the Truth. *They not only condemned the worshiping of Images, and* Germanus Constantinus, Georgius Cyprius, Jo. Damascenus, *and other Worshipers of them, as Idolaters; but destroyed the Reliques of Martyrs, and exacted an Oath of Men (by the Cross, and the holy Eucharist) that they would never adore Images, but execrate them as Idols, nor ever pray to the holy Apostles, Martyrs, and blessed Virgin*, saith *Baronius* and *Binnius*, p. 235. But the 15th and 17th definitions of this Council recited in the 2d *Nicene* Council, shew that they were not so free from praying to the Virgin *Mary* and Saints, as we could wish they had: For they decree we must *crave her intercessions, and theirs* ; but they forbad praying to their Images.

Sixtus Senensis & Pet. Crabbe f. 458. say it was at *Ephesus*, but *Binnius* confuteth them.

§ 25. The Acts of this Council (not pleasing the Adversaries) are not delivered fully to us ; but it fell out that their *Decrees* are repeated word by word in the 2d *Nicene* Council, and so preserved.

§ 26. There is one Doctrinal definition of this Council, owned also by their Adversaries the 2d *Concil. Nicen.* which by the way I will take notice of, about the glorified Body of Christ, (and consequently ours after the Resurrection) that it is a Body but not *Flesh*, Bin. p. 378. defin. 7. " [*Siquis* " *non confessus fuerit Dominum nostrum Jesum Christum post assumptionem* " *animatæ, rationalis & intellectualis Carnis simul sedere cum Deo & Patre,* " *atque ita quoque rursus venturum cum Paterna Majestate, judicaturum vivos* " *& mortuos, non amplius quidem* Carnem, *neque incorporeum tamen ut videa-* " *tur ab iis à quibus compunctus est, & maneat Deus extra crassitudinem car-* " *nis, Anathema.*] To which saith the *Nicene* Council by *Epiphanius*, [" *Huc usque recte sentiunt & Patrum traditionibus convenientia dicunt*, &c. _

Two sorts I would have take notice of this:

1. The *Papists*, who say that the Bread is turned into Christ's very *Flesh*, when he hath no very Flesh in Heaven: And therefore the meaning must be of the Sacramental Sign, that it is the Representation of that real *Flesh* of Christ which was sacrificed on the Cross.

2. Some

2. Some prejudiced *Proteſtants* that think he that ſaith, [*Our Bodies (and Chriſts) in Heaven, will not be Fleſh and Blood formally and properly ſo called, but ſpiritual glorious Bodies*] doth ſay ſome dangerous new aſſertion; ſuch groſs thoughts have groſs heads of the heavenly ſtate. To theſe I ſay, 1. You contradict the expreſs words of God's Spirit, 1 *Cor.* 15. *Fleſh and Blood cannot enter,* &c. That it is meant of Formal Fleſh and Blood, and not Metaphorical (Sin) is plain in the Context, ſee Dr. *Hammond* on the Text. 2. Give but a true definition of *Fleſh* and *Blood,* and it will convince you of itſelf. 3. You ſee here that you maintain an Opinion which theſe two (even adverſe) General Councils anathematized.

§ 27. By this Council we may ſee, how little General Councils ſignifie with the *Papiſts,* either as to Infallibility, Authority, or preſervation of Tradition, longer than they pleaſe the Pope. As to their Objection, that call it *Pſeudo-ſeptimum,* that the Pope was not there; I anſwer 1. No more was he by himſelf or Legate at the firſt of *Conſtant.* called the 2d General Council, as *Binnius* profeſſeth. 2. Is not the Church the Church, if the Pope be not there? Then he may chooſe whether ever there ſhall be more General Councils, (as indeed he doth.)

§ 28. CCXXIX. *An.* 756. King *Pepin* called a Council in *France,* declaring that things were ſo far out of order, that he could attempt but a partial Reformation, leaving the reſt till better times. The firſt Canon was, that every City have a Biſhop; of old πόλις, ſignified every ſuch Town as our Corporations and Market-Towns are: And by all the old Canons and Cuſtoms (except ſome odd ones) every ſuch Town of Chriſtians was to have a Biſhop; and in *Phrygia, Arabia,* &c. the Villages had Biſhops, ſaith *Socrates,* &c. And in many places the Villages had *Chorepiſcopos,* which *Petavius* (*Annot. in Epiphan. Arian.*) fully proveth *were true Biſhops.* And yet then the moſt of the People in moſt Countries were without the Church; ſo that then a Church was no greater than what was capable of perſonal Communion.

Here this King (being made by the Pope) ſo far gratified the Clergy, as to decree that Contemners of Excommunication ſhould *be baniſhed.* And now the *Keys* do ſignifie the Sword, and Church-Diſcipline is made another thing than Chriſt had made it.

The 13th *Cap.* is, That no vacant Biſhop meddle in another Biſhop's Pariſh without his conſent, (by what true authority then can the Pope meddle in other Mens Dioceſſes, ſince the foundation of his humane authority in the Empire is ſubverted?)

The 14th *Cap.* decreed, That Men may uſe Horſes and Chariots for Travel on the Lord's-day, and get Meat and Drink, &c. but not do common work.

The 17th, That no C'erk try his Cauſe before a Lay-Judge, without the Biſhop's leave.

§ 29. Pope *Stephen* dying, in the diviſion at the next choice, (by all the People) the ſtronger part choſe *Paulus* a Deacon, CCXXX. in his time a *German*

German Council condemned *Oathmarus*, Abbot of St. *Gallus*, for Incontinence, and put him in Prison, where he dyed of Famine; as Historians say, maliciously upon false accusation.

§ 30. At this time the *Greeks* accused the *Romans*, for adding the word [*Filioque*] to the Creed: And about that and Images, they say there was some Synod at a Village called *Gentiliace*.

§ 31. Pope *Paul* dying, and the People having still the choice, he that could get the greatest strength was in hope of so rich a Prey: And *Constantine*, Brother to one Duke *Toto*, getting the strongest Party, by fear compelled *George* Bishop of *Præneftine*, with two more Bishops, to make him Pope, (being first ordained Deacon,) he possessed the Popedom alone a year and a month: Then one *Christopher* the *Primecerius*, and his Son *Sergius* being powerful, got out to the King of the *Longobards*, and craved his help against *Constantine* as an Usurper; and gathering some strength got into *Rome*, killed *Toto*; and caused *Constantine* the Pope, and another Brother *Paffivus* to take Sanctuary. One *Waldipertus* a Presbyter was of *Christopher's* Party, and to make haste, without *Christopher's* knowledge, he gathereth a Party, and they make one *Philip* (a Presbyter) Pope. (So there were two Popes.) *Christophorus* incensed, swore he would not enter *Rome*, till *Philip* was pull'd out of the Bishop's house; which *Gratiosus*, one of his Party, presently performeth, and *Philip* returneth to his Monastery. *Christophorus* calleth the Clergy, People and Soldiers together, and (by his means) they chuse another *Stephen*, (and so there are three Popes.) The Actors being now in their zeal, go to *Theodorus* a Bishop, and *Vicedominus* that joined with Pope *Constantine*, and they put out his eyes, and cut out his tongue. Next they attempted the like excæcation on *Paffivus*. Bishop *Theodore* they thrust into a Monastery, and there (while he cryed for a little water) they famished him to death. *Paffivus* they put into another Monastery. They took all their Goods and Possessions. Pope *Constantine* they brought out, and set on Horseback on a Womans Saddle with Weights at his Feet, and put him into a Monastery, (How holy then were Monasteries!) Shortly after they brought him forth, and Pope *Stephen* and some Bishops deposed him. Then the Citizens were to make their penitent Confessions for owning him. Next the Army goeth to *Alatrum* in *Campania*, where *Gracilis* the Tribune that had been for *Constantine* is apprehended, brought bound to *Rome*, imprisoned, and after his eyes put out, and his tongue cut out. After this, *Gratiosus* and his Zealots go to the Monastery where they had thrust Pope *Constantine*, and drag him out, and put out his eyes, and leave him blind in the street. Next, they go to their own Friend Priest *Waldipertus*, and feign that he had laid a Plot with the *Longobards* to kill *Christopher*, and send to apprehend him, and when he fled for Sanctuary to a Temple, they drew him out with the blessed Virgins Image in his hand (even then when they were rebelling for the sake of Images;) but that would not save the Priest, (because he set up *Philip* for Pope;) they thrust him into a filthy Dungeon-hole, but that was too good for him: In a few days they drew him out, and casting him on the earth, put

F f

out his eyes, and cut out his tongue, and put him into an Hospital, where he dyed of the pain. And now Pope *Stephen* had, no doubt, a lawful calling to be Pope. He sends his Legats to the King of *France*. He brings forth blinded Pope *Constantine* to answer for his Crime, who falling flat on the earth, he lamenteth his sin as more than the Sands on the Sea-shore, and professeth that the People chose and forced him to be Pope, because of their sufferings under *Paul*: But at his next appearance he tells them, that he did no more than many other Lay-men did, who invaded Bishopricks; as *Sergius* Archbishop of *Ravenna*, *Stephen* Bishop of *Naples*, &c. when they heard this, all the Priests caused him to be busseted, and cast him out of the Church, and burnt his Papers, &c. And the most holy Pope *Stephen* cast himself on the earth, with all the Priests and People of *Rome*, and with tears lamented their sin, that they had taken the Communion from the hands of Pope *Constantine*, (it seems it is a sin to communicate with Bishops that are brought in irregularly by secular Power without due Election, and they are no Schismaticks that refuse it.) And so they all performed their Pennance for it, *Anastas. in ejus vita.*

§ 32. CCXXXI. On this great occasion Pope *Stephen* (being far unable now to call General Councils) sends to the King of *France*, to entreat him to send some wise Bishops to a Council at *Rome*, who sent him about a dozen, who, with some others, agreed against *Constantine's* Election, and such other for the time to come; and damned a Synod that *Constantine* had held; and also passed their judgment for Images.

§ 33. But here was a great difficulty, (such as often after happened) Whether *Constantine's* Papal Acts were valid; and the Council decreed that they should all be void except his *Baptizings*, and his *Consecrations*: And so those Priests that he Consecrated, when they were after duely chosen, officiated without a new Consecration. Either he was a real Pope, or no Pope. If a Pope, then by the Canons *Stephen* was no Pope, and so the Succession there failed. If no Pope, then, 1. How come his Consecrations to be valid? 2. Are not Presbyter's Ordinations better than a Lay-mans? 3. Then the Universal Church had no Head, and so was no Church (with them) while *Constantine* was Pope.

§ 34. A like Schism fell out at *Ravenna*: The power of the Magistrate made one *Michael*, *Scriniary* of the Church, (a Lay-man) Archbishop, the People being for one *Leo*, whom they imprisoned. He kept the place above a year; but by the help of the Pope, and the *French*, the People rose and cast him out, and brought him Prisoner to *Rome*, and set up *Leo*.

§ 35. *Christopher* and his Son *Sergius* were the Captains that had wrought this great deliverance to the Church: And now they plead with King *Desiderius* for St. *Peter's* Rights, as still zealous for the Pope. The King is angry with them, and jealous of their power, and seeketh to destroy them, and particularly to set their own Pope against them. They get the Citizens to stand by them, and the King cometh with an Army. The Pope seeing which was like to be the stronger side, in great wisdom went out to the King, and after
some

some days conference with him, sendeth to *Christopher* to render himself to the King. The Citizens hearing this, forsook *Christopher* and *Sergius*; *Gratiosus* (seeing they were deserted by the People through the Pope) went out first to the King and Pope, and *Sergius* next, and *Christopher* last. The Pope was so kind to them that made him Pope, that he made them Monks, and put them in Sanctuary in St. *Peter*'s Church to save their lives: But they had *Adonibezek*'s justice, and were soon drag'd out thence, and *Christopher*'s eyes put out, of which he dyed. But *Sergius* was awhile a Monk, and then thrust in the *Laterane* Cellar. Thus went the matters of the Universal Monarch at *Rome*.

§ 36. A little before the Pope's death, *Sergius* was fetcht blind out of the Cellar, and kill'd; the next Pope searcht out the Authors, and found them to be *Paulus Cubicularius*, and the last Pope's Brother, and other great Men; and he prosecuted some of them to Banishment, but the Archbishop of *Ravenna* caused *Paul* to be killed.

§ 37. It was *Adrian* (a Deacon) that was then chosen Pope (Son to the chief Man in *Rome*, ablest to effect it.) Upon these stirs, *Desiderius* desired friendship with the Pope; but he demanding the Cities which *Pepin* had given the Church (some of which *Desiderius* still kept) and doing the foresaid justice on the Friends of *Desiderius*, he came with an Army and killed many, and took many Cities. The Pope urgeth the restitution of all his Cities, (indeed the Emperor's) given him by *Pepin*; he still denieth; the Pope gets *Charles* of *France* to come with an Army, for fear of whom the *Longobards* flie. The Dutchy of *Spoletum*, and other Cities, yield themselves to the Pope, (and, as a token of subjection, receive tonsure.) *Charles* besiegeth *Desiderius* in *Papia*, and forceth his Brother *Carloman*'s Wife and Children that fled to the *Longobards*, to yield themselves to him; while the Siege continued *Charles* went to *Rome*, and was gloriously entertained by the Pope, and renewed to him *Pepin*'s gift of all the Exarchate of *Ravenna*, and many Dukedoms and Cities, (which were none of his own to give) and now the Pope is a Prince indeed. And *Charles* returning to the Siege, conquereth *Papia*, taketh King *Desiderius*, and winneth all the *Longobards* Kingdom: And thus Strength gave Right (according to the Atheists Opinion now stirring, that [*Right is nothing but a power to get and keep.*] *Pepin* and *Charles* make themselves Kings, and the Pope a Prince; that while they share the Emperor's Dominions between them, they might be a strength to one another. And *Desiderius* being himself but an Usurper, helped by the Pope into the Throne, no wonder if when interest changed, the same hand take him down. How *Charles* his Brother *Caroloman* dyed, and why his Wife and Sons fled from *Charles* to the *Longobards*, and what became of them, is not well known.

§ 38. Pope *Adrian* the 1st thus made a greater Prince than any before him, did greater works than they had done, and *ob nimium amorem Sancti Petri, & ex inspiratione Divina*, built many great and stately Buildings, made all places about his Palace, Baths, &c. fit for splendid pomp and pleasure, and all this from meer self-denial and holiness: Many Churches also he repaired and adorned, and did many other such good works.

§ 39. This great *Adrian* was before but a Deacon. I have oft marvelled to read that Deacons were so ordinarily then made Popes, (and sometimes Lay-men, when yet the old Canons required an orderly rising through the several degrees. It was no wonder that then a Deacon at *Rome* was a far higher preferment than a Bishop: For a Deacon (and a Priest) might be chosen Pope, but a Bishop could not: For of old (when Dioceffes and Parishes were all one) the Canons decreed that no Bishop should remove to another Church, (except being Confecrated by others, he never confented nor had poffeffion;) so that every Bishop must live and dye in the place where he was first Ordained; so that *Rome*, *Conft. Alex. Antioch*, &c. and all the great Seats chose either Deacons, Priests, or Monks to be their Patriarchs and Bishops. No wonder then, if as *Nazianzen* saith, *Orat.* 5. it was the custom to have almost as many Clergy-men in every Church as People, in regard of the present Honour, and the future hopes of Preferment. Indeed he carried it that had the greatest Friends, which was as commonly the Deacon, as the Priest or Archdeacon. By which we may conjecture, whether the worthiest Men were made Popes: For if they were the worthiest, why were they by former Popes never made higher before than Deacons? Did not the Popes know the worthiest men?

And if a breach of the Canons in Elections nullifie the regular Succeffion, by this it is evident, that the *Roman* Seat hath no such Succeffion.

§ 40. By the way the Reader must note, that in all the Writings of the Popish Clergy concerning these matters, there are certain terms of Art, or Interest, which must be understood as followeth, *viz.*

1. *Sanctiffimus Papa*, the most Holy Pope, signifieth any prosperous Bishop of *Rome*, how wicked soever in his life.

2. *Rex Pientiffimus*, the most Pious King, signifieth a King that took part with the Pope, and advanced his Opinions and Interest.

3. *Imperator Sceleratiffimus, & Hæreticus Nefandus*, &c. a most wicked Emperor, (or Patriarch, or any other) and abominable Heretick] signifieth one that was against the Pope, his Interest or Opinion. *Homo mendaciffimus*, a *Lyar*, is one that saith what the Papists would not have to be true. If you understand them otherwise, you are deceived (ordinarily.).

§ 41. About the death of *Paulus Cubicularius*, and others, note, that it had long been the way of the Church-Canons, to contradict God's great Law for humane safety, [*He that sheddeth Man's blood, by Man shall his blood be shed*;] and on pretence of being (more) merciful (than God) to entice Murderers, Adulterers, and all wicked Thieves and Criminals to make up the Church of Christ, by decreeing, that instead of being Hanged, or Beheaded, if they would but be Baptized, they should but be kept for a time from the Sacrament, or do Pennance; and what Villain would not then be a Christian?

§ 42.

§ 42. Here ariseth a great Controversie with *Sigibert*, (a Monk-Historian) and *Gratian* himself, which *Baronius* and *Binnius* take up, *viz.* the first say,. [*That Charles being at* Rome,*a Council there with Pope* Adrian *gave him the power of chusing the Pope,and ordering the Apostolick Seats; and all Bishops and Archbishops in all Provinces, to receive Investiture from him;and that none should Consecrate a Bishop unless he were praised and invested by the King; and that they Anathematize all that rebel against this Decree, and confiscate their Estates if they repent not: But,* say *Baronius* and *Binnius, this is a lye, and devised deceit to flatter the Emperor* Henry *a Schismatick.* And while Chroniclers may have the Lye given them so easily by Dissenters in matters of such publick Fact, we are left at great uncertainty in History, others as confidently giving the Lye to the Papal Flatterers, as they do those of their own Religion that do not please them.

One of the Reasons against this Decree, is the contrariety of the *French* Constitutions, *l.* 1. *c.* 84. saying, [*Not being ignorant of the sacred Canons we consented to the Ecclesiastick Order, to wit, that Bishops be chosen by the Election of the Clergy and* PEOPLE, *according to the Statutes of the Canons out of their own Diocess, without respect of Persons or Rewards, for the merit of their life, and their gift of wisdom, that by example and word they may every way profit those that are under them.*]

1. This indeed sheweth how Bishops by the Canons were to be chosen, even till these days of *Charles the Great* ; he was to be taken for no Bishop that came not in by the Peoples (as well as the Clergies) Election, or consent at least.

2. But this contradicteth not what *Sigibert* and *Gratian* say; the Emperor might still have a negative voice after all, especially as to a Pope: In very deed, the door is safe that hath divers locks. 1. It belongeth to the Clergy and Ordainers to judge who shall be [*A Bishop or Minister of Sacred things.*] 2. It belongeth to the Flock to discern whom they will accept for THEIR Bishop or Pastor. 3. It belongeth to the Magistrate to judge whom he will countenance or tolerate in that Office.

§ 43. *Paulus Diaconus* the Historian was Secretary to *Desilerius* the *Longobard* King;*Charles* in anger commanded his hand to be cut off, for doing somewhat for his own King against him ; the Courtiers added , *that his eyes should be put out* ; which made *Charles* consider and say, *If we do but cut off his hand, where shall we find such another Historian* ?

§ 44. *Constantine* the Emperor now dying, called *Copronymus* ; the *Papists* call us to take notice what a Leader we follow that are against the Worship of Images ; saying that he dyed with the *beginnings of Hell-fire*, convinced of his sin against the Virgin *Mary*, and that all his life he loved the smell of dung, and stinking things ; strong Arguments for Image-worship, as worthy as *Sigebert*'s and *Gratian*'s, to be suspected as Lyes, or of little certainty.

§ 45.

§ 45. While *Leo Isaurus* and *Constantine* lived, the Councils of Bishops went with them, and Images went down in the Eastern Empire: *Constantine* dying, his Son *Leo* succeeded him, saith *Binnius*, in his Heresie, Impiety and Sacriledge, that is, in his opposition to Image-worship, and such like. *Petavius* saith, he first feigned himself a Catholick, (that is, for Images) but after fell off: His Sacriledge was, that loving Jewels, he took for himself a rich Crown, which *Maurice* had devoted to the Virgin *Mary*; whereupon Carbuncles arose on him, and he dyed: but had not *Maurice* himself a sadder death? Thus partial Historians feign and apply Judgments.

§ 46. *Irene*, *Leo*'s Widow, with her Son *Constantine* a Child, next ruled, and, saith *Binnius*, God *by a Widow and an Orphan Child, by a Wonder, did tread down the Impiety that had been set up, and restored Religion*, that is, *Images*. And indeed *Rome*'s interest and proper way hath been chiefly advanced under *Women* and *Rebels*. And it is no wonder if *Irene* a *Woman*, and her *Child*, were more for *Images* than their Predecessors. *Children* use to play with *Images*, and Womens Fancies are oft not unsuitable to them. I think it as observable a matter, as *Binnius* doth, to note the Instruments.

☞ § 47. There are in *Binnius* the Titles of 44 at least Epistles of Pope *Adrian*'s recited: The 36th saith, [*He professeth that the Church of* Rome *doth embrace and reverence the Whole fourth* Calcedon *Council*. Remember then that the last Canon is approved, which declareth the reason of the *Roman* Priviledges to be because it was the Imperial Seat, and therefore that *Constantine* should have the like, and that it was *given it by the Fathers*.

Most or many of them are thanks to *Charles* for giving St. *Peter* so many great Cities and Dukedoms, and Exhortations to him to continue his bounty. By their ordinary language you would not suspect any Selfishness, Pride or Covetousness in the Popes; it is but for St. *Peter* that they desire all.

§ 48. In his Epistle to *Constantine* and *Irene*, (the Child and Mother) to entice them to be for *Images*, he tells a fabulous Story * of a Vision of *Constantine*'s sending him to *Silvester* as his Guide, to be baptized of him, and to be thereby cured of a Leprosie: It was *Peter* and *Paul* that appeared to him; and he asked *Silvester* whether there were left any Images of *Peter* and *Paul*, which he affirmed, and shewed him their Pictures; and the Emperor cryed out, *These are the Men that appeared to me*. And part of their Message to him was, that he should bring all the world into the subjection of the Church of *Rome*.] Was not here a strong Argument to a Woman and a Child to be for the *Pope* and for *Images*, contrary to current History, (that tells us *Constantine* was baptized at *Nicomedia* a little before his death,) and without any credible proof. Thus the Papal *Rome* was built. When *Adrian* had given away the Western Empire to *Charles*, yet he thus flattereth a Woman and Child in the East, as if he had done them no wrong at all.

* See *Hen. Fowlis* of Papists Treasons, P. 120. proving the whole Story false.

§ 49.

§ 49. *Paul* Bishop of *Const.* having sworn against Images, and repenting, is said to resign his place, and to tell them that they must have a General Council; and *Tarasius* succeeding him, being for *Images*, got a promise of a Council. It seems by their Epistles, though they agreed about Images, Pope *Adrian* and this *Tarasius* accused each other as suspected of Simony, see *Bin. p.* 262. and the Epistles. *Irene* knew that *Tarasius* was for her turn, and *Tarasius* knew that *Irene* was for Pictures; and so between them common notice was given abroad before-hand to the Bishops, (that lately had condemned Image-worship, and pull'd them down) that the Empress and the Patriarch were for restoring Images, and would call a Council to that end : and this was enough to prepare the majority of the Bishops for a sudden change.

§ 50. Besides a Council at *Wormes, An.* 772. to little purpose, *Velserus* hath published one of that year at *Dingolvinga* in *Bavaria* under Duke *Tassilo*, which had divers Canons of Equity, and some of Superstition; one was, that certain Bishops and Abbots agreed, that whosoever dyed first, the rest should sing so many *Psalms*, and get thirty Masses to be said. And a notable Priviledge is granted to all that will but seek liberty or shelter in the Church, that both they and their Posterity shall be free, unless they bring a debt undischargeable on themselves.

§ 51. There is by *Canisius* published an Epitome of the old Canons (except the *Nicene*) as gathered by this *Adrian*, and sent to *Charles Mag.* I will recite a few of them, *Ex Clem. c.* 23. " *Let a Bishop, or Presbyter,* " *or Deacon, taken in Fornication, Perjury, or Theft, be deposed, but not ex-* " *communicate.*

" C. 28. *That a Bishop who obtaineth a Church by the Secular Powers be* " *deposed.*

" Can. Antioch. 8. *Countrey Presbyters may not give Canonical Epistles, but* " *the* Chorepiscopi, (by which it is plain, that the *Chorepiscopi* were not Presbyters, but (as *Petavius* on Epiphan. Arrius hath well proved) " *true* " *Bishops.*

" C. 11. *That condemned Clerks shall never be restored if they go to the* " *Emperor.*

" Can. Laodic. c. 33. [*That no one pray with Hereticks or Schismaticks,*] (which seemeth to oblige us to separate from the *Roman* Prelates, who are grievous Schismaticks, by imposing things unlawful on the Churches, and silencing and persecuting those that obey not their sinful Laws.

Before the *Can. Sardic.* he mentioneth the weakness of old *Osius*, that said that they were both in the right, who used the word [*of one substance,* and [*of the like substance.*]

" Can. Sard. 2. *That a Bishop that by Ambition changeth his Seat, shall not* " *have* (so much as) *Lay-communion* (no not) *at the end.*

" C. 14. C. 15. *That no Bishop be above three weeks in another City, nor* " *above two weeks from his own Church,* (which implieth that each Bishop had then his own particular Church.)

" Can.

"Can. Afric. c. 15. *That there be no Re-baptizing, Re-ordaining, nor Tran-*
"*flations of Bishops.*

"C. 17. *That if a Bishop to be Ordained be Contradicted,* (that is, by any objected unfitness) "*he shall not after be Ordained as purged only by three* "*Bishops, but by many.*

"C. 19. *That Diocesses that wants Bishops, receive none without the consent of* "*the Bishop who hitherto held them,* (so it was) *not proudly; For if he* "*overheld them,* (that is, hold them under himself alone, when they need more Bishops) "*affecting to sit over the People, and despising his Fellow-Bishops,* "*he is not only to be driven from the retained Diocesses, but also from his own* "*Church:*] (so that no proud Bishops should have power to hinder the Churches from having as many Bishops as they need.)

"C. 60. *That Bishops that are of later Ordination, presume not to set or* "*prefer themselves before those that were before them.*

"C. 94. *If a Bishop, six months after admonition of other Bishops, neglect to* "*make Catholicks of the People belonging to his Seat, any other shall obtain them* "*that shall deliver them from their Heresie:* (that is, Donatism, or the like;) so that if one Bishop neglect the Souls of his People, and another that is more able and faithful convert them, they may be the Flock of him that converted them, without removing their dwelling.

"C. 105. *That a Bishop shall not Excommunicate a man on a Confession* "*made only to himself: if he do, other Bishops shall deny Communion to that* "*Bishop.*

§ 52. Several *German* Councils are mentioned, (at *Wormes, Paderborne, Daria,* in which (by a new example) *Charles Mag.* is confirmed to force the *Saxons* to profess themselves Christians, and to take an Oath never to revolt: who yet (doing it by constraint) were oft perjured and revolted, till at last their Heathen Duke *Witichind* became a voluntary Christian himself.

§ 53. There are 80 more Canons against Oppressors of the Clergy, said to be collected by *Adrian,* of which one is the old one, "*That no Bishop* "*judge the Cause of any Priest, without the presence of his Clergy; because the* "*Bishop's Sentence shall be void, if it be not confirmed by the presence of the* "*Clergy.*

Another, "*That no Bishop ordain or judge in another's Parish, else it shall be* "*void; For we judge that no one is bound by the sentence of any other Judge,* "*but his own:* (Who then is bound by the Pope, or any Usurper, who will Excommunicate those that are not of his Flock ?)

Another saith, "[*By a general Sanction we forbid* Foreign judgments, "*because it is unmeet that he should be judged by strangers, who ought to have* "*Judges of the same Province, and that are* chosen by himself.

Another, [" *That no Bishop presume to judge or condemn any of the Clergy,* "*unless the accused Person have* lawful Accusers *present, and have place for* "*defending himself by* answering to the Charge.

Another,

their Councils abridged.

Another, "*For Nullifying such Bishops judgments as are done without due* "*Tryal, by Tyrannical Power, and not by Canonical Authority.*

Another saith, "*Constitutions that are contrary to the Canons, and to the* "*Decrees of the Bishops of* Rome, *or to Good Manners, are of no moment:* (which nulleth even many of the Bishops of *Rome* also, as against *Good Manners.*)

Another notable Canon is, "[*Delatori aut lingua capuletur, aut convicto* "*Caput amputetur: Delatores autem sunt qui ex invidia produnt alios.*] That is, " *Let a Delator's tongue be pull'd out, or if Convict, his Head cut off: Dela-* "*tors are those that through envy betray others*; (or envious Accusers.) Alas! if our Delators, Calumniators and Informers were thus used now, what abundance would have suffered for wronging some one Man?

Another Canon is, "*If a Man be often in quarrels, and easie* (or forward) "*to accuse, let no Man receive his Accusation without great Examina-* "*tion?* (What then will be thought of the usual Accusations of Clergy Calumniators, that for Sects, and worldly Interest, can reproach others without shame or measure?)

Another is, "*That the danger of the Judge is greater than the danger of* "*him that is judged; therefore all care must be taken to avoid unjust judg-* "*ment and punishments.*

Another is, [" *Let no Man receive the witness of a Lay-man against a* "*Clergy-man.*] (And Door-keepers, and Clerks, and Readers, were then Clergy-men: Was not this a great priviledge to the Church?)

§ 54. CCXXXII. We come now to the great General Council at *Nice* 2d, called by the *Papists* the 7th, (that is, the 7th which pleased them.)

I have before noted that *Irene,* the Widow of *Leo,* now Ruled, her Son *Constantine* being Titular Emperor, a Child, under her Government. One *Stauratius* a Senator most swayed her, or ruled her. *Taurasius* the Patriarch joined with her for Images. They call a Council at *Constantinople.* A General Council and three Emperors (*Leo, Const. & Leb*) had lately condemned Images, and taken them down. The Pope and many *Italians* had resisted by force. This violence made the Emperor use severity against the Resisters. At *Ravenna* they killed *Paulus* the 14th Exarchate. In *Rome* they took *Peter* a Duke, and put out his eyes. In *Campania* they beheaded *Exhileratus* the Duke, and his Son *Adrian,* who took the Emperor's part. How the Emperor hereby lost *Italy,* is before shewed. But this Woman *Irene* will do as the Pope would have her: She is as much for Pictures as the Pope himself. She calling this Council at *Constantinople,* the old Soldiers bred up under the former Emperors being against Images, (*hæresin medullitus imbiberant,* saith *Binnius,* p. 396.) Would not endure them in *Constantinople,* but routed them. At which the Empress being troubled, dismissed the Bishops till they had purged the Army of those old Soldiers, and then she called the Bishops to *Nice*; and there (they knowing their errand before-hand) damned

G g them-

themselves and their Brethren that had held the former universal Synod, and set up Images again.

§ 55. By the way, I appeal from Pride and Ignorance, to Christian Sobriety and Reason, how the taking down of Images can (in the *Roman* sense) be called an Heresie, unless it be an Article of Faith, that Images must or may be used. And can any Man that ever read and believed the Scriptures, and the Writings of the first four hundred years, believe that having or worshiping of Images, or Saints by Images, is an Article of Faith, or necessary to Salvation? The best of them that any Man can plead with Modesty is, that they are *indifferent*, or *lawful*, and useful to some Persons. The *Papists* tell us now that they would not compel us to bow toward Images, but leave it to our liberty. Must it be Heresie, and the Christian world cast into distractions about it, when yet this Image-worship is Idolatry in the sense of one part of Christians, and but indifferent and convenient to the ignorant (that have other helps enow) in the sense of others? O what a Plague hath it been to the world, to have a worldly Clergy invade the Churches!

§ 56. At the meeting of this Council we have first the Call and Title, in which,

1. The Emperor and his Mother are called the Governors of *the whole world*, (*Orbis Terrarum*.) And yet our *Papists* (as *W. Johnson* in his *Novelty repress*, &c.) would make Men believe that if they find but such a saying of a Council, or of the Church, it must needs signifie more than the Empire, even all the Earth indeed.

2. It's expresly said over and over, that this Council was called by the Emperor, and by their Decree and Command.

Tharasius beginneth with telling them the need of Reformation (for Images,) and reporting how they were assaulted at *Constantinople*, when they met there, (and so removed to *Nice*,) &c.

§ 57. Next the Letters of the Empress and her Son are read, in which they are before made know what they must do. They are told what *Paul Const.* on his Death-bed said for Images, and that *Tarasius* would not take the Patriarchate till he had promise of a Council to restore them, and some hopes of it.

The Emperor here saith, that [*he called and Congregated the Synod*, and that *ex universo terrarum orbe, out of the whole earthly world* ;] and yet it was only out of the *Roman* Empire..

§ 58. When the Bishops business was so well made known by the Woman that called them, first three Bishops that had been lately forward speakers against Images in the former General Council under *Constantine*, did humbly confess their sin to the Council, and asked forgiveness; that is, *Basil. Ancyræ, Theodorus Myron*, and *Theodosius Amorii*. And first *Basil* Bishop of *Ancyra* gave them his Creed, in which he professed to " *believe in the Trinity, and* " *to embrace the intercession of the Mother of God, and of the heavenly Powers,* " *and of all the Saints, and with all honour to receive and embrace their holy* " *Reliques, firmly believing that he may be made Partaker of their holiness :*
" *Also*

"*Also that he embraceth the venerable Images, which* * *the Oeconomy of our* * The
"*Lord Jesus Christ*, &c. *and of the inviolate Virgin our Lady the Mother of* Verb is
"*God, and of the holy Apostles, Prophets, Martyrs, and all Saints; and giveth* left out.
"*them due honour: Rejecting and cursing with all his mind that called the*
"*7th Synod* (*), *that was gathered by a depraved mind and madness*——*a* (*) Where
"*false Council, as alien to all Piety and Religion, impiously barking against* lately a
"*Ecclesiastical Legislation*—*reproaching venerable Images, and commanding them* Leader.
" *to be taken out of the Churches*, &c.

And to shew his zeal, and lead others the way, he delivereth in nine Curses or Anathemas. One against those that demolish Images. Another against those that expound the Scripture words against Idols and *Gentile* Images, as against Christians Images. Next he execrateth all that embrace not Images, so it is now become necessary unto salvation.) Another Curse is against those that favour them that are against Images, &c. (Was not the Church ill used by her Bishops, when they are sure to be cursed by them; one year cursing all that be for Images, and another cursing all that be not for them? Was it such a cursing Clergy, to make a cursed Church, that Christ ordained?) And that the Council might not suspect that this Bishop was a Temporizer, and changed his Opinion with the Times, first he professeth to declare all this, [*With his whole Soul, Heart and Mind*;] and next he wisheth, [*That if ever by any means he revolt again from Images, he may be alienated from God the Father, Son and Holy Ghost, and the Catholick Church*.] And thus he renounceth Repentance, cursing himself if ever he repent.

§ 59. *Tharasius* and his Synod glorifie God for this excellent Confession: And next cometh *Theodore* Bishop of *Myros*, and he doth the like, and is joyfully received: And next cometh *Theodosius* Bishop of *Amorium*, and he more dolefully lamenteth, that [*being a sinner, and seduced, he had blattered out many evils untruly against venerable Images*; *and therefore confessing his fault, he condemneth and curseth* (or detesteth) *himself, resolving hereafter to do the same thing which he had cursed* (or spoken ill of) *and to teach it to the world, and begging to be received among Christians though unworthy*. Next he offereth his Libel, viz. " *First I approve, receive, salute and venerate before all*
" *things, the intemerate Image of our Lord Jesus Christ our true God, and the*
" *blessed Mother Virgins, who brought him forth without seed* *; *whose help, pre-* * How
" *tection and intercession I pray for night and day, that she may help me a sinner,* was he
" *as having that power from him whom she brought into the world*, *Christ our* then of
" *God. And I receive and venerate the Images of Saints, Apostles, Prophets,* stance.
" *Martyrs, Fathers, Eremites, not as Gods*, &c. *And with all my mind I be-*
" *seech them to intercede with God for me, that I may find mercy in the day of*
" *judgment*. On the same account I venerate the Reliques of Saints,
" &c.

So he proceedeth also to his Curses, and " *first he anathematizeth all that*
" *venerate not Images: Then he curseth those that reproach them: And next,*
" *that speak evil of them: And next he curseth those that do not from their*
" hearts

" hearts teach Christian People the veneration of holy and honourable Images of
" all Saints, which from the beginning pleased God.

Qu. 1. Where shall we have Painters enow?
2. Where shall we have Money to pay them?
3. Where shall we find room to hold them?
4. Is not here a new Article of Faith, and a new Commandment necessary to Salvation?
5. Was not their Church Universal, as it stood before all or most here cursed?
☞ 6. Was it not a hard matter to be saved, or be a Conformist on these terms, when a Man that did but doubt of Images, yea, *that did not teach them to the People, and that from his heart*, must be cursed?
7. Was not such a cursing sort of Bishops a great Curse, Shame and Calamity to the Church? Did they not tempt Infidels to curse or deride them all, while they thus cursed one another, even their Councils?

Tharasius joyfully received all this, and *Constantine* Bishop of *Constance* in *Cyprus* said, *That this Libel of* Theodosius *drew many tears from him*, (I suppose of joy;) And now they all saw the way.

§ 60. But now cometh a Crowd more to do their Pennance; *Hypatius* Bishop of *Nice*, *Leo Rhodi*, *Gregory* of *Pisidia*, *Gregory* of *Pessinunt*, *Leo* of *Iconium*, *Nicolas* of *Hierapolis*, *Leo* of *Carpathium*. And now *Tarasius* was sure of them, he groweth more upon them, and will know of them, *Whence it was that in the last Council they did what they did against Images? whether*
☞ *it was through meer Ignorance, or by any reason that drew them to it: If through Ignorance, he bids them give a Reason how they came to be so ignorant: If upon any Reason, to tell what that Reason was, that it might be refuted.*

Leo, Bishop of *Rhode*, answered, " [*We have sinned before God, and before*
" *the Church, and before this holy Synod*; *Ignorance made us fall from the*
" *Truth, and we have nothing to say in our own defence.*]

Tharasius would know what Reason now moveth and changeth them; some say, because it is the Doctrine or Faith of the Apostles and Fathers. Another alledgeth a saying as of the *Antioch* Council, and another as of *Isidore Pelas*, which the learned Reader examining, may see what proof it was that Images were brought into Churches by; it's worth the noting. But another alledgeth the Apostles and Prophets Tradition: But what's the proof? And did not the Council at *Constant.* nor the Bishops in the Reign of the three former Emperors know what Tradition was? Was it unknown till now?
☞ How came it now known then? Or who told it this Council, when the last knew it not? Or if the last were false Knaves, how shall we be sure that these were honest Men? Or that the same Men were suddenly become wise and honest?

Tharasius.

Tharasius asketh one of the Bishops (*Leo*) How it came to pass that he that had been ten or eight years a Bishop, never knew the Apostolical Tradition for Images till just now? He answered, *Because through many Ages, (or Times) Malice endured, and so wicked Doctrine endured; and when this persevered for our sins, it compelled us to go out of the way of Truth; but there is hope with God of our salvation.* But *Constantine Cypr.* answereth him, *You that are Bishops, and Teachers of others, should not have had need to be taught your selves.* *Leo* replied, *If there were no expression of sin in the Law, there would be no need of Grace.* Another (*Hypatius*) replied with the rest, *We received ill Doctrine from ill Masters.* Yea, but saith *Tarasius*, *The Church ought not to receive Priests from ill Teachers.* *Hypatius*, Bishop of *Nice*, replieth, [*Custom hath so obtained.*]

§ 61. Hereupon the Synod desired to be informed on what terms Hereticks were to be received, when they returned: so the Canons were brought and read. And though many Canons and Fathers have said, that no Repentance for some Crimes must restore a Man to the Priesthood, though it must to the Church; and there is an Epistle of *Tarasius* put by *Crabbe* before this Council, in which he determineth that a Simoniack may be received upon Repentance to Communion, but not to his Office; yet *Tarasius* here being desirous of their return, (knowing that these Penitents that renounced the errors of their Education, and former practice, would draw others to conformity with them) did resolutely answer all that was objected against their reception.

§ 62. Here (in *Crab.* p. 472.) a question fell in (upon their reading the Proofs, that repenting Hereticks were by the Church to be restored to their Bishopricks and Priesthood,) *What Hereticks these were?* And it was answered, that they were *Novatians, Encratists,* and *Arrians,* and *Manichees, Marcionists,* and *Eutychians.* And then one asketh, *Whether this Heresie (against Images) was greater or less than all those?* And *Tarasius* answereth, (like a Stoick) " [*Evil is always the same and equal, especially in matters Ecclesiastical, in the Decrees of which both great and small, to err is the same thing; for in both God's Law is violated.*] (O Learned Patriarch, worthy to be the setter up of Church-Images!) A venerable Monk that was Vicar of the Oriental Patriarch, answereth,[" *That this Heresie is worse than all Heresies, and the worst of all Evils, as that which subverteth the Oeconomy of our Saviour.*]

Note, Reader, how the Patriarchal Thrones did govern the Church and this Council, and by what reasons *Images* and *Saints intercessions* were set up: *Arrianism, Manicheism, Marcionism,* no Heresie that denied the essentials of Christianity, no evil was so bad with them as to deny Church-Images, &c. And so the late General Council, and Bishops, for three Emperors Reigns, had been under the worst of Hereses and Evils, worse than *Arrianism* itself.

§ 63.

§ 63. But here *Constantine* the Notary of the *Const.* Patriarchate, happily brought in so pertinent a Testimony, as much made for the pardon of the penitent Bishops: He read out of the Council of *Calcedon*, how the *Oriental* and other Bishops that had lately set up *Eutyches* and *Dioscorus* in the 2d *Ephesian* Council, cryed at *Calcedon*, [*We have all sinned, we all ask forgiveness.*] And how *Thalassius, Eusebius* and *Eustathius* cryed, [*We have all erred, we all ask forgiveness.*] And after them *Juvenal*, and after him the *Illyrian* Bishops cryed, [*We have all lapsed, we all ask pardon.*] And so the President was undeniable and effectual. These were not the first Bishops that went one way in one Council under one Prince, and cryed *peccavimus* for it, as Heresie, in the next.

§ 64. But *Sabas* the Monk starts yet a greater doubt than this, and that is, whether they had *true Ordination,* and so were *true Bishops.* For seeing they were bred in the times of Heresie, which had prevailed under so many Emperors, and had Heretical Teachers, it's like they had Heretick Ordainers, seeing the late Council shewed what the Bishops then were. And the Fact was confest, that they were Ordained by Bishops that were Hereticks, (that is, against Church-Images, and praying to Saints for their intercession, and using Reliques.) The Bishop of *Rome's* Vicars pleaded hard against their Ordination; but *Tarasius* knew what a breach it would make in the Church if a General Council, and all the Bishops that were at it, and all the rest that consented to it, and were bred up in that Opinion, should be degraded, and the new Conformity receive so great a stop ; and what confusion it would make among the People, (as they had seen in many former instances) and therefore he is against their deposition. And first there are two passages read in their favour out of *Ruffinus* and *Socrates*, and somewhat of *Athanasius*. And then when *Peter Vic. Rom.* alledged the instance of *Meletius* against it, *Tarasius* brought a notable expeditious Argument, *viz.* The Fathers agree among themselves, and do not contradict one another : ergo the rest consent to these that have been cited. Methinks I could make great use of this Argumentation to save time, labour and difficulty in disputing. *E. G. Nazianzen* wisht there were no difference of Bishops Seats (one above another) and said that he never saw Councils that did not more harm than good. The Fathers differed not among themselves; *ergo* the rest of the Fathers were of *Gregory's* mind.

In conclusion, they offered their Confessions, and were absolved.

§ 65. In the 2d Action, the Rulers send in the Bishop of *Neo-Cæsarea* to do his Pennance; and he also cryeth for mercy, and confesseth that his errors and sins were infinite, but now he believed as the Synod doth. *Tharasius* asketh him whether he be not ashamed to have been ignorant so long, and questioneth the sincerity of his Repentance, which he earnestly professeth, condemning his Sin, and promising Conformity.

Next a long Epistle of *Adrian's* to the Emperor and Empress, and another to *Tharasius* for Images are read: For Popes use not to travel to General Councils, but to send their Letters and Legates, lest in their present Disputes

they

they be found no wiser than other Men, and their Infallibility be proved less at hand, than at a distance, where they hear not the Debates. Here *Adrian* to the Empress relateth the foresaid Vision of *Constantine Mag.* to be healed of his Leprosie, a Fable fit to introduce Image-worship ; and for an Infallible Pope to use, fully confuted (as aforesaid) by *Henry Fowlis* (after many others) of Popish Treasons.

§ 66. *Tharasius* professeth his consent to *Adrian*'s Letters, yet professeth, [*That he giveth the Worship called* Latria *to God alone, and placeth his belief in him alone.*] Contrary to *Aquinas* and his Followers, and other such Roman Doctors. And the whole Council ecchoed their consent, and voted for Images ; so much can one Woman do in Power. Crab. p. 485.

§ 67. In the 3d Action, *Gregory* Bishop of *Neo-Cæsarea* is to receive his Absolution fully, and *Tharasius* puts in an Objection, that it's said that some Bishops in the late Persecution did scourge dissenting Bishops, and such were not to be received : But *Gregory* protested that he scourged none. But he is accused by others, to have been a Leader of the last Council against Images, and so he is deferred. And the Epistle of *Tharasius* to the Eastern Patriarchs is read, (and their Answers ;) in which it is to be noted, that yet Image-worship was not owned: For he professeth in his Creed to them, that [*We admit Pictures for no other use, but that they may the more perfectly be exhibited to the sight and eyes ; as the Lamb of God that taketh away the sins of the World,* &c.]

And the 4th Action containing all their Proofs from Scripture and Fathers, plead but for the memorative and instructing use of Images, by which they are to the eye, what words are to the ear : But they should have considered the danger of abuse, and foreseen how much further they were like to be carried, as with the *Papists* they are.

And in the fifth Action they proceed in reading more, to the same purpose, for commemorative Images ; till one read the *Itinerary of the Apostles,* which they voted to be a *cursed Book,* and said it was that Book that the Synod against Images made use of : whereupon *Greg. Neo-Cæs. & Theodos. Amorii,* are asked whether that Book was read in the false Synod, and *they sware by God,* that it was not, but only some recited words as out of it. *Pretorius* a Nobleman said, [*But they did all by the Royal Procuration.*] And they proceed to refell the Testimonies that were brought against Images. *Cosmas Cubicularius* brought out an Old Testament with *Scholia* blotted out, where was yet legible on the second Commandment, " [*If we make the Image of Christ, truly we do not for the similitude adore it, but that the mind might be raised upward by what is seen.*] The Expunction was said by *Tarasius* to be done by his Predecessors, *Anastasius, Constantine, Victor,* all Hereticks. And here they cursed Concealers and Cancellers of Writings. (Wo then to *Rome* !) Other rased Books were read, and Curses added against the Adversaries of Images, and those that communicate with them.

§ 68. In the 6th Action, the words of the 7th Council against Images are brought forth in a Book with a Confutation of them, which the Reader that hath

hath leisure may compare. *Greg. Neo-Cæsar.* read the Councils words. *Joan. Cancellarius* read the Confutation. It fell out well that this Confutation was undertaken, or else we had lost the Decrees of this Council, as the Acts, for ought I know, are buried.

In general every sober Reader may perceive a great deal of difference between the style of the Council of *Constantinople*, and the Answer. The Council speaks with as much temper and gravity, as most of the best Councils have done. The Answer aboundeth with such railings and reviling words, as are meeter for a common Scold, than for Divines. The common language of it, is to call the Bishops of the Council, Blinded, Ignorant, Fools, Wicked, Deceivers, Blasphemers, and such like. And if all the Bishops on earth be present, or represented in a General Council, what a Case then was the Church in? And how shall we know what Council is to be believed, unless the Pope make all the difference?

* At Constantinople.

§ 69. The number of the Bishops were * 338. They first shew how Satan hath brought in Idolatry. One of their chief Arguments against Images of Christ, is, that they savor of *Nestorianism*, representing Christ by his meer Manhood, when they cannot paint his Godhead; calling that Picture Christ, and overthrowing the Oeconomy and Union of his Person. I meddle not with the weight of their reason, but only recite it.

§ 70. It's again worth the noting, that the Answer to them saith, (For their charging Images, as drawing down the mind to Creature-worship; *Latria*) [*O insanien'em linguam, quam instar machæræ acutæ & veneno imbutæ possident*, &c. *O mad tongue, which they possess like a sharp sword, imbued with poyson*, &c. For no Christian ever gave Latriam *to the Image of those that are under Heaven*; *for this is the Fable of the Gentiles, and Devils invention, and the aggression of Satanical Action.*] — [*Our* Latria *is in Spirit and Truth.*] Other passages forbid us to think that they juggle here, and denying *Latriam* only to Creatures under Heaven, intend to give it to Creatures in Heaven; for they appropriate it elsewhere to God: by which they greatly differ from *Aquinas* and such *Papists*.

§ 71. Note also that (whether *well* or *ill*) both these adverse Councils curse Pope *Honorius* as an Heretick; see *Crab.* p. 560, &c.

§ 72. Another Argument which the first 7th Council (at *Const.*) useth against Images in Churches, is, that Christ himself hath chosen and instituted such an Image as he would be represented by, and that is the *Bread* and *Wine* in the Sacrament, and therefore we must not presume to make another, as if he had not done it well. This sheweth that this General Council and the Church then held that the *Bread* was not nullified, nor become Christ's Essence, but was the Image or Representation of his broken Body, and so called, *The Body of Christ*, as we say of E. G. *Cæsar's* Image, *This is Cæsar.*

But the adverse Council, or the Answer, raileth at this as an abominable Speech, (*Crab.* p. 567.) as if the Sacrament might not be called, *The Image of Christ*, (though *de re* they seem not at all to differ.) saith the *Constantine* Coun-

Council, [*Imaginem totam electam, viz. substantiam panis mandavit apponi, ne scilicet, humaná effigie figurata, idololatria induceretur.*] *A Deo ita...a Imago Carnis ejus panis scilicet Divinus impletus est Spiritu Sancto, cum poculo quoque sanguinis lateris illius vivificantis. Hæc igitur vera incarnatæ dispensationis Christi Dei nostri Imago sicut prædictum est, quam ipse nobis verus naturæ vividus Creator propriá voce tradidit.*

§ 73. Note also (*Crab.* p. 568.) that the *Constantin.* Council plead. "That this use of Images began neither by the Tradition of *Christ*, nor of the "*Apostles*, nor of the *Fathers*: And that the Answer saith, that "[*The Veneration of Images was delivered with many other things without Scripture, from the Apostles time*, &c.

Here note 1. How those *Papists* (in particular which I have elsewhere answered) are confuted, who say that [*Tradition is universal, sure, known, constant, and no Churches pleaded Traditions against each other, at least in necessary things or Faith; but if we have not the right now, it must be because the Councils went all to Bed in one mind, and rose in another.*] You see here that the 2d *Nicene* Council took the Doctrine of the former to be Anathematized Heresie; and that 338 Bishops in one of the Councils, (and the most under many Emperors) and 350 Bishops in the other Council, pleaded Tradition against each other. But sure any Man that hath read the Fathers of the first 300 or 400 years, will easily see which of them was in the right, excepting the sign of the Cross.

2. Note also that it is here confessed, that there is no Scriptural Tradition of this use of Images.

§ 74. In the Definitions of the *Constantine* Council it is to be noted,

1. That they are not so much against the intercession of the Virgin *Mary*, or Saints, as the *Protestants* mostly are, nor as the *Papists* make them: For (*Crab.* p. 589.) they say *Defin.* 15. [*If any confess not holy Mary ever a Virgin, properly and truly the Parent of God, and superior to every Creature visible and invisible* (*), *and doth not with a sincere Faith crave her Intercessions, as having this liberty with him that is born of her, God, let him be Anathema.*

And *Defin.* 17. [*If any confess not that all who from the beginning to this day, before the Law, and under the Law, and in the Grace given of God, being Saints are venerable in the presence of God in soul and body* (**), *and doth not seek their intercessions, as having liberty with God to intercede for the world according to Ecclesiastical Tradition, let him be Anathema.*] Were not these Men high enough in Creature-worship, to escape the Curse of Hereticks?

2. I noted before how they do *Defin.* 7. conclude, that Christ's Body glorified is not proper Flesh, and yet not incorporeal, but his true Body.

§ 75. That you may see that this Council were of one mind, in the conclusion they all say, *Omnes se credimus; Omnes idem sapimus; Omnes approbando*

(*) What! superior to Christ's Humanity? How prove you that she is superior to the highest Angels? (**) Are the bodies of all Saints already risen?

probando volentes subscripsimus, &c. *We all thus believe*, (againſt Images;) *We are all of one mind; We all subscribe willingly, as approving,* &c. Only *Germanus, George,* and *Manzurus,* (ſuppoſed to be *Damaſcene*) are found among the Anathematized Diſſenters, *Crab.* p. 592.

§ 76. The 7th Action of the *Nicene* Synod, containeth their Definition, in which they deny indeed *Latria* to Images, but yet ſay (more than before) "[*That they that ſee the Pictures, may come to the memory and deſire* " *of the Prototypes ; as by the ſight of the Croſs, and by the holy Goſpels, and* " *holy Oblations.—For the honour of the Image reſulteth to the Prototype, and he* "*that adoreth the Image, in it adoreth the deſcribed Argument.*] So that they that began lower, in the concluſion came up to *Adoration.*

They all profeſs full conſent, and curſe all that bring Scripture againſt Images, and that call them Idols, &c. They curſe the laſt Council, as *Regiens Conciliabulum* ; and three diſſenting Biſhops, and three former Patriarchs of *Conſt.* two more Biſhops they add. They curſe all that receive not Images, and all that *ſalute them not in the Name of the Lord and his Saints,* and that *care not for unwritten Tradition of the Church.*

Next they write an Epiſtle to the Empreſs, (and her Child) applauding them, and adding, that " [*Denying* Latria *to them , they judge them to be* " *adored and ſaluted , and pronounced every one Anathematized that is ſo* " *minded, as to ſtick at and doubt of the Adoration of Images , and this as* " *empowred by God's Spirit ſo to curſe them ; which Anathema* (ſay they) " *is nothing elſe but ſeparating them from Chriſt.*

Crab. p. 605.

Judge now what the uſe of ſuch Councils was, [*To curſe Men, and ſeparate them from Chriſt,*] and that if they do but *doubt of adoring Images.* Reader, if thou believe that in theſe Hereticatings, Separations and Damnations of ſuch, they were of Chriſt's mind, and did his work, and ſerved not his Enemy againſt him and his Church, I am not of thy mind, nor am ever like to be.

Another Epiſtle they wrote to the People, and one *Tharaſius* ſent to *Adrian.*

§ 77. Some Canons of theirs are added, of which this is the third.

"[*Every Election of a Biſhop, Prieſt, or Deacon, which is made by Magi-* " *ſtrates, ſhall remain void, by the Canon which ſaith, If any Biſhop uſe the* " *Secular Magiſtrates, to obtain by them a Church, let him be depoſed and ſepa-* " *rated, and all that communicate with him* *.

☞ *Alas!* Muſt all be Separatiſts from the Biſhops in *England, France,* &c ? *As by Interdicts

The 4th Canon is, " [*Paul* ſaith, *I have deſired no Mans ſilver or gold,* " &c. *If therefore any one exacting money, or any other thing, or for any af-* " *fection of his own, ſhall be found to drive from his Miniſtry, or to ſegregate* " *any one of his Clergy, or to ſhut the venerable Temple, forbidding in it the* " *Divine Miniſteries, ſhewing his madneſs even on that which hath no ſenſe* *, " *ſuch an one is truly ſenſleſs, and ſhall be obnoxious to the* Lex Talionis, *and his* " *work ſhall fall upon his own head, as being a tranſgreſſor of God's Law: For*

" *the*

" *the chief Apostle* P*e*ter *commanded, Feed the Flock of God, overseeing it, not
" by force, but freely and voluntarily, according to God; not for filthy lucre sake,
" but readily and chearfully; not as having a dominion over the Clergy,but as
" being examples to the Flock.*

The 15th Canon forbids one Man to have two Churches.
The 22d Canon forbids Canting, and Minstrels, and Ribald Songs at meat: But the 7th favors of their Superstition, forbidding any Temple to be Consecrated without Reliques, and ordering Temples that have no Reliques to be put down.

§ 78. In the Letter to *Adrian,Tharasius* tells him, that he had a year before attempted the like at *Const.* but was hindered a whole year by violent Men; which further sheweth how far the opposition to Images had obtained, when *Irene* began to set them up.

§ 79. So much of the 2d *Nicene* Council, in which by the power of one Woman, and *Stauratius* a Senator that ruled her, the judgment of the Universal Church (if the Council, or most of the Bishops in the Empire signifie it) was suddenly changed from what it had been during the Reign of the three last Emperors,and made that Church-use of Images(which some thought sinful, and no judicious Christian could judge necessary, but indifferent,and of use to some) to be henceforth so necessary, that the *Denyers* are sentenced for cursed Hereticks, yea the *Doubters* cut off from Christ.

§ 80. CCXXXIII. *Binnius* next addeth a Council at *Forojulium,An.*791. held by *Paulinus* Bishop of *Aquileia*: in which is a Speech of his to the Bishops, and an excellent Creed, and 14 Canons, written as by himself; all in a far more understanding, sober, pious manner, than is usual among the Patriarchs at General Councils. The 13th Canon is an excellent Precept for the holy observation of the Lord's-day, wholly in Holiness, and in Hymns of Praise to the Holy Ghost, that blessed it by his admirable Advent, calling it *God's Sabbath of delight,* beginning the 7th day evening, not for the honour of the 7th day, but of this Sabbath, *&c.*

§ 81. Yet rash and unskilful *words* set the Bishops into more divisions. *Fælix Urgelitanus,* and from him *Elipandus* Bishop of *Toletum,* taught that *Christ as the eternal Word was God's Natural Son, but that as Man he was his Adopted Son.* Hence his Adversaries gathered that he was a *Nestorian,* and held *two Sons.* A Council *An.* 792. at *Ratisbonne* was called to condemn this Heresie. Yea, *Jonas* Bishop of *Orleance* saith, *That it infected Spain for a great part,* (*and he knew their Followers to be certain Antichrists, by their faces and habits.*) But wise Men think that the Controversie was not *de re,* but *de nomine,* And that if one Christ be said to be *one Son of God in two*

natures,

natures, by a twofold *fundamentum* of the Relation of a Son, and that the *foundation* of the eternal Relation was the eternal Generation, and the foundation of the temporal Relation in the Humanity, was the temporal Generation and Union with the Deity, yet this proveth not *two Sons*; yea, or if it had been said that *two Generations being the* fundamenta, *two Relations of Sonship result from them*. If this be unskilfully and illogically spoken, it will not follow that the Speakers held *two Persons*, or made any more division of Chrifts natures than their Adversaries did; but only might think *that a double filiation from a double* fundamentum, *might be found in one Person*. Let this Opinion be wrong, I see not how the Hereticators could make it a damnable Herefie. But it's pity that *Fælix* had not taken warning by the Churches long and sad experience, to avoid such wordy occasions of Contention, and not to set again on work either the Heretical, or the Hereticating Evil Spirit.

§ 82. *Claudius Taurinensis*, a great and worthy Bishop at this time, did set in against the Worship and Church-use of Images, against whom *Jonas Aurelianensis* wrote, whose Writings are in the *Biblioth. Patrum* by *Marg. de la Bigne*; Read them, and judge as you see cause.

§ 83. About the time of the *Frankford* Council, came out a Book against Images, which is published as written by *Carolus Magnus* himself. A great Controversie it is, Who is the Author? No small number say, it was *Charles* his own indeed. Others, that it was written at his Will and Command. *Bin. p.* 288 *Bellarm. de Imag. lib. 2.* But *Binnius* and some others deny it, and say it was written by *Serenus Massiliensis* an *Iconoclast*, and his Disciples. How we shall know the Truth in such Cases, I cannot tell: But it is confessed that *Spain* and *France* were then much infected with the Doctrine which is against Church-Images. It is certain that Pope *Adrian* saith, that *Carolus Mag.* sent him such a Book by *Engilbert* an Abbot, and his Epistle against it is extant.

§ 84. CCXXXIV. We come now to a great Council at *Frankford*, called by *Charles Mag.* present, and by *Adrian*. And as late as it is, all the Historians cannot tell us whether it was *Universal*, or *what they did*. Some say it was a *General Council*, because *Charles* summon'd it as such, and 300 Bishops were there. Others say No, it was but Provincial, because none of *It was such a Western General Council as that at Trenk was for except* the Bishops of the East were there, (a sufficient reason; and the like may be brought to prove, that there never was a General Council in the World, so called from the *whole World*, but only from the *whole Empire*.) That they dealt with the Case of *Elipandus* Bishop of *Toletum*, and *Fælix Urgel*. is agreed on, but what they did about Images is not agreed on. *Ado, Rhegino, Aimonius Uspurg*, and many Historians say, *They condemned the Nicene Council that was for Images*. Even *Baronius* is of the same mind, thinking the *Liber Carolinus* deceived them. He proveth this to be the common judgment

of

their Councils abridged. 237

of Historians, and ancient Writers. *Bellarmine* * (his Brother) is of the * *Lib. 2. de*
same judgment. And is not their Concession more than twenty later Mens *Imagin.*
denial? Yea *Genebrard* concurreth; yet *Binnius* leaveth his Master *Baro-* *cap.* 14.
nius, and giveth his Reasons against them. And he doth well prove, that it Even
could not be by ignorance and surprize, that the *Frankford* Council should *Dion. Pe-*
condemn the *Nicene*; and he is loth to think that they were wilful Here- *tavius af-*
ticks, especially when they profess to follow Tradition: But he knew that the faith, *In*
7th Constantin. Council against Images, profest to follow Tradition. And if *which Sy-*
French Men will make us Hereticks for speaking *English*, it is no wonder if we *ned of*
make them Hereticks for speaking *French*. If Men will Hereticate others *ford, the*
for Images, or Ceremonies, or Words, others will measure the like to them. *7th Gene-*
This kind of Hereticating is circular, and hath no end. *ral Coun-*

Suarez will have either the Historians to have erred, or their Books to be *cil was re-*
corrupted; with what measure you mete, it shall be measured to you. You shall *the Bishops*
then give us leave to suspect your Books, where there is far greater cause. *that were*

§ 85. But the Synod , or *Paulinus Aquileiensis*, a learned worthy Bishop *ignorant*
in the Synod, (whom the rest follow) copiously write a Confutation of *Eli-* *of its De-*
pandus and *Fælix*. And the charges of Heresie are, *794. Hist.*

1. That they call Christ as to his Humanity, *God's Adopted Son*, (and his *l. 8. c. 7.*
eternal Person his *Natural Son*.)

2. Because they say he was *Adopted by Grace*.

3. Because they say he was a *Servant*.

Alas for the Church, that must thus by Bishops be distracted for want of skill in words! Is there no remedy? *Binnius* confesseth that some *Papists* think that they meant right, as *Durandus* did, and that the difference was but in words.

The Council supposeth *Elipandus* and *Fælix* to use the word [*Adoption*] exclusively, as to Christ's Filiation by *Generation*, as conceived by the Holy Ghost: whereas it is far likelier that they took both Conjunct to be the *fundamentum filiationis*. God adopting, that is, of his good Will freely creating Christ's Humane Nature, and uniting it to the Divine; called *Adoption*, because it was God's free act of Love, and not a communication of his Essence, as the eternal Generation is. The Humanity is not God's Essence. And I hope the name of [*The Son of Man*] used so oft by Christ of himself, is no Heresie. And there appeareth no reason to censure them as denying either the eternal or temporal Generation of Christ.

But they argue against them,

1. That he is said to be *Adopted*, that is, not Generated.

2. And that he merited it not, but was adopted of meer Grace, but so was not Christ.

Answ. 1. These Objections seem to confess that the difference was but *de nomine* ; and is the unapt use of such a word, an Heresie? How many Heresies then have most Councils, and Fathers, and all Authors?

2. Must we needs understand God's Adoption, just in the measure as mans?

3. We are Regenerate, and yet Adopted. Why then is it a Heresie, to say that Christ was *Generated*, and yet *Adopted*? 4. Grace

4. *Grace* is either that which is *against the merit of evil*, or only *without the merit of good*. It's doubtless that the first was not by them imputed to Christ: And it's undoubted to me, that it is consequentially Blasphemy, to say that Christ's Humane Nature, or any Angel had not the later. For the very being, and therewith all the good in the constitution and antecedent benefits of a Creature must go before his merits. Merit is too low a word for the Divine Nature as such before the Incarnation. And the Humane Nature did not merit *to be* before *it was, e.g.* to be conceived by the Holy Ghost, *&c.* As free Benefits are called Grace, Christ's Humane Nature had Grace.

But they object, that the two Bishops did not distinguish between *Christ's Adoption*, and ours.

Ans. 1. We have not their Writings to see that.

2. If they did not, it's like it was, because they thought it needless, being understood by all. They believed the Creed, *That Christ was conceived by the Holy Ghost, and born of the* Virgin Mary; and that the Godhead assumed the Humanity into personal Union. They knew that none dreamed that it was so with us.

The Council saith, *That it's Heresie to use the name Adoption of Christ.* The two Bishops seemed to think, *That God's free assuming of the Humanity into personal Unity with the Word eternally generated by the Father, might be called Adoption.* If the improper use of the word be *Heresie,* I leave it to the Reader to judge which were the Hereticks: But I think neither.

☞ But another part of the Heresie was, to say *that Christ was a Servant as Man.* And they think he was no Servant, because a Son. Some will think confidently that the Council were here Hereticks, but I think they did but strive about *words.* By [*Servant*] the Council seemeth to mean exclusively, [*One that is no Son.*] But the other meant inclusively, [*A Son and Servant.*]

They take him for a Servant, *that oweth Service and Obedience.* And Christ as Man owed Obedience to his Father on two accounts;

1. As a reasonable Creature to his Maker.

2. As one that had by voluntary Sponsion undertaken it. I might add,

3. As the special Law of Mediation was imposed on him, or given him, as Man, by which it was made his special duty to die for Man, *&c.* He saith, when he cometh into the world, *Here I am to do thy Will, O God; yea, thy Law is in my heart.* Did he not *take upon him the form of a servant?* Phil. 2. 7. which was *not a shew of that which is not, but of that which is.* Is he not called *God's righteous Servant justifying many,* Isa. 53. 11. Doth not God oft call him, *My Servant,* Isa. 49. 6. & 52. 13. Zech. 3. 8.

The Council seemed to think that the Bishops thought that Christ was born a Servant, and not a Son, and was adopted a Son only after for his merits: But there is no shew of reason to impute this to them that professed to believe the Creeds and Scripture, and said no such words. They seemed to intend nothing but to distinguish the natural eternal Generation of the second Person in the Trinity, from the temporal Generation of the *Man Christ Jesus*, which was an Act of free Beneficence.

Bin. p. 428. [*Ex quadam Elipandi confessione quæ in Bibliothec. Toletana reperitur in quodam libro à Beato & Heterio contra Elipandum scripto; aiunt nonnulli Fælicem & Elipandum non in mysterio Incarnationis, sed tantum abutendo voce Adoptionis, instar Durandi, aberrâsse: Idemque conjecturæ affirmant istis, quod nihil eorum quæ Nestorio objecta fuerant in Conc. Ephes. contra Elipandum attulerent, &c.* See the rest.

But they concluded that they were *Nestorians*, because they intimated *two Sons*, by saying that he was eternally begotten, and yet adopted a Son.

Ans. 1. It is not unlike that *Nestorius* himself, for want of more skill in speaking, was used as they were.

2. Why should that be imputed to them which they deny? They are told that as *Nestorius craftily denied two Persons, and yet inferred two*, so do they. But is not this a vindication of *Nestorius* by a Council? (Who knoweth what a man holdeth, better than himself?)

Obj. But by consequence Heresie will follow.

Ans. If all are Hereticks that hold any Error which such a greater Error would follow from as is called Heresie, I doubt not but every Council and Bishop, and Christian were Hereticks; the saying of some great Divines being true, *That Truths of Faith and Morality* are one, *that he that holdeth the least Error therein, doth by consequence* un— foundation. You may say that every man that tells a lye, or any known sin, is an Atheist, and that if he believed that there is a God, he would know that he must not sin against him; he that sins before his Face, denieth his Omniscience, and so denieth God, &c. At this rate all are Atheists and Hereticks.

3. But may not one that faith, [*Christ as the second Person in Trinity was the Eternal Son of God ; and as Man, was by Generation in time made the Son of God and Man :*] truly mean that it is but one Person that in one respect is the Eternal Son, and in another respect the Temporal Son? May he not hold that the personal Unity maketh it unmeet to say, *There are two Sons*, because *that would imply two Persons*, which they and *Nestorius* denied? But, again I say, what if they had said that there might be two *Filiations*, or filial *Relations in one Person*, resulting from two foundations, Eternal and Temporal Generation, and if this had been an unapt speech, (to say *ex duobus fundamentis duæ oriuntur relationes*) yet how comes it to be Heresie?

§ 86. I write not this, and such like, to justifie the accused; for I think the Council said well, (Bin. p. 418.) 1. *Cur nobis non sufficient quæ in Sanctorum Patrum dictis inveniuntur, & universali Catholicæ sanctionis consuetudine.*

intendine confirmant ur. 2. *Quare generationem Filii Dei vel æternam de Patre, vel temporalem de Matre quisquam hominum audeat investigare, dicente Scriptura, altiora te ne quæsieris!* O well said! Happy Church, if the Bishops had held to this: But here you see that they held a double Generation, Eternal and Temporal, and yet but one Filiation. I write this, because the Hereticating spirit yet reigneth; and by these old Weapons fighteth against Love and the Churches Unity, on pretence of Orthodoxness; and to this day the *Papists* reject a great part of Christ's Church as Hereticks, by the countenance of former Councils censoriousness, calling Christ's Members *Iconoclasts, Monothelites, Nestorians, Eutychians,* and many such names, some fetcht from indifferent things, (or duties) and some from quarrels about hard words.

§ 87. Note here that *Binnius* expresly saith, that *Adhuc nondum est certum qualis in particulari fuerit hæresis Fæliciana: It is not yet certain what this Fælician Heresie was.* And if so, I hope I shall not be censured for the same, notwithstanding you may say, the Council knew it.

§ 88. It's worth the noting as to the credit of Council Records, which *Binnius* there saith, (p. 427.) [*If this Council as it now is extant, may without temerity be rejected, all Councils by the same reason may be rejected which* Surius *hath gathered from the Catholick Libraries.*] : He confesseth that the rest are no surer than this, and yet that *Baronius, Bellarmine,* by the generality or number of Historians consent, do confess that there was by this Council a rejection of the *Conc. 2d Nicene,* which is now here to be found in it.

Vid. Not. Bin.p.428 § 89. The Council at *Frankford* determined *that Christ was not a Servant,* Servitute pœnali Deo subjectus, *subject to God by penal Servitude.* The present agreement of Christians, taketh this for Socinianism and Heresie: Christ suffered for our sins; his subjection to Poverty, Reproach, the Cross, and many works, (as Fasting, being carried about by Satan, and tempted, *Mat.* 4. 1. washing his Disciples feet, travelling on foot, being subject to his Mother, and to Princes, paying Tribute, &c.) we suppose were part of his Humiliation. The Holiness and Obedience was good, and no Penalty: But the matter of that Obedience was the Cross and Suffering, which is *Malum Naturæ.* And if this was no punishment (voluntarily accepted by his Sponsion) how was Christ our Surety, bearing our Transgressions? how suffered he for our sins? Is not suffering for sin, even of others, penal? Is not the denial of Christ's penal Service and Suffering, a denial of his Satisfaction and our Redemption? You see how easie it is to find Heresie and Infidelity itself in unskilful words; and yet it's like the Speakers meant better than they spake.

§ 90. Note that Pope *Adrian* first made himself Judge, and Anathematized *Elipandus* as an Heretick, and so the Council was byassed (with the Emperor;) and how great *Adrian's* power was (having made *Charles* Emperor, and *Charles* made him a Prince,) it is easie to conjecture.

§ 91. *Binnius* saith, p. 429. that *Fælix*, besides his other Heresie, impugned Images, and that this is said by the *Concil. Senonensin Decret. fid.c.14.*

Platina

Platina in *Adrian*. *Sabellic*. *Enead*. 8. *li*. 8. *Alph. de Castro verb. Imago.* And that *Claud. Taurin.* being his Disciple, and an *Iconomach*, he must needs be so himself: From whence I argue, that it is most probable that the Historians say true, that say *Charles* and the Council of *Frankford* were against the *Nicene* Council and Images. For else how could it come to pass, that they say not one word against *Fælix* and *Elipandus* for denying Images, when their Party was grown so great in *Spain* and *France* ?

§ 92. Pope *Adrian* dying, *Leo* the 3d succeeded. His Piety was so great, that *Anastasius* writes, as it were, a Volumn, in naming the good works which he did, that is, the Silks, Vails, Cloathing, Silver, Gold, and innumerable gifts which he bestowed upon Posts, Pillars, Altars, Walls, Floors, Utensils, it would tire one to read them, and the hard names of them; yea, he said seven Masses a day. Yet some Kinsmen of Pope *Adrian's, Paschal Primicerius, & Campulus Sacellarius, & Maurus Nepesinus*, laid Crimes to his charge; and assaulted him, and twice put out his Eyes, and cut out his Tongue, and put him in a Monastery; yet (saith the Story) his Eyes and Tongue were perfectly restored, and he fled to his Protector *Charles* into *Germany*; and *Charles* came to *Rome*, and judged his Accusers to Banishment, and restored him; and he crowned *Charles* then Emperor of the West, and perfected the Donation to him of all that had been the Emperor's. *Charles* gave him great Presents; and with his own Revenues and that, he laid out so much Silver and Treasure at *Rome*, and did so many new things in the Churches, that if you read but *Adrian's* life, and this *Leo's*, you will be ashamed to disgrace the Church of *Rome* with any Titles or Pretences of the ancient primitive state, but must say, *Old things are past away, behold all is become new*. *Charles* the Great, made the Pope Great.

§ 93. Some Historians say, that the kissing of the Pope's Foot, was brought in thus by this Pope *Leo*: A handsom Woman kist his Hand, which so inflamed his Heart with Lust, that he cut off the Hand that the Woman kist, and ordained that ever after the Pope's Foot should be kist instead of his Hand: But I rather believe with *Binnius*, that this is but a Fiction, because 1. There is mention before this of kissing the Pope's Foot. 2. And I do not think that such a Heart would so easily part with a Hand.

§ 94. To look back to the East; when *Irene* had kept up Images awhile, her Son *Constantine* grown up, is weary of her Government and *Stauratius*, and deposeth her; and when he ruled, the Bishops mostly were conformable to him: But in his youthful Folly and Rage, he put out the Eyes of his Uncle *Nicephorus*, and *Alexius* a Captain; he put away *Mary* his Wife, and took one *Theodota*, that better pleased him, in Marriage; one *Joseph* that married them, was preferred for it. *Tarasius* connived, and durst not gain-say. *Theodore Studita & Plato* therefore renounce the communion of *Tarasius*. At last, *An.* 797. his Mother *Irene*, and *Stauratius*, found means to apprehend him, and murder him, that is, put out his Eyes, of which he dyed, which some celebrate as a pious Act; it was done by her that set up Images. But

See *Petav. Hst. l.*S. *c.* 6.

within

within one year, *Nicephorus* depofed and banifhed her into *Lesbos*, where fhe dyed, and he took the Empire to himfelf.

§ 95. *Binnius*, p. 445. faith, " [*That the Emperor banifhed* Theodore " Studita , *for reproving his Marriage, and when he added crime to crime,* " *Merito juftu Matris quam imperio exuerat, zelo juftitiæ non regni, oculis,* " *imper'e, & vita orbatus eft. By the command of his Mother in her zeal* " *for juftice, he was defervedly deprived of his Empire, Eyes and Life.*] What is not juft with fuch Hiftorians, that maketh for their Intereft ? And how contemptible is their Cenfure of good or evil Men, which hath no better Meafures ?

§ 96. He tells us alfo, (p. 444.) that the *Spanifh* and *French* Bifhops at thefe times, of their own heads,without the Pope, added [*Filioque*] to the Creed, which hath to this day made fo great a ftir. It feems they thought that the Pope's Authority was not neceffary to it.

§ 97. He adds, that *Charles the Great* being dead, the People grew bold, and rofe up again againft the Pope ; which occafioned Rapines, Flames, and Murders, that *Ludovicus* the new Emperor was fain to take his Fathers Office, and come to *Rome* to fave the Pope, and fupprefs the Rebels.

§ 98. The *Venetian* Duke killing a Patriarch, *Johan. Gradenfis*, *Paulus* Patriarch of *Aquileia* called a Synod to crave aid of *Charles*.

☞ § 99. CCXXXV. An. 806. A Council was held at *Conftantinople*,in the Caufe of the forefaid *Jofeph* that had married the Emperor to his fecond wife, who had been ejected by *Tarafius* from his Bifhoprick, and the Emperor calling a Council, they reftored him ; wherefore *Theodorus Studita* called them a Council of Hereticks and Adulterants,becaufe they reftored the Caufer of the Emperor's Adultery. But how few Emperors have not found Councils of Bifhops ready to do their Will ?

§ 100. *Charles the Great* making his Will, divided his Empire between his three Sons, giving them Laws of Communion and Succeffion, (that if one dyed without Children, his Kingdom be divided between the other two; ☞ but if he have *fuch Sons as the People will choofe*, they fucceed their Father :) Commanding all three that they be the Defenders of the Bifhop of *Rome*, as he and his Father and Grandfather had been (to their commodity.)

☞ § 101. CCXXXVI. An. 809. Was another Council at *Conftantinople*, which was gathered to condemn honeft *Theodorus Studita, & Plato*, and fuch * This is as had been againft the reftoring of *Jofeph*,of which faith *Binnius*, " [*When* not the " *the Bifhops there Congregate had brought the moft holy* Plato *in Chains to* firft time " *be judged, and had paffed the Sentence of Anathema on the Univerfal Catho-* that Coun- " *lick Church* * *that was againft their Error, they made a moft wicked De-* cils have " *cree, that the Marriage of* Conftantine *with* Theodota, (*his Wife yet living,* curfed the " *thruft into a Monaftery*) *fhould be faid to be lawful by difpenfation. They* Catholick " *added for the Emperor's fake this wicked and fhamelefs Sentence, That the* Church.
" *Laws*

"*Laws of God* * can do nothing against *Kings*; and that if *any imitate* Chry- They
"foſtom, *and ſhed his Blood for Truth and Juſtice, he is not to be called a Mar-* mean by
"*tyr*: *That Biſhops have power to diſpenſe with all the Canons.*] Remember the Ca-
that *Papiſts* confeſs all this to be wicked. We have not the Acts and Speeches nons
of theſe Councils preſerved. of the Church.

§ 102. CCXXXVII. *An.* 809. A Council was held at *Aquiſgrana*, about
the Proceſſion of the Holy Ghoſt, and the word [*Filioque*] in the Creed *. *A new
Of which they ſent ſome Meſſengers to the Pope, who approved the thing, Contro-
but diſſuaded them from adding it to be ſung in the Creed; and after inſcri- verſie.
bed the Creed without *Filioque* in *Latin* and *Greek* in two Silver Tables, to
ſhew that it ſhould not be changed: which yet after it was by the Pope's
conſent.

The *French* Annals ſay, that in this Council they treated of the *ſtate of the*
Church, and converſation of the Clergy, but determined nothing for the great-
neſſes of the matter.

§ 103. CCXXXVIII. *An.* 113. (Yet under *Charles the Great*) a Council was held (by his Command) at *Arles*, where many very good Canons
were made for the Reformation of the Biſhops and Prieſts.

§ 104. CCXXXIX. The ſame year the ſame *Charles* had a Council at
Tours, which made 51 as honeſt Articles, as if *Martin* himſelf had been
amongſt them; even againſt all kind of ſin, and for all godly living. Among
others, the 37th Canon tells us, that the cuſtom of not kneeling in Prayer
on any Lords-day, (no not at the Sacrament) nor on any Week-day between *Eaſter* and *Whitſuntide*, was yet in force; on other days they required
humble kneeling.

§ 105. CCXL. Yet another Council did *Charles* call the ſame year at *Cha-*
lons (*Cabillonenſe*) in which he ordered Schools for the reſtoring of Learning, (our *Alcuin* being his Perſuader greatly eſteemed by him) Learning
then being almoſt worn away, (and Ignorance taking place) till he greatly
revived it: no leſs than 67 Canons were here made, moſt very good ones;
but praying for the Souls of the Faithful departed, and anointing the Sick, are
there enjoined.

§ 106. Among many good Canons, the 13th is againſt the *Oath of Obe-*
dience to the Biſhop, and to the Church. The words Tranſlated are theſe:
"[*It is reported of ſome Brethren* (Biſhops) *that they force them, that they*
"*are about to ordain, to ſwear, that they are worthy, and will not do contrary*
"*to the Canons, and will be obedient to the Biſhop that ordaineth them, and to*
"*the Church in which they are ordained; which Oath, becauſe it is very dange-*
"*rous, we all ordain ſhall be forbidden.*]

§ 107. The 15th Canon ſaith, "[*It is ſaid that in ſome places the Arch-*
"*deacons exerciſe a certain domination over the Pariſh-Presbyters, and take Fees*
"*of them; which is a matter of Tyranny, rather than of order of Rectitude:*
"*For*

" *For if the Bishops must not Lord it in the Clergy, but be Examples to the*
" *Flocks, much less may these do it.*

§ 108. The 25th Canon complaining how the old Excommunicating and Reconciling was grown out of use *, they desired the Emperor's help how they should be restored.

Council-Curies for Opinions take place.

§ 109. *Can. 33.* They say, "*That Confession to God and Man are both* "*good; but that Confession made to God, purgeth sin; and that which is made* "*to the Priest, teacheth how their sin may be purged.*

§ 110. The 45th Canon is against them, that by going to holy places, *Rome*, or *Tours*, think to have their sins forgiven.

§ 111. CCXLI. Yet another Council the same year 813, was held under *Charles M.* at *Mentz* in *Germany* to the like purpose, many godly Canons being made.

§ 112. CCXLII. Yet another under *Charles* at *Rhemes*, for Instructing and Catechising, and many good things, like the former.

§ 113. CCXLIII. But we have not done with Images yet, *An.* 814. There was a Council called at *Constantinople*, which damned the Council of *Nice* 2. *Irene* having set up Images, and murdered the Emperor her own Son, (as is aforesaid) was deposed by *Nicephorus*, who Reigned near ten years, with *Stauratius* his Son; he was no Friend to the Clergies power, and was killed in Fight by the *Bulgarians*, and his wounded Son Reigned a few months. *Michael Curopalates* succeeded, a Man of great Piety and Peace, but unfit for War, who being overcome by the *Bulgarians*, he consented to give up the Empire to *Leo Armenus*, a better and prosperous Soldier. This *Leo* the 5th, was of the mind of the former *Leo's* against Images, and his mind being known, the Bishops conformed presently, insomuch that in his 2d year this Council called by him, Anathematized the Bishops that would not renounce the *Nicene* 2d Council; and when they lay prostrate on the earth, it's said some trod on some of them, and they turned them at a Back-door out of the Council: For the Patriarch *Nicephorus*, that was for Images, was deposed, and *Theodorus Melissenus* that was against them put in his place, and led the rest. Thus did Council against Council thunder Anathema's, and curse each other by separating them from Christ, till few were left uncursed. The Rulers of the Monasteries also were called in, and those that would not consent against Images, were rejected. *Nicetas & Theodorus Studita* were the Champions for Images, and were both banished and imprisoned. *Theodore* wrote to the Council for Images, and tells them that " [*To take away the venerable* *Bin p. 470* " *Adoration of the Images of Christ, and of the Mother of God, and of all* *Epist.* " *the Saints, was to overthrow the Oeconomy of Christ.*] And he continued *Theod.* in Prison to preach and write for Images.

Those Councils that pleased not the *Papists*, we have not the Acts of, as we have of such as *Nic.* 2. that pleased them. Had we all the Speeches and Arguments used in this and other Councils against Images, as largely as those

their Councils abridged. 245

those that were for them, we might better see which had the better management.

§ 114. CCXLIV. The Clergy had for many hundred years abrogated God's Law, [*He that sheddeth Man's Blood, by Man shall his Blood be shed;*] and had put Pennance for the punishment instead of Death: But now at last the murdering of one *John* a Bishop (*inhoneste & inaudite mordidatus,* as they then spake) they were put to find some harder Penalty to save the Clergies Lives: And so they set great Fines of Money on the Murderers; and more than so, *He that wilfully murdered a Bishop must eat no flesh, nor drink any Wine as long as he lived.* If Murder now had no greater a punishment, Bishops would scarce be safe any more than others. This was at a Council at a Village called *Theorius,* or *Dietenhoven.*

§ 115. Next succeedeth Pope *Stephen* at *Rome*; *Platina* saith *Stephen* the 4th, *Anastasius* and *Binnius* say *Stephen* the 5th. *Platina* and others say that he Reigned but seven months; *Anastasius* and others say seven years, and seven months. *Platina* saith he was the Son of *Julius* a *Roman*; *Anastasius* saith he was the Son of *Marinus*.

Charles dying, the Empire came to his Son *Ludovicus* called *Pius,* his Brothers dying also. The Bishops of *Italy* (saith *Platina* and others) stir'd up *Bernard* to rebel against him; but he was conquered; and put to death: as also were the *Saxon* Rebels. *Paschal* first succeeding, *Stephen* is made Pope without the Emperor's knowledge; for which he excused himself, as forced by the People that chose him: The Emperor pardon'd it, but demanded obedience as to their Elections for the time to come. *Platina in Vit. Paschal. l.* 1. who saith that *Paschal* was suspected of the Rebellion of *Italy,* but disclaimed it; and that the Emperor re-assumed many Cities to the Empire, to prevent new Rebellions.

It's like Julius Martinus, as *Onuphrius* saith, was his name.

Some say that *Bernard* was but blinded: Among others banished for Treason, were *Anselm* Bishop of *Milan,* and *Theodulfe* Bishop of *Aurelia,* (*Orleance*) so that *Italy* and *France* joined in the Treason. See *Petav. Hist. Mund. li.* 8. *c.* 8.

§ 116. CCXLV. *Ludovicus Pius* was so careful to reform the Bishops and Clergy, that he raised their ill will against him, being too pious for them that should have been the Teachers of Piety; yea, so slothful did they grow, that though his Father and he had done extraordinary works for the promoting of Learning and Godliness, yet Learning in his days grew to such decay, that Learned Men became the common contempt, and few of them were to be found; but *Wealth* and *Jurisdiction* were the study, care, and interest of the Bishops.

Yet in his time at *Aquisgrane,* there was a Council that wrote, instead of Canons, the most excellent Treatise for the Teaching and Government of the Teachers and Governors of the Church, (besides the regulation of Monasteries) that ever any Council did before them: Not in their own words, but in the several Sermons, and passages of the chief Fathers, (*Isidore, Hierom, Gregory,*

Gregory, *Augustine* and *Prosper*,) that had written to the Clergy heretofore, which they collected into 145 Chapters and Canons.

But you must know that the excellency of the Canons of Provincial Councils in *France* and *Spain*, in these Ages, did not shew the excellency of the Bishops, so much as their Pravity and Necessity, as the Medicine doth the Disease. For such Canons were ordinarily drawn up by the will of the King, by some one or few choice Men, (such as *Paulinus Aquileiensis* in his time,) to whom the rest consented, because they knew the King would have it so*.

* Saith *Vita Ludovici in* Bin. p. 525. *Congregatis Episcopis, &c. fecit componi ordinarique librum Canonicæ vitæ normam gestantem, in quo totius illius ordinis perfectio continetur. In quo imperi jussit cibi petusque & omnium necessariorum summam. Quem librum per omnes Civitates & Monasteria Canonici ordinis sui imperii misit per manus missorum prudentium.* See the rest; so that it was the Emperor's Book, and not the Council's work.

§ 117. In these Chapters of this Council, they cite *Isidore* and *Hierom* at large, proving that it was Presbyters that were called Bishops in *Paul*'s Epistles, and *Acts* 20. and that in those times the Church was ruled by the Common-Council of Presbyters, till Schism shewed a necessity that one should rule among the rest.

They cite *Isidore*'s words, that [*Cæteri Apostoli cum* Petro *par consortium honoris acceperunt*] *Et* [*Non esse Episcopum qui præesse dilexerit, non prodesse.*] And *Hierom*'s on *Titus* maintaining the foresaid *Identity*, and his [*Sciat Episcopus & Presbyter sibi Populum conservum esse non servum :*] And his excellent Epistle *ad Nepotianum* : Many Sermons of *Augustine*'s describing his Collegiate Community of the Clergy. *Isidore*'s words, [*Plerique Sacerdotes suæ magis utilitatis causâ quam gregis præesse desiderant : Nec ut prosint, præsules fieri cupiunt, sed magis ut divites fiant & honorentur : suscipiunt sublimitatis culmen, non pro Pastorali regimine, sed pro totius regiminis vel honoris ambitione, atque abjecto opere dignitatis, solam nominis appetunt dignitatem. Dum mali Sacerdotes Deo ignorante non fiant, tamen ignorantur à Deo--sed hic nescire Dei, reprobare est.*] If *Isidore* say true, remember that I wrong not the Bishops in saying the same of them. And if this was the case of the *most*, as he affirmeth, what better than we find could be expected from General Councils, where it is carried by the major vote.

They cite *Gregory*'s words, [*Nemo amplius nocet in Ecclesia, quam qui perversè agens nomen vel ordinem sanctitatis habet : Delinquentem namque hunc redarguere nullus præsumit, sed in exemplum culpa vehementer extenditur, quando pro reverentia ordinis peccator honoratur.--Melius profecto fuerat ut hunc ad mortem sub exteriori habitu terrena acta constringerent, quam sacra officia in culpa cæteris imitabilem demonstrarent.* Much more such against ungodly Bishops they recite.

Cap. 46. They tell us that the Canons against Kneeling on the Lord's days were yet in force, [*Quoniam sunt quidam in Die Dominico genuflectentes, & in diebus Pentecostes; ut omnia in universis locis consonanter observentur, placuit sancto Concilio, stantes Domino vota dignissima persolvere.*

In

their Councils abridged.

In *Hierom*'s Epistle to *Nepotian* which they cite, there are most pungent warnings to Priests to take heed of familiarity or abode with Women; yea, even when they are sick. *Scio* (saith he) *quosdam convaluisse corpore, & animo ægrotare cæpisse; Periculose tibi ministrat, cujus vultum frequenter attendis.* He requireth Clergy-men to avoid fine Cloaths, curious Hair, pleasing the Appetite, and Riches. He saith of himself, [*Natus in paupere domo, & in tugurio rusticano, qui vix milio & cibario pane rugientem satiare ventrem poteram, nunc similam & mella fastidio.* He saith, the Mouth, Mind, and Hand of Priests must agree: Even a Thief may speak against Covetousness.-- *Multo melius est è duobus imperfectis rusticitatem habere sanctam, quam eloquentiam peccatricem: Multi ædificant parietes & columnas Ecclesiæ substruunt: marmora nitent, auro splendent laquearia, gemmis Altare distinguitur; & Ministrorum Christi nulla electio est. Portemus Crucem Christi, & divitias lutum putabimus.--Facile contemnitur Clericus qui sæpius vocatus ad prandium ire non recusat.* And his Epistle *ad Oceanum*, hath yet more against converse with Women. *Prima tentamenta Clericorum sunt Fæminarum frequentes accessus--Janua Diaboli, via iniquitatis, Scorpionis percussio, nocivumque genus est Fæmina. Cum proximat stipula, incendit ignem.----Mihi crede non potest toto corde habitare cum Domino, qui Fæminarum accessibus copulatur.* With much more the like.

It appeareth by *Cap.* 112. a Sermon of *Augustines*, that it was the custom then for the Preacher to sit, and the Hearer to stand, [*I will not hold you long*, (saith he) *because while I sit, you are weary by standing.*]

Augustine sheweth there how little he regarded the Appeals of his deposed Priests to *Rome*, [or Councils] *Interpellet contra me mille Concilia, naviget contra me quò voluerit, sit certè ubi potuerit; adjuvabit me Dominus, ut ubi ego Episcopus sum, illic Clericus esse non possit.*

§ 118. Yet I wonder that the Chap. 122 of this Council intimateth so strange a proportion of Meat and Drink to be the daily Commons of the Canonical Monks, I had thought they had lived in greater Abstinence. The proportion of Alms or Commons allowed them was, [*Every day four pound of Bread,*] (enough for me for near 4 weeks;) *and five pounds of Wine,* (more than I drunk, I think, in 20 years, in Wine;) *or else where Wine was scarce, they had three pounds of Wine, and three of Beer*; *or in great scarcity, one pound of Wine, and five of Beer.* I think our ordinary Ministers drink not so much Wine in a year, as these did in a day; I mean such as live in the Countrey, and were of my Acquaintance. I wonder how any Plowman's Belly can hold four pound of Bread one day, and live, without a present Vomit or Purge. I have tryed long *Cornario*'s and *Lessius*'s diet (12 or 14 ounces of *Panada*, and as much Beer only in a day, without tasting any other Meat,) and found no incommodity as to Health or Pleasure; but should I eat four pound of Bread in two days, I do not think I should ever eat more without a Vomit. And how can any Man drink five pound of any ordinary Wine, and not be drunk, or dead? yea, or three Pints either. What

Man's

Man's Belly will hold six pounds of Wine and Water every day, unless it pass as *Tunbridge* Waters, without present Suffocation, or a Dropsie. I would hope that I understand not this Chapter in the Council, but that these Canons had some Beggars that were to partake with them, but that I find no encouragement for my charity in the Text or History: But verily if it were as it is written, I wonder how these abstemious Monks did escape death by their Gluttony and Drunkenness one week or day without Physick; notwithstanding that the Council giveth you notice, *cap.* 122. *lin. ult.* that a pound hath but 12 ounces.

§ 119. We must not unthankfully omit what kindness *Anastasius* (saith Pope *Paschal*) shewed to the *English*: By negligence their House at *Rome* was burnt, and the Pope ran out bare-foot, and where he stood, the Fire stopt*; therefore he stood bare-foot there till morning, that the Fire might be fully quenched. But this he did for the love of St. *Peter*, whose Church was in danger by the Fire.

*Quæ si vera sunt, saith Binnius himself.

§ 120. The *Papists* here bring forth a Constitution out of their own Library, by which *Ludovicus* confirmeth to the Popes all that ever his Ancestors gave them, and addeth so much, that he was then made (if this be true) (as the *Geographia Nubiensis* calls him) *the King of Rome indeed*. And they meerly feign that *Charles* and *Ludovicus Pius* made none of these Laws of themselves, but by the Pope's advice, against plain evidence of History.

§ 121. A Convention of Abbots at *Aquisgrane*, and another of Bishops, and a Synod at *Engelheim* follow, and one at *Attiniac*, in which they say the Emperor penitently lamented his severity against his Nephew *Bernard*, and others, with open Confession and Penitence. And indeed his great endeavors to promote Piety, and to reform the Clergy; his frequent Councils, (in which it was he, by the advice of a few chief chosen Men, that did their business, and governed all) with the rest of his Life described by the Writer of it, and other Historians, do shew that he was justly called *Pius*, though Wars will cause many actions to be repented of.

§ 122. *Platina* saith, that *Anastasius* saith, that *Ludovicus* gave *Paschal* the power of freely chusing Bishops, *which before was not done without the Emperors*. (The Peoples consent still supposed.)

§ 123. The Pope being dead, two are chosen (which was the 11th Schism) but *Eugenius* the 2d carried it, the Emperor sending his Son *Lotharius* to settle the Peace of the City, *jamdudum Præsulum quorundam perversitate depravatam*, saith the Author of the Life of *Ludovicus*; where Murders of the chief Men had been committed in the Schism, and Mens Goods taken away, and much confusion made.

§ 124. In the East, the Party, that were against Images, prevailed ever since *Irene* the Woman that set them up was deposed and dyed; her Son *Constantine*, whom she murdered, being not for them before, nor *Nicephorus* that deposed her after; But *Leo* 5 *Armenus* that succeeded *Michael Curop-*

earneſt againſt them, and, as they called it, perſecuted the Worſhippers of Images. A Prince confeſſed to be very profitable to the Empire; *Michael Balbus* that is ſuppoſed the chief of them that murdered him, reigneth in his ſtead: he ſet himſelf earneſtly to have healed the Church-diviſions of the Eaſt about Images. To that end he ſent Ambaſſadors to *Ludovicus Pius* into *France* for his counſel, in the profeſſing his great deſire of Peace. *Ludovicus* called together ſome that he moſt eſteemed for Learning at *Paris*, (which ſome call a Council, but were like to be more learned than the Majority in Councils) to debate and conſider the buſineſs. The *Paris* Divines in this Debate drew up a Writing, in which they greatly ſinned, ſaith *Bellarmine*, in that they took on them to reprehend the Pope, and a General Council; (But do not they themſelves condemn many General Councils?) *In which*, ſaith Bellarmine, *they far exceeded the Author, who in the name of* Carolus Mag. *put forth a Book againſt the worſhiping of Images. For he (which alſo the Fathers of the* Frankford *Council did) diſallowed (or rejected) the 2d* Nicene *Synod, becauſe they thought it had been celebrated without the Pope's conſent* *: *An unlikely thing. But theſe Counſellors of the Emperor* Lewis, *confeſs the Council of* Nice 2d *for the worſhiping of Images to be called and approved by Pope* Adrian, *and yet they did not fear to examine, judge, and reprehend both the Synod itſelf, and the Epiſtle of* Adrian *to* Conſtantine *for the worſhip of Images, yea, and the defence of that Synod ſent by* Adrian *to* Charles M. *ſaying,* [*Indiſcretè neſcitur feciſſe in eo quod ſuperſtitioſè eas adorari juſſit.*] So (ſaith Bellarmine) *they were not aſhamed to judge the Judge of themſelves, and of the whole world, to feed the Paſtor of all* Chriſt's *Sheep, and to teach the Teacher of all men; than which temerity, no greater can be imagined.* Thus far Bellarmine.

§ 125. Here I deſire the Reader to take notice,
1. That even then when the Pope was advanced to his Kingly greatneſs, yet as the Eaſtern Empire was far from obeying him, ſo even that one Prince that ſet him up, and defended him, with his Doctors and Counſellors, were far from thinking *him Infallible*, but reproved him, and judged him as ſuperſtitious for Image-worſhip, and were not herein ruled by him.
2. And judge whether moſt Biſhops would not have judged accordingly, if they had had but the ſame countenance from Princes, as the Biſhops in the Eaſt and theſe now had?
3. And judge with what Face the Militant Doctors of *Rome* do pretend, that all the world was then ſubject to the judgment of the Pope, and bid us name any Churches that rejected it, when Eaſt and Weſt ſo far rejected it as is here confeſſed, even when they were grown ſo high, yea and Councils as well as Popes?

§ 126. Hereupon a Book was printed *An.* 1596. called, *The Council of* Paris *about Images*, containing,

1. The

1. The Emperor *Michael*'s Epistle, (*by which*, saith Bellarmine, *one would judge him one of the best Princes that ever was.*)

2. The *Paris* Doctors Collection of Testimonies, proving, (in the middle way) *that Images should not be broken contemptuously, as some would have them; nor be worshipped as the General Nicene Council, and the Pope would have them.*

3. An Epistle in the Pope's name, written, (saith *Bellarmine*, by the *French* Doctors) to *Michael* the Emperor, shewing, *that Images are neither to be wronged disgracefully, nor adored.*

4. An Epistle of the Emperor *Ludovicus* to the Pope, desiring him to write to *Michael* to further this Peace of the Churches.

5. An Epistle of *Ludovicus* to the two Bishops whom he sent to *Rome,*[*to direct them how to carry themselves wisely, to get the Pope's consent.*] Whether this at *Paris* was a Council, or only a select Convention of Men chosen by the Emperor, is a Controversie of no great moment. I take the latter to be the more honourable sort of Assembly, as the world then went; and should reverence more the judgment of 20 or 12 Men, selected by such an extraordinary Prince, than of the majority of the Bishops of all *Europe*: As I prefer the judgment of those Men that by King *James* were appointed to Translate the Bible, before the judgment of the major part of the whole *English* Clergy, of whom perhaps one in ten had a smattering in the *Hebrew* Tongue, and one of an hundred understood it, (at the most.)

§ 127. Our modern cheated *English Papists*, that are taught here in *England* to say that they worship not Images, might here see the Fraud of their Clergy, that fit them a Faith to their interests and occasions. We confess that it is but three sorts of Images that *Aquinas* saith we should worship with Latria (Divine Worship:) But yet the rest *are to be worshipped,* say their Doctors. Why else do they so commonly condemn this Book and Council of *Ludovicus Pius*, that forbiddeth both the breaking and the worshiping of them? Why doth *Bellarmine* purposely revile, and particularly confute this Book ? Why doth *Binnius* recite all *Bellarmine*'s Answer in his *Concil. Tom.* 3. p. 529, &c?

§ 128. *Bellarmine* is very loth that the Epistle here said to be written by Pope *Eugenius* the 2d, should be taken to be his, and supposeth that it was but sent to him to be subscribed: By whom? If by the Emperor *Ludovicus Pius*, and his Council of Divines, you may see of what reputation the Pope was then in the Church. One great Argument against it is, *That the Pope would not so impudently flatter the Emperor*, as to say, " O *venerable Princes of the world, seeing by God's disposal you govern all the Church,* &c. *And for uniting the Church which by God's Ordination you govern: What filthier Flattery* (saith Bellarmine) *could there be ?* Michael Balbus *a Murderer,* &c. *is said by the Pope to govern the Church by God's disposing. What then are Bishops for ?*

Ans.

Anſ. And 1. Did not even *Gregory Mag* as much flatter a worſe Man and Murderer, *Phocas*? and his Succeſſors him and many more?

2. Did not many, if not moſt of the Emperors, Heathen and Chriſtian, come in by Murder, or Invaſion, and Uſurpation? And were Men therefore diſobliged from obeying them, when they were ſetled, by ſubmiſſive implicite conſent?

3. But the venom of the Cardinal Jeſuite's anſwer is, that he taketh it to be baſe Flattery, to ſay that Princes are by God's diſpoſe the Governors of the Church: For then what are the Biſhops for? And muſt the world be ridden and abuſed by ſuch Men, that would turn Princes out of all Government of the Church, and underſtand not that the Government of the ſame Church, may belong to the Magiſtrate and the Paſtors reſpectively, (as the Government of an Hoſpital to the King, and to the Phyſician?) May not one rule and puniſh by the Sword, and another by the Word, by Teaching, and the Church Keys? Is it not one thing to Fine, and Beat, and Baniſh, and Kill a Man, and another to ſentence him unmeet for Church-Communion? Marvellous, that God permitteth the world to be deluded by ſuch a blinded or blinding Clergy, though as learned as *Bellarmine*, that would make theſe things ſeem inconſiſtent, and ſeparate what God hath conjoined!

See here to what the *Roman* Clergy would reduce Kings, they muſt be no Governors of the Church. And if all the Kingdom be Chriſtians, are they not all the Church? And ſo the Chriſtening of the Subjects depoſeth the King, and maketh the chief Prieſt King that Chriſteneth them.

If he had ſaid that Kings govern Churches, but not as Churches, but as parts of the Kingdom, he had ſaid falſly: For they govern *them as Churches*, though not by the ſame ſort of Government as the Paſtors do; as they govern not Hoſpitals by the ſame ſort of Government, as the Phyſicians.

§ 129. In *Eugenius*'s Epiſtle it is honeſtly and truly ſaid, that "[*If there had never been a painted or a forged Image, neither Faith, Hope nor Love, by which Men come to the Eternal Kingdom, would have periſhed.*] I am of *Bellarmine*'s mind now, that this was none of the Pope's Epiſtle, (but the honeſt Emperor's, and his Clergy Councils:) He thought it too bad for a Pope, and I think it too good for a Pope. He thinks that the Pope muſt be mad, if he would have ſo condemned his Predeceſſor *Adrian*'s Acts, as this Epiſtle doth; and I doubt he was not ſo honeſt as to do it. But did not *Bellarmine* know how much more ſharp and virulent Accuſations Popes have laid on one another?

§ 130. CCXLVI. So powerful was *Ludovicus Pius*'s Attempts to reform the Clergy, that it drove Pope *Eugenius* the 2d for ſhame to call a Council at *Rome*, (not from the *Antipodes*, but) of 63 Biſhops, (*An*. 826.) who repeated ſome old Canons, and, among other things, forbad ſuch Feaſts and Plays as our Wakes are on any Holy-days to be uſed.

§ 131. *Valentine* was next choſen Pope, (*Collectis in unum Venerab. Epiſcopis & Glorioſis Romanorum Proceribus, omnique ample urbis Populo in*

Pal. Later. faith *Anaſtaſius*) but he lived but 30 or 40 days, (Hiſtorians agree not of it.)

§ 132. *Gregory* the 4th ſucceeded, who, faith *Platina*, would not undertake the Papal Office,till *Ludovicus* the Emperor had conſidered of the choice, "and confirmed it: [*Which,*(faith *Platina*) Ludovicus *did not out of Pride,* * Mark that it is the Rights of the Empire. "*but left he ſhould loſe the Rights of the Empire*, being by nature gentle and "*moſt humane, and had ever upheld the Rights of the Church. He ſetled "*Benefices on every Prieſt, that Poverty might not hinder them.*] You ſee here that the great Friend of the Church yet took that for the right of the Empire, that none ſhould be Pope againſt his conſent.

§ 133. *Platina,* adding how he reformed the Clergy, forbidding them gay Attire, Ornaments, Sumptuouſneſs and Vanities, faith thereupon, "*Would* "*thou hadſt lived in our times,* O Ludovicus! *For the Church wanteth thy* "*holy Inſtitutions, and Cenſure, ſo much hath the Eccleſiaſtical Order poured ont* "*itſelf to all Luxury and Luſt.*] So deſcribing their abominable Pride and Vanity.

§ 134. Pope *Gregory* added ſo much to the good works of his Predeceſſors, by mending, building, adorning ſo many Temples, Pillars and Poſts, with Stones, Veſtments, Silver, &c. and removing the Bones of Saints, (if he miſtook not) that it is no wonder if *Rome* grew into greater pomp and ſplendor than ever before.

§ 135. This godly Emperor having three Sons by his firſt Wife, and marrying a ſecond, having two Sons by her; the Sons of the firſt Wife hated the ſecond Wife, thinking her Son *Charles* had too much favor. One Son (*Pepin*) apprehended his Father, and the eldeſt (*Lotharius*) came in and approved it, and the 3d joined with them, and wickedly depoſed him from his Kingdom: of which anon.

§ 136. *Ludovicus* called Councils at *Paris, Mentz, Lyons,* and *Tholouſe,*for Reformation; ſome ſay upon the warning of a Maid that being poſſeſſed of the Devil; and ſpeaking Latine,ſaid that this Devil executed Judgments on the Land for their Sins, Injuſtice, &c. CCXLVII. The Council at *Paris* wrote a large Book for Reformation, *An.* 829. with the reſt of this Emperor's Conſtitutions, worthy to be Tranſlated for the common good, that all might ſee the difference between Reformers and turbulent Hereticks and Hereticators, and proud aſpiring Prelates. The Book is a Treatiſe of pious Directions. The 50th Chapter,reproving the breach of the Lord's day,faith, that "[*By ſight and by certain relation they have notice, that many working* "*on that day have been killed with Thunderbolts, ſome puniſhed by ſudden* "*Convulſions, ſome by viſible Fire, their Fleſh and Bones being in a moment* "*conſumed and turned into aſhes, and many other ſuch terrible judgments.* Therefore they require that as the *Jews* keep their Sabbath, all Men much more do ſpiritually obſerve this day of the Lord.

The ſecond Book doth notably ſhew the duty of Kings and Magiſtrates.

The

their Councils abridged. 253

The last Chapter requireth those that are far from the Church, to meet for Prayer in other places, as being acceptable to God.

In the 8th *Capitul.* (*Bin. p.* 569.) the Bishops say, [*Beati* Petri *vicem indigni gerimus.*] So that the Pope is not *Peter's* onely Successor; others represent him, if this Council did not mistake.

§ 137. CCXLVIII. We come now to a Council which sheweth you, that the good Canons made by the Emperor for Church-Reformation, were far from reforming the generality of the Bishops. It is the Council at *Compendium*, which too compendiously deposed the godly Emperor, (of whom the world was not worthy.)

Calumniators pretended that one *Bernhard* a Courtier lay with *Judith* the Emperor's second Wife: The Sons of his first Wife hating her; *Pepin*, whom his Father had made King of *Italy*, on this pretence Trayterously raiseth Arms against his Father. *Lotharius*, the eldest Son, too much consenting, perswaded his Father to let a meeting without Arms, at *Neomagus*, prevent a War. At that meeting the Nobles, *Parentis Imperium legitimè prorogabant*, saith *Binnius, p.* 575, and *Pepin* took up Arms again. The Father conquereth his Son, and taketh him Prisoner, and might justly have taken away his life, but he was stol'n out of Prison in the night. *Ludovicus* depriveth him of his Kingdom of *Italy*, and divideth it between his two Sons by the second Wife, *Charles* and *Rodolphus*. Hereupon *Lotharius* the eldest rebelling, knew not how to conquer his godly and prosperous Father but by the Bishops: Them he draweth into his Conspiracy, that as *Binnius* himself saith, "[*Ut quem filii armis imperio deponere non possent, horum saltem nundinariorum Antistitum suffragio & judicio, honore ac potestate imperiali privaretur: successit impiis conatus impiissimus.*] The last means of Treason was a Council of the base mercenary Bishops; a wicked Attempt that served these wicked Men, and did the Feat. *Ebbo* the Archbishop of *Rhemes*, (of a base original) and enow more such Prelates were not wanting. The Emperor had before voluntarily lamented his putting out the eyes of his Kinsman *Bernard* a Rebel, (of which he dyed) as too cruel, (when now no Prince scrupleth Hanging, or Beheading open Rebels.) The Church had satisfaction by his voluntary Penance, for that which few Men will think a Fault. And what do these *Bishops now*, but become their *Sovereign's Judges*, yea, and that when he *was absent*, and *condemn him unheard*, for this former Fault. Note the Case.

1. They condemn their King to be deposed, who were Subjects.
2. Yea, Clergy-men, that had least to do with State Affairs.
3. Yea, and that for a Fault, which perhaps was but Justice, and no Fault.
4. Or if it were a Fault, was before judged and remitted. And did godly *Lewis* cherish Christian Bishops so zealously, for this use, so basely and trayterously to depose him?

5. Yea,

5. Yea, and to join in the horrid Rebellion of unnatural Sons, to accomplish their designs.

6. And to tempt Princes to hate Religion, when *in Nomine Domini*, the pretence of Religion shall do greater wickedness by Prelates, than the Rebels Arms was able to perform.

Saith the Author of the Life of *Ludovicus Pius*, [*This judgment some few gain-sayed, more consented to it : the greatest part, as it useth to be in such* (*a*) O. *cases* (*a*), *consented by word, for fear of offending their Leaders* (*b*). *They judged him, absent and unheard, neither confessing nor convict, before the Bodies of St.* Medard *Confessor, and St.* Sebastian *Martyr, to lay down his Arms* (*c*), *and forced him to lay them before the Altar; and cloathing him in a black garment, under a strict Guard, they thrust him into Prison. By this testimony,* saith Binnius, *it is certainly proved that the whole business was done by force and fear, and coloured with the false pigment of Religion.* Thus was the best of Princes, after all his services for the Prelates, and kindness to his Sons, deposed, and basely used by both, against Nature and Religion.

(*a*) O. wicked use of Bishops! (*b*) Whom should they have feared more than God and their King? (*c*) Is this the use of Reliques?

His first Restauration, when he had been before deposed, was by the *Germans :* How he was restored the second time, I find not certainly; some would give Pope *Gregory* the honour of it. It is likeliest that the interest which his goodness had got in the People, with the odiousness of his Sons and Bishops Acts, did it: But fully restored, after all this, he was. And being somewhat backward to forgive *Lotharius*, he filled *France* with new Wars, till the Emperor for Peace did pardon all. But *Ebbo,* Archbishop of *Rhemes,* and *Agobard,* Bishop of *Lyons,* were deposed, as Leaders of the Treason; and *Ebbo* banished, and restored by *Lotharius* when his Father dyed; yea, and sent as a fit Man to convert the *Normans* by Pope *Paschal's* mission , being made Bishop of *Hildesheim* in *Saxony,* by *Ludovic* King of *Germany,* see *Petavius* Hist. *l.* 8. *c.* 8.

Shortly after, *An.* 840. the Emperor (sollicited yet to more Wars by his own Sons, about dividing the Kingdoms) dyed, *a direful Eclipse of the Sun foregoing his death, the day before Ascension-day.*

§ 138. That you may see the base Hypocrisie of these Trayterous Bishops, I will recite their words in the Council that condemned the best of Emperors ; but his Imprisonment they leave out.

An. 833.

§ 139. The Bishops condemnation of the Emperor *Ludovicus Pius, An.* 833. after a Preface of the Duty of Bishops without Favor or Fear to judge Sinners, and the need of putting their Sentence in writing, to avoid the censure of bad Men, they say—

* Here is a High Court of Prelatical Justice against a good Emperor.

'*We hold it necessary to notifie to all the Sons of the Church, both present* '*and future, how we Bishops, set over the Empire* * *of our Lord and most* '*glorious Emperor* Lotharius, *An.* 833. *the first year of the said Prince in* '*October, did generally meet at the Palace at* Compendium, (Compeigne) '*and*

their Councils abridged. 255

' and humbly heard the said Prince *; And we took care, according to the
' Ministry enjoined us, to manifest to him or his Nobles, the generality of all
' the People, what is the Vigor, and Power, or Priestly Ministry, and with what
' Sentence of Damnation he deserveth to be damned, who will not obey the warn-
' ings of the Priests (a).

' And next both to the said Prince, (Lotharius) and to all the People, we
' studied to denounce, that they should study most devoutly to please God, and
' should not delay to appease him in whatever they had offended him : For ma-
' ny things were examined, (b), which by negligence hapned in this Empire,
' which manifestly tended to the scandal of the Church, and the ruine of the
' People, or the destruction of the Kingdom ; which must necessarily be quickly
' corrected, and by all means for the future prevented (c).

' Among other things we mentioned, and remembred all Men, how by God
' that Kingdom, by the administration of the most excellent Emperor Charles of
' good memory, and the Valor of his Predecessors, was peaceable, and united, and
' nobly enlarged, and committed to the Lord Emperor Lewis by God in great
' peace to be governed ; and by God's protection remain'd so preserved, as long as
' that Prince studied God, and used his Father's example, and was careful to
' acquiesce in the counsels of good Men : And how in progress of time, as is
' manifest to all, by his improvidence or negligence, it fell into so great ignominy
' and baseness, that it became not only the grief of Friends, but the derision of
' Enemies.

' But because the said Prince hath negligently managed the Ministry commit-
' ted to him, and did both do and compel others to do many things displeasing
' to God and Man, or permitted others to do it (d), and provoked God in
' many wicked counsels, and scandalized the Church ; and, that we may omit
' innumerable other things) at last drew all his Subjects to a common destructi-
' on, and by God's just judgment, suddenly his Imperial Power was taken from
' him (e). But we remembring the Commands of God, and our Ministry, and
' his Benefits, thought him worthy, that by the leave of the said Prince Lotha-
' rius, we should send a Message to him by the Authority of this Sacred As-
' sembly, to admonish him of his Guilts, that he might take sure advice for his
' safety (or salvation.) That he might in his extremity study with all his
' might, that being deprived of his earthly Power, according to God's Council,
' and the Churches Authority, he might not also lose his Soul. To the counsels
' of which Messengers, and their most wholsom warnings he willingly consented,
' he took time, and set a day in which he would give an answer to their whol-
' som Admonitions (f).

' And when the day was at hand, the same Holy Assembly unanimously went
' to the venerable Man, and took care to admonish him of all that he had of-
' fended God in, and scandalized the Church, and troubled the People com-
' mitted to him, and to bring all to his remembrance. And he willingly em-
' bracing their wholsom Admonition, and their worthy and congruous Aggra-
' vations, promised in all things to acquiesce in their wholsom council, and to un-
' dergo

*Lotharius accusing his Father
(a) No doubt but you made this known too far.
(b) By what Authority?
(c) Who made you the Governors and Judges of such matters? Are Rebellions of Sons, the Fathers fault?
(d) Must the King answer to a Court of Bishops, for all the evils that he permitteth the Bishops and others to do?
(e) Lotharius had got the Nobles to begin.
(f) O humble Prince! O traytorous Prelates!

dergo their remedying judgment (g). *And being glad of so wholsom an Admonition* (h), *strait we intreated his beloved Son, Lotharius Augustus, to be speedily present, that without delay, with his Nobles he might come, that there might be a mutual reconciliation between them according to Christian Doctrine, that if there were any blemishes or discords in their hearts, a pure and humble begging of Pardon* (i) *might expiate them, and thereupon before all the multitude, he might receive the judgment of the Priesthood as Penitents do, which soon after was done.*

'*Therefore the Lord Ludovicus coming into the Church of Holy Mary, God's Mother, where rest the Bodies of Saints, that is, of* Medard, *a Confessor of Christ and Bishop, and of Sebastian a most excellent Martyr (the Priests, Deacons, and no small multitude of the Clerks standing by, and his Son the foresaid* Lotharius *being present with his Nobles, and the generality of all the People, even as many as the Church could hold) and being prostrate on the earth upon Hair-cloth* (k) *before the Holy Altar, he confessed before all, that he too unworthily used the Ministry committed to him, and in it many wayes offended God, and scandalized the Church of Christ, and many ways troubled the People by his negligence: And therefore for the Publick and Ecclesiastick Expiation of so great Guilts, he said he would desire Penance, that God being merciful by their Ministry and Help, he might prosperously deserve (or obtain) Absolution of so great Crimes, God having given them the power of Binding and Loosing; whom also the Bishops, as spiritual Physicians, did wholsomly admonish, telling him that true remission of Sin followeth pure and simple Confession; that he should openly confess his Errors, in which he professed that he most offended God, left he should hide any thing within, or do any thing deceitfully before God, as it is known to all that he did heretofore in the Palace at* Compeigne, *when he was by another Holy Assembly reproved before all the Church: And that he come not to God now, as he did then, by dissembling and craft, with a double heart, and provoke him to anger, rather than to forgive his sin* (l); *for it is written, The dissemblers and crafty provoke the wrath of God. And after this Admonition he professed that he had chiefly sinned in all those things, whereupon he had been familiarly reproved by the foresaid Priests, by word or writings; that being by due rebuke reproved of the things they gave him a writing* (m) *of, containing the sum of his Guilts, of which they had specially reproved him; which he had in his hands, viz.*

'I. *As in the same Paper is fullier contained, incurring the guilt of Sacriledge and Murder, in that he kept not, according to his promise, the fatherly Admonition and terrible Contestation made to him with Divine Invocation before the Holy Altar in presence of the Priests, and the greatest multitude of the People; in that he had done violence to his Brethren and Kindred, and had permitted his Nephew to be killed* (n), *whom he might have delivered; and that being unmindful of his Vow, he after commanded the Sign of Holy Religion to be made for the revenge of his own indignation.*

'II. *That being the Author of Scandal, and Troubler of the Peace, and Vio-*
'*later*

(g) Its pity but he had better Judges
(h) Its like he lookt for better measures.
(i) Of a traytorous Son and Subjects.
(k) Was this keeping the fifth Commandement, and Honouring the King? O wicked Son, and wicked Prelates!

(l) O insulting Traytors!

(m) They wrote him his Lesson, & confessed his sins for him.

(n) A Traytor in open Rebellion

'later of the Sacraments, by unlawful Power he corrupted the Covenant which
'was made between his Sons for the peace and unanimity of the Empire, and
'tranquility of the Church, by common Council, and consent of all the faithful
'People, and confirmed by the Sacrament: and in that he compelled his faithful
'People in contrariety to the said first Covenant and Oath, to swear another Sa- (o) Or
'crament (o), and so fell into the guilt of Perjury, by the violation of the Oath.
'former Oaths. And how much this displeased God, is plain, in that the People
'subject to him had afterward no peace, but were all led into perturbation, bear-
'ing the punishment of their sins, and by God's just judgment.

'III. That against Christian Religion, against his Vow, without any pub-
'lick profit or certain necessity (p), deluded by evil counsel, he commanded a (p) Against
'general Expedition to be made in Lent, and in the extreme parts of his Em- the Arms
'pire appointed a general Meeting (or Council) at the time of the Lord's Sup- of his
'per, when the Paschal Sacraments were to be celebrated of all Christians (q). (q) Rebels
'In which Expedition, as much as in him lay, he drew the People into great must not
'murmuring, and against right put the Priests of the Lord from their Offices, and be resisted
'brought great oppression on the Poor. in the
Lent, or

'IV. That he brought violence on some of his faithful People, that for his Easter.
'and his Sons fidelity and safety, and the recovery of the shaking Kingdom,
'humbly went to him, and made known to him the snares prepared for him by
'his Enemies; And that against all Law Divine and Humane, he deprived (r) But a
'them of their Estates, and commanded them to be banished (r), and made Bishop
'them when absent judged to Death, and doubtless induced the Judges to false that doth
'judgment. And against Divine and Canonical Authority, raised prejudice but differ
'against the Lord's Priests, (or Bishops) and Monks, and condemned them from the
'absent. And in this incurring the guilt of Murder, he was a violater of the rest in
'Laws of God and Man. a word,
must be

'V. Of divers Sacraments (Oaths) contrary to each other, oft made un- banished.
'reasonably by his Sons or People, he commanding and compelling them;
'whereby he brought no small blot of sin on the People committed to him. He hereby
'incurred the guilt of Perjury, because these are rightly charged on him as Au-
'thor, by whom they were compelled. But in the purging of Women, in unjust
'Judgments, in false Witnesses and Perjuries, which have been committed in his
'presence by his permission, how much he hath offended God he himself know-
'eth.

'VI. Of divers Expeditions which he hath made in the Kingdom commit-
'ted to him, not only unprofitably, but also hurtfully without counsel and profit;
'in which many and innumerable heinous Crimes were committed in the Chri-
'stian People, in Murders and Perjuries, in Sacriledge and Adulteries, in Ra-
'pines, in Burnings, either in the Churches of God, or divers other places, in Plun-
'derings and oppressing of the Poor, by miserable usage, and almost unheard of
'among Christians; which all, as is aforesaid, reflect on the Author.

'VII. In the divisions of the Empire rashly made by him, against the com-
'mon peace, and the safety of the whole Empire, for his own will; and the
'Oath which compelled all the people to swear, that they would act against his

L l 'Sons

'Sons as Enemies, when he might have pacified them by Fatherly Authority, and
'the counsel of his faithful People.
'VIII. That so many Mischiefs and Crimes committed in the Kingdom
'committed to him, by his negligence and improvidence were not enough, which
'yet cannot be numbred, by which the Kingdom was evidently disgraced and
'endangered: but moreover to add to the heap of miseries, he lastly drew all the
'People of his power to their common destruction, when he ought to have been
'to his People the Captain of safety and of peace, when the Divine Piety had
'decreed to have mercy of his People by an unheard of and invisible manner,
'and by preaching in our ages.
'For these things therefore, and in all these things which are before recited,
'confessing himself guilty before the Priests, (or Bishops) or all the People, with
'tears, and protesting that in all these things he sinned, he desired publick Pen-
'nance, that so he might satisfie the Church by repenting, which he had scanda-
'lized by sinning; and as he was a scandal by neglecting many things, so he
'professed he would be an example by undergoing due Pennance.
'And after this Confession he delivered to the Bishops the Paper of his Guilts
'and Confession for future memorial, and they laid it on the Altar; and then
'he put off his military Girdle and laid it on the Altar, and stripping himself of
'his secular Habit, he took the Habit of a Penitent put on him by the hands of
*Here is a 'the Bishops, that after so great and such Pennance *, no Man after may return
new fort 'to a secular Militia.
of Com-
position 'These things thus done, it pleased them that every Bishop should write in his
of the 'own Papers how the matter was done, and should strengthen it by his own sub-
Bishops 'scription, and offer it to Prince Lotharius, thus strengthned in memory of the
hands, to 'Fact. To conclude, it seemed good to us all that were present, to put the sum
depose a 'of all the Papers, and of so great a business into one Breviate, and to roborate
King so 'it by the subscription of us all with our hands, as is hereafter demonstra-
as never 'ted.—
to be re-
stored: The Author of the Life of *Ludovicus* addeth, '[*Pulláque indutum veste,*
But it 'adhibitâ magnâ custodiâ sub tectum quoddam retrudunt.]
failed.
Here you see the Tryal of the godly Emperor, the Articles exhibited against
him in the High Court of Episcopal Justice, and the use of Penance, and of
laying on of the Bishops hands, in investing him in the Garb of perpetual
Penance. What wonder if the Pope ascended to such power, when ordinary Bishops in the best governed and instructed Countrey then in the world,
obtained such power; even by the name and abuse of the POWER OF
THE KEYS? Saith *Binnius*, [*Tháganus* therefore justly for this cause de-
claimeth against *Ebbo*, Bishop of *Rhemes*, the Leader, as *impudicum & cru-
delissimum Episcopum!*] And what were they that would thus follow him?

Ann. 835. § 140. CCXLIX. But the next Council was forced to do better, (for
usually the Bishops followed the stronger side;) in *Theodorus Villa* they caused *Ebbo* to depose himself from his Bishoprick, and the rest excused themselves that they did it by necessity and fear, and were all forgiven, *Bin.p.*575.
And yet will the Bishops say, that this Emperor was not humble and merciful?

§ 141.

§ 141. CCL. After his Restauration, *An.* 836. *Ludovicus* caused a Council at *Aquisgrane*, to renew the Laws for the Reformation of the Clergy and Abbots, with the Instructions and Rules for Kings themselves at large laid down. And here they determined, that all Bishops hereafter that were Rebels and Traytors, should be deposed, and Lay-men anathematized. But they sufficiently minded the Power and Dignity of the Bishops to be upheld.

§ 142. There is a Treatise in *Binnius*, p. 583. in which the Statutes of the Synods of *Aquisgrane* are opened and confirmed by Scripture.

§ 143. CCLI. *An.* 836. *Binnius* tells us, that in the deposing of the Emperor, *Agobertus*, Bishop of *Lyons*, and *Bernard*, Bishop of *Vienne*, having been Leaders with *Ebbo*, at the Council at *Theod. Villa*, fled, and the Emperor and all his Sons, save *Lotharius*, being here present at a Council at *Lyons*, they being summoned, appeared not, and Sentence was put off, because they were absent.

§ 144. *An.* 839. *Pepin* the Emperor's Son dying, he passed by his disobedient Nephew *Pepin*, and divided that Kingdom of *Aquitain* only between his Sons *Lotharius* and *Charles*; whereupon his Son *Ludovicus* was offended, and with them of *Aquitain* raised Rebellion again, and by a Convention at *Cabilone*, and after it, reconciliation was made.

§ 145. The Emperor *Ludovicus Pius* dying *An.* 840. aged 64, his Sons fell together in Wars for his Kingdoms.

Lotharius the eldest, that had used his Father so trayterously and unnaturally, sought too great a part for himself, and came to a War with *Ludovic* and *Charles*, who conquered him, and put him to a shameful flight, *An.* 841. in which Fight, say Historians, a greater slaughter was made of the *French*, than was ever known in the memory of man. This was the man that deposed his Father for the slaughter of the Subjects by his Wars against him. The next year they fought again, and he was again overcome.

§ 146. CCLII. It's easie then to conjecture which way the next Council (which was at *Aquisgrane*) would go: The conquering Princes made the Bishops their Counsellors, when they had made *Lotharius* flie out of the Countrey, what they should do with his Kingdom; and, saith *Binnius*, they received the answer which *Nithardus li.* 1. describeth in these words, ['*The* ' *Bishops considering the deeds of* Lotharius *from the beginning, how he had* ' *driven his Father out of his Kingdom; how he had made the Christian People* ' *perjured by his Covetousness; how oft he had frustrated the Oath he made to* ' *his Fathers, and his Brethren; how oft, since his Fathers death, he had at-* ' *tempted to disinherit his Brethren; how many Murders, Adulteries, Burnings,* ' *and all kind of heinous deeds the Universal Church suffered by his most wick-* ' *ed Covetousness: And that he neither had any knowledge of governing the* ' *Commonwealth, nor could men find any footsteps of goodness of will in go-* ' *verning. For which causes deservedly, and by the just judgment of God Al-* ' *mighty, they said he fled first in Battel, and then from his Kingdom: There-* ' *fore all (the Bishops) unanimously agree and consent, that for his wickedness* ' *God hath cast him out, and hath delivered his Kingdom to his Brothers that*

'*are*

' *are better than he. But the Bishops did not give them this liberty, till they*
' *openly asked them, whether they would govern it as their ejected Brother did,*
' *or according to the will of God. They answered, that as far as God should*
' *enable them, they would govern themselves and theirs according to God's will.*
' *By God's Authority (say they) we warn, exhort and command; that you un-*
' *dertake it, and rule it according to the will of God.*] So far *Nithard.*

§ 147. You see here that it is no wonder that the Pope took upon him to set up and take down, to make and unmake Kings, when the subject Bishops did it by their greatest Sovereigns. And you see here God's just judgment on a rebellious Son, and the shameful mutability of a temporizing Clergy. And how presumptuous Bishops have abused Religion, the use of the Keys and the Name of God, to the confusions and calamities of the world. But *Lotharius* after this Deposition reigned.

§ 148. All these times Images were cast out in the Eastern Empire, even all the Reign of *Leo* the 5th, and of *Michael Balbus,* (however he recalled *Theodorus Studita* from Prison) and of *Theophilus* that succeeded him ; *Petavius li.* 8. *c.* 9. saith, that *Theophilus* followed his Father in persecuting the Worshipers of Images, but yet was a most strict requirer of Justice, and reigning 12 years and three months, died *An.* 841. the next year after the death of *Ludovicus Pius.* He left his Son *Michael,* a Child, Emperor, under the Rule of his Mother *Theodora.*

In *France Claudius Taurinensis* set against Image-worship, and going to *Rome,* &c. And *Jonas Aurel.* writeth against him, citing some of his Sentences (too strong for the Answerer,) but in his Preface professeth that he never read or saw his Book : Was not this an excellent Confuter?

§ 149. And now come up Images again by a Woman, which ever since a Womans Reign almost had been cast out; she ruled 14 years, just as *Irene* did, and sped as she ; for when her Son came to age, he deposed her. In this time *Methodius* first, and *Ignatius* after, were made Patriarchs of *Constantinople.* And *Bardas* (made *Cæsar*) deposed *Ignatius,* because he would not excommunicate *Theodora* when she was deposed, and set up the learned *Photius* in his place, that came in as *Nectarius* had done from the Laity, by sudden Ordination : one honoured even by the Papists for his great learning, but reviled for being against them.

§ 150. CCLIII. *An.* 842. This Woman had presently so much power on the mutable Bishops, as in a Council at *Constant.* to turn them to be again for Images, and as *Theophanes* saith, [*Suddenly changing their judgment, they cursed those that opposed Images;*] and so after 120 years rejection they were restored, and the *Nicene* 2d Council owned without any great difficulty : And here all that were for Images accounted it *Godliness,* and called them *Ungodly* that were against it, and this Woman *Theodora* is stiled for it a very godly Woman, (though the other called it Idolatry ;) and so while one side was cryed down as *Profane,* and the other as *Idolatrous* ; the poor Church felt to its sorrow, that Images were not taken for *things indifferent.*

Theophanes railing at *John* the Patriarch of *Constant.* saith, that [*Seeing so sudden and unexpected a change, he that ruled impiously was struck with such a stupor and blindness of mind, that he was ready to have killed himself ; and being the head of all the wickedness, of an ungodly judgment, that had led the Emperors by lyes, and thrust them into the hell of impiety, he was with igno-*
miny

their Councils abridged.

miny caft out, and good Methodius *put in.*] I recite the words, to shew you what various Characters the intereft of Images gave to men, and what Godlinefs and Ungodlinefs, Good men and Bad men, are in the fenfe of many Hiftorians.

§ 151. The Pope dying, *Johan. Diaconus* feizeth on the place by force; but *Sergius* is chofen againft him, and prevaileth: In whofe beginning *Lotharius* fent his Son *Ludovicus* with an Army to *Rome* *, *Sigibert* faith to be the Confirmer of the Pope, and claim that right ; others fay, to be crowned. To *Lotharius* they fware obedience, but not to his Son. Some great debate *Anaftafius* tells us that a great company of Bifhops had againft the Pope and his Party, but he tells us not what it was, but that the Pope was too hard for them, and glad when the *French* were gone.

* Thinking they would have refifted him: The Pope fubmitted himfelf to all that was defired of a Subject, till *Ludovicus* was gone.

§ 152. It's before faid, that after the Bifhop's depofing him, *Lotharius* was reftored, the three Brothers agreeing, that *Ludovicus* fhould have *Germany*, and part of *France*, and *Charles* have *France*, and *Lotharius Narbon* and *Italy* as *Roman* Emperor.

CCLIV. The Archbifhopric of *Rhemes* had been ten years without a Bifhop, upon *Ebbo's* removal or flight, and two Presbyters fucceffively *Fulke* and *Hotho* had been the Governors of it, (fome will queftion the validity of their acts.) And a Council at *Bellovacum* makes *Hincmarus* Bifhop.

§ 153. Under *Carolus Calvus* the Church-Lands were much alienated, efpecially Abbots Lands, to Nobles and other Lay-men. Whereupon CCLV. a Council at *Melda* (*Meaulx*) did by *Anfegifus* and *Bernardus Levita* draw up a Book of feven Parts, lamenting the fins of Christians, and the Sacriledge of the Laity, and offered it to the King, who refufed it, the Nobles being againft it: For which (fay the bold Expofitors of God's Providences) the *Normans* by Invafion troubled the Land.

§ 154. *Leo* the 4th became Pope; they durft not confecrate him without the Emperor's authority, *Anaftaf. in Bin.* p. 618. This Pope wrought great Miracles, fay they. 1. He conquered a Bafilisk that killed men by his looks, (as St. *George* conquered the Dragon.) 2. By the Crofs he ftopt a fire in the City: But his good works contain a Volumn in *Anaftafius*, *viz.* the many Churches that he adorned, enriched, repaired; the filver Veffels and Ornaments that he gave, the Pofts and Pillars, and Altars that he beautified, and the glory that he added to the *Roman* City and Churches, &c. yea, when the *Saracens* came and fpoiled St. *Peter's* Church in the Suburbs of *Rome*, he caufed the faid Suburbs to be walled and fortified, as a new City, calling it *Leonina* from his name: And he made two or three Prayers of fix or feven lines long, to defire God's protection of it, by the interceffion of St. *Peter*. And he writeth a notable Homily, in which he comprizeth much of the Canons, teaching them all the Arts, Geftures, and Ceremonies of canting the Mafs; and precifely ordereth, that every Prieft do learn his Leffon; and that if any of them be illiterate, (that cannot read) he fhall be fufpended till he amend, (learn to read;) fo learned was the Clergy in that Age.

§ 155. By the way, the oft mention here of *finging* the Mafs, doth remember

ber me to note that which is much over-looked; *viz.* How Liturgies imposed first came up, or were mostly propagated without any exception or opposition: It was chiefly because they did *sing them,* and had fitted them accordingly to their *singing Notes,* like our Cathedral singing of our reading Psalms and Prayers: And we all know that the People or Minister cannot make Psalms *ex tempore,* but we must and do use forms in *singing*; but the Prayers that were *not sung,* but said, were longer left free to the Speakers present skill.

§ 156. CCLVI. *An.* 847. in a Council at *Paris, Lotharius* caused the cause of *Ebbo* to be reviewed; but after Summons, he would never appear to his death.

§ 157. CCLVII. A Council at *Mentz, An.* 847. repeated many Ecclesiastical Canons: Among others, Murderers still, instead of death, are but put upon long removal from the Communion, no, though they murder Priests.

In this Council a Woman called *Thiota,* was judged to be whipt, because she had professed to have Revelations foretelling the day of judgment that year, putting the People in fear, and even many Priests followed her as a Prophetess; she confessed that a certain Priest persuaded her to do it for gain.

CHAP.

CHAP. X.

Of the Councils about Ignatius *and* Photius, *and some others.*

§ 1. CCLVII. *A* N. 848. A Synod at *Mentz* under *Rabanus* condemned *Gotdescalcus* a Presbyter, and Monk of. *Rhemes,* as a Predestinarian Heretick. *Hincmarus Ep. ad P. Nicol.* reciteth his Hereties to be,

1. '[*That as* God *hath predestinated some to life eternal, so others to death eternal: That he would not have all Men saved, but only those that are saved, else he should have his Will frustrate, and not be Omnipotent.*

2. '*That Christ dyed not for all, but only for the Elect, who are the world that he redeemed; others he redeemeth by Baptism, but not by dying for them.*

3. ' *That no one shall perish that Christ dyed for.*

4. He addeth, (how truly I know not,) ' *That he asserteth a threefold Deity in the Trinity of Persons.*] They laid him in Prison, and *Hincmarus* wrote to the Pope to know what to do with him, saying, '*That he must employ a very able Man to keep him, for he wraps People, even the meanly learned, into admiration of him, reciting Scripture and Fathers distorted whole days together.* Some Bishops took his part.

§ 2. They say a Synod at *Tours* wrote an Admonition to one *Nomenoius* the King's Lieutenant in *Britany,* for Tyranny and Oppression, and casting out the just Bishops, and putting in Mercenaries, Thieves and Robbers; *Bin.* p. 638. and for despising the warnings of the Pope and Bishops.

§ 3. *Cavisius* tells us of a *Concilium Regiaticinum,* regulating Bishops, and *Cap.* 6. ordaining that the Arch-Presbyter examine every Master of a Family personally, and take account of their Families and Lives, and receive their Confessions: And *Cap.* 7. that a Presbyter in the absence of the Bishop, may reconcile a Penitent by his command. *Cap.* 13. That in the Villages Arch-Presbyters be set over the Lower-Presbyters. C. 12. That none that are denied Communion, may have any Military or Civil Office; and so every Bishop is Master of the Magistrates.

§ 4. CCLVIII. The *Saracens* in *Spain* persecuting the Christians, forced the Bishops to meet in Council at *Corduba,* and decree against Martyrdom, and the Memorial of Martyrs, saith *Binnius,* p. 643. ' [*Holding a Satanical Meeting, forbad Martyrdom, and took away the Honour of Martyrs, saying, That they that were not violently drawn to deny the Faith, but offered themselves to danger of their own accord, are not to be numbred with the Martyrs, not working Miracles as the Martyrs did, nor their Bodies remaining uncorrupt.*

§ 5. A Synod at *Mentz, An.* 852. did we know not what. But 853. CCLIX. one at *Soisons* was approved by Pope *Benedict,* and reprobated by Pope *Nicolas* (*Bin.* p. 648.) (yet both infallible.) And it is no wonder, for it is about a hard Point, and in which the Papacy is much concerned. When *Ebbo* was deposed and banished, *Lotharius* restored him for a while, and

and he intruded again, and ordained many Priests. *Hincmarus* succeeding in his life-time, rejecteth all those that he thus ordained. A Council is called to judge whether their Ordination was valid or null. The Council decreed, that ' *Whatever in Ecclesiastical Ordinations the said Ebbo had done after his damnation, according to the Traditions of the Apostolick Seat, as is read in the Deeds of the Popes, except Sacred Baptism, which is perfected in the name of the Trinity, shall be all void and null, and those ordained by him in whatever part of the world they shall be Fugitives or wander, because they cannot flie from God's judgment, let them be held deprived of all Ecclesiastical Degrees by the judgment of the Holy Ghost.*] And yet these Men had shewed Letters from the King and divers Bishops, for their reception as Presbyters, but the Synod said they were counterfeit.

Another Case was this, one *Halduinus* had been made Deacon by *Ebbo*, and Consecrated Presbyter and Abbot by *Lupus* Bishop of *Catalonia*. The Presbyter was ordained out of his own Jurisdiction to the Church of *Rhemes*: This being questioned, an Archdeacon shewed the King's Letters, commanding the Ordination of *Halduinus*. *Lupus* ordained him, in obedience to the King, without examining, (there being then no Bishop at *Rhemes*.) Whereupon the Synod decreed, according to the Canons, (say they) ' *That they that are made Presbyters without examination by ignorance, or by dissimulation of the Ordainers, when they are known, shall be deposed; because the Catholick Church defendeth (but) that which is irreprehensible*. And it was shewed in *Concil. Sardic. c.* 9. and other Councils and Decrees, ' *That the said Bishop touched nothing of his Ordination, but that he that leaped to the Priesthood without the degree of Deacon*, he ought to retire (*resilire*) to due degradation*.

* Because he was made Deacon only by *Ebbo*.

§ 6. Here you see the Nullification even of the Ordinations of an ejected Archbishop, yea, and of a lawful Bishop, when he makes a Presbyter of one that was by such an ejected Bishop made Deacon, and when he ordaineth unworthily without due examination. And if this hold, what interruptions have there been in the Succession of Bishops, especially in the *Roman* Seat!

§ 7. *Anastasius* a Cardinal, Presbyter of *Rome*, betook himself to the Emperor, solliciting him to depose Pope *Leo* the 4th, and to place him in his stead. The Pope hearing it, calleth him home to his charge, from whence he had been absent five years: but he would not return, nor appear, wherefore CCLX the Pope called a Council at *Rome*, which deposed him.

§ 8. CCLXI. *Ignatius* the Patriarch of *Constantinople*, called a Council to depose *Gregory* Bishop of *Syracusa*; They desired Pope *Leo*'s confirmation: He delaying it, dyeth. *Gregory* in the mean time prevaileth against *Ignatius*, who is cast out, and *Photius* put in, and a grievous Schism begun.

§ 9. CCLXII. *An.* 855. under *Lotharius Remigius Lugdun* and 12 other Bishops, are called a Council at *Valence*, who made 23 Canons or Decrees, with great Judgment and Piety, and shewed how much more venerable a Council of a few wise Bishops are, than greater Councils, where the most are weak. Their first work was against those that they called the *Predestinatianos*, where *Cap.* 2. they determine, ' [*Non ipsos malos Deum ideo perire velle quia*
' *boni*

' *boni esse non potuerunt, sed quia boni esse noluerunt.* Cap. 3. *Prædestinatio-*
' *nem electorum ad vitam,& prædestinationem impiorum ad mortem fidenter fa-*
' *temur: In electione tamen salvandorum misericordiam Dei præcedere meritum*
' *bonum, in damnatione autem periturorum meritum malum præcedere justum*
' *Dei judicium: Prædestinatione autem Deum ea tantum statuisse quæ ipse vel*
' *gratuita misericordia vel justo judicio facturus erat.---In malis vero ipsorum*
' *malitiam præscisse, quia ex ipsis est; non prædestinasse, quia ex illo non est.*
' *Pænam sane malum meritum eorum sequentem, uti Deum, qui omnia prospicit*
' *præsciviss & prædestinasse, quia justus est: apud quem est, ut S.* Augustinus
' *ait, de omnibus omnino rebus, tam fixa sententia, quam certa præscientia:* ———
' *Verum aliquos ad malum prædestinatos esse divina potestate, videlicet ut quasi*
' *aliud esse non possent, non solum non credimus, sed etiam si sunt, qui tantum*
' *malum credere velint, cum omni detestatione, sicut Arausica Synodus, illis Ana-*
' *thema dicimus.* The sum is, God's mercy goeth before Man's merit, but
his Predestination to punishment is only on the foresight of their sin, which
he decreeth not, because he causeth not.

Cap. 3. ' About Christ's death they like not those that say he dyed for
' all that from the days of Adam till then had been damned; but would have
' all take up with this simple Doctrine, that *God so loved the world, that he*
' *gave his onely begotten Son, that whoever believeth in him should not perish,*
' *but have everlasting life.*

Cap. 4. ' They conclude that all true Believers regenerate by water and the
' Spirit, have their sins washed by the blood of Christ: And they could not have
' true Regeneration, if they had not true Redemption. But of the multitude of
' the faithful and redeemed, some are eternally saved, because they persevere;
' others are lost, because they persevere not in the salvation of faith which they
' had received, and so make void the grace of redemption.

Cap. 6. ' About Grace and infirmed Free-will restored and healed by
' Christ, they exhort Men to stick to the Scriptures, and the Councils of Africa
' and Orange, and not to follow the Aniles penè Fabulas Scotorum, (I suppose
they mean the Followers of *Johan. Scotus Erigneuæ*, who was murdered by
his Scholars 833, whom *Godescalcus* followed). ' lest they should be corrupted
' from the simplicity that is in Christ: Remembring Christians that while they
' are vexed with the prevalency of the wicked in the world, they should not vex
' the sad Congregations with such superfluous things.

Cap. 7. ' They advise, that because Bishops were set over the Cities that were
' untryed and almost ignorant of Letters*, and unlike the Apostolick Prescript,
' by which means the Ecclesiastical vigor is lost, that they would petition the
' Prince, that when a Bishop was wanting, the Canonical Election by the Clergy,
' and the People, might be permitted, (because the King was used to thrust
his Favorites on the People,) ' *that Men of tryed knowledge and life, and not*
' *illiterate Men, blinded by covetousness, might be set as Bishops over the*
' *Flocks.*

§ 10. CCLXIII. *An.* 855. A Council was held at *Papia* in *Italy* by the
Order of the Emperor *Ludovicus*, for the Reformation of the corrupt Cler-

gy; where they ordered that the *Clergy* and *People* chuse the Bishops, and yet that the Laity on pretence of their Electing Power, trample not on the Arch-Presbyter; and that great Mens Chappels empty not the Churches: (with other old Canons recited.)

§ 11. *Lotharius*, that so mischievously sought for the Empire against his Father and Brethren, grew weary of what he had, and divided his 3d part, (which was the Empire of *Italy*, with *Burgundy* and *Lorrain*,) into three parts, and gave his Son *Lewis* the Empire in *Italy*; and his Son *Lotharius*, *Lorrain*; and his Son *Charles*, *Burgundy*; and entered himself into a Monastery: But *Charles* dying, the other two Brethren divided his Dominion, and *Lyons*, *Belanson* and *Vienna* fell to *Lotharius*.

§ 12. We come now to the Reign of Pope *Joane*, according to a great number of their own Historians; but *David Blondel* hath recited the Testimonies of multitudes on both sides, and after all impartially past his conjecture, that the Story was not true; whose judgment I reverence, and think most probable.

Whether at that time there was a *John* the 8th or none till him that some call *John* the 9th after *Adrian* the 2d, is uncertain.

§ 13. *Leo* dying, (if there was no *John* or *Joane* between) a Schism was made; the People most chusing *Benedict*, and the Agents of the Emperor, with part of the People and Bishops, chusing one *Anastasius* a Cardinal Presbyter, that had been Excommunicate by a former Pope. *Anastasius* thought his choice so sure, that entering *Leonina*, (the *Roman* Suburbs) he went into St. *Peter's* own Church, and broke down and burnt the Images, and with a Mattock cast down to the ground even the Image of Christ, and the Virgin *Mary*. They went on and imprisoned *Benedict*, (*quem omnis Romana Plebs eligerat*, saith *Anast. in Bin. p. 659.*) But while the great Men and Officers of the Emperor did their utmost to constrain the People to consent to *Anastasius*, they could not prevail, and so they were fain to yield to the multitude to end the Tumult and Confusion, and *Benedict* had the place.

§ 14. By this Story it appeareth, 1. That this *Anastasius* was against Images, and that was like enough to be part of the cause why he had five years left his Church in *Rome* before, and refused to appear before Pope or Council. 2. That when the Emperor and his Officers were so violent for his choice, even after he had broken down the Images in St. *Peter's* Church, it is apparent that the Party even about *Rome*, and in the West, which was against Images, was not small, though they made no stir.

§ 15. This Pope *Benedict* was he that confirmed *Hincmarus*'s Council, which nullified *Ebbo*'s Ordinations aforesaid, as is to be seen in his first Epist. *Bin.* p. 662, &c.

§ 16. *An.* 856. *Charles Calvus*, by a Synods concurrence at *Carissiac*, sent Orders against Church-Robbers very strict.

And 857, a Council at *Mentz* was held CCLXIV, where *Gunthar*, Bishop of *Colen*, sent a Letter, that '[*A terrible Tempest arose, in which the People*
'*for fear all ran into St. Peter's Church: And the Church-beams cracking*, *as*
'*they*

'they fell a praying to God for mercy, suddenly a mishapen Thunderbolt, like a
'fiery Dragon, pierced and tore the Church, and at one stroke killed three men
'among all the multitude, (though those three stood in several places) that is,
'one Priest that stood at St. Peter's Altar, one Deacon that stood at St. Denis's
'Altar, and one Lay-man at St. Mary's Altar: And six others were struck al-
'most dead, but recovered. At Trevirs also were many Prodigies.

§ 17. Pope Nicolas 1. is chosen by the Emperor Ludovicus consent, and all the People. He greatly advanceth the Roman Seat by his activity, and much by doing justice to the People that were oppressed by Tyrannical Prelates. He had a great conflict with John Bishop of Ravenna, who long despised him, and denied him his subjection: But the Emperor took the Pope's part, and so poor John was fain to submit, and cry miseremini mei, peto misereri mei, Anast. in Bin. p. 667. and to take an Oath of subjection to the Pope.

§ 18. The great Schism now rose at Constantinople, whether Ignatius or Photius should be Patriarch; Michael the Emperor deposing Ignatius by the counsel of his Uncle Bardas, and putting in Photius. The Pope kept up his power by interposing, uncalled, into all such matters. He sent some Bishops as Legates to counsel them by a Synod to decide the difference: When these Bishops came thither, they consented to Photius against Ignatius. The Pope said they were bribed, and false to their trust, and deposed them, (though he thought he chose the best he had;) of which more anon.

§ 19. Yet we have not done with worldly Prelates. King Lotharius was weary of his Wife, and loved a Whore (Waldrada.) He openeth his case to the Bishops. They call a Council, and approve of his Divorce, and his Marriage with Waldrada. The two great Archbishops of Colen and Triers, are the Leaders. The Pope is against it, and accuseth the Bishops of owning Adultery; They appear at Rome, and he condemneth them of Impudency, while (with some immodest words) they undertake to justifie the thing, (of which more anon.) He chargeth the Bishops of heinous Villany, and they despised him. He condemneth the Concilium Metense*, in which the Adultery was allowed. *At Metz.

§ 20. This Pope falls out with Hincmarus Bishop of Rhemes, justifying against him the cause of Rethaldus, whom he had deposed.

He sends Messengers to the King of Bulgaria converted in his days, whom the Emperor's Officers stop and abuse. The Adversaries of Images were still strong at Constantinople. Anast. & Bin. p. 670, &c.

Epist. 2. He useth a notable Argument for Images, viz. God is known only in the Image of his Works: Why then may we not make Images of the Saints? (But why must Men be compelled to do it, or else be Hereticks? and why must they be worshipped?)

Epist. 5. He is pitifully put to it, to justifie the Election of Nectarius and Ambrose, and yet to condemn that of Photius for being a Lay-man. And Ep. 6. the same again in the instance also of Tarasius.

§ 21. The 8th Epistle of this Pope Nicolas to the Emperor Michael, doth shew

shew that he had now shaken off the Imperial Power; and therefore chargeth his Letters as full of Blasphemy, Injury, Madness, &c. partly for being so sawcy as to bid the Pope, [*Send some to him.*] which he saith was far from the godly Emperors. Partly for blaming the deeds of the Prelates, when he saith, *Their words must be regarded, and their authority, and not their deeds.* Partly for calling the *Latine* Tongue *barbarous* and *Scythian*, in comparison of the *Greek*, which he saith is to reproach God that made it. Partly for saying, that the Council that deposed *Ignatius*, and set up *Photius*, was of the same number of Bishops as the first Council of *Nice*; where this high Pope's answer is worth the notice of our Papists, *Bin.* p. 689. ['*The small 'number hurteth not, where Piety aboundeth: Nor doth multitude profit, where 'Impiety reigneth. Yea, by how much the more numerous is the Congregation of 'the malignant, by so much the stronger are they to do mischief: Nor must men 'glory in numbers, when they fight not against the Rulers of the darkness of 'this world, and spiritual wickedness.---Glory not therefore in multitude,because 'it is not the multitude but the cause, that justifieth or damneth.---Fear not little 'Flocks*,&c.] This Doctrine was then fittest for the Pope in his Minority: But the Letter is a Book pleading for the *Roman* Grandure, and striving to bring the Emperor with others under his power.

§ 22. In his Answer and Laws to the *Bulgarians*,he disliketh their Severities against one that had pretended to be a Priest, when he was not, and had baptized many, concluding that he had saved many, and that they were not to be re-baptized, *Bin.* p. 772. No,not though he were no Christian that baptized them, as after *Consul. Cap.* 104. p. 782.

To the Case: Who are *Patriarchs?* he saith properly they only that have succeeded Apostles, which were only three, *Rome*, *Alexandria* and *Antioch*, but improperly only *Constantinople* and *Jerusalem.* (But why then are not *Ephesus, Corinth, Philippi,* &c. Patriarchates ?) And why had the rest of the Apostles no Successors ? Had they no Churches ?

§ 23. This Pope having Western security, threatned Excommunication to the Emperor of the East, unless he would depose *Photius*, and restore *Ignatius*; and threatned *Lotharius*, for the cause of his rejected Wife, and the Marriage of another, as aforesaid; and swaggered against *Hincmarus Rhemensis*, for his deposing *Rothaldus* a Bishop, and forced him to yield, and condemned his Synod at *Metz*, and would have proved that Pope *Benedict* had not confirmed it. He and other Popes did make the Contentions of Bishops as well as of Princes a great means of their rising,taking the part of him that appealed to *Rome* as injured, (and very oft of the truly injured.) By which means they had one Party still for them,and all injured persons were ready to flie to them for help.

He Excommunicated the Bishops of *Colen* and *Triers*. The poor Bishops that would fain be on the stronger side, began now to be at a loss, to know whether the Emperor or the Pope was the strongest. They followed the Emperor, and resisted the Pope awhile. The King and *Hincmarus* forbad *Rothaldus* going to *Rome*, and imprisoned him: But the Pope wearied them out,

out, by reason of the divisions of the Empire and Kingdom into so many hands of the *French* Line, that being in continual suspicion of each other, they needed the Pope's help.

Bin. p. 790. He ordereth Pennance (instead of just death) for one *Cumarus* that had murdered three of his own Sons, *viz.* That for three years he pray at the Church-door, and that for seven years he abstain from Wine three days in a week, and for three years to go without shoes, allowing him to eat Milk and Cheese, but not Flesh, and to enjoy his Possession, but not have the Sacrament for seven years.

§ 24. His Decretals begin, '*That the Emperor's Judgments and Laws are 'below the Canons, and cannot dissolve them or prejudice them.*

Tit. 4. 1. He saith, '[*All Patriarchal Dignity*, *all Metropolitical Prima-* '*cy, all Bishops Chairs, and the dignity of Churches of what Order soever were* '*instituted by the Church of* Rome : *But it's he only did found it, and erect it* '*on the Rock of Faith now beginning, who to St.* Peter, *the Key-bearer of eter-* '*nal life, did commit the Rights both of the Terrene and the Celestial Em-* '*pire.*

Reader, Had not the abuse of Humane Patriarchal Power, and of Excommunications got up very high, when this bold Pope made this Decree? What! All Churches in the World made only by *Rome* ? Was not *Jerusalem* , *Antioch,* and many another made before it ? Did Christ say any thing of *Rome* ? Did not other Apostles build Churches by the same Apostolick Commission as *Peter* had ? Is not the Church built on the foundation of Prophets and Apostles , Christ being the Head-corner Stone ? Did not others build the Church of *Rome* before *Peter* did it ? Did not *Peter* build other Churches before *Rome* ? Where and when did Christ give *Peter* the Imperial Power of Earth and Heaven ? Did he not decide the Controversie who should be the chief or greatest, with a prohibition of all Imperial Power, (*With you it shall not be so* ?)

§ 25. But the next Decree casteth *Rome* as low, as this over-raised it. ' *If any* ' *one by Money, or Humane Favor, or by Popular or Military Tumult, be intbre-* ' *ned in the Apostolick Seats, without the Concordant and Canonical Election of* ' *the Cardinals of that Church, and then of the following Religious Clerks, let* ' *him not be accounted a Pope, or Apostolical, but Apostatical.*] By which *Rome* hath had so few Popes indeed, and so many Apostates, that it hath no shew of an uninterrupted Succession to boast of.

§ 26. *Tit.* 4. *c.* 7. He claimeth Authority to absolve Men from Oaths, and all Obligations made by the violence and constraint of bad Men, and so absolveth the Archbishop of *Triers.* (A wicked Decree for Perjury :) (As if *in materia licita,* a Man that sweareth for Fear, were not bound ? And as if Man had not Free-will, when he is under Fear ?)

§ 27. C. 6. & 8. He decreeth that none can judge the Pope, nor retract his Judgments, nor judge of them, (contrary to many General Councils.)

He curseth from Christ all that contemn the Pope's Opinions, Mandates, Interdicts, Sanctions, Decrees, &c. c. 9.

Yet

Yet he faith that the Church of *Rome* may change, and mend its own Miſtakes and Decrees, *n.* 10.

'Tit. 5. C. 1. *No Cuſtom may occaſion the removal of any thing eſtabliſh-*
'*ed by full Papal Authority.* C. 2. *Other mens works approved or reprobate*
'*by the Pope's Decrees, muſt accordingly be judged, accepted or rejected.* C. 3. *They*
'*that have not the Decrees are to be reproved,* &c.

§ 28. *Tit.* 6. He brings down Emperors and Kings ſufficiently below the Prieſts, confining them to temporal things, and not to judge of Prieſts.

Tit. 7. He rebuketh the King for letting none be Biſhops but thoſe that he liked, charging him to admit none at *Colen* or *Triers*, till the Pope had notice. And before he told Emperors, that they muſt take no care what kind of Lords the Prieſts be, but what they ſay of the Lord; nor to note what Popes *be*, but what they *do* for correction of the Churches; For they are by *Conſtantine* called Gods, and God muſt not be judged of men, *Tit.* 3. *c.* 3. He queſtions whether *Lotharius* was to be called a King, becauſe he was an Adulterer.

§ 29. *Tit.* 8. *c.* 1. He decreeth that no Biſhops be ordained, but by the election or conſent of the *Clergy* and *People*.

☞ C. 3. That Primates and Patriarchs have no Priviledges above other Biſhops, but ſo much as the Canons give, and ancient cuſtom hath conferred.

☞ § 30. *Tit.* 11. *c.* 1. Is this, '[*Nullus miſſam Presbyteri audiat, quem ſcit*
'*concubinam habere aut ſubintroductam mulierem.*] That is, *Let no one hear*
'*the Maſs of that Presbyter, whom he knoweth undoubtedly to have a Concu-*
'*bine, or a Woman ſubintroduced.*

C. 2. *If Prieſts fall into the ſnare of Fornication, and the act of the crime*
'*be manifeſt or ſhewed, they cannot have the honour of Prieſthood, according*
'*to the authority of Canonical Inſtitution.*

(Yet our Canons will condemn him that refuſeth to take ſuch an one for the Guide of his Soul, or to hear him.)

Yet Can. 5. he ſaith, That we muſt receive the Sacrament from any Prieſt how polluted ſoever, and by the judgment of how many Biſhops ſoever he be Reprobated, becauſe bad men adminiſtring good things, hurt none but themſelves; and all things are purged by faith in Chriſt.

☞ *Tit.* 14. Lay-men muſt not judge of the lives of Prieſts, nor ſo much as ſearch into them.

§ 31. CCLXIV. *An.* 858. A Council at *Conſtantinople* placed *Photius* in the place of *Ignatius*, (of which before, and more anon;) *Ignatius* is baniſhed: we have not the Hiſtory and Reaſons of the Council.

§ 32. CCLXV. *An.* 869. A Council was called at *Tullum* of the Biſhops of twelve Provinces by King *Charles*, where, beſides other Clergy-mens miſcarriages, *Wenilo* Archbiſhop of *Sens*, was accuſed of Treaſonable Defection by the King. In which it's pity that Biſhops below the Pope ſhould have or pretend to the Power which the King doth intimate in theſe words, *Bin.* p. 798.

p. 798. [' *From which my confecration or fublimity of Kingdom, I ought
' not to be fupplanted or caft down by any one,without the hearing and judg-
' ment of the Bifhops, by whofe Miniftry I was confecrated King, and who
' are called the Throne of God,in which God fitteth, and by whom he decreeth
' his judgments, to whofe fatherly Correptions, and caftigatory Judgments, I
' was ready to fubject my felf, and at prefent am fubject.*]

You fee here to what power over Kings the common Bifhops (as well as the Pope) were got, by pretence of reprefenting Chrift, and of the Power of the Keys.

§ 33. CCLXVI. *An.* 859. A Council at *Conftantinople* condemned *Ignatius*, and again confirmed *Photius*, who with the Emperor *Michael* fent to the Pope to fatisfie him of all, and profefs enmity to Image-breakers.

§ 34. CCLXVII. *An.* 860. In a Council at *Confluence* the five prefent Kings of the *French* Line came to an agreement.

§ 35. CCLXVIII. A General Council was held at *Conftantinople*, An. 861. where 318 Bifhops (the fame number that was at the firft *Nicene* Council) depofed *Ignatius*, and fetled *Photius*, to which the Pope's Legates alfo fubfcribed, (the Papifts fay through fear;) fo that it was Papally confirmed. And yet here was much done for Images.

§ 36. CCLXIX. The Pope having condemned *John* Archbifhop of *Ravenna* who defpifed him, till the Emperor forfook him, in a Council at *Rome* he fubmitted himfelf to the Pope, and was reconciled.

§ 37. CCLXX. *An.* 862. In another Council at *Rome*, Pope *Nicolas* condemned the Herefie of the *Theopafchites*, that (they faid, made the Godhead to fuffer) it's like it was *Cyril* and the *Eutychians* old verbal Error by communication of Titles.

§ 38. CCLXXI. *An.* 862. A Council is held at *Aquifgrane*, in which King *Lotharius* defireth counfel about his Wife *Theutperge*; the Bifhops pronounce it his duty to put her away, fhe having confeffed Inceft with her own Brother, and allow him to marry *Waldrade*, he profeffing himfelf unable to contain. The Pope condemneth the action and them: The Papifts fay this was but a forged pretence. I only note 1. If they would deliberately forge fo heinous a thing on a Queen, what Heathens could be worfe than fuch Bifhops? 2. Did the Bifhops of that age think that they were bound to obey the judgment of the Pope, who thus oppofed him?

§ 39. CCLXXII. *An.* 862. In another Council in *France* (*in Villa ad fublonarias*) the three Kings again met for agreement.

§ 40. CCLXXIII. *Lotharius* appealing, defireth a Council in *France* by the Pope's confent : All the Bifhops of *France* and *Germany* meet at *Metz*, and the Pope's Legates with them: They and the Legates alfo fubfcrib* to the King's Divorce, and to more, which the Pope had before dec* red againft : (Did Bifhops then think the Pope Infallible, or not to be oppofed ?) The Papifts fay that the Pope's Legates were bribed.

§ 41.

§ 41. CCLXXIV. *An.* 863. The Pope calleth his own Council at *Rome*, and excommunicateth or curseth them all from Christ, and deposeth them *quantum in se.* But yet offereth forgiveness to all, save two, if they will subject themselves to him. The Bishops stand to it, that he cursed them unjustly: Must all the Kingdoms be thus ruled and confounded by one Priest, till matters between a King and his Wife be managed to his will and satisfaction?

§ 42. CCLXXV. In another Council at *Rome*, An. 863. the Pope curseth his Legates at *Constantinople* with *Photius* and *Gregory Syracusanus*, because they all crossed his will, which must everywhere bear rule.

§ 43. CCLXXVI. In a Council at *Senlis*, *Hincmarus Rhemensis* got *Rhotaldus* Bishop of *Soissons* deposed, and thrust into a Monastery, and another put in his place, notwithstanding the Pope's opposition, *An.* 863.

§ 44. CCLXXVII. Hereupon the Pope, in a Council at *Rome*, condemneth this Council at *Senlis*, and decreeth, That unless *Hincmarus* and the other Bishops do within 30 days restore *Rhotaldus*, they shall be forbidden their Ministery, and used as they used *Rhotaldus*: But they did not obey him, but put it to the venture.

And whereas the King had forbidden *Rhotaldus* to go to *Rome*, and the *French* Bishops pleaded this as a just restraint, the Pope answered, That no Imperial Laws must take place against Ecclesiastical. And so it came to the question, Whether the King or the Pope was King of *France*, or had more power over the bodies of the Subjects? Thus did the Papacy ascend.

§ 45. CCLXXVIII. A Council of Bishops and Lords together at *Pistis*, made Orders for Repentance, and restraint of Rapine and Plunder, *&c. An.* 863.

§ 46. CCLXXIX *An.* 864. In a Council at *Rome* the Pope deposed and excommunicated *Rodoaldus Portuensis* his Legate, with *Joh. Hicodensis*, for joining with the Synod at *Metz* against his Orders.

§ 47. CCLXXX. In another Council at *Rome*, An. 865. the Pope restoreth *Rhotaldus*: For *Hincmarus* at last let him out of Prison, and let him go to *Rome*, but would neither go nor send thither any Legates himself, as the Pope required, for his own and the Synod's defence.

§ 48. CCLXXXI. *An.* 866. A Synod at *Soissons* wrote to the Pope about *Hincmarus*, and against encouraging false Ordinations, unless after privately confirmed, *&c.*

§ 49. CCLXXXII. The Pope was so busie and troublesom with the *French* Bishops, making himself Judge in matters that he knew not, and restoring those that they deposed, that *An.* 867. a Synod at *Trecas* wrote to inform him of all that had passed for 33 years; how *Ebbo* and his Synod of Bishops had slandered and deposed the Emperor *Ludovicus Pius*, and how he did it to please *Lotharius*; and when *Ludovicus* was
restored

their Councils abridged. 273

restored how he fled; and when *Ludovicus* was dead how *Lotharius* with the base temporizing Bishops restored him, and after he had been condemned and resigned his place, returned to the exercise of it and ordained divers; and how upon the prevailing of *Charles* against *Lotharius* he was cast out again: and how after *Lotharius* got the Pope to appoint the hearing of all again when he was condemned, and how after this he was made a Bishop in *Germany*, and *Rhemes* was ten years ruled by two Presbyters, and how the Pope *Paschal* chose this Traytor to preach to the Heathens near him, and how *Hincmarus* was chosen, &c. as aforesaid. Such trouble did a *Usurper* put the Churches to.

§ 50. *Platina* saith that some say that after the death of Pope *Nicolas* the place was void eight years, seven months and nine dayes: But others say that it was void but seven dayes: so uncertain is the Papal History of succession. The next that we find inthroned is *Hadrian* 2d. [Saith *Harmar* to his in Bin. p. 876. *Ad hortos a Basilio spectante*]

§ 51. *Michael* at *Constantinople* having been long ruled much by *Bardas* (who was for *Photius*) at last giving up himself to drunkenness and other sins, by the perswasion of *Basilius* he killed *Bardas*, and made *Basilius* Cæsar: And after a while his vice gave *Basilius* the opportunity to kill the Emperor when he was drunk. See *Dion. Petavius* Hist. li. 1. chap. 12. Yet this *Basilius* washed his hands and made many Protestations that he had no hand in his blood. This made for the Popes advantage: Women and Rebels and Traytors and discordant Princes did much in raising him. This Regicide Emperor, as a second *Phocas* finds it useful to quiet his party by a change countenanced by the Bishop of *Rome*: And so he sets himself against *Photius* and sets up *Ignatius* again; and searching *Photius*'s servants, finds a book written of the Acts of the late great Council at *Constantinople*, which was for him and against *Ignatius*, and a defence of that Council against the Bishop of *Rome*, in which he dealt severely with the Pope. This Book the new Emperor sends to the Pope, and there it is read, stampt upon, stab'd with a knife, and openly burnt (and a miracle is said to be at the burning of it, some drops of rain that fell, not quenching the fire, but increasing it.) But their calling *Photius* a knave and burning his books, and condemning the council that was for him, will hardly keep the readers of his yet-preserved learned writings from suspecting that the Popes cause was not unquestionable, or at least, that the Pope was not taken for the universal Vice-Christ when *Photius* and his council did so little regard him. No wonder then if the Acts of a great council when they were against the Pope are called [*Nefardissimi Conciliabuli prophanata Volumina, quibus sanctissimum Papam Nicolaum susurrâ fauce latraverat.*] Yet our new Papists would make men believe that none but a few Hereticks refused subjection to the Pope before *Luther*. Were these Councils Hereticks?

§ 52. Here the Emperor *Basilius* was put to a hard strait about his Bishops: He wrote to the Pope (vid. *Bin*. p. 825. 826.) that almost all his Bishops had miscarried, both those ordained by *Photius* and those Ordained by *Ignatius*: they had turned with the times not knowing how the times would turn, and incurred such guilt that he desired the Pope to pardon them, lest he should want Bishops: silencing one party would not serve turn, while all had been so far guilty.

[*Tum à sanctissimo Patriarcha* Ignatio *consecrati secundum scriptura sua confessionem in veritate non permanserunt ; nec non et de his summis Sacerdotibus atque Abbatibus qui diversimodè scripserunt, quorum alii vi vel tyrannide, alii verò simplicitate aut levitate, quidam verò seductione et versutiis , quidam verò muneribus et honoribus diversimodè decepti sunt---Imò verò dicendum est quod pene omnes sacrati, tam priores quam posteriores qui sub nobis sunt, malè, et ut non oportebat, tractati sunt---Quatenus non Ecclesia nostra summis Sacerdotibus et Sacerdotibus, qui sub omni regimine nostro sunt, commune occurrat naufragium, propemodum universis illis de falsis et impotabilibus gustantibus iniquitatis Rheumatibus, Super his itaque postulamus compatientissimum Sacerdotium tuum, ut manum porrigat humanitatis et eorum dispenset salutem, &c.* saith *Basilius* ibid.

§ 53. Here also another difficulty arose (as there ever doth in ravelled works.) The Pope had been against *Hincmarus* and his Council for deposing the Bishops ordained by *Ebbo*. And yet to subdue the Greeks he was for the deposing of those ordained by *Photius*. This made him seem contrary to himself: *Anastasius Bibliothecarius* (who then lived and was employed at *Constantinople* in this matter) to reconcile the contradiction, saith that *Ebbo* was a true Bishop, but *Photius* was not, because he was a Lay-man before his consecration; and therefore his ordinations are nullities. This nullifying of ordinations maketh great disturbances in the Church. The present Bishops of *England* require those that were heretofore ordained by *Parochial* Pastors to be re-ordained, and on this and such other accounts about 2000 were silenced at one day (*Aug.* 24. 1662.) The silenced Nonconformists do some of them say that the Bishops have much less than *Photius* to shew for their authority to ordain. He had learning, he had the Emperors authority for him: He had lawfull Bishops to ordain him; He had a great Council or two to approve him and confirm him: And though he was a layman before, so is every one when he cometh to his first ordination. And though he was made Bishop *per saltum*, so was *Nectarius, Thalassius, Ambrose, &c.* And every Uncanonical irregularity nullifieth not the ordination. It hath been ordinary for Deacons to be made Popes: And is not that *per saltum*? why doth not that interrupt and nullifie the *Papacie*? But, say they, on this account 1. *Romes* succession is long agoe interrupted: There having been far greater incapacities in Simonists, common Adulterers, Perjured, Rebels, Hereticks, Infidels, (as Councils have judged.) 2. And (they say) that so the English Prelates are no Bishops, being chosen by the King, and wanting that choice of the Clergy and people, which the Canons have over and over again

made

made necessary to the validity of ordinations, are more null than those of *Photius*: And therefore we owe them (as such) no obedience nor communion.] Thus our nullifyings and condemnings proceed till most men have degraded if not unchristened one another. And he that is on the stronger side carrieth it, till death or some other change confute his claim, and then the other side gets up and condemneth him as he condemned them. And thus hath the Church long suffered by damning Divines, and domineering or censorious Judges.

§ 54. By the restoring of *Ignatius*, the Pope got to himself the reputation of some Supremacy, and obliged a party to him; which however it was not the greatest at the first, would be greatest when *Ignatius* his supremacy had advanced it: And with them he got the reputation of being just, indeed *Photius* seeming to possess the seat of one that was injuriously deposed by the meer will of the Prince, without sufficient cause.

§ 55. Pope *Hadrian* 2. (Epist. 4. ad *Ignat. Const.*) directeth *Ignatius* to forgive many others, but none of those that subscribed to *Photius* his great Council at *Constantinople*, because they reproached the Pope of *Rome*; where you may see 1. How dangerous it was then to be in a General Council, when, if they please not the strongest, they are ruined: And if they do, it's like enough the next age will damn them for it. 2. How much more dangerous is it for a Council to be against the Pope, than to be guilty of many other crimes; and how unpardonable it is.

§ 56. CCLXXXIII. *An.* 868. Besides the Popes Roman Synod that damned *Photius* and his Book and *Consi*· Council, there was a Council at *Worms*, which repealed many old Canons, of which the 14th. " is, *that if Bishops shall excommunicate any wrongfully or for light cause* "*and not restore them, the neighbour Bishops shall take such to their com-* "*munion till the next Synod.*

The 15. Canon is, *that because in Monasteries there are Thieves that* " *cannot be found, when the suspected purge themselves, they shall receive* " *the sacrament of Christ's body and blood, thereby to shew that they are in-* " *nocent.*] But this Canon the Papists are ashamed of.

" The 72. Canon alloweth *Presbyters (yea all Christians) to anoint the* "*sick, because the Bishops hindered with other business cannot go to all the sick.*] This intimateth that even then the Diocesses were not so great as ours that have one or many Counties, else other reason would have been given why the Bishop could not visit all the sick, than his hindering businesses: Would the Bishop, e. g. of *Lincoln* say, I would visit all the sick in *Lincolnshire*, *Northamptonshire*, *Leicestershire*, *Huntingtonshire*, *Rutlandshire*, *Hartfordshire*, *Bedfordshire*, *Buckinghamshire*, which are in my Diocess, but that I am hindered by other business? who would take this for the words of a sober man?

§ 57. CCLXXXIV. *An.* 869. was that *Constantinopolitan* Council which the Papists (damning some others) call the 4th. and the 8th.

General Council ended *An.* 879. in which but 102 Bishops condemned *Photius* and setled *Ignatius*, by the means of the Emperor *Basilius* and the Pope, who had before restored him. Here in Act. 2. The Bishops that had followed *Photius*, took the old course, and when they saw all turned cryed *peccavimus* and craved pardon, and themselves called *Photius*, *such a villain as there had never been the like.* (*Bin.* p. 882,) They said they *sinned through fear* and so were forgiven. Act. 3. Some Bishops that had turned, who were ordained by *Methodius*, were required to subscribe to a form proposed; But they told them that the late times had so vexed men with heinous subscriptions, that they had made a Covenant or Vow to make no more subscriptions but what they had done already, and the profession of their faith (like Nonconformists) and desired to be received on such terms without their new subscription. Act. 4. The Bishops of *Photius*'s party ordained by him were examined. And Act. 5. *Photius* himself, who would not enter till constrained, and then professed as in imitation of Christ to give them no answer to what they asked him; and is in vain exhorted to repentance. Act. 6. Many of the *Photian* Bishops repented and were pardoned: Others pretended that they had subscribed and sworn to *Photius*, where *Zachar. Calcedon.* shewed that the Canons were above the Patriarchs. Here *Basilius* the Emperor made a notable speech to exhort the Bishops to repentance, offering himself to lay by his honour and to lie on the earth, and let them tread on him confessing his sin, and asking mercy. Act. 7. *Photius* is again brought in, (and his staff that he leaned on taken from him) and he denyed to defend himself and to repent, but bid them repent. The Bishops of *Heraclea*, &c. rejected the Legates, and pronounced them anathematized that should anathematize *Photius*, and appealed to the Canons. Act. 8. They censured a Bishop that was against Images. Act. 9. They examined some great men that had sworn against *Ignatius*, who confest they had sworn falsely for fear of the Princes; but *Leo* would not damn or curse *Photius*, because he thought the Orthodox were not to be cursed. The 10th. Act. Containeth the Canons which they made; of which the Copies greatly differ.

§ 58. The 3 d. Canon saith that [*they ordain that the Image of Christ "be worshiped with the same honour as the Gospels; as teaching that by "Colours, which the Gospel doth by words:* saying, [*whoever adores not the " Image of our Saviour shall not see his face at his second coming*: adding "[*by the same reason we venerate and adore the Image of the Blessed Vir- "gin and the Holy Angels, as the scripture describeth them, and of all the "Saints. They that think otherwise, let them be cursed from Christ.*]

"Can. 6. *They anathematize* Photius *because he did excommunicate and " anathematize the Pope, and all that communicated with him.*

„Can. 7. *No excommunicate men are allowed to make Images.*

" Can. 8. Is too good for the Devil to let the Church enjoy viz. [*That whereas*

" *whereas it is reported that not only the heretical and usurpers, but some*
" *Orthodox Patriarchs also for their own security, have made men subscribe*
" *(to be true to them) the Synod judgeth that it shall be so no more, save*
" *only that men when they are made Bishops be required as usual to de-*
" *clare the soundness of their faith: He that violateth this Sanction let him*
" *be deprived of his honour.*

" The 10th Can. Condemneth them that hold, *That Man hath two*
" *Souls* (which they say *Photinus* favoured) *and cursed them from Christ.*

The 11th. Can. Tells us what men these Bishops were, and what they sought. It is [" *That all that are made Bishops bearing on earth*
" *the person and form of the Celestial Hierarchy, shall with all veneration*
" *be worshiped by all Princes and Subjects: and we will not have them to go*
" *far from the Church to meet any commanders of the Army or any Nobles,*
" *nor to light from their horses like supplicants or abjects that feared them,*
" *nor to fall down or petition them; If any Bishop hereafter shall neglect his*
" *due honour, or break this Canon, or permit it to be done, he shall be separat-*
" *ed for a year from the Sacrament; and that Prince, Duke, or Captain*
" *two years.*

" The 12. Can. *Princes as prophane men be not spectators of that which ho-*
" *ly persons do, and therefore Councils be held without them.* Either I understand them not, or it is in despite of truth that they say [" *Un-*
" *de nec alias reperimus Oecumenicis Conciliis unquam interfuisse: Neque*
" *enim fas est ut prophani Principes, rerum quæ sacris hominibus gerendæ*
" *sunt, gerunturve, spectatores fiant.*] *Binnius* noteth [*ex præscripto nempe Canonum*] turning an assertion *de facto* into one *de jure*, and an universal into a particular, by which licence of expounding what lye or blasphemy may not be justified! And why then have so many thousand been cursed from Christ by Councils for unskilfulness in words?

§ 59. The 14th. Can. secureth the Bishops admirably in despite of the old reforming honest Canons decreeing that [" *A Lay-man (not ex-*
" *cepting Kings or Parliaments) shall have no power to dispute by a-, rea-*
" *son of Ecclesiastical Sanctions, or to oppose the universal Church or any ge-*
" *neral Synod; for the difficulty of the things, and agitating them on both*
" *sides, is the office of Patriarchs, Priests and Doctors, to whom only God*
" *hath given power of binding and loosing.* For though a *Lay-man excel in*
" *the praise of piety and wisdom, yet he is a Lay-man and a Sheep and not a*
" *Pastor. But a BISHOP though it be manifest that he is destitute of*
" *ALL VIRTUE of Religion, yet he is a Pastor as long as he exerciseth*
" *the office of a Bishop, and the sheep must not resist the Shepherd.*] O brave doctrine for the *Roman* Kingdom! A Heathen, or Infidel, or Mahometan, or Arrian Bishop must not be opposed: He that is no Christian may be a Bishop. How much to be blamed were the General Councils that deposed Popes for Infidelity, Diabolism, Heresie, Simony, Perjury, Blasphemy, Sodomie, Fornication, Murders, &c. when a Pope that hath all these, and no virtue of Religion is not to be judged by Lay men, or opposed.

Q. 1. May a Prince save his crown from such? 2. May a man save his Wife from such, or a woman refuse their copulation, or defend her Chastity against them? 3. What if such are drunk in the Pulpit, are the People bound to be silently submissive? 4. Why did Pope *Nicholas* decree that none should hear Mass from a Priest that liveth in fornication? 5. Are Priests above Kings, or are they lawless?

Yet this very Synod of Bishops in their Epistle to Pope *Hadrian* sayes [*Cui consisti Synodo, qui tum imperitabant, Michael et Basilius noster, præsidebant,*] And *Basilius* and *Baanes* were now among them. And many Princes, especially in *France* and *Spain* have made strict Laws to amend the Bishops.

§ 60. One of the decrees of this Council was that *Photius should not be called a Christian*. *Bin*. p. 899. Col. 2. Yet the Apostle saith of the rejected; *account him not as an enemy, but admonish him as a Brother*. 2 *Thes.* 3.

§ 61. In *Bin*. p. 899. is an epistle of Pope *Stephens* to the Emperor *Basilius* which containeth the radical doctrine of all the Bishops rebellion and pride, viz. that Princes are only appointed for the things of the Body or this life, and prelates and Priests for the matters of the Soul and life eternal, and therefore that the Prelates Empire is more excellent than the Princes, as heaven is above earth. [" *Quandoquidem verbis qua ad usum vitæ, id est, rerum præsentium pertinent, Imperium a Deo traditum est, ita nobis per Principem Apostolorum Petrum, rerum divinarum procuratio est commissa: Accipe quæso in optimam partem qua subjicio* * --- *Hæc sunt capita curæque Principis imperii vestri. Nostri verò cura gregis tanto præstantior est, quanto altior est terra quàm cœlum. Audi Dominum--- Tu es Petrus--- de vestro imperio verò quid dicit--- Nolite timere eos qui corpus occidunt--- Obtestor igitur tuam Pietatem ut Principum Apostolorum instituta sequare, magna veneratione prosequare. Omnium enim in orbe terrarum, omnis ordo et Pontificatus Ecclesiarum, à principe Apostolorum Petro originem et authoritatem acceperunt*. (O horrid falshood, as before confuted!)

* i. e. I pray you give up your Crown.

§ 62. Yet this Council in *Breviar*. in *Bin*. p. 905. determine of the Pope, that being but one Patriarch, he cannot absolve one that is condemned by the other many Patriarchs.

§ 63. Laying all together I cannot perceive by historical notice, but that both *Ignatius* and *Photius* were both better Bishops than most were to be found; the first being a very pious man, and the other also a man of great learning and diligence. But the old contention WHO SHOULD BE CHIEF or greatest, made them both the great calamity of the Church.

I think it not in vain here to transcribe part of the summ of the life of *Ignatius* as written by *Nicetas, David, Paphlago* who was devoted to him, though somewhat said already be repeated. *Ignatius* (being of the blood Royal) was in quiet possession, when denying entrance or

Church

Church Communion to *Bardas Cæsar* for his reported Adultery, he provoked that indignation in him which depofed him. *Bardas* firſt perſwaded the Emperor *Michael* to aſſume the Government and not leave the Empire any longer to his Mother and Siſters. One *Gebo* then pretending to be the Son of Queen *Theodora*, and claiming the Crown, and many following him, *Ignatius* is accuſed as being then on *Gebo*'s ſide, The Emperor commandeth *Ignatius* to ſhear his Mother and Siſters, and put them into a Monaſtery: He refuſeth: The Emperor is angry and ſuſpecting him, cauſeth it to be done by others, and ſendeth *Ignatius* to the Iſland *Terebinth* and killeth *Gebo*. "*Within three dayes ſome* "*of the Biſhops who had ſubſcribed and ſworn to* Ignatius, *even that they* "*would ſooner deny the ſupream Majeſty of the Trinity, than without a* "*publick damnation they would ſuffer their Paſtor to be depoſed, became* "*agents to draw him to renounce his Place,* &c. *He refuſing*, Photius *is* "*made one day a Monk, the next day a Lector, the next a Subdeacon,* "*the next a Deacon, the next a Presbyter, and on Chriſts birth-day is* "*made Patriarch; a great and noble Courtier, the Emperors Secretary or* "*privy Councellor, famous for skill in things politick and civil, ſo flouriſh-* "*ing in the skill of Grammar, Poetry, Oratory, Philoſophy, Phyſick, and* "*the ſtudy of almoſt all Liberal Arts and Sciences, as that he was abſolute-* "*ly in them the Prince of his age, yea, and might contend with the ancients.* "*For he had a confluence of natural aptitude and force, of felicity, riches,* "*by which he got a library of all ſorts of books; and being deſirous of Glory* "*and Praiſe, ſpent whole nights in ſleepleſs Studies, and after ſtudied divi-* "*nity, and Eccleſtical Volumes.* Gregorius *Biſhop of* Syracuſe *(a cenſur-* "*ed Biſhop) ordained him:* Ignatius *is cruelly uſed, and its laid on* Photi- "us: *He ſendeth ſome Biſhops to* Rome, *and by them ſaith, that* Ignatius "*gave up his Place.* It's ſaid that ſome held *Ignatius*'s hand, and by force wrote his mark, and others wrote the reſt: but what's the truth is hard to know. A General Council is called: The Emperor and all his Princes, great ones, and almoſt all the City met at *Latin*'s poſſeſſion. *Baanes* and ſome of the baſer of the *Romans* are ſent to ſummon *Ignatius* to the Council, *(Bin.* p. 867.) He asketh them in what Garbs he ſhall come. "*Thy take time and the next day ſay*, Rhodoaldus *and* "Zacharias *Legates of Old* Rome *by us ſummon thee without delay to ap-* "*pear at the holy Oecumenical Council in what habit thou wilt according to* "*thy own Conſcience.* He goeth in Patriarchs habit. The Emperor commands him in the habit of a *Monk*. No leſs than ſeventy two witneſſes are brought into the Synod againſt him, Nobles and Vulgar; *Nicetas* ſaith perjured, of whom *Leo* and *Theodorus* two Noble men were chief; and ſome Anabaptiſts *(that is, ſuch as baptized men again, though not againſt Infant Baptiſm.)* Theſe ſwore that *Ignatius*, not juſtly ordained, had twelve years ago uſurped the place. And alas! there wanted not a Canon which would depoſe a great part of the Biſhops of the world, *viz.* that called the 30th. Apoſt. and oft renewed.

If

/ "If any Bishop using the secular power do by them obtain a Church, "let him be deposed."] They left out [*And those that Communicate with* "him] For which *Nicetas* accuseth the Bishops as falsly saving themselves. And alas! must all the ministers in England be deposed that communicate with any Bishop that gets a Church by the secular power? What a separation than must here be made. And would not this Canon depose *Photius* also? The Popes Legates, Bishops, *Rhodoceldus* and *Zacharias*, *aliique nefarii homines* faith *Nicetas*, cryed down *Ignatius* as *Unworthy*; then they beat and odiously abuse the good old man: And then cometh the foresaid forced subscribed confession (or forged.) After this its said that they sent men to kill him; but by old base cloaths and two baskets on his back, he past away unknown, begging his bread by the way. *Nicetas* faith that an Earthquake shook the City fourty dayes together, and frightned them to send abroad and proclaim security to *Ignatius*, who thereupon surrendered himself. *Bardas* convinced sendeth him safe to his own Monastery, and the Earthquake ceased; and the *Bulgarians* moved by famine and the Emperor's gifts, laid down armes and were baptized Christians. Pope *Nicholas* excommunicateth *Photius*, and the Emperor and all the Court. (*Bin.* p. 868.) A fire befals the Church of *Sophia*. The young Emperor groweth so drunken and prophane that he gets a pack of wicked ungodly men, and maketh them in mockery or play his Bishops, and consecrateth a Church for them, and maketh one *Theophilus* a jester their Patriarch, to turn Religion into a scorn, and then faith [' *Theophilus is my Patriarch*, " *Photius is Cæsars, and Ignatius is the Christians*.] And thus they by prophane witt derided the Bishops and Religion itself, to which alas, the Bishops ambition and odious strife did tend.

Photius was silent at all this. Another Earthquake frightned them again, the terriblest for a day and a night that had been there known. Upon this one *Basilius* a Bishop of *Thessalonica* went boldly to the Emperor and opened the sin of his prophanenefs disswading him from that wickedness that provoked God. The Emperor enraged struk out his Teeth, and caused him to be so scourged that he was like to dye. *Photius* cared for none of this, set his mind on the securing his seat and oppressing *Ignatius*, magnifying all that tooke his part, and encouraging false Stories and Calumnies against the best that were against him. One of the betrayers and accusers of *Ignatius* was one of his Disciples, and of his own name, made Arch-Bishop of *Hierapolis*, and then lost his Conscience and Fidelity. (*Bin*. p. 869.) It was but for presuming to Consecrate an Altar, cast down by the *Russians* and new built, which was taken after his deposition for a breach of the Law and Canons, and two Arch-Bishops, (ready at all times) were sent to pull down the Altar as Nonconformable, and to carry the stones to the Sea, and wash them, and then to set them up again. O that they would have washt their hearts from Pride and Worldly Ambition!

' O

'*Oh*, faith *Nicetas*, *What stupidity, what pravity of a perverse mind was
this? What excess of Envy? What study of ambitious Dishonesty? Did
thy daily meditation and night-watches, and innumerable Books teach thee
this? Did thy frequent reading and disputation, and striving for the
praise of learning teach it thee? Did the knowledge of the Old Testament
and the New, the sayings of the Wise, the Decrees of the Holy Fathers,
teach thee to persecute a poor man, and to vex and kill one of a broken
heart and spirit? Did not thy tyranical ejection of him satiate the im-
placable fury of thy mind*, &c? Thus *Nicetas*.

As much as to say, Much learning, and great power and places, are too often separated from Honesty, Charity and Conscience.

Here he mentioneth a terrible Dream of *Bardas*, and the murder of him by *Basilius*'s order, and the Emperor's consent; and how basely *Photius* cryed him down when he was dead, who was his onely Friend and Patron while he lived.

Next he tells us how the Emperor, by *Photius*'s perswasion, called a General Council, which deposed Pope *Nicolas*, as he had done *Phocas**. The other Patriarchs and the Bishops were assembled, and the Pope anathematized: And the Historian blames it as *causless*; but it was then commonly held, that a Council might judge and depose any Patriarch.

*Did the Church then hold that the Pope was the Supreme Ruler and Judge?

The Acts of the Council *Photius* sent to King *Ludovicus* and others in *Italy* and *France*, that they might depose the Pope (by two Bishops, viz. of *Calcedon*, and *Laodicea*.) It's said he spake evil to the Emperor of *Basilius*, and to *Basilius* of the Emperor. *Basilius* murdereth the Emperor, and the next day deposeth *Photius*, and thrusts him into an Hospital, and calls home *Ignatius*; and so gets *Ignatius*'s Party on his side, to which he resolved to add the Pope: Therefore sending to *Photius* for the Patriarchate Writings, and he saying he had left them all behind him, the Servants of *Photius* were seen striving about seven Bags of sealed Papers; which being surprized, were found to be the Acts of the Council, and the Condemnation of Pope *Nicolas*. *Ignatius* was odiously accused and abused in them. Many Pictures made of him: over one written *Diabolus*: over another *Principium peccati*: over another *Filius perditionis*: over another *Avaritia Simonis Magi*: over another, [*Qui se extollit supra omne id quod dicitur aut colitur Deus:*] over the sixth, *Abominatio desolationis*: and over the seventh, [*Antichristus*.] Reader, how shall a man know what History to believe that characterizeth Adversaries? and how little is the judgment and applause of man to be regarded, or their condemnation of us to be feared?

'*I would not* (faith *Nicetas*) *mention these things, but that I see the
Authors and their followers own them, and make* Photius *a holy man*.

The next part of the Book, faith *Nicetas*, ['*Syndicus in Nicolaum Pontificem Romanum tela torquebat, omnisque generis calumnias &
atrocia maledicta, in illius Sancti exaggerationem & damnationem com-*

'*plectebatur, impie ut tragico prope modo concinnitatus, sane quoque ipsius*
'*sygii doctoris magisterio &* Photii *ministerio dignus.* Gregory, Bishop of
Syracuse, wrote them out, and sent them to the King of France. Who
wrote truly, and who falsly, how should we now know? But this I
know,

☞ 1. That contending who should be greatest was the sin of the Prelates, and the plague of the Churches.

2. And that then it was taken for granted, that the Pope deserving it might be deposed.

The new Emperor Basil sent these Books to the Pope, who burnt them as you have heard (Great reason: but I would we saw them!) Ignatius being restored, excommunicateth Photius, and all that were initiated by him, and all that communicated with him. ('It seems they were 'much alike in the art of damning men, and separating them from 'Christ.) Then is Ignatius's Council called, where 102 Bishops damn 'Photius, depose him, and curse him from Christ; and the Bishops, to 'shew their holiness and constancy, would not write his damnation with 'Ink, but *with Christ's own blood*; (that is, the Sacramental Wine.)

☞ (And yet ere long they set up Photius again.) Nicetas blameth his Condemners, that went not so far as to prevent his Restoration. But how can Bishops rule God's Providence, or the mutable minds of Princes! saith he, ['*Nam qui per reconciliatos erat ejectus, & per hypocri-*
'*tas damnatus, is per eosdem quasi familiares postliminio recurrens, rursus*
'*Patriarchæ thronum per vim invasit----Cum omnes in sua testimonia &*
'*Chirographa perjuros, ut ipse erat, fieri coegisset, ut extrema primis dete-*
'*riora fecisset, omnium conscientias inquinavit & conspurcavit.*] Alas! if the Bishops will be perjured Weathercocks, and, as Hypocrites, cry *peccavimus* one year, and go contrary again the next, and change as Princes do, who can help it?

He saith now, new Earthquakes and terrible Whirlwinds did again afright men. He giveth us also many of Ignatius's Miracles, especially when he was dead. He saith Photius prosecuted him with malice when he was dead. He next tells us how after the death of Ignatius, Photius came to be restored; even by feigning a Pedegree of Basilius as from the King of Armenia, found by his skill in Antiquities; and by his great parts and elegancy winning upon him. He maketh Theophanes the instrument of the deceit. He won the hearts of all the Courtiers: so that within three days of Ignatius's death he was restored. Hereupon the Bishops turn round, and they that lately called him all that's naught,

☞ now magnifie him, (Bin. p. 875.) But all that Nicetas calleth *vero Christianos*, abhorred him.

(This maketh me remember the words of Erasmus in the life of Dr. Colet translated by Thomas Smyth, concerning the Bishop of London that then was) being an acute Schoolman, [*I have known*, saith he, *some such that I would not call Knaves, but never any that I could call a Christian.*]

stian.] Sad Prelates that *Nicetas* (and *Erasmus*) could not call Christians.

But the ambition of *Photius* tempted them to their mutability: He cast out the Bishops that were against him, and presently forgave and restored them if they would but conform. Yea, he dared to re-ordain those that *Ignatius* had ordained, supposing him no Bishop; but abhorring all that stopt him in it. But he proceeded to consecrate anew the Church Utensils, and say over certain Prayers (*If,* saith *Nicetas, they be not rather to be called Curses.*] *And* (saith he) *to make his sin out of measure sinful, when he ordained or preferred any, or changed Bishopricks, he made them conform by swearing and subscribing to him*; thereby binding all to him whom by Benefices he obliged *. So much out of *Nicetas*.

* How oft have such Oaths and Subscriptions been condemned in Councils! And yet alas!

§ 64. And now Reader, I leave it to thy judgment, whether *Gregory Nazianzen* knew not what he said, when he wisht there were no [*higher and lower*] among Bishops; and when he spake so much of their ambition, levity and temerity, and of the evil effects of their Councils in his time. Whether Patriarchal dignity was not a great temptation, when to the Son of a Prince on one side, and to the great and noble Secretary of the Emperor on the other side, it seemed a prize worth the striving for to the death? And whether it have not been the calamity of the Church, when two such extraordinary men, far above the common rank of Bishops, shall set an Empire and almost all the Christian Churches into Schism, Contention, mutual Persecution and Confusion, by so long striving Who shall be greatest? and drawing so many hundred Bishops into Faction, Schism, Perjury, and shameful mutations with them? And whether Christ did not (foreseeing such things) far otherwise decide this question, *Who shall be greatest?* in *Luke* 22. But if *Pride* turned *Angels* into Devils, it is not much to be wondered, if it turn the Angels of the Churches into the Ministers of the Prince of Pride and Darkness, and turn many Churches into a Theatre of Contention, and a Field of War.

§ 65. Yet here is one thing further to be noted, *viz.* the foresaid Contention that rose about the *Bulgarians.* These two great Patriarchs of *Rome* and *Constantinople,* were neither of them yet great enough, or satisfied with their jurisdiction, their desires being more boundless than *Alexander*'s for the Empire ; nothing less than *all the world* will satisfie one of them at least. *Nicetas* saith, it was by Famine, and a Treaty, and kind words of the Emperor, that the *Bulgarians* turned Christians. Some *Papists* would give the honour to the Pope, without proof, and cannot tell us any thing how the Pope converted them. But when they were converted, they sent to *Rome* for some Instructors: The Pope sent them two, and they received them. But they put the case themselves to the Council at *Constantinople*, Whether they were to be under the Bishop of *Rome*, or of *Constantinople*? The matter held a great debate. The Pope's Legates pleaded, that they had already received Bishops from *Rome*, &c. The *Greeks* pleaded, that their Countrey was part of the Empire, and under the Bishop of *Constantinople*, till they conquered it; and that they found there *Greek* Churches and Bishops, who were still there, and the Conquest did not translate them from the Bishop of *Constant.* to *Rome*. How the Controversie ended is hard to know: Some say that the Council gave them to the Pope, and some say otherwise. But this is confessed, that this *Roman* ambition so greatly displeased the new Emperor *Basilius*, that it turned him after against the Pope, and inclined him the more to restore *Photius*, which he did when *Ignatius* was dead.

§ 66. Here I would call the Reader to consider, whether the Pope's Universal Government was in those days believed? even by that Council which was supposed to be partial (by the Emperor's inducement) on the Pope's side. What place else could there be for such a strife, whether the *Bulgarians* were under the Government of the Bishop of *Rome*, or *Constantinople*; if all the World were under the Bishop of *Rome*? They will say that it was only questioned, whose Diocess or Patriarchate they were under? But *Rome* never pretended that they were of that Diocess or Patriarchate as anciently divided. But the question was, Whose Government they were now fallen under? And would any dispute whether *e. g. Westminster* were under the Government of the King, or of the Lord Mayor of *London*? when all the Kingdom is under the King. This Controversie clearly sheweth, that the Church then took the Pope to have but the first Seat and Voice in Councils, but not to be the Governor beyond his circuit.

§ 67. It is here also to be noted, that *Basil* the Emperor's revolt from the Pope was so great, that *Hadrian* is put to write sharply to him as accusing the Bishops of *Rome*, and derogating from them, admonishing him to repent; but we find not that this changed his mind.

§ 68. Yet one thing more is here to be observed. In the life of *Hadrian* the 2d (*Bin.* p. 882.) we find that the Pope taking the advantage of *Basil's* present state and mind, and the interest of *Ignatius* much depending on him, sent a new Libel to be subscribed by all the Bishops, before they should be permitted to sit in Council. The *Greek* Bishops grudged at this, and complained to the Emperor, [' *That the Church of* ' Constantinople *by these offered Libels, was brought under the power of* ' Rome, *by the doubtfulness of Subscriptions.*] But though *flebiliter conqueruntur*, they *complain with tears*, the Emperor was angry with them, and

and would have it; and some Bishops *non sine magno laboris periculo, libellos quidem vix tandem recipiunt,* with much ado were brought to subscribe, saying, It was *novum & inauditum.* The refusers *extra Synodum ingloril relicti sunt,* were shut out till they conformed: (Oh! that *Ingloril* was a cutting word.)

§ 69. The Emperor hiding his anger against the Pope's Legates (for the *Bulgarian* Usurpation) gave them great gifts, and sent them home. But at Sea they fell into the hands of the *Sclavonians,* who stripped them of their Riches, and the Subscriptions and Copy of the Council, and kept them Prisoners, and threatned their Lives: But by the mediation of the Emperor and Pope, they were delivered, and had some of their Writings again.

§ 70. CCLXXXV. *An.* 879. *Carolus Calvus* King of *France,* unjustly possessed the Kingdom of *Lotharius,* which by inheritance fell to *Ludovicus. Ludovicus* got the Pope to interpose, who sent his Legates to *Charles :* But the Bishops had not yet learned to obey Popes against Kings in power. A Council of Bishops called at *Metz,* give the Kingdom to *Charles,* because he was the stronger. This was called *Concilium Prædatorium,* a Council of Robbers and Traytors: And no wonder, when Bishops must be the Givers of Kingdoms. Was it not enough for the Pope, to usurp such power, to be over Kings, and dispose of Crowns, but ordinary Bishops must do the like?

§ 71. CCLXXXVI. Yet another Council against the Pope. King *Charles* had authorized *Northman,* a great man, to receive some Goods that were taken to belong to the Church. The Pope commandeth *Hincmarus,* Bishop of *Rhemes,* and the rest of the Bishops of *France,* to excommunicate *Northman. Hincmarus* and the Bishops refuse to obey him, only one *Hincmarus* Bishop of *Laon,* (*Laudunum*) obeyeth him, and publisheth the Excommunication. A Council is called at *Wormcia,* where *Hincmarus Rhem.* and the Bishops (the King consenting) condemn *Hincmarus Laudunensis,* for disobeying his Metropolitan, in obeying the Pope. He appeals to *Rome :* They will not let him go. He writeth. *Hincmarus Rhem.* writeth largely against him, (though his Nephew) shewing how he broke the Canons, how bad a man he was; how he had neglected his own Charge, left Children unbaptized, and for private quarrels excommunicated his Flock, and had silenced and suspended the Ministers under him tyrannically, &c.

Reader, Was the Pope's power yet fully received, when a Metropolitan was to be obeyed before him, and men condemned for obeying him?

§ 72.

§ 72. CCLXXXVII. Yet more sorrow. *An.* 870. a Council is called in *Villa Attiniaco* (*Attigny*) I will give you the Story in the very words of *Binnius* translated, [*When* Hincmarus *Bishop of* Laon, *for the cause in the foresaid Council expressed, had got the Rescript of Pope* Adrian *on his behalf, and had notified it to* Hincmarus Rhemensis, *and to King* Charles; *both of them, in hatred to the Bishop of* Laon, *decreed, That this Synod, called* Latrocinalis *, *should be called. There presided in it* , Remigius Lugdunensis *, Ardovicus Vesontiensis, Bertulfus Trevirensis, *with their subject Bishops. Herein* Hincmarus Rhemensis, *with King* Charles, *was the accuser of his Nephew* Hincmarus, *whom he had before consecrated Bishop of* Laon. *The Action brought against him was, That he had by Counter-writings defended the rights of the Apostolick Seat, which the Archbishop of* Rhemes *did endeavor to impugn and overthrow*. *And that, contrary to his Oath of Fidelity in which he was bound to the King, he had accused King* Charles *to the Pope of* Rome, *and had without his licence sent forth writings against him. And when* Hincmarus Laudunensis, *at the Pope's command, was ready for his journey to* Rome, *he was taken and spoiled by his Enemies, and brought into this false Council. Having heard the foresaid Complaints against him, he offered a Libel for his defence; but it was rejected, and not permitted to be read: of which when he again appealed to the Apostolick Seat, they did not only not accept of his Appeal, but also being prostrate on the ground, and pleading for leave to defend himself, he was not heard. Passing Sentence on him, they deposed him from his Bishoprick: and binding him in hard and iron bands, they cast him into banishment: And at last, which passeth all cruelty, his eyes pulled out; they perhaps blinded him that he might have no hope of returning to his Bishoprick.*] So far *Binnius*. And is it credible that such great and holy men as *Remigius*, and *Hincmarus* (even to his own Nephew set up by him) would do such things as these for nothing? Or that the Pope was then as high as since?

'By you.
'So great
and holy
a man also
against
the Pope.

*Luther was not the first.

§ 73. CCLXXXVIII. A Council at *Colen*, An. 870. for Discipline.

§ 74. CCLXXXIX. *An.* 871. A *Concil. Duzianse* was called of ten Provinces: where *Hincmar. Laudun.* subscribed a promise of obedience to the King and his Metropolitan. But this did not save him: Therefore he appealed to the Pope again, who interposed for him, but all would not do, nor serve his turn.

§ 75. Here falls in again the great Controversie of Pope *Joan* a Woman, but it is too hard for me to decide. He that will see what is said on each side, may read *Blondel* before cited. *John* the 8th is he that now reigneth, whom some late Writers are willing to believe some called Pope *Joan* in scorn for his failings. But he is after *Benedict* the 3d, Nicolas,

Nicolas, and *Hadrian* the 2d; whereas the *sere omnes*, faith *Platina*, the many Writers that mention Pope *Joan* place her before them all. And they make *John* to be a better man than these later do. *Platina* calling him *John* the 9th, faith, that *Carolus Calvus* being dead, Pope *John* laboured to have his Son *Ludovicus* succeed him; but the great men of *Rome* were for *Charles* King of *Germany*, and therefore laid hold on the Pope, and put him in Bonds in Prison (his Universal Sovereignty reached not far then.) But he escaping by the help of Friends, fled into *France* to the King, whom he unjustly pleaded for, (*Ludovicus Balbus*,) and there anointed him.

§ 76. Before this the Pope had anointed *Carolus Calvus* Emperor, unjustly confirming what the Bishops had unjustly done, as now he did unjustly stand for his Son. This contention among Princes, was the means of the Pope's power. Hear what *Binnius* himself faith of him, pag. 920. ['The Saracens *now depopulated almost all* Italy, *and all humane 'help failed in which the Pope trusted to expel them; and he was fain to 'buy peace of them by a yearly Tribute: which seemed to come by the righ-'teous judgment of God, that he might know that by the ill persuasion of car-'nal prudence, he had sinfully chosen, created and crowned* Carolus Calvus 'Emperor, *because he looked for more help against the* Saracens *from him, 'than from his Brother* Ludovicus; *whom, for invading another man's 'Kingdom, he should rather by Church-censure have exagitated, as* Hadr. 2d. 'did.] But when Pope *John* had stay'd a year in *France*, and the Saracens mastered *Italy* without help, he was glad to be Friends with the great men that imprisoned him, and to return to *Rome*, and take *Charles* for Emperor, after all. Yet is it noted as the rare Honour and Felicity of this Pope, that he crowned three Emperors, though he did it for two of them trayterously and unjustly, (the honour of a Pope!) *Platina* faith, he crowned *Charles* the rightful Heir, *Quo et liberius in urbe vivere liceret*, that he might live at *Rome* again (lest he should lose all.)

This *Charles* (faith he) also subdued the *Normans* in *France* and *Lorrain*, and forced them to become Christians, and be baptized: (And yet this is ascribed to the Pope's converting them.)

§ 77. This same Pope *John* the 8th, also at the desire of the Emperor *Basil*, and the Patriarch of *Jerusalem*, consented to the restoring of *Photius*, contrary, faith *Binnius*, to the Decree of his Predecessors, and of a General Council, and of all their Oaths.

§ 78. 'But what are Oaths to a dispensing Pope? faith *Baronius* and '*Binnius*. In his time *Ludov.* 11. the Emperor was compelled by *Aval-'gisus*, Duke of *Benevent*, to swear that he would never more invade 'his Confines, nor revenge his Wrongs: But the Pope absolved him
'from

'from this Oath, by the authority of God and St. *Peter*, affirming that
'which he did to save his life, was no hurt to him, and that it was not
'to be called an Oath, which was made against the good of the Com-
'monwealth, by how many Curses soever it was pronounced. *Bin*
'*p.* 920.

Epist.
2 for an-
her
murderer

§ 79. There are no less than 310 Epistles of this Pope inserted by *Binnius* in his Councils. The 12th is to plead with the Emperor, to forgive and restore *Modelgerus* a Murderer; and will you hear the motive? He had fled to *Rome*, and thereby merited pardon; ' *Nam pro tanti itineris labore durissimo, quem veniendo perpessus est, sicut credimus, aliquantulùm de peracto scelere indulgentiam meruit, ejus utique intercessionibus adjutus cui dictum esse à Domino constat*, Tibi dabo claves, *&c.* Accordingly *Epist.* 15. he writes to the Bishop to restore him all his Goods and Dignities, though it was contrived Murder, because God inspired him to go to *Rome*, &c.

§ 80. Many of his Epistles are to summon Bishops to come to *Rome*, and declare or threaten Excommunication against them if they come not; such an abused thing was Excommunication, by which the Pope made men his Subjects. *Epist.* 76, 77, 78, 79. He striveth to draw back the King of the *Bulgarians* from the *Greek* Church, to the Church of *Rome*, and denounceth Excommunication even to old *Ignatius*, and all the *Greek* Bishops of the Diocess of *Bulgaria*, for ordaining and officiating there, unless they give up the *Bulgarians* to *Rome*.

See also
Ep. 184,
185, 189,
9, 192.

Epist. 174. He writes to the said King, as if he were fallen from Christ, or his salvation lost, by submitting to the *Greek* Patriarch, rather than to him; as if the Converts of no Apostles but *Peter* were saved. And *Tibi dabo Claves*, and *Anathema's*, now are the two words that must subdue the world. The *Epist.* 175. to the *Bulgarian* Nobles, and *Epist.* 176. are to the same purpose. As the Religion of Saints tends all to Heaven, so did these Popes to the advancement of their Kingdom. And whereas we now take it justly for a suspicious sign of a proud hypocritical Preacher, that envieth the auditory and esteem of such as are preferred before him, as if other mens Preaching might not win Souls, as well as his; these Popes could not endure the crossing of their ambition, when Kingdoms took not them for their Lords.

Epist. 188. Is to justifie a man that baptized his own Child in danger of death, for which *Anselm* Bishop of *Lemovic.* judged him to be separated from his Wife. Were not these two Bishops judicious Casuists? Was either of them in the right?

After many other Epistles, striving with and for the *Bulgarians*, as belonging to his Diocess, he *Epist.* 195. chideth *Methodius* Archbishop of *Pannonia*, for turning from his Laws, and in special for celebrating Divine Service in the *Sclavonian* Tongue, which is barbarous, commanding him

him to do it only in *Latine* or *Greek*. You see how the Pope would edifie the *Barbarians* if he be their pastor. This is the first Papal decree that I remember against publick prayers in a known tongue.

But, alas! his neighbour *Italian* Bishops had not yet fully learnt the extent of his authority: sending for many Bishops on pain of excommunication to wait on him, and to obey him, old *Auspertus* Archbishop of *Milan* was one that disobeyed him; and being forbidden to officiate by him, conformed not to his silencing and suspending decree, but went on in his office as a Nonconformist. The Pope sent two Bishops as Legates to admonish him: He kept them at the dore, and set light by their message; for which the Pope chideth him, *Epist.* 196.

Epist. 197. He flattereth King *Ludovicus* to come to *Rome* and own him, in hope that he may be Emperor and all Kingdoms subject to him.

Epist. 199, 200, 201, 202, 203. He consenteth to the restoring of *Photius*, but chargeth him to give up the *Bulgarians* to his jurisdiction.

Many persons in many Epistles he exhorteth to break their Covenants with the *Pagans*, and chideth and threatneth them that did it not.

Epist. 247. The inclination of *Stentopulcher* a *Pannonian* Lord to the Church of *Rome*, brought down the Popes heart to dispense with *Methodius*, and changed his judgment to give very fair reason why Mass and Gospel and all might be used in the *Sclavonian* and all tongues; only to keep up the honour of the Latine tongue (and his authority) he commandeth that though the rest be done in the *Sclavonian*, yet the Gospel be first read in Latine, and then translated and read over again in the *Sclavonian*.

Epist. 250. 251. He approveth of *Photius*'s restitution.

Epist. 256. He is fain to chide *Auspert* Bishop of *Milan*; that Instead of fearing his sentence, he laid in prison two Monks sent by the Pope, and taken on the high way. But his heart came down at last, and he speaks *Auspertus* fair, and alloweth of his ordination of *Joseph* Episc. *Astensis*, though irregular.

Epist. 260 and commandeth his Arch-Deacon to obey him.

Epist. 261. After this he excommunicateth the Archbishop of *Ravenna*, and a great stir there was about that also.

Epist. 292. He had made one *Optandus* Bishop of *Geneva*: But *Opteramus* Archbishop of *Vienna* took it to be an usurpation on his right, and laid the Popes Bishop in a miserable prison; so far was he yet from being where he would be.

Epist. 294. Having excommunicated *Athanasius* Bishop of *Naples* for not breaking his Covenant with the *Saracens*, he absolveth him on condition that yet he will break it. The matter was that the *Italians* not able to resist the *Saracens*, those that lay next them under their power sought to save themselves by truce and tribute, by which means the *Saracens* had leisure to come further near to *Rome*; and so the Pope to keep them from himself compelled by excommunications the

Lords and Bishops of other parts to break their league, and stand up in arms to their own destruction.

That you may know what Bishops now ruled the Churches.

☞ *Epist.* 295. The foresaid Bishop of *Vienna* giveth one reason why he rejected *Optandus* ordained Bishop of *Geneva* by the Pope, *viz.* [" *Because he never was either baptized, made Clerk, acclamed, or* "*learned*] To which saith the Pope [*This should be covered in silence,* " *because* [*let us speak it with your charity*] *your holiness having nothing* " *of these was yet consecrated in the Church of Vienna.*] was not here good succession, and a holy Church. Bishops unbaptized that were no Scholars and no Christians.

Epist. 296. One Bishop by an armed band of men carrieth away another out of the Church, and the Pope interposeth.

Epist. 297. He again soliciteth *Michael* King of the *Bulgarians* to become his subject. The poor men that had chosen Christ, were so perplexed between the Priests that strove who should be their Vice-Christ, and King of Kings, that it seemed as hard to them to resolve the doubt, as it before was to be Christians.

Yet *Epist.* 307. sheweth, the Bishop of *Ravenna* being dead, that yet the Roman usurpation was not grown so high as to take the choice of the Bishop out of the People and Presbyters hands, except in long neglected vacancies (as *Geneva* aforesaid.)

Had not this Pope been kept under by Gods judgments, suffering the *Saracens* so to ruine *Italy* as that he still needed the help of Princes, he had been like to have overthrown *Rome* by his usurpations, setting both Princes and Prelates against him: But necessity made him a flatterer of the two Emperors of the West, the Emperor of the *East*, the King of *France*, the King of *Bulgaria*, the Princes of *Pannonia*, and all that he needed, as ambition made him still striving by *Tibi dabo claves*, and *Anathematizing* to affright the world to his obedience. I say not worse of him than *Baronius*, *Binnius*, &c. who have no other way to deny the Histories of Pope *Joan*, than by saying that this mans *baser compliance made him called Pope* Joan.

Baronius ad an. 879, *n.* 55. reciteth an Epistle of this Popes so greatly complying with *Photius* even against the [*Filioquen*] that *Binnius* would have us believe that *Photius* forged it. And [*"epistolam ipsam æterna obli-vione dignam nolui* (saith he) *hisce adjungi.*]

§ 81. CCXC. *An.* 876. *a Concilium Ticinense* maketh *Charles*Emperor when the Pope that had crowned *Ludovicus* before calleth*Charles*, *præscitum, prælectum et prædestinatum* hereto, with all honourable Elogies.

☞ And here cometh in a great controversie between the Papists, and the Protestants; *viz.* Whether Kings succeed by inheritance or by the election and making of the Pope. The Pope thought the craft of putting in a big usurping word, was as good as a Law to prove their own power to make Kings and unmake them. Accordingly this Pope when he
durst

durst stay from *Rome* in *France* no longer, lest he lost all, (being imprisoned for refusing the right Heir *Charles*) returneth, and speaketh some big words, and turneth forced consent into super-Kingly commands, and saith (*Bin.* p. 1010) *eligimus merito et approbavimus*] *solemniter ad Romani Imperii sceptra proveximus) et Augustali nomine decoravimus*,&c. And to disable the Kingly claim of inheritance he saith, [*Neque enim sibi honorem præsumptuose assumpsit, ut Imperator fieret, sed tanquam desideratus, et optatus, postulatus A NOBIS, et a Deo vocatus, et honorificatus ad defendendam religionem et Christi atque servos tuendos, humiliter et OBEDIENTER accessit,* &c. *Nisi enim talem cognovissemus ejus intentionem nunquam animus noster fieret tam promptus ad ipsius promotionem,* &c. So if the Pope had not liked him, the Emperor's hereditary right had never made him Emperor. And the flattering Bishops say to the Pope (*Bin.* p. 1010.) *ut non vos prius eligeret, sed contra vos eum et eligeretis et diligeretis: Et nos O Coangelice Papa, vestigia vestra sectantes et salubria monita recipientes, quem amatis amamus, quem eligistis eligimus,*&c.

And now comes in *Binnius* with his Comment and saith that [would our "refractory novelists, who with great temerity dare profess that the Roman "Popes in the crowning of Emperors have no other right then barely "ministerially to anoint and crown them, had but known these Acts (*)They (*) we "would from them have learned that that Pope John (*alias* Joan) did not now "only anoint and crown Charles, but also by Gods instinct did choose him know "to govern the Empire, and raised him to that sublime dignity honouring them. "him with the Augustal name, before he was anointed and crowned by him, "and that the Empire was conferred on him, not by hereditary right of suc- "cession, but by the will of the Pope who chose him and granted it to him.] *BE WISE* therefore *O YE KINGS, BE* instructed ye that are *Judges* of *the earth*:---Kiss the Popes foot lest he be angry and ye perish in the way; *If his wrath be kindled, yea, but a little,* &c.

§ 82. CCXCI. *An.* 879. *A concilium Pontigonense confirmed the choice* "of Charles where it's said (*Bin.* p. 1012) *et legit* Johannes Arietinus "Episcopus quandam schedulam ratione et authoritate carentem: Postquam "legit Odo Belgivacorum Episcopus quædam Capitula a Legatis Apostoli- "cis, et ab Ansegiso (*the Popes Vicar*) *et eodem* Odone *sine conscientia* "synodi dictata, inter se dissona, et nullam utilitatem habentia, verum et "ratione et authoritate carentia, et ideo hic non habentur subjuncta.]

§ 83. CCXCII. *An.* 877. A council in *Neustria* (*Normandie*) under *Hincmarus Rhemensis* rebuked *Hugo* base Son of *Lotharius* for rebellion and devastation of the Country.

§ 84. CCXCIII. *An.* 878. *a concilium Trecense* where the Pope was present excommunicated *Formosus Portuensis* (one of the former Popes preachers to the *Bulgarians*, and one that was after Pope himself,) Also *Hincmarus Landunensis* was restored blind, and joyned with the other that had his Place, (and so one Church had two Bishops in spite of his uncle *Hincmarus Rhemensis* that opposed it, and had both put him in and cast him out.

§ 85. CCXCIV. *An.* 879. Was a Council of the Popes at *Rome* for his unrighteous making *Ludovicus* 3. Emperor, the Pope challenging the first choice: But *Auspertus* Bishop of *Milan* came not and resisted, and though (as you heard) excommunicated by the Pope, did help to turn the choice to the right Heir.

§ 86. CCXCV. Besides some petty Council at *Rome*, there was *an.* 879. a General Council at *Constantinople* of 385 Bishops where *Photius* was confirmed, and the former General Council (called the 8th also) abrogated, and the word [*filioque*] taken out of the Creed: The Papists say that the Pope consented only to this as for *Photius*'s restitution, and not for the abrogation of the former Council; and that *Photius* corrupted his writing, and so they would make all writings uncertain. They say that Pope *John*'s epistle is by the wonderful providence of God found yet without some clauses added by *Photius*, whom they call the great architect of lyes: But the *Greeks* will no more believe the late found *Laterane* or other *Roman* Copies, than the *Romans* will believe the *Greek* Copies. And how shall we know which of them to believe? (And how little doth it concern us?)

§ 87. It must be a controversie also whether this Council must be called *Oecumenical*: I have oft proved that there was never any truly such as to all the world. There were 385 Bishops which is more than the first Council at *Nice* had, or most others: The Popes Legates were there; Oh but, saith *Binnius*, *It was not they but Photius that did preside: therefore it was not general.* *Ans.* 1. Let the world know then what maketh a general Council in the Papal sense: It doth not represent all the Church unless the Popes Legates preside. So much doth it import to know which Priest is the greatest.

2. But did *Binnius* forget that he himself affirmeth that at the first General Council at *Constantinople* the Pope did not preside by himself or any Legate. And yet that is one of the 4th. Councils equalled with the four Gospels; and the Pope dare not deny it left the *Greeks* further hereticate or anathematize him.

But saith *Binnius*, *It was no General Council because there was many frauds and impostures.* *Ans.* By that rule *Trent* had no General Council, nor *Florence*, &c. And so it is left to the judgment of all men to nullifie such Councils which they can prove to have had frauds and impostures. And must we also nullifie the Papacie of them that have had such frauds?

§ 88. Is it a grand question whether Pope *John* confirmed this Council. The approbation is extant. But the Reprobaters say 1. that he put in some terms of limitation (so far as his Legates went right) 2. that he after *ex umbone* condemned *Photius*, &c.

But 1. Is it not a General Council if the Popes Legates consent till he personally confirm it? Were all former Councils null, till the Popes personal confirmation? what are his Legates for then? 2. As his Legates

gates may miſtake, ſo may he himſelf: Is it null then till he rectifie his Error? 3. By this we ſee how impoſſible it is to know the new Goſple of the Papiſts; which is Canonical from the Apocryphal. For (as Pope *Martin's* *Conciliariter* after, ſo) here and elſwhere the Popes have ſo ambiguouſly given their conſent that no wit of man can tell what is conſented to by them, and what not (as their controverſies confeſſed, &c.

§ 89. At leaſt whether the Pope conſented or no, ſeeing in this Council the former 8th. General Council was condemned, and the *filioque* expunged the Creed, we ſee how ridiculouſly our late Papiſts argue from the conſent of Councils to prove the conſtant Tradition of the Church, ſaying, *Did the Council go to bed in one mind and riſe in another?* Did theſe 385 *Biſhops* do ſo? or did the former whom they condemned do ſo? Is this the ſmooth Current of Tradition? and may we know by it what our Fathers held?

§ 90. When the other Legates conſented, *Marinus*, who was after Pope, diſſenting, he was laid in priſon thirty dayes at *Conſtantinople*.

In the firſt Act of the Council, as *Baronius* tells us, *John* Biſhop of *Heraclea* ſpake much againſt the Church of *Rome*, which he ſaid was the original of all the miſchief that had befaln them; to overthrow and and cure which this Council was called. Much alſo againſt Pope *Nicolas* and *Hadrian* he ſpake, but for Pope *John* as being for them. In the 2d. Act was read an epiſtle of the Patriarch of *Alexandria*, to the Emperor for abrogating the former 8th. Synod: And *Thomas* one of the three Legates of the *Eaſtern* Patriarchs that conſented to the former Synod (the reſt being dead) made his penitent recantation. Then the epiſtles of the Patriarchs of *Jeruſalem* and *Antioch* for *Photius* are read, &c. In the third Act, Pope *John's* letters were read, as endeavouring the peace of the *Eaſtern* Church; which the Council took as a buſy pretending to more power than he had, and therefore ſaid *that "they had peace before his letters came, and that they were ſuperfluous.* And whereas he made it his buſineſs by this complyance, to get the *Bulgarian* Dioceſs; They ſaid this was to controvert the bounds of the Empire, and therefore left it to the Emperor. In the 4th Act the *Eaſtern* Patriarchs letters were read, diſclaiming their Legates at the laſt Council, as being not theirs but the *Saracens* Legates: and condemning that Council. The Papiſts think *Photius* forged theſe. Here alſo Lords profeſſed repentance, ſaying that the falſe Legates deceived them. In the 5th. Act *Metrophanes* Biſhop of *Smyrna* is accuſed of Schiſm, for being againſt *Photius*. Three Canons alſo were made. 1. That thoſe excommunicate by the Biſhop of *Rome* ſhould not be reſtored by the Biſhop of *Conſtantinople*. Nor thoſe that were excommunicated by the Biſhop of *Conſtantinople* be reſtored by the Biſhop of *Rome*: (and ſo *Rome* was ſhut out from troubling them with pretended juriſdiction.) 2. That thoſe that forſake their Biſhopricks ſhall not return to them. 3. Againſt Magiſtrates that enſlave and beat Biſhops. In the 6th. Act the Creed was recited (without *filioque*. And in the 7th. all those that should add to it or diminish are Anathematized.

§ 91. CCXCVI. A Council of the Popes at *Rome* excommunicated *Athanasius* Bishop and Prince of *Naples*, for not breaking his league with the *Saracens*.

§ 92. *John* dyed. *Marinus* is made Pope, commanded by his predecessor, called by *Platina*, *Martin*, who saith that he came to the Popedom, *malis artibus*, and therefore did nothing and soon dyed. But *Baronius* saith he lived long enough to do something, *viz.* 1. He condemned *Photius* again, and thereby provoked the Emperor *Basilius*; as if *Rome* did still set the imperial Church in contention, and hinder peace. The Emperor affirmed that he was no Bishop of *Rome*, because he had been ordained Bishop of another place. 2. He destroyeth what Pope *John* had done, who had deposed *Formosus* preacher to the *Bulgarians*, and Bishop *Portuensis*, and had made *him swear that he would never return to the Episcopal seat, but rest content with Lay-Communion*: But Pope *Marinus* recalled him to the City and restored him to his Bishoprick, and absolved him from his oath, which *Baronius* and *Binnius* doubt not but he had power to do; yea, and to dispense with the ill acts of the Pope, which he did out of private affects and partiality.

§ 93. In his time also the Church of *Rome* used Filioque, in opposition to *Photius*; Spain and *France* having used it before. Because, saith *Baronius* and *Binnius*, *Photius* had wrote about it to the *Ignorant and Schismatical* Archbishop of *Aquileia*. (There was it seems there so many of the greatest Bishops *Imperiti et Schismatici* in the Papal sense, as intimateth that as the Popes greatness rose in height, it did not grow equally in length and breadth.)

§ 94. *Marinus* having reigned a year and twenty dayes (a short pleasure to sell eternal happiness for) *Hadrian* the third succeeded him, and had longer part of the usurped Kingdom, *viz.* a year and three months and nineteen dayes. He also damned *Photius*, and was bitterly reproached by the Emperor *Basilius*, whose contumelious letters found him dead, and his successor answered them. (Was all the Christian world now (till *Luther*) subject to the Pope?)

Platina saith of this Pope, that[" He was of so great a spirit that in the
" very beginning of his Papacy, he straitway decreed that Popes should be
" made without expecting the Emperors authority, and that the suffrages
" of the clergy and PEOPLE should be free: which was before by Pope Ni-
" colas rather attempted than indeed begun. He was I suppose encouraged
" by the opportunity of Charles his departing with his army from Italy to
" subdue the rebelling Normans,] Rome was still on the rising hand.

§ 95. Stephen the 5th. *alias* 6th. succeeded him. In his time *Carolus Crassus* the Emperor is by a convention of Lords and Bishops deposed from his Empire as too dull and unworthy. (Kings were brought under as elective by the Pope, and now are at the mercy of their subjects

jects.) *Arnulphus* a base son of *Carolomannus* got an interest in the subjects, and they deposed the Emperor and set him up. *Baronius* and *Binnius* ascribe it to Gods judgment for *Charles* his wronging of *Richarda* a pure Virgin, yet repudiated by him. They say that he was reduced to such poverty that he was fain to beg his bread of *Arnulphus*, and dyed 888 in the 4th year of his Empire.

§ 96. The Letter against the Pope written by the Emperor *Basilius* the Papists will not let us see: But this Pope *Stephen's* answer to it they give us, which runs on the old foundation, trayterous to Magistracy as such. Telling the Emperor that ["*The Sacerdotal and Apostolical dignity is not subject to Kings, and that Kings are authorized to meddle only with worldly matters, and the Pope and Priests with spiritual. And therefore his Place is as far more excellent than Emperors, as heaven is above earth*] He tells the Emperor that in reviling the Pope of Rome *he blattered out blasphemy against the God of all the world, and his immaculate Spouse and Priest and the Mother of all Churches: And that he is deceived that thinketh [that the Disciple (Princes) is above his master (the Priests,) and the servant above his Lord. He wondereth at his taunts and scoffs against the holy Pope, and the curses or reproaches which he loaded the* Roman *Church with, to which he ought with all veneration to be subject, as King, who made him the judge of Prelates whose doctrine he must obey, and why he said* Marinus *was no Bishop,* &c. By this the reader may perceive whether yet all the Christian world obeyed the Pope, or judged him to be their Governor.

§ 97. How Pope *Formosus* set up *Wido* Duke of *Spoleto* trayterously as Emperor till he was forced to loyalty, is after to be said.

§ 98. CCXCVII. *An.* 857. A Council at *Colen* under *Charles Crassus*, made Canons against Sacrilege and Adultery.

§. 99. CCXCVIII. *An.* 888. A Council at *Mentz*,)while they were all in distress by the depopulations of the *Normans*) first decreed to pray for the King, and then tell him that "*Rex dicitur a Regendo: And if he rule piously, justly and mercifully he is justly called a King, but if impiously, unjustly, and cruelly he is a Tyrant.*

Can. 10. "*Whereas former Synods forbad all women to dwell in the house with Bishops, or Priests, or Deacons, except Mothers or Sisters; they now forbid these also, hearing oft of the wickedness committed by them, and that Bishops (or Priests) lay with their own Sisters, and begat Children of them.* But to secure them from all conviction for any such crime it is decreed Chap. the 12. "*that no Presbyter accuse any Bishop, nor any Deacon a Presbyter, nor any Subdeacon a Deacon,* &c. *And that no Prelate be condemned but under seventy two witnesses; and the chief Prelate be judged of no man. And a Cardinal Presbyter not under fortytwo witnesses; nor a Cardinal Deacon under twentysix: Subdeacons, Acolythes, Exorcists, Lectors, Doorkeepers, not under seven: and these without infamy having Wives and Children*] And indeed that Bishop that would lie with his own

own Sister in the presence of seventy two men that had wives and Children deserved to be blamed.

Chap. 15. *"One that wilfully murdered a Priest, was to forbear flesh and wine, and not to be carried in a Coach, and not come to Church in five years, and not to receive the Sacrament of twelve years after."*

§ 100. *Binnius* here addeth an observable note, that *Arnulphus* is called only King at first and not Emperor, it being *nefas* unlawful to assume the name of Emperor till it were given by the Pope] O brave Pope!

§ 101. CCXCIX. A Council at *Metz* under the same *Norman* calamities decreed such like things. *Chap.* 2. They decreed that no Presbyter should have more than one Church (unless a Chappel) and none take money for burials. *Chap.* 3. that Mothers or Sisters dwell not in the house with Bishops or Priests. But still capital crimes were punished but with excommunication and penance. *Chap.* 7. One that forced a widow: Another that killed his kinsman, and married his Wife, and swore to the Archbishop to forsake her and did not, was excommunicate. And so were some that gelded a Priest for reproving their filthiness,

§ 102. CCC. A Council at *Wormes* was called to end a controversie between two Prelates, Bishops of *Colen* and *Hamburg*, striving for *Bremen* (to have greater Dioceses and jurisdiction.)

§ 103. Next cometh the forementioned Pope *Formosus*, saith *Onuphrius* the first Pope that ever was made of one that before had been a Bishop. For the old Canons oft decreed that no Bishop remove from his first place: only when one was ordained against his will, and not consenting never possest the Place, sometimes he was accepted to another. Now was the fourteenth time that *Rome* had two Bishops at once by schism. *Sergius* got in to be Pope, but they forced him to resign, and banished him. *Formosus* was well esteemed of for his preaching to the *Bulgarians*; but Pope *John* 8 (some think for reproving his sin) deposed him (as afore said) and made him swear never to return to be a Bishop: But *Marinus* absolved him, and he came in thus perjured; notwithstanding the false pretence of Papists that the Pope can dispense with such oaths; the matter of them being a thing lawful, but not necessary.

Platina saith that he was suspected to have a hand in the tumult that imprisoned Pope *John*, and that he came to the Popedom *Largitione potius quam virtute*, *by gifts rather than virtue*, that is, by Simonie.

He did (lawfully if you will believe *Baronius and Binnius*) create, anoint, and consecrate *Lambert*, after his Father *Wido* Emperor (that was not Heir:) yet after consecrated *Arnulphus* (its like by constraint;) for such things the *Roman* Nobles hated him. But he got *Arnulphus* to *Rome*; who revenged the Pope by beheading many of the Princes that were hasting to meet him, which was not like to win mens love.

§. 104. He wrote an honest Epistle to the English Clergie, perswading them to keep up the ministry, and reproving them for indulging Pagan rites.

CHAP. XI.

The Progress of Counsels till Leo 9*th. especially in* Italy, France *and* Germany, *and their Behaviour.*

§. 1. CCCI. *Odo* Earl of *Paris*, having Usurped the Kingdom in the Minority of *Charles* the simple the right Heir, *Fulke* Bishop of *Rhemes* calleth a Synod and deposeth him, and sets up *Charles* (such Power had Prelates). Some say the *French* Chose *Odo* by *Arnulphus*'s Consent; and some say, that he dying, desired that *Charles* might have Possession. This was *Anno* 892.

§. 2. The great Devastations made by the *Normans*, burning Cities, Churches, Monasteries; and at last forcing Consent for a Habitation in *Neustria*, I pass over; and *Petavius* out of some Writers of their own will tell you, that when *Chartres* was besieged by them, the Virgin *Marys* smock, which King *Charles Calvus* had brought thither from *Besanson*, being carried, cast them into so great a Terror, that they fled away all in Confusion. Where they had this Smock, and how many Hundred Years after the Virgin *Marys* death it was found, and how they knew it to be hers, and how it was so long kept, and where, and why it did not many Miracles sooner, till above 900 Years after Christ, are Questions which I cannot Answer.

§. 3. *Italy* and *France* were all this while fill'd with Civil Wars. *Wido* and his Son *Lambert* being dead, *Berengarius* got Possession of *Italy*, whom *Lewis* after overcame, and was made Emperor at *Rome*, Crowned by the Pope: But three years after, taken by *Berengarius*, was Deposed, and had his Eyes put out. Yet after this *Berengarius* was cut off, and *Lewis* restored and Anointed by Pope *John* 10. *Rodulphus* King of *Burgundy* was set up by some Italian Nobles against *Berengarius*, and overthrowing his Army, was called King of *Italy*. *Berengarius* was kil'd by Treachery: *Rodulphus* was soon Deposed, and the Italians made *Hugo* Earl of *Provence* King. At last he joyned his Son *Lotharius* with him: The younger *Berengarius* prevaileth against him, driveth him to *Provence*; and is made King: Intending to marry his Son *Adalbertus* to *Adalcidis* the Widdow of *Lotharius*; she invited *Otho* King of *Germany* into *Italy* and marryed him, vvho after is made the first Germane Emperor: Of all which, more after in the particular Order and place. See *Petav. lib.* 8. *c.* 13.

§. 4. CCCII. *Anno.* 893. *Formosus* had a Roman Council, to Consult of some Relief of the Ruined Countries, in vain. For now men Secular and Ecclesiastical, Confounded all by striving for Rule.

§. 5. CCCIII. *Anno* 895. A Council at *Tribur* in *Germany* for Church Refor-

Reformation: Many of the Canons are to secure and advance the Clergy. The ninth decideth a doubt, if an Earl (or civil Ruler) Command the People ☞ to meet at one place (on Civil accounts) and the Bishop command them to meet at another on the same day, none shall obey the Magistrate (or Earls) but he and all his Company shall obey the Bishop and come to him. *Cap.* 10. No Bishop shall be Deposed but by twelve Bishops, no Presby- ☞ ter but by six Bishops, no Deacon but by three, *Cap.* 21. In Controver- ☞ sies, Lay-men must swear, but Clergy-men must not be put to swear, *Cap.* 22. There is allowed Tryal by fire, *Per ignem Candenti ferro Caute examinetur.*

§. 6. CCCIV. A Council at *Nantes* made more disciplinary Canons.

§. 7. Who was next Pope is not agreed: *Platina* and *Onuphrius* say, that *Boniface* was rightly Chosen, and Reigned but twenty six days, saith *Platina,* or fifteen saith *Onuphrius*; others (saith *Platina*) say twelve years: *Baronius* (and *Binius*) saith, that he was no Pope; and that he did but invade the Pope-dome, and was *homo nefarius, a wicked man, twice before this Degraded: First from his Deaconship, and next from his Presbyterate, Damned in a Romane Synod under* John *the Ninth: He addeth, that* (both *of them*) Boniface *and* Stephen *got the place by Force, Fear and Tyranny, and* ☞ *so it was but one Intruder, that thrust out another Intruder :* (But how then is the Succession secured. Why, it's added) *Yet* Stephen *is numbred with the Popes by the common Sentence* (or Opinion) *because to avoid the danger of Schisme, though he was* homo sceleſtiſſimus, *a most wicked man; yet all the Cler-* ☞ *gy approved him, and the whole Catholik Church, took him for* Christs *Vicar &* Peters *Succeſſor.* (How prove you that, why, because [*Fulke* Bishop of *Rhemes* owned him!] A Noble proof that all the Christian World did so!

§. 8. Say *Barronius*, and *Binius*, he began his Pope-dome with that Sacriledg, as to take the Corps of *Formoſus out of his Grave, and cloath-* ☞ *ing him in his Pontifical Robes,* (he set him in a Chair, and saith *Platina,* there judged him as no Pope, because he had been first a Bishop; which indeed, by the old Canons, nullified his calling; For *Formoſus,* was the first Pope that had been before a Bishop, as is said, unless the Emporour *Baſil* tru- ly charged *Macrinus* with the same): Having Expostulated with the dead man, * why he being a Bishop would take the *Pope-dome, he cut off his*
* *Luit-* *three four Fingers with which he had Anointed, and cast them into the River*
praud. l. *Tyber, and commanded, that all that he had Ordained should be Ordained*
1. c 8. *again :* (and so Conform to him.)

And they wonder with what face of Reason *Onuphrius* rejecteth all this as a Fable, when the Antient Monuments, Synodal Acts, and Historians testify it. Do you wonder at this? why it is because he was not willing it should be believed: a Reason that is not strange to your selves.

§. 4. CCCV. Pope *Stephen* called a Council, in which his usage of Pope *Formoſus* was approved, *Bin. ex Baron.* p. 1047. so ready were the Bishops
Anno 897 to follow the strongest side, in such things as the Papists mention with ab-
horrence. And (say they) this *portentum* attended the Synod, *That the Laterane*
☞ *Church, the chief Seat of the Pope, by the impulse of an evill Angel fell down*
quite

quite from the Altar to the doors: the Walls not being able to stand, when the Chief Cardinal Door was shaken with the Earthquake of so great a Villany.
§. 10. But here the Authors calling us *Novatores* (as if such Popes were of glorious *Antiquity*) are hard put to it to Vindicate against us the Popes infallibility! And how do they do it? Why 1ſt. They ſay that all that Stephen did againſt Formoſus, *a man ſtricken with Madneſs, did it fulfilling the perſwaſion of his boyling Rage. But in the lawful uſe of his Papal Authority, he defined nothing againſt Faith or good manners: For the Biſhops that were for this Cauſe called to the Council, and the Presbyters not unlike to* Stephen *himſelf, did proſecute* Formoſus *with the ſame hatred; and therefore pronounced that Sentence againſt him, which they foreknew would be pleaſing to a man ſmitten with Fury: ſo that we confeſs violent Tyranny, but no Errour in Faith defined or approved by him, Lawfully uſing his Papal Authority: And yet it were no prejudice to the Papal Seat, if we grant, that a falſe Pope, not lawfully Choſen, but invading and obtruded, did err in aſſerting Articles of Faith.* Thus the Author.

Anſ. 1. But if you grant this, is not your Succeſſion interrupted? 2. And was your Church a true Church, when an Eſſential part was Null? 3. However, was it the *Holy Church* when an eſſential Part was ſuch a Villain? 4. Will not your Argument as well prove every Biſhop, Prieſt, or man Infallible? For no one of them all can define falſly againſt an Article of Faith, as long as he lawfully uſeth his Power; For it is no lawful uſe of power that ſo defineth and believeth God. 5. But is all your foundation of Faith come to this? It is then but ſaying, when ever your Pope and Church Erreth, *that they did not uſe their Power lawfully:* And what relief is that to the deceived? How ſhall we know when your Popes have uſed it lawfully, and when not; and ſo what is true among you, and what falſe? 6. And were your Roman Council of Biſhops and Prieſts, all as bad as this Villainous Pope, and ready to pleaſe him in their Decrees: And was this a Holy Church, and like to be an Infallible Council: And muſt the World follow them? 7. And how then ſhall we know that it was not juſt ſo with many other former and following Councils; and that it will not be ſo with you again! O miſerable ſhifts againſt plain Truth!

§. 11. The ſame great Authors after *Luitprandus, l. 1. c. 9.* ſay, that *Stephen an Invader of the Papal Seat, by the faction of the Nobles againſt* Adelbert, *Prince of* Etruria, *was thruſt into priſon* An. 900. *and after he had been Pope Six Years, being ſtrangled in the ſame Priſon, ended his Days by Gods Vengeance in an infamous Death*]: Yet *Platina* ſaith, that he died the *firſt Year* and third month of his Reign; and *Onuphrius* ſaith, he ſate one year, two moneths, and nineteen days.

§. 12. It's ſtrang that *Luitprandus* ſaith, that *Stephen* condemned the Corps of *Formoſus* for being a Biſhop before, when *Platina* and *Onuphrius* ſay, that he himſelf was *Epiſcopus Anagninus*, when made Pope.

§. 13. And *Platina* ſaith, that [*This Controverſie* (againſt *Formoſus*) was great and of ill Examples; seeing that after this, it was almost always kept as a Custome, that following Popes did either Infring, or wholly undoe the Acts of those that went before them:] And yet were they Infallible?

§. 14. The next Pope was called *Romanus*, whose Life *Platina* thus Describeth: *Romanus as soon as he was Pope, presently Abrogateth and Condemneth the Decrees and Acts of* Stephen: *For these Popes thought of nothing, but to Extinguish the Name and Dignity of their Predecessors, than which nothing can be worse, or the part of a narrower mind: For they that trust to such Acts as these, having no Virtue themselves, endeavor to rase out the men of Desert, whom through sloth and malice they cannot match. You shall never find any to envy anothers Fame, but one that himself is Contaminated with all disgrace, and despaireth that his own Name should ever be Famous with Posterity: These are they that by Fraud, Malice, Craft, and evil speaking, do Bite, Tear, Accuse, and Worry those that deserve well of Mankind; like cowardly, or slothful, and useless Dogs, that dare not set upon wild Beasts themselves, but will bite those that are tyed, or in their Dens.]* So *Platina*. --- *Romanus* Ruled but three Months.

§. 15. Next Succeeded in the Popedome *Theodorus* 2. who saith *Platina followed the steps of the Seditious: For he restored the Acts of.* Formosus; *and preferred his followers: and Reigned but Twenty days.*

Next came *John* 9. (or 10. as others) saith *Platina.* [*He restored the Cause of* Pope-Formosus, *many of the People being against it: whence arose such a Sedition, that they hardly scaped a Battle. Baronius* saith, that *Ludovicus* 4. was deposed and blinded now by *Berengarius*, who assumed the Empire; and this Pope Crowned him, through fear! Yet after he was gone, he called *Lambert* to *Rome*, and with a Synod concurring with him, declared the Coronations both of *Berengarius* and *Arnulph* to be Null, as being extorted; and so took *Lambert* for King and Emperour: Did not the Crowns of Princes sit very loose, when it was but a Popes pretending that he Crowned them through Fear, and they were presently Deposed? Would these Popes have been Martyrs, or were they *Christians* or *Gnosticks*, that would sin, if they were but put in fear? And would not fear have made them own a Heresy, as well as other sin? On this occasion all was cast into Confusion: the Pope was fain to fly to *Ravenna* for protection, to him whom he had Crowned.

§. 16. CCCVI. This Pope called a Synod at *Rome* (that called *Overensis*, I pass by as of small moment) *An.* 904. in which he condemned the fact of Pope *Stephen*, decreeing that the Dead are not to be judged by men. But what became of the Synod of Bishops that had joyned herein with Pope *Stephen*? Why (*Bin.* p. 10.9.) they turn'd with the times, and did as such had used to do; *They asked forgiveness, and said, they did it for Fear*; and so, he that hath power by *Fear* or *Hope*, can make such Bishops and Councils Sin and Repent, and Sin again, and Repent again, as Interest altereth. They were pardoned. But *Formosus* preferment from a Bishoprick to the Popedome was Voted to be against the Canons, excusable

cusable only by necessity, and not to be imitated but in cases of necessity: His Ordained Clergy were Restored, and Re-ordinations and Re-baptizations, forbidden as unlawful.

§. 17. CCCVII. Another Synod he called at *Ravenna* for the same use, when he fled thither from *Rome*; of 74 Bishops. *Baronius* saith, He was another *Jeremias* sent of God, to pluck up and pull down what *Pope-Stephen* had done. *Platina* saith [*I think this came to pass because Popes were deprived from St. Peters steps; and chiefly, because the Christian Common-wealth had idle slothful Princes that would have Peters ship thus tossed, lest the Ruler if he look about him, should cast them out as evil Pilots.* Arnulphus was given to pleasure, and Charles *the simple or rather foolish of* France, *was little better; and so the* Hungarians *destroyed and killed in* Germany *and* France, *and the* Affricans *in* Calabria, *and had little resistance; Blood and Misery being the common Lot.*

He addeth, [*That this Pope John dying in the 2d. Year and 15th. day of his Reign, left nothing worthy of Memory behind him, but that He revived some Seditions that before were almost extinct.*

And it is a sad question, that *Herveus* Bishop of *Rhemes* put to him (*Bin.* p. 1048) "*What to do with these that are Baptized and Rebaptized, and yet after Baptism live as the Heathens, kill Christians, yea the Priests, sacrifice to Idols, eat things offered to them?* The *Pope* durst "not use Discipline on these, because they were Novices, lest he af-"fright them from the Church to Heathenisme again; but left them to "the Bishops Discretion and Experience, to do as he saw best.

§. 18. This *Pope* had a Corrival, which was the 15. Schisme: *Sergius* that had been made *Pope* with *Formosus*, and was put out and Banished, did now get in again; but *John* had the stronger part, and cast him out, and Banished him once again: *Onuphr. Chron.* p. 28. But had he been but strong enough, the succession had come down from him, as right.

§. 19. *Benedict* the 4. came next: "Nothing saith *Platina*, was done "in his time that is much to be praised; because both *Princes, Popes,* and *Clergy* were grown Debauched; bad Princes making *Popes* by Tyranny: Now the Line of *Charles* the Great, lost the Empire, *Ludovicus* the Son of *Arnulphus* being slain by *Berengarius*; and so they lost both *Italy, Germany,* (and after *France*) by their own, and the *Clergies* Wickedness.

§. 20. *Leo.* 5. Came next, *Anno* 907. Who thrust him in, I find not; but when he had Reigned but 40. days, his familiar friend *Christopher* had list to be *Pope*, and cast him out, and laid him in Fetters; where, it's said he dyed of Grief: where *Platina* well noteth, that ["*The saying is certainly true, that* Dignities (or places of preferment) "*receive more honour from the Men, than the Men do from the Dignities (or places)*]

§. 21. *Christopher* thus got in by sudden invasion, kept it longer than

Leo did, even near seven Months; and then he that had been twice *Pope* before, did once again try for it, and was too strong for *Christopher*, and put him into a *Monastery*. A Holy place then, no doubt, For saith *Platina* [*This was the only refuge of the Calamitous: For in those times bad Clergy Men were thurst into* Monasteries, *by way of Banishment, as heretofore into* Islands]

§. 22. The Man that did this and got the *Popedom*, was *Sergius* 3. who had been twice before cast out: faith *Baron*, and *Bin.* (p. 1052.) [*That wicked* Sergius (Nefandus) *by* Albertus *Armes got in: A Man that was the servant of all Vices, and of all Men the most wicked* (Facinorosissimus) *invaded the* Popedom, *and so was by all Men taken for no lawful* Pope: *To his horrid Sacriledge, he added the most impudent filthyness; and by* Marozia *(a great Whore) the Daughter of that most famous Whore* Theodora, *he begot his Son* John *(after Pope.)*] For many Historians tell us, how these two famous Whores did rule *Rome*, and make and unmake *Popes*.

§. 23. This *Pope* undid again all that had been done for *Formosus*, and against *Stephen*: For both the King of *France*, and *Sergius*, were Enemies to *Formosus*, for setting up other powers against *France*; and because his party was against *Sergius*: But I wonder that *Platina* tells us, that both *Stephen* and *Sergius* took *Formosus* out of his Grave, and the one cut off his three Fingers, and the other his Head; and both cast into *Tyber*! If this be true, he was taken up again the first time, and buried again. But I suppose that it was but his Fingers that were cast in the first time, and the Corps after; or else he was found after the first time. *Platina* faith, *It is reported, but not of any certainty; that some Fisher-men found the Corps, and buried it at St.* Peters *Church,* and that while it was doing, the Church *Images bowed to it* (It's well *Uncertainty* was put into the Story:) and that some thought this moved *Sergius* to envy; but that indeed it was, because *Formosus* party were against his Papacy. It seems by this that the Fisher-men found him after the first casting into *Tyber*; or else his burial by them could not be called the occasion of *Sergius* fact. So little rest had this *Popes* Carkass, being twice buried, twice taken up, twice judged, and executed after death, and twice cast into *Tyber*. But faith *Platina*, [*Popes now seeking and getting the Popedome by liberty and ambition, disregarding Gods Worship, exercised enmity against one another; no otherwise than do the cruellest Tyrants, glutting their own lusts the more securely, when there are none left to restrain Vices.* This wicked Man for almost seven Years enjoyed the fruits of his iniquity.

§. 24. Here *Baronius* and *Binius* forget to answer the great difficulty. 1ft. How the Roman succession escaped from being interrupted. 2. And also, where was the Roman Church while such Reigned as were no *Popes*. 3. And also, where was its Holiness and Infallibility, when it had the *worst of Men* (as they say themselves) thus set over them as

their

their Heads: But they are careful, [*Nequis pusillanimus ex hoc facto scandalum accipiat*, left weak minded persons should be scandalized by this: And they tell us as a wonderful providence of God, *that so great was the reverence to the Church of* Rome, *that even when such Men invaded the Popedome unlawfully, being even in the Churches censure rather Apostatical than Apostolical; yet those that did but hear who was* Pope (*especially the Northern Countries that were far off*) *obeyed them: so that any Man may understand by how great a providence God Governeth the universal Church, which when it was set on Fire at the will of Whores, and all mischiefs and scandals did increase, and it was feared it would be divided by a great schisme; yet God defended it from all heresy and schisme, all Nations persisted in one bond of Faith, and Covent of Obedience.*] Indeed Gods providence is wonderful that saveth his true Church from such wicked usurpers; and keepeth a Union of all in Christ: But this is no honour to the wicked usurpers; when now fifteen schismes had divided them, and many more afterward; nor was it any honour or blessing, to them that gave up their Kingdoms to such usurpers. If these were no *Popes*, but intruding Whore-mongers; was it a blessing to the World to be deceived, and to take those for *Popes*, that indeed were none. But had not they then a *seeming Church*, and indeed *none*, when an essential part was Null.

§. 25. CCCVIII. They say that *Anno* 909. A Council at *Soissons* ordered some Reformation.

§. 26. *Leo* called Philosophus Son to *Basilius Macedo*, this while was Emperour in the *East*, who being formerly suspected and imprisoned by his Father, upon some suggestion of *Photius*, and *Santabacenus* was revenged on them, when he Reigned, and deposed *Photius*, and put him into a *Monastery*. This is the rest, that Ambition procureth. Thus Sin is the misery of the Sinner. *Alexander* his Unckle was Gardian to *Constantine Prophyrus Leo*'s Son, the Father being Dead: *Nicholas* had before been made *Patriark*, and upon offence deposed, and *Euthymius* put in his place. But *Alexander* deposed *Euthymius*, and restored *Nicholas*: and having spent thirteen Months in Drunkenness and Lust, Bled to Death; and *Constantine*, seven Years old, with his Mother *Zoe* Reigned alone: *Constantine Ducas* rebelling, is subdued: The *Bulgarians* Conquered by *Leo Phocas* General; who thereupon aspiring to the Crown, was slain. Eight Years after, *Zoe* is removed, and one *Romanus Licapenus* made Guardian; and *Cæsar*, He advanced three of his Sons to the like honor, to strengthen himself, and made his other Son *Theophilact* Patriark, instead of *Stephen*, though he was but sixteen Years old. He Married his Daughter to the *Bulgarian* King; and then began to despise the Emperour, and prefer himself. God punished this, by permitting his own Son *Stephen*, to depose and banish him into an *Iland*: At last *Constantine* awaked, and deposed them all, and ruled himself, in Drunkenness, and Debauchery fifteen Years, and then dyed,

dyed; or as some say, was killed by *Romanus*'s Sons.

After him *Nicephorus Phocas* a successful Warrior, but a bad Man, Ruled; The Church called him bad for oppressing them with Taxes: His Wife *Theophanon*, and *John Trimisces* (who succeeded) killed him. Thus hath the World been Governed; and this is the profit of Ambition.

§. 27. The next *Pope* is *Anastasius* the 3d. who sate two Years, and two Months. In this time the *Eastern* Emperour *Leo* published *Constitutions*, which *Baronius* and *Binius* (p. 1053) deride as ridiculous, in imitation of *Justinian*, because he presumed to make Church Laws.

§. 28. *Lando* was the next *Pope*, *Anno* 912. and sate 6. Months and 22. Days; say *Baronius* and *Binius*, [*This Man at the importunate instance, of that most potent, most noble, and most impudent Whore* Theodora, *(who had prostituted one of her Daughters* Marozia *to Pope* Sergius, *and the other* Theodora *to* Aldebert *Marquess of* Tuscia, *and hereby had obtained or kept the Monarchy of the City,* (who was Pope if this Whore was Monarch) *did create* John *whom she most filthily doted on, a Presbyter of* Ravina, *the Bishop of* Bononia, *and Peter Arch-Bishop of* Ravenna *being Dead, he made him there Arch-Bishop. And a little after so filthy an act, he Died.* Luitpraud. *l.* 2. *c.* 13.

§. 29. Next cometh this same Man, *Anno* 912 *John* 10. saith *Platina* and others, the Son of Pope *Sergius* (by the Whore *Marozia* say some, but its not like, because *Marozia* killed him.) But its more probable, as *Onuphrius* noteth, that it was not this *John*, but the next that was Son to *Sergius* and *Marozia* This Pope saith Baron. and Bin. is he that the famous Whore *Theodora* for great comeliness of person doted on; and saith *Luitpraud*, got him made *Arch-Bishop of* Ravenna, *and after* Pope of Rome, *that she might not lye with him so seldome, as the distance between* Rome *and* Ravenna *would necessitate.* So [*say they, this impudent Man being powerful at* Rome, *by the strength of a Whore, is made a false Pope and wicked invader of the Seat*] where they shew how this Whore obtained her power. But was this no interruption of the succession neither, nor a nullifying of the Papal Church, while he sate 13. or as *Onuphrius,* 14. Years and more. No saith *Baron.* (and *Bin.*) He that was an *Invader, Theif,* and *Robber, by the after Consent of the Roman Clergy,* became *the lawful Pope of* Rome. 1. We see then, what the Romane Clergy were, that would have such a *Pope.* 2. But they give no proof of any such Consent; but say, It is *verisimile.* 3. And where was the Church till that Consent, or at least its Holiness. 4. Can such Mens Consent make a *Pope* of an *uncapable* person? Will no Wickedness incapacitate?

§. 30. Say the foresaid Authors, in this *Popes* time *Sisevandus* Bishop of *Compostella,* finding the great diversity of the *Roman* and *Mozarabick* Liturgy, altered his by the *Popes* consent.

After

After *Herveus*, one *Seulphus* was Arch-Bishop of *Rhemes*. *Heribert* Earl of *Aquitane*, considering that the Bishop of *Rhemes* Anointeth the King of *France*, bargained to have his Son made next Bishop, that thereby he might get the Crown. In haste *Seulphus* is Poysoned, because they could not stay till he dyed. *Heribert's* Son, not yet Five Years old, is made Arch-Bishop. (*O see'm in auditum*, say *Baronius* and *Binius*.) *This monstrous Election, (say they) never before seen or heard of in the Christian World, nor perhaps thought of,* Pope John *did not only not disallow, but ratifyed.* —— *And by this Fact, the Infamous* Pope *gave an Example to many Princes, not only in that, but the following Ages, (Alas, for Grief !) to procure Lads that were their Kindred, to be thrust into the Chief Seats, (or Bishopricks) to the great Mischief of the Church.*] *A Work (say they) indeed, worthy such a Pope, whom an Infamous Woman, by an Infamous Work, had thrust into St.* Peter's *Chair*.

Qu. Were such Villaines as Infallible as others? Did their Love, Honesty, and Chastity fail; and yet, Were they secured against the Failing of their Faith? Or, Had they a Sincere Faith, that had no other Grace? And, Could these forgive Sins, and deliver Souls out of *Purgatory* ?

When he had sate Fourteen Years, or Sixteen, (saith *Baronius* and *Binius*) Marquess Wido, *by the Persivasion of his Wife* Marozia, (Pope Sergius *Whore*) *for the sake of his Brother* Peter, *whom they hated, cast him out of his Seat into a Prison; where shortly after, he was Choked with a Pillow: And so the Invader, and unjust Deteiner of the Apostolick-Seat, had an End worthy of his Wickedness. And he, that by the Impudent Mother,* Theodora, *had violently seized on the Holy Seat, by her as Impudent Daughter, was by* God's *just Judgment Ejected, Imprisoned, and Deprived both of it, and of his Life.* Ex Luitpr. & Frodoaldo, *Baron*.

§. 31. CCCIX. *Anno* 912. A Synod at *Confluence*, decreed as against Incest, That none Marry within the seventh Degree of Kindred. Was that Divine Law?

§. 32. Two or Three other *Synods* at *Trosleium* are mentioned, about small Matters ; and One at *Duisburge*, to Excommunicate some that put out the Bishops Eyes.

§. 33. The next *Pope*, is *Leo* the Sixth ; and Dyed after Seven (or Six) Months, and Fifteen Dayes.

§. 34. Next, *Anno* 929. succeeded *Stephen* the Eighth, (or Seventh) and sate but two Years, one Month, and fifteen Dayes. How they were so fast dispatched, I omit.

§. 35. Next comes the Son of *Marozia*, Pope *Sergius* his Bastard, call'd *John the Eleventh :* His Mother, and Father-in-Law. *Wido*, got him in *Anno* 931. even when he was a Lad under Age. His Brother *Albericus*, (saith *Baronius*) did keep this *Pope* in Prison to his Death. But the Case was this, (vid. *Ein.* p. 1055.) [*Wido being Dead*, Marezia rozia *offereth the Dominion of* Rome *to his own Brother* Hugo, *on condition he would Marry her: He accepteth the Condition; and secretly entering the Castle of St.* Angelo, *after he had committed Incest with her, his Brother's Widow, he despised the* Romans. *When his Son-in-Law* Albericus, *by his Mother* Marozia's *Command, poured out Water to wash his Hands, he stroke him on the Face for pouring too much. To Revenge this Wrong,* Albericus *stir'd up the* Romans *to a Defection; and having by Assaults of the Castle, put to Flight his Father-in-Law* Hugo, *he commanded his Mother* Marozia, *and his Bastard-Brother, the Counterfeit Pope* John, *to be kept in Prison; in which the violent Invader dyed, being violently cast out, after for five Years, and some Months, he had rather filthily Defiled, than Ruled the Apostolick Seat.*] Saith *Binius* out of *Luitprandus* and *Baronius:* Calling him a Monster; and yet Magnifying *Rome,* because such were Obeyed.

§. 36. CCCX. *Anno* 932. A small Council at *Erford* in *Germany*, under King *Henry,* decreed, 1. That Holy-Dayes be kept for an Honourable Commemoration of the Twelve Apostles, and Fasting on the Evens. 2. That no State-Meetings be kept on the *Lord's-Dayes*, or other *Holy-Dayes*; nor Christians then cited to the Courts of Justice. 3. Nor when he is going to Church. 4. That scandalous Ministers be tryed. 5. That no private Christian make, or impose any Fast on himself, without the Bishop, or his Missionaries Consent. *(*An unreasonable Usurpation! Must the Bishop needs know all the Reasons that every Man hath for Fasting, and be Judge of them? But sure, the *Bishop's Diocess* had not then so many hundred Parishes, and so many Counties, as they have now: Else, by that time, the Bishop and his Commissary had heard a Hundred Thousand, or Fifty Thousand Persons, tell him, what Reasons they had to Fast besides the common Fasts, at any time, or on any special Occasions, much of his time would be taken up.

§. 37. *Anno* 935. A Council at *Rhemes* against Church-Robbers, &c.

§. 38. *Anno* 936. *Leo* the Seventh was made *Pope,* after *John* the Eleventh. In that time *Hugo,* that was got away from *Albericus,* had got an Army, and Besieged *Rome.* A Match was made for *Albericus* to Marry *Hugo's* Daughter: And so *Marozia's* Husband and Son were agreed, by the means of *Odo,* Abbot of *Cluniac.*

§. 39. *Henry,* King of *Germany, the Glory* (saith *Baronius* and *Binius*) *of Christian Religion, dyed at this time; who, after many other Nations, Converted also the King of* Denmark *to the Christian Faith: and left his Son* Otho, *the Heir of his Piety and Valour.* Yet are not other *Papists* ashamed to say, That all these Nations were Converted by the *Pope*; who was the great Scandal, that hindred the Conversion of the World.

§. 40. But (say the same Authors) Manasses, *Bishop of* Arles, *now troubled the Church: Being an Ambitious Man, not contented with his Seat, by the means of* Hugo *King of* Italy, *he also invaded the Bishopricks of*
Verona,

and their Councils abridged.

Verona, *and of* Trent, *and of* Mantua, *and of* Milan *it self!* (O now the Church prosper'd!) *Saying, That he did it by the Example of the Prince of the Apostles; who at once possessed* Rome, Antioch, *and* Alexandria.] Ex *Luitprand.* (And could the *Pope* blame him, that would be Bishop at the *Antipodes*, and have all the World?) But its strange, that Men should talk of Bishops Ambition, as of a strange thing, in the Year 937.

§. 41. *Anno* 939. Pope *Stephen* the Nineth was chosen by *Otho* of *Germany*, without the *Cardinal-Clergy*, who had neither Power, nor Virtue enough, to choose: And the City was under the Power of *Albericus*, who Tyrannized over them: And because he had not the Choice he caused some Fellows so to cut and mangle the Face of the *Pope*, that he would never after be seen abroad, but kept close till he dyed; which was after Three Years. This *Otho* resolved to Revenge on *Albericus* : And also, the War between *Hugo*, and *Albericus*, broke out again. *Platina* saith, That *Hugo* was *about to Revenge the* Pope, *but then Dyed.*

§. 42. A Synod was at *Narbon*, to end the Contention of two Bishops, about the Extent of their Dioceses, and Jurisdiction.

§. 43. CCCXI. If yet you perceive not the sad State of the Church, by Men's striving for Church-Dignities ; a Council at *Soissons*, *Anno* 940. will tell you more. You heard before, how the Earl of *Aquitane* had got his Son to be made Arch-Bishop of *Rhemes :* The Child in coats, was but Five Years old: It happened, that he was put out again for his Infancy, or Non-Age; and *Artaldus*, a *Monk*, chosen in his stead. This Council of Bishops, was to decide the Case between the two Arch-Bishops. The Objection against one, was his Infancy, and his Father's ill means to bring him in: The Objection against the other, was *Perjury*; He had sworn, that he would never accept an Arch-Bishoprick: (Alas! Must the Church of *France* be Headed by one of these ; an Infant, or a Perjured *Monk!*) The *Synod* cast out the Perjured *Monk*, and judged the Seat to the Infant, as being lawfully Chosen ; (Power made it a Lawful Call.) And the Bishops went to *Rhemes*, and Consecrated him.

Binius,
p. 1057.
Frodoard.
in Chronic.

§. 44. In the Year 920. the *French* Nobles, by consent at *Soissons*, had Revolted from King *Charles*; because he took *Haganon*, a Man of low Quality, into his Privy-Council, and made him Great: *Herveus*, Bishop of *Rhemes*, had partly healed this Breach. But, *Anno* 922. it broke out again ; and the Nobles chose *Robert* King, and *Herveus* Consecrated him: But this Rebellion was their Ruin. Three Years after dyeth *Herveus :* And the next Year, *Robert* Fighting against *Charles*, was slain at *Soissons*; yet his Army conquered the King's. Shortly after, *Rodolph Duke* of *Burgundy*, is called in by the Nobles, and made King; as if the Kingdom had been void. *Charles*, on pretence of a Treaty, is led by *Heribert* to a Castle; and thence carryed

323

to *Perone*, where he dyed, *Anno* 929. leaving a Son *Lewis* to Fight for the Kingdom. And when *Charles* was in Prison, *Hugo* rejected *Rodulph*, and called *Lewis* out of *England*, to be King, *Anno* 936. But *Hugo* and *Heribert* would be his Masters, and gave him little Quiet. *Heribert* dyeth miserably, and Repenteth. *Hugo* Domineering, the King craveth Aid of *Otho* out of *Germany*, against him: But shortly dyeth himself, by a Disease got by a Fall in Hunting a *Wolf*. *Lotharius* his Son, succeedeth him. In his Third Year, *Hugo* the Great Duke of *Orleance*, dyeth; and *Lotharius* the King, *Anno* 986. His Son *Ludovicus* succeeded; who dyed Childless, *Anno* 987. And in him ended the Line of *Charles* the Great: For *Charles* Duke of *Loraine*, that was next, was by the Treachery of a Bishop, taken by *Hugo Capet*, the Son of the fore-said Duke *Hugo*, and imprisoned to Death: And this *Hugo* got Possession of the Crown. So much briefly on the By of these Matters; that they after interrupt us not too much: See *Dion. Petav. lib.* 8. c. 16.

§. 45. *Marinus* 2. (alias, *Martin* 3.) is made *Pope*, *Anno* 943. and Reigned three Years, and some Months (the common Time of *Popes* in that Age.) In his time, *Artaldus* strove again for the Seat of *Rhemes*.

§. 46. CCCXII. When Bishops would needs be Princes, they taught Princes to resolve to be Bishops: And as *Heribert* did at *Rhemes*, so did the Emperor at *Constantinople* put in a Patriark, *Trypho*, a *Monk*; on condition, that he should hold it but till his own Son *Theophylact* came to Age. When the time came, *Trypho* would not Resign: A Council is called; where *Bin. ex Curopal.* tells you the State of that Church also, as too like the *Western*. The Council being met, *Tryphon* makes a Speech to them, and saith; That his Adversaries, that had a mind to cast him out, gave the reason, that he knew not Letters: But that they might all see that this was false, and that he could Write and Read, he call'd for Pen and Paper; and (having been taught thus much before) wrote his Name thus: [Tryphon, by the Mercy of God, Arch-Bishop of Constantinople, New Rome, and Universal Patriark,] (for that was then the Title.) The Emperor receiving the Paper, (it seems, knowing that he could not Read) writeth over head [Knowing myself Unworthy, I Resigne the Throne to any that will.] And so sent the Paper to the Council; and the Bishops (wise and Good Men, you must suppose) Dethron'd *Tryphon*. The Seat staid void five Months, till *Theophylact* came to Age; who then was chosen.

§. 47. *Anno* 946. *Agapetus* the Second is made *Pope*, in a time when Wars (between the *Hungarians*, and *Henry Bavaria*, *Berengarius* and *Otho*, &c.) made Miserable the Countries, and Ignorance and Ambition the Churches.

§. 48. CCCXIII. A Council at *Virdun* in *France*, again tryed the Cause between the fore-said Infant, and the Perjured Bishops; *Hugo* and *Artald*; and they undid what the last had done, and Deposed *Hugo*, and gave the Seat to *Artald*. Yet we have not done with *Doing* and *Undoing*: For Pope *Agapete* now took *Hugo*'s Part; and wrote to the Bishops of *France* and *Germany*, that *Hugo* that was in Possession, was to be kept there. But the *Papists* say, he mistook by *Hugo*'s Mis-information.

§. 49. CCCXIV. *Anno* 948. Another Council at *Mesume* was called for the same Business: *Hugo* would not come in, but sent the *Pope*'s Letters; which being not Canonical, but his bare Command, they rejected them, cast out, and Excommunicated *Hugo*, till the next General-Council.

§. 50. CCCXV. *Anno* 948. A General-Council of *France* and *Germany* is called at *Engelenheim*, for the same Cause; almost all *France* being disquieted about two Mens striving, who should be the Great Arch-Bishop: The *Pope's* Legate *Marinus*, proved *Hugo*'s Letters false; and *Hugo* was Excommunicated, and *Artald* setled. But the Presence of two Kings, *Ludovicus* and *Otho*, did much there-to.

The Bishops thence removed to *Triers*, (called another Council) where they judged for King *Ludovicus*, against Duke *Hugo*; and Excommunicated some Bishops Ordained by Bishop *Hugo*, (that was Ordained in his Child-hood.)

And another Council at *Rome* confirmed these things.

§. 51. Now cometh the Famous *Pope John* the Twelfth, the Son of Prince *Albericus*, the Son of the Famous Whore: A Child too. Saith *Baronius* and *Binius*, (p. 1060.) *Quanquam huic Legitima ætas aliaq; omnia deessent quæ inlegitimo Pontifice requiruntur, tamen accedente postea consensu totius Cleri, visum est hunc potius esse Tolerandum quam Ecclesiam Schismate aliquo, quod alicquin exortum fuisset, dividendam* He wanted Natural and Moral Endowments; even *All Things necessary to a Legitimate Pope*, say they: And yet, the After-Consent of the *Clergy* made him Tolerable, &c. *Qu*. 1. But, Did that After-consent make him a true Bishop? 2. If not, Where is their Succession? 3. Did *God* authorize the *Clergy*, to consent to such a Man? Where? Prove it. 4. If not, Could their Consent make him a Bishop? Is not all Power of *God*? And, Doth *God* give it contrary to his Word? 5. Were not those *Clergy*-Men wicked themselves, that would do so? 6. Did those Doctors presume, that their *Readers* were such Fools, as not to know, that *Forma non recipitur nisi in materiam dispositam*? And that *Ex quovis ligno non fit Mercurius*. An Illiterate Man cannot be a School-Master: He that is no Christian, cannot be a Bishop; nor he that hath not the Qualifications essentially necessary. All the World cannot make a Physician, a Lawyer, a Divine, a true Pastor or Bishop, of an Ideot, an Infant, or a Man that wanteth Essential Dispositions. To say, he *wanted all requisite Qualifications*, and yet that he was a Bishop, is a Contradiction: *Materia Disposita & Forma*, being the Constitutive Causes.. What if they had made a Bishop of a *Turk*, an *Infidel*, a Corps,

&c.? Had it not been a Nullity, and prophane Mockery? 7. What else signify all the Canons, that nullify Ordinations for less Faults? But the Image of a Bishop, will make but the Image or Carkass of a Church.

§. 52. But, say they, *Cum Universa Ecclesia Catholica sciret minus malum esse caput quantum libet monstrosum proferre quam unum corpus in duo secari, & duobus capitibus informari, eundem toto orbe terrarum tanquam verum & legitimum Pontificem venerata fuit.* *Answ.* 1. What a shameless Dream do you impose on us, under the Name of, *Totus orbis Terrarum?* What had the *Ethiopians,* the *Armenians,* yea, or the *Greek-Church,* to do with Pope *John?* Or, What was it to them, how he was called, or what he was? Did not the *Patriark* of *Constantinople* then write himself, the *Universal Patriark?* (even *Tryphon,* that they said, could not write any thing else.) Where is your Proof of this Universal Concession? Which way did the *whole Catholick-Church* (or the Tenth or Hundredth Part of it) signify their Consent? 2. Who taught you to feign the State and Necessity of such a Church, as must have another Universal Head besides *Christ?* You know, that it is the Being of such a Church or Head, (be he never so Good) that we deny: And you have never proved, nor can prove it. He only is the Universal Head, who maketh Universal Laws, and undertaketh Universal Teaching, and is an Universal Judge and Protector; none of which any Mortal man can perform. The very Fiction of such a Head and Body, is Monstrous, and your Capital Error. 3. How small a part of the Christian World was subject to the *Pope,* at that time; though within his reach, he was almost at the Height of his Presumption? 4. He that wanteth what is Essential to a true Bishop, is no true Bishop: But Pope *John* the Twelfth wanted what was Essential to a true Bishop: *Ergo.* He was none. The *Minor* is proved: He that wanteth the necessary *Disposition of the Receptive Matter,* and is not *Subjectum Capax,* wanteth that which is Essential to a true a Bishop: (For the *Materia Disposita* is an Essential Constitutive Cause; a *Subjectum Capax* is Essential to a Relation.) But *John* the Twelfth wanted the Necessary Disposition of the Matter *ad Formam Recipiendam,* or was not *Subjectum Capax:* Proved. He that wanted capable Age, and *all other Things necessary to a lawful Pope, was not Subjectum Capax; but wanted the necessary Disposition Receptive.* But all these, you say your selves, Pope *John* wanted: *Ergo,* &c.

5 If then the Universal Church had so erred, as to take him for a Bishop that was none; that Error would not make him a Bishop, no more than it would make a dead Man alive, or an illiterate Man learned. But this is the *Roman-Catholick* kind of Proof: You say your selves, That a Whore, and a wicked Son of that Whore, got Power enough to over-top the Citizens of *Rome,* and the *Clergy,* (yet too like them) and to thrust a wicked uncapable Fellow into the Chair.
When

and their Councils abridged 327

When that is done, it's known, all good Men diffent and abhor it. But when he hath Poffeffion, they muft know that he hath Poffeffion: And, What can they do to help it? What Power have the *Ethiopians, Armenians, Syrians,* or other Nations of the Earth, in choofing the *Pope* of *Rome?* And if they have none in Choofing him, What Power have they to examine the Choice, and Depofe him? And if they have no Power, Why or how fhould they fignify their Confent or Diffent? If they leave your own Matters to your felves, What is that to the *Confent of the Catholick-Church?* But fome men think, that big Words to the Ignorant may ferve for Proof, even of a Right to Govern at the *Antipodes,* and all the World.

§. 53. His Father *Albericus,* being Governour of the City, defigned the Succeffion to his Son *Octavian:* To which he added the Ufurped-Papacy, calling himfelf *John.* The firft (fay *Baronius* and *Binius*) that changed his Name, (though others fay *Sergius* was the firft.) Saith *Platina; From his Youth, he was Contaminated with all odious Crimes, and Filthinefs: When he had any time to fpare from his Lufts, it was not fpent in Praying, but in Hunting.* Two of the Cardinals, moved with the Shame of fuch a Pope, fend Letters to Germany, to Otho, to intreat him to fave Rome *from* Berengarius, *(that Plundered all the Country)* and *from Pope* John *the Twelfth; or elfe* Chriftianity *was loft.* John *having notice of this, catcheth t e* Cardinals, *and cutteth off the Nofe of one, and a Hand of the other.* Otho *cometh into* Italy, *and took* Berengarius, *and his Son* Albertus, *and Banifhed them.* Yet *Baronius* and *Binius,* out of *Luitpraudus,* fay, That the Pope *himfelf fent for* Otho, *to Help him.* However that was, the *Pope* received him as with Honor, and Crowned him the Emperor of *Germany, (*the Firft) and *Hungary.* The Pope, and all the Great Men of the City, fwore over the Body of St. *Peter,* that they would never help *Berengarius* or *Adalbert:* and the Emperor departed. But the *Pope* quickly broke his Oath, and joyned with *Adelbert:* Which the Emperor hearing, faid, *He is a Child; perhaps Reproof, and Example, may yet reclaim him.* He returned to Rome, and Adelbert, and the Pope *fl.d: The Citizens received the Emperor, and promifed him* Fidelity; *and took an Oath, that they would never Choofe or Ordain a* Pope, *without the Confent and Choice of the Emperor* Otho, *and his Son* Otho. John *fled into a Weed, and lay there like the Wild-Beafts.* (Saith *Platina.*)

§. 54. CCCXVI. *Otho* called a Council at *Rome;* where the Bifhops depofed *John,* and made *Leo* Pope: By which we ftill fee, how obedient the Bifhops were to the ftronger Side; or elfe, that really even thofe near *Rome,* did not confent to *John;* much lefs the whole *Catholick-Church,* as *Baronius* immodeftly affirmeth.

The Council was called, *Anno* 963. out of *Italy, France,* and *Germany,* befides *Roman* Cardinals and Nobles. The Emperor firft asked, *Why* Pope John *was not there?* The Roman *Bifhops, Cardinals, Prefbyters,*

byters, and Deacons, and all the People answered, We wonder your Holy Prudence should ask us this Question; seeing he so openly manageth the Works of the Devil, that it is not unknown to the Babylonians, Iberians, or Indians. The Emperor required particular Accusations: Then Peter, a Cardinal-Presbyter, said, That he saw him Celebrate Mass, and not Communicate. A Bishop, and a Cardinal-Deacon said, That they saw him Ordain a Deacon in a Stable of Horses. Benedict, and many others said, That he Ordained Bishops for Money; and Ordained a Boy of Ten Years old, Bishop of Tudortine. Of Sacriledge, there needed no Witness but Eyesight: Of Adultery, they said, that they saw it not; but they certainly knew, that he abused the Widow of Ragnerius, and his Father's Concubine, and Anne, a Widow, and her Neece; and made the Holy-Palace a common Bawdy-House, and Stews. That he put out the Eyes of his Spiritual Father Benedict, and kill'd him thereby: That he killed John, a Cardinal Sub Deacon, by cutting off his Virilia: That he set Fire on Houses, went Armed and Harnassed as a Souldier. They all (both Clergy and Laity) cryed out, that he Drunk a Health of Wine to the Devil, (Diaboli in Amorem.) That he at his Play at Dice, would crave the Help of Jupiter, Venus, and other Demons, &c. The Emperor said, That Bad Men often accuse the Good; and lest Malice or Livor should move them, he adjured them, as before God, to speak nothing untruly against the Pope, and without certain Proof: His Adjurations were most Vehement. The Bishops, Deacons, Clergy, and all the People of Rome, answered as one Man, and said, [If both the Things read by Benedict the Deacon, and filthier and greater Villainies were not committed by Pope John, Let not St. Peter Absolve us from the Bond of our Sins: Let us be found tyed with the Bonds of Anathema, (or Cursed from Christ); and be set at Christ's Left-Hand, at the Last Day, with those that said to God the Lord, Depart from us, we would not have the Knowledge of thy Wayes. If you believe not Us, believe your Army that saw him, &c.] The Emperor being satisfyed by his Armies Witness also, the Council moved, that Letters of Summons might be sent to the Pope, to appear and answer for himself. A Letter was written, as from the Emperor and Bishops; telling him, That the things charged on him were such, as it would be a Shame to hear of Stage-Players; which, if all were numb'red, the Day would fail: That not a Few, but All, (both Clergy and Laity) accused him of Murder, Perjury, Sacriledge, and of Incest with his own Kindred, and with two of his own Sisters. They say also, (Horrid to hear!) That you drunk Wine in Love to the Devil; ask't Help of Jupiter, Venus, and other Demons, at your Dice, &c. We crave you would come, and answer for your self; and swear, nothing shall be done to you besides the Canons.

The Pope reading this, sent this Answer; [We hear, that you will make another Pope: If you do so, I Excommunicate you from God Almighty, that you may have no License to Ordain any, nor to Celebrate Mass.]

After

After this, more Bishops came out of Germany; *and they write again to the Pope, telling him, That if he will not appear and answer, they shall despise his Excommunications, and turn it upon himself. He would not be found. The Emperor seeing he would not appear, told the Council, how treacherously he had dealt by him, intreating him to come, and help him; and after broke his Oath, and joyned with his Enemies. The whole Clergy, Bish. ps, and all the People, cry out, An un-heard-of Wound must be cured with an un-heard-of Cautery; and declaring the Mischief he had done, craveth that this Monster of incurable Vice, might be cast out of the* Roman-Church; *and another put in his Place, that will go before them with good Example. Then they all cryed up* Leo *the Proto-Sozintarius; which thrice repeating, upon Consent, they Ordained him, and swore Fidelity to him.*

§. 54. If now *Baronius* and *Binius* say, That the Clergies Consent can make an uncapable Monster a true Bishop, let any one tell us: 1. Whether this Council did not prove, that the Church did not consent to *John*? 2. Or, Whether his utter Incapacity, many expresi Canons, and the Bishops and Councils Consent, did not Eject him, and Authorize *Leo*?

§. 55. But here we come to the Core of all the *Papists* Cheats: When they tell us themselves of all this Wickedness, they cry out, *O the happy Church of* Rome! *that though it fail in* Manners, *yet never faileth in* Faith. *Ansv.* 1. If General Councils are sufficient Witnesses, that judged *Popes* Hereticks, it hath failed in Faith. 2. Hath that Man true Faith, that *wanteth all things requisite to a Lawful Bishop, and that drinketh to the* Devil, *and prayeth to* Jupiter *and* Venus; *and Liveth in all Wickedness?* What a thing is *Popish* Faith? 3. Did *Christ* mean to pray only, that St. *Peter* might have such a Faith, as will stand with Wickedness and Damnation? What the better is any Man of a wicked Heart and Life, for a dead Opinion call'd *Faith,* that will damn him the more deeply for sinning against it? 4. It is not possible, but that serious true Belief of so great Things, as *God,* and *Christ,* and *Glory,* will bring a Man to serious Repentance and Reformation.

§. 56. Here *Baronius* and *Binius* become this Monster's Advocate, and say, [*That there never was a Council of Orthodox Men, that sinned more against the Canons and Traditions, than this false Council.*] (How false is a Devil-worshipping - *Pope,* a Murderer, and common Adulterer, and incestuous Villainies, in comparison of all his Neighbor-Bishops?) 1. They say, They could not call a Council without him. *Ansv.* 1. He was no *Pope.* 2. It's a Travterous Fiction to say, That an Emperor may not call his Subject-Bishops together, to a Council. 3. VVhat if Devilish Villains will make Murders, and Perjury, and Rebellions, to pass for Duties, and never call Councils; Must the *Devil* therefore be made Lord of the *Catholick - Church,* without Remedy? 4. VVho gave your *Pope* that Priviledge? If Council or Princes, they can take

it from him: If *Christ*, prove it, or Shame be to him that yieldeth it.
5. That Man is so ignorant of Church-History, or Impudent as not to be worthy to be disputed with, that denyeth, That Princes have called Councils, even the Greatest, and most Honored.

II. They say, *There should be Seventy-Two Witnesses; and there was scarce one, besides the Accusers.*] *Answ.* 1. The whole Council, and People of *Rome*, and Army, are Witnesses, under the most direful Imprecations. 2. The *Pope* may go on safely, till God take him in Hand, if he must pass for Innocent till he will lye with his own Sisters, or murder Men, and cut off their *Virilia, &c.* before Seventy-Two Witnesses! O shameful *Holy-Church*, that is thus Essentiated!

III. They say He should have been thrice cited. *Anf.* 1. What! When he would not be found? 2. Is that necessary to the being of the Sentence?

IV. They say, No delay was granted! *Anf.* He was not to be found: And to what was *delay* necessary, when the *Babylonians, Iberians*, and *Indians* had notice of his Diabolical Life.

☞ V. They say, contrary to all Councils, the Emperour Condemneth him, who may not Condemn any Clerk. *Anf.* But you may Condemn Kings and Emperours! Is not this Heresy, contrary to *Rom.* 13. and the 5. Commandement; How shall Mens Lives, Wives, and Estates be saved from Clergy-men, if Kings may not judge and punish them. This Doctrine calleth for timely restraint.

VI. They say, Execution went instead of Sentence. *Anf.* Is not a plain Sentence here expressed?

VII. The *Pope* is exempt from all humane judgment: The whole Council therefore were impudent or ignorant to Condemn a *Pope*, *How many Ca-* which none ever did but a Heretick or Schismatick. *Anf. 1st.* That is, such *nons did* as you are able to call General Councils, Emperours and Kings, He-*John and* reticks and Schismaticks; if they presume to judge a Heretick, Schis-*his perju-* matick, or devillish *Pope*. But your faculty proveth not another cul-*red adhe-* pable. 2. Did not *Solomon* judge *Abiathar*? Did not many Councils *rents vi-* Condemn *Honorius*, and many other *Popes*. 3. What a case is your *olate?* miserable *Catholick Roman* Church in then; when *Popes* may kill, ravish, blaspheme, and destroy, and no Man can judge them, neither King nor Council? 4. Why said you, that the whole Church did consent to your *Pope*, when all this Council, and all the Clergy, and People at *Rome* thus begged for another. 5. If all your Bishops of *Italy, Germany*, &c are utterly *impudent or ignorant* as you call these; What an honour is this to the *Prelacy* of your Church? And is it not because your *Popes* ordained them, and like will generate its like. Such other trifling objections they frame.

§. 57. But now we have two *Popes, John* and *Leo*: and to this Day it is not known, nor agreed among the *Roman* Doctors, which was the true *Pope*. Most say *Leo: Baron.* and *Bin.* say, *John*; and call
Leo

Leo a Schifmatick; confeffing yet, that *Scriptores in finiti numeri* call him *Leo 8th*. and own him. How then fhall we derive their fucceffion? *John's* Kindred got the better, when the Emperour was gone, and called him again, and caft out *Leo*. Now we have two Heads, and fo two Churches; the Church of *John*, and the Church of *Leo*.

§. 58 CCCXVII. *Anno* 963. A Council at *Conft*. gave the Emperor *Nicephorus Phocas* leave to marry *Theophanes*, the Widdow of *Romanus*.

§. 59. CCCXVIII. *Ann.* 964. The monftrous Beaft Pope *John* got up again, call'd a Synod of Bifhops: And what will not Bifhops do? He is here ftill called, *The moft Godly and moft Holy Pope*. The Bifhops at his motion Condemn *Leo*, and thofe that Ordained him, and thofe that were Ordained by him. And this Council *Binius* juftifieth, and cryeth down *Leo 8th*. as no Pope. But he confeffeth, that by the common confent of Writers, *Leo* was the true Pope; but *Scriptorum error veritati nihil prajudicare poteft*. *Anf*. 1. How then fhall all the world that knew not the Cafe, be fure that *Binius* and *Baronius* are to be believed before all their own Writers, whofe common Sentence is againft them, and that *Romes* Succeffion from *John* is good? 2. Remember this when you plead for your fuppofed Tradition, that *infinite Writers prejudice not the Truth*.

§. 60. But faith *Platina, Its reported, that juft then* John *was punifhed by Gods juft judgment, left a Schifme fhould have followed*. And it is commonly agreed, that being in bed with a mans Wife, the Devil ftruck him on the head and killed him. But fome think it was rather the VVomans Husband that did it.

§. 61. But yet we are never the nearer conceding, ftill there are two Roman Popes and Churches. *John* being dead one *Benedict* is Chofen by the parties. *Totius cleri & populi Romanæ Confenfu*, faith *Bin*. p. 1067. Yet had this Clergy and People fworn before to *Otho*, to Choofe no Pope without his Confent and Choife, and tied themfelves to *Leo*. But to to be Perjured, and change with the Ruling Power, alas how common was it!

§. 62. The godly Emperor *Otho* was offended at thefe Villanies, and brought an Army again to *Rome*: *Benedictus* made them ftand out a Siege till Famine forced them to yield, and the Emperor fet up *Leo*, and carried away *Benedict* to *Hamburgh*, where he died. And think you but this Pope is therefore by *Binius* and *Baronius* made a Martyr, that by Rebellion and common Perjury was thus fet up.

§. 63. While *Otho* was at *Rome Anno* 964. He and *Leo* 8. called another Council of Bifhops, *Italian*, *Roman*; from *Loraine*, *Saxony*, &c. and all the Roman People: Pope *Bene ict* is brought forth, *Benedict* the Deacon tells him of his Perjury, having broken his Oath to *Leo* and to *Otho*: Pope *Benedict* faid, *If I have finned, have mercy on me*. The pittiful Emperour with Tears intreated the Bifhop to have mercy on the man: Whereupon, he fell down at the feet of *Leo* and the Emperour, and confeffed that he had finned and invaded the Papacy: and delivered

red the *Insignia* to *Leo:* (yet our foresaid *Annalist* and *Historian* make him and not *Leo,* the true Pope still.) The Council Deposed and Banished him, but continued him a *Deacon* as he was before. They removed him to *Hamburgh* to prevent new broiles.

§. 64. Here *Baronius* and *Binius* cry out on the History of *Luitfrandus* as Forg'd, on *Cranizius, &c.* But there is a great reason why *Leo* must not be taken for a Pope: It is because by a Canon of this, his Council they gave *Otho* the same power for choosing Popes as *Charles* the great had. O how much Interest prevaileth with these Historians judgments.

But alas, Reader, is it not a sad thing to read how fast Bishops and People did thus Swear and Forswear, and do and undo, making Councils as weather-cocks that turn with every Wind that is strong? Is this the honour of Prelacy, and their stability in governing the Church?

§. 65. Next comes another *John* 13th. who was not Chosen till *Leo* dyed, and expresly chosen to succeed him; and so by that Account of *Baronius* and *Binius* the Succession was interrupted, *Leo* being no Pope whom he Succeeded. But, alas, had it not been for the great Zeal of *Otho*, that came so oft with Armies to defend them, and to cast out intolerable Popes, what had become of the Roman Papacy? This *John* was a Bishop before, (as *Formosus* was) and so by the Canons his Election was Null on that account. Almost as soon as he was setled, saith *Platina*, the *Romans* having now got a Custome of Expelling their Popes, (yet *Baron.* saith, the Universal Church owned them,) did by Seditions tire out this also. *By the help of* Jofred *Earl of* Company, *they brake into the* Laterane *House, and took him, and first imprison him, and then send him Banished into* Campania: *But* John *Prince of* Campania *killed* Jofred *and his only Son; and delivered Pope* John *the Eleventh month after his Banishment: And the Emperour* Otho *again bringeth an Army to* Rome, *with speed, and casts the Governour, the Consuls, and the Dearebones into Fetters; The Consuls he sendeth into* Germany *banished; The Dearebones he Hanged: Peter the Praefect of the City, some write (saith* Platina) *that he delivered to the Pope to have his flesh torn off; his Beard and Head being Shorn, and he hanged a while at the head of the Constantinian-Horse, he was set on an Asse naked, with his face backward, his hands tyed under the taile, and so whipt through the Streets till he was almost Dead, and then Banished into* Germany. *The Corps of* Jofred *and his Son he caused to be taken up, and to be vildly cast away into divers filthy places.* Thus did the blind Zeal of a good Emperour Revenge and defend Usurping Popes.

§. 66. A Council at *Revenna*, of small importance, and one at *Rome*, to confirm *Glassenbury-Monastery* I pass by: and all the *English* Councils which *Spelman* hath given us by themselves. But it is worth the noting, that the famous *Dunstan* that banished Priests Marriage out of *England,* was the Favourite of these two Popes, *John* the 12. and 13th.

even

and their Councils abridged.

even much countenanced by the monstrous Pope that lay with two Sisters of his own, and made his House as a common Whore-house, if a Council under solemn Appeals to God, and Execrations, said true.

§. 67. The next Pope according to *Platina*, is *Benedict* (though *Onuphrius* and *Binius* put *Donus* next: *faith* Plat. Cintius *a potent Citizen of* Rome *took him and laid him in Jayle, and there strangled him: He wondred that neither* Otho *nor any other ever Revenged it:* But *Otho* was now near Death, and could not have leasure to bring an Army out of *Germany* to *Rome*, every time that wicked Citizens and Popes fell out: Did the Universal Church own this man also? But (*faith* Plat.) Benedicts *Merits were such as* Cintius *his reward importeth. But yet it was not well done of* Cintius *to meddle with the Pope were he never so bad: But alas* (faith he) *how the World is changed! For in our Age, Popes lay Citizens, faulty or suspected, in the same Prison, and then Macerate them.*

§. 68. *Donus* 2. was Pope but three months: In his short time, the *Bulgarians* had almost taken *Constant.* faith *Platina.* And *Anno* 972. a Council was held at *Ingelheim* in *Germany*, to compose Church matters.

§. 69. The next Pope (*faith* Plat.) was *Boniface* the 7th. who ill got the Popedome, and so lost it. *Onuphrius* and *Bin.* say, *that* Cintius *by his command strangled his Predecessors, and that he Succeeded him. Saith* Plat. *in the beginning of his Magistracy (for a Magistracy it thus was) by the Conspiracy of the good Citizens, being forced to leave the City, taking away all the pretious things out of* S. Peters *Church, he fled to* Constantinople*; where he stayed, till selling all that he had sacrilegiously gotten, he got a great mass of Money, with which he returned to corrupt the Citizens by Bribes. But good men resisted him, especially* John *a Cardinal-Deacon, whom* Boniface *caucht and put out his Eyes: And the Sedition increasing more and more, either for fear or remorse, he next made away (or kill'd) himself:* He was Pope 7 months and 5 days faith *Platinus.* But *Onuphrius* faith (one year, one month and 12 days.) But other Popes came in between before he died, and he got in again.

§. 69. *Baronius* and *Binius* say, that *Boniface* is not to be numbred with the Popes; If so, 1. Why not many score also? 2. Where then is their uninterrupted Succession? And where was their Church then?

§. 70. *Binius* maketh *Benedict* 6. next after *Donus*, and faith, He was imprisoned and kill'd by *Boniface*, who Usurped the place.

§ 71. *An.* 973. A Council at *Mutina* was to reconcile two Brethren.

§. 72. *Benedict* 7. *An.* 975. drove away *Boniface*, and was Pope himself: And so here were again two Popes: Now *Otho* 2. had a great Overthrow by the *Greeks* in *Calabria*; and flying by Sea, was taken Prisoner by Pyrats, and Redeemed by the *Sicilians*, dyed at *Rome*: And *Otho* the 3. was Chosen in his place by the *Germanes*. Writers agree not of the time of *Benedicts* Reign. In his time they feign, that at a Council at *Winchester* in the midst of their Disputes, the Image of our Lord spake out for the Monks against the secular Clergy, and so decided all the Controversies.

And a Synod was at *Rome*, about the Bishop of *Magdeburg*, accused.

§. 73. CCCXIX. *Anno* 975. At a Council at *Constantinople, Basil* the Partiarch is Accused as Criminal, and *Antonius Studita* put in his place.

§. 74. Pope *John* 14. (*alias* 15.) is next at *Rome, Anno* 984. *Binius* maketh him succeed *Boniface* that had killed Pope *Benedict*, and was fled to *Constantinople*; and *saith, that when* Boniface *knew that* Otho *the Emperour was dead, he returned to* Rome, *and seized on the Papacy again; and finding* John *in it, did not only turn him out, but cast him in Bonds in the Tower of St.* Angelo, *which was kept by men of his own faction; and with great Tyranny kept him there four months, and as a violent and sacrilegious Robber, at last Murdered him cy Famine. And left any hope should be left to the Emperours Party, he exposed the Corps of the dead Pope (for all the Citizens to behold) before the doores of the Prison: And the People seeing the bare body of the Pope consumed by Hunger, buried him with Sorrow. In the mean time, the Invader of the Seat, and the cruel Murderer of two Popes, the odious Paricide, and turbulent thief* Boniface *the Anti-Pope, (Oh Horrible!) by Tyranny Invaded St.* Peters *Chair: But after four months, by Gods Revenge, he suddenly dyed (he killed himself* said Plat. *When he was dead, even the factious persons on whom he had trusted, Wounded his dead Carkass, and Drag'd it through the City.* This Bin. out of *Baron.* and he *exantiquis Vatican-Codicibus.*

And must a Governour of all the World be thus Chosen.

But *Platina* faith, that some say, that *Ferrucius, Bonifaces* Father, a great man, murdered *John*; and others say, he was cast out for Impotency and Tyranny; *and others say, by malevolent Seditious Men. So confused* (faith he) *are the Histories of those times.*

§. 75. Next comes *John* 15. (alias 16) *Binius* faith, that for fear of the like usage that had befallen his Predecessors, he left *Rome* & dwelt in *Tuscany*; one *Crescenius* a great man, having got the Castle of St. *Angelo:* till the Pope sending to *Otho* 3. afrighted the *Romans*, and made them intreat him to return. But *Platina* faith, That [*He burned against the Clergy with a wonderfull Hatred, and therefore was deservedly hated by the Clergy: especially, because he bestowed all things Divine and Humane on his kindred, disregarding the honour of God, and the Dignity of the* Romane *Seat ; which Errour* (faith he) *he so Traditioned (or delivered down) that it remaineth to this day* (This is Romane Tradition) *a Comet then appear'd, Famine, Pestilence, Earthquakes, which were thought to be for the Pride and rapacity of the Pope, and his contempt of God and Man.*] So *Platina.*

Platina speaks this of John 16. called by him the 17th.

§. 76. An Instance was given of a Bishop of the contrary Spirit: *Adelbert* Bishop of *Prague* in *Bohemia* found the People so contrary to him, and

and bad, that he forfook them, and Travelled firſt, and then entred into a Monaſtery: And when he had lived there five years, the people defired him again, and promiſed Obedience. A Council at *Rome* defired his return, vvhich with grief he did; But they ſtill proved incorrigble, and he again forſook them and vvent to Preach to the *Hungarians*, when he Bapzed the King *Stephen*, and did much good. *Bin. p.* 1071.

§. 77 CCCXX. *Arnulphus* Arch-Biſhop of *Rhemes* fufpected of Treafon, for delivering up the City of *Rhemes* to *Charles*: Called a Synod at *Seulis*, to purge himſelf, Excommunicating them that did it. *Anno* 990.

§. 78. CCCXXI. *Hugo Capet* having now got the Crown of *France*, and defirous to deſtroy all the *Carolines* line, upon the aforefaid fufpition got a Synod at *Rhemes*, to caſt out *Arnulphus* a Baſtard of that Line; faying, a Baſtard muſt not be a Biſhop: One Biſhop refufed; The reſt for fear of that King confented, and caſt him out; (fo conſtant were the *French* Biſhops.)

§. 79. CCCXXII. Six Biſhops, and Nine Presbyters, and Four Deacons made a Council at *Rome*, to Canonize *Udalric* Biſhop of *Auguſta*, *Anno* 993. upon the reports of his Holineſs and Miracles.

Here let me at once tell the Reader, that he hath no cauſe to think the moſt of thefe Canonizations wholly caufelefs. But that while Pope and Patriarcks, confounded all by wickedneſs and contentious pride; God had many faithful Biſhops and Presbyters that lived holily in quieter and privater kind of Life; And the *Popes* that would not endure themſelves to live a Godly life, thought it their honour to have fuch in the Church that did, and to magnifie them when dead, and paſt contradicting them. Juſt like the *Phariſees, Mat.* 23. that killed the living Servants of God, and honoured the dead, and built them Monuments, faying, *If we had lived in thoſe days, we would not have killed them.*

§. 80. CCCXXIII. A Synod was called at *Moſon*, to debate the Cafe between *Arnulph* and *Gerbert* fubſtituted at *Rhemes*, who fo pleaded his caufe, that it was put off to another Synod. *Baron* revileth fome Writings afcribed to the former Synod at *Rhemes*, faying, they were this *Gerberts*, as being Blafphemous againſt the *Pope*: The *Centuriators* of *Magdeb.* mention them at large. Did *Rome* then govern all the World?

§. 81. CCCXXIV. Another Council is called at *Rhemes*, and *Gerbert* (that wrote fo Blafphemoufly againſt the *Pope*) is depoſed by the *Popes* means, and *Arnulphus* reſtored: which *Gerbert* obferving, flyeth to the Emperour to *Germany*, feemeth to repent (as *Baron.* but furmizeth) and gets higher, to be *Pope* himſelf, by the Emperours means, as you ſhall hear anon.

§. 2. Can any Man think that *Popes*, that themſelves came in by Tyranny and meer Force, and lived in Wickedneſs, could have fo great a Zeal as is pretended to do Juſtice for all others, unlefs for their own ends? §. 83.

§. 83. *John* the 16*th.* (*alias* 17) is passed over by *Binius: Onuphrius* saith, that he Reigned four Months: *Platina* saith, he died the tenth Year, and sixth Month, and tenth Day (a great difference.)

§. 84. *Gregory* the 5*th.* is next, made *Pope* (saith Plat.) by *Otho* 3*d* his Authority for Affinity: *But* (saith *Plat.*) *The* Romans make Crescentius *Consul with chief Power; who presently made* John *Bishop of* Placentine Pope*; who came to it by the consent of the* Roman Clergy *and People, to whom the choice belonged, though some leave him out :* Otho *cometh to defend his own* Pope*;* Crescentius *fortifieth City and Castle against him : The People dare not resist, but open the City Gates :* Crescentius *and* Pope John *flyeth to the Castle ; and in hope of Pardon, yields :* Crescentius *is Killed by the People in his passage ;* John *hath first his* Eyes put out, *and then his* Life*; and* Gregory *the Eleventh Month is restored : Binius* faith, *that* Johns *Hands were cut off, his Ears cut off, and his Eyes pulled out ; and after set on an Ass, holding the Tail in his Hand, was carried about the Streets.*

§. 85. This *Pope* and *Otho* the 3*d.* agreed to settle the Election of the Emperour, as now it is on the 7. Electors. The cause of great Confusions, and Calamities was, that the Emperours did not dwell at *Rome;* and so left *Popes* then to fight, strive, and sin, that else would have lived submissively under them. *Constantine, Carolus Mag.* or *Otho*, might have done much to prevent or cure all this.

The *Papists* would fain prove this the work of a *Roman* Synod, (to settle the Electors) that they may prove that it is they, that must make and unmake Emperours. But they can shew us no such Council.

Onuphrius hath written a Treatise to prove that this was after done by *Greg.* 10*th.* For which *Binius* reprehends him, as believing *Aventinus.*

But this is a Controversy handled by so many, that I shall refer the Reader to them: and whether the seven Electors only, or all the Feudatories chose.

Baronius and *Binius* maintain, that all came from the Authority of the *Pope*; that *Greg.* 5*th.* Ordained the choice of the Emperour to be by all the Feudatories of the Empire; that the Council at *Lyons*, under *Innocent* 4*th.* setled it upon Seven, but not all the same that are now Electors; and that the Princes after setled it on these same Seven, they know not who nor when.

For the right understanding of many such matters; I only mind the Reader of this one thing, that as the contention of Princes, and the superstitious fear of *Anathematizing* had made the Papal, and Prelatical Power then very great, in setting up, and taking down Princes; so it was usual for their Assemblies, even those called Councils, to be mixt of Men Secular and Clergy; Kings and Princes, and Lords being present with the Bishops, as in our Parliaments; and usually the greatest Princes ruled all. Therefore, to ascribe all to the *Pope* and *Prelates*,

that

that was done in such conventions, and thence to gather their power to dispose of Empires and Kingdoms, is meer deceit.

§ 86. *Platina* next nameth *John* 17th. *alias* 18th. but saith he was no true Pope (its impossible to know who was,) but that he corrupted *Crescentius* with money, and it cost them both their lives: How he was mangled, shamed, and killed (though a Bishop before) you heard before.

"He had, saith Pla-
na, been School-
master to Otho, and the King of France and other great men.

§ 87. Next *an.* 999. cometh that French Bishop *Gerbert* (*) before mentioned, that wrote so blasphemously (as they called it) against the Pope (as *Æneas Silvius* after did) till he saw some hope of being Pope, himself, by the Emperor's favour first made Arch-Bishop of *Ravenna*, and then Pope, *Formosus*'s Case and the Canons that forbid a Bishop to be chosen, were now forgotten or dispensed with. He had won the Emperor's favour by a rare Clock that he made, being a good Mathematician: And the People and Clergie were taught that it was the Emperor's Will that they should choose him, which to please the Emperor they did: Historians say that he sold his Soul to the Devil by Covenant, to be made Pope, which accordingly the Devil distrained and took him away. But *Baron.* and *Bin.* say that Cardinal *Benno* was the first author of this and many fouler accusations of the Popes than I have here mentioned; and that he was Schismatical (as taking the Emperor's part) and so not to be believed. And indeed I am not apt to believe any that accused men of Magicks in that ignorant age of the Roman Church; whenas *Erasmus* saith, He that did but understand Greek or Hebrew was suspected to be a Magician.

Platina after others tells a terrible story of his Covenant with the Devil and his confession; But I rather believe O-nuphrius's vindication from that ignorant age.

Otho 3d. that preferred this Pope gave him two Counties to his Church, *Vercellis* and St. *Agatha*: A heresie *Glebar* and *Baron.* mention in his time, soon extinct. *Stephen* King of *Hungary* it's said converted the *Transylvanians* (which yet the Papists ascribe all to the Pope.) An hundred fifty nine Epistles of *Gerbert*'s written before he was Bishop of *Rhemes* (or Pope) are found with *Nicol. Faber.* saith *Bin.*

This Otho was but a Child of ten years of age when he was made Emperor.

§ 88. CCCXXV. In a Council at *Rome*, *an.* 999 *Giefler* Archbishop of *Montz* is accused for having two Parishes; but struck with a Palsie could not appear, and the matter referred to a German Council. *Bin,* p. 1079.

§ 89. Next cometh *John* 16th. as *Bin.* or 19th. as *Plat.* who dyed the fifth month. But though no good be said of him, *Plat.* noteth the great happiness of *Italy* by the good Government of *Hugo* the Emperor's Lieutenant.

§ 90. Next is *John* 17th. as *Bin.* or 20th. as *Plat.* who saith *Nil dignum memoriâ gessit*. But what was wanting in the unhappy Bishops God made up in good Princes. *Robert* King of *France*, and *Henry* the new Emperor of *Germany* (*Otho* being dead) being men of very great piety and justice: Holiness was now placed Eminently

§ 91. *Lambert* recordeth that *Leutherius* Archbishop

begin the Heresie of *Berengarius*. It seems then, neither *Luther*, nor *Zuinglius*, nor *Berengarius*, nor *Bertram* (alias *Ratram*) began it. But where will the reader find that *Transubstantiation* was yet named, or by any consent received? so that this is but to confess that yet the doctrine contrary to Transubstantiation did still obtain: And the name of heresie from *Baron*. or *Bin*. signifies no more against this Archbishop than the name of Magick and Diabolism against *Silvester* 2. from many Historians.

§ 92. In a Council at *Frankford* the Emperor *Henry*, having a great love to *Bamberge*, would endow it and make it an Archbishoprick. The Bishop of *Wirceburge* would not come to the Council unless it might be joyned to his Bishoprick. It seem'd a hard controversy. The good Emperor (oft prostrate before them) first, having no Children, dedicateth all that he hath to Christ, and then desireth them to consider, that [*It was not for the Lord, but for ambition, and to get more dignity that this Bishop did resist his desire*] (his agent speaking for him.) (Oh that Princes had sooner discerned the evil of such ambition and aspiring!) At last the Emperor (being present) carried it, and chose an Archbishop who was ordained to *Bamberge*.

§ 93. Next *Peter* Bishop of *Abbane* is made Pope and called *Sergius* 4th (The Canons are here again violated) Now saith *Bin*. "*was a great* "*prodigie, in a Church at Rome rose a spring of oyl, of which a vessel full* "*was sent to King Henry, no doubt to call him to take the Empire.*]

§ 94. CCCXXVI. *An.* 1011. A Council at *Bamberge* endeavoured to end some quarrels among Bishops that strove to get more, and accused one another unjustly to the Pope; for which the King reproved some of them.

§ 95. *An.* 1012. Two Popes were chosen and set up; which is the 19th. schism or double-head of the Roman Church. The Emperor's party chose *Benedict* the 8th. The City Party chose *Gregory*. The Citizens were the stronger at present (and so long their's was the true Pope.) The Emperor proved strongest at last, and therefore *Benedict* became the true Pope (for *Hobbes* his Law ruled among them,) [*that Right is nothing but Power to get and keep*] *Gregory* had no power to keep his Place: *Ergo* he had no right to it: *Benedict* fled to *Germany*, and the good Emperor *Henry* came to *Rome* with an Army, and made *Gregory* fly, and set up *Benedict*. Here *Henry* first instituted the Golden Globe and Cross as fit for an Emperor's hand and aspect. *Bin*. out of *Glab. li.* 3. *c.* 8. speaketh of the Jews injuring Christ's Image by a ludicrous crucifixion, and that after the adoring of the cross the same day, a whirlwind cast down the Houses [*omnesque pene Romanos occisos esse*] and almost all the Romans were killed (that's scarce credible,) and that it ceased not till the Pope had put the Jews to death. *Platina* saith, that this Emperor *Henry* and his Wife were so pious that they omitted nothing that might do good. He overthrew the *Saracens*, and giving his Sister in marriage to the King of *Hungary* converted him and his People to the Faith: And *Baron*. giveth you the copy of his large grant of Cities and Principalities to the Pope, by way of confirmation of former grants.

§ 96.

§ 96. They call it a Council at *Legio* in *Spain*, where the King and Queen and Nobles with the Bishops and Abbots, made some Laws for Church-priviledges.

§ 97. CCCXXVII. *An.* 1017. A Council was called at *Orleance* in *France*; where, by the Zeal of the religious King *Robert* and the Prelates, the burning of Hereticks were set on foot. *Bin.* out of *Glaber* thus reciteth the matter. One Italian woman revived the heresie of the Manichees, and two Clergie men (yet called *Palatii proceres et Regi familiares*) received and spread it abroad with confidence. The opinions are thus recited by *Glaber*. 1. That the Doctrine of the Trinity delivered in scripture, is a deceit. 2. That Heaven and Earth are from eternity without a maker. 3. That the crimes of sensual pleasure shall have no punishment. 3. That there is no reward for any Christian works, save of Piety & Justice. The two leaders *Lisoius* and *Heribertus*, and eleven more were burnt to ashes; and afterwards as many more as were found guilty of the same errours. *Bin. p.* 1083. Here consuming zeal began.

§ 98. CCCXXVIII. *An.* 1022. A Council at *Salegunstad* in *Germany* made many ceremonious Canons; but decreed *c.* 16. that none go to *Rome* without the consent of the Bishop. and *c.* 17. that the Popes pardons shall not profit them that have not fulfilled the time of their pennance.

They tell us also of a Council at *Mentz*, and *Gothard*'s curing a Dæmoniack woman.

§ 99. *Benedict* dying, went to purgatory saith *Bin.* as some apparitions proved, but he was delivered out of that pain by St. *Odilo*'s prayers, and his Brother's Alms. (you see how much better it is to be a Saint than a Pope) you need not question the credit of their intelligence from purgatory.

§ 100. This Pope's own Brother, Son to the *Tusculane* Earl, by his power presently seizeth on the Papacie. But *Bin. ex Baron.* would perswade us that this invaded Pope afterward repented, resigned, and was new chosen by the Clergy. He was very like to have their votes when he had gotten such power and advantage: But where was the Roman Church that while?

Now dyed the pious Emperor *Henry*, and when he dyed gave up his religious wife to the Bishops and Abbots, as a Virgin, as he received her; who entered a Monastery accordingly: *Conrade* his General succeeded him, and the Pope (*John* 21 as *Plat.* 18 as *Bin.*) being driven away by the People, *Conrade* restored him. (So far was the Pope obeyed.)

§ 101. A Council at *Lymoges*, *an.* 1029. gave an Apostolical title to *Martial* their founder.

§ 102. *An.* 1032. Another at *Pampilone* was about a Bishop's seat.

§ 103. Princes in this age are commended for their piety (especially their zeal for *Rome*.) But did the Popes yet amend? The next man that cometh in by the same power as the former, is *Benedict* the 9th Nephew

phew to *John* and Son to *Albericus*; most say he was but ten years old, "some say 18. capable, saith *Baron* and *Bin.* of Impudence and luxury; by "the tyranny of his Father intruded, *An.* 1030. And (say they) being given "over to lust and pleasure, and by humane frailty rushing into impudence, "and living to great scandal of the faithful, he was by the Romans, the Consul *Ptolemy* favouring it, rejected, or at least gave it up by the per- "swasion of the holy Abbot *Bartholomew*. Whereupon *Silvester* the 3d. "came into his place, who had been Bishop of *Sabine*, even by bribery and "evil arts; and did rend the Church by a new Schism: But he had scarce "Sate three months, but *Benedict* by the help of the *Tusculanes* returned "and cast him out, as an invader. In the mean time a third man, *John* "*Arch-Presbyter* of *Rome* invading the same seat, brought yet a greater "deformity on the Church: And so A THREE-HEADED BEAST ARI- "SING FROM THE GATES OF HELL did miserably infest the holy "Chain of St. *Peter*.] These are the words of the Popes grand flatterers: "And they tell us that one *Gratian* a Presbyter pitying this miserable state "of the Church, went to all the three Popes, and gave them money, to "hire them all to resign; And so *Benedict* as the most worthy being se- "cured of the Revenues of *England*, deposed himself; and that he "might the more freely execute his lusts betook himself to his Fathers house, when intruded by force and tyranny he had held the Papacy eleven years. And when the rest by his example had done the like, each being contented with his assigned portion of the Revenue, the Church *An.* 1044. was restored to its ancient union, peace and concord, the Schism be- "ing expelled, and the tyranny by which it was oppressed taken out of the "way.] Thus *Bar.* and *Bin.* But how came this Presbyter to be so honest and so rich? you must know that when he had got out the three Popes he was made Pope himself, of which more anon.

§. 104. But though these Authors tell us but of four Popes at once, as credible writers of their own tell us there were six: *Wernerus* in *Fas-*
(*) *Onu-* *ciculo Tempor.* saith [The 14. * Schism was scandalous and full of confusi-
phr. will 'on between *Benedict* the 9th. and five others; which *Benedict* was whol-
tell you 'ly vitious, and therefore being damned, he appeared in a monstrous and
better 'horrid shape, his head and tail were like an Asses, the rest of his body
that it 'like a Bear, ** saying, I thus appear because I lived like a beast. In this
was the 'Schism there were no less than six Popes at once: 1. *Benedict* was expulsed.
20th. '2. *Silvester* 3d. got in, but is cast out again, and *Benedict* restored. 3. But
** So say 'being cast out again *Gregory* the 6th. is put into his place: who because
Platina he was *ignorant of Letters* caused another Pope to be consecrated with
and many him, to perform *Church-Offices*, which was the fourth: which displeased
others many, and therefore a third is chosen instead of those two that were fight-
also. ing with one another. 6. But *Henry* the Emperor coming in deposed them
'all and chose *Clement* the 2d.] the sixth that were alive at once. There is great difference between *Wernerus*, *Onuphrius*, *Platina*, *Baronius*, but all confess that there were three or four at once. And the three were secured

red of the revenues before they refigned to the fourth ; no doubt leaving him his part: This it is for Bifhops to be great and rich, which will afcertain wicked men to feek them. But if *Werverus* fay true that this *Johan. Gratianus*, made *Gregory* 6th. was illiterate, he was a ftrange *Roman* Arch-Presbyter before, and a ftrange Pope after, but greatly to be commended that would ordain a fellow Pope that could read.

§ 105. This horrid monftrous villain called *Benedict* the 9th. Canonized *Simeon* an *Anchorite* at *Trevirs*. Do you think he was not a good judge and lover of Saints? He crowned *Conrade* the Emperor who came into *Italy* to mafter the Bifhop of *Milan* that rebelled, fay *Baron*, and *Bin*. and many other great things he did.

§ 106. Even in thefe times there were Councils held. 1. One at *Lymoges*, to judge St. *Martial* to be an Apoftle, and to agree to excommunicate the fouldiers that robbed and plundered, and to curfe their horfes and arms, and deny Chriftian burial to all the Countrys where they prevailed, fave the Clergy and poor, &c. Another at *Beauvois* on the fame occafion. And another at *Tribur*, unknown for what.

§ 107. This Pope *Gregory* 6th. (who was *Johan Gratian* the Roman Arch-Presbyter, that *Werner* faith was illiterate and made him a fellow Pope) is very varioufly defcribed: *Baron*, and *Bin*. and fome others make him an honeft man that ended the Schifm. Cardinal *Benno* maketh him Simoniacal that hired them out to get the Papacie: *Baron*, and *Bin*. for this revile him as a malicious lyar. They fay that *Gregory*, for punifhing facrilegious villains by the fword that cared not for Anathema's, was accufed by the Romans that now lived by theft and rapine, as a Simonift and a murderer. *Conrade* being dead and *Henry* his Son made Emperor, he being in *Italy* held a Synod at *Sutria* near *Rome* where all the four Popes caufes were examined: And the three former were depofed, that is, deprived of the revenue which was parted among them, and this *Gregory* 6. (fay moft authors, and even *Hermannus* that wrote in thofe very times) was depofed, (but faith *Baron*. he honeftly refigned.) And the Roman *Clergy* being found fo bad, that none were fit for the place, the Emperor chofe (fay moft, or *caufed* to be chofen faith *Bin*.) the Bifhop of *Bamberge* in *Germany* called *Clement* the 2d.

§ 108. The Emperor fetling the Bifhop of *Bamberge*, *Clem*. 2. in the chair, returned and took the laft Pope *Gregory* with him to avoid contention; and *Clement* went after with *Hildebrand* and dyed by the way the 9th. month after his Creation. *Benedict* hearing this invadeth the Papacy again, the third time, even that villain that was firft of the four, and held it eight months after this, fo yet we have divers Popes.

§ 109. *An*. 1067. A Council is held at *Rome* by *Clem*. 2. againft Simony.

§ 110. *Poppo* Bifhop of *Brixia* is made Pope, by the Emperor and the common fuffrage, fay *Bar*. and *Bin*. (*an*. 1048.) But faith *Platina* "and others, it is reported that he made the poyfon with which the

Citizens

"Citizens poysoned his predecessor *Clem.* 2. And that he seized on the
"place by violence without any consent of Clergy or People, it being
"now the custom for any ambitious man, that could, to seize on the
"Popedom; but God, saith *Plat.* as a just revenger resisted him, for
"he dyed the twenty third day of his Papacie. Yet the Romans had
"again taken an oath in *Clem.*2d's. time to choose no Pope without the
"Emperor's licence. For the Romans were become so wicked and
factious that they were not to be trusted in such a thing.

§ 111. Upon these horrid villanies and schisms *Baron.* and *Bin.* again
cry out on the *Novatores,* for casting these things in the teeth of
the *Roman* Church, as impudent men. And they say still, 1. That it
" was not the Church that chose these Popes (as *Benedict* 9.) but Tyrants
" obtruded them. 2. "That yet so great was the power of the Roman
" Church that even false Popes were obeyed by all the Christian world."]

Ans. 1. When yet they tell us themselves that even the City of *Rome*
was so far from obeying them, that they imprisoned, deposed, killed
them. And the whole *Greek* Church excommunicated them since *Photius*'s dayes; only the horrid contentions between the Sons and off-spring
of *Charlmain* and the *Germane* Princes, gave them advantage to Lord
it by *Anathema's* in *France, Germany,* and *Italy,* and such nearer parts;
whilest the contenders would make use of them, and they of the contenders. And horrid ignorance had invaded the clergy, and consequently the Laity, and subjected them in darkness to this Ruler that
maketh so great use of darkness.

2. And if these men uncalled were true Popes, why might not the
Turk be one, or any man that can get the place or Title? Why were
not all the 4 or 5 or 6 at once true Popes? If not, Where was the
Catholick Church this while, if a Pope was a constitutive head or
part? and what is become of your Succession? will any possession *jure vel
injuria* serve for a Succession? If so, Why tell you the Protestants that
they want it? If nor, What pretence have you for it? I think the Protestants can prove a far better succession.

§ 112. *Berengarius* rose in these horrid dayes; and it is no wonder
if such a monster as Pope *Benedict,* and his companions condemned him,
and set up the monstrous doctrine of Transubstantiation. As *Tertullian*
saith it was an honour to Christians to be first persecuted by such a
one as *Nero,* so was it to the doctrine of the Sacrament to be condemned by such a one as *Benedict* 9. and in the time (as *Baron.* and *Bin.*
speak) *of the three-headed monstrous beast.*

§ 113. *Rome* was now so wise as to be conscious a little of their badness and unfitness to choose themselves a Pope, and therefore sent to the
Emperor *Henry* to choose them one. He chose them *Bruno* a good Bishop of *Tullum*; who in his way, at the Abby of *Cluny,* met with *Hildebrand* that went from *Rome* thither, who told him that the Emperor
being a Lay-man had no power to make or choose a Pope (*) but the

Clergy

Clergy and people; but if he would follow his advise, he should in a better way attain his end: so *Hildebrand* went with him and perswaded him to put off his purple, and to go in a common habit, and confess that he is not their Bishop till they choose him, and that he taketh not the seat as given by the Emperor but by them; whereby he won the Romans hearts, and they readily chose him. And he being called *Leo* the 9th, after so many monsters, went for a very excellent Pope. But yet he commanded an army himself against the *Normans*, and proved no good or happy Captain, his Army being wholly routed, and himself taken Prisoner: whom the *Normans* in reverence released and returned safe. *Pet. Damianus* and others lament his Souldiery as his great sin, but *Baron*.and *Bin*. excuse him,and say,all the world now alloweth it: You see what arguments serve at *Rome*: where it was but lately that the first article that a Roman Council before *Otho Mag*. brought in against Pope *John* was that he went sometimes in Arms: And to be formerly a Bishop was heretofore an incapacity by the Canons: Yet *Rome* covereth her innovations by pretending antiquity,and calling others *Novatores*.

King may not ordain a Bishop: Question whether he may remove an ordained Bishop from one Church to another, the people only accepting him by free consent?

§ 114. But how militant a defender of the Roman grandure this *Leo* was, may be seen in his Epistles in *Bin*. p. 1096. &c. In the first long one to the Patriarch of *Constantinople* and another *Greek* Bishop, he reproveth them for bold damning of the Church of *Rome*, and tells them that they were members of Antichrist,and forerunners of him that is King over all the Children of pride; and saith, who can tell how many Antichrists had have been already?He tells them how many heretickBishops they have had at *Const*. and of above ninety heresies in the East; and how by force they raged against the *Joannites* (the Nonconformists that followed St. *Chrysostome*;)what a heretick their Bishop *Eutychius* was,that said,the body at resurrection will be impalpable,and more subtil than the wind and air (He believed *Paul* that said it should be a *spritual body* (though not a Spirit.) And how his Books were burned.He reprehendeth their title of Oecumenical Patriarch;and saith that no *Roman*Bishop to that day had ever accepted or used that Title (*) Yet he reciteth the forged grant of *Constantine*, saying, that as far as Kings are above Judges, so all the world must take the Pope for their Head; and that he gave the Palace and all *Rome*, &c. to *Silvester*, and said it was unmeet that they should be subject to any earthly Prince that were by God made Governors of Heaven. At large he thus pleadeth for the Roman *Kingdom of Priests*, chiding them that had put down all the Latine Churches and monasteries in the East.] (yet *Baron*. and *Bin*. tell you all the Church on earth obeyed the Pope.)

* Remember that.

In his 4th. Epistle he laments that in *Africa* there was "205. Bish-
"ops at a Council, now there were scarce five in all; and he sheweth
"that all Bishops were of one order, but differenced as the Cities were
"for primacie, by the Civil Laws or the Fathers reverence. That
"where the Pagans Arch-Flamins were, there were instituted Arch-
"Bishops to be over the Provinces; where a Metropolis was, Metro-
"poli-

"politans or Arch-Bishops were placed; and Bishops in lesser Cities "where had been Flamins and Counts. But in *Africa* they were diversifyed " only by the times of their ordination; the Bishop of *Carthage* being " the chief."]

In his Epistle 5. he hath a good confession of faith, where among other things he well faith, [*"That God predestinated only things " good, but foreknew both good and evil; and that Grace so preventeth and "followeth man, that yet mans free will is not to be denied: that the Soul " is not part of God, but created of nothing.* He anathematizeth every He- " resie, and every one that receiveth or venerateth any Scriptures but * what are received by the Catholick Church, &c.

In the 6th. again he chides the Patriarchs of *Constantinople* for the title *Universal*; saying that *Peter* himself was never called the *Universal Apostle*, nor did any of his Successors take so prodigious a title. For he is no friend to the bridegroom that would be loved in his stead, but a *Bawd of Antichrist*, &c.

His 8th. Epistle is to the *Greek* Emperor to flatter him, to help him with *Henry* against the *Normans*; In which (to prove the Romans succession) " he faith, [The holy Church and Apostolick Seat hath been too long usur- " ped by *Mercenaries* that were no Pastors, that sought their own, and " not the things of Christ.]

"This Pope and *Michael* Patriarch of *Constantinople*, were so unreconci- "lable that they continued mutual condemnations. *Michael* is condem- ned with his *Greeks*. 1. For rebaptizing the Papists. 2. For saying that they had no true Sacrifice or Baptism. 3. For holding Priests marriage, for rejecting the *Filioque*, &c. Bin. p. 1116.

§ 114. CCCXXIX. *An.* 1049. A Roman Council was fain upon pen- nance to pardon Simoniacal Bishops and Priests, because the Cry was, that " else almost all the Churches would be destitute, and the Church ser- " vice omitted to the subversion of the Christian Religion, and the des- " peration of all the faithful. (Where was the holy Church of *Rome* now, and its Succession, if the Canons for nullifying Simoniacal ordinations hold good?)

§ 115. CCCXXX. The Pope resolved to go to *France*, and Preside in a Council, which he did, at *Rhemes*: But many Nobles and Bishops told the King that it was an usurpation and a Novelty and would enslave his Kingdom : The King forbad him, yet the Pope came whether the King would or not ; And the King went away about his military affairs, and some Bishops with him, and others stayed.

The Arch-Bishop of *Rhemes*, and others were accused of heinous Crimes : The Bishop of *Laugres* was charged with [*entring by Simoniacal* " heresies, selling orders, bearing Armes, Murder, Adultery, Tyranny to " his Clergy, and Sodomy: Many witnesses testified all this: One Clergy- " man witnessed, that while he was yet a Lay-man this Bishop violently " took his Wife from him, and when he had committed adultery with her,

he

"he made her a Nun.] A Presbyter witnessed that this Bishop took
"him and delivered him to his followers, who tormenting him by ma-
"ny torments, which is more wicked, did with sharp nails pierce his
"genetals, and by such violence forced him to give them ten pounds
"of denaries: The Bishop hearing these accusations desired time and
"Council, and going to the Arch-Bishops of *Besanzon*, and *Lyons*, o-
"peneth his secrets to them and desireth them to plead his cause. But
"the man involved in the guilt of such villanies (who but the day be-
"fore had been the accuser of a faulty Brother, and seeing the mote in
"anothers eye, had not seen the beam in his own, but moved for
"the other mans damnation being himself deservedly to be condemned,)
"was not only unable to excuse himself from the objected crimes, but
"also the tongue of his advocate (the Arch-Bishop) was by God so si-
"lenced that he was not able to speak a word for his defence. For
"the Arch-Bishop of *Besanzon* where he prepared himself to plead for
"him and excuse his crimes, suddenly found himself disabled in his voice
"by God. And when the Arch-Bishop of *Besanzon* found himself so dis-
"abled by miracles, he gave signs to the Arch-Bishop of *Lyons* to speak
"for this his Brother in his stead; who rising up said that the accused
"Bishop doth confess that he sold Orders, and that he extorted the mo-
"ney from the said Priest, but that he did not do the tormenting acti-
"ons mentioned by him; other things he denyed, but before the next
"day he fled from the Council. And another Bishop (of *Nevers*) con-
"fessed that his Parents bought his Place, and deposed himself: and
"some other Bishops confessed Simoniacal entrance. The Pope excom-
"municated many that fled from the Council. He renewed some old
"neglected Canons, as 1. *That no man be promoted to Church-Govern-*
"*ment without the ELECTION of the CLERKS and the PEOPLE*, &c.

Y y   CHAP.

The continuation of the history of Councils and their Bishops till the Conucil at Constantinople.

§ 1. CCCXXXI. Under *Leo* 9. *an.* 1049, a Synod at *Mentz,* some accused Bishops were questioned and other little matters done.

§ 2. CCCXXXII. In a Council at 1050. *Berengarius* his Letters to *Lanfrancus* were read, and he condemned (in a blind age.)

§ 3. CCCXXXIII. *An.* 1050. A Synod at *Vercelli* condemned *Johannes Scotus* and *Berengarius* and some that defended them.

§ 4. CCCXXXIV. *An.* 1050. A Council at *Cojaca* contained the King *Ferdinandus* of *Castile*, and his Queen, Bishops and Nobles (like our Parliaments, and so were many Councils then:) It is said to be for restoring Christianity (so low was it grown in the height of Popery and ignorance) having several orders for reformation. The 3d Title saith, that *wine*, *water* and the *host* in the eucharist signifie the Trinity. The 5th. saith, that Priests must so eat at the feasts of the dead, as to do some good for their souls, &c.

§ 5. CCCXXXV. *An.* 1051. A Roman Council excommunicated *Gregory* Bishop of *Vercelli* for Adultery with a widow espowsed to his Uncle, and for perjuries: But he was after restored to his office on promise of satisfaction: Also all the whores of Priests were decreed to be made servants at *Laterane. Pet. Damian. et Bin. p.* 1124.

§ 6. CCCXXXVI. In another Roman Synod the Pope Canonized a Bishop *Gerhard,* and decided a quarrel between two Bishops for extent of their Diocesses,

§ 7. *Victor* the 2d. is next Pope *an.* 1055. *Leo Hostiensis* saith that no man at *Rome* was found worthy. *Plat.* saith that they feared offending the Emperor: However the Romans sent to the Emperor to choose one for them, and some say desired this might be the man.

§ 8. CCCXXXVII. *Platina* saith that in a Council at *Florence* he deposed many Bishops for Simony and Fornication.

§ 9. CCCXXXVIII. In a Council at *Lyons, Baronius* (after others) saith a miracle was done, *viz.* saith he [" The heresie of Simonie having seiz-
" ed on all *Italy* and *Burgundie,* the Pope sent *Hildebrand* a sub-Deacon
" to call a Council, where an Arch-Bishop accused of Simony bribed all
" his accusers the next day into silence: *Hildebrand* bid him say [*Glory*
" *be to the Father, Son and Holy Ghost*] He said the rest, but was not
" able to name the Holy Ghost: Whereupon he confest his crimes, and
" besides seven and twenty other Prelates of the Churches, forty five
" Bishops confest themselves Simoniacks and renounced their places.]
What

their Councils abridged.

What a case was the Church in when Popery grew ripe? *Pet. Damian.* mentioneth six Bishops deposed by *Hildebrand* for divers crimes.

§ 10. By the way it is worthy enquiry whether *Hildebrand* being neither Bishop, Priest, nor Deacon, but a sub-Deacon only, was any of the Clergy or Church-Pastors to whom Christ gave the power of the Keys *(*Yea, if he had been a Deacon.*)* And therefore whether he had any power from Christ to preside before Arch Bishops and Bishops in in Councils, and to depose and excommunicate Bishops. If it be said that he did it by the Pope's commission, the question recurreth, whether God ever gave Pope or Prelate power to make new Church-officers whom he never instituted *de specie*, that should have the power of the Keys, yea, and be above the Bishops of the Church? And whether Popes or Prelates may commit preaching or Sacraments to Lay-men? if not, how can they commit the Keys of Church-Government to them, or to any as little authorized by Christ? Indeed baptizing is but using the Key of Church-entrance; And therefore he that may so let men into the Church may baptize them *(*which Papists unhappily allow the Laity.*)* And if *per se* or *per alium* will salve all, whether Priests may not preach, pray, and give Sacraments by Lay-men: And so Lay-men at last put down both Prelates and Priests as needless?

§ 11. CCCXXXIX. *An.* 1055. They say that this great Subdeacon *Hildebrand* (the grand advancer of the Roman Kingdom) did call a Council at *Tours*, which cited poor *Berengarius* and forced him to recant *(*whether it be true I know not.*)*

§ 12. To this Council the Emperor *Henry* sent his Agents to complain that *Ferdinand* the great, King of *Castile*, refused subjection to the Emperor, and claimed some such title to himself, and (now ignorance, superstition, and interest having made the Clergy the Rulers of Kings and Kingdoms) the Emperor desireth that King *Ferdinand* may be excommunicate unless he will submit and surcease, and all the Kingdom of *Spain* be interdicted *(*or forbidden Gods worship.*)* The Prelates perceived how they were set up by this motion, and made Kings of Kings, and they thought the Emperor's motion reasonable, and without hearing King *Ferdinand* made themselves judges and sent him word that he must submit and obey or be excommunicated and bear the interdict. The King took time to answer, and calling his own Bishops together found them of the same mind and spirit, and so was forced to promise submission. This *Baronius, an.* 1055. writes *ex* ?*o. Mariano;* and *Binnius p.* 1126.

§ 13. CCCXL. They say that the Emperor dying, left his Son *Henry* but five years old, and knew no better way to secure his succession than to desire Pope *Victor* to take the care of it: who therefore called a Council at *Colen* to quiet *Baldwin* and *Godfrey* Earls of *Flanders* that else would have resisted him. Thus Bishops in Councils now were as Parliaments to the Kingdoms of deluded men.

§ 14. CCCXLI. At *Tholouse, an.* 1056. A Council of 18 Bishops attempted

tempted reformation, forbidding (alas! how oft) Bishops to sell orders, and other acts of Simony, and Priests using their wives, and the Adultery, Incest and perjury of Bishops and Priests; bidding them that are such, repent, and forbidding communion with men called hereticks.

§ 15. CCCXLII. Though Adultery, Incest, Perjury and Simony of Bishops was so hardly restrained, it seems they would pay for it by superstition; for a Council at *Compostella* decreed (saith *Baron. ad an.* 1056.) that 1. All Bishops and Priests should say Mass every day. 2. That at fasts and Litanies (which were perambulations in penitence) they should be cloathed in sackcloth.

§ 16. *Stephen* the 9th. alias 10th. is next made Pope: In his time saith *Platina* the Church of *Milan* was reconciled to *Rome*, that had withdrawn itself from it two hundred years. Was all the world then subject to the Pope when his Italian neighbours were not?

§ 17. This Pope lived after his entrance but 6 or 7 months, and they say made them promise him to choose none in his place till *Hildebrand* came home to counsel them: (A great Subdeacon that *Rome* must be ruled by.) But in the mean time the new Emperor being but five or six years old, the great men of *Italy* turned to the old game and brought in one by strength *(Mincius)* whom they called *Benedict* the 10th. alias 9th. a Bishop; he reigned 9 months, 20 dayes. But when *Hildebrand* came home he got him cast out. This was the twenty first schism in the Papacie.

§ 18. *Hildebrand*'s crafty counsel was to send to the Emperor to consent to *Gerard* Bishop of *Florence* whom they chose in *Italy* and called *Nicholas* the 2d. Lest *Benedict* should get the Emperor on his side; and so *Nicholas* made *Benedict* renounce and banished him: But how shall we be sure which was the true Pope?

An. 1059.

§ 19. This Pope's first epistle is to the Arch-Bishop of *Rhemes* to advise him to admonish the King of *France* for resisting the Pope.

§ 20. CCCXLIII. The Pope's Council at *Sutrium* deposed *Benedict*.

§ 21. CCCXLIV. *An.* 1059. A Council of 113 Bishops at *Rome*, they say, made *Berengarius* recant, but not repent; but as soon as he came home he wrote against them and their Doctrine.

§ 22. In this Council, saith *Platina*, the Pope made a decree very profitable to the Church of *Rome. Bin.* saith these were the words (translated) ["*p.* 1666. *First, God being the Inspector it is decreed that the election of the Roman Bishop be in the power of the Cardinal Bishops: so that if any one be inthroned in the Apostolick seat, without the foregoing concordant and Canonical election of them, and after the consent of the following religious Orders, Clerks and Laity,* (*) *he be not accounted Apostolical but Apostatical.*]

(*) But others say, the Emperor's consent also was put in.

Here it is much to be noted, 1. That this is a new foundation of the Papacy (by *Hildebrand*'s Council) without which it was falling to utter confusion. How then doth the Roman sect cry down Innovation and boast

boast of Antiquity? 2. Either the Bishop of *Rome* is to be chosen as the Bishop of that particular Church, and then the members of that particular Church should choose him, or else as the Bishop of the universal Church (pretendedly) and then the universal Church should choose him. But the Cardinal Bishops of other particular Churches are neither the particular Roman Church, nor the universal, nor their delegates: and so have no just pretence of power.

3. Either this decree was new, or old and in force before: If new, their Church foundation is new and mutable, as is said: If old, all the Popes that were otherwise chosen were no Popes.

4. And if it be but necessary for the future, all that after were otherwise chosen were no Popes.

5. If several wayes and parties or powers making Popes may all make them true Popes, then who knoweth which and how many of those there are and which is the true Pope if ten were made at once ten several wayes?

6. This confesseth that Christ hath appointed no way for choosing Popes, nor given any sort of men power to choose them: else what need Pope *Nicholas* begin it now anew? And if so, it seemeth that Christ never instituted the Papacy: For can we suppose him so Laxe a Legislator, as to say, a Pope shall be made, and never tell us who shall have power to do it. Then *England* may choose one, and *France* another, and *Spain* another,&c.the Bishops one,the Priests another, the Prince another, and the Citizens another.But if Christ have setled a Pope-making power in any,it is either the same as Pope *Nicholas* did,in Cardinal Bishops, or nor: If not, the Pope changeth Christ's institution: If yea, then all those were no Popes that were otherwise chosen, and so where is the Roman Church and its succession.

7. What power hath Pope *Nicholas* to bind his successors? Have not they as much power as he? and so to undo it all again? If the King should decree that his Kingdom hereafter shall not be hereditary but elective, and that the Bishops should be the choosers of the King, were this obligatory against the right of his heirs?

8. By this decree, if the Laity and Clerks consent not after, he is still no Pope.

§ 23. In this same Council (saith *Bin.* ibid.) it was decreed [" that no one hear the *Mass* of a *Presbyter*, whom he knoweth undoubtedly to have a Concubine, or Subintroduced Woman.] *Quær.* Whether they that make him a Schismatick that goeth from a scandalous, wicked, malignant, or utterly insufficient Priest, and dare not commit the care of his soul to such a one, be not looser than Pope *Nicholas* and this Roman Council was?

§ 24. A Council at *Malphia* and another at *Paris* for Crowning King *Philip*, and one at *Jacca* in *Spain*, of small moment.

§ 25. *An.* 1061. Was the 22d. Schism or two Popes of *Rome*, for
five

five years continuance. The Cardinal Bishops, for fear of the Emperor, chose one that was great with him, *Anselm* Bishop of *Luca*: but the *Italian* Princes perswaded the Emperor that it was a wrong to them and him, and chose *Cadolus Palavicinus* Bishop of .... *Honorius* the 2d. The Sword was to determine who .... *Cadolus* came with an Army to *Rome*; the Romans, ..., and in the Fields, called *Nero*'s; a great .... *in which many of both sides fell*, but *Cadolus* .... He shortly returned with a great Army being called by a .... *Romans*, that were men of pleasure, and by force seized on .... and St. *Peter*'s Church: But the Souldiers of *Gotifred* put his Souldiers to flight; and he himself narrowly scaped, the Prefect of *Rome*'s Son with him breaking through the Romans got possession of the Tower, where they besieged him till they forced him to yield, and buy his liberty of the besiegers for 300 pound of Silver. Then the Bishop of *Colen* having the education of the young Emperor came to *Rome* to rebuke *Alexander* as an Usurper, but by *Hildebrand* was so overcome (that the choice belonged not to the Emperor) that he called a Council which confirmed *Alexander* and deposed *Honorius*. The Emperor consented on condition that *Cadolus* be pardoned, and *Gibert* (his promoter, Chancellor of *Parma*) made Arch-Bishop of *Ravenna*, which the Pope consented to and did. Thus then were Popes and Bishops made.

Q. How shall we be sure, for *Cadolus*'s five years, who was the Pope?

§ 26. A woman called *Mathildis* a Countess was then the great Patroness of the Papacy, who furnished military *Hildebrand* (that did all) with Souldiers to conquer several Great Men that opposed them, and to set up *Alexander* and defend him.

§ 27. This Pope *Alexander* is said by *Bin.* and *Baron* to judge King *Harold*, of *England*, an Usurper, to dispose of the Crown to *William* of *Normandy*, and declare him lawful Successor, and send him a Banner that he might fight for it and possess it. Thus did this Prelate give Crowns and Kingdoms, as the supreme judge (made by himself.)

Bin. p. 1132.

He after required Rent (*Peter-Pence*) from *England* of *William*.

§ 28. He made some constitutions for his old Church at *Milan*. Three thing are the summe of them and many other Councils. 1. Against Simonie. 2. Against the Clergies fornication (no Canons cured them of either of these.) 3. That no Lay-Man judge any Clerk for his crimes: only if Priests live in fornication he alloweth Lay-Men to tell the Arch-Bishops, and if they will do nothing, then to withhold their duties and benefits till they amend. (But this *Binnius* noteth was but a temporary extraordinary concession, for the hatred that this Pope had to fornicating Clergy-Men.) But if they did but now and then lie with a woman by chance, and did not obstinately still keep them, they must not so trouble them.

§ 29.

§ 29. CCCXLV. The foresaid *Cadolus* or *Honorius* 2d. was setled Pope by a Council at *Basil, An.* 1061. where, say some, many Simoniacal, incontinent, wicked Bishops decreed that no Pope should be made but out of *Italy* (which they called Paradise, that is, *Lombardy*.)

§ 30. CCCXLVI. A Council at *Osborium, An.* 1062. contrarily condemned him and set up *Alexander*. Though before *Platina* faith that *Cisalpini omnes* all on the *Romans* side of the *Alpes* obeyed *Honorius* except *Mathildis* a good woman.

§ 31. Here *Binnius* thought a Dialogue of *Pet. Damian* worthy to be inserted, to prove that Princes may not make Bishops of *Rome*. In which he would prove that the Decrees that gave the Emperor such power may be changed, because God doth not alwaies perform his own word for want of mans duty; And he faith, that some men have been sinners and perished for obeying Gods own Law, and some rewarded for breaking it; which he proveth by a profane quibble. 1 In *Judas*; as if Chrifts words *what thou dost do quickly*, had been a command to do the thing. 2. In the *Rechabites* that drank not Wine when *Jeremy* bade them; As if Gods Command to *Jeremy* to try them, had been his Command to them to do it.

A Council was at *Arragon* in *Spain* for we know not what.

§ 32. CCCXLVII. *An.* 1063. *Peter* Bishop of *Florence* being accused of Heresie and Simony, and deposed, a Council at *Rome* renewed Pope *Nicolas* 2d's. Canons, not to hear *Masse* of a Priest that liveth with a Concubine or introduced woman: To excommunicate Simoniacks, &c.

§ 33. CCCXLVII. In a Council at *Mantua* (to quiet some that yet took *Cadolus*'s part and accused Pope *Alexander* of *Simony*) *Alexander* is owned, and *Cadolus*, not appearing, cast out; who after tryed it out (as is aforesaid) by an Army.

§ 34. CCCXLIX. In a Council at *Barcelon* the *Spaniards* abrogated their old *Gothish* Laws and made new ones, but would not change the *Gothish* Church rites: Here also *Alexander* was owned.

§ 35. *An.* 1065. A Council was at *Rome* against incest.

§ 36. Another for the same, the former not prevailing.

§ 37. In a Synod at *Winchester, William* the Conqueror puts down and imprisons Bishops and sets up others, for his own interest.

§ 38. CCCL. A Council at *Mentz* was to have separated the young Emperor and his Queen, but the Popes Legate hindred it.

§ 39. CCCLI. In a Council at *Mentz* the Bishop of *Constance* is cast out for Simony and many crimes; the Emperor being for him.

§ 40. *An.* 1072. They say an English Council subjected *York* to *Canterbury* and owned *Wolstan* Bishop of *Worcester* accused for being unlearned as he was.

§ 41. CCCLII. *An.* 1073. In a Council at *Erford* the Emperor got the Bishops to fulfil his will about some Tythes, threatening them that appealed to *Rome*.

§ 42.

§ 42. Now cometh in the Foundation of the new Church of *Rome*, *Hildebrand* called *Gregory* 7th. *An.* 1073. a man of Great wit, and for ought I find in the most probable History not guilty of the gross immoralities, or sensuality of many of his predecessors; but it's like blinded with the opinion which the Papists Fifth-monarchy men have received (and *Campanella de regno Dei* opened and pleaded for) *viz.* that Christs Kingdom on earth consisteth in the Saints judging the world, that is, the Pope and Prelates ruling the Kings and Kingdoms of the earth, he did with greatest animosity set himself to execute his opinions. And withal, the factions of *Rome* and tyranny of their petty Princes and Whores and debauched Citizens, having long made the Papacy the scorn of the world and the lamentation of all sober Christians, constrained the better part to beg help from the Emperors against debauched monstrous Popes and their upholders: And by this means sometimes the choice fell into the Emperors hands, and sometimes when they were far off, the City-prevailing-part rebelled, and chose without them, or pulled down them that the Emperors set up: And then the Emperors came and pulled down the Anti-Popes, and chastised the City faction; and thus between the *Italian* and the *German* powers the City was a field of war, and the richer by bribes, and the stronger by the sword, how monstrous villanies soever were set up. It was no wonder then if *Hildebrand* first by Pope *Nicholas* 2. and *Alexander* and then by himself did resolve to run a desperate hazard, when he had two such great works at once to do, as first to recover the debauched and shattered shamed Papacy from this confusion, and then to *subdue all Kings and Kingdoms* within their reach to such a *Priest-King* as was then under so great disgrace. And *tibi dabo claves* must do all this.

§ 43. *Hildebrand* however had the wit to settle himself at first by seeking the Emperor's consent: And being settled he got *Agnes* the Emperor's mother and Guardian mostly on his side. He then began to claim *presentations and investitures* and to take the power over the Bishops out of the Emperor's hands, and to threaten him as Simoniacal, and for *communicating with the excommunicate*. The Emperor after some treaty submitted, and was reconciled to the Pope; but the Pope said *he did not amend*. The Pope calls a Council at *Rome*, where he excommunicated Simoniacks, openly saying that he would excommunicate the Emperor unless he amended. *Guibert* Arch-Bishop of *Ravenna* being there accuseth the Pope for such threats against the Emperor, and got *Cincius* the Prefect's Son to apprehend him *and imprison him*. The People rise up in arms and deliver the Pope, and pull down *Cincius*'s house to the ground, and cutting off their noses, banish his family out of the City. *Cincius* got to the Emperor. *Guibert.* Arch-Bishop of *Ravenna*, *Theobald* Arch-Bishop of *Milan*, and most of all the other Bishops on that side the *Alpes* conspire against the Pope. (And yet they say that all the world were his subjects.) He calls another Synod of his own Bishops (for Synods

nods were still the great executioners) where *Gibert* and *Hugo* (one of his Cardinals that was against him) are deposed and curst from Christ. This Emperor also calls a Council at *Wormes*, where by the means of *Sigifred* Arch-Bishop of *Mentz*, it is decreed that no man in any thing obey the Pope of *Rome*. *Roland* a Clerk is sent to *Rome* to command the Pope to meddle with the government no more, and the Cardinals are commanded to forsake *Gregory* and seek for another Pope. Now the War began between the Sword and the Keys. *Gregory* by sentence deposed the Arch-Bishop of *Mentz*, and the other Clergy that were for the Emperor; and he Anathematized the Emperor himself, having first *deprived him of all Regal Power and administration* (as far as his decree would do it.) The form of his curse and deposition *Platina* reciteth, where are these words:[" *I cast him down from his Imperial and Regal Administration;* " *And I absolve all Christians Subject to the Empire, from that Oath, by* " *which they have used to swear Fidelity to true Kings: For it is meet that* " *he be deprived of dignity, who endeavoureth to diminish the Majesty of* " *the Church.*] (Mark O ye Kings and be wise.)

Some told the Pope that the Emperor should not be so hastily Anathematized: To whom he answered, " *Did Christ except Kings when he* " *said to* Peter [*Feed my Sheep ? when he gave him the Power of binding and loosing, he excepted none from his power.*]

The Emperor wrote Letters to many Christian Princes and States to acquaint them with the Papal Injuries; and the Pope wrote his accusations of the Emperor and his own Justification. The Empire was presently all in Division. One part was for the Emperor, and another for the Pope: Most of the Bishops of *Germany* obeyed the Emperor, and some were against him, as excommunicate. Some Councils were for him, and some against him. And, as *Abbas Urspergensis* said, they did so often swear and forswear according as Power and Interest moved, one time for the Emperor, and another against him, that Perjury was become a common thing both with the Bishops and the Laity. He that will see the many treatises that Learned men then wrote for the power of Princes against the Papal tyranny and rebellion may find them in the Voluminous Collections of *Michael Goldastus de Monarchia*.

The party that obeyed the Pope chose another to be Emperor, *Rodulph* Duke of *Suevia*: The Emperor requireth the Pope to Excommunicate *Rodulph*: He refuseth: The Emperor calleth a Council of Bishops at *Brixia*: They depose the Pope, and make *Gibert* of *Ravenna* Pope called *Clement* the 3d. who, saith *Onuphrius*, sate, 21 years, so long had they two Popes, at this 23d. Schism or doubling.

But did the Emperor nothing to prevent all this? Yes, at the motion of the *German* Princes to avoid contention, he made an Oath to ask the Pope forgiveness, if the Pope would come into *Germany*. The Pope on his way fearing that the Emperor coming toward him with an Army would apprehend him, turned back again, and betook him to a strong

City of his Patroness one *Mathildis* a woman: The Emperor with his Army travelled to him, and came to the Gates of the City; and in a great and sharp winter frost, putting off his Royal Ornaments, came barefoot to confess his fault and ask forgiveness of the Pope. The Pope would not suffer him to come in; He patiently stayed three daies in the Suburbs continually begging pardon, and the Citizens moved with Compassion; At last the woman *Mathildis*, and *Adelai* a *Savoy* Earl, and the Abbot of *Cluny* became petitioners for him, and prevailed for mercy with the Pope, and he was absolved and reconciled to the Church, having sworn a peace and promised Obedience.]

I give you the words of *Platina* all along. And now whether *Hildebrand* or *Henry* was the better man in common morals, I that knew them not, must refer you to the Historians of that age, of whom some extol the Pope and depreciate the Emperor, and others honour the Emperor, and deeply accuse the Pope; But if an Emperor that travelled so far into another Country, and put off his ornaments, and with his Army waited three daies patiently in the Suburbs of a womans City barefoot in a great frost, begging mercy and pardon of a Priest before he could be let in, and after this swore obedience to him, I say, If this Prince did not yet sufficiently submit, but deserve to be turned out of his Empire, though at the cost of blood and desolation to the innocent Countries, it will be hard to know when the Obedience and Submission of Kings is enough to satisfie an ambitious Prelate.

But the Popes Historians say that the Emperor brake his Covenant. It is a hard thing for a King that promiseth Subjection and Obedience to a Pope to be sure to keep his word, unless he foreknew what would be commanded him: when he hath taken away his Power and Kingdom by parts, he may command his life. It's a great doubt to me, when God hath made Princes the Rulers of Prelates, and Procurators of his Church, whether it be not a sin against God and their undertaken office, for these Princes to cast off this trust and work, because a Pope or Prelate claimeth it. The Pope still charged him with sacriledge. But I doubt he expounded his meaning when he *deposed him for diminishing the Majesty of the Church*, that is, of the *Pope* and *Prelates*.

To proceed in the History: In the 3d. or 4th. battle it was that *Rodulph* was slain; and It was the Popes denial to disown or excommunicate *Rodulph* after so low a submission of the Emperor, that enraged *Henry*, and made him think of another remedy than to be a Prelates slave. The Pope called all the Bishops that cleaved to the Emperor *seditious*: He condemneth *Roland* the German Legate and sendeth into *Germany* Legates of his own with a *Mandamus*, *We command that no King, Arch-Bishop, Bishop, Duke, Earl, Marquess, or Knight dare resist our Legates*, &c. And the Penalty to the disobedient is terrible, viz. [*We accurse him from Christ, and take from him his part of Victory by Arms.*] Sure if Popes had the power of Victory, they need not so oft have fled to Castles, nor to have rid on an Aſs with the face backward, nor to have ſuffered what many of them have done. All this he doth, [*Interpoſitâ Dei et B. Petri authoritate, quâ nulla poteſt eſſe major.*] Did *Peter* ever think that his name would have thus ſubdued Emperors and Kings?

-The Pope again in a prayer to God and St. *Peter* reciteth the 2d. *Pſalm,* and telleth them how the Emperor would caſt off his yoke, and again curſeth him from Chriſt, and depoſeth him from all his Government, and abſolveth all his Subjects from the Oath of Obedience; ſaying, that "he that may bind and looſe in Heaven hath power to take away on "Earth, both Empires, Kingdoms and Principalities, and whatever "men have to give or take away: *If we Judge the ruling Angels, how* "*much more their Servants? Therefore* (ſaith he to the Biſhops) *Let Kings* "*and all ſecular Princes underſtand by the example of this man, how great* "*your power is in Heaven, and how much God eſteemeth you, and let them* "*fear hereafter to break the commands of the Church.*] Paſs this ſen- "tence preſently on Henry, *that all may underſtand that this Son of iniquity* "*fell not from his Kingdom by Chance, but by your endeavor.*] Plat. p. 180.

Rodulph being killed, the Rebels ſet up the Emperors Son, a Lad, a- gainſt his own Father: But at that preſent he was quieted, and the Em- peror went with an Army into *Italy*, and firſt Conquered the Army of *Mathildis* the Popes Patroneſs, and brought his own Pope *Clement* the 3d. to the Chair, and was crowned by him: He beſieged *Gregory* in the Caſtle : *Guiſcard*, a Norman cometh with an Army to fight for the Pope : The Citizens reſiſt him, (the Emperor being drawn out to *Sens*.) *Guiſcard* burnt and deſtroyed that part of the City which is between the Laterane and the Capitol, and took the Capitol and deſtroyed it. He gave the prey of the City to his Souldiers, and delivered *Gregory* and carried him away to *Caſſinum* and *Salernum*, where he dyed, having reigned 12 years. *Bin*. ſaith, that *Henry* beſieged *Rome* three years be- fore he took it. When *Robert Guiſcard* had delivered the Pope, he de- poſed (*quantum in ſe*) all the new Cardinals made by *Clement* 3. and curſed the Emperor again. *Gregory* himſelf ſaith that *Italian, French*, and *German* Biſhops were for the Emperor, and they were alſo for *Clement* 3. How ſhall we know then which was the true Pope?

§ 44. No leſs than ten Books of *Hildebrand's* Epiſtles are added by *Binnius* to his life. Moſt of them for the Papal Intereſt. In *lib*. 2. *Ep*. 5. He talketh of *Philip* King of *France* as he did of the Emperor, ſaying he was no King but a Tyrant, and declaring that he was reſolved to take his Kingdom from him if he did not amend his wicked life. One of his crimes was reſiſting the Pope that would ſet Biſhops in his Kingdom without his conſent.

Epiſt. 13. He tells *Solomon* King of *Hungary*, that his Kingdom is the propriety of the Church of *Rome*, devoted to it by King *Stephen* ; and reproveth him for diminiſhing the Roman Kingdom, by accepting *Hun-*
gary

gary as from the Germans; and exhorts him to repent and amend.

Epist. 18. He again threatneth the King of *France* to cut off from the Church, both him and all that give him any *Regal Honour or Obedience* (O heinous crime! to keep the 5th. Commandment and *Rom.* 13. 1,2,3.) *And that this excommunication shall be oft confirmed upon* St. *Peter's Altar.*]

Epist. 28. He suspends (*quantum in se*) the Arch-Bishop of *Breme* as an Enemy to the Church of *Rome* and for hindering his Legates from gathering a Council, and refusing to come to *Rome* to answer it.

Epist. 32. He calls the King of France a ravening Wolf, and unjust Tyrant.

Many great persons he forced to separate after Marriage, because they were in the fourth degree of Consanguinity.

Epist. 51. He tells the King of *Denmark*, that not far from *Rome* there was a Province possest by *vile and sluggish Hereticks*, and desireth him to send his Son with an Army to conquer them. What Province he meaneth, I am not certain; unless it was the *Waldenses*.

☞ § 44. Reader, we are greatly beholden to *Binnius* who hath recorded, as Oracles, 27 sentences called THE POPES DICTATES, by which you may partly know what Popery is.

1. "That the Roman Church was founded only by our Lord.
2. "That only the Bishop of *Rome* is rightly called Universal.
3. "That only the Pope can depose Bishops and reconcile them.
4. "That his Legates must preside in Councils, though they be of "inferior degree, before all Bishops; and may pass on them the senten-"ce of deposition.
5. "That the Pope may depose those that are absent.
6. "That with those that are excommunicated by him, among other "things, we may not dwell in the same house.
7. "That to him only it is lawful to make new Laws for the necessity "of the time; and to congregate new people; of Canonical to make "an Abbaty; and contrarily to divide a rich Bishoprick, and unite poor "ones.
8. "That only he may use Imperial Ensigns or Escucheons.
9. "That all Princes must kiss the feet of the Pope only.
10. "That only his name may be recited in the Churches.
11. "That it is the one only name in the World.
12. "That it is lawful for him to depose Emperors.
13. "That it is lawful for him in case of necessity to remove Bishops "from seat to seat.
14. "That he may ordain a Clerk from any Church, whither he "will.
15. "That one ordained by him may govern another Church; and "must not take a superior degree from another Bishop.

16. That

16. "That no Synod without his command may be called Universal.

17. "That no Chapter, nor no Book may be accounted Canonical without his authority.

18. "That his sentence may be retracted by none: and he alone may retract all mens.

19. "That he ought to be judged of no man.

20. "That no man must dare to condemn any one that appealeth to the Apostolick Seat.

21. "That the Greater causes of all Churches must be referred to him.

22. "That the Roman Church never erred, nor, as the Scripture witnesseth, will ever err.

23. "That the Bishop of *Rome*, if he be Canonically ordained, is undoubtedly made Holy by the merits of St. *Peter*, as St. *Ennodius* Bishop of *Papia* witnesseth, and many holy Fathers confess, as is contained in the Decrees of Pope *Symmachus*.

24. "That it is lawful for subjects to accuse by his Command and licence.

25. "That he may depose and reconcile Bishops without Synodal meetings.

26. "That he is not to be accounted a Catholick who agreeth not with the Roman Church.

27. "That he may absolve the Subjects of unjust men from fidelity.

These are put by *Bin.* among *Gregory's* Epistles, *p*. 1196. as the Popes Dictates. If I had not translated them from such an unquestioned Author that followeth *Baronius*, some would have thought they had been but the forgeries of some Protestant accuser, and that the Popes have no such tenents. What one is here that is not false? and how many of them are horridly arrogant? The reading of them would tempt a doubting man to think that the Pope is the Eldest Son of the Prince of Pride, exalting himself above all that is called God, and arrogating Christ's prerogatives, and therefore Antichrist. If any would know what Popery is; A great part of the description is here given you by their greatest Pope himself, and by their chief Historians.

§ 45. Much of his 4th Book of Epistles is to require Princes, Prelates, and People to forsake the Emperor and choose another, and to excommunicate all that will communicate with him: yet in his 11th. *Epist.* he reciteth himself, how lamentably with tears, three dayes in the frost barefoot, he begged for pardon, and how the compassionate People thought the Pope hard-hearted and tyrannical for not yielding; and that at last two Ladyes and an Abbot overcame him to absolve him.

§ 46. *Lib.* 4. *Epist.* 28. He tells the *Spaniards* also that their Kingdom was St. *Peter's* property: But why did he trouble himself to lay

claim

claim to particular Kingdoms? Would not his claim to all the world serve turn for the particulars?

Lib. 5. *Epist.* 4. He claimeth the Isle of *Corsica*.

§ 47. That it may appear that the presumptuous usurpations of the Pope were not consented to by many Bishops, he oft complaineth that many Bishops of *France*, *Italy*, and *Germany* were against him: He abundantly chideth and threatneth several particular Bishops for resisting and disobeying him. *Lib.* 6. *Epist.* 4. he writeth thus to the Bishop of *Liege*. [" *Having read the Letters of your Brotherhood, we did not a lit-* " *tle wonder that you wrote that which became you not, in reverence of the* " *Apostolick seat: but that you did with biting invective reprehend me, for* " *absolving your Parishioner, that lately came to us; as if the Apostolick seat* " *had not authority to bind and absolve whomsoever we will and wheresoever* " *we will: Know therefore that we are greatly moved against your temerity*.]

Indeed one of the tricks of the Papal ambition was to be the Asylum of all wicked fugitives that fled from Church justice in all Countries near them; to shew favour to all condemned sinners that would but fly to *Rome*, and appeal to them from the Justice of their Pastors, yea, and of their Princes too, which made their friends to be rather many than good.

§ 48. And the Church of *Rome* was not yet rich enough with all the Principalities it had got: They still kept on the trade of enriching the Pope to save their souls. *Binnius.* p. 1233. honoureth us with a record among *Gregory* 7th. *Epistles*, viz. [" *In the name of the Father, Son and* " *Holy Ghost, in the* 6th. *year of the Pontificate of Gregory* 7th. *I* Marro " *Son of* Gislet *dwelling in the Dukedom of* Spoletane, *for the Redemption* " *of my own and my Parents souls do give, deliver and offer to St.* Peter " *Prince of the Apostles, and on his Altar, all that belongeth to me of the* " *Castle called* Moricicla, *&c*.] Did Christ think how easily Rich men might be saved (by giving to the Pope in the name of St. *Peter*) when he said, *It was harder for a rich man to enter into the Kingdom of Heaven, than for a Camel to go through a Needle's Eye?*

§ 49. *Lib.*7. *Epist.* 3. He saith [" *They that are Latines do all of them,* " *except a very few, praise the cause of* Henry, *and defend it, and charge me* " *with too much obstinacy and impiety against him*.] And if the Latines did so, what did the *Germans*, *French*, &c? You see here that it was far from all the world that was subject to the Pope, and took his part in his usurpations.

Epist. 4. He commandeth a General no more to fight against the King of *Dalmatia*, as belonging to St. *Peter*].

§ 50. Yet this Pope doth teach them the truth against deceitful pennance or repentance, *Lib,* 7. *Epist.* 10. viz. [*We say that it is a fruitless* " *pennance, when men remain in the same fault, or in the like, or in a worse* " *or in one little less: He therefore that will worthily repent, must have re-* " *course to the Original of his Faith, and be solicitous watchfully to keep that*
which

their Councils abridged.

" which in his Baptism he promised, viz. to renounce the Devil and his
" pomps and to believe in God, that is, thinking rightly of him, to obey his
" Commands.

§ 51 Epist. 11. He tells the Duke of *Bohemia* that it is customarily and doubtfully that he saluteth him with [*Apostolical Benediction.*] Because
" he communicated with the excommunicate : And he denieth his request of
" using or translating the Divine Service or Offices into the Sclavonian
" tongue ; because there were many mysteries in it. Thus come up the Prohibition to the peoplee, to pray understandingly.

Epist. 14. He absolveth the Bishop of *Liege* from an Oath because, he took it by force : And commandeth him to rise up against the imposer with all his power, he being St. *Peter's* enemy.

Epist. 21. He tells the King of *Denmark* of an ill custom among them, that whatever ill weather or calamity befell them, they imputed all to the *ill lives of Priests*.

Epist. 23. He tells our King *William* the Conqueror that seeing he was on his side, and is charged by some with all his bloodshed, that now he must be very obedient to him as his Pastor, and *Peter's* Successor.

And *Epist.* 25. He tells them that the Papal or Apostolick power is greater than the Kingly ; and must rule it, as the Sun is greater than the Moon.

Lib. 8. *Epist.* 1. He laments the Corruption of the Church in *Armenia*:
"[1. Because they mixed not *Water with Wine in the Sacrament, when all
" men know that Blood and Water came from the side of Christ.* 2. *Because
" they made not their Chrysm of Balsom, but of Butter.* 3. *Because they
" honoured the memory of* Dioscorus.] O what Heresies !

Pag. 1254. in *Bin.* There is an Oath that *Robert* Duke of *Apulia, Calabria* and *Sicily* to be true to the Pope, and defend him as holding all these from him ; and there is the Popes grant of them to him, laying claim also to his other dominions ; the denyal of which he patiently beareth at the present.

§ 52. But lest you think that at least the Kingdom of *Spain* was fast, all this while to the Church of *Rome*, *Lib.* 8. *Epist.* 2. He writeth thus himself. [" *By the Letters of my Legate* Richard Abbot *of* Marseilles
" *you may know how great impiety is gone out of your Monastery* (*of* Cluny)
" *by the presumption of* Robert *a Monk, who imitating* Simon Magus,
" *feareth not to rise up against the Authority of* St. Peter, *with all the craft
" of his malignity, and to reduce by his suggestion into their old error an hun-
" dred thousand men, who by our diligence began to return to the right way:*]
the hopes that the Abbot thinks as he, for the honour of the *Roman*
urch. He chargeth the Abbot to cast out this man that had so engred *Spain*, adding [" And by your Letters diligently acquaint the
" King who is deceived by his fraud, that he hath greatly provoked St.
" *Peter's* wrath and indignation against him, and his grievous Revenge
" against him and his Kingdom unless he repent, because he undecently
hand-

" handled a Legate of the Roman Church, and believed falshood rather
" than truth. Of which that he may worthily make satisfaction to God
" and St. Peter, as he hath disgraced our Legate, so let him by due humility
and condign Reverence, make himself commendable and devout.
" For we think meet to signifie to him by you, that we will excommunicate
him if he correct not his fault, and will solicite all the faithful
' in the parts of *Spain* to his confusion : And if they be not obedient to
" my command, I will not think much to travel into *Spain* my self, and
" there to endeavour *dura et aspera*, Things hard and sharp against him as
" an enemy of the Christian Religion.] O brave Pope! had not these men
" a notable Knack or hap that could sit and talk down Emperors, and
Kings, and subdue and dispose of Kingdoms, by sitting at home and talking
big, and telling them that St. *Peter* was angry with them?

And who was this King but the great *Alfonsus*, to whom he writeth
himself, *Epift*. 3. to put away his evil counsellors, and hearken *in all things
to the Popes Legate, Richard*?

§ 53. *Epift.* 6. *l.* 8. He commandeth Souldiers to help *Michael* the
Emperor of *Constant* against the Usurper, to make himself judge, and
get an interest again in the Empire : But in vain.

§ 54. *Epift*. 7. He declareth that divers Princes having sworn and
promised him help, he resolved to come with an Army to recover *Ravenna*
to the Church.

*Epift.*8. He rejoyceth that they had newly found St. *Matthew*'s body,
and bids them now take him joyfully for their patron. These are the
grounds of Popish superstition : The body of St. *Matthew* that preached
to the *Abassines* in another part of the world, is found at *Salerno* in *Italy*,
a thousand years after he is dead. O that one knew how to be sure that
it was his body, and how it came thither ! Divers such findings they glory
in.

§ 55. *Epift*. 10. He writeth to *Orzocens* Prince of *Calaris* or *Sardinia*,
to require him as a note of his obedience to St. *Peter* and concord
with the Church of *Rome*, whose use it is, to let his Arch Bishop shave
his Beard, and to command all the Clergy of his dominion to shave their
Beards; and if they obey not, to force them to it, or exclude them. And
to be sure of success he lets him know, (how truly I know not) that
many Princes importuned him to give them leave to invade his Countrey,
but (this righteous ruling Pope) denied leave to them all, till he
had tryed whether he would obey him, which if he would do, he would
not only deny them leave to invade him, but also protect him. Reader,
think here. 1. Whether Princes held not their kingdoms loosely when
they where to lose them if they obeyed not the Pope in so small a thing
as the shaving of a Priests Beard. 2. Whether it were not a hard thing for
the Catholick Church then to have concord, when so small a difference
as the *shaving* or *not shaving* of Beards were put into their terms of Union

on and Peace? Who were the Schifmaticks then? was it not the makers and impofers of fuch laws and terms? 3. Is it not a high power that is claimed by Popes, when no Prieſt in all the Chriſtian world may have fo much as his Beard in his own power, in which nature hath given him a propriety? How much more might the Pope then command all mens purſes? 4. May way we not ſee here on what weighty reafons, thefe men condemn God's word of infufficiency, and plead for traditions, and a neceſſity of their additional Laws? When Scripture hath left out the ſhaving of mens Beards, and we had never had fuch a Law, if fuch power as the Papal had not made it? O what difcord and diforder would there be in the Church if we had not fo neceſſary a government! and what confuſion would toleration introduce, if mens Beards were left at liberty! But if *Paul* called the heathen Phylofophy *Vain* and [*Science falſly fo named.*] 1 *Tim.* 6. 20. as befooling the world with pedantick trifling, and calling them off from their great concernes, may we not ſay then that this is *vain Government and Order falſly fo named*, which thus calleth the Church from its primitive purity, fimplicity and unity, when Chriſtians were known by loving one another, to thefe childiſh games, that the Prelates and Prieſts of the Catholick Church muſt be known by their being without Beards? One would fufpect this had its original from Pope *Joane*, if there were indeed fuch a perfon; and that it is a Symbol of the Churches fex, as it is called *Our Mother*; or at leaſt that *Marozia* or *Theodora* inſtituted it. 5. And do you know which were the more inexcufable, for filencing and perfecuting the preachers of the Gofpel? The *Jews* that did it becauſe they thought it took down Gods Law, and would bring the Roman Power on them; Or the Roman heathens that thought the Gofpel deſtroyed the worſhip of their forefathers Gods; or the Roman Papiſts, that filenced and perfecuted men for wearing Beards? 1 *Theſ.*2.16.

§ 56. *Epiſt.* 11. When fome French Preachers had revived Religion in *Sweden*; the Pope, defirous to reap where they had fowed, fends to the King of *Sweden*, to tell him his joy; and that what the French taught them they recieved from *Rome*, and to defire him to fend one of his Biſhops to *Rome*, to acquaint him with their cuſtoms, and to receive his Laws and Mandates. You fee by what means *Rome* was raifed.

Epiſt. 15. A Biſhop gave up his Biſhoprick: The Pope chides him and commands him to a Monaſtery; Rather than do fo, he returneth to his feat again: The Pope chargeth him with the *Idololatriæ ſcelus* the Crime of *Idolatry*, for not *obeying him*; and writes to them not to recieve him or be ruled by him, as ever they loved the *Grace of God and* St. Peter.

The like he doth, *Epiſt.* 16. by the difobedient Biſhop of *Narbon*, and *Epiſt.* 17. by the difobedient Arch Biſhop of *Rhemes*, and *Fpiſt.* 18. 19, 20. of the fame; and all this in St. *Peter's* name. Yea *Epiſt.* 20. he requireth the King of *France* (*Philip*) to joyn againſt the Arch-biſhop of *Rhemes* as excommunicate, as ever he would have St. *Peter's* Grace, becauſe his *Kingdom and his Soul* were in St. *Peter's power*. And it is no wonder that they that believe that the Pope is St. *Peter*'s Vicar and Secretary, and that their souls are in his power, will give him all their Lands or Kingdoms to save their souls.

§ 57. When the Pope sentenced the Emperor *Henry* to be excommunicate and deposed, and was charged to have done this without authority, he wrote his 21 *Epist. l.* 8. to the Bishop of *Metz* to prove that he had power to do it; and to absolve his Subjects from their Oaths of fidelity; saying, that the *Scriptures were full of certain documents* to prove it. And his certain documents are *Tibi dabo Claves*, &c. *and Feed my Sheep*; *And Kings are not excepted.* They are St. *Peter*'s Sheep. Bin. p. 1262. he saith, that *the Head of Priests is at the right hand of God*; *but who knoweth not that Kings and Dukes had their beginning from them that knew not God, and affected by blind lust and intolerable presumption to domineer over others, the Devil the Prince of the world acting them, in Pride, Rapines, Perfidiousness, Murders and all wickedness? who while they would have the Priests of the LORD to stoop to their footsteps, are rightlyest compared to him who is head of all the Sons of pride, who said even to Christ, All this will I give thee, if thou wilt fall down and worship me. Who doubteth but that the Priests of Christ are the Fathers and Masters of Kings and Princes, and of all the faithful? And is it not notorious miserable madness for a Scholar to endeavour to subjugate his Master, and a Son his Father, and by wrongful obligations to subject him to his power, by whom he believeth that he may be bound or loosed both in Earth and Heaven? Did not Pope* Innocent *excommunicate* Arcadius *the Emperor? and Pope* Zachary *depose from his Kingdom the King of France, not so much for his iniquities, as because he was not meet for so great power; placed* Pepin *in his stead, and absolved all the French from the Oath of fidelity?* Ambrose *sheweth that Gold is not so much more pretious than Lead, as the Priestly Dignity is higher than the Kingly Power.* Pag. 1263. *Yea even the exorcists have power over Devils: How much more over those that are Subject to the Devils, and are his members? And if the exorcist excel so much, how much more the Priests? And every King when he cometh to his end, doth humbly and pitifully beg the Priests help, that he may scape the prison of Hell, and Darkness, and at the judgment of God be found absolved. But is there either Priest or Lay-man that when he is dying begs help of the King for the saving of his soul? What King or Emperor can by his Office, take a soul by baptism from the power of the Devil, and number him with the Sons of God, and fortifie him with holy Chrism? And (which is the greatest thing in the Christian Religion) can with his own mouth make Christs body and blood? Or which of them can bind and loose in Heaven and earth? By all which it may be plainly gathered by how great power the sacerdotal dignity excelleth. Which of them can ordain one Clerk in the holy Church? How much less can they depose him for any fault? For in orders ecclesiastical, to depose is an act of greater power than to ordain: For Bishops may ordain Bishops, but in no wise depose them without the authority of the Apostolick seat: Who then that hath any knowledg can doubt but that Priests are preferred before*

fore Kings? In a word, we must know that all good Christians are more fit- (*) And
ly Kings than evil Princes: For these by seeking the Glory of God do strenu- are Pre-
ously rule themselves: But the other seeking their own, and being enemies to bad too
themselves do tyrannically oppress others: These (good Christians) are the body that rule
of Christ. The other (bad Princes) are the body of the Devil. These so rule them- the
selves, as that they shall reign eternally with the highest Emperor. But the Church?
power of the other brings them eternally to perish by eternal damnation, with it a mark
the Prince of darkness, who is King over all the Sons of Pride. And it is not of a repro-
to be wondered at that (*) bad Prelates consent to an unrighteous King, whom bate to o-
for their ill got preferments by him, they love and fear, who Simoniacally or- bey the
daining any, do for a base price sell even God himself. For as the elect are insepe- gainst the
rably united to their head, so the reprobate are pertinaciously confederate a- Pope?
gainst the good with him that is head of their militia. (**) Let Emperors and (b) And
Kings see then how much the Imperial and Kingly dignity is to be feared, in are there
which very few are saved (b) and those that by Gods mercy come to salvation Popes sa-
are not made so good (or eminent) as many of the poor, the Spirit of God being ved?
judge: For from the beginning of the world to these times of ours, we find not (c) How
in all the authentick Scripture any Emperors or Kings whose lives were so ador- few Popes
ned with great (c) virtue and miracles, as were an innumerable multitude of wrought
the contemners of the World; though I believe that by Gods mercy many of them miracles?
have been saved: For to say nothing of the Apostles and Martyrs, what Empe- (d) It's
ror or King, was ever famous for miracles, like Martin, Anthony or Benedict? worth the
what Emperor or King did raise the dead? cleanse the Lepers? illuminate the what is
Blind? Constantine of pious memory, Theodosius, Honorius, Charles, Lewis, the reason
propagators of Christian Religion, defenders of the Church, are praised and that we
honoured by the Church, but not noted to have shined with such glory of mi- have no
racles. Moreover to what Kings or Emperors names (d) are Churches or Al- Churches,
tars dedicated? or hath the Holy Church appointed Masses to be celebrated? or Masses
Let Kings and other Princes fear lest by how much in this life they would be named for
preferred before other men, by so much the more liable they be to eternal bur- the honor
nings. As it is written: Wisd. c. 6. Great men shall be greatly tormented, save a
For they have as many men to be accountable for, as were Subject to them. few of
(*) And if one religious man find it so great a work to keep his own soul, how late that
great a labour belongeth to Princes, for so many thousand souls? (*) And if were de-
the judgment of holy Church so bind a man for killing one; what will become the Pope.
of them that for this worlds honour murder many thousands? Who though (*) Ah
they sometime cry Mea Culpa for killing many, yet are glad at the heart for poor Pope
the extension of their honour, and are not sorry that they did what is done, nor then! that
that they have driven their Brethren into Hell. must an-

The rest of the Epistle exhorteth Kings to avoid Pride and Tyranny: As all the
I cite it historically to shew you the Spirit of Papacy, so far as it at al hostile world or
doceri. There is somewhat in it worthy the remembering, that greatness Church,
prove not pernicious to themselves and others, for want of goodness. even for

§ 158. But sure these Papal arguments favour not of infallibility: the Anti-
May not a mean wit discern, 1. That goodness giveth not right to pla- *p. des*

Pope Zachary believed not.
(*) But you use to say that Kings are not for souls but for the body.

ces of Government without a call, else the best man must be always King: And then what Pope had Title to his Seat? Right to Heaven, will not prove a right to Kingdoms: Nor, è contra, Power to cast out Devils will not prove that the exorcist may cast out the King, nor give him Laws. 2. What though the King be a Scholar to a Grammarian, a Musician, a Physician? Is it therefore absurd that he be King over these Masters? What though he must obey his *Physician* for his life? May he not command that Physician for the common peace? What though he cannot do that which a Physician, a Musician &c. can do? May he not rule them for all that? 3. What a discontented mind have such holy Prelates, that cannot be satisfied with their Title to Heaven, their Miracles, Sanctity, Church-Keys &c. unless they may also be above Kings, and have the secular power also? 4. And what cause have Kings and States to look to themselves, that are under such Priests, where every Clergy man is their Master? And how many superiors then hath every Popish King? Even as many as he hath Prelates, Priests or exorcists. Yet I will confess that if Princes had been as bad still as some of them have been, and as such Popes pretended; and Popes and Prelates, and Priests had been as *Infallible, Holy, Wise* and *Peaceable as they have pretended*, and had not proved the shame of Religion and Incendiaries of the Christian World, in so many generations, it would have tempted men strongly for the interest of Religion and mankind, to wish that all power had been committed to the Clergy, and that *Campanella*'s *Regnum Dei*, or *Fift-Monarchy*, by *Priestly Government* of the World, had taken place. But when their own historians make fourty Popes together Monsters of wickedness, and piety at the same time to be translated to the Princes, this turneth our thoughts another way: Especially when we find still that a proud, worldly, wicked Clergy, are the great confounders of the World.

§ 59. *Epist.* 23. He sends to his Legates to demand of the King of France, that *every house do give a penny to St. Peter, if they take him for their Father and Pastor*. It seemeth the Roman Peter must have *money*, *Rule* and *Honour* of all the world, though he cry it down in others.

§ 60. *Lib.* 9. *Ep.* 1. He suspendeth the Arch-Bishop of *Rouen* in *Normandy*, from consecrating any Bishop or Priest, or Church, because he *had not visited the Pope at Rome, when as men and women came to him from the remoter parts of the Earth*; (The Pope loved much company, and loved not privacy so well as I do.) and because he had not sought his *pallium*; though he wrote submissively to him.

§ 61. Even this Pope *Ep.* 2. *l.* 9. Professeth to the King of Spain [*that a Lye is a sin though it come from a pious intention for peace; but in Priests it is a kind of Sacriledg.*] And if so, Priests had need to take heed that they *Lye* not, by *swearing, subscribing, declaring or professing any falshood* though a Pope should command *them*.

§ 62. In the same *Ep.* he congratulates that *Spain* received his *Order of service* or *Liturgie, because that which they used hitherto had some things contrary*

contrary to the Christian Faith. What? Was the old Spanish Liturgy, heresie?

§ 63. *Ep.* 3. *l.* 9. The Pope upon the death of *Rodulph,* fearing the Emperors coming into *Italy,* pretendeth that now all men advised him to receive the Emperor, for peace, into his favour and mercy; saying, that *almost all the Italians were for him,* and that his Patroness *Mathildis was counted mad by her own Subjects, who would not fight for her and him; and therefore sends to try whether he could get any help from others;* charging them to see that the next chosen King be one true to St. *Peter,* and to that end sends them an *Oath of obedience* to Saint Peter and his *Vicar* which the King must take.

§ 64. *Ep.* 4. He employeth his agents to engage the Norman Duke *Robert* to help him with an Army.

And *Ep.* 5. His Legate having deposed all the Bishops of *Normandy* that refused to come to his Synod, he tells him that *William* King of *England,* and *Duke* of *Normandy,* though he was not so good as he should be, was more useful and better to the Church than other Kings, and therefore must not be offended, and therefore bids him restore the Bishops: and also to pardon some Soldiers, excommunicated for not paying tythes, because they must not lose the Soldiers.

Ep. 8. He writeth to the Duke of *Venice,* by all means to avoid all excommunicate persons, and *their friendship* and *favour* left they came into the snares of the same *damnation*: For Anathema's were the arms by which he subdued Emperors, and was to do his work.

The like to others in other Epistles. And *Ep.* 12. He brought one Count *Bertran* to swear him fidelity, and to give him all his Countrey, and honour as Earl of *Provence,* and this for the pardon of his own and his Fathers sins.

§ 65. *Ep.* 14. He congratulates to the Kings of the *Visigoths* their conversion to Christianity; but tells them they must oft send to Rome for further instruction.

How frequently he made Arch-Bishops and Bishops travel to him out of other Kingdoms when his Legates wronged them, many other Epistles shew.

Ep. 17. The Norman Duke, *Robert,* acquainteth the Pope with a Victory which he had got: He returneth him this answer, *that he had but done his duty* and *now as it was Saint Peter that had given him, this victory, if he would not make him angry, he must now be thankful to Saint Peter, and* remember what he owed him, to help him against the Emperor, *Henry,* and all his other enemies.

§ 66. *Ep.* 20. He writes to the Arch-Bishop of *Canterbury* that he had shewed himself guilty of *disobedience which is as Idolatry* in that he had not travelled to *Rome* to visit the Pope when he commanded him; and *tells him that if he come not by All-Saints day next he shall be deposed;* for many weak men that could scarce rise out of their beds, came from other much farther Countreys: and he should lose Saint Peter's grace if he failed (must they do so also from the Antipodes?) *Epist.*22.

Ep. 22. He tells the Count of *Angiers* (or *Anjou*) that he should have obeyed the sentence of his Bishop, though it was unjust. And so every wicked Prelates power over Princes and all others shall be absolute.

He flattered our King *William* the Conqueror more than other Kings; but *ep.* 2. *l.* 11. He complaineth of his punishing a Bishop, telling him that God taketh them as the apple of his eye, and saith, Touch not mine anointed; and though they are naught and very unworthy they must be honoured, and being called *Gods, men must not meddle* with them.

Ep. 1. *Append.(Bin.p.*1278) he tells Lan— Arch-Bishop of *Canterbury*, how far the Church was from purity in —— *viz.* that [*The* Bishops and *such as should be Pastors of Souls*, do with insatiable desire hunt after the *Glory of the World*, and the *pleasures of the flesh*. And do not only themselves confound all things that are holy and religious, but by their example draw their *Subjects to all wickedness*; *And that to let them alone is unlawful, and to resist them how difficult!*

So much of the Epistles of *Greg.* 7th. who seemeth to be much more against vice than his predecessors for many ages, but more for tyrannical usurpation and rebellion than ever any that was before him: And if the better sort of them be such, what may be expected from them?

§ 67. CCCLIII. *An.* 1074. In a Council at *Rome* Priests were forbid marrying, and all that were married commanded to put away their Wives: The Arch-Bishop of *Mentz* trying to do the same in *Germany*, the *whole party of the Clergy* (saith *Lambert, an.* 1074) raged against it, and called the Pope a *downright* Heretick *that opposed Christs Law, who forbad putting away Wives except for fornication, saying, all men cannot receive this saying*; *and as driving men to fornication*: *They went from the Synod, and some were for casting out the Archbishop of Mentz and putting him to death*: But he spake them fair. But the Pope went on.

§ 68. CCCLIV. In a Synod at *Genesius*, the Popes Legate and *Anselm Lucens.* excommunicated many that had been against *Anselm*: whereupon the whole City was enraged, and forsook *Mathildis*, and joyned with the Emperor, and expelled the Bishop, one *Peter* a Canon leading them.

§ 69. CCCLV. *an.*1075. a Council at *Rome* excommunicated five of the Emperors Family; unless they travelled to *Rome* and made satisfaction: It excommunicated *Philip* King of *France* unless he satisfied the Nuntii of the Pope: It suspended the Arch-bishop of *Breme*, the Bishop of *Strasburg*, the Bishop of *Spire*, the Bishop of *Bamberge*, and in *Lombardie* the Bishop of *Papia*, the Bishop of *Turine*, the Bishop of *Placentine*, and also *Robert* Duke of *Apulia*, and *Robert de Roritello.* &c.

§ 70. *an.* 1075. Was the foresaid Synod at *Mentz* where the Arch-Bishop seeking to bring the Clergy to obey the Pope in putting away their Wives, was fain to put it off to save his life from the Clergies rage.

The English Councils I omit referring you to *Spelman*, of which one deposed *Wulstan* (they say *injuriously*) &c.

§ 71. CCCLVI. *an.* 1076. A Council at *Worms* sentenced the Pope deposed. Two Bishops awhile refused consent, but at last yielded: And they

they sent to the Pope, that thenceforth all that he did as Pope was void.

§ 72. CCCLVII. Hereupon the Pope calls a Council at *Rome*, which excommunicated all the German Bishops that deposed him, and the Bishops of *Lombardy* as conspiring against St. *Peter*, and many French Bishops: And with them the Emperor *Henry*; and deposed him (*quantum in se*) from all his dominions: and absolved his Subjects from their oaths (as aforesaid.)

§ 73. CCCLVIII. The excommunicate Bishops had a Council at *Papia*, where they retorted the Popes Anathema on himself, and excommunicate him.

§ 74. CCCLIX. The Pope calls another Council at *Rome*, where the Arch-Bishops of *Millan* and *Ravenna* (the Antipope) are excommunicate, and the Emperor's cause and party again condemned.

§ 75. CCCLX. Another Synod at Rome *an.* 1078. decreed divers things for defence of the Clergies priviledges. And it is observable that to that day the old Canons were in force for nulling all ordinations not made by the *Common Consent of the Clerks and People: Ordinationes quæ interveniente pretio vel precibus, vel obsequio alicujus personæ ea intentione impensò, vel quæ non Communi consensu Cleri & populi secundum Canonicas sanctiones fiunt, & ab his ad quos consecratio pertinet, non comprobantur, infirmas & irritas esse dijudicamus; quoniam qui taliter ordinantur non p.r ostium, id est, per Christum intrant, sed ut ipsa veritas testatur, fures sunt & latrones.* Therefore it is no sinful separation to disown and avoid such obtruded Bishops or Pastors as are not so ordained by the Common Consent of the Clergy and the People.

§ 76. In this Council the Pope, to keep up some pretensions yet to a power in the *East*, excommunicated the new made Emperor *Nicephorus Betoniates* for deposing wrongfully the Emperor *Michael* and his Wife *Mary*, and his Son *Constantine Porphyrus*, and putting them into a Monastery and invading the throne, whom the Patriarch *Cosmas* lately set up by *Michael*, had Crowned: But thus matters were then often carryed.

§ 77. That we may a little take along some of the Greek affairs, note here, that *Zimisces* being dead *an.* 975. the Empire returned to *Basil* and *Constantine* the Sons of *Romanus jun. Basil* held it 50 years; and *Constantine* three more. Against them rose first *Bardas Scleros*, and then *Bardas Phocas*. *Basil* overcame and subjected the *Bulgarians: An.* 1028. *Argyrus Romanus* took the Empire with *Zoe Constantine*'s daughter (putting away his Wife for her and the Empire.) After five years *Zoe* killed him, and took her adulterer and the agent *Michael Paphlago* to her bed and Empire. He being afflicted in body penitently turned Monk, and reduced *Zoe* to some order: But being dead, she took *Michael Calephate* who sware to obey *Zoe*; but breaking his Covenant, she deposed him and put out his eyes. And *an.* 1042. She took to her bed and the Empire *Constantine Monomachus*, in whose times the Greeks had divers losses by the *Sueves*, and by the *Normans* that got *Apulia*. At which time the Turks being Soldiers under the *Persians*, revolted and oft overcame them. *Zoe* and her Sister *Theodora* having ruled all, dye. In *Constantine's* time *Michael Cerular* Patr. of *Const*. wrote

against

Church-History of Bishops and

against the Church of *Rome*. *Theodora* being dead, *Michael Stratonicus* reigned one year: who was forced to resign to *Isaac Comnenus*: 1057. Who being diseased turned Monk, and made *Constantine Ducas* Emperor: *an.* 1059. He dyed 1067 swearing his wife *Eudocia* not to marry and make a Father in Law to his three Sons; but she brake her oath and married *Romanus Diogenes* and made him Emperor: He is taken in fight by the *Sultan*, and released, and when he came home his eyes put out by his own Subjects; of which he dyed *an.* 1071. and *Eudocia* is thrust into a *Monastery*. *Michael* Paripinacius, the Son of *Const*. *Ducas* is chosen Emperor: The Turks and others greatly weaken the Empire: Two *Nicephori* usurp: One called *Botoniates*, helped by the Turks, getting possession, him *Alexius* entred a *Monastery*, and the other *Nicephorus Byennius* is overcome and his eyes put out: *Botoniates* after three years, is deposed and made Monk by *Alexius Comnenus*, who was made Emperor, *an.* 1081, and being worsted by *Robert* D. of *Apulia*, and having dealt ill with *Godfrey* and his army going for *Palestine*, and beaten by them *an.* 1096. living 70 years and reigning 37 he dyed *an.* 1118. forsaken first of all, and succeeded by his son *Calojohannes*.

Sect. 78. CCCLXI. A Roman Council *an.* 1079. Forced *Berengarius* to recant, and to own Transubstantiation.

Sect. 79. CCCLXII. *An.* 1080. Another Roman Council renewed the deposition of the Emperour, and gave his Empire to *Rodulph*, the Pope excommunicating *Henry*, and saying [*Confidens de judicio & misericordia Dei ejusque piissimæ matris semper Virginis Mariæ, fultus vestra authoritate, sæpe nominatum Henricum, quem Regem dicunt, omnesque fautores ejus excommunicationi subjicio, & anathematis vinculo alligo: & iterum Regnum Teutonicorum & Italiæ ex parte omnipotentis Dei & vestra, interdico: ei, Omnem Potestatem & dignitatem illi regiam tollo, & ut nullus Christianorum ei sicut Regi obediat, interdico: Omnesque qui ei juraverunt, vel jurabunt de regni dominatione a juramenti promissione absolvo: Ipse autem Henricus cum suis fautoribus in omni congressione belli, nullas vires, nullamque in vita sua victoriam obtineat.* Then he giveth *absolution from all their sins to all that take part with* Rodulph, and *blessing in this life and that to come*. Adding [Go on then holy Fathers and Princes I beseech you, that the whole world may understand and know, that if you can bind and loose in Heaven, you can on earth both take away the Empires, Kingdoms, Principalities, Dukedomes, Marquisates, Earldoms, and Possessions of all men, according to their merits, and grant them (to others) for you have often taken away from the evil and unworthy, Patriarchates, Primacies, Arch-Bishopricks, Bishopricks, and given them to religious men: For if ye judge spiritual things, what must men believe that you can do about things secular? and if you judge the Angels that rule over all Proud Princes, what can you do with their servants? Let Kings and all secular Princes now learn, how great you are and what you can do; and let them hereafter be afraid to set light by the Command of your Church: And exercise your Judgment so speedily on the said Henry, that all may know, that he falls not by chance, but by your power; I wish he be confounded to repentance, that his Spirit may be saved in the day of the Lord.] O brave Pope!

From this Council the Pope sent *Rodulph* a Crown with this inscription------
Petra dedit Petro Petrus diadema Rodulpho. But all this was but as *Balaam's* attempt; It destroyed not *Henry*, nor saved the life of *Rodulph*, that was after killed.

Sect. 80. CCCLXIII. *An.* 1080. The Emperor called a Council at *Brixia* which deposed Gregory as [a *false monk, the pestilent Prince of all villanie, the invader of the Roman Seat, never chosen of God, impudently intruding himself by fraud and money, subverting all Church-order, perturbing the Kingdom of a Christian Empire; designing the death of Soul and Body to a quiet Christian Emperour: defending a perjured King; sowing discord where there was concord, and strife, where there was peace, scandals among brethren, divorces between Husband and Wife, and shaking all that seemed to be in quietness among godly men*; a *proud preacher of Sacriledge and flames, defending perjuries and murders, questioning the Catholick doctrine of Christs body and blood, an old Disciple of* Berengarius (*) a *follower of divinations and dreams a manifest Conjurer, possessed with a divining evil Spirit, and so swerving from the true Faith*.] And they made *Guibert* Pope in his stead (as was aforesaid.)

(*) These were no Protestant Bishops, and either wronged him, or he was greatly changed.

Sect. 81.

their Councils abridged.

§ 81. CCCLXIV. A Council at *Lyons*, *An.* 1080. deposeth *Manasse* Bishop of *Rhemes*, for refusing to give account to the Pope, &c.

§ 82. CCCLXV. Another at *Avenion*, maketh *Hugo* Bishop of *Gratianople*.

§ 83. CCCLXVI. Another at *Meaulx*, maketh *Arnulph* Bishop of *Soissons*.

§ 84. CCCLXVII. Another at *Rome*, *An.* 1081. Excommunicateth the Emperor again.

§ 85. CCCLXVIII. *An.* 1083. another at *Rome*, the Pope kept three days in sighs and groans, being besieged, and then dismist it.

§ 86. CCCLXIX. *An.* 1084. in another, the besieged Pope again excommunicated the Emperor, and the new Pope *Clement* (*Guibert Raven.*)

§ 87. CCCLXX. *An.* 1085. A Council at *Quintilineburg* condemned two Heresies: The first was the Royalist Heresie of Loyalty, called the *Henricians*, from *Henry* the Emperor, who thought that the Pope and Prelates had not authority to depose Kings and Emperors, but were to be Subjects to them. An Heresie, if such, that most Kings are very much inclined to, as taught them by St. *Paul, Rom.* 13. and by St. *Peter* himself. You see, O Princes, if you will be the Popes and Prelates Executioners, that you must come at last to the Stake your selves, and fall under the Law *de Hereticis comburendis*, unless you will be Servants your selves, or trust to some peculiar chalibeate remedies.

The great argument of the Pope was [*The Disciple is not above his Master*. One *Guibert* undertook to prove, *That the Pope had no such power, but what he had usurped, and taken to himself, but might be judged*. But the foresaid Argument struck all dead. But might not these Prelates have understood, 1. That the Pope himself may have a Master in Philosophy, Physick, &c? And is he not for all that, *Above his Master* ? 2. Is the King above no Master that teacheth him in any Art or Science? 3. Are not Christ's words plainly to be understood, of *Superiority* and *Inferiority in eodem genere*? The Disciple as such is not above his Master ; but as a King he may : or else Princes give up their Kingdoms to every Schoolmaster that they choose. 4. This Doctrine sets not only Popes and Prelates, but every *teaching Priest* or *Preacher* above the King ; for *to such* the King may be a *Disciple*. 5. This tendeth therefore to tempt Princes to be utterly ignorant and brutish ; for fear lest by learning any thing of any Master, they should give away their Kingdoms. And if Children be Kings by inheritance , what a snare is here laid to undo them ? 6. Doth not the Holy Ghost say, *Let every Soul be subject* ; and were not *Peter* and the Apostles some of these Souls? Did not Christ himself and *Peter* pay Tribute ?

But remember again you that are Subjects to such Councils and Prelates, that it is by them judged *Heresie* to be *Loyal*, and to plead for the Clergies subjection to Kings.

§ 88. The *Heresie* of *Wecilo* was here also condemned, that said (as they report him) *That when the secular Men were spoiled of their Estates and Goods,* (it's like by the Ecclesiasticks) *they were not bound to obey the Ecclesiasticks,*

B b b

and might be received by others, when they were Excommunicate. It was therefore decreed, [That whoever was Excommunicate by his Bishop, that Bishop not being himself Excommunicate, or deprived of his Office, though it were unjustly done, should by no means be received to Communion (by any other) unless absolved in the Ecclesiastical manner.] And so God must be disobeyed, that commandeth the Faithful to worship him in Sacramental Communion, whenever any proud, malicious or drunken Prelate will forbid him: And must so live and die, unless his Masters will repent of their injuries. When as it is usual for one injury to engage a Man to more, or to continue it, for the justification of the first.

§ 89. Another Decree of this Hereticating Council was, *What days to keep the Spring and Summer Fasts on; and that none eat Cheese or Eggs in Lent.* This is the *Roman* holiness, and way to Heaven.

Many Archbishops and several Cardinals were here Excommunicate also, for being for the Emperor against the Pope.

§ 90. CCCLXXI. But the Wars of Councils continuing, a Council was called by the Emperor at *Mentz,* where the deposition of *Gregory,* and the substitution of *Clement* (whose Legates were present) was confirmed, and the Condemners again condemned.

And so we have done with the *Life, Letters and Councils of Hildebrand.*

§ 91. Pope *Gregory* dying, *Clement* alone was Pope one year, and then the *Italians* chose *Desiderius* an Abbot, called *Victor* the 3d. This was the 23d Schism, or two Popes at once. *Victor* lived but a year and three months, and 24 days. Historians tell us of Famines, and dreadful Prodigies in those days. In that little time he raised an Army which beat the *Saracens* in *Africk.*

§ 92. CCCLXXII. A Council at *Capua* chose this *Victor, An.* 1087. and when he was brought to *Rome,* they found Pope *Clement* in possession, and keeping it by Arms: but when they had fought, *Victor*'s Soldiers proved Victors, and his Title to be best.

§ 93. CCCLXXIII. *Victor* had a Council at *Benevent,* where he damned Pope *Clement* and his Bishops, *An.* 1087. The grand Controversie of those times of the Pope against the Emperor and other Princes was, about Presentations to Bishopricks, or Investitures, which the Pope said, belonged to no Layman: *Victor*'s Council again judged such Presentations or Collation of Bishopricks to be Sacriledge, and such Simoniacs that used them: And here it's worth the noting that they decree, (*Bin.* p. 1293.) *That Penance and Communion may be received from none but a Catholick: And if no Catholick Priest be there, it is righter to persist without visible Communion, and to communicate invisibly with the Lord, than by taking it from a Heretick to be separated from God. For there is no Communion of Christ and Belial; nor of a Believer with an Infidel: But every Heretick is an Infidel: And a Simoniac because an Heretick, is an Infidel: For though Catholicks because of the Hereticks being over them, cannot have visible and corporal Communion, yet while in mind they are joined to Christ, they invisibly receive his Communion.*]

Let

Let it be here noted, 1. That this Council confesseth that the Sacrament and visible Communion is not of necessity to salvation: And why not the same of visible Baptism, when it cannot be had on lawful terms? 2. That therefore it is no sinful Separation to refuse such Church-Communion as cannot be had on lawful terms, or but from Hereticks, Simoniacs, or Sacrilegious. 3. That this sheweth that the Church of *Rome* hath their Succession oft interrupted: For by the testimony of their most flattering Historians, and of General Councils, many Popes have been *Simoniacs*; *Ergo*, saith this Council, *Hereticks and Infidels*; *Ergo* no Popes: *Ergo* their *Faith failed*. 4. That this maketh their Bishops, Priests, and Churches in all their own Kingdoms where Princes have the presenting and investing of Bishops, to be all void and null, as being Infidels. And that not only among Protestants none should communicate with any Bishops that have their Presentation and Investiture from Kings, but must separate from them as Infidels, but even in Papists Kingdoms they must do the same.

§ 94. *Victor* commended *Odo*, or *Otho Ostiensis* for his Successor; who is chosen in his stead against *Clement*, and called *Urban* the 2d. He made their old Patroness *Mathildis* in her age to marry with an *Italian* Duke *Welpho*, on condition that they should never have Carnal Copulation. The Emperor came to *Rome*, and set up *Clement*: Urban (or *Otho*) being one that before had published the Excommunication of the Emperor, Excommunicateth him again, and goeth from *Rome*, into *Italy* and *France*; and sets the Princes upon the recovering of *Jerusalem*, Listing 300000 Men, and so reconciled most of their Strifes at home. The History of this Expedition, *Platina* briefly, and many Authors largely give us, to whom I refer you.

Conrade the Emperor's Son rebelleth against his Father, encouraged by the Pope. The Papal Historians pretend that his Father would have forced him to Incest, but others think otherwise.

It was this Pope (saith *Bin.* p. 1293.) that appointed the horary Prayers, called *the Office of the Blessed Virgin*, to be used by Clergy and Laity, for success against the *Saracens*. Having Reigned eleven years, and four months, he died.

§ 95. CCCLXXIV. *An.* 1089. *Urban* in a Council at *Rome*, repeateth against the Emperor and Pope *Clement* what was done before by *Greg*. the 7th. *Clement* is expelled *Rome*, and driven to renounce. The Holy Wars breed reconciling thoughts. The Papal Party offer the Emperor his Crown, if he will depose *Clement*. His Bishops dissuade him, and he refuseth; being otherwise for Peace inclined to it.

§ 96. CCCLXXV. A Council at *Troy* in *Apulia* about marriage of Kinsfolk.

§ 97. *An.* 1090. A Council at *Tolouse* deposed the Bishop as criminal, &c.

§ 98. *An.* 1090. A Council of *Urban's* at *Melsi* decreed again, that no Bishop receive Investiture from any Lay-man; and that no Lay-man have right or authority over any Clerk. Also against false Penance (*Hildeb.* and before had decreed that *Penance*, and *Baptism*, (and so *Absolution*) profit not impenitent undisposed Receivers.)

§ 99. CCCLXXVI. A Council at *Benevent* condemned Pope *Clement* again.

§ 100. CCCLXXVII. Another at *Troy* did consult for *Urban*'s interest.

§ 101. CCCLXXVIII. Another at *Constance*, *An*. 1094. against married Priests and Simoniacs, and about the number of *Easter* and *Whitsun* Holy-days. And the Empress *Praxes* departed from the Emperor, accusing the Court of most filthy Fornication; perhaps the cause of their Calamities.

§ 102. CCCLXXIX. *An*. 1094. A Council at *Ostio* in *France* Excommunicated their own King *Philip*, for putting away his Wife, and marrying another; and again Excommunicateth the Emperor and Pope *Clement*.

§ 103. CCCLXXX. *An*. 1095. A Council at *Placentia* heard the Cause of the Emperor of *Const*. begging help against the Infidels; and of the King of *France*; and the Empress complained how filthily she had been forced by her Husband's command. It repeated damnations, and decreed that no money be taken for Baptizings, Chrysms or Burials.

§ 104. CCCLXXXI. A Council at *Clermont* for the same Causes. It decreeth, *That if one injure another on Monday, Wednesday or Thursday, it shall not be reputed a breach of Peace: but if it be done on any of the other four days, it shall be judged a breach of holy Peace, and be punished as shall be judged*. C. 1.

And that no Clergyman shall receive any Honour (or Preferment) *from the hand of Lay-men*. C. 15.

And C. 16. *That no Kings or Princes make investiture of any Ecclesiastick Honour*.

And C. 17. *That no Bishop or Priest make any promise of Allegiance to a King, or to any Lay-man* (*Ne Regi, vel alicui Laico in manibus Ligium fidelitatem faciat*.) *Ligius* is Liege, or *Ligatus*, a Vassal or full Subject.

And C. 19. *That no Lay-labourer keep the tenth of his labour*, (from the Clergy;) *or receive* (from the Clergy) *the tenth of his wages*.

§ 105. It sheweth you that ever the Sacrament in one kind was not introduced, in that the 28th Canon of this Council decreeth, that [*None communicate at the Altar, unless he receive the Body by it self, and the Blood by it self, unless through necessity, or with cautelousness*.]

Can. 29. Any one that fled from his Enemies to any Cross, was to be there protected as in a Church.

But the *Jerusalem* War was the main business of this Council, by which the Pope cunningly turned away Animosities and Jealousies from himself, and got the repute of a Holy Defender of the Church.

§ 106. But in an English Council all the Bishops in the Kingdom save one (*Rochester*) would force Archbishop *Anselme* to renounce the Pope; which *Anselme* refusing, and reasoning against, they said that he blasphemed the King, setting up any in his Kingdom without his consent; and so *they jointly renounce their subjection and obedience to the Archbishop, and abjure the unity of brotherly society with him*, Bin. p. 1302. You see *Luther* was not the first that renounced the Pope.

§ 107.

§ 107. CCCLXXXII. A Council at *Tours*, for the Holy War: where the King of *France Philip* was reconciled, promising service to the Pope.

§ 108. CCCLXXXIII. *An.* 1097. A *Concilium Barense* was held, for winning the Greek Church in their necessity; where *Anselme* of *Canterbury* got the honour in disputing of the Procession of the Holy Ghost. The sum of which Disputation is in his Works.

§ 109. CCCLXXXIV. *An.* 1098. A Council at *Rome* gave the King of *England* time to repent till *Michaelmas*, the former Council had Excommunicated him, if *Anselme* had not desired delay.

§ 110. *An.* 1099. Another *Roman* Council for the Holy War, and Reexcommunicating Pope *Clement*, (but what *Clement* did all this while, is past over here.)

§ 111. *An.* 1099. Some little Council at *Jerusalem* put out *Arnulph* the Archbishop of *Jerusalem* as a wicked Man and Usurper, and gave it to the Pope's Legat.

§ 112. *An.* 1099. *Paschal* the 2d is made Pope; a little after Pope *Clement* dieth, who had Reigned with his Competitors 21 years: Being buried at *Ravenna* after five years, a Council caused his Carkass to be dig'd up and burnt: Decreeing, *That all the Bishops of the Henrician Heresie,* (that is, who were for Emperors being above the Pope, or not deposable by him, and for his power of Presentations or Investitures) *if they were alive should be deposed ; if dead, should be dig'd up and burnt,* (which were most of the Bishops of the West, if *Hildebrand* himself mistook not.) O Military Bishops! that can overcome the dead. No wonder if the Church and Nations be confounded by you, that cannot let each others Carkasses rest in their Graves; but will dig up the bones of the Prelates of many Kingdoms, even the greatest part. How many Princes and Prelates now Papists, are guilty of the *Henrician Heresie* ? Should not their bones also be burnt if you durst ?

§ 113. But the Schism continued, three persons successively being made Anti-Popes by the Emperor's party ; but all of them one after another overcome by *Paschal*, who being a Military Pope, did most of his work by his Army, which he frequently had on foot. In his time *Jerusalem*, and the Cities about, were won by *Godfrey* of *Bullen*, his Brother *Baldwin*, *Boemund*, *Tancred*, and the rest of the Christians; and *Godfrey* made first King, and *Baldwin* next ; *Boemund* and *Tancred* having *Antioch*, and after suffering great losses, &c. as you may read in the Histories.

§ 114. Never did the Papal Rebellion work more unnaturally, than in setting up the Emperor's Son *Henry* against his own Father, as excommunicate and deposed ; who being chosen in his stead by the Papal Faction, overcame him, and took him Prisoner, and kept him till he dyed (naturally, or violently, I know not) at *Liege*.

§ 115. Yet was the Pope deceived of his hopes: For this *Henry* also was of the *Henrician Heresie*, and having by the Pope's order kept his Fathers Corps five years unburied, because Excommunicate, he came with an Army after to *Rome* to be crowned Emperor, and getting into the City, (the Pope's

Historians

Historians say by perfidiousness, and others lay the perfidiousness on the Pope) he took the Pope and Cardinals (that were for him) Prisoners, for denying him to confirm the Bishops which the Emperor had promoted; and he kept him till he made him confirm them, and grant him Investitures under his hand and seal, and promise: But when the Emperor was gone, the Pope took his promise to be null, and brake it, (he that can dispense with others, may dispense with himself.)

§ 116. *Binnius*, after many such others, doth not only justifie the Pope's deposing of the Emperor; but shamelesly saith, that even the *Novatores Hæretici*, (as he calleth the Loyal and Orthodox) will not deny but that he was justly deposed, because (saith he) in a Letter to *Hildebrand*, he said himself *he might justly be deposed if he fell from the Faith*; and he was deposed for Heresie, viz. *for defending Priests Marriage, selling Benefices, contemning the Popes Excommunication, and saying that he ought not to regard it.*

Ans. 1. Doth every word in a Letter that you can distort, forfeit a Crown?

2. Did not the Apostles and ancient Christians obey Heathens, and command it?

3. Was it to the Pope that he forfeited his Crown? How prove you that?

4. Were these Apostolic Doctrines, (that Priests may have Wives, as *Peter* had, &c.) a falling from the Faith?

5. Is every Princes Crown and Life at the Pope's mercy, because he may judge him to be an Heretick?

6. Are not the chief Christian Kings now that are Papists (especially the King of *France*) of that which is called, *The Henrician Heresie*? And may they be so deposed?

☞ § 117. But one thing I desire may be noted of this *Henrician Heresie*, that the Emperor did not take away the old liberty of the Clergy and People in chusing their Bishops: Investiture was not *Election*, or any determining *Nomination*, but like our *Inductions* an *after-consent*, and a delivery of possession by a Staff and Ring, as may be seen in the form of Pope *Paschal's* Grant in *Nauclerus*, Gen. 38. p. 738. [*We grant and confirm to you, that you may bestow Investiture by a Staff and Ring to the Bishops and Abbots in your Dominion, FREELY ELECTED WITHOUT FORCE AND SIMONY.*] And it medled not with the Presbyters, but was only a Negative power of freely chosen Prelates induction, who was still chosen by the inferior Clergy and the People.

☞ § 118. How the old Emperor was basely deprived by the three Bishops of *Mentz*, *Colen* and *Wormes*; how he charged their Oaths of Allegiance on them; how he denounced the Revenge of God against them; how he was kept in such poverty, that he desired for his relief to have been but an Assistant in the Monastery of *Spire* which he had built himself, and was by the ungrateful Bishop of *Spire* denied; how in his misery he confessed it was the justice of God for the sins of his youth (Lust) you may see in *Sigon. de Reg.*

Reg. Ital. An. 1106. *Helmold. Hist. Sclav. c.* 32. *Sigebert An.* 1106. *Albert. Xrantz. Hist. Sax. li.* 5. *c.* 20, 21, 22, 23, 24. compared. As also how his Body was digged up out of his Grave, and kept five years by his unnatural Son in an unconsecrated place, and after buried. Thus ended one that had fought (as Historians say) with honour, Sixty two Battels (more than *Cæsar* had done) a Man (had he duly mastered his youthful lust) credibly described as of laudable endowments, and one that shewed much zeal for the Clergy, though he was not willing to be absolutely their Subject.

§ 119. CCCLXXXV. Of the Councils that were in *Paschal's* days, the first was at *Rome, An.* 1102. where the old Emperor *Henry* the 4th.was again Excommunicate, and a form of Anathematism made against all Heresies, and in special against that Heresie that then troubled the Church,which was [*That the Churches Anathema's and Bonds are not to be regarded.*] It was time for Pope and Prelates to call that a Heresie, when by *Cursing* they had got their Dominions, and conquered so many Emperors and Kings: But it's a wonder that when *Tibi dabo Claves*, would not keep up the credit of the Cursers, that Cursing again should be able to do it.

Two Councils at *London* , partly against the Clergies Incontinence, and against Sodomy, and partly to depose several married Priests, I pass by.

§ 120. CCCLXXXVI. *Fluentius*, Bishop of *Florence*,published *that Antichrist was come.* Whether he told them who he was I know not : But *An.* 1105. A Council of 340 Bishops was there called, to try him for that dangerous doctrine ; and finding that Prodigies and Calamities drew him to believe it, they chid him as a weak Man, and warned him to talk so dangerously no more, (you may know why.)

§ 121. CCCLXXXVII. When the young *Henry* began his Rebellion against his Father, he called *An.* 1105. a Council at *Quintilineburg*, where he solemnly called God and Angels to witness, that it was not out of desire to Reign that he did what he did, nor to depose his Father, but to restore them to the Obedience of the Church, lamenting his Father's obstinacy against it : And he profest his Obedience to the Pope, and drew divers revolted Archbishops to do the like.

§ 122. CCCLXXXVIII. *An.* 1106. A Council with the Nobility or Princes was called by *Henry junior* at *Mentz*,where the old Emperor was again Excommunicated, and forced to resign his Scepter to his Son ; and this by those Princes, Prelates and Nobles, that had sworn Allegiance to him,supposing themselves absolved from all their Oaths by the Pope. Now it was that the three Archbishops violently divested him. When he asked them, what was his fault, and they said, *Simony, in the Collation of Bishopricks and Abbies,* he adjured them (the Bishops of *Mentz*, and *Colen*, with the Bishop of *Wormes*) by the name of the Eternal God, to say *whatever he took of any of them :* And they said, *Nothing*. He thanked God that so far their own tongues justified him, when their Bishopricks might have brought him no small Sum.

§ 123. CCCLXXXIX. The Pope in a Council at *Wastallis* in *Lombardy*, took in some submitting Bishops.

§ 124.

§ 124. CCCXC. Two Bishops at *Jerusalem* striving for the place; one put out by the King, but restored by the Pope, died in his return; the other by a Synod at *Jerusalem* was put out, but made Bishop of *Cæsarea*.

§ 125. CCCXCI. In a Council at *Trecæ*, the Emperor's Investitures are forbidden.

§ 126. CCCXCII. Another at *Benevent, An.* 1108. of the same, decreeing, *That if any take a Benefice from a Lay-man's Presentation, the Giver and Taker shall be Excommunicated.*

And one at *London* to the same purpose, made King *Henry* consent against investing Bishops or Abbots.

Another at *Luge*, for St. *Cuibert's* Elevation.

§ 127. CCCXCIII. But the Pope's *Lateran* Council of 100 Bishops is more considerable, where the Pope breaketh his Oath and Covenant to the Emperor as being constrained, and this by their approbation. The History of the occasion before-mentioned, is here again recited by *Binnius* out of the *Chron. Cassinens.* at large; where you may see that the Emperor sware to the Pope, and the Pope was thereupon to crown the Emperor as in his proper Rights. The Emperor claimed to be crowned as to the same Rights that had been granted to *Charles, Lewis, Henry,* and other former Emperors: This the Pope denied to do, and so they went to fight; where on both sides, between the *Romans* and *Germans,* so many thousands were slain, that *Tyber* was coloured with their blood. How the Earl of *Millan* that interposed his person to save the Emperor's life was slain, and his flesh cut in pieces, and given the Dogs by the *Romans,* and what other bloody work was there made, the said Chronicle mentioneth.

The Pope when he crowned the Emperor, and made the Covenant with him, *took the Body of Christ and brake it, taking part himself, and giving the Emperor the other part, and said, so let him be divided from the Kingdom of Christ and the Lord, that breaketh this Covenant*] which now by the consent of the Bishops in Council he brake.

§ 128. CCCXCIV. A Council at *Benevent* , to decide a quarrel about Church-lands.

§ 129. CCCXCV. In a *Cyperan* Council an Archbishop complained, that he was put out by the Prince *Roger* of *Sicily,* and made a Monk against his will; and was delivered, because *God will have no involuntary Service* : Another Archbishop accused, fled.

§ 130. CCCXCVI and CCCXCVII. A Council at *Beauvois,* not known for what.

One in *Syria* against *Arnulp.* Archbishop of *Jerusalem,* for his Crimes.

§ 131. CCCXCVIII. *An.* 1116. A Council at *Colen* Excommunicate the Emperor, (or declare the Popes Excommunicate;) but he forced some to receive him.

§ 132. CCCXCIX. *An.* 1116. In a *Lateran* General Council (as they call'd it) it unhappily fell out, that the Pope who had before call'd the Emperor's claim an Heresie, (as Councils had before named it , *The Henrician Here-*

Heresie) could not here disclaim and revoke his Act, without confessing his fault, in granting that power to the Emperor, and confirming it by Covenant and Oath. He tells them that he is but a Man, and so a Sinner, and lamenting his sin, begs their prayers to God for pardon, and then anathematizeth all that he had written, and desireth them to do the like. Hereupon a crafty Bishop (*Bruno Signinus*) said, *Let us give thanks to God, that we our selves have heard the Pope condemn that Priviledge that containeth Pravity and Heresie: And if that Priviledge contain Heresie, then he that made it was an Heretick.*] This put them all to their shifts; and *Joh. Cajetan* angerly said, [*Dost thou call the Pope an Heretick here, and in our hearing? The writing that our Lord the Pope made was Evil, but not Heresie.* Another Bishop said, [*Nay it ought not to be called Evil; For to deliver the People of God is good, by the authority of the Gospel, which commandeth us* animas ponere, *to lay down our Souls for the Brethren: And that which the Pope did, was to deliver the People of God.*]

O holy Bishops and Councils, that take it to be no sin to lye and forswear, if it do but *deliver the People of God!* But the Pope's patience would not hold at the charge of *Heresie*, but after great expectations, he told them that [*That Church had never had Heresie: yea, the same Church had quelled all Heresies.* And Ego rogavi pro te, Petre, *secureth it.* As much as to say, *Though I confess an Heresie before I was aware, now I tell you, the same thing is an Henrician Heresie in others, and none in me.*

§ 133. CCCC. *An.* 1116. A *Roman* Synod to end a strife between the two Monasteries, *Cluniacens. & Cassinens.*

§ 134. *Platina* tells us how the Pope sent the *Pisans* to fight against the *Saracens* at Sea; and when they were absent, the *Lucenses* sought to take their City, but the *Florentines* honestly came and repelled them; for which the *Pisans* gave them two *Porphyretice Columns*.

Also that *Mathildis* (*Maud*) the Pope's great Defender now dying, enriched the Pope, with bequeathing her Principalities to *Rome*. And that *Incentius*, an excellent Author, saith, *That she was burnt with two thousand more in a great Fire that hapned at* Florence. *And being Sainted*, divers places say, they have her Body.

Bernard was the glory of this Age.

Platina tells us also of a bloody War and Sedition in *Rome*, upon the Pope's denying a Boy of ten years old, to succeed his Father as Prefect of the City, the Pope being forced to remove: That the Emperor came with an Army again to *Rome*, where a Bishop crowned him again, the Pope being in *Apulia*, who after returned and dyed.

§ 135. Now cometh the 24th Schism, or two Popes at once; *Joh. Cajetan* Cardinal is chosen at *Rome*, by the CLERGY, SENATE, and PEOPLE of *Rome*, Bin. p. 1315. The Emperor sends to demand the confirmation of Pope *Paschal*'s Covenants: He denieth, and as at his choice a great Citizen, *Cincius Frangipanis*, offended at the choice, threw him down, trod on him, and imprisoned him, till the People rose and forced *Frangipanis* to restore him safe; so the Emperor now set up another Pope, *Gregory* VIII. And *Cajetan*, called *Gelasius* the 2d, got some *Italian* Princes to help him, and when the Emperor was gone he came to *Rome*, and scuffling awhile, was fain to go to *France*, and dyed after a year and five days, *Gregory* reigning three years, and some being for one, and some for the other.

In this time King *Baldwin* and *Tancred* had a great overthrow near *Jerusalem*.

§ 136. CCCCI. Pope *Gelasius* with a Synod at *Capua*, Excommunicateth the Emperor and Pope *Gregory* (who, it's like, requited him.)

After at *Vienna* in *France* he called a Synod, and dyed.

§ 137. The Bishop of *Vienna* in *France*, (kin to the Emperor and the King of *France*) is chosen Pope in *France*: He prevaileth with the Emperor to give up his Investitures, and so maketh a joyful Peace. He overcometh Pope *Gregory* VIII. and imprisoneth him in a Monastery. In his time *Baldwin* was again overthrown, and the *Venetians* took many Islands from the *Greek* Emperor, for hindering them to relieve *Jerusalem* by Sea.

§ 138. CCCCII. The first Council under *Calixtus* the 2d was at *Rhemes*, whither went *Turstan* chosen Archbishop of *York*, upon promise to King *Henry*, that he would *not receive the Pope's blessing*: But he stuck not to break his word; therefore the King banished him, or forbad him his Dominions.

Here four Tenents of *Guilbert Porretane* a Schoolman were condemned.

☞ 1. *That* Divinitas *and* Deus *are not the same* (in signification.)

2. *That the three Persons are not* unum aliquid.

3. *That besides the Persons there are eternal Relations, which are not the same as the Persons*, &c.

4. *That it was not the Nature of God that was incarnate.*

These they condemned, whether rightly understanding *Porretane* I know
not:

not: But if Schoolmens Quirks muſt make work for Councils, and Councils will be their Judges, what work will there be?

§ 139. CCCCIII. Another at *Colen, An.* 1119. the Emperor was Excommunicated.

§ 140. CCCCIV. In a *Lateran* Council called General, the Emperor (ſaith *Otto Friſing.*) ſeeing the People fall from him when he was Excommunicate, and fearing his Fathers caſe, yielded to reſign Inveſtitures, which he after performed, *An.* 1122.

And *An.* 1122. CCCCV. A *Roman* Council ſetled the *Caſſine* Monaſtery of *Benedictines* in their Independency, ſave on the Pope alone, againſt the envy and complaints of the Biſhops.

§ 141. CCCCVI. A *Roman* Council finiſhed the Peace with the Emperor.

And *An.* 1124. one at *Tholouſe* call'd ſome Religious men Hereticks.

§ 142. *Caliſtus* dying, *Theobaldus*, called *Cæleſtine*, is choſen by the Fathers; but *Lambert* called *Honorius* the 2d, by the help of *Leo Frangipauis*, a great man, came after him, and got the greater power, and got and kept poſſeſſion. This was the 25th Schiſm, which the Emperor's reſignation of Inveſtitures prevented not.

§ 143. CCCCVII. *An.* 1127. A *French* Council about the Templars Habit: And one at *London* 1125, and another 1127. where becauſe *Mat. Paris* openeth the ſhame of the Pope's Nuncio, and others, *Binnius* revileth him.

§ 144. *Arnulphus*, a famous Preacher, was murdered in *Rome*, for Preaching againſt their Pride, Covetouſneſs and Luxury. *Platin.*

§ 145. Two Popes are next choſen: (the 26th Schiſm.) 1. *Gregory* called *Innocent* the 2d. 2. *Peter* called *Anacletus*. *Onuphrius Panninus* ſaith, that *Innocent* had but 17 Cardinals Votes, and *Anaclet* had 21. And yet *Innocent* being the ſtronger, is by them taken now for the true Pope, and the Succeſſion is from him.

§ 146. Pope *Innocent* preſently becometh a Soldier, and gets an Army to fight with *Roger* Prince of *Sicily*, for claiming *Apulia*: The Pope and Cardinals at the ſecond Battel are taken Priſoners, by the coming of *William* Duke of *Calabria* to his Father. *Roger* gently releaſeth them: They come to

Rome, and find Pope *Anaclet* in poffeffion; who got *Reger* of *Sicily*, and the People of *Rome* that were for *Innocent*, to be for him, (faith *Platina*.) *Innocent* dares not ftay, but goeth into *France*; thence into *Germany*, where *Henry* being dead, and *Lotharius* made Emperor, the Pope got him to fwear to help him: The Emperor and Pope come againft *Rome* with two Armies. The Anti-Pope *Anacletus* is not to be feen; till the Emperor was gone home, and *Innocent* at *Pifa*, and then he appeareth as Pope again. *Lotharius* cometh with another Army, and driveth away *Anacletus*, and *Roger* of *Apulia* into *Sicily*.

§ 147. The *Romans* now rofe up againft the Pope, and claimed the Civil Government of *Rome* by a Senate. The Pope hereupon deprived them of their Votes in the Election of Popes, and deprived all the Clergy alfo of theirs except the Cardinals, and confined the power to the Conclave of the Cardinals alone. This was the firft time that the old way was overthrown, and all the Canons broken by one Pope in revenge againft the *Romans* for rebelling againft his Civil Government, and helping *Anaclet*. Till now, Clergy and People chofe the Bifhops. *Hildebrand* began to fet up the Cardinals power, but denied not the Clergy and People their Votes *in Comitiis*.

§ 148. The *Greek* Emperor's Legat now had a difpute with the Pope's Party, to prove the *Roman* Church erroneous for the *Filioque*, of which fee *Plat. in Innoc.* 2.

§ 149. CCCCVIII. and CCCCIX. and CCCCX. The Pope *Innocent* being above feven years in *France* and *Germany*, damned Pope *Anaclet* and his Fautors in a Council at *Clermont*, and in another at *Rhemes*, and in another at *Liege*. And 411, another at *Pifa* did the like. And 412 one at *Mentz* was about a Bifhops quarrels. And 413, one at *Eftampes* condemned *Anaclet*; *Innocent*'s prefence prevailing there, and *Anaclet*'s prefence at *Rome*.

§ 150. *Lotharius* dieth, and *Conrade* is Emperor. CCCCXIV. *Innocent*, *An.* 1139. calleth a great Council called General upon his return at *Rome*, to condemn *Anaclet* again.

§ 159. *Anaclet* dying, another Pope called *Victor* is chofen againft *Innocent*, and the Schifm continued: and after five months being too weak, giveth it up.

§ 160. In *England*, faith *William Malmsbury*, and *Binnius* out of him, *p.* 1325. two Bifhops (of *Salisbury* and *Lincoln*) built the great Caftles of *Newark*, *Shirburne*, *Devifes*, *Malmesbury*, and held the Caftle at *Salisbury*, &c. The Nobles complain'd to the King of the Bifhop's greatnefs, and building fo many Caftles, as of ill defign. At an Affembly or Parliament at *Oxford*, the
Servants

Servants of some Earls and these Bishops fought for Quarters: The Bishops Servants prevailed, and Blood was shed, and the Nephew of an Earl wounded near to death, and all was on an uproar. The King (*Stephen*) took the advantage, and made the two Bishops deliver up the Keys of their Castles, lest they prepared to be for the Empress *Maud* in time. The Bishop the King's Brother was the Pope's Legat; he calls a Council at *Winchester*, and summoneth the King, where he and other Bishops pleaded against the King, that he violated the Canons, wronged the Church, invaded the Bishops Propriety, &c. But a *French* Bishop of *Rouen* pleaded for the King, that no Canon allowed them those Castles, and that in danger of Wars all Princes would secure such places; and so far got the better, as that they durst not proceed against the King, who told them that if any went to *Rome* to complain against him, they must not think easily to return into *England*.

§ 161. CCCCXV. *An.* 1140. A Council at *Soissons* condemned *Peter Abailard's* Books to the Fire; but saith *Otto Frising.* (& *Bin.* ex co) they would not hear him speak for himself, suspecting or fearing his skill in disputation, his great acuteness being famous. His Heresie was, *That whereas* (saith *Otto*) *the Church holdeth the Three Persons in the Trinity to be* res distinctas*, distinct things* ; Peter used an ill similitude, and said that [*As the same argument or speech is Proposition, Assumption and Conclusion, so the same Essence is the Father, Son and Holy Ghost*] and this was judged Sabellianism. But sure, 1. *Peter* never meant this similitude should hold in all respects. 2. Sure this asserteth unhappily such a difference as is between the *Whole* and the *Parts*, if he had meant it to be fully *simile*. And that maketh a greater difference *inter personas*, than the Schools allow. But be the Man Heretick or not, what justice was in these pitiful Prelates that condemned him, and durst not hear him speak? Is such Hereticating much regardable?

See in the Schoolmen what they hold, particularly Mestrisse de Trinit. And Petavi. de Trinit.

§ 162. CCCCXVI. Another Synod (*Senonensis*) got St. *Bernard* among them, who debated the case of *Peter*, and he appealed to the Pope, who condemned him, and yet saith that *Peter* denied many of the *words*, *and all the sense that was charged on him*: but nameth five Errors, worthy his condemnation, if his indeed.

§ 163. *Binnius* from *W. Malmesbury* (who was present) reciteth another Council at *Winchester*, King *Stephen* being taken Prisoner by some Lords, and the *Londoners* pleading for his liberty, his Brother the Pope's Legat was against him, and accused him, Excommunicating divers Lords that were for him.

§ 164. CCCCXVII. A Synod at *Jerusalem* against the Patriark of *Antioch*, the Prince, and the Pope's Legat being against him : Accused of many Crimes he would not appear, and was deposed and imprisoned, and scaping out went to *Rome* for help, and was there poisoned. An unlearned bad Man *Haymericus* is put into his seat. § 165.

§ 165. *Innocent* dying, *Cælestine* the 2d was the first Man that ever was ordained or made Pope without the Peoples Election, saith *Binnius* himself *ex Onuphr.* by the Cardinals privately alone, according to Pope *Innocent's* Order. *An.* 1143. in *Conrade's* Reign; he dyed within six months. In his time the Christians lost *Edessa* to the *Turks.*

§ 166. Pope *Lucius* the 2d cometh next, and liveth but 11 months. In which he set the Emperor *Conrade* on a fruitless Expedition towards *Jerusalem,* to the death of multitudes.

§ 167. A *Gallican* Council against *Abailardus,* who is said by *Plat. & Pet. Cluniac.* to repent and dye a holy death.

§ 168. *Eugenius* the 3d, a Companion of *Bernards,* is next Pope: The *Romans* rising for their Civil Government, expel him: He goeth into *France,* maketh an Archbishop against the King's will, who sweareth he shall not enter the City. *Bernard* persuadeth the King to repent, and to expiate his sin by an Expedition (with *Conrade*) to *Jerusalem,* where both lose men, time and cost. The Pope overcometh the *Romans,* and maketh them promise that the Senators shall hold of him: he again withdraws, and dyeth.

§ 169. 1. Note here, that the Civil Government of *Rome* it self fell not till lately into the Pope's hands, and that by the same means as he conquered Kingdoms.

2. Note how far he was from ruling all the World, when for so many Ages the City of *Rome* it self contended against him. But the dependent Prelates in all Nations of *Europe* were his strength, who perceived that *Tibi dabo Claves,* might be abused for themselves, as well as for the Pope; and the Policy of Popes was in those days to do all or most by Synods, and thereby to make the Prelates perceive that it was their Power, Interest and Rule as well as his. But now the case is quite changed with this unchangeable Church; Councils now are needless, because scarce to be trusted.

§ 170. Passing by a Council at *Wesel* for the *Jerusalem* War, a (CCCCXVIII) Council at *Paris* fell again upon the Scholastic Bishop of *Poictiers, Gilbert Porretane.* In his Visitation he spake some words too hard for his Hearers, and his two Archdeacons getting *Bernard* on their side, (a Man more devout than Scholastically acute) they accuse the Bishop of Heresie again; having had success lately against *Peter Abailard,* the Bishops were ready to receive the Charge. The Articles of Accusation were these:

1. That he said, *Divinam Essentiam non esse Deum.*
2. *Quod Proprietates personarum non essent ipsæ personæ.*
3. *Quod Theologicæ personæ in nulla prædicarentur Propositione.*
4. *Quod*

4. *Quod divina natura non esset incarnata.*
And some lesser, as 1. *That attenuating mans merits,* he said *None merited but Christ.* 2. *Evacuating the Sacraments of the Church,* he said *None were truly baptized, but those that were to be saved:* And such like other things. The Pope and the Prelates heard the Charge: Two Masters are brought out against him, who sware that they heard some of these things from his mouth; many wondering that learned Men used Oaths instead of Arguments, (saith *Otto Frising.*) After many Charges and Urgencies, he said, [*Andater confiteor Patrem alio esse Patrem, alio Deum, nec tamen esse hoc & hoc.*] that is, *it is one thing to be God, and another to be the Father,* (or the words are not of the same signification) *and yet God is not one thing, and the Father another thing.*] The hardness of these words seeming a prophane Novelty, provoked the Bishop of *Soissons* to say, [*What say you, That the Being of God is nothing?*] having not read or understood *Austin,* that saith, [*Sic aliud est Deo esse, aliud subsistere; sicut aliud Deo esse, aliud Patrem esse, vel Dominum esse: Quod enim est ad se dicitur: Pater autem ad Filium, & Dominus ad servientem creaturam.*]

The Bishop of *Soissons* misusing a saying, [*Cum quis diceret,* Socratem *esse nihil diceret.*] He turned the Auditory against himself; and they asked *Porretane* to open why he so distinguished the Persons; who answered, [*Quia omnis persona est per se una.*] which puzled or amazed them, and ended that days work.

The next day he was accused of Novelty, for saying that [*The three persons were tria singularia.*] The Archbishop of *Rouen* aggravating it, said that [*God should rather be called unum singulare, than tria singularia.*] At which many were offended, because *Hilary* saith, [*Sicut duos Deos dicere profanum est, ita singularem & solitarium dicere sacrilegum est.—Et nihil solitarium ex divinis Sacramentis ad suspicionem audientium & occasionem blasphemantium proferamus.*] But *Porretane* told them, that by *singular,* he meant nothing but excellent and incomparable. In this manner *Porretane,* Bishop of *Poictiers,* was examined, and modestly answered them many days; till the Pope perceiving that these School-niceties being too hard for him, durst not determine them, nor gratifie *Bernard* (though his Friend) and the Hereticating Bishops and Clergy, but craftily put it off to a General Council. This is all out of *Otto Frising.* recited by *Bin. p.* 1332.

You may see here what work Hereticating Prelates and Councils were inclinated to make. If all the Schoolmens subtile Assertions (sound and unsound) must thus be tryed in General Councils, and all that was disliked, called Heresies, though it would have shamed the Prelates ignorance, it would have afrighted daring Wits from their presumption; and since I have seen the tendency of *Cartesianism, Gassendianism,* and other Epicurean Follies, I did not care much if we had some such ignorant Prelates to afright these bold Philosophers also.

I have oft marvelled why General Councils that understood not the *Hebrew*

brew Tongue, (nor the Pope's Western Councils the *Greek*) have no more exercised themselves in Councils to judge of *Scripture, Copies,* and *Translations.* And I have thought in what words and manner they would have prosecuted such debates : sure falsifying Scripture is of as dangerous consequence as these School presumptions. Some will think it is well that the Councils for above 1000 years had so few that understood the original language, or else they would have so tost and torn, and sensed and nonsensed the Scripture, that they would have made it quite another thing.

§ 171. CCCCXIX. Yet we have not done with Heresies. A Council at *Rhemes*, called by the banished Pope, tryed a mad man, an illiterate Rustick, called *Eum*, one unworthy to be called an Heretick, saith *Otto Frising*, who said he was the Son of God, &c. whom they sent to Prison, where he dyed.

In the same Council *Gib. Porretane*, Bishop of *Poictiers*, is again called, where their Subtilties were disputed over again; and *Bernard* Abbot *Clareval.* being his chief Adversary, upon *Porretane*'s exception to some of his words, saying, *Scribantur*, went and drew up some Articles of Faith, seeming contrary to *Porretanes*, and got many Bishops to subscribe them. The *Roman* Cardinals took this heinously, and came all together to the Pope, and told him, *That it was they that of a private Man made him Pope, and that he must know that it was they that were the* Cardines, *en which the Axis of the whole Church did turn, and that he must not now be his own, but theirs, and not prefer private and new Friends before his old common ones.* And that his Abbot Bernard *with the Gallicane Bishops, had audaciously presumed to lift up their Necks against the primacy and top of the* Roman Seat, *which only doth shut and no man opens, and opens and no man shuts; which only may discuss matters of Faith: And even when absent, may not receive prejudice of this honour from any.* But, behold these French-men, contemning our faces, (or presence) have presumed to write their Belief, without consulting us, as if they would pass a definitive Sentence on the matters that have been handled before us : which had it been done at Antioch or Alexandria, had been void--How then durst these usurp in our presence--We will therefore that you presently rise up against this temerarious Novity, and delay not to punish their Contumacy.] And so they had like to have run into a Schism : But the Pope and *Bernard* spake them fair, and *Bernard* said, *They wrote not as Determiners, but to give account of their own Faith, when provoked*; and so pacified the Cardinals. But this Tumult hindered the deciding of the Case : But, saith Otto, *whether Bernard was decived by humane infirmity, or* Porretane *escaped by hiding any thing by his great learning, I must not determine.*

§ 172. CCCCXX. Another Council *An.* 1150. the banished Pope held at *Trevers*, where *Bernard* told him of the Revelations of a Woman Abbess called *Hildegardis*: The Pope sent some to her; she returns him a writing of
her

their Councils abridged.

her Revelations, which he read, admired, and by *Bernard*'s perſuaſion returne her with a Letter: But what they were is not mentioned.

§ 173. *Conradus*, called *Anaſtaſius* the 4th, is next Pope, and dyeth after a year, four months, and 24 days. The glory of his time is ſaid to be *Ricardus de Sanēlo Viētore*, a famous Writer, ſpecially *de Trinitate*, and *Gratien*. *Lombard*, and *Comeſter*.

§ 174. *Hadrian* the 4th, an Engliſh man, is next Pope. The *Romans* by requeſt and threats, importune him to permit their Conſuls to govern them as heretofore. He reſolutely denieth them. They wound one of his Cardinals. He Excommunicateth and Curſeth them. (*Quære, Whether Rome was the Catholick Church when it was Excommunicate?*) They had before deſired him to come to the *Lateran*, which he refuſed, till they ſhould turn out one *Arnoldus Brixianus*, called by him a Heretick and Diſciple of *Abailard*. The People (ſaith *Platina*) took this ill, and ſo hurt the ſaid Cardinal (I doubt the *Romans* themſelves were for Hereticks.) The Pope curſeth *William* of *Sicily* for invading the Church-lands. The Greek Emperor offereth to help the Pope, and to give him much Gold alſo, if he ſhall but have three Maritime Cities in *Apulia*, where he hath won them. This afrighteth *William* to offer the Pope all again, if he may but be called King of *Sicily*. The Pope denieth it. *William* angry, over-runneth *Italy*. The Pope repenting, granteth him his deſire. The new Emperor *Frederick* alſo coming with an Army into *Italy*, took ſome Cities belonging to the Church, and gave them up to the Pope: But when he came into the City to be crowned, the Citizens enraged at the Pope for denying them their Civil Government, ſhut the Gates (the Emperor's Army being without) and fell on many of the Pope's Followers, and the *Germans*, beat ſome, and killed many. The Emperor hereby provoked got in his Army, and killed many of the Citizens, and had done more, but that the Pope diſſuaded him: Yet was the Pope and he fain to go round about to the *Lateran*, to avoid another Battel.

Platina mentioneth the Pope's Curſing *William* of *Sicily*, and abſolving his Subjects from their Oaths that they might Rebel, but ſaith nothing of the Emperor's after-quarrel with the Pope, occaſioned by a Letter of the Pope's rebuking him, for not helping the Biſhop of *London*, ſaith *Binnius*, and refuſing an offered Biſhop of *Ravenna*.

The Pope's Epiſtles againſt the Emperor, &c. *Binnius* leaveth out. At laſt the *Romans* again riſing againſt him, he goeth to *Anegria*, and dyeth.

§ 175. *An.* 1160. *Reland* is made Pope, called *Alexander* the 3d; and *Oētavian*, called *Victor* the 4th, is made Pope by others, and ſate four years, and ſeven months. This is, ſaith *Onuphrius*, the 27th Schiſm, or double Papacy.

pacy. Three more succeeded *Clement*, to keep up the duplicate before *Alexander* dyed, of whom one Reigned five years, and another seven.

Alexander addresseth himself to the Emperor *Frederick* to heal the Schism; who therefore bids both the Popes come to him, that he may hear the Case: But *Alexander* himself refuseth, and gets away. The Emperor sendeth two Bishops to him to summon him to a Council; *Alexander* refuseth to appear. The Bishops go to *Octavian* (*Victor*) and the Emperor calleth a Council, and this Council with the Emperor make *Octavian* the confirmed Pope. (Quer. *Whether this was not as good Authority as* Alexander's *greater number of the Cardinals?*) Hereupon *Alexander* curseth the Pope *Victor*, and the Emperor, and sendeth Letters to Christian Princes to tell them that he did it justly: (Wonderful! that Empires and Kingdoms could be then disposed of by Cursing?) The Emperor seizeth on many of the Church-Cities. *Alexander* returneth to *Rome*, but findeth so many against him that he durst not stay there, but flieth into *France*, invited by King *Philip*; and there again at a Council, curseth the Emperor. The Emperor *Frederick* destroyeth *Milan*, and translateth thence to *Colen* the supposed Bodies of the *Magi*, or three wise men that came to *Bethlehem*! (Is it not strange what brought them to *Milan*? and how they came all to dye there together? and how all their Bodies came to be known? O the wisdom of *Rome*!) The rest of the *Italian* Cities and States raise an Army against him; he sendeth to the King of *France* to end the Schism, by bringing Pope *Alexander* with him to a Council, where he would meet him with *Victor*. *Divo* is the appointed place between *France* and *Germany*: The Emperor with *Victor* and some Kings cometh to the Council; *Alexander* refuseth, because he call'd it not, and calls another at *Tours* in *France*. The Emperor angry returneth to *Germany*, and sendeth *Victor* into *Italy*, where he dyeth, and *Guido*, called *Paschal* the 3d, is chosen after him. The *Romans* chose Consuls that were *Alexander*'s Friends, and send for him to *Rome*, and receive him. The *Italians* then arm against the Emperor; who cometh with an Army into *Italy*, and taketh *Ancona*. The *Greek* Emperor is drawn to promise the Pope a great Army against *Frederick*, so he would unite the Empire and Churches again. This affrighteth the Emperor. The *Tusculanes* and the *Abanes* had a War with the *Romans* that oppressed them with Tribute, and gave the *Romans* a grievous overthrow. The Emperor besiegeth *Rome*; *William* of *Sicily* sends help to the Pope. The People of *Rome* intreat the Emperor for Peace, which he promiseth, on condition the worthier Pope may be chosen, and the Schism ended. The Pope *Alexander* hearing of this, flieth secretly by Ship. The Plague driveth the Emperor from *Rome*; he goeth into *Germany*. The Pope's Friends in *Italy* get strength. The Greek Emperor *Emanuel* sendeth yet larger offers to the Pope, if he would restore him the Western Empire by Re-union. Pope *Paschal* dyeth. The *Tusculane* Cardinal, called *Calistus* the 3d, is chosen in his stead, and reigned seven years, (saith *Onuphr*.) But the *Tusculanes* refusing him, he goeth to

Alexan-

Alexander, and refigneth to him all his right in *Tufculum*. Whereupon the *Tufculanes* receive *Alexander*, who there heard the Ambaffador of *Henry* King of *England*, purging him of the guilt of the death of *Tho. Becket*; and fent into *England* two Cardinals with power to examine all the matter; who impofed on the King, though fwearing he was innocent, that for Penance he fhould maintain Soldiers for *Jerufalem*, and for three years fhould have an Army againft the *Barbarians*, and defend the Church-liberties in his Land, and not hinder Appeals to *Rome*; All which he fware : [*By which*, faith *Platina*, *he merited that the Title of the Kingdom of* England *fhould be transferred on him, and his Heirs, by the Pope's confent : whence it is obferved that all the Kings of* England *do recognize* (or acknowledge) *the Rights of the Kingdom from the Pope of* Rome.] A juft Reward for their ferving the Titular Servant of Servants in his peftilent Ambition ! That he fhould thence take them for his Vaffals, and take himfelf for the difpofer of their Crowns ; ftooping to fuch Priefts, doth make them Kings of Kings.

Yet *Alexander* hath not got poffeffion of *Rome* it felf, fo far was he from being received by all the world ; and fo low did he condefcend as to offer the Citizens, [*That if they would receive him, he would come in peace, and meddle with nothing but Divine matters, leaving to them the care of fecular things : And when they would not grant him this much, he went to* Signia.] Was this man truly the Bifhop of *Rome*, that had no more of the Citizens confent fo much as to dwell among them? There he Canonizeth the Archbifhop of *Canterbury, Tho. Becket*, for a Saint. The Emperor entereth *Italy*, and taketh many Cities, but the *Venetians* owning the Pope, and he being wearied with Wars, at *Papia* treateth of a Peace. But this not taking, the Emperor fhortly returned with another Army into *Italy*, but was fo hard put to it by the *Millanois* and others in one fight, that he narrowly efcaped death himfelf. This one lofs made the Nobles that followed him fay, *That they fuffered this, becaufe they fought unlawfully againft the Church ; and if he made not his peace prefently with the Pope, they would go home :* So that the Emperor was forced to fubmit to the Pope, for fear of being forfaken by his Subjects and Soldiers. At *Venice* they met, and the Emperor kiffing the Pope's feet, credible Hiftorians fay, That the Pope trod on his Neck fcornfully, and profanely repeating the words of the Pfalm, [*Thou fhalt tread on the Lion and Adder*, &c. Pf. 91.13.) But *Baronius* and *Binnius* will not believe this, though as *Fowlis* noteth, p. 261. it is recorded by *Ciaconius, Maffon*. and abundance more of their own Hiftorians, and preferved in the Archives of the Library at *Venice*, and the Picture of the Story hang'd publickly in the Senate Houfe.

The Emperor's feverity againft them of *Milan* was not for nothing : They not only brake their Oath by Rebellion, but when his wife *Beatrix* came to fee the City, fet her on a Mule backward with the tail in her hand, and fo led her in fcorn from one Gate out at the other : What may not fuch provocations do to an Emperor ?

The ſtir that there was about the Emperor's holding the Stirrup to Pope *Urban*, is recorded by divers Historians: And how the Kings of *France* and *England* did the like by *Alexander*; And how this on debate was ſaid to be their due.

The truth is, the Papiſts Princes of *Europe* themſelves are beholden to the Proteſtants, for redeeming them from Servitude, and their Kingdoms from the meer will and mercy of the Pope.

§ 176. The Pope having conquered the Emperor by Curſing, is paſt doubt now of Conquering *Rome*, (for ſuch Men were Biſhops by Conqueſt, and not by Conſent.) To *Tuſculum* he goeth, and now demandeth of the *Romans*, that they abrogate the Office of the Conſuls: But finding this too hard a task to be done at once, he maketh a bargain with them, that none ſhould by the People be choſen Conſuls, till they had taken an Oath of Fidelity to the Pope, in his own propoſed words, and that they would never do any thing againſt his dignity. And ſo *Alexander* goeth the third time to *Rome*, and calls a Council; but quickly dyeth, when after twenty years contention, he thought he was new ſetled in peace, *An.* 1185.

§ 177. *Onuphrius*, after *Radavicus Friſing. Joan. Cremon. Abb. Urſperg.* &c. ſaith that it was this Pope *Alexander*, that firſt ordained that the Clergy and People being excluded from the Election of the Pope, (and ſo he was no true Biſhop) the choice ſhould be in the Cardinals ſhut up in Conclave, and go by two third parts of their Votes, to avoid Schiſms for the time to come. *Onuphrius* ſaith, that he had the writing of Pope *Lucius* the 3d, that ſaith, he was the firſt that was choſen by the Cardinals ſcrutiny, (though the Cardinals in a looſer way were lately made Electors before.)

☞ He that is no Biſhop, is no Univerſal Biſhop or Pope: But he that is not choſen by the Clergy or People of that Church, is no Biſhop. The *Minor* is proved by the Canons of many Councils.

§ 178. The Epiſtles of *Alexander* are ſo full of Uſurpation and Treaſon againſt Princes, that *Binnius* thought it beſt to omit them, and give you but the Titles: But thoſe that concern *England* are in *Mat. Paris*, whom *Binnius* referreth you to, though he oft reproach him for ſpeaking truth. Many are about *Tho.* Becket Archbiſhop of *Canterbury*, and againſt the Emperor and the King of *England*, forbidding the Coronation of *Henry* the 3d, and ſuſpending *Roger* Archbiſhop of *York* for Crowning him, and ſuch like, to ſhew how he was King of Kings.

§ 179. CCCCXXI. Of the Councils in *Alexander*'s time recorded by *Binnius*, the firſt is *An.* 1160. at *Papia* called by the Emperor which voted *Victor*

Victor Pope, and condemned *Roland*, called *Alexander*. The Letters of the Emperor and the Bishops tell us, that this Council consisted of *innumerable* Bishops and Abbots, and that the Emperor, after a good Speech, departed, and left all to their judgments: And that it was there proved by the Oaths of many Witnesses, that *Victor* was chosen by the full consent of the People and Clergy, and some Cardinals, and that, twelve days before *Roland* was chosen; and that *Roland* was present and contradicted not, but bid them obey him that was chosen: And that after being Chancellor he stole out of the City, and the major part of the Cardinals having before the death of the last Pope entered a Confederacy, to choose none but one of themselves that confederated (against the Emperor) they secretly chose *Roland*; the People and Clergy (a multitude subscribing) all desiring *Victor*: Three or four Kings also consenting to accept him, when the Council declared him the onely true Pope, and *Roland* a perfidious Usurper.

Here is all the *Romans*, Clergy and People, the Emperor and many Princes, and a Council of innumerable Prelates of *Germany, Italy*, &c. against the major Vote of an upstart sort of Men called Cardinals, that had confederated treacherously before: And yet the *Roman* Papacy is by Succession from this Man, that was no true Bishop himself.

CCCCXXII, CCCCXXIII, CCCCXXIV, CCCCXXV. *An.* 1161. *Alexander* got a Council at *Clermont*, and another at *Newmarket*, and another at *Belvacum*; and *An.* 1164. another at *Tours*, to curse the Emperor and Pope *Victor*. The *French* taking his part, (and the *English* at last) kept up the Schism and Contention.

The Reader must take this notice by the way, that such Meetings as we call Parliaments, the Popish Historians often call *Councils*, that they may draw Men to think that what Parliaments did was done by Clergy Power; And when Lords, Commons and Bishops met in the same Assembly, some called them Parliaments, and some Councils; And as *Spelman* saith, *pag.* 529. The same Assemblies were indeed mixt, and partly Civil or Royal (as he calleth them, because called by the King) and partly Ecclesiastical. But among the *Romanists*, Councils are greatly advanced by this ascribing to them the Acts and Power of Parliaments.

Accordingly the Parliament at *Clarendon* is called a Council by *Binnius*, (CCCCXXVI) by the reproachful name of *Conciliabulum*, because they setled the Rights of the King as Ruler of the Clergy, and would not let the Pope be King of *England*, (which is the *Henrician*, or Royal Heresie, to be punished by Fire or other death on Kings themselves, when the Pope is big enough to do it.) In this Council or Parliament, *Thomas* of *Canterbury*, and the rest of the Bishops concurred with the rest (for fear.) But *Thomas* when

he

he came home repented, and imposed so strict Penance on himself, that the Pope hearing of it, was fain to absolve him.

§ 180. CCCCXXVII. *An.* 1171. *Binnius* saith, that *Ireland* being given to the Pope as soon as they became Christians, the Pope gave it to King *Henry* the 2d, as soon as he had conquered it; and a Council at *Cassel* was called for Reformation.

Note here, 1. That the Pope hath great reason to seek the Conversion of the Kingdoms of the world, if they are his when they are converted.

2. That it is no wonder if five parts of six of the world be still Infidels, or at least that they are unwilling to yield to Popish Christianity, when Heathen and Infidel Kings must lose their Kingdoms, and become Subjects to the Pope, if they turn to Popish Christianity.

3. That it hath long been a cunning way of Bounty with Popes, to give Princes their own Kingdoms and Conquests, when they cannot take them from them.

CCCCXXVIII. *An.* 1179. was the Synod at *Venice* for reconciliation.

§ 181. CCCCXXIX. *An.* 1180. *Alexander* being at peace, called a Council at *Rome*, which they call General, or the 11th General Council approved at *Lateran*: In which are many reforming Canons, and many for the Papal power. The first is (as aforesaid) to confine the power of Pope-making to two third parts of the Cardinals only. Another to degrade those ordained by the three Anti-Popes. Another that no one have many Churches, *&c.* And the last against some called *Cathari*, *Patrini*, or *Publicani* as Hereticks, giving those Indulgences that will fight against them, and absolving all Inferiors from all Fidelity and Duty to them, *&c.* Some think that these were the *Waldenses*, some the *Albigenses*. But I have elsewhere shewed (against Mr. *Danvers*) that there were several sorts then in those Countries, some *Manichee* Hereticks, and some good Christians called *Waldenses*, and *Albigenses*, but against the Pope and his Superstitions, whom the Papists would jumble together to disgrace the best: who were, as some of their own Writers (*e. g. Sanders lib. 7. de vis. Monar.*) say, *A portion of the Henricians*, that is, of the Emperor *Henry*'s Heresie, that held the Pope's false usurping Excommunications were to be contemned (not as from *Henry* their Teacher) that is, they were Royalists, and against the Pope's ruling the abused world by the *Cursing way*.

§ 182. To this Council, *Crab* and *Binnius* have annexed a voluminous Appendix of Decrees, of which many are notable. As *that no Bishop may suspend*

suspend a Presbyter without the judgment of his Chapter. That a *Perjured Clergy-man is to be perpetually deprived, and may not govern a Church.* That *in case of ambiguity of words, we must have recourse to the common understanding of them,* with divers others.

§ 183. *Alexander* dying, *Lucius* the 3d is the first chosen by the Cardinals, according to *Alexander's Lateran* Council, (as is aforesaid.) And to perfect the Papacy, having got the choice of the Bishop out of the hands of the Clergy and People of *Rome,* his Flatterers next persuade him to put down the *Order* and *Name* of *Senators,* which attempting, his Party by the Cities insurrection had their eyes put out, and the Pope forced to leave the City; and at *Luca,* while he provoked Princes to send Soldiers to *Jerusalem* and *Asia,* he dyed.

§ 184. CCCCXXX. One Council this Pope had at *Verona,* as they say, where the Emperor *Frederick* met him, and sollicited him to restore all the Bishops and Clergy deposed that had adhered to him and the Anti-Popes. The Pope consented, but said he could not do it without another Council: (By which it appeareth, that this at *Verona* was no true Council.)

§ 185. *Urbanus* the 3d is next Pope, called *Turbanus,* as an Incendiary, by *Ab. Urspergens.* but better spoken of by *Platina* ; he sate above one year. It's said that he dyed of grief for the loss of *Jerusalem* in his time.
CCCCXXXI. A Council he had at *Paris,* they say, for *Jerusalem,* too late.

§ 186. *Gregory* the 8th succeedeth him two months, and dyeth.

§ 187. *An.* 1187. *Clement* the 3d succeeded him, who importuneth the Christian Kings to recover *Jerusalem.* The Emperor *Frederick,* the King of *France,* and *Richard* King of *England,* go in person. The Emperor was drowned in *Asia,* as he was washing himself in a River. The rest do much, but all to little purpose, but to the great destruction of many Christians. The Pope sendeth an Army into *Sicily* to claim it for the Church, because the King dyed childless : There also bloody havock is made.

An. 1188. An Assembly at *Paris* furthered the Holy War, (*Binnius* will call it a Council.)

§ 188. Though this *Clemens* sate but three years, and five months, he ended the long War between the *Romans* and the Pope, granting them their Senators, but deposing their *Patricius* or Head, that Union might not strengthen them.

§ 189. *Cælestine* the 3d cometh next, who to get *Sicily* from *Tancred,* gets out

out of a Nunnery a devoted Virgin that was the Heiress, and marrieth her to the young Emperor *Henry* the 6th, and giveth him with her the Kingdoms of *Sicily* and *Naples*, (when he can get them) and so wholly obligeth him to the Church; and to surrender *Tusculum*, which the *Romans* utterly demolish. *Sicily* the Emperor gets, and puts out *Tancred*'s eyes, but *Naples* was too hard for him, his Soldiers dying of the Plague.

How the King of *France* and the King of *England* disagreed in *Palestine*; and how the King of *France* returned home, and treacherously joined with *John* the King's Brother, to invade the King of *England*'s Dominions, and so called him from attempting the Siege of *Jerusalem*, and how he was taken Prisoner by the way home, many Histories acquaint you.

§ 190. *Binnius* out of *Urspergens*. tells us, how this Pope that had sent the King of *France* into *Palestine*, for his repudiating his Wife after, interdicted the whole Kingdom of *France* the use of holy thing. O horrid Villany, worse than Heathenish! For one Man's Family-sin, to forbid so great a Kingdom to worship their God and Saviour. *Saladine* when he had taken *Jerusalem*, dealt better with the Christians. O bewitched Princes and People, that by their degenerate Prelates would be brought to suffer or submit to such a wickedness, contrary to the nature of all Religion! O wicked Prelates and Clergy, that would obey an Usurper in such a wicked Interdict! But the King of *France* grievously punished his Clergy for the Fact. For it was done by the Pope's Legat and the Bishops at a Council at *Divion*: (the CCCCXXXII. here.)

§ 191. Next cometh the great Pope *Innocent* the 3d, (a young man of 30 years old called *Lotharius*) An. 1198.

§ 192. The Duke of *Saxony*, *Otho* the 4th, succeedeth the Emperor *Henry* the 6th. But *Philip* of *Suevia* is his Competitor, and the King of *France* was for *Philip* (*Henry*'s Brother) and the Pope for *Otho*, hating *Frederick*'s Line. Some say *Philip* conquered and deposed *Otho*, but *Petavius*, after divers others, saith, that they agreed that *Philip* should Reign quietly during his life, and *Otho* afterward succeed him. After ten years *Otho*, a Palatine of the *Rhine*, killeth *Philip*, and *Otho* again Reigneth quietly, marrying *Philip*'s daughter. But seeking to possess *Apulia* and *Calabria* by Arms, and not obeying the Pope's Prohibition, the Pope Excommunicateth him first, and after sentenceth him deprived or deposed, which at his command, the Archbishop of *Mentz* publisheth; which *Otho* despising, the Pope to shew that he can make and unmake Emperors and Kings, sets up *Frederick* King of *Sicily*, *Henry* the 6ths Son by *Constantia*, (the Nun formerly, saith *Binnius*, which *Petavius* denieth) and commandeth all to take him for Emperor. The King of *France* stands for *Frederick*, and the King of *England* for *Otho*. *Otho* is overcome being forsaken,

forsaken and dyeth for grief; and *Friderick* (a young man twenty years old) prevaileth.

§ 193. Passing by the English and Scottish Councils, (for the Sabbath or Lords day.) CCCCXXXIII. The Roman Council that deposed the Emperor *Otto* for rebellion against the Pope was, *An.* 1210.

§ 194. This Pope excommunicated our King *John* for rejecting *Stephen Laughton* Arch-Bishop of *Canterbury*: Yea, he deposed him *quantum in se*, *and interdicted Gods worship to the whole Kingdom*, for six years three months and fourteen dayes. (O wicked Bishops and Priests that would give over the worship of God because an Usurper forbad it!) The Pope gave the King of *France* commission to seize on *England*. King *John* is constrained to please the Pope. What wars were hereupon in *England*, and how he gave up his Kingdom at last to the Pope, and to hold it as of him, our own Historians certifie us, yea, and how he offered the King of *Morocco* to turn *Mahometan* for his help.

§ 195. CCCCXXXIX. Next cometh the famous 4th. *Laterane* Council called by the Papists the 12th. General, approved of 400 Bishops and 800 other Fathers (for others they have) *an.* 1215. *Regn. Frider.* 2.

In the first *Cap.* is the Creed and their Transubstantiation asserted, as 'the way of Union between Christ and us, we taking his flesh as he 'took ours: and that no one can make this Sacrament but a Priest 'ritely ordained according to the Keyes of the Church which Christ gave 'to the Apostles and their successours. But the Sacrament of Baptism sav-'eth by whom soever it is ritely done.

'The 2d, *Cap.* condemneth Abbot *Joachim*'s doctrine who opposed *Lom-*'*bard* as making a quaternity for saying that *Quædam summa res est Pater* '*Filius et Spiritus Sanctus, et illa (res) non est generans, nec genita, nec* '*procedens*, which the Council owneth.

'The 3d. *Cap.* is this [We excommunicate and anathematize every 'Heresie (*) extolling itself against this holy Orthodox Catholick faith 'which we before expounded, condemning all Hereticks by what names 'soever called: having indeed divers faces, but tails tyed together, be-'cause they agree in vanity in the same thing.

'And being damned let them be left to the present secular power or 'their Bailiffs to be punished by due animadversion: the Clerks being 'first degraded from their orders; so that the goods of such damned 'ones if they be Lay-men be confiscated, but if Clerks, let them be ap-'plied to the Churches from which they had their stipends.

'But for those that are found notable only by suspicion, unless they 'shew their innocency by a congruous purgation, according to the con-'siderations of the suspicion and the quality of the person, let them be 'smitten with the sword of anathema (cursed from Christ)(a) and avoid-'ed by all till they have given condign satisfaction: so that if they re-'main a year excommunicate, they be then condemned as Hereticks.

'And let the secular powers be warned and induced, and if need be

(*) That is localled by themselves so that not only the denying of transubstantiation but also the Henrician heresie, that is, Royalty, or that Kings are not to be deposed by Popes is here included; and all Royalists to be exterminated or else the King to be deposed for not doing it. (a) what upon suspicion?

'com-

'compelled by ecclesiastical censure, what offices soever they are in,
'that as they desire to be reputed & taken for believers, so they publickly
'take an oath for the defence of the faith, that they will study in good
'earnest to exterminate to their utmost power, from the lands sub-
'ject to their jurisdiction, all Hereticks, denoted by the Church; so that
'every one that is henceforth taken into any power either spiritual
'or temporal, shall be bound to confirm this Chapter by his oath.

'But if the temporal Lord required and warned by the Church, shall
'neglect to purge his countrey of this Heretical filth, let him by the Me-
'tropolitane and other Comprovincial Bishops be tyed by the bond of
'excommunication: And if he contemn to satisfie within a year, let
'that be signified to the Pope, that he may denounce his vassals thence-
'forth absolved from his fidelity (or allegiance) and may expose his
'countrey to be seized on by Catholicks who exterminating the Here-
'ticks may possess it without any contradiction, and may keep it in the
'purity of faith, saving the right of the principal Lord, sobeit he him-
'self put no obstacle hereto nor oppose any impediment: The same Law
'notwithstanding being kept about them that have no principal Lords.

'And the Catholicks that taking the badge of the Cross shall gird
'themselves for the extermining of Hereticks, shall enjoy that indul-
'gence, and be fortified with that holy priviledge which is granted to them
'that go to the help of the holy land.

'And we decree to subject to excommunication, the believers and re-
'ceivers, defenders and favourers of Hereticks; firmly ordaining, that
'when any such an one is noted by excommunication, if he contemn to
'satisfie within a year, let him thenceforth be *ipso jure* made infamous,
'and not be admitted to any publick Offices or Councils, nor to
'chose any to such, nor to be a witness; and let him not have power to
'make a Will, nor to witness, nor have succession to any inheritance. And
'no man shall be compelled to answer him in any business (or suit) but
'he shall be compelled to answer others: And if he be a judge, his sen-
'tence shall be void, and no Causes shall be brought to his hearing: If
'he be an Advocate, his plea (or defence) shall not be admitted: If a Re-
'gister, the instruments made by him, shall be of no moment at all, but
'be damned with the damned Author. And the like we will have observ-
'ed in the like cases. But if he be a Clergyman, let him be deposed
'from all office and benefice, that as he is in the greater fault, the great-
'er vengeance may be exercised on him.

'And if any, after such are marked by the Church, shall contemn to
'avoid them, let them be smitten with the sentence of excommunicati-
'on till he give due satisfaction. And let no Clergyman give such pesti-
'lent persons the ecclesiastical Sacraments, nor presume to give them
'Christian burial, nor receive their alms or offerings: otherwise let
'them be deprived of their offices, and never be thereto restored with-
'out the especial indulgence of the Apostolick seat. And so the Regulars on
'whom this shall be inflicted, that their priviledges be not kept in that
'Diocess, in which they presume to commit such excesses.   'And

'And becaufe fome under pretence (or form) of Piety, *denying* (as
'the Apoſtle faith) the *virtue* (or power) thereof, challenge to them-
'felves the authority to preach, when the fame Apoſtle faith [how
'fhall they preach unleſs they be fent:] Let all thofe be tyed with the
'bond of excommunication, who being prohibited, or not fent do pre-
'fume publickly or privately to ufurp the office of preaching without
'authority received from the feat Apoſtolick or the Catholick Biſhop of
'the Place : And if they fpeedily repent not, let them be puniſhed with
'other competent puniſhment.

'And we moreover add, that every Arch-biſhop or Biſhop by himſelf
'or his Arch-Deacon, or fit honeſt perfons fhall twice or once in a year,
'go about his pariſh where Fame faith that Hereticks dwell, and fhall
'there compel two or three men of good teſtimony, or if he fee fit, the
'whole neighbourhood to fwear, that if they know any Hereticks there
'or any that feek fecret conventicles, or that differ in life or manners
'from the common converfation of the faithful, he will ſtudy to tell
'them to the Biſhop. And let the Biſhop himſelf call the accufed to his
'prefence, who unleſs they purge themſelves of the guilt objected, or
'if after purgation made, they relapfe into the former perfidie fhall be
'Canonically puniſhed. And if any of them refuſing by damnable obſti-
'nacy the bond of an oath, will not fwear, let them be for this very
'thing reputed Hereticks.

'We will therefore and command, and ſtrictly command in the ver-
'tue of obedience, that the Biſhop do watch diligently through their
'Diocefs, for the effectual execution of thefe things, if they will Efcape
'Canonical revenge. And if any Biſhop be found negligent and remiſs
'in purging his Diocefs from the leaven of Heretical pravity, when
'this appeareth by certain ſigns, let him be depoſed from his Epiſco-
'pal office, and another fit man be fubſtituted in his place, who will and.
'can confound heretical pravity.

The 4th. *Chap*. is againſt the *Greeks* for rejecting the *Roman* Pope, and
'and fo far abhorring the *Latines*, that if *Latine* Prieſts did but celebrate
'at their Altars, the *Greeks* would not ufe them again till they had waſh-
'ed them, as being defiled:: yea, they rebaptized thofe that the *Latine*
'Prieſts baptized (the world did not then obey the Pope, how infolent-
ly foever he trod on the divided Princes of the *Weſt*, by the confpiracy
of their Prelates.) And here he was ufed in his kind, and hereticated and
excommunicated, and curfed as he did by others.

The 5th. *Chap*. ['was to confirm the old Patriarchate (*) on conditi- (*) O
'on they receive the Pall from the Pope, and fwear fidelity and obedi- bountiful
'ence to him, and make thofe under them to do the like] O daring chal- Pope!
lenge and innovation !

And yet *Chap*. the 9th. they grant that diverſity of Rites by Biſhops
of their own languages and cuſtoms be ufed, fo they will but be the
fworn vaſſals of the Pope.

And

And yet *Cap.* 8 'in their direction for inquisition, even this Council 'decreed that the accused be admitted to speak for himself, and not on-'ly the words of the witnesses but their names also to be told him and 'published, and the exceptions and replyes admitted;' left by sup-'pressing their names, men be emboldned to defame, and by excluding 'exceptions emboldned to swear falsly.]

Because the supposed Hereticks got ground by preaching, the *Cap.* 10. decreed the setting up of Preachers instead of the Bishops or to help them, because they wanted ability or time.

The 13. *Cap.* was to forbid making any more new Religions, there were so many made in their Church before.

The 17. *Cap.* was against Bishops that sate up feasting, drinking, or prating till after midnight, and lie in bed the next morning and come not four times in a year to Mass, and then talk with Lay-men at the time of worship.

Cap. 43. forbids all Clergy men that have not temporal estates under them, to take any oath of allegiance (or fidelity) to any Lay-man.

The 44. is to invalidate Lay-Ruler's Laws about ecclesiastical matters (as *Glebes, Mortuaries,* &c.) the rest I pass by.

§ 196. In this Council besides the *Albigenses* and Abbot *Joachim, Almaricus* a learned man was condemned; they say he said that '*All Christ-*'*ians were Christs members,* and (they add, how truly is doubtfull) *suffer-**ed by the Jews with him: that Christ's body was no more in the sacrament than**in another thing: That Incense as offered in the Church is Idolatry: That**every Christian is bound to believe that he is a member of Christ: That if**Adam had not sinned there should have been no generating in Paradise nor**difference of sexes.*] We must take these things on the report of such as *Sanders,* with some other that they charge on him; for which when they had killed him with grief, they dig'd up his corps and burnt it, as they were then burning multitudes of the living.

§ 197. In this Council *Stephen Laughton* Arch-Bishop of *Canterbury* was deposed for taking part with the Barons of *England* against King *John;* whose case was now become the Pope's when he had given him his Kingdom: in so much that when the Arch-Bishop confessed and begged absolution, his Holiness answered ['*By St. Peter, Brother, thou* '*shalt not so easily get absolution, who hast done so many and so great inju-*'*ries, not only to the K.* of *England, but to the Church of* Rome.].

§ 198. Let the Reader note, that 1. General Councils are the Papists religion. 2. That this is one of their greatest approved General Councils. 3. That therefore by their Law and Religion, they are bound to exterminate all Protestants, and that all Princes must be deposed that will not execute it, and their dominion given to others that will. 4. That all Protestants and others called Hereticks are dead men in Law and want

but

but judgment and execution where their Law is in force. 5. That the *Henrician heresie* is one that is judged such by their Councils. 6. That therefore not only all Protestant Kings, but all Papists that are for the safety and power of Kings against the Popes pretended power of condemning and deposing them, are Hereticks to be exterminated and burnt (by many Canons.) 7. Therefore Kings are beholden to the Protestant reformation (disabling the Pope to execute his Laws and Religion) for their Crowns and lives. 8. That when ever any King or others set up Popery and the power of their Laws and Councils in a Kingdom that is reformed, the subjects are presently dead men in Law, being to be destroyed as Hereticks, (though Policy or want of power may hinder the execution.) 9. *Qu.* Whether it be lawful for any King (or in his authority) so to destroy his Kingdom, or to make all (or the generality of) his subjects dead men in Law? 10. Whether by these Laws the Pope and his consenting Bishops have not published themselves to be *hostes Regnum et Regnorum*, if not *humani generis*; and are not so to be esteemed?

§ 199. Note also that D. *Heylin*, in his *Certamen Epistolare* against me, answereth, that it is not Kings but *temporal Lords* that are mentioned in this Council; and that he and Bishop *Taylor*, and Bishop *Gunning*, and Bishop *Pearson* in their dispute published by *Terret* or *Johnson*, and others before them, have maintained that these Canons were but proposed by Pope *Innocent*, and not consented to and passed by the Council. But to the first It is clear 1. that by *Domini Temporales* Councils ordinarily mean Emperors and Kings as well as any others. 2. That the words of the Council are express ['eâdem nihilominus lege servatâ circa eos qui non habent Dominos principales.]

And to the 2d. I answer 1. The Church of *Rome* actually taketh this for one of their approved General Councils, and will not be beholden to our Bishops for their friendly favour and excuse: And therefore it is all one to us whether the Council consented or not. 2. Mr. *Henry Dodwel* in his late *considerations how far Papists may be trusted by Princes*, &c. pag. 167 & pag. 174 &c. hath fully answered all the reasons given by these Bishops (as *Terret* did in part before;) and hath added abundant proof that these Canons were passed in that Council. 1. From the Council at *Oxford* where *Stephen Laughton* himself was. 2. From *Mat. Paris* who is alledged for the contrary. 3. From *Gregory* 9th's decretals. 4. From the case of *John Blunt* elect Bishop of *Canterbury* recited by *Mat. Paris an.* 1233. 5. From *Otto* the Pope's Legate. in *M. Paris an.* 1237. and that *London* Council. 6. From the Popes Letter to *Otto an.* 1238 in *M. Paris*. 7. From *Honorius* the 3d's condemnation of *Rich. de Marisco* Bishop of *Durham*. 8. From P. *Clement* the 5th's Bull for King *Philip* the Fair. 9. From the Council of *Tarragon*. 10. From the Council at *Vienna* under *Clement* 4th. 11. From the General Council at *Lyons* under *Gregory* 10th. 12. From the

the *Sabine* Council in *Spain.* 13. From a Council at *Toledo* under *Benedict* 12th. 14. And from the Council of *Trent.* 15. From the Common sense of the Case of *Abbot Joachim.* 16. And of the word Transubstantiation. 17. And of annual confession: All taken as setled by this Council.

So that as the Papists will not accept of this Charity of our Bishops in excusing their Religion from this part of guilt, so there is little place indeed for an excuse.

§ 200. The Papists themselves though they have many other Councils and instances to prove the Popes Claim and Practice of deposing Princes, yet will not let go this as being a famous General Council: But when here in *England* they would excuse their Religion from Rebellion, they use to say, that this being not an 'Article of Faith,' but a Canon of " Practice, they are not bound to take it as *infallible.* To which the said Mr. *Henry Dodwell* ibid. pag. 185. hath largely answered, to which I refer the Reader; adding only, that That which must be *Believed to be of God is not alway matter of practice, yet what must be done as by the will of God, must alwaies be, first the matter of faith: we must believe that it is God's will before we can obey it as his will.* The full answer see as aforecited.

§ 201. In the performance of the Laws of this Council multitudes called hereticks were burnt: Their St. *Dominick* preaching to the people to perswade them to take arms under the Sign of the Cross to destroy the Hereticks, for to get pardon of their sins, so that from first to last many hundred thousand (some say two millions, but that seemeth too much) were killed in *France, Savoy, Germany, Italy,* and other Countreys: see *Sam. Clerk* Martyrol. and Arch-Bishop *Usher de succeff. Ecclef.* Thus hath Papal *Rome* been built and maintained by Blood, Rebellion and Confusion, under pretence of Church Purity, Unity and Government, and all by the pretended KEYES.

§ 202. *Honorius* 3d. succeedeth *Innocent*: He confirmeth the *Dominican,* and *Franciscan* Religions and Sainteth *Francis.* He procureth a new expedition towards *Jerusalem,* and the destruction of many. The Emperor *Friderick* followeth his predecessors, and invadeth *Italy,* conquereth *Sicily* and *Apulia* (being his own by his Mothers title.) But the Pope excommunicateth him, and by the mediation of *John* King of *Jerusalem* (in title) he is absolved.

§ 203. CCCCXL. *Stephen Laughton* being restored, a Synod at *Oxford* passed many general excommunications, and there numbered all the Holy-dayes to be kept, and made several Canons; One good one was, [*that every great Parish have two or three Presbyters,* because of the greatness of the work, and if one should be sick, &c. Another (repeated many ny old Canons) that no *fees be taken for Sacraments or Burials* : &c. Another that no *Clergy-men should keep their Concubines PUBLICKLY in their lodgings, nor else where go to them with scandal*] (A good caution! for their credit.)

§ 204. CCCCXLI. A German Council lamenting that Clergy-men kept their Concubines publickly and would not dismiss them, forbids this publick keeping of them, *C.* 1, 2, 3, 5. But dealeth gently with them. But *C.* 6. those that preach when the Bishop silenceth them, it [*maketh infamous and intestable, casting them out without hope of mercy or restitution, ab officio et beneficio*, and rendering them uncapable for the time to come.

Here the Popes Legate demanded out of every Cathedral two Prebends to be given to *Rome* (And great reason that he that giveth all, even Bishopricks and Kingdoms should have some again, even what he will.) But it was denied.

§ 205. CCCCXLII. Also in a Synod at *Westminster An.* 1226. the Pope demanding two Prebends out of every Cathedral, the King answered that the matter belonged to all *Christendom*, and when he saw what other Kingdoms did herein, he would give his answer.

§ 206. *Gregory* 9th. is next Pope: He commandeth the Emperor *Friderick* 2d. to go recover *Jerusalem*, and excommunicateth him as a dissembler for his delaies: He re-Sainteth St. *Francis* and St. *Dominick*. He absolveth the Emperor upon his payment of an hundred and twenty thousand ounces of Gold for damage. The greatest sedition and heresie (saith *Platina*) rose at *Rome* that ever was there, so that the Pope was banished; But a plague ended it that left scarce the tenth man alive. Again the Senators and the Pope agree not about Legislation, and the Pope is fain to be gone again, and gets the Emperor to promise him that their conjunct forces should assault the Romans. The Emperor faileth, and bids his Souldiers help the Romans, himself departing, the Pope by mony hireth them to help him, and recovereth *Rome*. He sendeth preachers abroad to call men to the holy War: He Sainteth *Elizabeth* daughter to the King of *Hungary*. An Army goeth into *Asia* with *Theobald* King of *Navarre* and others, and is overthrown. He would go to *Rome*, but is kept out: The Emperor taketh many Cities in *Italy*: *Gregory*'s party get him into the City: He again curseth the Emperor, and deposeth him from his Empire (by his presumptuous sentence.) The *Venetians* help the Pope. The Emperor afflicteth them: The *Italians* are divided. In *Pistoria* two brothers, one called *Gaelph* was for the Pope, and the other called *Gibel* was for the Emperor, the City was distracted and

The Emperor faith Mat. Paris was forced to return from Jerusalem, and make a truce, because the Pope took his Cities in his absence and fought to betray him to the Soldan.

and the name of *Guelphs* and *Gibellines* filled *Italy* with confusion. The Romans were again falling off from the Pope, but he went among them *Carrying the heads of the Apostles* (you must believe it,) and by supplication and speeches moved the People to pity him, and got them to fight against the Emperor; which cost them and others of the Church party in *Italy* dear. The Pope calleth a Council to depose the Emperor again (to kill one man twice.) But the Emperor way-layeth them, and taketh many Cardinals and Bishops, and Imprisons them by the *Pisanes* help: *Gregory* dyed for grief in his 14th. year (or 15th.)

This is that Pope that by the help of *Raymund* made the Books of *Decretals*. So much out of *Platina*. *Binnius* addeth that the Emperor went with an Army into *Asia* in performance of his vow and received *Jerusalem* yielded to him: And made ten years truce with *Saladine*, and therefore was again excommunicated by the Pope.

☞ § 207. In this Popes time, saith *Bin.* the Divines of *Paris* after long disputation defined, *that it is a mortal sin for any man to have two benefices, when one of them sufficeth to sustain him*.

208. Multitudes of the *Albigenses* were burnt and killed as Hereticks.

§ 209. CCCCXLIII. A Council at *London* under *Otto* the Popes Legate was held *An.* 1237. the King sending first to charge them to do nothing against his rights, and leaving one to see to it. The Legate was in danger for opposing *Pluralities*, the Bishop of *Worcester* and multitudes threatning resistance, and it was suspended.

§ 210. *Cœlestine* the 4th is next Pope, but not by the Laterane Canon by two third parts of the Cardinals: some say he lived 18 daies, some 17 some 14, some say two Schismaticks were between.

§ 211. The seat was void a year and eight months and more: the Emperor keeping many Cardinals in prison, but at the request of *Baldwin* of *Constantinople* he released them.

§ 212. *Innocent* 4th. is next chosen, who of a Cardinal-friend became by interest a Pope-enemy to the Emperor; and daring not to stay in *Italy*, fled into *France*, and there calleth a Council of Bishops (with these he hunted Princes,) and excommunicateth or curseth the Emperor: where saith *Matth. Paris An.* 1245 one Priest being commanded to publish the curse, he doth it thus. ['*Good People, I am commanded to pronounce excommunication against the Emperor Frederick, the Candles put out and Bells ringing: But not knowing the reason, though I know the hatred between them, & that one doth the wrong, but which I know not; as far as my power reacheth, I excommunicate & anathematize him that doth wrong, & absolve him that suffers the wrong*

wrong, which is so hurtful to all Christendome. And at *Lyons* the Pope curseth him again: The Emperor despised the Popes deposition, and would not give up his Crown, for fear of his curse. The Popes party choose *Henry Landgrave* of *Thuringe* Emperor, who is quickly killed beseiging *Ulm*, (as some say) that party chose *William* Earl of *Nassau* after him: *Henry* the Son of *Friderick*, was drawn to rebel, and being overcome by his Father soon after died. And the Emperor not long after him, by what death it is not agreed, some say poysoned, others say stifled by *Mansfred* his base Son; some say, he continued impenitent; others that he repented of his opposing the Pope (not probable): some speak ill of him; others extol him for Learning and worthiness.

§ 193. *Frederick* being dead, the Pope travels *France*, and *Matth. Paris* saith, that at his leaving *Lyons*, a Cryer called the Citizens (who had long entertained him) to his farewel; and that Cardinal *Hugo* made his fare-
'wel Speech, telling them *what good they had done the City: For when*
'*they came thither they found three or four bawdy houses, but at their depar-*
'*ture they left but one: But that one reached from the East Gate of the City*
'*to the West gate.*

§ 194. The Pope returneth into *Italy*, and seeketh to get men to ruine *Conrade* the late Emperor *Fridericks* Son: The King of *Englands* brother *Richard* is first invited, but denied due help, and refuseth; King *Henry* the third himself at last is drawn in, and furnisheth the Pope with a great deal of money, and the *Croisado* Souldiours are turned against *Conrade* from the relief of *Palestine*: Bitter accusations against him are published by the Pope, which *Conrade* answereth: He and *Robert Grosthead* the famous Learned holy Bishop of *Lincoln* dying near together, the Pope biddeth all that *Mat. Paris* belong to the Church of Rome to rejoyce with him, because these two their great- *an. 1254.* est enemies are gone. And if such wise and holy men as this Bishop, were *p. 853.* numbred with the enemies of the Pope, we may conjecture what he was and did, and whether all the Christian World were then his Subjects, and whether *Rome* then needed reformation.

§ 195. But though the King of *England* had so far served him, it was not enough: Nothing less than all would serve, as *Matth. Paris*, tells us, when the King would yet be King, and did not fully obey the Pope: which he manifested in his rant against this rare and excellent Bishop of *Lincoln*, the occasion of which I think well worthy of our recital; as it is in *Matth. Paris Anno* 1453. *pag.* 871. 872. (A credible Monk though oft reviled by *Baron.* and *Bin* for telling truth.)

This Bishop was one of the famousest men in the whole world for knowledge, piety and justice: The Pope had sent him an order (as saith *Matth. Paris*, he often did to him and other English Bishops) to do somewhat which the Bishop judged to be unjust. It was not so bad as an interdict to silence Christs Ministers; but whether it was the promoting of bad Ministers, or hindering or excommunicating good men, some such thing it was as you may see by
' what followeth: The Bishop writeth a Letter to the Pope and Cardinals

'in which he tells them [*That he would obey the Apostolical precepts: but
'that was not Apostolical which was contrary to the doctrine of the Apostles;
'Christ saying, he that is not with us is against us: And that cannot be A-
'postolical that is against Christ: as the Tenour of the Popes Letters were:
'His non obstante so often repeated, shewed his inconstancy and his blotting the
'purity of the Christian Religion, and perturbing the peace and quiet of So-
'cieties; a torrent of audaciousness, procacity, immodesty, lying, deceiving, hard-
'ly believing or trusting any one; on which innumerable vices follow. And
'next after the sin of Lucifer, which in the end of time will be that also of
'Antichrist, the son of perdition, whom the Lord will destroy with the Spirit
'of his mouth, there neither is nor can be any other sort of sin, so adverse and
'contrary to the doctrine of the Apostles and the Gospel, and so hateful, dete-
'stable and abominable, as to kill and destroy souls by defrauding men of the
'care of the Pastoral office and Ministry: which sin those men are known by
'the most evident testimonies of the sacred Scripture to commit, who being pla-
'ced in power of pastoral care, do get the salary of the pastoral office and mini-
'stry, out of the milk and the fleece of the sheep of Christ, who are to be quic-
'kened and saved, but administer not to them their dues: For the very not ad-
'ministring of the Pastoral ministeries, is by the testimony of Scripture, the killing
'and destroying of the sheep: And that these two sorts of sins, though unexpectedly
'are the very worst, and beyond all comparison exceed all other sort of sin, is manifest by
'this, that they are, in the two existent fore'aid things, though with disparity and dis-
'similitudes, directly contrary to the best things: And that is the worst, which is contrary
'to the best: And as for these sins, as much as in them lieth, one of them is the destructi-
'on of the Godhead it self, which is supressentially and supernaturally best: and the
'other is the destruction of that conformity and deification (of souls) by the gra-
'cious participation of the Divine beams, which is the best thing essentially and
'naturally. And as in good things, the cause of good is better than the effect,
'so in evils, the cause of evil is worse than the effect is manifest, that the in-
'troducers in the Church of God, of such most mischievous destroyers of (holy)
'formation and deification in the sheep of Christ, are worse than the destroyers
'(or murderers) themselves; the nearer to Lucifer and Antichrist, and in the
'greater degree of mischief (or priority) by how much the more superexcelling,
'and by the greater and diviner power, given by God for edification and not for
'destruction, they were the more bound to exclude and extirpate such most mis-
'chievous murderers (or-destroyers) from the Church of God: It cannot be
'therefore, that a holy Apostolick Seat, to which all power is given by our
'Lord Jesus Christ the holy of holies, for Edification, and not for destruction
'as the Apostle testified, should command, or require any thing that bordereth on
'or tendeth towards so hateful, detestable, and abominable a thing to Jesus Christ
'and so utterly pernitious to mankind, or by any way endeavour any thing that
'tendeth thereunto. For this were either a defection or a corruption or an a-
'buse of Christs own power, which is evidently most holy and most full; or it
'were an absolute elongation from the Throne of the Glory of our Lord Je-
'sus Christ, and the next sitting together of the two to 'Princes of darkness,
'and

'and of hellish punishments, in the chair of pestilence. Nor can any one with
' unspotted and sincere obedience (who is a subject and faithful to that same
' Seat, and not by schism cut off from Christ, and that holy Seat) obey the
' said mandates and precepts, or any endeavours whatever, and whensoever
' they come, yea though it were from the highest order of Angels, but must ne-
' cessarily contradict them and rebel with all his strength (or power): And
' therefore Reverend Lords, from the duty of obedience and fidelity, in which I
' am bound to both the parents of the holy Apostolick Seat, and from the Love
' which I have to Union in the body of Christ with it; I do only, filially and
' obediently disobey, contradict and rebel, to the things which in the foresaid
' Letter are contained, and specially, because as is before touched, they do most
' evidently tend to that sin which is most abominable to our Lord Jesus Christ,
' and most pernitious to mankind, and which are altogether adverse to the San-
' ctity of the holy Apostolick Seat; and are contrary to the Catholick Faith. Nor
' can your discretion for this hint conclude (or decree) any hard thing against
' me; because all my contradiction and action, in this matter, is neither contra-
' diction, nor rebellion, but the filial honour due to the Divine Father, and of
' you. Briefly recollecting all I say; the sanctity of the Apostick Seat can do no-
' thing, but what tendeth to edification and not to destruction: For this is the
' plenitude of power, to be able to do all to edification: But these things which
' they call provisions, are not to edification, but to most manifest destruction. There-
' fore the blessed Seat of the Apostle cannot accept them, because flesh and blood
' hath revealed them which possess not the things that are of God, and not the
' Father of our Lord Jesus Christ, who is in Heaven.

§ 196. When the Pope heard this Letter, saith Mat. Paris p. 872. Not
' containing himself through wrath and indignation, with a writhen aspect and
' a proud mind, he saith; who is this doting old man, deaf, and absurd, who
' boldly and rashly judgeth my doings? By St. Peter and St. Paul, if our in-
' nate ingenuity did not move us, I would precipitate him into so great confusi-
' on that he should be to the whole World, a Fable, a Stupor, an example and
' a prodigy. IS NOT THE KING OF ENGLAND OUR
' VASSAL. AND I SAY MORE, OUR SLAVE. WHO
' CAN WITH OUR NOD IMPRISON HIM. AND EN-
' SLAVE HIM TO REPROACH.
' These things being recited among the Cardinal brethren, with much ado af-
' swaging the rage of the Pope, they said to him, It is not expedient, O Lord,
' that we decree any hard thing against this Bishop himself: For that we may
' confess the truth, the things are true which he speaketh: We cannot condemn
' him. He is a Catholick; Yea a most holy man; more religious than we are,
' more holy and excellent than we, and of a more excellent life; so that it is
' believed that there is not among all the Prelates a greater, no, nor any equal to
' him: This is known to the whole Clergy of France and England: Our con-
' tradiction will not prevail: The truth of this Epistle, which perhaps is alrea-
' dy known to many, may stir up many against us; For he is esteemed a great
' Philosopher, fully learned in Greek and Latine, a man zealous for justice

'*Reader of Theology in the Schools, a Preacher to the people, a Lover of cha-*
'*stity, a persecutor of Simonists: These words said the Lord Ægidius, a Spa-*
'*nish Cardinal and others, whom their own Consciences did touch. They coun-*
'*selled the Pope to wink at all this, and pass it by with dissimulation, lest tu-*
'*mults should be raised about it: especially for this reason, that,* IT IS
'KNOWN THAT A DEPARTURE WILL SOMETIME
'COME.] so far *Mat. Paris.*

§ 197. Yet neither this Bishop nor the Historian flattered Princes, but both of them sadly lament the oppression and other sins of King *Henry*: And the Bishop commanded his Presbyters to denounce excommunication against all that should break the *Magna Charta*, the Charters heretofore granted, foreseeing, saith *Mat. Paris*, what the King would do. And he sharply reprehended the Fryar Minors, that would not tell Great men of their sin, when they had nothing to lose (*Cantabit Vacuus*, &c.) having chosen poverty that they might be freer from hindering temptations.

§ 198. When he lay on his death bed at *Bugden* in *Huntingtonshire*, he told *Joh. Ægidius* his learned friend, that he took them for manifest He-
'reticks, that did not boldly detect and reprove the sins of great men,
'and thereupon reprehended and lamented the sins of Prelates, but e-
'specially the Roman; reciting their putting unworthy and bad men in-
'to the Pastoral office, for kindred or friendship sake. The third day be-
'fore his death, he called to him many of his Clergie, and lamenting
'the loss of souls by Papal avarice, groaning he said, Christ came into
'the world to win souls, *Is not he then deservedly to be called Antichrist, who*
'*feareth not to destroy souls?* God made all the World in six dayes; but to
'repair man he laboured above thirty years: And is not a destroyer of souls
'then judged an enemy of God and Antichrist] &c.

Next he goeth on to shew how sinfully the Pope by his *non obstante* overthrew even the rights that his Predecessors had granted, vainly pretending that they bind nothing because *par in parem non habet potestatem*, and what evils to the Churches he had done, and addeth [*I saw a Let-*
'*ter of the Popes, in which I found inserted, that they that make their Wills,*
'*or that undertake the Crisado, and to help the holy land, shall receive just*
'*so much indulgence* * *as they give money,* &c. And so goeth on, naming his imposing men that cannot preach, or strangers of other languages as Pastors on the people, and his covetous and greedy devouring all the wealth he could get, concluding

* Or pardoning.

> *Ejus avaritiæ totus non sufficit orbis,*
> *Ejus luxuriæ Meretrix non sufficit omnis.*

And that he drew Kings in for his own ends, making them partakers
'of the prey. Prophecying [*that the Church will not be freed from Egyp-*
'*tian servitude, but by the mouth of the bloody Sword: These things are small,*
'*but*

'but *worſe will follow within three years*] ſighing and weeping out theſe
'words, his ſpeech failed him and he died.

And *ibid. Mat. Paris* ſaith, that the ſame night that he died wonderful
Muſical ſounds and Ringings were heard near in the Air by ſeveral friars,
and by *Fulk* Biſhop of *London* (then not far off) who ſaid when he heard
'it, that he *was confident their reverend Father, Brother and Maſter, the Venerable*
'*Biſhop of* Lincoln *was paſſing out of the World to Heaven.*   *Id. ibid.*

The Biſhop being dead, the Arch-Biſhop of *Canterbury* and the Dean and
Chapter of *Lincoln* fell out in ſtriving, who in the vacancy had the power of
giving Prebends: wherein the Arch-Biſhop by Power utterly oppreſſed them.

And *M. Paris p.* 880. affirmeth that Miracles were done after the death of
this Biſhop by his virtues at *Lincoln*, and yet confeſſeth ſome of his faults
and his ſharp thundring againſt Monks and Nuns, &c.

§ 199. The ſame Author tells us, *p.* 883. *anno* 1254. that the Pope was
'*ſo unmeaſureabley wrathful againſt this holy Learned Biſhop*, that when
'he was dead, he would have taken up his bones and caſt them out of the
'*Church*, and purpoſed to precipitate him into ſo great infamy, that he ſhould
'*be proclaimed a Heathen, a rebel and diſobedient to the whole world*; and he
'*commanded a Letter to that purpoſe to be written to the King of* England,
'*knowing that the King would be mad enough againſt him* * *and ready enough
'to prey upon the Church*: But the next night the ſaid Biſhop of Lincoln ap-   * *The Bi-*
'*peared to him in his epiſcopal attire, with a ſevere countenance, an auſtere look*   *ſhop was*
'*and terrible voice, he came and ſpake to the Pope that was reſtleſs in his bed,*   *for Magna*
'*pricking him in the ſide with a violent thruſt with the point of his paſtoral*   *Charta and*
'*ſtaffe which he carried, and ſaid*; miſerable Pope Senebald! *Doſt thou purpoſe in*   *the coun-*
'*diſgrace of me, and the Church of* Lincoln *to caſt my bones out of the Church.*   *treys liber-*
'*Whence did this temerity befal thee. It were better that thou, advanced and*   *ties.*
'*honoured by God, ſhould honour thoſe which are zealous for God, even when
'*they are dead: Henceforth God will give thee no more power over me: I wrote
'*to thee in the ſpirit of humility and love; that thou ſhouldſt correct thy many
'*errours: But with a proud eye and a bewitching heart thou haſt deſpiſed
'*wholeſome warnings: Wo to thee that deſpiſpeſt: Shalt thou not be deſpiſed.*]
'And the Biſhop Robert departing, *ſtriking as with a lance, the Pope, who when
'*as is ſaid he was pricked, groaned aloud, he left him half dead, and with a
'*mournful voice groaning with ſighs; His Chamberlains hearing him, being aſto-
'*niſhed, asked him, what the matter was. The Pope anſwering with ſighs and
'*groans, ſaid; The terrours of the night, have vehemently troubled me; nor ſhall
'*I ever be well again as I was! Oh, alas, how great is the pain of my ſide!
'*A ghoſt hath pierced me with a lance: And he neither eat nor drank that day,
'*feigning that he was inflamed with feavours that ſtreightened his breath; And
'*Gods revenge and wrath did not ſo leave him.*

'Not long *after the Pope, not ſenſible of Gods warnings by his Servants, but
'*ſetting about warlike and ſecular matters, he proſpered not in them, though he
'*laid out great care and labour and coſt: But Wars, yea, the Lord of hoſts
'*being againſt him, his army which at great charges he had ſent againſt the*
                         * *Apuli-*

'Apulians, under the conduct of his Nephew William, being scattered, conquered
' and confounded, perished with their Captain mortally wounded. They say there
' were there slain of Souldiours and valiant stipendiary's of the Pope, four thousand
' men: And the whole Countrey of the Romans lamented the shedding of so
' much Christian blood. The Pope then went to Naples, though weakened as with a
' plurisie in his side, or as wounded with a lance: And Cardinal Albus physick
' could not help him. For Robert of Lincoln spared not Sinebald of Genoa;
' And he that would not bear him warning him when alive, felt him peircing him
' when dead. Nor did the Pope ever after enjoy one good day till night, nor
' one good night but sad day, but sleepless and molested. Thus M. Paris.

§ 200. M. Paris, p. 896 anno 1254. saith that Henry the third of England
' obliged himself and his Kingdome unjustly * to the Pope, under pain of
' being disinherited to pay all the treasure which the Pope should lay out
' in his War for the King (that is, to have made him King of Sicily).
' And that the Pope having no mercy on England prodigally wasted its
' money, but those vast sums got by rapine were all lost.

*Quod tamen (saith be) nec facere potuit, nec debuit.

§ 201. The same Author saith p. 897. that when Pope Innocent lay dying
(after the stroke of the Bishop of Lincoln and the loss of his Army) and his
followers lay crying about him, he opened his dying eyes, and said, what do
' you mourn for you wretches? Do I not leave you all rich? what would you have
more? And so he died.

§ 202. CCCCXLIV. Anno 1245. Innonocent calls a Council called General (their 13th. Approved) at Lyons of 140 Bishops, where he heaped up accusations against the Emperour, whom Thaddeus his agent defended: And at last pronounced himself an excommunication and deposition, absolving all his Subjects from their Oaths and Allegiance, and excommunicating all that should own and help him.

Here you see that more than one of their approved General Councils are for Rebellion and perjury, and the Popes deposing Christian Emperours.

In the same Council sad Complaints were made from England of the pillaging or woful impoverishing of the land by the Pope and King, but the Pope heard all silently and would give no answer.

§ 203. At this Council the Pope importuned the Electors to choose another Emperour: some refused and stuck to the Emperour, saying that it belonged not to the Pope to make or unmake Emperours: Others obeyed him, and set up Henry of Hassia. * But the Emperour while he lived kept up his possession, so far as to make the Pope repent, and saith Trithemius was a weary of his life: But all Germany, Italy, &c. were confounded by the schim, or contention, one half (as is aforesaid) called Guelphes following the Pope and Henry, the other called Gibelines cleaving to the Emperour Frederick, to the shedding of abundance of Christians blood, and the desolation of Countreys, and the shame of Papal tyranny.

* Or Nassau or Holland, as they diversly called him.

§ 204. Anno 1254. Alexander the 4th was Pope. Matth. Paris tells us of a terrible dream that he had of Pope Innocents damnation, or misery:
But

But the fault of his writing is that he was too credulous of dreams and visions. He tells us also of twenty Miracles done at *Lincoln* for the fake of the late Bishop *Robert*. And that at a Parliament in *London*, the greatest which hath been seen, all the Nobles Ecclesiastical and Civil, demanded of the King that the *choice of the Lord Chief Justice, the Lord Chancellor, and the Lord Treasurer should be in the Parliament (or their common Council) as of old was usual, and just; and that they should not be removed without notorious faults, which the Kings secret Councellours perswaded him to deny.* Prelates and Nobles being grieved by exactions express it, &c.

Mat. Paris p.924. 905.

§ 205. Here the said Monk, *Matth. Paris*, exclaimeth *O the steril solicitude of the Roman Court! their blind ambition! Though holy, yet often deceived by the Council of bad men: Why dost thou not learn to moderate by the bridle of discretion, thy violence, being taught by things past, and so often chastised by experience. In thy losses we are all punished, &c*

Thou now endeavourest to make two German Emperours, which must cost inestimable treasure whence soever taken, and both uncertain of the dignity, &c.

§ 206. At that time the Lords and Prelates of *England* crying out of the King *Hen. 3d.* as false and oppressive, and pillaging Churches and People to maintain his profuseness, the Bishop of *Hereford* laid a Plot which the King accepted, that getting the hands and seals of a few Bishops he would go to *Rome*, and get power from the Pope to gather the King as much money as he needed. So to *Rome* he went, and there found the Pope in great grief and care himself for money, to pay vast debts that his Wars had cost him: The Bishop told him that the King who had engaged his Kingdom to be forfeited, if he paid not the Popes debts, would help him to money if he would be ruled by him, and write to the Bishops and Churches to grant the King such help as they could well do. The Pope gladly gave leave to the Bishop to write what he would. And home he went, and *Rustandus* a Legate was sent from *Rome* to see all done: faith, M. *Paris*, p. 911. *anno* 1255. *The Legate was prepared and ready in all things to the destruction of all* England *to obey the will of the King which was tyrannical, and to bind the oppressed contradictors in the bonds of Anathema.* *Rustandus* cometh with the Arch-Bishop of *Canterbury*, and the Bishop of *Hereford* is empowred by the Pope to gather moneys, for the Pope or King: A Parliament is called at *Westminster*: They refuse and go home. The Popes Letters press the Collection: A Council of Bishops is called at *London*, so much money is demanded, faith M. *Paris*, as would have enslaved or undone all the Kingdome. The Bishop of *London* protested he would lose his head rather than consent: The Bishop of *Worcester* said he would be hang'd first: The rest follow them. The King is angry and threatneth. The Earl *Marshal* in anger, when the King called him Traytor, answered, *thus liest, I never was a Traytor nor will be:* The King threatned to send men to thresh out his corn and sell it to humble him: The Earl told him, if he did so he would

would cut off the threshers heads and send them him: some interposed for the time: The Lords refused to meddle with the Kingdomes business, or to impoverish themselves, and were dissolved.

Rustandus again Congregateth the Bishops at *London*. They did nothing 'again: saith M. *Paris*, too boldly, *p. 917*. [*Si enim sive juste sive injuste per 'dictum Magistrum Rustandum suspenderetur quis, vel excommunicaretur, Rex 'quasi Leo in abscondito, quærens quem devoraret post 40 dies omnia direperit in-'sisceata: Papa & Rex velut Pastor & Lupus, in ovium exterminium confœderati, 'omnibus ruinam minabantur.* And then saith he, *like blind men groping for 'the wall, the Council were divided, and as English men are used to do, every one 'shifteth for himself (or seeketh to save himself.)* Tithes are now *paid by the 'Clergy to the Laity*; *They are granted for the Magna Charta which was not kept*: *'They are granted as for the holy land and turned against Christians in* Apulia: *'Many lies and false oaths are imposed,* saith M. Paris, *p. 919*.

The next year the Clergy were called again, 1256. *Rustandus* the Le-'gate said, *All Churches are the Popes*: Leonard *the Prolocutor answered, yes,* ☞ *'to defend; not to enjoy and appropriate; as we say, All things are the Prince's; 'that is to defend; and not to disperse; And this was the intent of the founders.* 'The Legate angry at this answer, commanded that henceforth without 'a Prolocutor *every man should speak for himself, that they might be known*; 'which astonished and silenced all. *He* commanded them to *subscribe a 'Lie, that they had received such sums of money of forreign Merchants and 'Usurers*; which they said, it was good *Martyrdome to die for the refusing 'of. Pag. 920.*

Here is annexed by M. *Paris*, A charter of King *John* confirmed by Pope *Innocent* 3*d*. ordering that all Bishops be freely elected without the Kings hinderance by the Church vacant, and cursing all that otherwise come in, *pag. 921.*

But *Platina saith this was done in* Victor *the* 4ths. *days.*

§ 207. At that time the Romans imprisoned a great Citizen *Braucaleo* for his justice. The Bononians detain many Romans pledges for him: The Bononians are interdicted sacred things: but they yield not, till *Braucalco* is delivered. M. Paris anno 1256.

The Letters of Pope *Alexander* and his many exactions, see farther in M. *Paris* this year.

§ 208. *Anno* 1257. saith M. *Paris*, some went to *Rome* for the Bishoprick of *Ely*, and the Church of St. *Edmunds*, and gave and promised so vast sums of money as astonished men with wonder. Whereupon the Pope made a new Law that every Elect Bishop should come personally to *Rome*, hoping to have the like prey from others.

☞ § 209. *Anno* 1258. saith M.*Paris, p.* 910. The Pope that claimed the Kingdomes of the World was mastered in *Rome*, by the foresaid Senator *Braucaleo*, who being delivered from Prison, was beloved of the people, executed the Malefactors and his enemies; forced the Pope to stay his excommunication and humble himself, and beg his mercy.

§ 210. The same year the Pope pretends anger to the King of *England* for

and their Councils Abridged, 418

for not tempering his excesses; and threatneth to excommunicate him: The King is afraid, and sends him money, and stops his mouth, *p 910.*

§ 211. Against the Parliaments will the King again hearkeneth to the Pope, that offereth now the Kingdome of *Apulia* to *Edmund* his younger Son, as he did before to *Edward* the Elder. But the Parliament denieth him money, which he screweth from the Abbeys and Churches.

§ 212. saith *M. Paris*, *Sewale* Arch-bishop of *York* now died a Martyr (though without blood as many do) having constantly fought against the Tyranny of the Roman Court oppressed by the Pope, wrote earnestly as *Rob.* of *Lincoln* had done to the Pope to cease his tyranny. In his sickness (saith *M. P.*) he called for water which was fetcht out of the Well, and it was turned into excellent Wine. *p. 969.*

§ 213. How the Parliament of Barons at *Oxford* this year 1258. entered their Confederacy and resolution to stand against the King for their Liberties, Charter and Justice, *M. Paris*, *p. 972* and many others tell you. And *p. 974* how the Londoners joyned with them; and how many of the Lords were poysoned.

§ 214. *Brancaleo* the Roman Senator having humbled the Pope, pull'd down the Castles of the Tyrants and Rebels, put to death the kindred of many Cardinals, and died. The Pope forbade the Citizens choosing another without his consent. They laugh at him and choose *Brancaleo's* unkle. *M. P. p. 984.*

§ 215. This Pope *Alexander* of whom *M. Paris* speaketh so much evil, saith *Binnius post obitum suavem sui memoriam reliquit,* dying 1260. And *Platina* praiseth him, in whom you may see more of his life, and Wars against *Maufred, &c.*

§ 216. Next cometh *Urban* 4th. Patriarch of *Jerusalem*: of whom no great matters are recorded. He ordained *Corpus Christi* day.

217. Next cometh *Clem.* 4th. a French Lawyer a Widdower, and then Bishop. His first good work was to go to *Perusium* in the habit of a beggar: His life is praised by *Platina, Onuphius, Binnius, &c.* How he made a Frenchman *Charles* King of *Scicily,* and *Apulia,* and how *Maufred* was kill'd and conquered, *&c.* I need not trouble the Reader in reciteing.

§ 218. CCCCXLV. In his daies *Canisius* hath found a small Council at *Vienna* for reforming some things in the Clergy, Bin *p. 1492.*

§ 219. Next cometh *Gregory* 10th. But the Seat was vacant first almost three years: So long the Church of *Rome* was extinct, if the Pope be an essential part (as they would have him even of the Universal.)

§ 220. CCCCXLVI. In his time a Council at *Lyons* (called the the 14th. Universal approved one by them) was held: in which the poor Emperour of *Constantinople, Michael Paleologus* being in danger at his wits end came in person to flatter the Pope in hope of help. There also was decreed the shutting up of the Cardinals at Elections for fear of vacancies

Hhh as

as had happened by discord and delays. The Pope interdicted the Florentines, because the *Guelphes* refused to receive the Gibelines, which quarrel still cost bloody Wars. *Rodulph* is made Emperour, and the Pope dieth.

Onuphrius further openeth the Reasons and Rules of the Cardinals being shut up; viz. *Clem.* the 4th. being dead, the Cardinals (as is aforesaid) were all so desirous to be Popes themselves, that they were two years and nine months contending, and could not possibly agree. *Philip* King of *France* and *Charles* King of *Sicily* came themselves to *Rome* to intreat them, but departed without success. Yet they invoked the Holy Ghost every day to help them. At last the Cardinal Bishop *Joh. Portuensis* deridingly prayed them to uncover the houses, for the Holy Ghost could not come in through so many covered roofs: At last by *Bonaventures* intreaty, they chose *Theobald* a Viscount and Archdeacon that was with our Prince *Edward* going to fight in *Palestine*: And the said Cardinal *Portuens.* made these Verses ou their choice, anno 1271.

> *Papatus munus tulit Archidiaconus Unus,*
> *Quem Patrem patrum fecit discordia fratrum.*

§ 221. *Innocent* the 5th. cometh next; the first after the shutting up of the Conclave. He sought to end the Italian Wars, but died before six moneths reign.

§ 222. CCCCXLVII. A Council at *Saltzburge* is published by *Canisius*, as in *Greg.* the 10ths. days, but it seemeth liker to be after; which condemned Pluralities, nonresidence of Priests, and their being in Taverns (or Alehouses) and playing at Dice, and their wearing long Hair and fine Cloaths, and restrained supernumerary begging Schollars, and ordered that the Bishop should imprison such as prophaned holy things after they were excommunicated or suspended: It seemeth that Bishops had by this time got coercive power; but they used it not to bring the unworthy to the Sacrament, but to keep the unworthy from it and from other profanations.

§ 223. Next *Ottobonus*, that was Pope *Innocent* the 4ths. Nephew, and Legate of *England* at the Barons Wars, is chosen Pope, but died before his Consecration, within forty dayes, but got the name of *Hadrian* the 5th.

§ 224. Next cometh Pope *John* the 22th. as *Platina*, the 19th. as *Binius*, and the 21st as most, the 20th. by *Onuphrius*, 1276. He was a Physitian, made Bishop, *inverecundi & focordis ingenii*, saith *Platina*, so foolish that he boasted how long he should live, when presently the house fell on his head, and he died by it in seven days after. *Suffridus* (saith *Binius*) saith that he was writing an heretical perverse book, when the room fell, and cryed out after, O, what is become of my book? Who will finish it? which saith *Binius*, if true, sheweth the wonderful Providence of God for his Church. But had this Pope been infallible, had he been in a Council?

He died the first year.

His

and their Councils Abridged. 419

His Predecessor purposed to revoke the decree for shutting up the Cardinals in Conclave, and this man finished the revocation, and till the dayes of *Celestine* 5*th.* that renewed it, it stood revoked, saith *Onuphrius.*

§ 225. Next came *Nicholas* 3*d.* after six months contention and vacancy. King *Charles* as Senator presiding and pleading for a French Pope. He is commended much, save that he set up all his own Kindred too much.

§ 226. After three years Reign, eight months and fifteen dayes of *Nicholas* came *Martin* 2*d. vulgo* 4*th.* saith *Binius* and *Onuphrius* a Frenchman : In his time, the Greek Emperour *Paleologus* (not keeping his promise to the Pope) joyned with *Peter* King of *Arragon*, who claimed *Sicily* as his Wives inheritance; and though the former Pope had set him on, this was against him, restoring King *Charles* to be Senator at *Rome*, and siding with him, because he was a Frenchman : But the fatal *Sicilian* Vespers killed all the French, and *Peter* overcame *Charles* and took his Son, and *Charles* and the Pope shortly died of Fevers.

But before he died the Pope played the old Game, excommunicating and cursing King *Peter*, and gave his Kingdom for a prey to any one that would get it, and absolved all his Subjects from their Oath of Allegiance, and signed Croisado's (Soldiers under the sign of the Cross) to fight against him.

§ 227. *Honorius* the 4*th.* cometh next (his Brother being Senator at *Rome*) He confirmed the same Anathema against *Peter* King of *Arragon*, who shortly after died of a wound received in fight by the French. The Pope dieth (and the seat is void ten moneths) 1287. after two years Reign.

§ 228. *Anno* 1287. CCCCXLVIII. A Council was held at *Herbipolis* by the Popes Legate, endeavouring to have got the tenth penny of the Estates of the Clergy for the Pope, and of the Laity for the Emperour (by their joynt consent.) But *Siphridus* Arch-Bishop of *Colen*, and *Henry* Arch-Bishop of *Trevers* stoutly opposing, frustrated both their Conciliary designs.

§ 229. *Anno* 1288 came P. *Nicolas* 4*th.* a Religious Man, General of the Minors, when he had four years together laboured in vain to stay the blood in *Italy*, between the *Guelphes* and *Gibellins*, and to reconcile the French and English, and to relieve the Christians in *Palestine*, he died : And the Cardinals, though for liberty they went to *Perusium*, kept the Church headless two years and three months by contention, though Princes in vain endeavoured to perswade them to agreement. (Are these no intercessions of the Succession?)

In this time died *Mich. Paleologus* Emperour of *Constantinople*, and the Clergy and Monks would not suffer him to be buried in holy ground, because in the Council at *Lyons*, he had consented to the Church of *Rome*, *Platina*. Was this a true Reconciliation of the Greek Church?

§ 230. *Anno* 1286. CCCCXLIX. A Council at *Ravenna* (in *Honorius* time) made some Canons for Reformation.

§ 231. *Anno* 1291. CCCCL. A Council at *Saltsburg* for reconciling some Christians.

§ 232.

§ 232. *Anno* 1292. CCCCLI. The Arch-bishop of *Mentz* held a Council at *Aschaffenburge* which they say did many good things; It is not known what.

§ 233. *Anno* 1294. After two years and four months vacancy *Celestine* the 5th. a Religious man of solitary life is chosen Pope; If ever there was a good Pope it is likely this was one: But he was no sooner setled by common applause, but the Cardinals, especially Bened. *Cajetanus* a subtile man perswaded him that his simplicity and unskilfulness would undo the Church; and urged him to resign. King *Charles* and the people disswade him, and are only for him: But the Cardinals prevailed, and he resigned; And going to his solicitude again, the Cardinal *Ben. Cajetane* that got him to resign, sent him Prisoner to the Castle of *Fumo*, where (at best) he died of grief: Some write that Cardinal *Cajetane* got a way to speak through a Pipe put into the Wall as if it were some Angel, to charge him to resign; He was too good to be a Pope.

§ 234. The deceiver that got him out, succeeded him, called *Boniface* the 8th. (by *Bin.* 7th.) 1294. This is he of whom it is said, *Intravit ut vulpes, regnavit ut Leo, exivit ut Canis.* He raised Wars to prosecute some Cardinals and the Gibelines: While he lived wickedly he set up a Jubilee, proclaiming Pardon of all sins to them that would visit *limina Apostolorum*, that is, himself: A terrible Earthquake made him for fear set up a hut of boards in an open Meadow, lest the houses should fall on him: He digg'd up the body of one *Hermane*, that had twenty years been honoured as a Saint, and burnt it as a Hereticks. He sent a Bishop to *Philip* King of *France* to intreat him to go fight in *Palestine*, and threatened him when he could not intreat him. The King imprisoned the Bishop. The Pope sent to require him to release him, saying openly, that the Kingdome of *France* was divolved to the Church, for the contumacy of *Phillip* and his violating the Law of Nations; and bid him Anathematize him, and absolve all Frenchmen from the Kings Oath. The King let go the Bishop, but forbad all his Subjects going to *Rome* or sending any money thither, and not enduring his insolency, he assembled his Nobles and declared the Popedome void by Usurpation and unjust enterance of *Boniface*, and appealed to a Council: He Coyned money with this Inscription [*Perdam Babilonis nomen*] The Pope called a General Council, where he gave the Kingdom of *France* to *Albert* the Emperour, Anathematizing the King. The King would not play with him, but sends *Sciarra* and *Nogarete* to *Italy* to proclaim his Appeal: But *Sciarra* in a mean habit gets together many friends, that the Pope had oppressed and surprizeth him in his Fathers-house, breaketh open the doors, carrieth him from *Avignia* to *Rome* a Prisoner, where the thirtieth day he died of grief, of whom saith *Platina* [*Thus died Boniface, who endeavoured more to put terrour than Religion into Emperours, Kings, Princes, Nations and People; and to give Kingdomes and take them away to expel men and reduce them at his pleasure, unspeakably thirsting for gold, which way ever to be gotten.* Let all Princes Ecclesiastical and Secular (saith he) learn by this mans
example

example to go before the Clergy and people, not proudly and contumaciously, as he did, but holily and modestly as Christ and his disciples, and true imitators, and choose rather to be loved than feared, from whence the ruine of Tyrants deservedly cometh.

§ 235. *Anno* 1297. CCCCLII. Bin. faith, a Council (*Lugdunense*) decreed that Princes should not tax their Clergy, nor the Clergy pay them without the Popes Consent.

§ 236. *Anno* 1302. CCCCLIII. The Popes General Council at *Rome* excommunicateth the King of *France* as aforesaid. His Army follow their Captain Pope.

§ 237. *Benedict* the 11th. alias the 10th. alias the 9th. is next chosen Pope, (much praised): who excommunicated *Sciarra*, and absolved King *Philip*, and died before nine Moneths.

§ 238. *Anno* 305. Entreth *Clemens* the 5th. the Bishop of *Bourdeaux*, who called the Cardinals to *France*, and setled the Popes Court there, where it continued seventy years, till the Church and great buildings at *Rome* were desolate and ruinous, saith *Platina*. In his time *Albert* the Emperour was kill'd by his Nephew: *Italy* confounded by Wars: The Pope curseth and interdicteth the Venetians, the Florentines, the Lucenses: Requireth the new chosen Emperor of *Luxemburge* to come to *Rome* for Coronation; He entereth *Italy*; some Cities fight against him, some yield: At *Rome* demanding money, they resist, and it cometh to force, and he is driven back: After many bickerings and Cities taken, he dieth, as is said (faith *Plat.*) Poysoned in the Eucharist by a Monk. Two fight for the Empire, *Lodovic. Bavour* and *Frederice. Austriæ*: *Lodovicus* conquereth and maketh himself Emperour. *Clement* burneth two as Hereticks, maketh P. *Celestine* the 5th. a Saint, writeth his *Clementinus*, and dieth, and again there was no Pope, for two years, three moneths and seventeen dayes.

§ 239. CCCCLIV. A Council at *Saltzburge* to get money (Tenths) for the Pope.

§ 240. CCCCLV. Another there *Anno* 1310. declaring some penalties.

§ 241. CCCCLVI. Another at *Mentz*. to extirpate the Templars, where some of them rusht in and appealed to the next Pope, protesting they were killed and burnt wrongfully, without being heard speak for themselves.

§ 242. CCCCLVII. But the great Council called by them the 15th. General Council approved, was at *Vienna* near *France*, on this occasion. King *Philip* having got the Popedome, for *Clem*. the 5th. made him promise to condemn Pope *Bonif*. the 8th. and all his Acts: When he had possession, he found himself in a streight, and *Nicholas* Cardinal *Pratensis* advised him to please the King with the hopes that a General Council would do it most effectually, and to get the Council out of his Country and power: which being done the Council frustrated the Kings expectations: The King accused Pope *Boniface* of Simony, Heresie, and Perjury, in forty Articles.

titles. His crimes were not denyed, but they juftified him to be a true Pope, and found him not an Heretick.

In this Council the Templars were condemned and put down, and their Lands given to the *Jerufalem* Hofpitalers, or Knights of *Rhodes* (which they fay King *Philip* thought to have got) fome fay the Templars were falfly accufed of Herefies (and the Mafters and others burnt): Others fay, truely. The moft probable is, that fome particular Men of them (no new thing among Soldiers) committed many Villainies, and the reft fuffered for their fakes.

In this Council the Herefies of *Petrus Joann.* is a Difciple of Abbot *Joachim*, were condemned, which were three. 1. *That the rational Soul, as rational, is not the form of humane bodies.* 2. *That habitual grace is not infufed in Baptifm* (that is alwayes and to Infants). 3. *That Chrifts fide was pierced with the Launce before he was dead.*

In this Council the Fratricelli and Dulcinifts were Condemned, and alfo eight Herefies of the Beguines and Beguards; which were thefe (all for *perfection*, which Quakers and fome Fryars now feem to be too much for in profeffion, as we all are in defire) 1. That man in this life, may get fuch a
' degree of perfection, as that he may become impeccable (or finlefs) and fo
' to *rife* to no higher a degree of grace: Elfe, fay they, if one might ftill in-
' creafe he might grow better than Chrift.

2. 'That when one hath atteined that degree, he ought not to faft or
' pray: Becaufe then fenfuality is perfectly fubject to the Spirit and reafon,
' fo that a man may then freely grant his body what pleafeth him.

3. ' That they that have got this degree of perfection and the Spirit of li-
' berty, are not fubject to humane obedience, nor bound to any precepts of
' the Church, for where the Spirit of the Lord is, there is liberty.

4. ' That thus a man may get final beatitude in all degrees in this life, as
' well as in that to come.

5. ' That every intellectual nature is naturally bleffed in it felf, and the
' foul needeth not the light of glory for the feeing and enjoying of God.

6. ' That to exercife virtues is a note of imperfection.

7. ' That to kiffe a Woman is fin, becaufe nature needs it not ; but copu-
' lation is not, becaufe nature requireth it, when one is tempted.

8. ' That one ought not to rife and do reverence at the elevation of Chrifts
' body, becaufe he muft not defcend from the altitude of his contemplations
' fo as to to think of the Sacrament or Chrifts humane body.

It feems thefe were fuch fanatiks as fome Fryers are.

In this Council the decrees called Clementines were paffed ; in which are fpecially noted by *Binius*, fome things *de fide*, as followeth.

I. ' That it is herefie to call in doubt, or affent that the fubftance of the
' rational or intellective foul is not truly and perfect the form of mans body.

II. ' That whereas Divines differ about the effect of Baptifme, fome fay-
' ing that to Infants fin is remitted, but not Grace conferred; others faying that
' the fault is remitted and virtues or informing Grace infufed as to the Ha-
' bit,

'bit, though not yet for use, we attending the general Efficacy of Christs
'de..h, which by Baptisme is equally applyed to all, judge the second opini-
'on more probable and agreeable to the sayings of the Saints and modern
'Doctors of *Theologie*, the sacred Council approving this, which saith, that
'both to adult and infants in baptisme informing grace and virtues are
'given.

III. 'If any one fall into this errour that as pertinaciously to affirm that
'*Usury is no sin*, we decree that he be punished as an Heretike, and the ordina-
'ries and inquisitors for heresie may proceed against such as against hereticks.

IV. 'And it is decreed that if any Communities or Officers shall presume
'to write or dictate that usury should be paid, or being paid should not be
'fully and freely restored, let them be excommunicate, and they shall in-
'cuir the same sentence that do not as far as they can blot out such statutes
'out of the bookes of the said Companies, that shall keep such customes.
Also that Usurers be compelled to shew their books of accounts.

§ 243. Here the *Pope and the Bishops in a General Council* have judged
divers points to be heretic, and consequently their contraries to be Articles
of faith: And for Heresie they curse, burn and damne men.

1. I overpassed their Article that Christ was dead before his side was
pierced, which is true: But whether an Article of our Creed necessary to
be understood to Salvation, let the Church Creed be witness.

2. Its well, that the possibility of sinless perfection is made a heresie by
them (for we must daily pray for pardon): But why then do they talk so
much of the possibility of keeping all Gods Law, that is of never sinning,
and talk of perfection, and works of Supererogation?

3. Do not they make an Article of Faith of a Logical Arbitrary Notion
(*that intellectual Souls being the Bodies form*) who knows not how ambiguous the word *form* is? An *Aristotle* supposeth a *Corpus organicum*, besides the
Soul; and that *Corpus* hath its form *quà Corpus*. I imagine, that these Bishops meant the same thing, that I do, and that our difference is but of
the fitness of words; but I will so far venture on their heretication as to say,
that *forma Corporis*, *forma Animæ*, and *forma Hominis*, are divers: That *Corpus organicum quà tale* hath its proper form, which denominateth it such;
which is not the Soul: That the Soul being a *substance* hath its *proper
form* which denominateth it, and which it retaineth, when separated from
the Body: And that the *intellectual Soul* is *forma Hominis*, but improperly
called *forma Corporis*: I will venture on their Heretication, to tell them my
opinion, and I think their Errour and Presumption to thrust such things
on Men under the penalties of cursing, burning, and damnation.

4 Their Article of Faith about the effect of Baptism (*That all that are
baptized at Age* and *Infants have both pardon and infused informing habitual
Grace*, I take for unproved, and have elsewhere proved it to be false in all
probability, as *universally* taken.

5. The Article of Faith, That *Usury is a Sin*, doth hereticate many great
Divines, more Lawyers, and most *Cities*, *Corporations*, and *Companies* in the
World

World: No doubt, but all Usury is a sin that is against either *Mercy* or *Justice*: But that some Usury may be an Act of *great Charity*, many wise men think past doubt: We have known some get estates of many thousand pounds a year by trading with money taken upon Usury, when perhaps some that Leant that money, had nothing but the Use to buy them bread and course cloathing, and keep them from perishing. How many thousand Great Men, Lawyers and Citizens are to be cursed, burnt, and damned by this Canon, for holding some Usury to be Lawful: Nay, how many for *not restoring* it when taken; when perhaps, an Orphan took it of a rich man to save them from famine. This is the benefit of hereticators.

§ 244. *Anno* 1311. Was a Council at *Ravenna* CCCCVIII. for Discipline and Reformation of the Churches manners, with many superstitions.

§ 245. CCCCLIX. *Anno* 1314. Another at *Ravenna*, was like the former.

§ 246. Next cometh Pope *John* the 20th alias 21th. alias 22th. alias 23th. He lived at *Avinion*: He thought souls were kept in some receptacles from the sight of God till the Resurrection: He damned those that held that Christ and his Apostles possessed no propriety (*Platina* thinks contrary to the Gospel.) He tormented to death *Hugo* Bishop of *Cature* for being against him. He cursed and excommunicated the Emperor *Lewis* of *Bavaria*, and many other great men: *Italy* was all in Wars in his days. The Emperor set up another Pope in *Italy* against him, *Nicol.* the 5th. which was saith, *Onuph.* 28th. Schism at *Rome*, was not he that was at *Rome* liker to be Bishop of *Rome*, than he that was in *France*.) But the Pope *Nicolas* after three years Reign was catched by one that would merit of Pope *John*, and sent to him, and put in Prison, where he soon died: and *John* died at Ninety years Old after Nineteen years Reign, leaving more money behind him, than any Pope that ever went before him.

Toes forbad any below a Bishop to examine or judge a Priest at his ordinat.

His process against *Lodov.* the Emperor, you may see in *Freberus* History *Rer. Bohem.* and others more at large.

§ 247. CCCCLX. Another Council at *Ravena*, *Anno* 1317. to the same purpose with the former, where the manners of those times may be noted in the crimes forbidden: The 3*d. Can.* sheweth that men had then the place of Archdeacons before they were ordained Deacons, and the places or benefices of Abbots, Deans, Archpresbyters, Prelates, (*Prepositi*) before they were ordained Priests: And the Cannon requireth such to be after ordained within a year.

Can. 18. Excommunicateth all Lay Magistrates, that take a Priest or Clerk in arms or in any excess or sin, and keep him, (that is imprison him or punish him) and do not send him to his Bishop; or that sending him to the Bishop do openly shame him, by sending him with trumpets or armed men, or with his arms hang'd about his neck.

§ 248. CCCCLXI. *Anno* 1322. A *Concilium Sabinense* had many of the like

like orders to reſtrain the vicious Clergy, and yet *Can.* 3. excommunicate ſecular Judges that compel them to anſwer at their Bar. Eſpecially they are large in impoſing penalties on thoſe that publickly keep Concubines in their houſes (and have not the modeſty to fornicate more ſecretly.) If they put not away their Concubines in two Moneths they muſt loſe the third part of their tythes, and after other two months another third part, and at laſt the other third part, and after be uncapable of preferment, &c. Theſe are gentler penalties than a differing opinion is puniſhed with under the name of a hereſie.

§ 249. CCCCLXII. *Anno* 1324. A Council at *Toletane* to the like purpoſes.

§ 250. CCCCLXIII. The two Popes called two Councils againſt each other as Hereticks (were neither in the right.) *John* in a Council at *Avignion* proved *Nicolas* the 5*th.* a heretick for holding that Chriſt poſſeſſed nothing as Proprietor; *Nicolas* called a Council in *Italy* which condemned *John* as a heretick for holding the contrary: Thus the hereticators were hereticated.

§ 251. The French now got the Power of the Papacy, and another Frenchman was choſen Pope *Anno* 1334. called *Benedict.* 11. alias 12*th.* He renewed the excommunication and depoſition of the Emperor *Ludov.* and claimed the Empire to himſelf, concluding that being vacant it fell to the Church (ſee to whom Kingdomes eſcheat): whereby he ſet all *Italy* in Wars in all the Cities, giving them to the Rulers as the Popes Leiutenants, and perſwading the Romans alſo to depoſe the Senatorean power as of the King, and to exerciſe it themſelves under the Church: He lived above ſeven years Pope.

This Pope contrary to his Predeceſſor deſined that ſouls ſufficiently purged enjoy the clear viſion of God before the reſurrection.

§ 252. CCCCLXIV. *Anno* 1339. A Toletane Council decreed among other things that *every Rector of a Church and their Vicars under pain of excommunication do every year write the names of all their Pariſhioners that come to years of diſcretion, and conſign* (confirm) *all that are confeſſed, and excite them to come to the Sacrament;* But *if they have not received it, let them abſtain unleſs it be by the Counſel of their own Prieſt.* And *thoſe that confeſſe not, after a year to expel from the Church, and deny them eccleſiaſtical burial.*

§ 253. *Anno* 1342. Another Frenchman (Biſhop of *Roven*) is made Pope at *Avignion: Clem.* 6. All *Italy* and *Naples* was put into the flames of Wars. He forced the Germanes to ſet up another againſt the Emperor, *Lodov. Bavarus,* which was *Charles* Son of *John* the 11. of *Bohemia. Charles* ſends bound to the Pope, a new Senator *Nicolas Rentii* that ruled all at *Rome.* He made a new Jubilee; he laboured in vain to reconcile King *Edward* of *England* to the French, the Engliſh conquering their Navies and taking *Calis,* &c. The Colenſes and Trevinuſes having contributed money as to a Turkiſh expedition, that Pope liberally rewarded them, by granting them licence to eat Eggs and Milk-meats on any faſting dayes out of Lent.

§ 254. CCCCLXV. *Anno* 1347. A Toletane Council againſt Simony, &c.

The Empe-rour Lodo-vic. died,

§ 255. Anno 1352. *Innoc.* the 6*th.* is made Pope of *Avignion*: All *Italy* was still kept in blood: One *Barnacellus* Lorded it as Ruler at *Rome*: The Pope craftily lets *Nicolas Gencii* out of Prison to set up against him; *Nicolas* gets the better and killeth him: but domineering too much is next kill'd himself. 1347. The new Emperor *Charles* is Crowned in *Italy*. The Romans put the power into seven Citizens called *Reformers of the common wealth*. The Pope sets *Hugo* King of *Cyrus* against the Reformers, and bids him pull them down. But trouble came near him: Our King *Edward* conquered the French, and took the King and his Son *Philip* Prisoners, nobly releasing the Prisoners upon promise that they would fight against him no more, which they presently brake; The Pope dieth.

§ 256. Having long said nothing of the Greek affairs, I here only briefly say, that the utter confusion of their imperial Successions by murders and usurpations, and the continued confusions of their Church affairs ever since the divisions of the Orthodox Nestorians, Eutychians, Monothelites, &c. maketh it both a hard and unpleasant task to give any exact account of their Bishops, Synods and manifold contentions, which furthered the ruine of the Empire. Their divisions gave the Latines opportunity to take *Constantinople* 1204. which they kept 58 years, and then lost it. *Baldwin* was the first Latine Emperour whom the *Bulgarians* conquered, and took Prisoner *Anno* 1205. and kept sixteen months, and then put him to death. *Henry* his brother succeedeth him, 1206 and died 1216. *Peter* succeedeth him that married his sister (or daughter) and is quickly slain by *Theodorus Lascaris*. Robert succeedeth his Father *Peter* 1261. *Theodore Lascaris* was Emperor chosen by the Greeks and kept Court at *Nice*: He defeated the Turks, and slew their Sultan, and died, 1222. *John Ducas* his Son in Law succeedeth him, and 1255. his Son *Theodore Lascaris* succeedeth him and died 1259. leaving a Son *John* of six years old: *Michael Palcologus* putting out *Johns* eyes at ten years old, usurpeth the Empire, and by a stratagem of *Alexius Cæsar* with 800 men taketh *Constantinople*; and feigned a reconciliation with *Rome*, and died 1282, and for his seeming reconciliation with *Rome* his Son *Andronicus* and the Clergy denied him Christian burial. *Andronicus* succeeded: His Son *Michael* dying, his Grandson *Andronicus* deposeth and banisheth him, and taketh the Throne: he reigned 8 years, and died 1341. He committed his two Sons to *Joh. Cantacuzenus*: The Eldest Son *John* reigned 27 years, and *Manuel* his brother succeeded him 1384. and his Son *John* succeeded him 1419. *Constantine* the 8*th.* began 1445, and *Anno* 1453, *May* 29*th.* the Turks took *Constantinople*; and set up their Empire.

§ 257. *Anno* 1355. Under *Innocent* the 6*th.* was another Toletane Council: short and sweet; worth the noting: (by authority of *Blasius* Arch-Bishop of *Toletan. Viz.* [*Lest faithful Christians should be burdened with the weight of sin (or faultiness) by transgressing provincial Constitutions, when Divine piety hath mercifully put them under an easie yoke and light burden, we ordain, the holy Council approving it that the Provincial constitutions of our Predecessors* *dcessors* and *that shall be made hereafter, unless it be otherwise expresly ordained in such as shall be made, shall oblige the transgressours only to the penalty of them, but not* (ad culpam) *to faultiness* (or sin.)

It's worth the Inquiry how far all other Canons and humane penal Lawes are thus to be expounded.

§ 258. *Anno* 1362. Another French man is made Pope, called *Urban* the 5*th*. He sent *Ægidius* to fight for him in *Italy* (still broil'd in Wars,) and died.

§ 259. *Anno* 1370. *Petrus Bellfortis* that was made Cardinal before he was 17 years old is made Pope of *Avignon*, and called *Greg.* the 11*th*. So far was all the world from obeying the Pope, that *Italy* still fought against him: Thither he sends an Army, bloodshed and misery overspreadeth the Country. The Pope at last saw that his absence gave his Enimies advantage, and not daring to let the *French* know lest they should have stopt him, he slipt away to *Rome*, and thither removed his Seat, that had been at *Avignion* 70 years, to the great joy of the City, impoverished by the absence of the Court.

§ 260. *Anno* 1378. *Gregory* the 11*th* being dead, the People of *Rome* flock to the Cardinals, and cry to them to choose no more Frenchmen least the Seat be again removed, but an Italian, and the best man that could be found, least all should run to utter confusion. Thirteen Cardinals were Frenchmen and four Italians: The French were for a French Pope; but they fell out among themselves, while part of the French were for one, and part for another, by which it fell out that *Barthol. Epise. Barensis*, a Neapolitane was chosen, an extraordinary good Pope. The Cardinals cryed out that the People of *Rome* had by tumult, force, and arms constrained them to the choice of this man (*Urban* 6.) and they fled to strong holds; but at last came to *Rome* and owned the Pope: But when he told them, that he would not go to *France*, and reproved their wickedness, and told them how severely he resolved to punish them if they amended not, they got away and declared, that *Urban* was a false Pope, chosen by the Peoples tumults and force, where the Cardinals were not free, and that the Seat was void, and they chose another (Cardinal *Gebennensis*) and called him *Clement* 7*th*; And so whereas for seventy years there had been a Pope at *Avignion*, and none at *Rome*, now for forty years more there were two, one at *Avignion*, and one at *Rome* (and sometimes three). And indeed it passeth my skill to know how the *Avignion* Popes were Bishops of *Rome*, who never saw *Rome*, nor any of the People, any more than he is a true Schoolmaster that never saw the School or Scholars.

And now the two Popes fall to fighting for it; and the French Pope sending an Army of Britons against the Italian Pope; at first they beat the Romans, but next were so destroyed by them, that few scaped home to bring the news.

The *Italian* bloody Wars still continue, especially between the *Venetians* and *Genonefes*. Then had the *Venetians* the first Guns: The *Neapolitans* also

also were ruined by Wars, their Queen siding with one Pope *(Clement)* was destroyed by *Charles* that was for the other (justly strangled, as she had used her own Husband). The Duke of *Anjou* also came with a great Army into *Italy* from Pope *Clement* to destroy Pope *Urban*; but the General died, and the Souldiers scattered and returned home: The Pope then desired of King *Charles* that his Nephew might be Prince of *Naples*; and being denied, threatned *Charles*, and cited him to *Nucena*, who came at his Summons, but with an Army: The Pope escaped to *Genoa*; and King *Charles* upon his Fathers death called home to *Hungary*, was murdered.

☛ The Pope putteth seven of his old Cardinals in five Sacks, and drowneth them in the Sea: But to be strong enough, he maketh no fewer than twenty nine new ones in one day. He went to *Naples*, thinking to surprize and deject the Kings two Sons, but was defeated. *Italy* still flamed with War: He made 54 Cardinals, of which he killed five, and deposed seven, and died, saith *Platina*, little lamented, as his Epitaph sheweth, as being rustick and inexorable, though one of their best: He died after eleven years, *An.* 1389.

§. 261. CCCCLXVI. *An.* 1388. A Council is held at *Palentine* in *Spain*, under the Cardinals of the Antipope *Clement*, about Shavings and Church-Orders.

§. 262. *An.* 1389. *Boniface* 9. alias 8. is chosen at *Rome*, and *Clement* dead in *France*, *Pet. de Luna* is chosen there, called *Benedict* 13. The *Italians* were still the furthest from Unity and peace, all the Cities almost in war against each other: so far were they from Eminency in Religious love and concord, that they had not the common quietness of Heathens. The Pope went to *Perusium* to reconcile them there; where to shew what his power was over them, the people killed fourscore of the Nobles before the Popes face, which he took ill, and departed. He got possession of the Government of *Rome*; he required Annals, that is, half a years value of every Benefice of him that received it: All, saith *Platina*, save the *English* granted it; and they would yield it of no Benefices but Bishopricks. Had the Pope indeed been Head of all the World, Annals would have come to a considerable Rent: But going so far as the *Antipodes* to gather it, would have made it come shorter home than the *Spanish* Gold and Silver doth from the *West-Indies*.

Instead of winning men by Preaching, the Popes Arms now subdue *Perusium* and many *Italian* Cities to him: *Platina* saith, that his own Father, that saw the man, told him, that a Priest cloathed in white, carrying a Crucifix, with certain Hymns to the Virgin *Mary*, came from the *Alps* with a grave and pious look, so preaching, that all the people followed him, even Nobles as well as others; and that he pretended that he went to visit the ☛ Holy Fathers at *Rome*; but the Pope suspected that he meant to be Pope, or get too much interest, and sent Souldiers and took him, and burnt him to death; some saying that he had some error, others saying no such thing was ever proved by him, but it was reported by the Pope to hide his cruelty.

In

In these times, saith *Platina*, *Chrysoloras Byzantinus* brought *Greek* Learning into *Italy*, that had been silent five hundred years.

§. 263. *An.* 1404. *Boniface* dying, *Innocent* 7. is chosen at *Rome*, one part of *Europe* being for him, and another for the *Avignion* Pope. *Tumultuante tota Italia*, saith Platina, *Tota Italia ad arma respiciebat*: Five and twenty Cities revolted from the Viccecomites, and set up new Governments. (What Concord did the Pope keep in the World?) *Platina* saith he was not only slothful, but could not endure to be told of his duty. The Citizens of *Rome* petitioned him to endeavour the ending of the Schisme, the King of *France* and the *Avignion* Pope being inclined to peace: For answer he sent them to his Nephew *Ludovicus* to be murdered, who presently killed eleven that came to consult with him, casting them out at a window, saying *that was the only way to cure Sedition and Schisme:* Upon this the City takes Arms for revenge; the Pope and his Nephew fly to *Viterbium*; *Ladislaus* King of *Apulia* helps the Citizens, they fall upon the Courtiers, take the Capitol, and other places, &c. The Pope sends an Army against them that overcometh them, and forceth them to beg his return: He dieth 1406. after two years and 23 days Reign; and so there was only the *Avignion* Pope.

§. 264. *An.* 1406. *Gregory* 12. is chosen at *Rome*, taking an Oath (as *Innoc.* 7. did) to resign, if the Unity of the Church required it: The Princes of *France* had made their Pope *Benedict* 13. take the like Oath: The Princes and Cardinals ashamed of two Popes, and two Churches, prest them both to summon a Council; they cunningly would not agree of the place, and so forced the doing it without them.

§. 265. CCCCLXVII. To put a shew on the business, *Greg.* calleth a Council at *Aquileia*, whether by long delays he creepeth with a few to do nothing.

§ 266. CCCCLXVIII. And the other Pope. *Bened.* 13. *Anno* 1409. also calleth his Council in *Arragone* of his Subjects: which calleth it self a General Council, and pronounce him the true Pope, and no Schismatick or Heretick, and *Greg.* to be the Usurper, but exhort him to endeavour Unity.

§. 267. CCCCLXIX. The two Popes giving no better hopes, some of the Cardinals of both sides slipt from them, and by the Countenance of the *Florentines* and King *Ladislaus*, chose *Pisa* for a General Council, where they met and summoned both the Popes, who scorned them; and they deposed them both as *Hereticks* and *Schismaticks*, saith *Binius*, forbidding all Christians to obey them, and they chose a third, *Alexander* 5. and the two old ones kept up still; and so there were three Popes at once.

§. 268. *An.* 1409. *Alex.* 5. is chosen, much commended, but died in eighteen Months, some say; saith *Antoninus*, poysoned by a Clyster: But to shew himself a Pope, in that little time he deposed King *Ladislaus*, and gave his Kingdome to *Lewis* Duke of *Anjou*.

§. 269. *Balthasar Cossa* is next chosen, called by some *Joh.* 21. by others 22 by others 23. and by *Platina Joh.* 4. (So little are they agreed of their succession)

succession) *Platina* saith the Cardinals of *Greg.* were yet poor, and he hired them with Money to Create him: He got *Sigismund* King of *Bohemia* chosen Emperour, and would have had the Council to be at *Rome. Italy* continued still in blood, the Popes having parcelled it into so many small Principalities, to secure it against the Emperours; no part of the whole World lived from Age to Age in such continual War and confusion. This Pope, saith *Onuphrius Panvinus*, viz. *fuit bello & armis quam Religioni aptior, utpote qui neque fidem norat neque Religionem, rebus profanis magis quam Divino cultu accommodatus.* How he was accused, deposed, imprisoned; how the other two Popes *Greg.* 12. and *Bened.* 13. were all deposed with him, and *Martin* 5. chosen; the next Chapter sheweth.

CHAP. XIII.

The Council of Constance, Basil, *and some others.*

§. 1. CCCCLXX. AN. 1414. the Council of *Constance* was called by the means of the Emperour *Sigismund*, and the consent of Pope *John*, who the more trusted the Emperour because he had promoted him: There were then three Popes, *Bened.* 13. in *France*, whom the Kingdomes of *France, Spain, Arragon, England*, and *Scotland* followed; and *Greg.* 12. and *John* 23. at *Rome*, that divided the rest of the *Papalines.* It was not certainly to represent the *Trinity*, but to profane the Name, and abuse the Kingdome of the blessed Trinity. *Oct.* 28. P. *John* called by them *Sanctissimus Dominus Noster*, entereth the City, *Nov.* 5. The Pope began the Council. *Nov.* 16. was the first Session, the Pope speaking to them, and his Bull being read, shewing that he would have had the Council at *Rome*, but the miserable case of *Rome* (by contention and confusion) hindering, it was agreed with the Emperour to be at *Constance*, commanding to be there for the peace of the Church, and appointing a Weekly Mass to be said for obtaining Gods blessing, and pardoning a years penance for every Mass to every Mass-Priest that said it, exhorting all to fasting and prayer for good success, charging them to look after Errours, especially those that rose from one *John Wickliff*, and also to reform the Church, &c.

March 2. 1415. The Pope took an Oath, for the peace of the Church, to lay down his Popedome, if the other two Popes would do the same, and the Emperour kist his feet.

The Cardinal of *Florence* read these Decrees: 1. That the Council was lawfully called. 2. That it will not be dissolved by the departure of the Pope, or other Prelates. 3. That it be not dissolved till the present Schisme be healed, and the Church reformed in *Faith* and *Manners*, in *Head* and *Members*. 4. That it be not removed but on just cause. 5. That the Bishops depart not.

§. 2.

§ 2. In the fourth Session they decreed that the general Council repre-
'senting the *militant Catholick Church*, hath its power immediately from Christ,
'to which every man of what State or dignity soever, though it be Papal, is
'bound to obey in the things that belong to Faith, and the extirpation of
'the said Schism and the general reformation of the Church in head and mem-
'bers. 2. That the Pope withdraw not himself or the Officers, and if he
'should, or should thunder out Church censures against them or any adhering
'to the Council, they are void. 3. That no Translations, Promotions, or
'Cardinals be made to the prejudice of the Council. 4. That three of each
'Nations be chosen to judge of departures, &c. But the Pope fled and sent
'them word that it was not for fears, but for his health.

§ 3. Sess. 5. The Emperor being among them, they decreed again the
Power of the Council as immediately from Christ, which the Pope and all
must obey; and that the Pope is punishable if he disobey; that he is bound
to surrender in any case of great and evident profit to the Church; that
he unlawfully departed; that if he will return and perform his promise,
he shall be safe.

Next, they proceeded to condemn the Books of *John Wickliff*, and to
prosecute *John Huss*.

Next they applied themselves to the Emperour to reduce the Pope; who
told them he was in the hands of the Duke of *Austria*; but if they pleased
he would write to him, or try to fetch him by force, &c.

§. 4. Sess. 6. They order the Procuration for the Popes Resignation to be
demanded, and Process to be made against *John Huss*, and *Hierome* of
Prague. A Letter is read from the University of *Paris* to the Pope, to submit to the Council.

§. 5. Sess. 7. They accused *Hierome* of *Prague* for not appearing, and summoned the Pope, promising him safe Conduct, *sed salva Justitia* &c.

§. 6. Sess. 8 They condemned *Wickliff's* Bones to be dig'd up, upon 45
Articles, instead of 260 which they had gathered. *Art.* 1. was:

'1. That the substance material of Bread and Wine remain in the Sa-
'crament of the Altar.

'2. The Accidents of Bread remain not without the substance.

'3. Christ is not identically and really in his proper bodily presence in
'the Sacrament.

'4. If a Bishop or Priest live in mortal sin, he Ordaineth not, Baptizeth
'not, Consecrateth not.

'5. The Gospel saith not that Christ instituted the Mass.

'6. God ought to obey the Devil. *   * *A ca-*

'7. If a man be contrite aright, outward confession is needless and un- *lumny.*
'profitable

'8. If the Pope be a Reprobate, and wicked, and so a Member of the
'Devil, he hath no power over the faithful given him by any but *Cæsar*.

'9. Since *Urban* the 6. none is to be taken for Pope, but we must live as † *Under*
'the *Greeks*, † under our own Laws.   *the Turks.*

'10. It

'10. It is against Scripture that Church-men have possession (that is, *they should not labour to be rich.*)

'11. No Prelate should excommunicate any one, unless he know that God hath first excommunicated him: And he that so excommunicateth, is thereby a Heretick or Excommunicate.

'12. A Prelate that excommunicateth a Clerk who appealed to the King, or to the Council of the Kingdome, is thereby a Traytor to the King and Kingdome.

☞ '13. They that give over Preaching, or hearing Gods Word, for mens Excommunication, are Excommunicate, and in the Day of Judgment shall be judged Traytors to Christ.

'14. It is lawful for a Deacon or Presbyter to preach the Word of God without the Authority of the Apostolick Seal, or a Catholick Bishop.

'15. No one is a Civil Lord, or a Prelate, or a Bishop, while he liveth in mortal sin. *(The meaning of this is, no open wicked man is a Subject capable of such Authority given by Christ, as shall warrant him to use the place, but his acts may be valued to others in many cases) Dispositio materiæ est necessaria ad formam recipiendam:* As an Infidel can be no Bishop or Pastor.)

'16. Temporal Lords may take away temporal goods from the Church, from a Possessor habitually criminal, and not only in act. *(Not from the sacred use in general, but from that man that forfeiteth them.)*

'17. The people may correct their Delinquent Lords *(This is not to be believed to be Wickliff's sense, till they cite his own words, which no doubt limit it to the cases.)*

'18 Tythes are meer Alms, and the Parishioners may take them away for their Prelates sins.

'19. The special prayers applied by Prelates and Religious men to one person, profit him no more than the general ones, *cæteris paribus.*

'20. He that giveth Alms to Fryars is thereby Excommunicate (that is, *he sins by cherishing wilful idleness.*)

'21. He that enters the private Religion, either of the *Possessing* or the *Mendicant* Fryars, becomes less fit and able to keep the Commandments of God.

'22. Holy men that made private Religions, thereby sinned.

'23. The Religious living in private Religion, are not *(therein)* of the Christian Religion.

'24. Fryars are bound to get their living by the labour of their hands, and not by begging.

'25. They are Simoniacal that bind themselves to pray for others for a temporal reward (or price.)

'26. The prayers of Reprobates *(wicked men) availeth* not to any.

'27. All things come to pass by necessity.

'28. The Confirmation of Youth, the Ordination of Clarks, the Consecration of Places, are reserved to the Pope and Bishops for covetousness of temporal gain and honour.

'29. Univer-

'29. Universities, Studies, Colledges, Degrees, and Masterships in them, 'are introduced by vain Gentility, and profit the Church as much as the 'Devil doth.

'30. The Excommunication of a Pope, or any Prelate, is not to be 'feared, because it is the Censure of Antichrist.

'31. They that found Cloysters sin, and they are Diabolical that enter them.

'32. To enrich the Clergy is against Christs Rule.

'33. Pope *Sylvester*, and the Emperour *Constantine*, erred in inriching the Church.

'34. All the Order of Begging Fryars are Hereticks; and those that give 'to them are Excommunicate.

'35. They that enter Religion (*as Fryars*) or any Order (*of them*) are 'thereby disabled from keeping Gods Commands, and so of coming to 'Heaven, unless they forsake them.

'36. The Pope, and all his Clergy that have Possessions, are therefore He-'reticks, and the Secular Lords and Laicks that consent to them (*to their 'great riches.*)

'37. The Church of *Rome* is the Synagogue of Satan; and the Pope is 'not the immediate and nearest Vicar of Christ and the Apostles.

'38. The Decretal Epistles are Apocryphal, and seduce from the Faith 'of Christ, and the Clerks that study them are fools.

'39. The Emperour and Secular Lords were seduced by the Devil to in-'rich the Church (*excessively he meaneth*) with temporal goods.

'40. The Election of the Pope by Cardinals was introduced by the 'Devil.

'41. It is not necessary to Salvation to believe the Church of *Rome* to be the Supreme among other Churches.

'42. It is foolish to trust to the Indulgences of the Pope and Bishops.

'43. Oaths made to strengthen humane Contracts and Civil Commerce, 'are unlawful.

'44. *Augustine*, *Benedict*, *Bernard* are damned, unless they repented of ha-'ving possessions, and instituting and entering (*private*) Religions; and so 'from the Pope to the lowest Religious (*Fryar*) they are all Hereticks.

'45. All Religions (*that is Orders of Fryars*) were introduced by the 'Devil.

This Article about *Necessity of Events*, I see in *Wickliff*'s Books is his own, and many here cited are true; but no doubt but many of them are perverted by their wording them, and leaving out the Explicatory Context.

The Council forbad his Books, and condemned them to be burnt, and reprobated every one of all these foresaid Articles, with all the 260.

The Duke of *Austria* most humbly begged the Emperours pardon for receiving the Pope.

§.7. Sess. 9. The Citation of the Pope is read, and Commissaries and Judges

Judges appointed; and a Letter read from the University of *Paris*, instigating the Council to their duty (for their honest Chancellour *Gerson* was here.)

§. 8. Sess. 10. The Popes Suspension was read. The *Sess.* 11. the Articles against the Pope are read, which were proved; which were in sum as followeth.

Art. 1. That the Pope *John* from his Youth was of a naughty disposition, impudent, a lyar, rebellious against his Parents, given to most Vices, and so was, and still is accounted of all that know him; Cardinals, Arch-Bishops, Bishops, &c. witness it.

2. He gathered riches by Symony, and wicked means.

3. By these Symoniacal riches he purchased a Cardinals place at great rates.

4. Possessing *Bononia* as Legate by tyranny and cruel exactions, inhumanely and impiously he ruined the people, without all Justice or Piety, &c.

5. Getting thus to be Pope, like a Pagan he contemned all Divine Offices.

6. That he is the oppressor of the poor, the persecutor of Justice, the Pillar of the unjust, the Statue of Simoniacks, the servant of the Flesh, the dregs of Vices, a stranger to Virtue, flying publick Consistories, wholly given to sleep, and other fleshly desires; wholly contrary to Christ in life and manners, the Glass of Infamy, and the profound Inventer of all wickednesses (or malice) so scandalous to the Church, that among faithful Christians that knew him, he was commonly called THE DEVIL INCARNATE.

7. That as a Vessel of all sins, he repulsed the worthy, and gave all Offices, Benefices and Church-promotions to the bad that would give most Money for them. *

* *What was the Church then.*

8. Hereby the whole Church, Clergy and People, fell under infamy and scandal.

9. That of all these he was oft admonished and humbly intreated.

10. That he was worse after than before, laying all pretence of Justice, and openly selling all to the worst that would give him money.

11. That growing yet stronger in Vices, he made divers Officers purposely to manage his Simony (as his Bailiffs) for all fat Cathedrals, Abbeys Monasteries, Priories, and vacant Benefices reserved, &c.

12. That he charged his Registers to receive all the money before they granted, &c.

13. That he appointed certain Merchants to put vacant Benefices in the Balance, and grant their Petitions that offered most for them.

14. He ordered that no Petition for a Benefice be offered him, till it were signed by the Refundary, who then was to pay it out of his own Estate if he took too little.

15. That against God and his Conscience he oft sold his Bulls to Eminent men, in which he wrote, that they that had Benefices had resigned them to him, and that by lying forged Resignation, which never was made, sold them again for great sums, and beggar'd many. 6. By

16. By this it came to pass, that without all difficulty he that gave most, carried it: And the same course was held in Sacraments, Indulgences, Dispensations, and other Ecclesiastical and Spiritual Gifts.

17. That he usually sold the same Benefice divers times over to divers persons, or to the same, silencing Claims of Right; whereby the *whole Church* was defiled with Simony, * filled with the unworthy, both in higher and lower Prelacies, &c.

<small>* Which Councils have judged Heresie.</small>

18. That he refused to Confirm those that were Canonically Elected, unless even to satiety they glutted him with Money, putting the unworthy in their stead, and translated men against their wills from their Churches, that he might sell them dearer.

19. That promising Church-Reformation in the Council at *Pisa*, he called one at *Rome*, and being there publickly admonished, being incorrigible by the Devils instinct, did worse.

20. That he sold for Money Indulgences at the hour of death, the Predication of the Cross, Absolutions from fault and punishment, Concessions of Churches and portable Altars, Consecrations of Bishops, Benedictions of Abbots, Relicks of Saints, Holy Orders, power in Confession to absolve from sins, and Acts that may be ministred only by the Operations of the Holy Ghost for Grace.

21. That one *Nic. Pistorius*, a *Florence* Merchant, and the Popes Secretary, a Lay married man, was made by the Pope his Legate Apostolical, sent into *Brabant* to exact and receive a Subsidy, which was the tenth part of the fruit of all Benefices in divers Cities and Diocesses, and to excommunicate the refusers by a certain deputed Sublegate, † and suspend Colledges, Covents, Chapters, &c.

<small>† Like a Lay Chancellour and his Surrogate.</small>

22. That he authorized this *Nicholas* to grant to all persons, of each Sex, for Money to choose their Confessors, that might absolve from fault and punishment, by which the Merchant got vast sums of Money, seducing the people.

23. That all the premises are known, true, proved, &c.

24. That *Anno* 1412. Ambassadors from the King, Bishops, and Universities of *France*, admonished him charitably of this scandalous, infamous Simony.

25. That he amended not by it, but did worse.

26. That he is defamed of all this in all Kingdomes of the Christian World.

27. That he abused *Rome* and the Churches Patrimony, exhausting the people, and imbursing it himself, by Taxes, Gabels, &c. *Many instances are added.*

28. For these things many Crimes, Sacriledges, Adulteries, Murders, Spoils, Rapine and Thefts were committed in *Rome*, through his fault.

29. It is the common voice, opinion, assertion and belief, that in these, and innumerable other evils, he is the greatest Dilapidator and Dissipator of the Church Affairs that ever was, scandalous to the Universal Church, a

Kkk 2 Witch,

Witch, a Murderer, a Killer of his Brethren, Incontinent, in all things serving the Vices of the flesh, of infinite crimes, called infamously *Balderinus*.

30. That all this is notorious by common fame, repute, &c.

31. That he hath sold the goods of Cardinals, Bishopricks, Parishes, Colledges, Priories, &c.

32. And this not only in the City about (many instances named.)

33. That he destroyed University Studies, by taking the Salaries to himself.

34. Besides, he laid such burdens on the Parsons, as forced them to sell the Church-goods, Ornaments, and Books.

35. That hereby the whole Church was notoriously scandalized.

36. The Infamy was so great, that Princes and the Emperour besought him to amend.

37. Hereupon he promised to amend, and to call this Council.

38. But he went on, and did worse than before.

39. He forbad the righting of the injured in judgment.

40. That the Bishop of *Salisbury*, and other *English* Embassadours, admonished him to amend, and he gave them ill words, and threatned, and abused them.

41. That at *Constance* he swore to resign for Peace.

42. And he promised to submit to the judgment of the Council.

43. He bid all say what they would against him.

44. He was humbly intreated by the Council to perform his word.

45. Yet thought by hiding himself to evade.

46. Yet he professed before that he intended not to depart.

47. And when the Church longed for peace, by the Council he plotted to dissolve the Council, and so fled in a disguized habit.

48. He fled to *Schafhausen*, and commanded some Cardinals and Bishops to come to him.

49. Thence he fled to *Lauffenberge*, and towards *Brisac*.

50. The Council desired his return.

51. He denied to answer, but fled to *Nurenburg* to frustrate the Council.

52. He is an obdurate sinner, and incorrigible Fautor of Schism, &c.

53. That all this is notorious, and the common repute of men.

54. And all the premises are the common fame and voice. Here somewhat is left out.

And they begin as anew ; 1. Declaring his wickedness from his Youth.

2. That he is notoriously suspected to have poysoned Pope *Alexander*, and his Physitian *Daniel*.

3. That he committed Incest with his Brothers Wife, and with the holy Nuns, and ravished Maids, and committed Adultery with Wives, and other crimes of Incontinence.

3. That he Simonaically sold six Parish Churches in *Bononia* to Lay men, who set Priests in them at their pleasure.

4. That

4. That for Money he sold the Mastership of the Order of S. *John* of *Jerusalem* in *Cyprus* to a Child of five years old, Bastard to the King of *Cyprus*, with the fruits of Vacancies, and spoils of the last Master, &c.

5. That he would not recall this, but on condition.

1. That the K. of *Cyprus* should be paid (by them that succeeded) all the Money back which he gave to the Pope.

2. That the Pope should have more, six thousand Florins of Gold, which the Prior of *Rhodes* paid, and for which the Hospitallers are yet in debt.

3. He reserved for the said Bastard the Magistral Chamber, worth two thousand Florins.

4. That the said Pope *John* gave Fryar *Jacobus de Vitriaco*, an ancient man, and expresly professing the Hospitallers Religion, an Absolution from his Vows, Rule and habit of Religion, and reduced him to a Secular life, and Marriage, &c. for six hundred Ducats.

Many other Articles I pass by, as tedious to be repeated: One was, *That he was a notorious Simoniack, and a pertinacious Heretick*: Another was, *That often before divers Prelates, and other honest men, by the Devils persuasion he pertinaciously said, asserted, dogmatized, and maintained, that there is no Life Eternal, nor any after this: And he said, and pertinaciously believed, that mans Soul dieth with the body, and is extinct, as are the Bruits: And he said, that the Dead rise not, contrary to the Article of the Resurrection,* &c.

He sent an Epistle to the Emperour to beg mercy &c.

§. 9. Sess. 12. The Articles being shewed the Pope, his Answer is recited: Viz. *That he repented of his filthy departure, and ratified all the Councils Process against him, and would give no other Answer to their Charge, affirming, that the Council of* Constance *was most holy, and could not err ; and was the Pisane Council continued, and he would never contradict the Council, but publickly confess that he had no right in the Papicy: That he would be much pleased that the Sentence against him might be quickly passed, and sent him, which with all reverence he would receive, and as much as in him lay confirm, ratifie, approve, and divulge; and did then ratifie, approve, and confirm all their Process against him, and promise never to gainsay them.*

The Council decreed, that when the Papacy was void, none should be chosen without them, and they that attempted it should be punished, and the Election be void.

Next the Definitive Sentence of Deposition was past against him.

Next they decreed, that none of the three present Popes should ever be elected again.

§. 10. Sess. 13. The Council decreed, that though Christ after Supper instituted. and to his Disciples administred the Sacrament in both kinds, Bread and Wine, &c. 'And though in the Primitive Church the faithful received it in both kinds, &c. yet the contrary custome of the Church should 'be a Law, which may not be reprobated without the Churches Authority, 'or changed: And to say that this is sacrilegious and unlawful, is erroneous,

and

'and the pertinacious Assertors to be proceeded against as Hereticks (that
'is, burnt.)

Thus they take power to change Christs Sacrament, and that when they suppose it to be his very blood that they deny men, and make it Heresie and death to obey God before them. This was the Reforming Council.

Next they decree, that any Priest that giveth the Sacrament in both kinds shall be excommunicated, and used as a Heretick, even by Secular Power, that is, burnt.

§. 11. Sess. 14. *Carolus de Malatestis* recited in the name of *Gregory* 12. his Renunciation of the Papacy, and *Greg.* approved the Council. The Council absolveth all men from his obedience, &c. confirm some of his Acts, require the third Pope to resign, and declare him, if he refuse, a notorious Schismatick, and pertinacious Heretick.

§. 12. Sess. 15. After a severe Decree for silence, and no contradiction, the Articles of Heresie charged on *John Huss* were read, the sum of many is as followeth.

1. *As Christ is both God and Man, so the consecrated Host is the Body of Christ, at least in Figure, and true Bread in Nature.*

2. *That he declareth to the heretical lyars about the consecrated Host, that they can never declare or understand an accident without a subject.*

3. *This is my body, is such a figurative speech, as* John *was* Elias.

4. *The madness of feigning an accident without a subject, blasphemeth God, scandalizeth the Saints, and deceiveth the Church.*

5. *Its foolish and presumptuous to define, that the Infants of the faithful are not saved, dying without the Sacrament of Baptism.*

6. *The light and brief Confirmation by Bishops, solemnized only by the Rites said over, was introduced by the Devil, and to delude the people in the belief of the Church, and that the solemnity and necessity of Bishops may be the* more believed.

7. *Against Oyl, anointing Children, and the Linnen Cloth, as a light Ceremony,* &c.

8. *Vocal Confession made to a Priest, introduced by* Innocent, *is not so necessary as he defineth: He that by thought, word or deed offendeth his Brother, it sufficeth him to repent by thought, word or deed.*

9. *The Priest hearing Confession as the Latines do, is grievous and groundless,* &c.

A good life is a good sign of a true Minister.

The ill life of a Prelate substracteth the Subjects acceptation of Orders, and other Sacraments; and yet in case of necessity they may receive of such, piously praying that God will make up himself by these his Diabolical Ministers, the work or end of the Office which they are sworn to.

Ancient persons that despair of children may lawfully marry for temporal commodity, or mutual help, or to excuse Lust.

Words of Marriage, de præsenti, I take thee for my Wife, frustrate words de futuro, to another, I will take thee for a Wife.

The

The Pope that falsly calls himself the servant of the servants of God, is in no degree of Evangelical service, but worldly; and if he be in any order, it is in that of Devils, serving God more culpably by sin.

The Pope dispenseth not with Simony, being the Capital Simonist, running rashly to keep a most damnable state.

That the Pope is summus Pontifex is ridiculous: Christ never approved such a Dignity in Peter, or in any other.

The Pope is the Patron of Antichrist; not only that single person, but the multitude of Popes from the time of the Churches Donation, the Cardinals, Bishops, and other their Complices, is the compounded monstrous person of Antichrist: And yet Gregory, and other Popes that did good in their lives fruitfully repented at last: Peter, and Clement, and other helpers in the Faith, were not Popes, but Gods helpers to edifie the Church of Christ.

That this Papal Preeminence had its rise from the Gospel, is as false, as that all Errour arose from the first Truth.

There are twelve Procurators and Disciples of Antichrists, the Pope, Cardinals, Patriarchs, Arch-bishops, Bishops, Arch-deacons, Officials, Deans, Monks, forked Canons, false Fryars, and Questors.

Its as clear as the light, that he is greatest, and next Christ in the Church Militant, that is most humble, most serviceable, and most loveth the Church in the love of Christ.

He that unjustly possesseth any good thing of God, taketh anothers by theft.

Grace is necessary to dominion: (He meaneth, 1. Not of right before men, but God. 2. Nor of special grace only, I suppose.

Without the Law of Christ inwardly, Charters and Papers give not ability and justice.

We must not by gifts cherish a known sinner, being a Traytor to God.

Divers are against temporal power or right in wicked men in mortal sin: But I suppose that he meaneth only such a defect as will disable himself before God to receive his approbation and reward, but not such as will disoblige the Subject, or lose his property in foro humano.

Many more there be, that Fryars and the foresaid twelve Orders of Antichrist are not of God, and some Philosophical Opinions; which how far Huss held them, I take this Catalogue for no proof without his words, the Context and Explication.

All these are mentioned as taken out of *Wickliff*; but *Huss* is condemned for these following Articles.

§. 13. 1. *That there is one holy Universal Church of all the Predestinate.*

2. *That Paul was never a Member of the Devil.*

3. *That Reprobates are not parts of the Church, for no part of it finally falleth away, Predestinating Love never forsaking him.*

4. *Two Natures, the Divinity and Humanity, are one Christ.*

5. *The same as afore.*

6. *Taking the Church for the Predestinate, it is an Article of Faith.*

7. *Peter was not, nor is the Head of the Catholick Church.*

8. Priests

8. Priests of wicked lives pollute the Priestly power.

9. The Papal dignity arose from the Emperour, and the Popes præfecture and institution flowed from Cæsars power.

Divers of Popes and Priests that live wickedly are not the Apostles Successors.

Delivering men to Secular powers (because excommunicate) is to imitate the Scribes and Pharisees above Christ.

Ecclesiastical obedience is obedience after the Priests invention without any express authority of Scripture.

All humane Acts are distinguished into virtuous and vicious.

A Priest of Christ living after his Law and understanding the Scripture, and desirous to Edifie the people, ought not to obey the Pope or any Prelate that forbids him to preach, and excommunicateth him.

Every one made a Priest hath a command to preach and must obey it, notwithstanding excommunication.

By Church Censures of excommunication, suspension and interdict, the Clergy keeps the Laity under their feet for their own exaltation, and multiply avarice, protect malice, and prepare the way to Antichrist; It is an evident sign that such Censure, proceed from Antichrist, in which the Clergy principally proceed against those that open the nakedness of Antichrists wickedness, which the Clergy will for themselves usurp.

If the Popes be wicked men and reprobates, then as Judas an Apostle was a thief and traitor and son of perdition, so they are no heads of the Church, when they are no members.

The grace of predestination is the bond of the Churches union with the head.

A wicked and reprobate Pope and Prelate is equivocally a Pastor, and truly a thief and robber.

The Pope should not be called most holy.

Right election makes not him that cometh not in by Christ to have right.

Wickliffs 40 Articles were unjustly condemned.

There is no spark of appearance that there must be one head in spirituals to rule the whole Church, that must alwayes converse with it, and be conserved.

Christ Ruled his Church better throughout the world by his true Disciples dispersed, than it is by such monstrous heads.

The Apostles and faithful Priests of the Lord, did strenuously regulate the Church in things necessary to salvation, before the Office of a Pope was introduced, and so would do, were there no Pope, to the end of the world.

There is no Civil Lord, no Prelate, no Bishop, while in mortal sin. (Of which oft before.)

These Articles are mentioned which they say were proved against him.

It is to be noted that *Huss* called God to witness that he never preached nor owned many of these Articles which false witnesses brought in against him, and yet renounceth nothing that he held. And whether he or his accusers, better knew his mind and faith its easie to conjecture.

They

They condemned *Huss* to be burnt; and condemned another Article, *that any Subject may kill a Tyrant* (that is, an Usurper) by any secret or open means.

Then they made an Order against Robbers of such as came to the Council, and went back.

§. 14. Sess. 16. Deputies are appointed to go to *Arragon* to the third remaining Pope *Bened*. 13. to resign; and other matters.

The Sess. 17. was an honourable dimission of the Emperour.

The Sess. 18. about the Councils Bulls, &c.

The 19. Sess. was against *Hierome* of *Prague*, where they recite a long Recantation which they say he made, and from which they said he afterward revolted.

Also the Council decreed that they might proceed against Hereticks, notwithstanding the safe conducts and promises of the Emperour, Kings, or Princes, by what Bond soever they tyed themselves therein, though the Hereticks had not appeared, but trusting herein: And that the said Emperour, Kings, &c. having done what in them lieth, are no way obliged by their promises.

The 20. Sess. Decreed a monitory against the Duke of *Austria* on behalf of the Bishop of *Trent*, about estate.

The rest was about the Ejection of Pope *Benedict* the 13th. They swore to certain Capitula about it.

§ 15. *Hierome* of *Prague* having recanted through fear, repented and openly professed, that he dissembled and stood to his former doctrine and was condemned.

§ 16. Many following Sessions are against *Pet. Luna*, or *Bened*. the 13th. and treating with the *Arragonians* about him: He refused to resign, being left sole Pope (I think chosen by more Cardinals than the rest) in the 37 Sess. they pass Sentence against him.

§ 17. Sess. 39. It is decreed that there should be henceforth General Councils celebrated, *One five years after this, another seven years after that, and thence forward every ten years one: Or if there fall out another Schism, then within a year, none of the contending Popes being presidents*; with much more about the Councils.

Next they frame a Profession which every Elected Pope must make, *viz.*
'[That he firmly believeth and holdeth the holy Catholick Faith, according
'to the Traditions of the Apostles, of General Councils, and other holy
'Fathers, especially the eight holy General Councils, *viz. Nice, Conf.* 2.
'*Eph*. 3. *Calced*. 4 *Constant*. 5 and 6. *Nic*. 7. *Constant*. 8. As also the *Laterane, Lugdune*, and *Vien*. and to hold that faith unchanged in every title,
'and to contain even to life and blood, defend it and predicate it, and every
'ry way to prosecute and observe the rite of Ecclesiastical Sacraments delivered the Catholick Church.

Sess. 40. There are eighteen heads of reformation named: And the form of Electing Popes decreed. Sess. 41. An Oath for the Electors.

Otho Columna Cardinal is made Pope: *Wickliffes* errors again repeated, and *Huffes*, some Constitutions of *Frederic.* 2. Confirmed, and the Council dissolved.

§ 18. *Platina* tells us, that Pope *John* was deposed only by those that had adhered to him, before the other parties came. He was kept Prisoner three years, none but *Germanes*, whom he understood not, attending him: *Gregory* died of grief, that *Carolus Malatesta* had too hastily published his resignation, which he hoped to frustrate by delay. *Benedict* refusing to resign, the *Arragonians* and *Spaniards* forsook him as obstinate. The *Scot* stuck last to him: *Platina* saith *Huss* and *Hierome* were burnt for saying that Church men *should imitate Christ in poverty*, when their wealth and luxury was the common Scandal. There was great joy at the choice of *Martin.* 5. but *Rome* and *Italy* were still in Wars and confusion.

§ 19. *Gregory* was preferred till he died, and this P. *John* so odiously described by the Council is yet after some years imprisonment made Cardinal Bishop of *Tusculum.* O what Bishops then had the Church!

§ 20. For all the confirmations of this Council the decrees of a Council being above the Pope, are said by most Papists to be *unapproved*, because the Council of *Florence* and *Laterane* judged the contrary to be true.

§ 21. Pope *Martin* found *Rome* decayed, *Italy* in Wars, and at five years end summoned his promised Council at *Papia*: Few came, and the plague forced them to remove to *Senæ*, when *Alphonsus* King of *Arragon* sent Orators to plead the Cause of *Bened.* 13. whereby *Martin* for fear of a Schism was fain to dissolve the Council; and appointed the next seven years after at *Basil*, not trusting *Italy*; where he had long Wars himself, as afterward he stirred up against the *Bohemian Huffites*, after 14 years, aged 63 died of an Apoplexy; much praised.

§ 22. CCCCLXXI. This *Concilium Senense* we need say no more of.

§ 23. One would have thought that after this stir one more sober Pope should have been chosen: *Eugenius* 4th. was the next, of whom more after. He hath presently a War and much bloodshed in the streets of *Rome*, with the *Columnenses*. *Italy* is still in Wars: The Pope is again assaulted: The *Romans* set up seven agistrates: *Eugenius* flyeth: they pursue him with stones; he escapeth to *Florence*; leaveth the Castle garded, which continued the City-War a while. The Emperor coming into *Italy* he would have resisted but could not, who peaceably came and went. It were tedious to relate all his and others Wars in *Italy*; *Platina* and many others do it.

The Council at *Basil* beginning, he would have removed it to *Bononia*: The Emperour and Council resist, and threaten him, and he confirmeth it; for, saith *Platina*, he had scarce breathing time from vexing Wars. He recovereth *Rome* (and other places) *Pulcellus* a Leader he hanged, when he had pull'd off his flesh with hot Pincers: He turneth his War against *Alphonsus*

phonsus King of *Arragon*; the City of *Preneste* he utterly destroyed, as rebellious: The Council at *Basil* frightened Him; but *Sigismund* dying, and *Albert* D. of *Austria* chosen Emperour, he ventured to call it away to *Ferraria*. *Joh. Paleologus* contrived thither, in false hope of succour from the *West*, put some Reputation on his Council: The Plague drove them to *Florence*; there the pretended Reconciliation of the *Greeks* and *Latines* was made, of which many Histories speak at large, especially the *Greek* Edition of that *Flor.* Council. The Wars still continued round about him: The Council at *Basil* deposed *Engenius*, and made *Amadeus* D. of *Savoy* (a Pious man) Pope, called *Felix* 5. *Engenius* held on and yielded not; Blood and Murders still filling *Italy*: He died aged 64. *An.* 1447. making first twenty seven Cardinals, &c.

§. 24. CCCCLXXII. This great Council at *Basil* began 1431. and ended 1442. the History of it is too large to be much recited. The *Bohemians* exasperated by the *burning of their Teachers*, and the *Popes Excommunications*, and the *Decrees to burn them*, defended themselves by Arms under *Zisca*, and were usually victorious: They were therefore invited to the Synod, which they received with tears of joy; but for the sake of the case of *Huss* and *Hierome*, durst not trust their safe Conduct, till after the promise of many Princes, and the Synod. They sent fifteen; the *Bohemians* four daies pleaded their four Articles: '1. For the Sacrament in both kinds. 2. For 'correcting and eliminating publick sins, or crimes. 3. For liberty to preach 'Gods Word. 4. Of the Civil Power of the Clergy.

Joh. Ragusinus answered the first, calling them Hereticks; and others tediously (many daies upon one point) answered the rest; and dispute begat dispute, and so some motioned a reconciling Conference: But they could not agree, and the *Bohemians* returned, and the Council sent many of their Members with them to *Prague*, whom the City received civilly, and heard them, exhorting them to their Opinions; but they still desired satisfaction in their four Articles. Many Debates there were, and by explication of the terms they came to understand each other, and a fair beginning of reconciliation was made; but the first Article of the Sacrament in both kinds stuck so, that they could not get over it, though the Council confessed that they had power to dispense in it. But though there be reason enough for all these requests (for the opposing publick wickedness, for leave to preach Gods Word, and for Church-m.ns forbearing Civil coercive Government, unless made the Magistrates Officers) yet such reasonable things are hardlier obtained than more disputable matters; because flesh and blood, worldly interest, and the Devil, is most against them: And of this great famous Council of Bishops, after Petitions, and some good words, and hopeful approaches, they could *never one of them be obtained*, but tricks were devised to elude their hopes, and inconveniences pleaded that would follow such Concessions; (the ordinary way of the carnal Clergies hindering Reformation.)

§. 25. The first Session being for introduction, to shew their lawfulness, in the second Session they decreed, as did that at *Constance*, that a General Council is above the Pope, in matters of Faith, Schisme, and Reformation: And Sess. 3. that the Council may not be dissolved: And they admonish the Pope to retract his Revocation, and to own and assist the Council.

After they declare, that the Pope may not make Cardinals, &c. during the Council.

§. 26. Sess. 22. They condemned a Book of *Augustinus de Roma*, a Bishop of *Nazareth*, that had many Phanatick Expressions; as that Christ daily sinneth in us, because of our Union with him, though sinless in himself; that only the Elect, and not all the Justified, are Members of Christ; that besides the Union of Love, there must be another Union with Christ; that the Humane Nature in Christ is truly Christ, and the Person of Christ, and the Person of the Word; that Christ loveth his Humane Nature as much as his Divine; that the two Natures are equally lovely; that the Soul of Christ seeth God as clearly as the Godhead, &c. Thus worketh the temerarious mind of man.

§. 27. Sess. 24. There is a Treaty for a more General Council and Union with the *Greeks*; and the place assigned at *Basil*, *Avignion*, or *Savoy*; and to defray the charges, money to be gathered of Christians, who, if they give as much as will keep their houses a Week, are rewarded with the pardon of all their sins, where the liberality of their Pardons is expounded; viz. it is only the pardon of such sins *de quibus corde contriti, & ore confessi fuerint*, which their hearts are contrite for, and their mouths confess; and these are pardoned on a further condition, that besides this money given, they do for a year fast one day every Week more than else they were obliged to do by the Church; and if they be Clerks, say every such day seven Psalms, or a Mass; if Laicks, seven *Pater Nosters*, and seven *Ave Maries*: And if it had not been for the Bishops, might not a *contrite Confessor* have been certainly pardoned without such formalities.

§. 28. In divers following Sessions they prosecute Pope *Eugenius*, and declare the Council at *Ferrary* to be but a Schismatical Conventicle, and they establish these *Catholick Verities*, or Articles of Faith.

Sess. 33. 1. *That a General Council representeth the whole Church, and hath its power immediately from Christ, and that over the Pope, and every other person; and that this is a truth of Catholick Faith.*

2. *That such a Council lawfully congregate, may not without their own consent be dissolved, prorogued, or transferred; and that this is an Article of Catholick Faith.*

3. *That a pertinacious repugner of these Verities is to be judged a Heretick.*

§. 9. Sess. 34. They depose Pope *Eugenius* as a sentenced, *notorious, obstinate persisting Rebel against the Precepts of the Universal Church, and a daily violater and contemner of the Canons, a notorious perturber of the Peace and Unity of the Church of God, and a notorious scandalizer of the whole Church, a notorious Simonist, incorrigible perjured person, devious from the Faith, a pertinacious Heretick, with much more such.*

§. 30. Here

§. 30. Here I would crave the Readers confideration : 1. If this extraordinary Great Council erred in all thefe matters of fact, whether the judgment of a Council be a good proof of the Papifts fort of Tradition ?

2. If they erred in thefe Articles of Faith, whether it weaken not both their Tradition and grounds of their faith ; and whether fuch an heretical perjured Popes confent would have made them Infallible ?

3. Whether their General Councils be not contradictory *de fide*, as this, and that at *Florence* and *Lateran* exprefly are.

4. Whether a great part of the Church of *Rome*, and their laft named Councils, be not Hereticks in the judgment of this Council?

5. Seeing Pope *Eugenius* continued when the Council had depofed him as a Simonift, and perjured pertinacious Heretick, and all their following fucceffion is from him, is there not a nullity in that fucceffion ?

§. 31. Seff. 36. They decreed the Immaculate Conception of the Virgin *Mary*, as a point of Faith ; and yet many of their Doctors take it yet as undetermined, and many ftill are of the contrary mind.

§. 32. After this follow Decrees about Election of a Pope, and they make the Duke of *Savoy* Pope, *Felix* 5. and fo we have two Popes again.

Onuphrius calls this the thirtieth Schifme: He continued Pope above nine years, and then refigned to *Eugenius* for Peace. Seff. laft : They recite the Herefies of Pope *Eugenius*, as againft the forefaid Verities.

§. 33. Next is added the Bull of Pope *Nicholas* the 5. approving the Acts and deeds of the Council at *Bafil*: And then are divers Synodical Epiftles and Anfwers, fpecially proving Councils above the Pope, and againft his Crimes, and of the juftnefs of his depofition, very large; as alfo againft his Conventicle Council, and againft his Adherents, that is, moft of their Church fince, with Anfwers to his Invectives, and Monitories to draw men from his obedience. In the *Appendix* are many more Epiftles and Orations, and a Treatife of the Patriarch of *Antioch*, to prove the Pope above Councils. There are many Epiftles of the Pope againft the Council, and of the Emperour to the Council, and of many other Princes.

§. 34. The *Bohemians* Epiftles place their main caufe upon the four forementioned Articles : ' I. *The Sacrament in both kinds*. II. *That the Word of* ' *God may be freely, publickly, and truly preached by thofe that it belongeth to.* ' (for they were filenced, &c.) III. *That Civil Dominion* (they mean not all ' Propriety but *Power of the Sword* or force over mens Eftates and perfons, ' which is the Magiftrates) *as a deadly poyfon be taken from the Clergy,* (they ' fpake from feeling.) IV. *That publick, and great or heynous fins, may be ex-* ' *tirpated from among the vulgar of the faithful by lawful Powers.* This was the Religion of the *Bohemians*, and the denying of thefe was the caufe of all their cruel Perfecutions, and the blood there fhed.

§. 35. In confutation of thefe Demands are adjoyned four Treatifes of the four Preachers that fpake againft them : What Caufe fo great or plain, that men cannot talk againft with many and confident words. I. *Joh. Ragufius* acknowledged the regulating fufficiency of the Scripture, hath

hath an Oration (a Treatise) against the Sacrament in both kinds.

II. *Ægidius Carbrerius Decanus Cameracensis* hath a Treatise (four days Oration) against their request, for *correcting heynous publick sins*; where much learning and reading is poured out, to save sin: And in particular it is maintained, that the Clergy may not be punished by the Laity (some few cases excepted) not being therein their Subjects. (It seems the *Bohemians* would have had wicked Priests punished) And it is specially pleaded, that no wickedness of Clergy or Laity will warrant any Nation to separate from their Unity (that is, *Roman* Government;) and to that end, the badness of the Church Militant to be endured is described.

When he cometh to the Popes pardons, he denieth that Pardons *à culpâ & pœna* are usually the Popes stile; whereas I have before cited their express words so speaking often: And he honestly maintaineth out of the School-men, that God only can give pardon *à culpâ*, save as any Priest as *instrumentum animatum* may *vi clavium* dispose the receiver, and declare *Gods pardon, and remit part of the temporal punishment; but sometimes the Pope remitteth part of the Church penances, and so it is that Priests are said to forgive sins.* (Mark this, against our present Papists, that reproach the Protestants for this Doctrine.)

Bin p.13. 319.

III. Next is *Henr. Kalteisen*, a *Dominican* Inquisitors Oration against the *free preaching of Gods Word by Ministers*: (for this would have undone the Pope and his Clergy:) The *Bohemians* whom he confuteth, maintained: '1. That Gods Word is so perfect, that nothing should be added or diminished. 2. That the wickedness of Priests is the great cause of the peoples ruine. 3. Against Venial sin as against Gods Counsels differing from 'Laws. 4. That every Priest and Deacon is bound to preach Gods Word 'freely, or else sins mortally; and after Ordination he should not cease '(that is, when he was forbidden by silencing Bishops, or others) no not 'when excommunicated, because he must obey God rather than man; and 'that Bishops are bound to preach as well as Presbyters.

See the old Reformers Doctrine.

The Answer first noteth, that *Papa non est nomen Ordinis sed Jurisdictionis*; that Gods Word is *Incarnate, inspired, written*; that it is expounded by the same Spirit that inspired it: (But hath the Pope the same gifts of that Spirit?) That the *Inspired Word* is publick or private; that the Bishops Decrees in Councils are Gods *publick inspired Word*: (see here the Enthusiastical pretence of Episcopal Inspiration, is the ground of all the *Roman* Usurpations and tyrannies, and deposition of Princes) to them he applieth, *He that heareth you, heareth me*; whence he gathereth the danger of disobeying that Council (and so the Popes Heresie.) The rest is worth the reading, but too long for me to repeat: Much of it is to shew, that Reading and Massing is more needful than Preaching, and that every Priest that Masseth is not bound to Preach; there needeth many Mass-Priests, and not so many Preachers; and that silenced excommunicated Priests are bound to cease preaching, and obey the Prelates: But he had the wit to add *(if silenced for a reasonable cause)* and to confess that *Sententia injustè lata à suo judice si errorem*

rorem inducat, vel peccatum mortale afferet, nec timenda est nec tenenda.

Pag. 364. He denieth that it is any Precept of Christ: 1. To receive the Cup, 2. Or that Priests Preach, 3. Or to abolish all mortal sin, 4. Or for the Clergy not to be Civil Governours, &c.

IV. *Joh. de Polecnar Archdiacon. Barcinon.* hath a Treatise of three days speech for the Civil Power of the Clergy, in which he mis-spendeth much time in disputing for their *Propriety*, when as the *Bohemians* took *Dominion for Empire*, or *civil forcing power of Government*, and for *inordinate possessions* of *Lordships* and *great wealth*.

§. 36. The Papists confess that this Council was *Universal*, and rightly called and confirmed; but they pretend that it was *partly reprobate* by the Popes removal of the Council, and that Pope *Nicholas* 5. approved it but in part. It began 1431. and continued above eleven years.

§. 37. CCCCLXXIII. *An.* 1438. A Council at *Bridges* concurred with this at *Basil*, making the Pragmatical Sanction, decreeing that a General Council be called every ten years, and confirming the Council at *Basil*.

§. 38. CCCCLXXIV. Next cometh the Anti-Council at *Ferrary* and *Florence*, where the attempt for Union with the distressed *Greeks* was made, all the passages whereof are so fully opened in the *Greeks* History, published by Dr. *Creighton*, that I shall say no more of it.

Here note, that there were two *General Councils* at once; and how could they both (or either of them) be truly Universal: The Papists call it the sixteenth.

§. 39. After many Wars, *Eugenius* the deposed Pope died, *An.* 1447. (having made twenty seven Cardinals (against the Council of *Basils* Decrees) from whom is their succession) and *Nicholas* the 5. succeeded him: *Italy* still continued in bloody Wars; Pope *Felix* at last resigned; and so there was once more but one Pope. And that yo may see still how far the Pope was from governing all the World, the City of *Rome* was again seeking to recover their Liberties, and had a Plot against him, one *Steph. Hircanius* being the Chief, and the Pope secured himself by hanging many of them.

§ 40. The Emperour of *Constantinople*, and those Bishops that pretended a Union with *Rome*, in hope of help, found the people and Clergy there utterly averse to come under the Pope, and they had no help from him, nor any of their desired successes; for now the *Turks* took the City, and killed the Emperour, and many thousands more, and 1455. the Pope died.

§. 41. CCCCLXXV. A Council at *Tours* about Church Orders decreed praying oft for the dead, forbad Clandestine Marriages, and Masling in unconsecrated places, &c.

§. 42. CCCCLXXVI. A Synod at *Lyons* to end the Schisms between the two Popes done by the Emperour *Frederick*, who desired King *Charles* concurrence.

§. 43. *An.* 1455. *Calixtus* the 3. is made Pope; he raiseth a Sea Army against the *Turks*, the Patriarch of *Aquileia* being Captain: *Rome* was still in War: He claimed the Kingdome of *Naples* to the Church for want of Heirs; an Anti-Pope was also made, called *Clement* 8. but being perswaded to resign, he accepted a Bishoprick: Many Cities in *Italy* ruined by Earthquakes, whose ruines *Platina* saith he saw with admiration: He made a new Holy-day for Christs Transfiguration.

§. 44. Next cometh *Æneas Sylvius*, called *Pius* 2. one of the most learned of all the Popes, especially an Orator: He was against the Pope for the superiority of Councils at *Basil*; but when he was made Pope, he recanted it. In his Epistle to his Father he excuseth himself for having a Bastard, and for fornication, (particularly with an *English* Woman that lodged in the same house with him) telling him, that he was not an Eunuch, and remembring his Father what a Cock of the Game he had been himself; but among the Popes he was a wonder of worthiness: He was vehement for a War with the *Turks*, but could not so far quench the flames of War at his own doors in *Italy*, and other Christian Countries, as to accomplish it. *Platina* recordeth many of his Sentences, among which are: [*Every Sect established by Authority, is void of humane reason: If the Christian Religion had not been approved by Miracles, it should have been received for its honesty: The Mortals measures of Heaven and Earth are more bold than true: Astronomy is more pleasant than profitable: The Friends of God are happy here and hereafter: There is no solid joy without virtue: They that know most, doubt most: Artificial Orations move fools; not wise men: As all Rivers flow into the Sea, so all Vices into great mens Courts: Flatterers rule Kings as they list: Princes hear none so readily as accusers: The tongue of a flatterer is the worst plague to a King: He that ruleth many, is ruled by many: He is unworthy the name of a King, who measureth the publick affairs by his own commodity, &c. Ill Physitians kill bodies, and unskilful Priests souls: Virtues enrich the Clergy, Vice impoverisheth them: Marriage was for great reasons forbidden Priests, and for greater is to be restored to them: He that too much pardoneth his Son, cherisheth his Enemy: The covetous never please men, but by dying: Lying is a servile vice, &c.*

You may see his Recantation in *Binius*, where his Dignity raised him so high as to say, *That the Greek and Latin Doctors with one voice say, that he cannot be saved that holdeth not the Unity of the Roman Church, and all those Virtues are maimed to him that refuseth to obey the Pope, though lying in sackcloth and ashes he fast and pray day and night, and seem in other things to fulfill the Law of God, because obedience is better than sacrifice, and every soul must be subject to the higher power; and it is manifest that the Pope of* Rome *is placed in the top (or Crown) of the Church, from which (his power of Government) we know that no Sheep of Christ at all is exempted.*

O then how much worse is the case of the *Abassines, Armenians, Greeks, Protestants*, even three fourth parts of the Christian World, than of the Heathens, being all certainly damned for not believing in the Pope: How much more necessary to Salvation is it to please and honour the Pope, than any Angel or Saint in Heaven? But how false is it that the *Greek* and *Latine* Fathers all agree in this?

§. 45. *Paulus*

§. 45. *Paulus* 2. succeedeth *Pius*, a man just and clement, saith *Platina* himself; yet, saith he, before he was Pope, he could get what he would by begging, even with tears, of the Pope and great men: And when he was Pope, all about him sounded with Wars, and Benefices were theirs that would give most for them; and in his fears some-body muttering, that one *Callimachus* had a Plot against him, he set all on tumult to find out the Conspirators, when there was no such thing: He had before cast out of their places all the Colledge of *Abbreviates* that had bought their places under *Pius*, of whom *Platina* being one, and not getting Audience and relief, wrote him a Letter, that *they would go to Princes, and get a Council called to relieve them*: For this he was accused of Treason, and laid in Irons by a long imprisonment: And after his release, upon this Dream of a Plot, he and many more were not only imprisoned, but tortured and tormented to force them to confess that which never was: Many died of the torments, even of the worthiest young men of the City. After a long time poor *Platina* with a broken body is delivered, but the Prisoners at last were accused of Heresie, that they might not seem to have suffered for nothing: *Platina's* Heresie was, that he had praised *Plato*, and the *Gentile* Learning, and had disputed about the Godhead, which was a questioning it; and the Pope himself was so much against Learning, that he used to call studious men Hereticks, and to perswade men that their Sons must learn no more than to read and write. Here *Platina* endeth his History; and had he known other Popes as well as he did this, perhaps he would have praised their *Justice* and *Clemency*, as he doth this Pope, by the effects.

§. 46. *Sixtus* 4. is next, who also spent his days in *Italian* War and bloodshed: Wonderful! that our late Papists think that all the Christian World hath still obeyed the Pope, when none have so much fought against him as the City of *Rome*, and the *Italians*: *Onuphrius* (who here beginneth the Supplement of *Platina*) tells you modestly of his Wars, and his horrid treachery against the *Florentines*, when to get his will on them, he appointeth Conspirators to murder the two Brothers, *Julian* and *Laurence Medices*, of whom the Archbishop of *Pisa* was one: They assault them in Gods Worship in the Temple, and kill *Julian*; but *Laurence* wounded, is lockt up by the Church-Wardens in the Vestry; The Citizens rose before the Execution could be finished, and hanged the Archbishop, and *Poggius* and all their Companions in Ropes out at the Windows, strangling also the rest of the Conspirators. The Popes Plot being disappointed, he maketh War against the *Florentines*, and interdicteth them all publick worship: (the Popes ordinary profane Usurpation, forbidding whole Cities and Kingdomes all such publick worship of God, which *Robert Grosshead* said was the part of Antichrist, and the Devil.) The wisdome of *Laurence Medices* ended the War when it seemed near the consuming flames; and the *Turks* invading *Italy*, terrified the Pope into a peace with the *Florentines*: But still *Italy* was imbrued in Wars.

§. 47. Though the Council of *Basil* had determined the Immaculate

Conception of the Virgin *Mary*, yet this Pope to reconcile the *Dominicans* and *Franciscans* that preached against each other as Hereticks for differing about it, did decree, that on pain of Excommunication neither Party should call one another Hereticks for it: By which it appeareth how little indeed the Decrees *de fide* of General Councils signifie with Popes themselves when their Interest is against them.

§. 48. CCCCLXXVIII. A *Toletane* Synod renewed divers good Canons for reforming the Clergy; as that none be ordained that cannot speak Latine; to diminish the Priests maintenance that still publickly keep Concubines; that Clergy-men play not at Tables, and such like.

§. 49. Next comes *Innocent* 8. the *Italian* Wars continuing: He raised an Army to get the Kingdome of *Naples* as his own; but being beaten, and repenting, he made peace; yet after again deposed the King for not paying him his Rent: He ruled those at *Rome* and *Italy* that he could conquer, as the rest of the Popes did before him.

§. 50. *Alexander* the 6. is next, who (saith *Onuphrius*) having four Bastard-Sons, and two Daughters, set himself wholly to make them great: The Cardinals bribed, chose him that was the worst of them all, and justly were destroyed by him: The old *Italian* Wars now ran in the proper Channel: *Cæsar Borgia*, one of the Popes Bastards, being a Cardinal, laid by his holy Order, and set himself to conquer all the Princes of *Italy*: Historians fill a Volume with his Acts, the cruel murders of Princes and people, surprize of Cities, basest treachery, too long to be by me recited: He murdered his own Brother, many of the chief of *Rome*, and got possession of most of *Italy*, killing the former Lords, and their Sons: The *Ursin* overthrew his Army, and the Pope flattered them with confident promises into a Peace, till they foolishly trusting him, he got them into his power, and murdered them: Some Cardinals the Pope commanded to drink poyson, and at last having more great men to dispatch, Cardinals and Citizens at a purposed Feast, the Pope ordered his Butler to prepare poysoned Wine for them, and mistaking the Cup, he gave it to the Pope, and his Son *Cæsar*: The Pope died of it; but *Cæsar* being young, and diluting his Wine, was recovered, but his Army hereby scattered. If you would see the History of this Monsters cruelties, read *Paulus Jovius*: I recite now but what *Onuphrius* saith, who concludeth that this Popes Virtues were equal to his Vices, (so far goeth a little in a Pope) and yet that *he had the greatest perfidiousness, savage cruelty, unmeasurable covetousness and rapacity, inexhausted lust of getting Empire to his Son by right or wrong, when business permitted, giving up himself to all pleasure without difference, but most given to Women, by whom he had four Sons, and two Daughters;* the chief was Vannocia Romana. *whom he kept as his lawful Wife, for her beauty, alluring manners, and marvellous fruitfulnes:* His Comedies, Sports, Gladiators, he mentioneth more fully: *Never was there greater licence to Hackers and Murderers, and never less liberty to the people: A huge number of Informers (or Accusers;) death was the punishment of the least ill word* (against him;) *all places were full of robbers or assaulters,*

See Paul. Jovius, and Guicciardine.

so

and their Councils Abridged.

so that there was no safe going in the City by night, nor out of it by day; Rome *that was the refuge and sanctuary of all other people heretofore, was now become a Slaughter-house, or Butchery.* Thus *Onuphrius* of *a virtuous* Pope.

§. 51. The Pope being dead, *Cæsar Borgia* seizeth on the Castle, and would have forced the Cardinals (being yet sick of his poyson himself;) but by the rising of the people his Souldiers are stopt, and he agreed to depart, and *Pius* 3. is chosen, said to be one of the better sort, but lived but 26 days, and died of a sore Leg, suspected to be poysoned.

§. 52. Next cometh *Julius* 2. a Military Pope, who spent his days in *Italian* Wars, especially against *Alphonsus* Duke of *Ferrary*, and *Ludovicus* King of *France*: In a cruel Battel 20000 are said to be slain near *Ravenna*, the *French* having the Victory, but losing their General, and multitudes of Nobles and Commanders, and were so weakened, that by hired *Helvetians*, and the *English* and *Spanish* that invaded them at home, they were driven and drawn back.

§. 53. CCCCLXXVIII. A Council at *Tours* in *France* met against the Pope.

§. 54. CCCCLXXIX. A General Council at *Pisa* 1511. gathered against him to call him to account: He had sworn to call a Council within two years, and did not; and so some Cardinals call it, by the Emperour *Maximilian* and *Ludov.* K. of *France* his will (as they said.) The Pope excommunicateth the King of *France*, and calleth an Anti-Council to *Rome*; this of *Pisa* removed first to *Millan*, and then to *Lyons* in *France*.

§. 55. CCCCLXXX. Now cometh the great Anti-Council at the *Lateran*, which they call the seventeenth approved General one, 1512. begun by *Julius* against the *Pisane* Council, and ended 1517. under *Leo* 10. The Pope thought *Rome* the safest place to rule them, and obtain his will; and for all the numerous Bishops of *Italy*, this General Council had but 114. Bishops: *Qu.* Whether any of them came from *Abassia*, *Egypt*, *Armenia*, *Greece*, or the *Antipodes*, and were the Representatives of all the Christian World? yet they had a dull cheat herein to deceive the ignorant, and put the name of the *Alexandrinian* and *Antiochian* Patriarch on two Fellows of their own, as in a Play the parts of Princes are acted by the Stage-players: But when the *Monothelites* had a Council of *innumerable Bishops* under *Philippicus*, that was not to be called General. He that is so idle may read a Volumn of the twelve Sessions of this Council, and there find who said Mass such a day, and who such a day, and who sung a Gospel and *Te Deum*, and such like: And he may read divers Orations, among which their great learned *Cajetane*'s is the chief, condemning the *Pisane* Council, and confessing that of the three Popes, *Nullus eorum aut certus quidem aut absque ambiguitate verus Petri successor existimaretur* : Another Oration by *Christopher Marcellus*, Sess. 4. tells the Pope that he is, [*Unus Princeps qui summam in terris habet potestatem, idque omnis ævi, omnium sæculorum, omnium gentium Principem & caput appellat*] *tantæ reipublicæ unicus & supremus Princeps es, cui summa data potestas, ad divinum injunctum imperium, tuum est.* He calls the

Church *his Spouse*, and faith, he hath given *salutem vitam & spiritum*, and faith, that he is *alter Deus in terris*. You see what Popes are.

Stephen, Archbishop *Patracens*, and Bishop *Torcellan*, doth Poetize in *Saphicks*.

> *Omnium splendor, decus & perenne*
> *Virginum lumen, genitrix superni,*
> *Gloria humani generis Maria,*
>   *Unica nostri.*
> *Sola tu Virgo Dominaris astris,*
> *Sola tu Terræ, Maris atque. Cœli*
> *Lumen, inceptis faveas*
>   *Inclyta nostris,*
> *Ut queant sacros resecare sensus,*
> *Qui latent chartis nimium severis;*
> *Ingredi & colsæ, duce te, benigna*
>   *Mænia terræ.*

The business of that Council was to frustrate that at *Pisa*, and condemn it; and so to save the Pope, and to condemn the *French* pragmatical Sanction, as injurious to the *Roman* power; to which end they read a Renunciation of it, of *Ludovicus* 2. to Pope *Pius* 2.

Pope *Julius* died, and *Leo* 10. was chosen in the midst of the Councils Sessions: They pretended War against the *Turks*, but in vain.

§. 56. One Decree here past which nulleth utterly the Papal Succession, *viz:* Sess. 5. (*That a Simoniacal Election of a* Roman *Pope is plainly null, and doth confer no Right or Authority to the elected*) which is plainly declarative; therefore when they confess the Simoniacal Election of so great a number of their Popes successively, where is the true succession.

§ 57. In the eighth Sess. a Decree past against them that say the *Soul is mortal*, or that it is but one in all or many: And they confute the truth, by pretending to confirm it, saying, that the Soul is *per se & essentialiter forma corporis*: For then the separated Soul loseth its essence, and so is no Soul, or else is *forma corporis*, when *corpus* is not *corpus organicum*.

For the cure of this, they decree that none study Philosophy above five years, unless they joyn Divinity with it: And they forbid Printing and Preaching unlicensed.

§. 58. This *Leo* the tenth was excellently prepared for the Papacy; Wars had dispossest his Father at *Florence*, and the King of *France*; *Lewis* 11. for his Fathers sake, had honoured (or dishonoured) him with an excellent and rich Archbishoprick, when he was a Child: You may conjecture at what age, when as he was scarce thirteen when *Innocent* 8. made him a Cardinal, to gratifie his Father *Laurence Medices*, who had given his Daughter to *Francis* the Popes Son; but because of his Non-age, he staid yet from *Rome*: When he was Pope, he would fain have had peace in *Italy* if he could, being

ing wholly addicted to ease and voluptuousness: He hired the *Helvetians* for his *Militia* against *Francis* King of *France*, but they were destroyed by the *French* and the Pope was glad at last to beg a peace. Having unbounded desires of Empire, he pickt a quarrel with the Duke of *Urbane*, and assaulted him with Arms, and dispossest him of his Country, whence he fled, and ungratefully banished *Doristaus*, and his Brother *Alphonsus* a Cardinal, who studying revenge, was destroyed by him: The Pope sought to insnare the Duke of *Ferrary*, but failed; the *French* in *Italy* conquer the Emperour and *Helvetians*; the *Turk* winneth *Syria* and *Egypt*; the Pope sits bare-foot to pray against him, bringing forth all the Consecrated Dishes, the Saints Relicks, Images, &c. in pomp, and the Tyrant presently died of a Cancer: The Pope falleth on divers Cardinals; Cardinal *Alphonsus* he imprisoneth, and appointeth a *Blackmoor* to break out his Chamber, and strangle him: Having hereby lost the love of many of the old ones, in one day he maketh one and thirty new Cardinals, that he may be sure of help; *Paulus Balcon* he beheaded, *Amadeus Ricinatius* he harg.d: It was this Pope that is commonly said to have said to *Pet. Bembus* his Secretary, *What profit doth this Fable of Jesus bring us in.*

§. 59. But now begins the fatal time, Anno 1517. *Martin Luther* began to cry down their sin, and draw the people of *Germany* from them; and *Zuinglius*, and many others doing the same, the light brake forth, and the darkness vanished. I need not write the History of it, which is so commonly known or published: The Pope published a Bull against him, in which he numbereth his supposed Errours; you may see them in *Binius*, pag. 653. in *Leo* the tenths life, how *John Frederick* Elector of *Saxony* bore *Luther* out, how *Philip* of *Hassia* seconded him, how the University of *Wittenberge* clave to him, and especially *Philip Melancthon*, that excellent man; how the Free Cities, with many Princes, came in to them, and joyned; how many Petitions and Disputations there were about; how the *Augustine* Confession was written, and the Apology for it; how it turned to a War; how the Elector of *Saxony*, and *Philip* Landgrave of *Hassia*, were taken prisoners; how *Maurice* of *Saxony*, siding with the Emperour, was made Elector, and *John Frederick* dispossest; how the same *Maurice* after, to vindicate *Philip* of *Hassia*, took Arms against the Emperour, and forced him to flight, and finally to some degree of toleration for the Protestants. All these things the History of the Reformation, written by divers, telleth you at large; as also how many, great and excellent Divines were suddenly raised up for Reformation, as soon as Tyranny was so far abated as that men might shew their minds, it soon appeared that most had been long subjugated to the Pope more by violence than by consent: when the Emperour was necessitated to a Toleration, he consulted for some abatement to procure Concord, and by *Agricola*, *Sidonius*, and *Julius Pflug* (an *Antinomian* turned back to Popery) drew up a middle form of worship, called the *Interim*, which he would have all conform to till a General Council, which divided the Reformers among themselves, while some as moderate

and

and to avoid total ruine of the Church, yielded to part, and others refused, and multitudes of Ministers were therefore rejected and persecuted. This great Emperour, *Charles* the Fifth, after long Wars, and many Victories, and sharp Persecutions, was at last weary of all, and resigned his Empire, and betook himself to a private life in *Spain*, where he died, strongly suspected of repentance and inclination to the Reformed Doctrine himself: He bequeathed nothing (as was usual) to any Religious House, or Order: There were found papers about him for the Protestant Doctrine of Justification; his Confessor, and another Doctor that attended him, were hereupon suspected of Heresie, and one persecuted, and the other put to death by the Inquisition. Thus errour, sin, and worldly violence are never true to themselves, but must be repented of at last, and none can stand to them when the light prevaileth.

See the History of Charles, Prince of Spain's death.

§. 60. But to return to Pope *Leo*, when he had made above forty Cardinals, exercised many cruelties, and made a League with the Emperour against the *French*, to drive them out of *Italy*, when his Arms had prevailed, and the *French* were expelled, and *Milan* recovered, and some Cities restored to the Church (that is, to the Pope) the excessive joy for the Victory so moved him, that (saith *Onuphrius*) he fell into a Fever, of which he died, but not without suspition of poyson. The same *Onuphrius* (whom I follow) saith, that (*he was a diligent observer of divine things, given to the sacred Ceremonies, but he was profusely given to Voluptuousness, Hunting, Hawking, Luxury, splendid Feastings, Musick, and to get money sold Cardinalships, invented Offices, &c. and yet was the most liberal of all the Popes that ever had lived to that day, excessively loving Musick,* &c.) This was Papal Piety, by which he merited a Monument inscribed OPTIMO PRINCIPI LEONI X. &c. saith *Onuphrius*: (*In all his life he desired nothing more ardently than the highest glory of liberality, from which other Priests use to be very far off.*) Perhaps for this glory *Tecelius* must get money by selling Pardons, which began his fall: *Verily they have their reward,* saith Christ of Hypocrites, that do their Alms to be seen of men.

§. 61. It is to be noted, that as the great ignorance and wicked lives of the *Roman* Clergy were the great advantage to *Luthers* success, (as the gross idolatry and wickedness of Heathens was to Christianity of old) and the *Learning* and *Piety* of the Reformers were the means of their common acceptance; so hereupon the Papacy perceived a necessity of greater Learning, and some Reformation, for its own defence from utter ruine: whereupon many were awakened, and addicted to seek Learning, and some Provincial Councils made some Canons for amending the Clergies lives; so that their encrease of Learning, and some amendment of manners, was occasioned by the Protestants; yea, the Popes themselves have since then been far less vicious and turbulent than before.

§. 62. And all Christian Princes have cause to be thankful to the Reformers, and to acknowledge that from them they have now the safety of their Crowns and Dignities, and their peace; and by them, of Subjects,

they

they are restored to a great degree of freedome, I mean even those that yet are Papists, the Pope dare not now damn them as *Henrician Hereticks*, as he long had done; he dare not be so bold in taking away, and giving Kingdomes; he dare not execute his Laws against Princes Investitures, nor excommunicate them, and depose them, and absolve their Subjects, nor interdict whole Kingdomes, and shut up Church doors, nor so much as openly profess that he hath power from God, and S. *Peter*, to depose Kings according to their Merits, and to set up others in their stead. O how much quieter is *Italy, Spain, France, Germany, &c.* since the Reformation, and how much less troubled with Papal terrours and wars, than heretofore; and all is for fear lest if the Pope should anger them, the rest of the Princes should forsake him. Heretofore if one Kingdome stood up against the Pope, the rest were ready blindly to obey his Commands, to fall upon them and destroy them: But now the Reformed Nations have more strength to defend themselves, and those that shall joyn with them: The truth is, *it is Reformation that hath made even the Papists Princes Free-men.*

§ 63. The History of all the *Roman* horrid bloody cruelties, by which they laboured to suppress Reformation, I here omit, because (as it well deserveth) it is written in many large volumns by it self: I mean the bloody murders of the *Albigenses, Waldenses, Bohemians*, the cruelties of the Inquisition in *Spain, Belgia* and other parts: The Massacre in *France*. The burning people in *England* and the murders in *Ireland*, and in other countries: you may read them at large in many Histories: In *Thuanus, Sleidan, Illericus, Mornay, Perin, Moreland*, the *Belgian*, and *French* Histories: *Foxe's* Acts and Monuments, and summarily in Mr. *Sam. Clerks* Martyrology: And *Carion, Melancthon, Micrelius, D. Pareus, Vignerius, Scull.tus, Buchoicer, Fustinus*, and many others give you an account of the Reformation. And the Lives of the *German* Divines, written by *Melchior Adamus*, yea and of their Lawyers, Physicians and Philosophers, giveth not an unpleasant light into that History: So that for me here to treat of the Reformation in a large volumn (to do what is so often done already) would be incongruous.

The making of *Urban* the 6th. the Emperours Schoolmaster Pope, and the Wars in his time; The Succession of *Clement* the 7th. and the *Italian* Wars in his time, between the Emperour and the *French* and others, and the taking of *Rome* by the Emperour (*Charles* the 5th.) army under *Charles* Duke of *Bourbon*, and all the progress of their broils, Historians have at large recorded; and therefore I shall pretermit.

§ 64. The day before *Charles* the 5th. was chosen Emperour, the Senate of *Electas* chose *John Frederick* Duke of *Saxony*; but he *ingenti animo recusavit*, refused it; and being asked whom he thought most eligible, he said none but *Charles* was fit. For this noble mind, he was offered 30000 Florens of money, which he constantly rejected: And when they urged him that 10000 might be given to his servants, he said, let them that will take it, but he that taketh any shall not stay to morrow with me, and taking horse went his waies, lest they further troubled him: Thus saith *Erasmus, Epist. l* 13.

ep. 4. I was assured of by the Bishop of *Liege* that was present] See *Bucholtzar Chronol. p.* 553.

§ 65. The Reformation forced the *German* Bishops to make many reforming Canons, at *Colen, &c.* Among those of an *Augustine* Synod our own strife about communicating maketh me think of no loss of time to recite their Catalogue of persons that were to be denied the Sacrament of Communion, *viz.* as followeth.

1. Heathens, Infidels and Hereticks. 2. The Excommunicate. 3. All men at a time of common Interdict. 4. Men that go from their own Parishes for it. 5. Those that are under age: And distracted, possessed, Ideots. 6. Those that are troubled with crudity of stomacks (till cured.) 7. Infamous persons, as Juglers, Players, Jesters, &c. 8. Women that wear Mens apparel. 9. Separatists and Conventiclers. 10. The Sect of the Beggars of *Lyons*. 11. The superstitious. 12. Those that have not contrition and confession, living in sin. 13. That live in notorious wickedness, as Adultery, Usury, &c. till their actual reformation. 14. Deserters of Marriage unallowed. 15. Those that play much at Dice. 16. That are given to drunkenness, gluttony, comessations, spend daies in Taverns; And if they amend not they are to be put to death. 17. That detain other mens goods. 18. That break and spoil Temples. 19. That encroach on others lands and grounds. 20. Servants that being corrected refuse their duty to their Master after it. 21. They that use false weights and measures. 22. That pay not Tythes. 23. That delay to execute Testaments. 24. That obstinately despise the Customes of the Church, and meet elsewhere. 25. That disturb the Preachers, or go out of Church contemptuously. 26. That will not hear Mass and stay the end. 27. That use unnecessary labour on the Lords day or holy daies. 28. That marry secretly. 29. That slothfully or contemptuously refuse to learn the Lords prayer, and Creed. 30. That blaspheme or prophanely swear. 31. That reproach and dishonour Priests. 32. Murderers, Enemies, revengeful and oppressors. 33. That preserve not carefully their Childrens Lives. 34. That make Laws against Church Liberties, or Judge by such Laws, or lay burdens and exactions on Churchmens persons or goods. 35. Those that judge that money received on Usury is not to be restored.

§ 66. The Reformers accusations of the Popish Clergy had this effect, to make them confess many of their faults, especially drunkenness, and Whoredome, as being the cause of the peoples distaste and desertion; see the Orations at the Councils of *Augusta*, and *Trevers*; and the Council at *Trevers* made strict Canons against them, especially for removing Concubines from the Priests. And one at *Colen* 1549. is large for some reformation; but especially careful to keep out true Reformation, forbidding the books of Protestants by name. Among other things they forbid baptizing Children in private houses, except Kings Children, &c. And another Council at *Mentz* hath the whole sum of the *Roman* Doctrine and Discipline at the best, save the matters of the Papacy; and these late provincial Councils made Canons

in

in the frame of them, not much of our *English* Canons and our Articles of Religion set together. And another Council at *Trevers* repeateth their disciplinary Canons in part, and addeth more.

§ 67. The History and Canons of the Council of *Trent* are sufficiently published; and Pope *Pius* his Oath conjoyned; so that I need not speak of that which I intend not to make any part of the matter of this Epitome, which extendeth but to the time of *Luthers* Reformation.

68. Even after the Reformation, the Pope could not live in *Italy* without fighting: Pope *Julius* the 3d, fought with *Octavius Farnesius* at *Parma*; Pope *Paul* fought with the King of *Spain*: but was beaten: He set sixteen Cardinals over the Inquisition (the defence of his Kingdome): He imprisoned Cardinal *Morrovius* suspected of heresie, absolved after by Pope *Pius* the 4th. who yet strangled *Caraffa*, and beheaded Cardinal *Leonard*, Count *Montarius*, &c.

§ 69. Cardinal *Charles Borrhomeus* (sainted by them) at divers Millane Councils shewed a great deal of Reforming, and some deforming zeal. In the first Council I shall note that they decreed that men once admitted to the Communion, and returning to their sin, be no more admitted till the Priest see that they have actually reformed their lives. And that before any young persons first receive, they shall some dayes be *examined*, and taught the use and reason of the Sacrament, Priests notoriously criminal must not say Mass till they amend their lives. No Physician must give physick to any after four dayes sickness that is not confest to the Priest (on pain of excommunication). Bishops are forbidden to stand when Princes sit, no not for saying Grace at meat: nor otherwise to depress and abject themselves to Princes. Parish Priests must have a book of the Names, Sex, Age, and State of every Parishioner. Whores are to dwell in their assigned places, and to be known by their apparel from others. Dancing, Playes, Dice, Selling, &c. forbidden on the Lords dayes and holydayes. Indeed the *Roman* Religion was never set out with greater advantage of piety and reformation than in the copious Decrees of *Carolus Borrhomeus* in the *Milan* Councils: To which a Council at *Aquileia* added, endeth *Binnius* his History of Councils.

§ 70. In all this History of Councils, Bishops and Patriarchs it appeareth that *Corruptio optimi est pessima*; As the sacred Ministry in pious humble wise, peaceable and sincere men hath been Gods great means of planting, ordering, preserving and encreasing his Church, and converting, edifying, and saving Souls, and such to the day are as *Paul* called *Timothy* (not the Church) (*A Pillar and Basis of the truth in the Church, which is the House of the Living God*) the Husbandmen that still cultivate the Vineyard of the Lord, while with self-denial, and faith, and heavenly minds, they labour to promote holy WISDOME, LOVE, SPIRITUALITY and PEACE, abhorring pride and worldly designs, and being mostly little noted in the Histories of the Church, as not appearing in the turbulent and publick affairs of the world: so contrarily Pride, and *worldliness*, seeking Dominion, favour and wealth, to feed also sensuality with fleshly pleasure, by Satans great diligence have corrupted sacred Societies, Doctrine, Worship, Discipline and Conversation; and when the Prince of pride and darkness, the God of this World, could not directly expugne Christianity, he hath under pretence of Government, Unity, and Advancement to the Church, set his Malignant Ministers in the Chairs and Pulpits of the Church to do his work, and fight down piety, love and peace in the name of Christ, and as it were by his Authority; and instead of persecuting Heathens, Satan hath set up *contentions*, *dividing*, and *silencing*, and *persecuting Prelates*, to finite the true Shepherds, and scatter the Flocks; and as for *Faith* and *Order*, to tread down the true life of *Faith*, *Love* and *Order*, and to be the Capital Enemies of the Church, while they would make themselves its Heads, Advancers and Defenders; so that the *chief good* and the *chief mischief* hath come to the Church by the means of the Pastors: And no Schismes, no Heresies, no Persecutions have been more grievous, than those that have been caused by a tyrannical and contentious Clergy; witness all the Conciliary Episcopal Schismes, Wars, and Bloodshed mentioned in this Collection; witness the many hundred thousand *Albigenses*, *Waldenses*, and *Bohemians* murdered, as for the *Faith* and *Church*; witness the 30000. or 40000. at once murdered at the *French* Massacre; witness the horrid cruelties of the Inquisition; witness the Volumes of burned and otherwise murdered Protestants; and witness the *Irish* Zeal stirr'd up by their Clergy, that murdered two hundred thousand in so narrow a room as that small Country, and in so few Weeks: And whoever is the Antichrist, certainly in *Rome*, and the Militant Tyrannical Church-Clergy is found *the blood of the Saints*, and Martyrs of Jesus; and as proud *contentious Patriarchs* and *Prelates* ruined Religion and the Empire in the *East*, and gave it up to *Mahometan* darkness and cruelty, so have they under the name of Christianity impugned the Christian Interest in the *West*. I end with G. Herbert:

> Only the *West* and *Rome* do keep them free
> From this contagious infidelity:
> And this is all the Rock whereof they boast,
> As *Rome* will one day find unto her cost;
> Sin being not able to extirpate quite
> The Churches here, bravely resolv'd one night
> To be a Church-man, and to wear a Mitre,
> The old debauched Ruffian would turn Writer:
> I saw him in his Study, where he sate
> Busie in controversie sprung of late:
> A Gown and Pen became him wondrous well,
> His grave aspect had more of Heaven than Hell;
> Only there was a handsome picture by,
> To which he lent a corner of his eye:
> As Sin in *Greece* a Prophet was before,
> And in old *Rome* a mighty Emperour;

So now being Priest, he plainly did profess
To make a Jest of Christs three Offices;
The rather since his scattered juglings were
United now in one, both time and sphere:
From *Egypt* he took petty Deities,
From *Greece* Oracular Infallibilities;
And from old *Rome* the liberty of pleasure,
By free dispensing of the Churches Treasure:
Then in memorial of his Ancient Throne,
He did sirname his Palace *Babylon*:
Yet that he might the better gain all Nations,
And make that name good by their transmigrations,
From all these places, but at divers times,
He took five Vizards to conceal his Crimes.
From *Egypt* Anchorisme, and retiredness,
Learning from *Greece*, from old *Rome* statelinefs;
And blending these, he carried all mens eyes,
While Truth sate by, counting his Victories;
Whereby he grew apace, and scorn'd to use
Such force as once did captivate the *Jews*;
But did bewitch, and finely work each Nation
Into a voluntary transmigration:
All post to *Rome*; Princes submit their Necks,
Either to his publick Foot, or private Tricks:
It did not fit his Gravity to stir,
Nor his long Journey, nor his Gout and Fur;
Therefore he sent out ABLE MINISTERS,
States-men within, without door Cloysterers;
Who without Spear, or Sword, or other Drum,   Councils
Than what was in their Tongue, did overcome;   by *Ana-*
And having conquer'd did so strangely rule,   *thema's.*
That the whole World did seem but the Popes Mule:
As new and old *Rome* did one Empire twist,
So both together are one ANTICHRIST;
Yet with two Faces, as their *Janus* was,
Being in this their old crackt Looking-glass:
How dear to me, O God, thy Counsels are!
         Who may with thee compare!
Thus Sin triumphs in *Westerns Babylon*,
Yet not as Sin, but as Religion;
Of his two Thrones he made the later best,
And to defray his journey from the *East*,
Old and new *Babylon* are to Hell and Night,
As is the Moon and Sun to Heaven and Light.

CHAP. XIV.

LEst this treatise be mistaken & abused to the dishonour of the Christian Religion, Church or Ministry I adde two papers which I long agoe published for the Ministry 1. Against profane Malignants, 2. Against Sectarians, especially those called Seekers, as also Papists & others that for interest or faction, deny or vilifie the Pastors.

One sheet for the Ministry; Against the Malignants of all sorts.

AS mans first felicity was attended with the malice of the Serpent, so is the wonderful work of his Restauration. The promise of Reconciliation by the seed of the woman, is joyned with a proclamation of open war with the Serpent and his seed. The enmity was hottest in the Devil and his seed against Christ himself, who bare and overcame it; and is become the Captain of our salvation, that his Church may overcome by his Cross and Strength, and Conduct; The next degree of malice is against his officers: the most eminent, the General Officers had the hottest assault; and his ordinary Officers bear the next: That we shall be hated of all men for the name of Christ, (*Mat.* 10.22.) is still verified to our experience. Not only the openly prophane abhor us for our work sake, but false-hearted professors that turn from the truth, do presently turn Malignants against the Ministry; and many weak ones that are better minded, are dangerously seduced into a guilt of the sedition. To all these I here proclaim in the name and word of the Lord, *Numb.* 16.26. [*Depart I pray you from the tents of these wicked men, and touch nothing of theirs, lest ye be consumed in all their sins.*] Which I shall now open to you.

1. The office of the Ministry is an undoubted Ordinance of God, to continue in the Church to the end of the world. No man can pretend that they ceased with the Apostles, for it is Gods will that ordinary fixed Presbyters shall be ordained in every Church, *Acts.* 14.23. *Tit.* 1.5. 1 *Tim.* 3.1. 2 *Tim.* 2.2. And Pastors and Teachers are appointed for the perfecting of the Saints, for the work of the Ministry, and edifying of the body of Christ, till we all come to a perfect man, *Ephes.* 4.11,12,13. A Ministry authorized to Disciple the Nations, baptize and teach them, is instituted by Christ as King and Saviour, and have his Promise to be with them alway to the end of the world, *Mat.* 28.18,19,20. The same necessity and work continueth; still souls are born and bred in darkness, and how shall they be saved without believing, or believe without hearing, or hear without preaching, or we preach without sending? *Rom.* 10.13. 14,15.

14, 15. There is a clearer word in the Gospel for the Ministry then the Magistracy; though enough for both. Our own call I shall speak of anon.

2. These Malignants set themselves against the Principal members of the body of Christ, that are in it as the eyes and hands to the natural body, 1 *Cor.* 12. 16, 19, 27, 29. *Ephes.* 4. 11, 15. The Ministers of Christ, and Stewards of the Mysteries of God, 1 *Cor.* 4. 1. The Over-seers of the flock that is purchased with Christs blood, *Acts*. 20. 28. They are the chief members, 1. in office, 2. ordinarily in gifts for edification of the body: 3. and in grace. Now a wound in the stomack or liver is more mortal to the body, then in the hand: and the loss of an eye or hand is worse then the loss of an ear.

3. These Malignants are therefore principally enemies to the Church it self. They take on them to be only against the Ministers, but it will prove most against the people and whole Church. If they smite the Shepherds, the sheep will be scattered. How can they more surely ruine Christs family, then by casting out the Stewards, that must rule, and give the children their meat in due season, even milk to the babes, and stronger meat to them of full age, *Heb.* 5. 12, 13, 14. *Luke*. 12. 42. *Mat*. 24. 45. What readyer way to ruine the Schools of Christ, then by casting out the Teachers that he hath appointed under him? Or to ruine his Kingdome, then to reject his officers? Or to wrong the body, then to cut off the hand, and pull out the eyes, or to destroy the principal parts? Was it not Ministers that planted the Churches, and converted the world and have ever born off the assaults of enemies? Where was there ever Church on earth that continued without a Ministry? The great Kingdom of *Nubia* fell from Christianity for want of Preachers. The Nations that have the weakest and fewest Ministers, have the least of Christianity; and those that have the most and ablest Ministers, have the most flourishing state of Religion. All over the world the Church doth rise or fall with the Ministry: Cut down the Pillers, and the building falls. He is blind that sees not what would become of the Church, were it not for the Ministry? Who should teach the ignorant, or rebuke the obstinate, explain the word of truth, and stop the mouths of proud gain sayers? What work would heresies, and division, and prophaneness make, if these banks were cut down; when all that can be done is still too little. It must needs therefore be meer enmity against the Church, that makes men malignant against the Ministry.

4. The design of the maligners of the Ministry is plainly against the Gospel and Christianity it self. They take the readyest way in the world to bring in Heathenism, Infidelity and Atheism, which Christianity hath so far banished, For it is the Ministry that Christ useth to bring in light, and drive and keep out this damnable darkness, *Acts* 26: 17, 18. [*I send thee to open their eyes, and turn them from darkness to light, &c.*] Why are so many Nations Infidels, Mahometans, and Idolaters, but for want of
Ministers

Ministers to preach the Gospel to them? These Malignants therefore would take down the Sun, and banish Christianity out of the world.

5. And they hinder the Conversion of particular souls, and so are the cruellest wretches on earth. Though an Angel must be sent to *Cornelius*, it is not to be instead of a Preacher, but to send him to a Preacher, *Acts* 10. Though Christ would wonderfully appear to *Saul*, it is to send him to *Ananias* for instruction, *Acts* 9. Though the Jaylor must feel an Earth-quake, and see Miracles, it is but to prepare him for the Ministers words, *Acts* 16. *Philip* must be carried by an Angel to expound to an Eunuch the Word that must convert him. The Ministry is Gods instituted settled way, by which he will convert and save the world, as truly as the light is the natural way by which he will corporally enlighten them *Acts* 2. 18. 1 *Tim.* 4. 16. *Mat.* 5. 14. *Rom.* 10. 14. Do you think so many souls would be converted if the Ministry were down? Do you not see that the very contempt of them, that the scorns of the ungodly, and opposition of Malignant Apostates have occasioned, doth hinder most of the ignorant and prophane from receiving the saving benefit of the Gospel? How many millions of souls would these wretches sweep away to Hell, if they had their will? While thousands are in damnation for want of the light, they would take it from you, that you might go there also. Do you not understand the meaning of these words, against Christs Ministers? Why the meaning is this: They make a motion to the people of the Land, to go to Hell with one consent, and to hate those that are appointed to keep them out of it. They would take the bread of life from your mouthes. They are attempting an hundred times more cruelty on you, than *Herod* on the Jews when he killed the Children, or the Irish that murdered the Protestants by thousands; as the soul is of greater worth then the body.

6. These Malignants against the Ministry are the flat enemies of Christ himself, and so he will take them and use them. He that would root out the inferiour Magistrates, is an enemy to the Soveraign; and he that is against the officers of the Army, is an enemy to the General; Christ never intended to stay visibly on earth, and to Teach and Rule the world immediately in person; but he that is the King will Rule by his Officers; and he that is Prophet will Teach us by his Officers; and therefore he hath plainly told us, [*He that heareth you, heareth me; and he that despiseth you, despiseth me; and he that despiseth me, despiseth him that sent me, Luke* 10. 16.] O fearful case of miserable Malignants! Durst thou despise the Lord thy Maker and Redeemer, if he appeared to thee in his glory! to whom the Sun it self is as darkness, and all the world as dust and nothing? Remember when thou next speakest against his Officers, or hearest others speak against them, that their words are spoken against the face of Christ, and of the Father. I would not be found in the case of one of these Malignants, when Christ shall come to judge his enemies, for a thousand worlds.

He

He that hath said, [*Touch not mine annointed, and do my Prophets no harm;* *and hath rebuked Kings for their sakes*, Pſal. 105. 15. will deride all thoſe that would *break his bands*, and will *break them as with a rod of iron, and daſh them in pieces as a potters veſſel*, Pſal. 2. 3, 4, 9. And as he hath told them plainly, [*Who ſo deſpiſeth the Word ſhall be deſtroyed*, Prov. 13. 13.] And [*he that deſpiſeth, deſpiſeth not man, but God*, 1 Theſ. 4. 8. So he hath told us that *it ſhall be eaſier for Sodom and Gomorrah in the day of Judgement, then for ſuch*, Mat. 10. 15. Many a thouſand prouder enemies then you hath Chriſt broken; and look to your ſelves, for your day is coming. If you had but *ſtumbled on this ſtone, it would have broken you in pieces*; but ſeeing you will ſtrive againſt it, it will *fall on you, and grind you to pouder*, Mat. 21. 44. And then you ſhall ſee that he that made them his Embaſſadors, will bear them out and ſay, [*In as much as you did it to theſe, you did it to me.*] And you ſhall then ſay, *Bleſſed are they that truſt in him*.

7. It is apparent that theſe enemies of the Miniſters are playing the Papiſts game. Becauſe the juſt diſgrace of *their* Miniſtry, was the ruine of *their* Kingdom; therefore they hope to win of *us* at the ſame game. They know that if the people were brought into a hatred or ſuſpicion of their guides, they might the eaſier be won to them. They tell us in their writings, that not one of ten of our people but taketh his faith on truſt from their Teachers, and therefore take them off from them and they will fall: but they delude themſelves in this: For though the ungodly among us have no true faith of their own, and the Godly muſt lean on the hand of their ſupporters, yet there is in them a living principle; and we do not as the Papiſts prieſts, teach our people to ſee with our eyes, and no matter for their own: but we help to clear their own eye-ſight. Doubt not but the moſt of the ſects in the Land that fall againſt the Miniſtry, are knowingly or ignorantly the agents of the Papiſts. For the principal work of a Papiſt is to cry down the Miniſtry and the Scripture, and to ſet all they can on the ſame work.

8. Theſe ſects that are againſt the Miniſtry do all the ſame work as the Drunkards, Whore-mongers, Covetous, and all ungodly perſons in our Pariſhes do: And therefore it ſeems they are guided by the ſame ſpirit. It is the work of Drunkards and all theſe wicked wretches to hate, and deſpiſe, and revile the Miniſters, and to teach others to ſay as they. And juſt ſo do Quakers, Seekers, Papiſts and all other Malignants reproach the ſame Miniſters: And yet the blind wretches will not ſee that the ſame Spirit moveth them.

9. It is apparent that it is the Devils game they play, and his intereſt and Kingdom which they promote. Who fights againſt Chriſts Officers and Army, but the General of the contrary Army? What greater ſervice could all the world do for the Devils, then to caſt out the Miniſters of Chriſt? and what more would the Devil himſelf deſire, to ſet up his Kingdom and ſuppreſs the Church? Wretches! you ſhall ſhortly

see your Master, and he will pay you your wages contrary to your expectation. Read God's word to a Malignant, *Acts* 13. 10.

10. These Enemies do reproach as faithful a Ministry as the world enjoyeth, and their malice hath so little footing, as that the result must be their own shame. Among the Papists indeed there are Mass-Priests that can but read a Mass, whose Office is to turn a piece of Bread into a God: And yet these the Malignants either let alone, or liken us to them. The *Greeks*, and *Ethiopians*, and most of the Christian World, have a Ministry that seldome or never preach to them, but read Common-prayer, and Homilies. The most of the Protestant Churches have a learned Ministry that is so taken up with Controversies, that they are much less in the powerful preaching and practise of godliness: Above all Nations under Heaven, the *English* are set upon Practical Divinity and Holiness, and yet even they are by Malignity chosen out for reproach. Alas, scandals in the Ministry, (as drunkenness, swearing, &c.) among other Nations are but too common: but in *England* Magistrates and Ministers combine against them. Ministers are still spurring on the Magistrates to cast out the insufficient, negligent and scandalous; and desire and use more severity with men of their own profession, than with Magistrates, or any others in the Land. In nothing are they more zealous, than to sweep out all the remnant of the scandalous: And for themselves, they are devoted to the work of the Lord, and think nothing too much that they are able to perform, but preach in season and out of season, with all long-suffering and Doctrine; and yet Malignants make them their reproach.

11. It is abundance of pride and impudency, that these Malignant Enemies are guilty of. They are most of them persons of lamentable ignorance; and yet they dare revile at the Teachers, and think themselves wise enough to rebuke and teach them: Many of them are men of wicked lives; and yet they can tell the world how bad the Ministers are. A Railer, a Drunkard, a covetous Worldling, an ignorant Sot, is the likest person to fall upon the Minister; and the Owl will call the Lark a Night-bird. Alas, when we come to try them, what dark wretches do we find them! and should be glad if they were but teachable: And yet they have learnt the Devils first Lesson, to despise their Teachers.

12. And O what barbarous ingratitude are these Malignant Enemies of the Ministry guilty of! For whom do we watch, but for them and others? Can they be so blind as to think a painful Minister doth make it his design to seek himself, or to look after great matters in the world? Would not the time, and labour, and cost that they are at in the Schools and Universities, have fitted them for a more gainful trade? Do not Lawyers, Physitians, &c. live a far easier, and in the world a more honourable plentiful life? Have not the Ministers themselves been the principal Instruments of taking down Bishops, Deans and Chapters, Arch-deacons, Prebends, and all means of preferment? And what have they got by it, or ever endeavoured? Speak malice, and spare not. Is it any thing but what they had before? Even the

maintenance

maintenance due to their particular charge. Unthankful wretches! It is for your fakes and souls that they study, and pray, and watch, and fast, and exhort, and labour, to the consuming of their strength; and when they have done, are made the Drunkards Song, and the scorn of all the wicked of the Country; and when they spend, and are spent, the more they love, the less they are beloved. In the times of this greatest prosperity of the Church, they live under constant hatred and scorn, from those that they would save, and will not let alone in sin. And what do they endure all this for but Gods honour, and your salvation? Would we be Ministers for any lower ends? Let shame from God and man be on the face of such a Minister! I profess, were it not for the belief of the greatness, and necessity, and excellency of the Truths that I am to preach, and for the will of God, and the good of Souls, I would be a Plow-man, or the meanest Trade, if not a Sweep-Chimney, rather than a Minister. Must we break our health, and lay by all our worldly interest for *you*, even for *you*, and think not our lives and labours too good or too dear to further your Salvation; and must we by *you*, even by *you*, be reproached after all? God will be Judge between you and us, whether this be not inhumane ingratitude; and whether we deserve it at your hands?

13. Yea, it is *Injustice* also that you are guilty of: *The labourer*, faith Christ, *is worthy of his hire, Luke* 10. 7. (Mark that, you that call them *Hirelings*) *The Elders that rule well are worthy of double honour,* 1 Tim. 5. 17. *Especially they that labour in the Word and Doctrine.* And will you throw stones at their heads for endeavouring to save your souls? Will you spit in their faces for seeking with all their might to keep you from Hell? Is that their wages that you owe them? But blessed be the Lord, with whom is our reward, though you be not gathered, *Isa.* 49. 5. But as you love your selves, take heed of that Curse, *Jer.* 18. 20. [*Shall evil be recompenced for good? for they have digged a pit for my soul: Remember that I stood before thee to speak good for them, and to turn away thy wrath from them, &c.*] O how many a time have we besought the Lord for you! that he would convert you, and forgive you, and turn away the evil that was over you: And when all these our prayers, and groans, and tears shall be remembred against you, O miserable souls, how dear will you pay for all!

14. And is it not a wonder that these Malignants do not see what evident light of Scripture they contradict; and how many great express Commands they violate? They break the fifth Commandment, which requireth honour as well to spiritual Ecclesiastical Parents, as to Civil and Natural. And he that curseth Father and Mother, his Lamp shall be put out in darkness, *Prov.* 20. 20. The eye that mocketh at his Father, and despiseth to obey his Mother, the Ravens of the Valley shall pick it out, and the young Eagles shall eat it, *Prov.* 30. 17. Did these wretches never read, 1 Thes. 5. 12. *We beseech you brethren, to know them which labour among you, and are over you in the Lord, and admonish you; and to esteem them very highly in love for their work sake, and to be at peace among your selves.*] And Heb. 13. 17.

O o o [*Obey*

[*Obey them that have the rule over you, and submit your selves, for they watch for your souls as they that must give account, that they may do it with joy, and not with grief; for that is unprofitable for you.*] And Heb. 13. 7. *Remember them which have the rule over you, who have spoken to you the Word of God.*] And so ver. 24. And 1 Tim. 5. 17. *The Elders that rule well are worthy of double honour, &c.*] with abundance more such passages as these? Do not you feel these fly in your faces when you oppose the Ministers of Christ? Doth a Thief or Murderer sin against plainer light than you?

15. These Malignants sin against the consent and experience of the Universal Church of Christ till this day. The whole Church hath been for the Ministry, and instructed by them; and as the Child doth seek the Breast, so did new-born Christians, in all Ages, seek the Word from the Ministers, that they might live and grow thereby. And all the Nations of the Christian World are for the Ministry to this day! Or else they could not be for Christ, and for the Church, and Gospel. Is it not plain therefore that these Malignants are dead branches, cut off from the Church, that are so set against the Spirit and interest of the Church?

16. Moreover they sin against the experience of all, or almost all the true Christians in the world. For they have all experience, that Ministers are either their Fathers, or Nurses in the Lord: And that by their means they have had their life, and strength, and comforts; their sins killed, their graces quickned, their doubts resolved; the taste of the good Word of God, and of the powers of the world to come? May we not challenge you as *Paul* oft doth his Flock, Whether you did not receive the illuminating sanctifying Spirit by the Ministry, if ever you received it? I tell you, it is as much against the new and holy nature of the Saints to despise the Ministers of Christ, as it is unnatural for a Child to spit in the face of his Father or Mother. And the experience of sound Christians will keep them closer, and help them much against this inhumanity, what ever Hypocrites may do.

17. And if these Malignants had not *Pharaohs* heart, they would sure have considered, that the experience of all Ages tells them, that still the most wicked have been the Enemies of the Ministry, and the most godly have most obeyed and honoured them in the Lord; and that this Enmity hath been the common Brand of the rebellious, and the fore-runner of the heavy wrath of God; and that it hath gone worst with the Enemies, and best with the Friends of a godly Ministry. Do I need to prove this, which is so much of the substance of the Old Testament, and the New? Was it the Friends or Enemies of all the Prophets, Apostles and Ministers of Christ, that Scripture and all good Writers do commend? Do not the names of all Malignants against the godly Ministry stink above ground, as the shame of mankind, except those that are buried out of hearing, or those that were converted?

18. Nay such as are noted for the *highest* sort of the wicked upon Earth; worse than Drunkards, Whoremongers, and such filthy Beasts! The Persecutors

cutors of Gods Ministers have been ever taken as walking Devils: And the hottest of Gods wrath hath faln upon them. Take two instances; 1. When the *Jews* went into Captivity, this was the very cause, 2 *Chron.* 36. 15, 16. [*But they mocked the Messengers of God, and despised his words, and misused his Prophets, till the wrath of the Lord arose against his people, till there was no remedy.* 2. And when the *Jews* were cut quite off from the Church, and made Vagabonds on the Earth, this was the very cause, *Acts* 28. 28. *Be it known therefore to you, that the salvation of God is sent to the* Gentiles, *and that they will hear it.*] 1 *Thes.* 2. 15, 16. These Jews [*both killed the Lord Jesus, and their own Prophets, and have persecuted us: and they please not God, and are contrary to all men, forbidding us to speak to the* Gentiles, *that they might be saved, to fill up their sin alway; for the wrath is come upon them to the uttermost.*]

19. It is the Devils own part that these Malignants act: For it is he that is the great Enemy of Christ, and the Saints, and he that is *the Accuser of the Brethren, which accuseth them before God day and night*: And is not this the work of Quakers, Drunkards, Papists, and all Malignants? But the Lord will rebuke them, and be the glory of his servants, *Zach.* 3. 1, 2. [*He shewed me* Joshua *the High-Priest standing before the Angel of the Lord, and Satan standing at his right hand to resist him. And the Lord said unto Satan; The Lord rebuke thee, O Satan, even the Lord that hath chosen* Jerusalem.]

20. These Malignants do most of them condemn themselves; for they honour the Ancient Ministers of Christ that are dead, even while they oppose and hate the present that are living, who are the nearest Imitators of their Doctrine and life that are on Earth! The name of *Peter*, and *Paul*, and *John* they honour, and some of them keep Holy-days for them; and at the same time hate and reproach those that preach the same Doctrine, and that because they tread in their steps. They honour the names of *Austin*, and *Chrysostom* and *Hierom*, and other Ancients; and hate those that preach and live as they did. They speak honourably of the Martyrs that were burned to death for the Doctrine of Christ; and at the same time they hate us for doing as they did. What difference between the Calling, Doctrine and lives of those Martyred Ministers, and these that are now alive? O wretched Hypocrites! do you not know that these Apostles, Fathers, and other Ministers did suffer in their time from such as you, as we now do, and more? Hear what Christ saith to such as you, *Mat.* 23. 29, 30, 31. [*Woe to you Scribes, Pharisees, Hypocrites; because ye build the Tombs of the Prophets, and garnish the Sepulchres of the Righteous, and say, If we had been in the days of our Fathers, we would not have been partakers with them in the blood of the Prophets: Ye are witnesses to your selves, that ye are the children of them which killed the Prophets: fill ye up then the measure of your Fathers: Ye Serpents, ye Generation of Vipers, how can ye escape the damnation of Hell?*]

21. Moreover, these Malignants do harden themselves against the freshest of the Judgments of God, which some of their own hands have executed; and justifie the Persecutors, and succeed them in their fury. Have you forgotten what God hath done here against the Papal Enemies of the Gospel

and Ministry, in 88. and the Powder-plot, and many other times? Have you already forgotten how the persecutors of a godly Ministry have sped within these sixteen years in *England* and *Ireland*? And dare you now stand up in their room and make your selves the heirs of their sin, and punishment, and justifie them in all their Malignity? What do you but justifie them, when you rave against and revile the same sort of Ministers, and many of the same persons, whom the former Malignants persecuted? and oppose the same sort of Ministers that the Papists burned? And would not you do the like by them if you had Power in your hands? Can any wise man doubt of it, Whether Papists, and Quakers, and Drunkards, that now make it their work to make the Ministry odious, would not soon dispatch them if they could? Blessed be the great Protector of the Church, for were it not for him, our lives would soon be a prey to your cruelty.

22. And indeed if these Malignants had their wills, they would undo themselves, and cut down the bough they stand upon, and destroy the little hope and help that is yet left for their miserable souls: It is for the sake of Gods servants among them that judgements are so long kept off them. And as long as the Gospel and Ministers remains, salvation is offered them: the voice of mercy is calling after them, *Repent and live*. They have the light shining in their eyes, which may at last convince them, as *Paul* was convinced of his persecution: the voice which they despise may possibly awake them. Though they have less hope then others; yet there is some, But if they had their will, and were rid of the Ministry, alas, what would the forlorn wretches do? Then they might damn themselves without disturbance, and go quietly to hell, and no body stop them, and say, [*Why do you so?*]

23. And I pray you consider what it is that these men would have? What if the Ministers were all cast out? would they have any to do Gods work in their stead, or none? If *none*, you may see what they are doing: If *any*, Who, and where are they? Is it not horrible Pride if all these silly souls do think that they can do it better themselves? And what else do Quakers and all these sects that are the enemies of the Ministry? Do they not go up and down the Land, and say to the wisest holyest Teachers, as if they took them by the sleeve, [*Come down and let me preach that can do it better: Come down thou deceiver and ignorant man, and let me come up that am wiser, and better, and known more: Out with these proud Lordly Preachers, and let us be your Teachers, that are more holy, and humble, and self-denying then they.*] Is not this the loud language of their actions? And can you not hear the Devil in these words of highest Pride and Arrogancy? But really Sirs, do you think that these men would teach you better? And is there enow that are wiser and better then we to fill up our rooms, if we were out? Do but prove that, and you shall have my consent to banish all the Ministers in *England*, to some place that hath greater need of their labour, that they may no more trouble you that have no need of them, and keep out better.

24. Lastly,

24. Lastly, consider on what senseless pretences all this enmity against the Ministry doth vent it self. You shall hear the worst that they have to say against us, (though but briefly) and then judge.

1. The Quakers say, We are *idle drones that labour not, and therefore should not eat. Answ.* The worst, I wish you, is, that you had but my ease instead of your labour. I have reason to take my self for the least of Saints, and yet I fear not to tell the accuser, that I take the labour of most Tradesmen in the Town to be a pleasure to the body in comparison of mine; (though for the ends and the pleasure of my mind, I would not change it with the greatest Prince) Their labour *preserveth* health, and mine *consumeth* it: They work in ease, and I in continual pain: They have hours and dayes of recreation: I have scarce time to eat and drink: No body molesteth them for their labour; but the more I do, the more hatred and trouble I draw upon me. If a Quaker ask me, what all this labour is, let him come and see, or do as I do, and he shall know.

2. They accuse us of *covetousness and oppression, because we take tithes or hire,* (as they call it.) *Answ.* 1. Is it not malice or sacrilegious covetousness that frameth this accusation? *Whose* are the Tithes? are they *ours* or *theirs?* The same Law of the Land that makes the nine parts theirs, doth make the tenth ours. If we have no title to the tenth, they have none to the rest. We ask none of our people for a farthing. They *give* it not to us: It was never *theirs*. When they buy or take leases of their Land, it is only the nine parts that they pay for, and if the tenths were sold them, they should pay themselves a tenth part more. And would these men make all the people thieves and covetous, to take or desire that which never was their own? Nay would they have them rob God, to whom for his service the Tithes were devoted? Read, *Mal.* 3. 8, 9, 10. *Rom.* 2. 22. *Gen.* 14. 20. *Heb.* 7. 6, 9. And whether Tithe it self be of Divine institution still, is more then they are able to disprove. Sure I am, when Christ told them of *tithing mint, and cummin,* he saith, *These ought you to have done, and not to leave the other undone, Mat.* 23. 23. 2. But most certain I am that God hath made it our duty to *meditate* on his word, and *give our selves wholly thereto,* 1 *Tim.* 4. 15. and that we may [*Forbear working, and not go on warfare at our own charge; and sowing to men spiritual things, should reap their carnal things: Do ye not know that they which minister about holy things, live of the things of the Temple; and they which wait at the Altar, are partakers with the Altar? Even so hath the Lord ordained, that they which preach the Gospel should live of the Gospel.*] 1 *Cor.* 9. 6, 7, 13, 14. 3. And know you not that the primitive Christians gave not only the tenths, but all that they had, and laid it at the Apostles feet? to shew that the Gospel teacheth more clearly then the Law, the necessity of Dedicating our selves and all that we have to God. 4. And yet I must say, that we are content with *food and rayment*. Most Minist. in *England* would be glad to give you all their tithes, if you will but allow them food and rayment

for themselves and families, and such education for their children as is fittest to make them serviceable to God. And I hope it is no sin to have mouths that must be fed, or backs that must be cloathed. What! must Gods Ministers above all others be grudged *food and rayment*, and that of the Lords portion, which none of you pay for? I fear not to imitate *Paul* stopping the mouths of malicious accusers, and to tell you, that the Ministers, whose expences I am acquainted with, do give 500. pence, for 50. that they receive by gift from their people: and that they take all that they have as Christs, and not their own, and if they have never so much they devote it wholly to him, and know he's not beholden to them for it: and some of them lay out in charitable uses, much more then all the tithes that they receive for their Ministerial maintenance. And if the Quakers that accuse them of covetousness, would cast up accounts with them, I doubt not but it will be found that they receive more by gift then Preachers, and give not the fourth part so much when they have done.

3. Another accusation is, that we *preach false Doctrine, and deceive the people. Answ.* It's easie to say so of any man in the world: But when they come to prove it, you will see who are the deceivers.

4. Another is, that we are *persecutors, and like the Priests of old, and so all the reproofs of them and the Pharisees belong to us. Answ.* This is soon said too: but where's the proof? For themselves we have no mind to be troubled with them. Let them let us alone, as long as we will let them alone. But yet they shall be taught one day to know, that if the Magistrate stop the mouths of such railers and abusers of God and men, he doth no more persecute them, then he persecuteth a thief when he hangeth him; or then *Paul* persecuted *Hymeneus* and *Philetus* when he delivered them up to Satan; or *Elymas*, *Acts* 13. 11. or then *Peter* persecuted *Ananias* and *Sapphira*, *Acts* 5. or then God would have had the Churches be persecutors against the woman *Jezebel* that was suffered to teach and seduce the people, or against the Doctrine of the Nicolaitans which God hated, *Rev.* 2. 15, 20. If *hindering sin*, be *persecuting*, the *calling* of a *Magistrate* is to be a persecutor, *Rom.* 13. 4. and all parents must persecute their own children.

5. Another accusation is, that we are *against the preaching of any but our selves. Answ.* Who doth not desire that all the Lords people were Prophets? But yet we know all are not Prophets, 1 *Cor.* 12 29. nor Teachers. We would have none of Gods gifts in our people buried, but all improved to the uttermost for his glory. But we would not have men turn Ordinary Teachers, that are neither sound, nor able, nor sent; nor every self-conceited ignorant man, have leave to abuse the name and word of God, and the souls of men. What would you have more then is granted you? When any unordained man that is judged competent by the Commissioners of Approbation (of whom some are Souldiers) may be a constant preacher, and have fullest maintenance, as well as Presbyters?

6. Another

6. Another Charge is, that *we are some weak, and some scandalous.* *Answ.* We do all that we are able to cast out such; and I think never more was done. The Magistrate sets his Guard at the door, and lets in none but whom he pleasè: and sure if he knew where to have better than those that are in, he would put them in, or else he is too blame: If he do not know, will you blame him for using the best that he can get? But if you will come and help us to cast out any that are vicious and unworthy, we will give you thanks.

7. Another Accusation is, that *we differ among our selves, and one saith one thing, and another another thing.* *Answ.* 1. And are all these Sects that oppose us better agreed among themselves? Enquire and judge. 2. Do not all preach one Gospel, and the same Essentials of the Christian Faith? And we expect not perfect Unity, till we have perfect Knowledge and Holiness; which we dare not boast of, whatever *Quakers* do.

8. Another Accusation is, that *we are not true Ministers.* And why so? Because we have not an uninterrupted succession of lawful Ordination. *Answ.* This Objection is the Papists, who have little reason to use it, while it is so easie a matter to prove so many interruptions of their Papal succession. At large and often have we answered them, and are still ready to deal with any of them herein, and to prove; 1. That an uninterrupted succession of right Ordination, is not of necessity to the being of the Ministry. 2. And if it were, we have more to shew for it than they. If others stick on this, let me tell them, that Magistracy is as truly from God as the Ministry: And let ever a King on Earth shew me an uninterrupted succession giving him Title to his Crown, and I will shew him a more undoubted succession or Title to my Ministry. But here's no room to discuss this Question.

9. Object. *But you are Parish Priests, and no true Ministers; because you have not true Churches.* *Answ.* All the Christians in our Parishes that consent are our Flock: And we undertake to prove the truth of such Churches, not only against scorn, but against all the Arguments that can be brought.

10. Object. *But you have not the Spirit, and therefore are no true Ministers.* *Answ.* And how prove you that we have not the Spirit? The approvers admit none but such as they think have the Spirit. He that is sanctified hath the Spirit: Prove us unsanctified, and we will resign our Office. Object. *You read your Sermons out of a Paper; therefore you have not the Spirit.* *Answ.* A strong Argument! I pray you take seven years time to prove the consequence. As wisely do the *Quakers* argue, that because we use Spectacles, or Hour-glasses, and Pulpits, we have not the Spirit. It is not want of your abilities that makes Ministers use Notes; but it's a regard to the work, and the good of the Hearers. I use Notes as much as any man, when I take pains; and as little as any man when I am lazy, or busie, and have not leisure to prepare. It's easier to us to preach three Sermons without Notes, than one with them. He is a simple Preacher that is not able to preach all day without preparation, if his strength would serve; especially if he preach at your rates.

11. Object.

11. *Object:* But the true Ministry is persecuted; but so are not you, but are Persecutors of others. *Answ.* 1. For our persecuting others, be so merciful as to prove it to us, that we may lament it. If punishing wicked men and Seducers be persecuting, not only *Paul* was such, that wished *they were cut off that troubled the* Galatians; but God himself would be the greatest of all persecutors, that will lay you in Hell without repentance, and then you will wish your old persecution again. And if we be not persecuted, what means the reproaches of you and all the Drunkards and Malignants about us? But I pray you envy us not our lives and liberties, and a little breathing time. Do you not read that [*The Churches had rest throughout all Judea, and Galilee, and Samaria, and were edified, and walking in the fear of the Lord, and in the comfort of the Holy Ghost, were multiplied?* Acts 9.31.] Envy not a little prosperity to the Church. Doth not *Paul* pray that the Gospel *may run and be glorified, and that we may be delivered from unreasonable wicked men,* 2 *Thess.* 3.1. Sometimes you can say that more glorious days are promised, and that the Saints shall rule the world. Unmerciful men! It is but a while ago since we had our share of sufferings! Since that the Sword hath hunted after us! Many of our Brethren are yet in *America,* that were driven thither: at this time in *Spain,* and *Italy,* and *Germany,* and *Savoy:* Alas, what do our Brethren suffer in the same Cause and Calling that we are in! And do you reproach us with our mercies, if we be out of the Furnace but a little while, in one corner of the world?

Object. 12. *You work no Miracles to confirm your Doctrine.* *Answ.* It is true; nor do we need: It is confirmed by Miracles long ago. If we brought a new Gospel, or as the Papists, gave you not our Doctrine on the credit of Scripture, but Scripture and all on our own credit, then you might justly call for Miracles to prove it: But not when we have nothing to do but expound and apply a Doctrine sealed by Miracles already.

Again, I say, *Let any Prince on Earth that questions our Calling, shew his Title to his Crown, or any Judge or Magistrate to his Office; and if I shew not as good a Title to mine, let me be taken for a Deceiver, and not a Minister.*

Christian Reader, as ever thou wouldest be *sanctified, confirmed, and saved,* hold fast to *Christ, Scripture, Ministry,* and *Spirit,* and that in the *Church* and *Communion* of *Saints,* and abhor the thoughts of separating them from each other.

A second Sheet for the MINISTRY; *Justifying our Calling against* Quakers, Seekers, *and* Papists, *and all that deny us to be the Ministers of Christ.*

THe corruption of the *Romish* Church being most in the Errours and Vices of the Priests, which made men abhor the offering of the Lord (*1 Sam.* 2. 17.) the reproach which they brought upon themselves, did much prepare men to hearken to the Reformers: The observing of this, and of the necessary dependance of the people on their Pastors, hath caused the Papists to bend their force against the Ministers of the Reformed Churches, and to use all their wit to defame their Persons and Callings, and make them seem ignorant, unworthy, or no Ministers to the people. On this Errand they send abroad their Agents; this is the saving Gospel that the *Seekers*, *Quakers*, and their Brethren preach; that the Scripture is not the Gospel, or Word of God, and that we are no true Ministers. Whatever Doctrine we are preaching, the Opposers work is to call us Deceivers, and ask, How we prove our selves true Ministers? My work therefore at this time, for the sake of the ignorant in our Assemblies, shall be, to acquaint them with our answer to this demand. And I shall give it you in order, in certain Propositions.

Prop. 1. *Both in the Old and New Testament there is mention of two distinct sort of Ministers of Gods appointment.* First, such as received some *new Revelation* (either a Law, or a particular Message) *immediately from God*; so that the people could not be sure that their Doctrine was true, till they were sure that the men were sent of God. These were called *Prophets* in the Old Testament, and *Apostles, Prophets,* &c. in the New. So *Moses* received the Law from God; and the following Prophets their particular Messages. So the Apostles received the Gospel from Christ; and so did the Seventy, and other Disciples that conversed with him; and other Prophets and Evangelists had it by immediate inspiration. All these were necessarily by Miracles, or some Infallible Evidence to prove their own Call, before the Hearers could receive their Doctrine: for this was their Message; [*The Lord hath commanded me to say thus or thus to you*] or [*The word which the Lord spake to me is thus or thus*] This sort of Ministers the Papists and Seekers do confess.

But besides these, there is a second sort of true Ministers, whose Office is not to receive from God any new Doctrine, Law, or Message; but to *proclaim the Laws already delivered*, and *teach men the Doctrine already revealed*, and to *oversee and govern the Churches of Christ* according to his Laws, and to go before the people in the worship of God: The Prophets and Apostles did both these; both reveal the Doctrine which they received from Christ, and teach and guide the Church by it when they had done; but the latter sort of Ministers do but the latter sort of the work. The Papists and Seekers

P p p   cheat

cheat men by jumbling all together, as if there were no Ministers of Gods appointment, but those of the former sort; and therefore they call for Miracles to prove our Ministry. Here therefore I shall first prove, that the *second sort* of Ministers are of Gods Institution. 2. That such need not prove their Calling by Miracles, though yet God may work Miracles by them if he please. 3. That *we are true Ministers of Christ, of this sort.*

1. Christ found such Ministers under the Law that were to teach and rule by the Law before received, and not to receive new Laws or Messages; I mean the ordinary *Priests* and *Levites*, as distinguished from *Prophets.* These Priests were to keep the Law, and teach it the people, and the people were to seek it at their mouth, and by it they were to judge mens Causes: and also they were to stand between the people and God in publick worship, as is exprest, *Deut:* 31.26. *Josh.* 23.6. *Neh.* 8.1,2,3,8,18. & 9.3. *Levit.* 1. & 2. & 4. & 5. & 7. & 13. & 14. throughout, *Num.* 5. & 6. *Deut.* 17.12. *Mal.* 2.7. *Jer.* 18.18. The Prophet had Visions; but the Priest had the Law, *Ezek* 7.26. *Isa.* 8.16,20. *Hag.* 2.11,12. *Num.* 1.50 1 *Chron.* 9.26. & 16.4. 2 *Chron* 19.11. & :0.19.& 30.17,22. He was called, *A Teaching Priest,* 2 *Chron.* 15.3. *Lev.* 10.10,11. *Deut.* 24.8, 2 *Chron* 17.7 9. *Ezek.* 44.23. 2 *Chron.* 35.3. And Christ himself sends the cleansed to the Priest, and commandeth *them to hear the Pharises that sat in Moses Chair*, though they were no Prophets: so that besides the Prophets that had their message immediately from God, there were Priests that were called the *Ministers of the Lord,* Joel 1.9.2.17. and Levites that were not to bring new Revelations, but to *teach*, and *rule*, and *worship* him according to the old. *For Moses of old time hath in every City them that preach him, being read in the Synagogues every Sabbath day,* Acts 15.21. The *Jews* rejected Christ because they *knew him not, nor the voice of the Prophets which are read every Sabbath day,* Acts 13.27. *And even unto this day, when Moses is read, the Vail is on their heart,* 2 Cor. 3.15. And they that *would not believe Moses, and the Prophets* (thus read and preached) *neither will they be perswaded, though one rose from the dead,* Luke 16. 29, 31.

2. And as Priests and Levites were distinct from Prophets before Christ, so Christ appointed besides the Apostles and Prophetical Revealers of his Gospel, a standing sort of Ministers, to 1. Teach, 2. Rule, 3. And worship according to the Gospel which the former had revealed, and attested, and proved to the world. These were called *Overseers,* or *Bishops, Presbyters,* or *Elders, Pastors* and *Teachers*; and also the *Deacons* were joyned to assist them, *Acts* 14.23. *They ordained them Elders* (not Prophets or Apostles) *in every Church,* Tit. 1.5. *Titus* was to *ordain Elders in every City: Timothy* hath full direction for the ordaining of Bishops, or Elders and Deacons, 1 *Tim* 3.

That their work was not to bring new Doctrine, but to teach, rule, and worship according to that received, I now prove, 2 Tim. 2.2. *The things that thou hast heard of me among many witnesses, the same commit thou to faithful men, who shall be able to teach others also*] Mark, that its the *same*, and not a *new* Doctrine; and that as *heard from* Paul *among many witnesses*, and not as received immediately from God: and others were thus to receive it down from *Timothy.* And v. 15. *Study to shew thy self approved unto God, a workman that needeth not be ashamed, rightly dividing the word of truth.*] It is not to bring new Truths, but rightly to divide the old. And 2 *Tim.* 1. 13. *Hold fast the form of words which thou hast heard of me* (not which thou hadst immediately from God) *in faith and love which is in Christ Jesus; that good thing which was committed unto thee, keep, by the Holy Ghost which dwelleth in us.* The Holy Ghost is to help us in keeping that which is committed to us, and not to reveal more, 2 *Tim* 6. 13, 14. [*I give thee charge in the sight of God, that thou keep this Commandment without spot, unrebukable, till the appearing of our Lord Jesus Christ.* There was a *form of Doctrine delivered to the Church of Rome,* Rom. 6. 17. And 1 *Tim.* 5. 17. *The Elders that rule well are worthy of double honour, especially they that labour in the Word and Doctrine.* You see their work was to rule and labour in the Word and Doctrine, 1 Tim. 4. 13, 14, 15, 16. *Till I come, give attendance to Reading, to Exhortation, to Doctrine; meditate upon these things: give thy self wholly to them; that thy profiting may appear to all: Take heed unto thy self, and unto the Doctrine: continue in them; for in doing this, thou shalt both save thy self and them that hear thee.*] 1 Tim. 5. 6. [*If thou put the brethren in remembrance of these things, thou shalt be a good Minister of Jesus Christ, nourished up in the words of faith, and of good doctrine, whereunto thou hast attained.*] Mark here the description of a good Minister of Christ; one that's nourished up in the words of faith, and good doctrine, (which is the use of Schools and Universities) and having attained it, makes it his work to teach it, and put others in remembrance of it, *Tit.* 1. 7, 9, 10, 11. *For a Bishop must be blameless, as the Steward of God---holding fast the faithful word as he hath been taught,* (mark that) *that he may be able by sound doctrine, both to exhort and convince the gainsayers: For there are many unruly and vain talkers and deceivers, whose mouths must be stopped, who subvert whole houses, teaching things which they ought not, &c.*] So 1 *Tim.* 3. 1, 5. The Office of a Bishop is to *rule and take care of the Church of God:*] *To take heed to themselves, and to all the Flock, and feed the Church of God;* and to *watch hereunto,* according to the *word of Gods grace,* which is *fully* and wholly delivered by his Apostles, and *is able to build us up, and give us an inheritance among the sanctified:* as Act. 20. 28, 20, 27, 35, 32. 1 Thes. 5. 12, 13. *We beseech you brethren to know them which labour among you, and are over you in the Lord, and admonish you* (this is their Office) *and to esteem them very highly in love for their works sake* (and not revile them as the servants of Satan do) *and be at peace among your selves,* Heb. 13. 7, 17, 24. *Remember them which have the rule over you, which have spoken to you the word of God: Obey them that have the rule over you, and submit your selves, for they watch for your souls, as they that must give account, that they may do it with joy, and not with grief: for that is unprofitable for you. Salute all them that have the Rule over you: The Elders of the Church* are to pray with, and for the sick, Jam. 5. 14. They must *feed the Flock of God among them, taking the oversight of it,* 1 Pet. 5. 1, 2. Thus you see their Office and work.

2. And that they were not to bring any *new Doctrine*, further appears, in that they have a charge to *Preach no other doctrine*, 1 Tim. 1. 3. Nor *to be tossed as children with every wind of doctrine*, Eph. 4.14. Nor *carried about with divers and strange doctrines*, Heb. 13. 9.

3. Yea, if any *man bring not the doctrine of Christ, we must not receive him into our houses, or bid him God speed, lest we be partakers of his evil deeds, for he that abideth not in this doctrine hath not God*, 2 John 9.10, 11. Gal. 1. 8, 9. [*Though we or an Angel from heaven, preach any other Gospel to you, then that which we have preached unto you, let him be accursed. As we said before, so say I now again: If any man preach any other Gospel to you then that ye have received, let him be accursed.*] And Rom. 16. 17, 18. *Now I beseech you Brethren, mark them which cause divisions and offences, contrary to the Doctrine which ye have learned, and avoid them*] 1 Tim. 6.3. *If any man teach otherwise, and consent not to wholsome words, the words of our Lord Jesus Christ, and to the Doctrine which is according to Godliness, he is proud, knowing nothing, but doating.*]

4. And if all Ministers must be receivers of new Doctrines, the Church would never know when it hath all, but would be still obeying an imperfect Law. 5. And it would be an oppression to the Church instead of a Direction, to be so overwhelmed with new Doctrines and Precepts. 6. And it would accuse Christ, the Lawgiver, of such mutability, as wise Princes are not guilty of; to be still changing or adding to his Laws. 7. There was great occasion for the New Testament or Gospel, upon the great work of our Redemption: but there is no such cause for alterations since. 8. The Priests before Christ were not to receive new Laws, as is said.. 9. The Companions of the Apostles that wrought Miracles, had not all new Revelations; but did it to seal up this Gospel. 10. What need we more then actual experience, that God doth not give New Revelations to the world, and none since the Scripture times, have sealed any other by Miracles.

And thus I have proved to you the two sorts of Ministers: as *Paul* plainly distinguisheth them, 1 Cor. 3.10, 11, 12. Eph 2.20. There are *Planters* and *Waterers, Master builders that lay the foundation, and others that build thereon: Other foundation can no man lay then that which is laid: but every man that buildeth hay or stuble and loseth his work, doth not nullifie the Ministry. We are built on the foundation of the Apostles and Prophets, Jesus Christ being the head corner-stone*: but we are not built on the *foundation* of every Pastor, Teacher, Elder, Bishop or Deacon: Though both in their places (Apostles, Prophets, Evangelists, Pastors and Teachers) *are given for the perfecting of the Saints, for the work of the Ministry, for the Edifying of the body of Christ*, Eph. 4. 11, 12. That we might be one united Body, having one fixed standing doctrine, ver. 14. 15, 16. And *how shall we escape if we neglect so great salvation; which at the first began to be spoken by the Lord, and was confirmed unto us by them that heard him*: (mark whence the Church receiveth it) *God also bearing them witness* (but not every Elder or Teacher) *both with signs and wonders, and with divers Miracles, and gifts of the Holy Ghost according to his own will*, Heb. 2. 3, 4. Prop. 2. And

Prop. 2. And now that *these Later Ministers need not prove their calling by Miracles,* I prove thus: 1. God never imposed such a task upon them, nor commanded the people to require such a proof, and not to believe any but worker of Miracles. 2. God gave not all the gift of Miracles, that were employed in his work even in the Apostles daies: *Are all workers of Miracles?* saith *Paul;* some had by the Spirit, the *word of wisedom, and of knowledge,* and others *Tongues,* and others *Interpretation,* and others *Miracles.* 1 Cor. 12.29,7,8.9,10. 3. They that have the Holy Ghost are owned by Christ, and so have many without working Miracles. See *Rom.*8.9. 1 *Cor.*12 5. *Gal.* 5. 18,20,23,24. 1 *Cor.*6.11. *Eph.*3.16.& 5.9,18. 1 *Pet.*1.2,22. *Rom.*15.13, 15. *Tit.*3.5. 4. The Law of *Moses* was kept and taught by Priests and Levites that wrought not Miracles. 5. If the Laws of all Nations may be kept without Miracles, so may the Laws of Christ. 6. If humane writings are kept without Miracles, (as *Homer, Virgil, Ovid, Cicero, Livy,* &c.) so may the Laws of God much more, as being the daily subject of the belief, meditation, conference, preaching, controversies, devotions of Christians through the world, and translated into so many Tongues. 7. There is nothing in the Nature of the thing that requireth ordinary Miracles. Cannot men sufficiently prove without Miracles, that there have been such men as *Cæsar, Pompey, Aristotle,* or which be *Calvins* or *Bellarmines* writings, &c. Much more evidently may they prove what doctrine is essential to Christianity, and the Scripture that contains the whole. 8. Else Parents could not teach their children, nor *bring them up in the Nurture and admonition of the Lord,* Eph.6.4. Nor teach them with *Timothy, from a child to know the Scriptures, which are able to make men wise to salvation through faith in Christ,* 2 Tim.3. 15. Must no Parents teach their Children to know Christ, but such as can work Miracles? 9. The Doctrine which we preach is fully confirmed by Miracles already, by Christ and his Apostles: There needs no greater then Christs own Resurrection, nor more then were done; which Universal unquestionable History and Tradition hath brought down to our hands. 10. It is a ridiculous expectation, that every person should see the Miracles before they do believe. Then if Christ had done Miracles before all *Jerusalem,* save one man, that one man should not be bound to believe: Or if I could do miracles in this Town or Country, none must believe me ever the more but those that see it. And so you may as well say, I should not believe that there is any Sea or Land, City or Kingdom, *France, Spain, Rome,* &c. but what I see. Are these men worthy to be talkt with? that believe no body, and confess themselves such Lyars that they would have no body believe them. It was not *all* that saw *Corists Miracles* or *Resurrection,* or the Apostles. miracles! It seems the rest were not bound to be Christians? Even as *Clem: Writer* told me, that *no man is bound to believe that Christ did Rise again, or the rest of Christianity, that seeth not Miracles himself to prove it :* adding withall, that *indeed Antichrist may do Miracles;* and so it seems for all the talk, miracles themselves would not serve if they saw them. 11. Is it not to put a scorn on God Almighty, to say that the Glory of all his most miraculous

works

works should be buried to all that saw them not; and that Parents should not tell them to their Children, or Children should not believe them if they do? 12. Its injurious to Posterity, that the knowledge of the most wonderful works of God shall be only for the good of them that see them; and that all ages after shall be never the better. 13. It tends to make men mad and as Ideots, that must know and believe no more then they see: what kind of folks must these be, that know not that there is either Prince or Parliament, City or Countrey, or any folks in the world but those they have seen? This will stand with trading, converse, Subjection, Societies; and its doubtful whether such are capable of managing estates; or should not be put under others as Ideots? 14. Children cannot learn to read nor speak without some kind of belief of them that teach them: nor can they obey their parents nor learn any trade, nor obey Physitians: so that this conceit of incredulity is against the Nature, livelihood, and life of man. 15. And they would tie God to be at the beck of every unreasonable Infidel; that shall say, [*Though all the Town have seen thy Miracles, yet I will see my self, or else I will not believe.*] 16. They expect that God should overturn the course of Nature: for if Miracles be as ordinary as the operations of Nature, they are confounded. 17. And by this they would cross themselves, and make Miracles uneffectual: For if they were ordinary; few would be moved by them *as* any proof of a Divine Testimony: were it as ordinary for the Sun to go backward as forward, who would take it for a Miracle? To this *Clem: Writer* answers me, that [*Miracles were convincing in the first Age when they were common*] *Answ.* How common? Not as natural operations: Nor so as for all Countreys or persons to see them; 500 saw Christ at once after his Resurrection: 5000. were once miraculously fed: but as this was not every day's work, so what was this to others? And in that it was but for an age, and rarely in after ages, shews that they were not for every mans eyes. 18. What need we more proof then actual experience, that God doth not often now work miracles! And he that saith the Gospel, and Christian faith, and Church, and Ministry are therefore ceased, its like will not take it ill to be taken himself for an Heathen or Infidel. 19. And we have experience of millions that still do actually and stedfastly believe in Christ without Miracles: and many have laid down their lives on that belief: therefore without miracles men may believe. But to this *Clem: Writer* saith to me, [*These believers of all sorts condemn each other as Hereticks.*] *Answ.* But not as *Infidels.* None but the ignorant or passionate condemn all other sorts as Hereticks. The sober do not. And it is not enough to prove you a bastard, if an angry Brother call you so. 20. Because this sheet alloweth me not room, I intreat the Reader to peruse these Texts, which tell him aloud that the word and works of God must be believed by Tradition, though without Miracles, *Exod.* 10.1, 2. & 12.14,17,26,27,42. *Deut.* 11.2. to the 22. & 29.22. to 28. *Josh.* 4.6, 7. & 22.24. to 32. *Psalm.* 48.13. & 78.1. to 9. & 102.18. & 145.4. & 89.1. *Joel.* 1.2, 3, 4. *Acts* 1.8. & 2.32 & 5.30, 31, 32. & 10.38. to 42. & 13.

30, 31. & 1.22. & 4 33. & 22.15. & 26.16. & 23.11. 2 Tim.2.2. *John.* 20. 29. & 19.35. & 15.27. & 12.17. & 5.33. & 1.15, 32.34 *Luke* 4. 22. 1 *Pet.* 5. 1. And that you would read my Determination of this very Question in my Book against Infidelity: I proceed to the next.

Proposition 3. *This ordinary Ministry for teaching, ruling, and publick worship, was ordained by Christ to continue till his coming, and doth yet continue, and did not cease when the extraordinary Ministry ceased.* I prove it, Matth. 16.18. *Upon this Rock will I build my Church, and the Gates of Hell shall not prevail against it.*] The Church never did nor can subsist without its Officers, who are an Essential part of it, as it is a *Political Body,* and the first and most eminent part, as it is a *Community.* And therefore if the Ministry be extinct, the *Gates of Hell have prevailed* against the Church: And then Christ is overcome, or hath broke his promise; and then he were not Christ: So that if Christ be Christ, the Church and Ministry continue. So Luke 1.33. *He shall reign over the House of* Jacob *for ever, and of his Kingdome there shall be no end,* Isa. 9.6, 7. *Of the encrease of his government and peace there shall be no end,* Psalm 145. 13. *Thy Kingdome is an everlasting Kingdome, and thy Dominion endureth throughout all Generations.* Christ ruleth by his Officers in his Church; if Church or Ministry had an end, his Kingdome had an end, and he reigned not for ever, Matth. 28 20. *Lo, I am with you alway, even to the end of the world.* To this express promise, *Clem. Writer* hath no wiser an answer, but that, [*it is conditional. If they teach men to observe all things that Christ hath commanded, then he will be with them, else not.*] *Repl.* This is your forgery: here is no such words, but an absolute promise. His being with them, is to support and help them in his work: And will you feign Christ to promise them help on condition they do it without? The further Cavils against this Text and others, the *London* Ministers in their Vindication have answered at large, Eph. 4. 11, 12, 13. *The Pastors and Teachers are given to the Church for the perfecting of the Saints for the work of the Ministry, for the edifying of the body of Christ, till we all come in the unity of the faith, and of the knowledge of the Son of God to a perfect man, &c.*] Extraordinary and ordinary Officers are here conjoyned, who between them are to perfect the building, the first *laying the foundation,* and the others *building thereon,* 1 Tim. 6. 13, 14. *I give thee charge in the sight of God---- that thou keep this Commandment without spot, unrebukable, unto the appearing of our Lord Jesus Christ*] which must needs extend to his Successors. *The faithful and wise Stewards that give the children their meat in due season, will be found so doing by the Lord at his coming,* Luke 12. 42, 43. And it is not till the last day that Christ will *give up the Kingdome to the Father,* 1 Cor. 15.25. 2. The Apostles actually setled an ordinary Ministry in their time, as is proved. 3. There are Commands for setling Successors of these, as 2 Tim. 2.2. Tit. 1. 5. as is proved. 4. These Ministers are described, and the way of their Ordination setled by Canons, 1 Tim. 3. Tit. 1. 5. We find the several Angels of the Churches in their places, *Revel.* 2. & 3. and promises to some of them for the future, with a Command [*Hold fast till I come,* 2.25.] and

3. 10. [*I will keep thee from th. hour of temptation which shall come on all the world: Behold, I come quickly.*] 6 Christ hath commanded the Ministerial *work* to continue to the end: As the *Preaching of the Word* must be to all Nations, and every Creature, *Matth.* 28. 19. *Mark* 16. 15. And these most cruel men would have all the Preachers give over their work, and leave the world to perish in Infidelity. So for the *assembling of our selves together, and exhorting one another,* we are commanded *not to forsake it, as is the manner of some*; and so much *the more, as we see the day approaching,* Heb. 10. 23, 24, 25. So that the nearer we are to Christs coming, the closer must we stick to Church Communion, and holy Assemblies; considering, that its but *a little while, and he that comes will come, and shall not tarry,* ver. 37. God doth on purpose forbear his coming, because he is *long-suffering,* and will continue the means to call men to *repentance,* and then the day of the Lord will come suddenly, 2 Pet. 3. 9, 10. [*The Word of the Lord endureth for ever: and this is the word which by the Gospel is preached to you,* 1 Pet. 1. 25. The Lords Supper is Instituted to be used to *shew the Lords death till he come,* 1 Cor. 11. 26. Church government or Discipline is a fixed Ordinance, *Mat.* 18. 15, 16, 17. And if the *work* continue, the *workmen* must continue. 7. The mercy of God, and the Efficacy of Christs Blood, and the necessities of the Church continue: we still need a Teaching Ministry, Heb. 5. 11. and for *our need* it is Instituted till the Church be perfect, that we be not as children toss'd up and down, *Eph.* 4. 13, 14. What enemies to us, and to the love and mercy of God are they that would perswade men, that he so quickly withdrew so great a mercy, when the *gifts and calling of God are without repentance?* 8. The Law and its Priesthood was not removed but by the glory of a better Law and Ministry: And Christ is the Mediator of a *better Covenant* and *Promises,* Heb. 7. 22. & 8. 7, 8. Therefore he will not deal so much worse. 9. Christ telleth us that a wise man will consider whether he can go through with it, before he build or make War: Therefore he would not himself begin to build his Church, and enter himself the Captain of our Salvation, and presently let his Enterprize fall. 10. If the Ministry continue not, then the Church continueth not; for as the Head, Liver, and Stomack, or Lungs are to the Body, so is the Ministry to the Church, 1 *Cor.* 12. 13, 19, 20, 28, 29. They *plant* and *water it,* 1 *Cor.* 3. 6. and *build it,* ver. 10. *For how shall we believe on him of whom we have not heard? and how shall we hear without a Preacher? and how shall they preach unless they be sent?* Rom. 10. 14. But the Church doth continue: for first, else Christ were no longer the *Head* of it, the *King, Prophet,* or *Priest,* and so not Christ: But he is a *Priest for ever, abiding continually: he continueth ever, and hath an unchangeable Priesthood; he ever liveth to make intercession for those that come to God by him,* Heb. 7. 3. 22, 24, 25. 2. Those that deny the Church, must needs deny themselves Christians and Members of that Church. 3. There is no Salvation promised but to the Church; *Eph.* 5. 23, 25, 26, 27. *Mark* 16. 16. 4. *Blindness is on the* Jews *but till the fulness of the* Gentiles *be come in, and so all* Israel *shall be saved*: Therefore it is most evident that the *Gentile* Church shall not cease till

till the fulness have prepared for the re-ingraffing of the *Jews*, Rom. 11. 25, 26. 5. It is an *everlasting Kingdome, which cannot be moved and the City of the living God, the heavenly* Jerusalem, *whereof even the Angels and perfected Spirits of the Just are a part*, to which we come by Faith: therefore it ceaseth not, Heb. 12. 22, 23, 28. 6. *When that which is perfect is come, then that which is in part shall be done away*, 1 Cor. 13. 10. but not before. 7. If nothing can separate us from the love of God, no not any distress or tribulation, then are not all the Ministers and Church cut off, Rom. 8. 34. to 39. Yea, those that in all Ages suffer for his sake, are not cut off from him; but so many faithful Ministers do. 8. But what should I say any more against that Assertion which carrieth stark Heathenism or Infidelity in its Forehead, reproaching Christ as no Christ, and teaching men that they are not bound to be Christians, and believe the Gospel, and perswading the world to despise Christs Messengers and Ordinances; and Ministers to cast off their Masters work; which in two words is, to turn Infidels, or Apostates. I must refer you for my fuller answer to such men, to my Book against Infidelity.

Prop. 4. *God hath in his Law appointed a standing way for the calling of these ordinary Teaching, Ruling, worshipping Ministers, in all Ages; and doth himself call them in this way.* 1. He instituteth the Office. 2. He commandeth that fit persons be ordained to this Office. 3. He describeth them by their necessary Qualifications. All this is at large, 1 Tim. 3. Tit. 1. Act. 20. 1 Pet. 5. &c. This is his work by his standing Law: By which also he commandeth the people to chuse, consent to, or accept the fit, and to hear and obey them, Act. 14. 23. 2 Thes. 5. 12. Act. 6. 3, 5. Heb. 13. 7, 17. And then by Providence, 1. He giveth them those gifts of the Spirit that may competently qualifie them for their Office. 2. He assisteth the Chusers and Ordainers to discern those Qualifications, and do their duties. 3. He causeth some special fitness of a Minister to the special Province or Charge which he is to undertake, and special inviting occasions and opportunities, and oft-times causeth Necessity to make the choice. 4. He boweth the heart of the person called to consent, and usually to desire the work (for the right ends.) 5. And if he be called to be the Pastor of a particular Church, he moveth the people to consent or accept him. And thus God according to his appointed Order doth call his Ministers: Besides which, he afterward 1. Helps them in his work: 2. And procureth them liberty, and often furtherance from Christian Magistrates. 3. And giveth them success.

Proposition 5. *The faithful Pastors of the Reformed Churches, are these ordinary Ministers of Christ, approved by him, and given in great mercy to his people, who are bound to know honour, and obey them in the Lord.*

I exclude not all others, but I now prove that *these are true Ministers*. Argument 1. They that have all that is essential to true Ministers are true Ministers: But such are these Pastors of the Reformed Churches; as I prove thus: If the Office it self be of Gods Institution, and their Qualifications competent, and their entrance right in every point of flat Necessity, then they

have

have all that is essential to true Ministers: But the former is true, as I shall prove in the three several parts. 1. That the *Office* it self is of Gods appointment, is proved fully before, and confessed by all Christians that ever I knew, *Acts* 14.23. 1 *Tim.* 3. *Tit.* 1. 1 *Pet.* 5. 1, 2. 1 *Thes.* 5. 12. *Heb.* 13. 7, 17, 24. *Acts* 20. 28. 2. For *Qualifications*, they have 1. competent *Knowledge*, 2. and *Utterance*, 3. and *Godliness*: and these are the Qualifications that God accepteth 1 *Cor.* 12. 8. 1 *Tim.* 2. 15. 1 *Tim.* 5. 17. Mark the Canons of the Holy Ghost, 2 *Tim.* 2. 2. They must be 1. *Faithful men,* 2. *Able to teach others*: But such are those in question, 1 *Tim.* 3. *A Bishop must be blameless (that is, not scandalous) the husband of one Wife; vigilant, sober, of good behaviour, given to hospitality, apt to teach, not given to Wine, no striker, not greedy of filthy lucre, but patient, not a brawler, not covetous, one that ruleth well his own house having his children in subjection, with all gravity.*] To which is added, *Tit.* 1. 8, 9. *A lover of good men, sober, just, holy temperate, holding fast the faithful word as he hath been taught, that he may be able by sound Doctrine both to exhort and to convince the gain-sayers.*] Let all here note: 1. That here is not only the mention of the Vertues necessary to the *Being*, but to the *well-being* also of a Minister: 2. And yet through the great mercy of God, all these are the qualifications of multitudes of the Pastors of the Reformed Churches, as malice it self must be forced to confess: But if any deny it of any particular men, as that is nothing to the rest; so an unproved accusation is not by honest men to be believed. The world knows that the Act for rejecting scandalous, insufficient, negligent Ministers is very strict, and Commissioners in each County forward to execute it, and Ministers have enemies enough to search out their faults, and yet none are more forward than Ministers themselves to have the Act put in execution; so that their standing justifies them before the world: Or, if any will yet deny them the necessary Qualifications, I here challenge and provoke them to accuse all that are guilty, and cast them out; or else to confess themselves meer slanderers, and back-biters, and learn more truth and modesty hereafter. 3. And for the third point, *their entrance into the Office: They have all that God hath made necessary to a just entrance,* as I prove: *They that have a true Ordination, and the Peoples consent, and the Magistrates allowance, have all that God hath made necessary to a just entrance, and more than all: But the said Pastors of the Reformed Churches have true Ordination, and the Peoples consent, and the Magistrates allowance*: That they have *true Ordination,* I shall shew anone in answering all that can be said against it. The *Peoples consent,* by *Electing,* or *Accepting,* is known by the *fact*; and so is the *Magistrates* by *Law* and *fact*: I put in all this, though *more than necessary,* that all Objections may be satisfied at once: So that the Enumerations being unquestionable, the Conclusion is so to. In short; *All those are true Ministers, that are in an Office of Gods own Institution, and are competently fitted for that Office by Knowledge, Godliness, and Utterance, and have all, and more than all that God hath made necessary to a right entrance or admission, even true Ordination, consent of the Flock, and the Magistrates allowance. But such are the said Pastors of the Reformed Churches, therefore they are true Ministers of Christ.* Argu-

Argument 2. *Those that have not only the Essentials, but excel all other Ministers on Earth (that are known to the world) are certainly the true Ministers of Christ. But such are the Ministers before-mentioned of the Reformed Churches; Ergo.* This will be proved at once with the next, which is,

Argument 3. *Either these Pastors of the Reformed Churches are the true Ministers of Christ, or else there are none such visible in the world: But there are such visibly and certainly in the world, as* was proved; else there is no Church, no Ordinances, no Christianity, no Christ: For he can be no King without Subjects and Laws; no Master without a School and Scholars; no Physitian without Patients; no Husband without his Spouse; no Head without a Body; no Intercessor without a Church to intercede for. And to *believe the holy Catholick Church, and the Communion of Saints,* is part of our Belief; and therefore the Christian Faith is gone, if these be gone: And that either *we,* or *None* are Christs true Ministers, I prove thus: 1. We challenge the Adversary to name us the true Church and Ministry; if these be none of them, where be they, and who are they? speak out, or give up your wicked Cause. If you know not who they be, or where, then how know you that there are any such? True Ministers are like a *light that shineth to all the house,* even *the lights of the world, and like a City on a Hill that cannot be hid,* Mat. 5. 14, 15, 16. 2. But let us try the particulars: 1. The *Seekers* have no Church or Ministry. 2. The *Quakers* have no Ordination, that we know of, and are every way so unworthy, and had no being in the world till a few years ago, that he is either no Christian, or of a crazed brain, that thinks Christ hath no Church or Ministry but them. 3. The *Anabaptists, Socinians, Swenkfeldians, Familists, Paracelsians, Weigelians,* and such like, have no more to shew for their Ministry and Churches than we, but their Errours; and are so few, and so lately sprung up, that of them also I may say, that he that takes them for the only Church, or Ministers, is either out of the Faith, or much out of his wits. 4. The Eastern and Southern Churches have no more to shew for their Ministry and Churches than we; but are incomparably more ignorant, and erroneous: few of them doing more than read their Liturgies and Homilies, and so administer the Sacraments. 5. All the Controversie therefore lieth between us and the Papists; either they are true Ministers, and a Church, or not; if *not,* then its left to *us:* if *they are,* then *we are so much more;* for we have *much more* unquestionable Evidence of our Title. 1. The Office of a Teaching, (Guiding, Worshipping Presbyter which we are in, is beyond all question, and yielded by themselves to be of Divine Institution. But the office of a Mass-Priest, to make a God of a piece of Bread, and turn Bread into Flesh, so that there shall be quantity, colour, taste, *&c.* without bread, or any subject; and a mans eyes, taste, or feeling, shall not know that its bread or wine, when we see, taste, and feel it; as also to celebrate publick worship in an unknown tongue; this office is more questionable than ours. 2. It remaineth a great doubt, whether the Pope be not the Antichrist: but of our Ministry there's no such doubt. 3. For Knowledge, Godliness and Utterance, and all true Ministerial abilities, as its well known what an ignorant Rabble their common secular Mass Priests are; so those Military Fryars and Jesuites that are chosen of purpose to play their Game among us, and credit their Cause, if they have any relicks of truth or modesty, will confess, that the generality of our Ministers are much beyond theirs for Parts and Piety; or at least, that we cannot be denied to be true Ministers for want of necessary abilities: We should rejoyce if their Ministers, Priests or Jesuites were near of such Piety as those of the Reformed Churches. Some of their Jesuites and Fryars are learned men; in which also we have those that equal the best of them: but for the learning, ability, or Piety of the common Ministers on both sides, there is no comparison to be made. 4. All the question then is of the way of entrance: And there 1. The Papists seek not the *Peoples consent* so much as we do. 2. They despise the *Magistrates consent*, in comparison of us. 3. And for *Ordination*, which is it that all the stress must be laid on, we *have it*, and nearer the *Rule* of God than they. Are they ordained with Fasting, Prayer, and Imposition of Hands? so are we. Must it be by one of a Superiour Order? Who then shall Ordain or Consecrate the Pope? And yet a multitude of our Ministers are ordained by Bishops, if that be necessary: But the great Objection is, that we have not an *uninterrupted succession* from the Apostles, and so those that ordained us had no power; and therefore could not give it to us.

Proposition 6. *The want of an uninterrupted succession, and so of Power in the Ordainers, doth not disable our Title to the Ministry, or set us in a worse condition than the Papists.* For if it be only the *succession of possession of the Office*, there is no man of brains can deny, but *we have an uninterrupted succession down from the Apostles*. But if it be a *succession of Right Ordination* that is questioned, 1. The Papists have none such themselves. 2. We have more of it than they. 3. It is not necessary that this be uninterrupted. All these I prove: 1. The Popes themselves, from whom their power flows, have been Hereticks, denied the Immortality of the Soul. Whoremongers, Sodomites, Simonists, Murderers; so that for many of them successively, the Papists confess they were Apostatical, and not Apostolical. See in their own Writers the Lives of *Sylvest.* 2. *Alexand.* 3. & 6. *John* 13. & 22. & 23. *Greg.* 7. *Urban* 7. and abundance more, *Joh.* 13. was proved in Council to have ravished Maids and Wives at the Apostlick doors murdered many, drunk to the Devil, askt help at Dice of *Jupiter* and *Venus*, and was kill'd in the act of Adultery. Read the proofs in my Book against Popery, pag. 269, 270, 255, 101. The Council at *Pisa* deposed two Popes at once, called them Hereticks departed from the Faith. The Council at *Constance* deposed *John* May 25. as holding that there was *no Eternal Life, Immortality of the Soul or Resurrection*: The Council at *Basil* deposed *Eugenius* 4. as a *Simonist and perjured wretch, a Schismatick, and obstinate Heretick.* Now these men are uncapable of the Ministry as an Infidel is, for want of Essential Qualifications: As Copper is no currant Coyn, though the stamp of the Prince against his will be put upon it: Undisposed matter cannot receive the form: A ht

man.

man unordained is nearer the Ministry, than such a man ordained: So that here was a Nullity. 2. And all the following Popes were the Successors of *Eugenius* that was deposed, and thus judged by a General Council; but by force brought them to submit, and held the place. 3. Either the *Election*, *Ordination*, or *both*, is it that giveth them the Essence of their Papacy: If *Election*, then there hath been a long interruption: for some-while the *People* chose, and in other Ages the *Emperours* chose, and in these times the *Cardinals*; and therefore some of them had no lawful choice: And for *Ordination*, or *Consecration*; 1. There have been three or four Popes at once, and all were *Consecrated*, that yet are now confessed to have been no true Popes. 2. *Inferiours* only Consecrated. 3. And such as had no power themselves. Besides that, the See hath been very many years vacant, and some score years the Pope hath been at *Avignion*, and had but the name of *P.* of *Rome*. And when three or four have been Pope at once, *Bellarmine* confesseth, learned men knew not which was the Right; yea, General Councils knew not. The Council at *Basil* thought *Felix* the fifth was the right Pope, but it proved otherwise; so that many palpable Intercisions have been made at *Rome*.

2. Our *Ordination* hath been less interrupted than theirs.

Object. *But you are not ordained by Bishops.* Ansr. 1. Almost all in *England* are till of late, if that will serve. 2. *Presbyters* may ordain in case of necessity, as the generality of the Old Episcopal men grant, and their Ordination is not null. 3. *Presbyters* have power to Ordain, and were restrained only from the *exercise* by *humane Laws*, as many of the Schoolmen confess. 4. *Presbyters have still ordained* with the Bishop; therefore they had *Authority* to it, and the work is not Alien to their Function. 5. Our *Parish Presbyters* are Bishops, having some of them Assistants, and Deacons under them; or as *Grotius* notes, at least they are so, as being the chief Guides of that Church: Their own Rule is, that every City should have a Bishop; and every Corporation is truly a City, πόλις, and therefore must have a Bishop. 6. The *Jus Divinum* of Prelacy is *sub judice*. 7. Bishop *Usher* maintaining to me the validity of the Ordination of the *Presbyters* without a Bishop, told me how he answered King *C.* who askt him for an instance in Church-History, *viz.* That *Hierom ad Evag.* tells us *of more*; *that the Presbyters of Alexandria, till the days of Heraclas and Dionysius, took one from among themselves, and made him Bishop*; therefore they may make a Presbyter, which is less. 8. Its at last confessed, that in Scripture-times there were no *Presbyters* under Bishops, but the single Churches had single Pastors. 9. No man can prove Ordination by fixed Bishops over many Churches (now called *Diocesan*) in the first Age: The fixed Bishops had no more at first but single Churches. Object. *But you never received power from the Bishop to ordain; and therefore cannot have that which was never given you.* Ansr. If they put men into that *Office*, to which God hath affixed the *power* of Ordination, then they do their part to convey the power. As if you marry a couple, and express not the mans authority over the woman, yet he hath it nevertheless by being made her Husband. So he that is made a Pastor in City or Country, may do the work of a Pastor, though each particular was not named.

Proposition 7. *Ordination is ordinarily necessary as a means of our right entrance, but not absolutely necessary to the Being of our Office or Power.* For 1. God having already setled the *Office, Duty,* and *Power,* and what *Qualifications* shall be necessary, and *giving* these Qualifications to men, he hath left nothing to man but mutual *consent,* and to *judge* of the person qualified, and *solemnly introduce* him. 2. God hath not tyed himself or us absolutely to the judgment of Ordainers. If a Bishop ordain a Heathen, or any man void of Essential Qualifications, its null, as being against a flat Command of God: And if Bishops *refuse* to ordain us Pastors, the people must take them without; because the *Command of Preaching, Hearing, Sacraments, &c.* is greater than that of *Ordination,* and *before* it. Positives yield to Natural Morals, and matters of *Order* to the *substance* and *end* of the Duty ordered. See my *Christian Concord,* pag. 82, 83, 84. 3. *Ordination* is no more necessary to the *Ministry,* than *Baptism* to *Christianity:* As those that are first Princes by Title must be Crowned, and those that are Souldiers by Contract, must be listed, and take Colours, and those that are Husband and Wife by Contract, must be solemnly Married, which are celebrating, perfecting actions; so they that are first heart-Christians by believing, or by Parents dedicating them to God, must be solemnly entred under the hand of the Minister: And those that are by approbation and consent initially Ministers, must by solemnization have the Office publickly delivered them by the Ministers of Christ. So that as a man is a Christian indeed before Baptism initially, and is justified initially before, and in case of necessity may be saved without it (the Papists confessing that the Vow will serve) so is it in the case of Ordination to the Ministry.

Proposition 8. *It is only Christ, and not the Ordainers, People or Magistrates, that give us our Office and Power:* Only the people and approvers design the person which shall receive it from Christ; and our own consent, and the peoples, is of necessity thereto (and our own as much as theirs) and the Ordainers do instrumentally invest us in it; but the Power and Duty arise directly from Gods Institution, when the person is designed. Now I proceed to prove our Calling.

Argument 4. *We have a far clearer Call than the Priests before Christ had to the Priesthood*: For they were not of the true Line; they bought the Priesthood; they corrupted Doctrine and worship, and were of wicked lives. And yet Christ commanded submission to their Ministry: Ergo.

Argument 5. *If we have as clear a Call to our Office as any Magistrates on Earth have to theirs, then we are true Ministers of Christ*: For they are true Magistrates; and God is the Fountain of their Power too; and its impossible they should have any but from him: Or from him but by his means: Officers have no power but from the Soveraign. The Prince was at first chosen by God immediately, as well as the Apostles were by Christ, yet no.
Prince

Princes can plead an uninterrupted succession thereto; and if they may Reign without it, we may be Pastors without it: and yet I can prove that we are without it, though Princes be. Kings were formerly anointed by inspired Prophets, and were Prophets themselves: And as the continuance of this is not necessary to them, so neither to us. The differences between *their power* and *ours*, makes nothing against this Argument: If *Conquest*, or the *peoples consent*, or *Birth*, or *directing Providences* can prove their Title, then *Consent*, *Ordination*, *Providence*, with *due Qualifications*, will sure prove ours: were it not for fear, they should soon hear the Arguments more set home against themselves, that are now bent against the Ministers.

Argument 6. *If besides all this God own us by such a blessing on our labours, that he maketh us the means of propagating and continuing his Gospel and Church, and brings most of his chosen to Union with Christ, Reconciliation, Holiness, and to Heaven by our Ministry, then certainly we are his true Ministers:* But experience assureth us of the former: therefore--so much for Argument.

Proposition 9. *If a Minister be in quiet possession of the place, and fit for it, the people are bound to obey him as a Minister, without knowing that he was justly ordained or called.* Argum. 1. We must obey a *Magistrate* without assurance of his Call and Title, *Rom.* 13. therefore a *Minister*. 2. Christ commanded hearing and obeying them that were not called as God appointed, because they were Priests, or sat in *Moses* Chair, and taught the truth, *Luke* 16. 29. *Matth.* 23. 2. *Luke* 5. 14. *Matth.* 8. 4. *Mark* 1. 44. 3. Else the people are put upon impossibilities: Can all the poor people tell before they submit to a Minister, what is Essential to his Call, and whether he have all that is so, and whether his Orders be true or forged, and whether they that ordained him were truly ordained, or chosen themselves: Not one of twenty thousand knows all this by their Pastors.

Proposition 10. *The Ordinances are valid to the people when the Minister is uncalled and unordained, if they know it not:* He that hath no just Call, shall answer for what he doth as an Intruder; but the people shall have for all that the fruit of his Ministration; and Preaching, and Baptism, and other acts, shall not be null to them. 1. The Papists themselves confess this. 2. Else scarce a man could tell whether he be baptized, or may use any Ordinance, because he cannot have an exact account of the Ministers Call, no nor know that he is indeed a Christian. I knew divers in the Bishops days that forged themselves Orders, and acted long before it was discovered. 3. It is the *Office* which is *Gods Ordinance* that is blest, and valid to the people, and not his Call only. 4. It is he that sinneth that must suffer, and not the Innocent; therefore his sin depriveth them not of their due. 5. As an usurping Magistrate oweth us protection, though he shall answer for his Usurpation; so an usurping Minister oweth us his labour; so that the people are bound to *hear and obey* men, when they are uncertain of their due Call, if they possess the place; and shall have the blessing of such Administrations: For we are sure the Office and work is of God.

Proposition 11. *The truth of our Doctrine depends not on our Calling.* Were we no Ministers, we can prove the Gospel true which we deliver. And any man must be believed, that brings a truth that concerneth our peace. Therefore let Quakers, and Seekers, and Papists first disprove our Doctrine if they can; and not cheat the people, by perswading them, that our Calling must first be proved; as a Prophets must be.

Object. *But you have your learning only from Books, and Universities, and so have not true Ministers.* Ansir. We have it from God in the use of his means, even by prayer, reading, study and learning his works and word of our Teachers, whether at Universities, or elsewhere. And we are commanded to *study* and *meditate on these things, and give our selves wholly to them, and to meditate on Gods Law day and night*, Psal. 1. 2. 2 Tim. 2. 15. 1 Tim. 4. 13. 15. Christs Ministers must be Teachers or Tutors to others, and *commit the things which they have heard to faithful men, who shall be able to teach others also*, 2 Tim. 2. 2. *Good Ministers of Christ are nourished up in the words of faith and good Doctrine, and so attain to it*, 1 Tim. 4. 6. All should learn according to their *time* of teaching, Heb. 5. 11, 12, 14. We study nothing but the *Word*, and works of God: And is not that a Wretch, and not a man, that will reproach us as no Ministers, for doing that which we have our Reason for, and which must be the work of our lives: Poor Christians, as you love God and your Souls, and would not cast off Christ and Heaven, let not Deceivers draw you to cast off the Ministry, Scripture, or the Ordinances of God.

FINIS.

www.ingramcontent.com/pod-product-compliance
Lightning Source LLC
Chambersburg PA
CBHW022106300426
44117CB00007B/605